Oracle SOA Suite 11*g* R1 Developer's Guide

Develop Service-Oriented Architecture Solutions with the Oracle SOA Suite

Antony Reynolds

Matt Wright

BIRMINGHAM - MUMBAI

Oracle SOA Suite 11*g* R1 Developer's Guide

Copyright © 2010 Packt Publishing

All rights reserved. No part of this book may be reproduced, stored in a retrieval system, or transmitted in any form or by any means, without the prior written permission of the publisher, except in the case of brief quotations embedded in critical articles or reviews.

Every effort has been made in the preparation of this book to ensure the accuracy of the information presented. However, the information contained in this book is sold without warranty, either express or implied. Neither the authors, nor Packt Publishing, and its dealers and distributors will be held liable for any damages caused or alleged to be caused directly or indirectly by this book.

Packt Publishing has endeavored to provide trademark information about all of the companies and products mentioned in this book by the appropriate use of capitals. However, Packt Publishing cannot guarantee the accuracy of this information.

First published: June 2010

Production Reference: 1220610

Published by Packt Publishing Ltd.
32 Lincoln Road
Olton
Birmingham, B27 6PA, UK.

ISBN 978-1-849680-18-9

`www.packtpub.com`

Cover Image by Sandeep Babu (`sandyjb@gmail.com`)

Credits

Authors

Antony Reynolds

Matt Wright

Reviewers

John Deeb

Hans Forbrich

Bill Hicks

Marc Kelderman

Manoj Neelapu

ShuXuan Nie

Hajo Normann

Acquisition Editor

James Lumsden

Development Editor

Swapna Verlekar

Technical Editors

Gauri Iyer

Hyacintha D'Souza

Smita Solanki

Alfred John

Copy Editor

Leonard D'Silva

Editorial Team Leader

Aanchal Kumar

Project Team Leader

Priya Mukherji

Project Coordinator

Prasad Rai

Proofreader

Aaron Nash

Indexer

Hemangini Bari

Graphics

Geetanjali Sawant

Production Coordinator

Shantanu Zagade

Cover Work

Shantanu Zagade

Foreword

First and foremost, let me say what an honor it is to participate in the great work that Antony Reynolds and Matt Wright are doing through this Oracle SOA Suite Developer Guide. The original edition of the book provided SOA developers with practical tips, code examples, and under-the-covers knowledge of Oracle SOA Suite and has received extremely positive feedback from our developer community. This edition carries forward all of those benefits, but is completely updated for the 11gR1 release of Oracle SOA Suite, which brings with it not only new features and APIs, but also some very significant architectural changes.

The original edition filled a very important need for the developer community, going beyond basic documentation to provide best practices and tips and tricks for Oracle SOA Suite developers. Antony and Matt were just the right people to create such content, each having many years hands-on experience of enabling Oracle SOA Suite implementations for customers and partners, as well as a close working relationship with Oracle's SOA engineering and product management teams. However, I believe this update for the 11gR1 release will be even more valuable to the developer community.

With 11gR1, Oracle invested a tremendous amount of engineering work to not just integrate, but unify the components that make up the Oracle SOA Suite. This was done across many areas - adapters, service bus, routing, process orchestration, business rules, B2B / partner integration, business activity monitoring, and complex event processing. To achieve this unified experience, new micro-kernel based run-time architecture was created, called the Service Infrastructure, and new standards such as SCA (Service Component Architecture) were implemented. These advances bring great benefits to customers around ease-of-use, manageability and scalability; however, there is naturally a learning curve with the new features and also new architectural factors that come into play. For example, architects and developers will now consider not just how to decompose their requirements into Services and Processes, but also determine what level of granularity their SOA Composites should be at.

As such, besides the many updates and descriptions of new components, Antony and Matt have also added critically valuable new content on advanced SOA architecture considerations. I believe that this alone will make this book uniquely useful for Oracle SOA Suite developers.

Especially coming so soon after the 11gR1 release, the updated content in this book, including areas such as exception handling, testing, security and operational automation, will surely be invaluable to anyone working with Oracle SOA Suite. But even more difficult to find is the information that Matt and Antony have from working with customer implementations around edge cases, design patterns, and how these products best fit into the full development lifecycle. This kind of information comes only from real-world project experience, such as Antony and Matt have.

I believe that this book will help developers realize their goals with the Oracle SOA Suite, helping them increase productivity, avoid common pitfalls, and improve ROI through more scalable, agile, and re-usable implementations. On behalf of the Oracle SOA Engineering and Product Management team, as well as all the customers and partners who have asked for this book, we heartily thank Antony and Matt for the investment of their time and energy and hope that this updated edition help you achieve your goals with the Oracle SOA Suite.

David Shaffer
Vice President, Product Management
Oracle Integration
`david.shaffer@oracle.com`

About the Authors

Antony Reynolds has worked in the IT industry for more than 25 years, after getting a job to maintain yield calculations for a zinc smelter while still an undergraduate. After graduating from the University of Bristol with a degree in Mathematics and Computer Science he worked first for a software house, IPL in Bath, England, before joining the travel reservations system Galileo as a development team lead.

At Galileo, he was involved in the development and maintenance of workstation products before joining the architecture group. Galileo gave him the opportunity to work in Colorado and Illinois where he developed a love for the Rockies and Chicago style deep pan pizza.

He joined Oracle in 1998 as a sales consultant and has worked with a number of customers in that time, including a large retail bank's Internet banking project, for which he served as the chief design authority and security architect.

After the publication of his previous book, the SOA Suite 10*g* Developers Guide, Antony changed roles within Oracle, taking a position in the global customer support organization. As part of this change of position he moved from a small village outside Bristol, England to a small town outside Colorado Springs, Colorado. He is now acclimatized to living at 7,500ft and has learnt to survive on less oxygen.

Within support, Antony deals with customers who have problems with large complex SOA deployments, often working as an advisor to other support analysts. Antony also has a role in training support analysts in SOA principles and details of the Oracle SOA Suite.

Outside of work Antony helps with scouting at church, which gives him the opportunity to spend time with his two eldest sons. His wife and four children make sure that he also spends time with them, playing games, watching movies, and acting as an auxiliary taxi service. Antony is a slow but steady runner and can often be seen jogging up and down the trails in the shadow of the Rocky Mountains.

Acknowledgement

I would like to thank my wife Rowan, and my four very patient children, who have put up with my staying at home on family trips and working late nights in my basement office. My colleagues in support have often volunteered to be reviewers of material and have been the unwitting guinea pigs of new explanations. The reviewers have provided invaluable advice and assistance, challenging me to explain myself better and expand more on key points.

Matt has been a constant source of enthusiasm and energy and with Prasad and Swapna at Packt has helped keep me to some sort of schedule.

Finally, thank you to the development team at Oracle under Amlan Debnath, who have enhanced and improved the SOA Suite product significantly in this release. I would particularly like to mention Clemens Utschig, who has expanded my understanding of SOA Suite internals and without whom Chapter 15 in particular would be much less complete.

Matt Wright is a director at Rubicon Red, an independent consulting firm helping customers enable enterprise agility and operational excellence through the adoption of emerging technologies such as Service-Oriented Architecture (SOA), Business Process Management (BPM), and Cloud Computing.

With over 20 years experience in building enterprise scale distributed systems, Matt first became involved with SOA shortly after the initial submission of SOAP 1.1 to the W3C in 2000, and has worked with some of the early adopters of BPEL since its initial release in 2002. Since then, he has been engaged in some of the earliest SOA-based implementations across EMEA and APAC.

Prior to Rubicon Red, Matt held various senior roles within Oracle, most recently as Director of Product Management for Oracle Fusion Middleware in APAC, where he was responsible for working with organizations to educate and enable them in realizing the full business benefits of SOA in solving complex business problems.

As a recognized authority on SOA, Matt is a regular speaker and instructor at private and public events. He also enjoys writing and publishes his own blog (`http://blog.rubiconred.com`). Matt holds a B.Sc. (Eng) in Computer Science from Imperial College, University of London.

Acknowledgement

Well, this is the book that Antony and I originally intended to write, when we first put pen to paper (or finger to keypad) back in May 2007. At this point the 11gR1 version of the Oracle SOA Suite was still in the initial stages of development, with the *goal* being to time the publication of the book with the release of 11gR1. Then in early 2008 Oracle announced the acquisition of BEA, which it finalized in July; at this point future timings around the release of 11gR1 were very much up in the air.

By this stage a significant amount of the book was already written, and we had received some really positive feedback from the initial reviews. With this in mind, Antony and I took the decision to retarget the book for the current 10gR3 release and bring in the Oracle Service Bus (formally known as the BEA Aqualogic Service Bus).

The first version of the book was published in March 2009, almost two years after our original start date, and much to the relief of anyone closely connected with Antony or I. Then in July, Oracle announced the release of the Oracle SOA Suite 11gR1, Antony and I blinked and then decided to write the 11gR1 version of the book, in many ways it was unfinished business!

So while this edition has been produced significantly quicker, it's still almost three years since we began this journey; a journey that we would not have been able to complete without the support of many others. First, I would like to express my gratitude to everyone at Oracle who played a part; in particular to David Shaffer, Demed L'Her, Prasen Palvankar, Heidi Buelow, Manoj Das, Neil Wyse, Ralf Mueller, Mohamed Ashfar, Andy Gale and all the members of the SOA Development Team.

I would also like to express my deep appreciation to everyone who has reviewed this book, the original reviewers: Phil McLaughlin, Jason Jones and James Oliver. Also the reviewers who helped with this edition: Bill Hicks, Normann Hajo, Manoj Neelapu, Hans Forbrich, Shu Xuan Nie, Marc Kelderman and John Deeb. Their invaluable feedback and advice not only helped to validate the overall accuracy of the content, but more importantly ensure its clarity and readability.

A book like this doesn't make it into print without a lot of work from the publisher. I would like to thank the team at Packt Publishing for all their support; especially James Lumsden, Swapna Verlekar, and Prasad Rai.

A special mention must go to John Deeb, for his continual encouragement, input and above all support in ensuring that I found time to write the book. I couldn't ask for a more supportive friend and business partner.

Finally, I would like to say a very, very special thank you to my wife Natasha and my children Elliot and Kimberley, who for the past three years have been incredibly patient and supportive in allowing me to spend far too many evenings and weekends stuck away in my office writing these books.

About the Reviewers

John Deeb is a director at Rubicon Red, an independent consulting firm helping customers enable enterprise agility and operational excellence through the adoption of emerging technologies such as Service-Oriented Architecture (SOA), Business Process Management (BPM), and Cloud Computing.

Prior to Rubicon Red, John held senior product management positions at Oracle and TIBCO Software. His areas of focus include enterprise integration, business process management, and business activity monitoring. John has worked with organizations to educate and enable them in realizing the full business benefits of BPM and SOA in solving complex business problems.

John holds a Bachelors degree in Cognitive Science from the University of Queensland and a Masters degree in IT from the Queensland University of Technology. He is a regular speaker on middleware vision, strategy, and architecture.

Hans Forbrich is a well-known member of the Oracle Community. He started with Oracle products in 1984 and has kept abreast of nearly all of Oracle's Core Technologies. As ACE Director, Hans has been invited to be present at Oracle Open World and various Oracle User Group meetings around the world. His company, Forbrich Computer Consulting Ltd., is well established in western Canada. Hans specializes in delivering Oracle University training through Oracle University and partners such as Exit Certified.

Although his special interests include Oracle Spatial, OracleVM, and Oracle Enterprise Linux, Hans has been particularly excited about the advances in Oracle SOA, Oracle Web Logic, and Oracle Grid Control.

Hans has been technical reviewer for a number of Packt books, including *Mastering Oracle Scheduler in Oracle 11g Databases*, *Oracle 10g/11g Data and Database Management Utilities*, and *Oracle VM Manager 2.1.2*.

I wish to thank my wife Susanne, and the Edmonton Opera, for their patience while I worked on these reviews as well as on my own book.

Bill Hicks is a Senior Sales Consulting Manager for Australia and New Zealand, specializing in Oracles' Middleware products.

Over the last 11 years at Oracle, Bill has held various positions within Sales Consulting and Support.

His current focus is on Service-oriented Architecture and Cloud Computing and how the varied Oracle Middleware product offerings can be utilized to deliver flexible, cost effective, and complete business solutions.

Marc Kelderman is working for Oracle Netherlands as a solution architect. He started his career at Oracle in 1995 working in consulting. His broad knowledge of Oracle products and IT technology helped making the projects he is involved to be successful. Since 2005, he is implementing and has designed projects based on Oracle SOA technology. From that period he started to share his solutions to a broader audience via his blog (`http://orasoa.blogspot.com`). Marc is often called for as a speaker at seminars.

I would like to thank Matt and Antony for giving me the opportunity to review their book. Good work!

Manoj Neelapu has around nine years of experience in Java/J2EE/SOA technologies. He started his career as contractor engineer for Hindustan Aeronautics Limited (Helicopter Division) and later worked for BEA Systems as Developer Relations Engineer handling level3/4 support. Before joining Oracle, he had experience working with open-source technologies at Sudhari.

As a Principal Engineer in Oracle, Manoj has expertise in various components of Oracle Fusion Middleware stack, including Oracle Service Bus, Financial Service Bus, JCA Adapters, and Oracle WebLogic Integration. He currently works for SOA product lines as part of the engineering team. Among other activities, he actively participates on Oracle Technology Network evangelizing, trouble-shooting, and solving customer issues.

ShuXuan Nie is a software engineer specializing in SOA and Java technologies.

He has more than eight years of experience in the IT industry that includes SOA technologies such as BPEL, ESB, SOAP, XML, Enterprise Java technologies, Eclipse plugins, and other areas such as C++ cross-platform development.

Since 2007, he has been working as part of the Oracle Global Customer Support team and focuses on helping customers solve their Middleware/SOA integration problems.

Before joining Oracle, he worked for IBM China in their Software Development Lab for four years as a staff software engineer. She participated in several complex products involving IBM Lotus Workplace, Websphere, and the Eclipse platform before joining the Australia Bureau of Meteorology Research Center where she was responsible for the implementation of the Automated Thunderstorm Interactive Forecast System for Aviation and Defense.

He holds an M.Sc. in Computer Science from Beijing University of Aeronautics and Astronautics.

When not reviewing SOA books ShuXuan enjoys swimming, dancing, and visiting new places.

Hajo Normann is SOA/BPM architect at HP Enterprise Services since 2005. He helps motivating, designing, and implementing integration solutions using Oracle SOA Suite and BPA Suite (a BPM-ready version of ARIS from IDS Scheer) and works on SOA/BPM principles, design guidelines, and best practices.

Since 2007, Hajo is the Oracle ACE Director. Since 2008, he leads together with Torsten Winterberg from OPITZ Consulting, the special interest group "DOAG SIG SOA". Hajo is a co-founder of the "Masons-of-SOA", an inter-company network, consisting of architects of Oracle Germany, Opitz Consulting, SOPERA, and HP ES - with the mission to spread SOA knowledge and support projects/initiatives across companies. The masons meet regularly for thought exchange, have written a multi-article series on *Yet Unshackled SOA Topics*, have contributed to Thomas Erl's book *SOA Design Patterns* and are giving whole day advanced SOA workshops on conferences.

Websites: `http://hajonormann.wordpress.com/`, `http://soacommunity.com/`

Table of Contents

Part 2: Putting it All Together

Part 3: Other Considerations

Preface

Service-Oriented Architecture is not just changing how we approach application integration, but the mindset of software development.

Applications as we know them are becoming a thing of the past, in the future we will increasingly think of services and how those services are assembled to build complete, "composite" applications that can be modified quickly and easily to adapt to a continually evolving business environment.

This is the vision of a standards-based Service-Oriented Architecture (SOA), where the IT infrastructure is continuously adapted to keep up with the pace of business change.

Oracle is at the forefront of this vision, with the Oracle SOA Suite providing the most comprehensive, proven, and integrated tool kit for building SOA based applications.

This is no idle boast. Oracle Fusion Applications (the re-implementation of Oracle's E-Business Suite, Siebel, PeopleSoft and JD Edwards Enterprise as a single application) is probably the largest composite application being built today and it has the Oracle SOA platform at its core.

Developers and Architects using the Oracle SOA Suite, whether working on integration projects, building new bespoke applications or specializing in large implementations of Oracle Applications will need a book that provides a "hands on" guide on how best to harness and apply this technology, this book will enable them to do just that.

What this book covers

Part 1: Getting Started

This section provides an initial introduction to the Oracle SOA Suite and its various components, and gives the reader a fast paced hands-on introduction to each of the key components in turn.

Chapter 1: *Introduction to Oracle SOA Suite*: Gives an initial introduction to the Oracle SOA Suite and its various components.

Chapter 2: *Writing Your First Composite*: Provides a hands-on introduction to writing your first SOA composite. We then look at how we can expose this as a proxy service via the Oracle Service Bus.

Chapter 3: *Service-enabling Existing Systems*: Looks at a number of key technology adapters, and how we can use them to service-enable existing systems.

Chapter 4: *Loosely Coupling Services*: Describes how we can use the Mediator to loosely couple services within a composite and Oracle Service Bus to loosely couple services within the Enterprise.

Chapter 5: *Using BPEL to Build Composite Services and Business Processes*: Covers how to use BPEL to assemble services to build composite services and long-running business processes.

Chapter 6: *Adding in Human Workflow*: Looks at how human tasks can be managed through workflow activities embedded within a BPEL process.

Chapter 7: *Using Business Rules to Define Decision Points*: Covers the new Rules Editor in 11*g*R1, including Decision Tables and how we can incorporate rules as decision points within a BPEL Process.

Chapter 8: *Using Business Events*: Introduces the Event Delivery Network (EDN), a key new component in Oracle SOA Suite 11*g* that provides a declarative way to generate and consume business events within your SOA infrastructure.

Chapter 9: *Building Real-time Dashboards*: Looks at how Business Activity Monitoring (BAM) can be used to give business users a real-time view into how business processes are performing.

Part 2: Putting it All Together

This section uses the example of an online auction site (oBay) to illustrate how to use the various components of the SOA Suite to implement a real-world SOA-based solution.

Chapter 10: oBay Introduction: Provides a blueprint for our SOA architecture, highlighting some of the key design considerations and describes how this fits into our architecture for oBay.

Chapter 11: Designing the Service Contract: Gives guidance on how to design XML schemas and service contracts for improved agility, reuse, and interoperability.

Chapter 12: Building Entity Services Using Service Data Objects (SDOs): Details how to use ADF-Business Components to implement Service Data Objects (SDOs) and embed them as Entity Variables within a BPEL Process.

Chapter 13: Building Validation into Services: Examines how we can implement validation within a service using XSD validation, Schematron, and Business Rules, as well as within the service.

Chapter 14: Error Handling: Examines strategies for handling system and business errors, with detailed coverage of the Composite Fault Management Framework.

Chapter 15: Advanced SOA Suite Architecture: Covers advanced SOA Architecture, including message delivery to asynchronous / synchronous composites, transaction handling, and clustering considerations.

Chapter 16: Message Interaction Patterns: Covers complex messaging interactions, including multiple requests and responses, timeouts, and message correlation (both system and business).

Chapter 17: Workflow Patterns: Looks at how to implement workflows involving complex chains of approval and how to use the Workflow Service API.

Chapter 18: Using Business Rules to Implement Services: Looks at the Rules Engine's inferencing capabilities, and how we can use them to implement types of business services.

Part 3: Other Considerations

This final section covers other considerations such as the packaging, deployment, testing, security, and administration of SOA applications.

Chapter 19: Packaging and Deployment: Examines how to package up SOA applications for deployment into environments such as test and production.

Chapter 20: *Testing Composite Applications*: Looks at how to create, deploy, and run test cases that automate the testing of composite applications.

Chapter 21: *Defining Security and Management Policies*: Details how to use policies to secure and administer SOA applications.

What you need for this book

1. Oracle WebLogic Server 11gR1 (10.3.3) + Coherence + OEPE - Package Installer

   `http://www.oracle.com/technology/software/products/ias/htdocs/wls_main.html`

      `wls1033_oepe111150_win32.exe`

2. Repository Creation Utility (11.1.1.3.0)

   `http://www.oracle.com/technology/software/products/middleware/htdocs/`

      `fmw_11_download.htmlofm_rcu_win_11.1.1.3.0_disk1_1of1.zip`

   SOA Suite (11.1.1.2.0)

      `ofm_soa_generic_11.1.1.2.0_disk1_1of1.zip`

   SOA Suite (11.1.1.3.0)

      `ofm_soa_generic_11.1.1.3.0_disk1_1of1.zip`

3. Oracle Service Bus (11.1.1.3.0)

   `http://www.oracle.com/technology/software/products/osb/index.html.`

      `ofm_osb_generic_11.1.1.3.0_disk1_1of1.zip`

4. Oracle JDeveloper 11*g* (11.1.1.3.0) Studio Edition

   `http://www.oracle.com/technology/software/products/jdev/htdocs/soft11.html`

      `jdevstudio11113install.exe`

5. XE Universal database version 10.2.0.1 or 10*g* database version 10.2.0.4+ or 11*g* database version 11.1.0.7+.

6. Enterprise Manager requires Firefox 3 or IE 7.
    - Firefox 3 - get it from `http://portableapps.com` if you want it to co-exist peacefully with your Firefox 2 installation (keep Firefox 2 if you use Rules Author in 10*g* R3.)
    - Firefox 2 and IE 6 do not work in 11*g*.
7. BAM requires IE 7
    - IE 7 without special plug-ins (some plug-ins may cause problems).
    - IE 8 does not work. IE 6 has a few UI issues. Firefox does not work.

Who this book is for

The primary purpose of the book is to provide developers and technical architects with a practical guide to using and applying the Oracle SOA Suite in the delivery of real world SOA-based applications.

It is assumed that the reader already has a **basic** understanding of the concepts of SOA, as well as some of the key standards in this space, including web services (SOAP, WSDL), XML Schemas, and XSLT (and XPath).

Conventions

In this book, you will find a number of styles of text that distinguish between different kinds of information. Here are some examples of these styles, and an explanation of their meaning.

There are three styles for code. Code words in text are shown as follows: "Each schema can reference definitions in other schema's by making use of the `xsd:import` directive."

A block of code will be set as follows:

```
<types>
  <schema xmlns="http://www.w3.org/2001/XMLSchema">
    <import namespace="http://xmlns.oracle.com/Echo"
            schemaLocation="Echo.xsd"/>
  </schema>
</types>
```

When we wish to draw your attention to a particular part of a code block, the relevant lines or items will be made bold:

```
<types>
  <schema xmlns="http://www.w3.org/2001/XMLSchema">
    <import namespace="http://xmlns.oracle.com/Echo"
            schemaLocation="Echo.xsd"/>
  </schema>
</types>
```

New terms and **important words** are introduced in a bold-type font. Words that you see on the screen, in menus or dialog boxes for example, appear in our text like this: "The deployed test suites will appear in the EM console in the composite **Unit Tests** tab, as shown in the following screenshot".

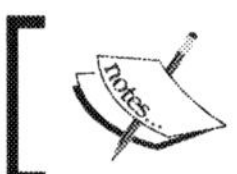

Warnings or important notes appear in a box like this.

Reader feedback

Feedback from our readers is always welcome. Let us know what you think about this book, what you liked or may have disliked. Reader feedback is important for us to develop titles that you really get the most out of.

To send us general feedback, simply drop an email to `feedback@packtpub.com`, making sure to mention the book title in the subject of your message.

If there is a book that you need and would like to see us publish, please send us a note in the **SUGGEST A TITLE** form on **www.packtpub.com** or email `suggest@packtpub.com`.

If there is a topic that you have expertise in and you are interested in either writing or contributing to a book, see our author guide on `www.packtpub.com/authors`.

Customer support

Now that you are the proud owner of a Packt book, we have a number of things to help you to get the most from your purchase.

> **Downloading the example code for this book**
>
> You can download the example code files for all Packt books you have purchased from your account at `http://www.PacktPub.com`. If you purchased this book elsewhere, you can visit `http://www.PacktPub.com/support` and register to have the files emailed directly to you.

Errata

Although we have taken every care to ensure the accuracy of our contents, mistakes do happen. If you find a mistake in one of our books—maybe a mistake in text or code—we would be grateful if you would report this to us. By doing this you can save other readers from frustration, and help to improve subsequent versions of this book. If you find any errata, report them by visiting `http://www.packtpub.com/support`, selecting your book, clicking on the **Submit Errata link**, and entering the details of your errata. Once your errata have been verified, your submission will be accepted and the errata added to the list of existing errata. The existing errata can be viewed by selecting your title from `http://www.packtpub.com/support`.

Piracy

Piracy of copyright material on the Internet is an ongoing problem across all media. At Packt, we take the protection of our copyright and licenses very seriously. If you come across any illegal copies of our works, in any form, on the Internet, please provide us with the location address or website name immediately so that we can pursue a remedy.

Please contact us at `copyright@packtpub.com` with a link to the suspected pirated material.

We appreciate your help in protecting our authors, and our ability to bring you valuable content.

Questions

You can contact us at `questions@packtpub.com` if you are having a problem with some aspect of the book, and we will do our best to address it.

Part 1

Getting Started

1

Introduction to Oracle SOA Suite

Service-Oriented Architecture (**SOA**) may consist of many interconnected components. As a result of this, the Oracle SOA Suite is a large piece of software that initially seems to be overwhelmingly complex. In this chapter, we will provide a roadmap for your understanding of the SOA Suite and provide a reference architecture to help you understand how to apply SOA principles with the SOA Suite. After a review of the basic principles of SOA, we will look at how the SOA Suite provides support for those principles through its many different components. Following this journey through the components of SOA Suite, we will introduce Oracle JDeveloper as the primary development tool that is used to build applications for deployment into the SOA Suite.

Service-oriented architecture in short

Service-oriented architecture has evolved to allow greater flexibility in adapting the IT infrastructure to satisfy the needs of business. Let's examine what SOA means by examining the components of its title.

Service

A service is a term that is understood by both business and IT. It has some key characteristics as follows:

- **Encapsulation**: A service creates delineation between the service provider and the service consumer. It identifies what will be provided.
- **Interface**: It is defined in terms of inputs and outputs. How the service is provided is not of concern to the consumer, only to the provider. The service is defined by its interface.

- **Contract or service level agreements**: There may be quality of service attributes associated with the service, such as performance characteristics, availability constraints, or cost.

The break-out-box uses the example of a laundry service to make more concrete the characteristics of a service. Later, we will map these characteristics onto specific technologies.

A clean example

Consider a laundry service. The service provider is a laundry company, and the service consumer is a corporation or individual with washing to be done.

The input to the company is a basket of dirty laundry. Additional input parameters may be a request to iron the laundry as well as wash it or to starch the collars. The output is a basket of clean washing with whatever optional, additional services such as starching or ironing were specified. This defines the interface.

Quality of service may specify that the washing must be returned within 24 or 48 hours. Additional quality of service attributes may specify that the service is unavailable from 5PM Friday until 8AM Monday. These service level agreements may be characterized as policies to be applied to the service.

An important thing about services is that they can be understood by both business analysts and IT implementers. This leads to the first key benefit of service-oriented architecture.

SOA makes it possible for IT and the business to speak the same language, that is, the language of services.

Services allow us to have a common vocabulary between IT and the business.

Orientation

When we are building our systems, we are looking at them from a service point of view or orientation. This implies that we are oriented or interested in the following:

- **Granularity**: The level of service interface or number of interactions required with the service are typically characterized as course-grained or fine-grained.
- **Collaboration**: Services may be combined together to create higher level or composite services.

- **Universality**: All components can be approached from a service perspective. For example, a business process may also be considered a service that, despite its complexity, provides inputs and outputs.

Thinking of everything as a service leads us to another key benefit of service-oriented architecture, namely **composability**, which is the ability to compose a service out of other services.

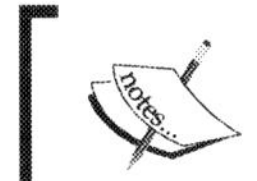

Composing new services out of existing services allows easy reasoning about the availability and performance characteristics of the composite service.

By building composite services out of existing services, we can reduce the amount of effort required to provide new functionality as well as being able to build something with prior knowledge of its availability and scalability characteristics. The latter can be derived from the availability and performance characteristics of the component services.

Architecture

Architecture implies a consistent and coherent design approach. This implies a need to understand the inter-relationships between components in the design and ensure consistency in approach. Architecture suggests that we adopt some of the following principles:

- **Consistency**: The same challenges should be addressed in a uniform way. For example, the application of security constraints needs to be enforced in the same way across the design. Patterns or proven design approaches can assist with maintaining consistency of design.
- **Reliability**: The structures created must be fit to purpose and meet the demands for which they are designed.
- **Extensibility**: A design must provide a framework that can be expanded in ways both foreseen and unforeseen. See the break-out-box on extensions.
- **Scalability**: The implementation must be capable of being scaled to accommodate increasing load by adding hardware to the solution.

Extending Antony's house

My wife and I designed our house in England. We built in the ability to convert the loft into extra rooms and also allowed for a conservatory to be added. This added to the cost of the build, but these were foreseen extensions. The costs of actually adding the conservatory and two extra loft rooms were low because the architecture allowed this. In a similar way, it is relatively easy to architect for foreseen extensions, such as additional related services and processes that must be supported by the business. When we wanted to add a playroom and another bathroom, this was more complex and costly as we had not allowed it in the original architecture. Fortunately, our original design was sufficiently flexible to allow for these additions, but the cost was higher. In a similar way, the measure of the strength of a service-oriented architecture is the way in which it copes with unforeseen demands, such as new types of business process and services that were not foreseen when the architecture was laid down. A well-architected solution will be able to accommodate unexpected extensions at a manageable cost.

A consistent architecture, when coupled with implementation in "SOA Standards", gives us another key benefit, that is, inter-operability.

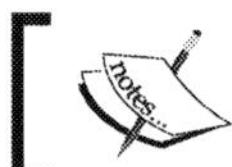

SOA allows us to build more inter-operable systems as it is based on standards agreed by all the major technology vendors.

SOA is not about any specific technology. The principles of service orientation can be applied equally well using an assembler as they can in a high-level language. However, as with all development, it is easiest to use a model that is supported by tools and is both inter-operable and portable across vendors. SOA is widely associated with the web service or WS-* standards presided over by groups like OASIS (`http://www.oasis.org`). This use of common standards allows SOA to be inter-operable between vendor technology stacks.

Why SOA is different

A few years ago, distributed object technology, in the guise of CORBA and COM+, was going to provide benefits of reuse. Prior to that, third and fourth generation languages such as C++ and Smalltalk (based on object technology) were to provide the same benefit. Even earlier, the same claims were made for structured programming. So why is SOA different?

Terminology

The use of terms such as services and processes allows business and IT to talk about items in the same way, improving communication, and reducing impedance mismatch between the two. The importance of this is greater than what it appears at first because it drives IT to build and structure its systems around the business rather than vice versa.

Interoperability

In the past, there have been competing platforms for the latest software development fad. This manifested itself as CORBA and COM+, Smalltalk and C++, Pascal and C. However, this time around, the standards are not based upon the physical implementation, but upon the service interfaces and wire protocols. In addition, these standards are generally text-based to avoid issues around conversion between binary forms. This allows services implemented in C# under Windows to inter-operate with Java or PL/SQL services running on Oracle SOA Suite under Windows, Linux, or Unix. The major players Oracle, Microsoft, IBM, SAP, and others have agreed on how to inter-operate together. This agreement has always been missing in the past.

WS basic profile

There is an old IT joke that standards are great, there are so many to choose from! Fortunately, the SOA vendors have recognized this and have collaborated to create a basic profile, or collections of standards that focus on interoperability. This is known as WS basic profile and details the key web service standards that all vendors should implement to allow for interoperability. SOA Suite supports this basic profile as well as additional standards.

Extension and evolution

SOA recognizes that there are existing assets in the IT landscape and does not force these to be replaced, preferring instead to encapsulate and later extend these resources. SOA may be viewed as a boundary technology that reverses many of the earlier development trends. Instead of specifying how systems are built at the lowest level, it focuses on how services are described and how they inter-operate in a standards-based world.

Reuse in place

A final major distinguishing feature for SOA is the concept of reuse in place. Most reuse technologies in the past have focused on reuse through libraries, at best sharing a common implementation on a single machine through the use of dynamic link libraries. SOA focuses not only on reuse of the code functionality, but also upon the reuse of existing machine resources to execute that code. When a service is reused, the same physical servers with their associated memory and CPU are shared across a larger client base. This is good from the perspective of providing a consistent location to enforce code changes, security constraints, and logging policies, but it does mean that the performance of existing users may be impacted if care is not taken in how services are reused.

Client responsibility in service contracts

As SOA is about reuse in place of existing machine resources as well as software resources, it is important that part of the service contract specifies the expected usage a client will make of a service. Imposing this constraint on the client is important for efficient sizing of the services being used by the client.

Service Component Architecture (SCA)

We have spoken a lot about service reuse and composing new services out of existing services, but we have yet to indicate how this may be done. The Service Component Architecture in SOA Suite is a standard that is used to define how services in a composite application are connected. It also defines how a service may interact with other services.

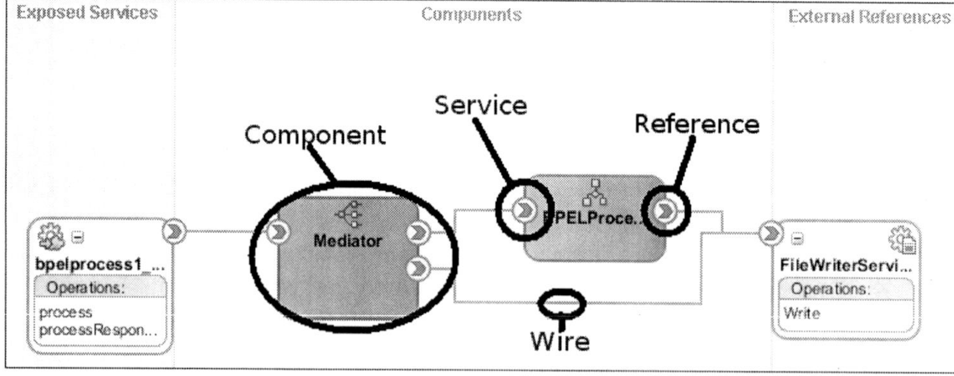

As can be seen in the preceding screenshot, an SCA composite consists of several different parts.

Component

A component represents a piece of business logic. It may be process logic, such as a BPEL process, routing logic, such as a mediator, or some other SOA Suite component. In the next section, we will discuss the components of the SOA Suite. SCA also supports writing custom components in Java or other languages, but we will not cover that in this book.

Service

A service represents the interface provided by a component or by the SCA Assembly itself. This is the interface to be used by clients of the assembly or component. A service that is available from outside the composite is referred to as an **External Service**.

Reference

A reference is a dependency on a service provided by another component, another SCA Assembly, or by some external entity such as a remote web service. References to services outside the composite are referred to as **External References**.

Wire

Services and references are joined together by wires. A wire indicates a dependency between components or between a component and an external entity.

> It is important to note that wires show dependencies and not flow of control. In the example, the **Mediator** component may call the **FileWriteService** before or after invoking BPEL, or it may not invoke it at all.

Composite.xml

An SCA Assembly is described in a file named `composite.xml`. The format of this file is defined by the SCA standard and consists of the elements identified in the preceding screenshot.

Properties

The components in the SCA may have properties associated with them that can be customized as part of the deployment of an SCA Assembly. These properties are also described in the `composite.xml`.

SOA Suite components

SOA Suite has a number of component parts, some of which may be licensed separately.

Services and adapters

The most basic unit of service-oriented architecture is the service. This may be provided directly by a web service-enabled piece of code or it may be exposed by encapsulating an existing resource.

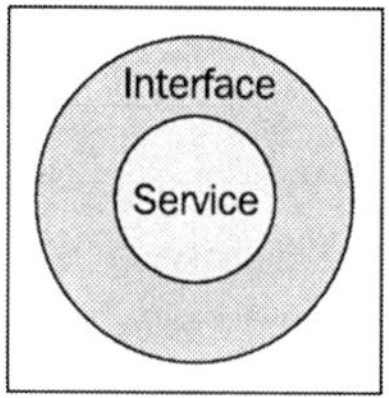

The only way to access a service is through its defined interface. This interface may actually be part of the service or it may be a wrapper that provides a standard-based service interface on top of a more implementation-specific interface. Accessing the service in a consistent fashion isolates the client of the service from any details of its physical implementation.

Services are defined by a specific interface, usually specified in a **Web Service Description Language (WSDL)** file. A WSDL file specifies the operations supported by the service. Each operation describes the expected format of the input message and if a message is returned it also describes the format of that message. Services are often surfaced through adapters that take an existing piece of functionality and "adapt" it to the SOA world, so that it can interact with other SOA Suite components. An example of an adapter is the file adapter that allows a file to be read or written to. The act of reading or writing the file is encapsulated into a service interface. This service interface can then be used to receive service requests by reading a file or to create service requests by writing a file.

Out of the box, the SOA Suite includes licenses for the following adapters:

- File adapter
- FTP adapter
- Database adapter
- JMS adapter
- MQ adapter
- AQ adapter
- Socket adapter
- BAM adapter

The database adapter and the file adapter are explored in more detail in *Chapter 3, Service-enabling Existing Systems*, while the BAM adapter is discussed in *Chapter 9, Building Real-time Dashboards*. There is also support for other non-SOAP transports and styles such as plain HTTP, REST, and Java.

Services are the most important part of service-oriented architecture, and in this book, we focus on how to define their interfaces and how to best assemble services together to create composite services with a value beyond the functionality of a single atomic service.

ESB – service abstraction layer

To avoid service location and format dependencies, it is desirable to access services through an **Enterprise Service Bus (ESB)**. This provides a layer of abstraction over the service and allows transformation of data between formats. The ESB is aware of the physical endpoint locations of services and acts to virtualize services.

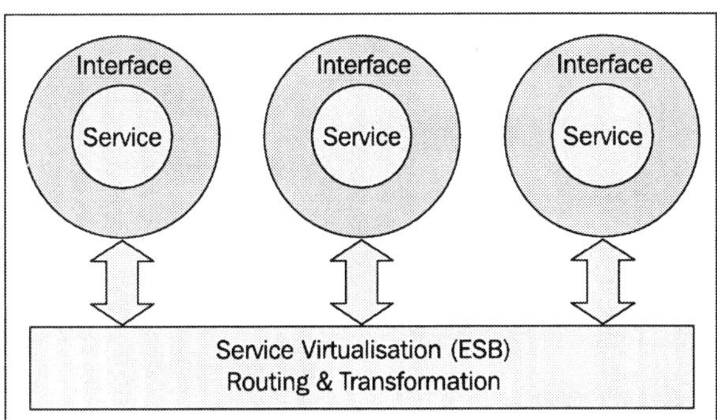

Services may be viewed as being plugged into the Service Bus.

An Enterprise Service Bus is optimized for routing and transforming service requests between components. By abstracting the physical location of a service, an ESB allows services to be moved to different locations without impacting the clients of those services. The ability of an ESB to transform data from one format to another also allows for changes in service contracts to be accommodated without recoding client services. The Service Bus may also be used to validate that messages conform to interface contracts and to enrich messages by adding additional information to them as part of the message transformation process.

Oracle Service Bus and Oracle Mediator

Note that the SOA Suite contains both the Oracle Service Bus (formerly AquaLogic Service Bus, now known as OSB) and the Oracle Mediator. OSB provides more powerful service abstraction capabilities that will be explored in *Chapter 4, Loosely-coupling Services*. Beyond simple transformation, it can also perform other functions such as throttling of target services. It is also easier to modify service endpoints in the runtime environment with OSB.

The stated direction by Oracle is for the Oracle Service Bus to be the preferred ESB for interactions outside the SOA Suite. Interactions within the SOA Suite may sometimes be better dealt with by the Oracle Mediator component in the SOA Suite, but we believe that for most cases, the Oracle Service Bus will provide a better solution and so that is what we have focused on within this book. However, in the current release, the Oracle Service Bus only executes on the Oracle WebLogic platform. Therefore, when running SOA Suite on non-Oracle platforms, there are two choices:

- Use only the Oracle Mediator
- Run Oracle Service Bus on a WebLogic Server while running the rest of SOA Suite on the non-Oracle platform

Later releases of the SOA Suite will support Oracle Service Bus on non-Oracle platforms such as WebSphere.

Service orchestration – the BPEL process manager

In order to build composite services, that is, services constructed from other services, we need a layer that can orchestrate, or tie together, multiple services into a single larger service. Simple service orchestrations can be done within the Oracle Service Bus, but more complex orchestrations require additional functionality. These service orchestrations may be thought of as processes, some of which are low-level processes and others are high-level business processes.

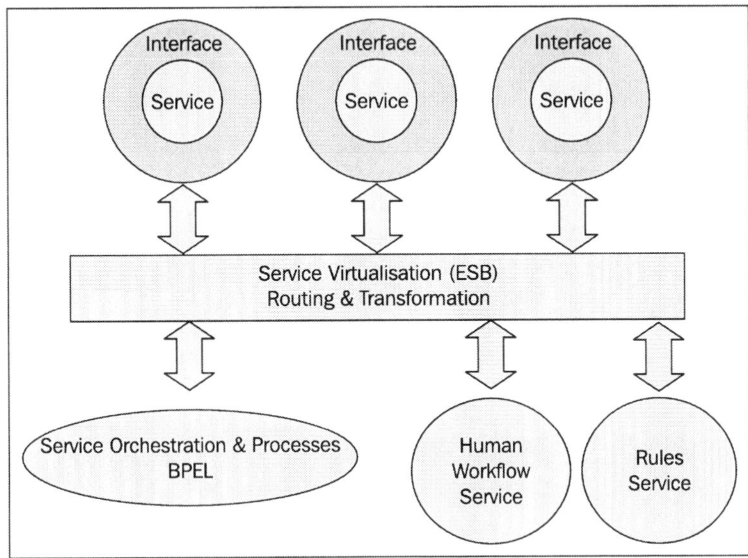

Business Process Execution Language (BPEL) is the standard way to describe processes in the SOA world, a task often referred to as service orchestration. The BPEL process manager in SOA Suite includes support for the BPEL 1.1 standard, with most constructs from BPEL 2.0 also being supported. BPEL allows multiple services to be linked to each other as part of a single managed process. The processes may be short running (taking seconds and minutes) or long running (taking hours and days).

The BPEL standard says nothing about how people interact with it, but BPEL process manager includes a Human Workflow component that provides support for human interaction with processes.

The BPEL process manager may also be purchased as a standalone component, in which case, it ships with the Human Workflow support and the same adapters, as included in the SOA Suite.

We explore the BPEL process manager in more detail in *Chapter 5, Using BPEL to Build Composite Services and Business Processes* and *Chapter 14, Error Handling*. Human workflow is examined in *Chapter 6, Adding in Human Workflow* and *Chapter 17, Workflow Patterns*.

Oracle also packages the BPEL process manager with the **Oracle Business Process Management (BPM)** Suite. This package includes the former AquaLogic BPM product (acquired when BEA bought Fuego), now known as Oracle BPM. Oracle positions BPEL as a system-centric process engine with support for human workflow, while BPM is positioned as human-centric process engine with support for system interaction.

Rules

Business decision-making may be viewed as a service within SOA. A rules engine is the physical implementation of this service.

SOA Suite includes a powerful rules engine that allows key business decision logic to be abstracted out of individual services and managed in a single repository.

In *Chapter 7, Using Business Rules to Define Decision Points* and in *Chapter 18, Using Business Rules to Implement Services*, we investigate how to use the rules engine.

Security and monitoring

One of the interesting features of SOA is the way in which aspects of a service are themselves a service. Nowhere is this better exemplified than with security. Security is a characteristic of services, yet to implement it effectively requires a centralized policy store coupled with distributed policy enforcement at the service boundaries. The central policy store can be viewed as a service that the infrastructure uses to enforce service security policy.

Enterprise Manager serves as a policy manager for security, providing a centralized service for policy enforcement points to obtain their policies. Policy enforcement points, termed interceptors in SOA Suite 11*g*, are responsible for applying security policy, ensuring that only requests that comply with the policy are accepted.

Security policy may also be applied through the Service Bus. Although policy management is done in the Service Bus rather than in the Enterprise Manager, the direction is for Oracle to have a common policy management in a future release.

Applying security policies is covered in *Chapter 21, Defining Security and Management Policies.*

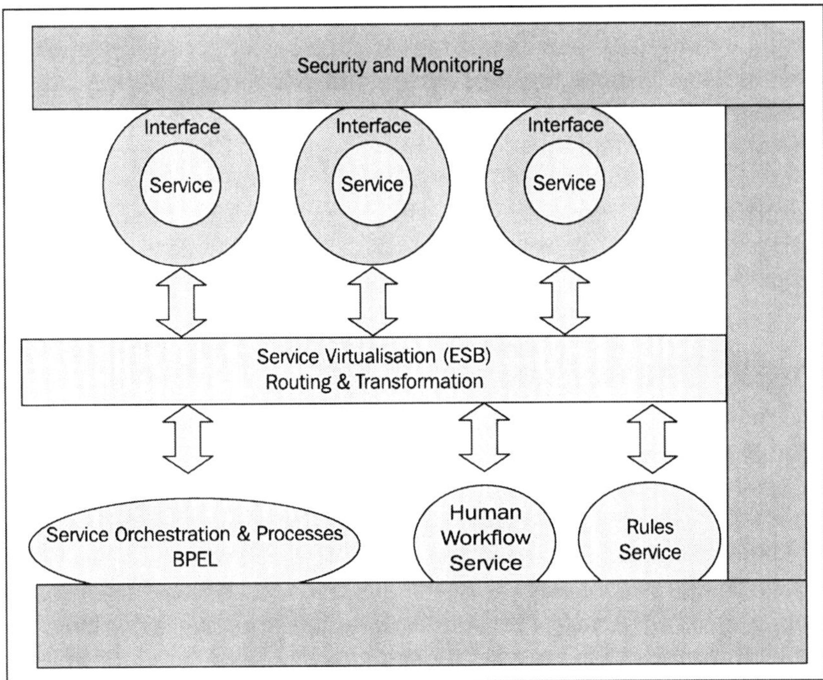

Active monitoring – BAM

It is important in SOA to track what is happening in real time. Some business processes require such real-time monitoring. Users such as financial traders, risk assessors, and security services may need instant notification of business events that have occurred.

Business Activity Monitoring is part of the SOA Suite and provides a real-time view of processes and services data to end users. BAM is covered in *Chapter 9, Building Real-time Dashboards.*

Business to Business – B2B

Although we can use adapters to talk to remote systems, we often need additional features to support external services, either as clients or providers. For example, we may need to verify that there is contract in place before accepting or sending messages to a partner. Management of agreements or contracts is a key additional piece of functionality that is provided by Oracle B2B. B2B can be thought of as a special kind of adapter that, in addition to support for B2B protocols such as EDIFACT/ANSI X12 or RosettaNet, also supports agreement management. Agreement management allows control over the partners and interfaces used at any given point in time. We will not cover B2B in this book as the B2B space is a little at the edge of most SOA deployments.

Complex Event Processing – CEP

As our services execute, we will often generate events. These events can be monitored and processed using the complex event processor. The difference between event and message processing is that messages generally require some action on their own with little or minimal additional context. Events, on the other hand, often require us to monitor several of them to spot and respond to trends. For example, we may treat a stock sale as a message when we need to record it and reconcile it with the accounting system. We may also want to treat the stock sale as an event in which we wish to monitor the overall market movements in a single stock or in related stocks to decide whether we should buy or sell. The complex event processor allows us to do time-based and series-based analysis of data. We will not talk about CEP in this book as it is a complex part of the SOA Suite that requires a complementary but different approach to the other SOA components.

Event delivery network

Even the loose-coupling provided by a Service Bus is not always enough. We often wish to just publish events and let any interested parties be notified of the event. A new feature of SOA Suite 11*g* is the event delivery network, which allows events to be published without the publisher being aware of the target or targets. Subscribers can request to be notified of particular events, filtering them based on event domain, event type, and event content. We cover the event delivery network in *Chapter 8, Using Business Events*.

SOA Suite architecture

We will now examine how Oracle SOA Suite provides the services identified previously.

Top level

The SOA Suite is built on top of a **Java Enterprise Edition (Java EE)** infrastructure. Although SOA Suite is certified with several different Java EE servers, including IBM WebSphere, it will most commonly be used with the Oracle WebLogic server. The **Oracle WebLogic Server (WLS)** will probably always be the first available Java EE platform for SOA Suite and is the only platform that will be provided bundled with the SOA Suite to simplify installation. For the rest of this book, we will assume that you are running SOA Suite on the Oracle WebLogic server. If there are any significant differences when running on non-Oracle application servers, we will highlight them in the text.

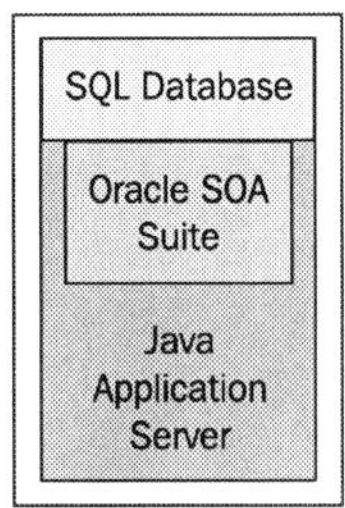

In addition to a Java EE application server, the SOA Suite also requires a database. The SOA Suite is designed to run against any SQL database, but certification for non-Oracle databases has been slow in coming. The database is used to maintain configuration information and also records of runtime interactions. Oracle Database XE can be used with the SOA Suite, but it is not recommended for production deployments as it is not a supported configuration.

Component view

In a previous section, we examined the individual components of the SOA Suite and here we show them in context with the Java EE container and the database. Note that CEP does not run in an application server and OSB runs in a separate container to the other SOA Suite components.

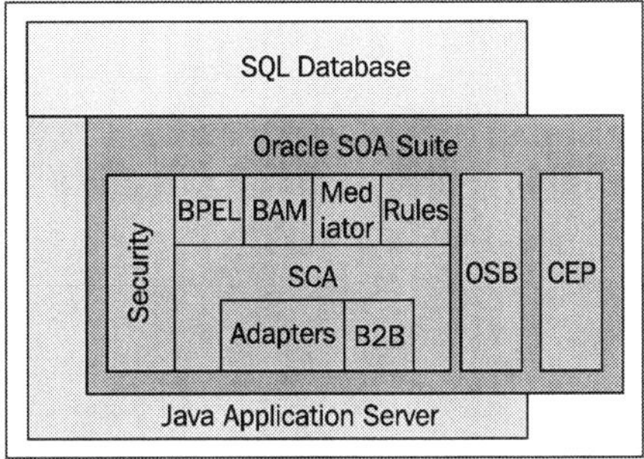

All the services are executed within the context of the Java EE container, even though they may use that container in different ways. BPEL listens for events and updates processes based upon those events. Adapters typically make use of the Java EE containers connector architecture (JCA) to provide connectivity and notifications. Policy interceptors act as filters. Note that the Oracle Service Bus (OSB) is only available when the application server is a WebLogic server.

Implementation view

Oracle has put a lot of effort into making SOA Suite consistent in its use of underlying services. A number of lower-level services are reused consistently across components.

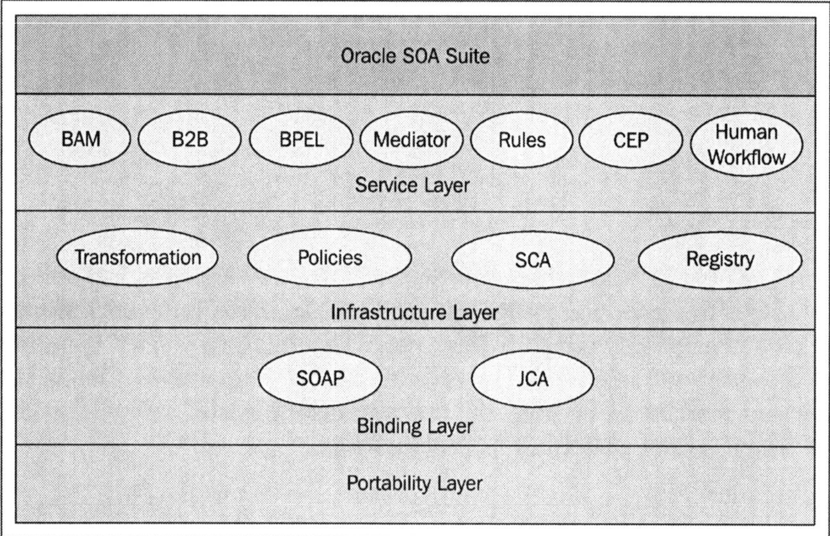

A **Portability Layer** provides an interface between the SOA Suite and the specifics of the JEE platform that hosts it.

At the lowest level, connectivity services, such as SCA, JCA adapters, JMS, and Web Service Framework, are shared by higher-level components.

A **Service Layer** exposes higher-level functions. The BPEL process manager is implemented by a combination of a BPEL engine and access to the Human Workflow engine. **Rules** is another shared service that is available to BPEL or other components.

A recursive example

The SOA Suite architecture is a good example of service-oriented design principles being applied. Common services have been identified and extracted to be shared across many components. The high-level services such as BPEL and ESB share some common services such as transformation and adapter services running on a standard Java EE container.

JDeveloper

Everything we have spoken of so far has been related to the executable or runtime environment. Specialist tools are required to take advantage of this environment. It is possible to manually craft the assemblies and descriptors required to build a SOA Suite application, but it is not a practical proposition. Fortunately, Oracle provides JDeveloper free of charge to allow developers to build SOA Suite applications.

JDeveloper is actually a separate tool, but it has been developed in conjunction with SOA Suite so that virtually all facilities of SOA Suite are accessible through JDeveloper. One exception to this is the Oracle Service Bus, which in the current release does not have support in JDeveloper but instead has a different tool named WebLogic Workspace Studio. Although JDeveloper started life as a Java development tool, many users now never touch the Java side of JDeveloper, doing all their work in the SOA Suite components.

JDeveloper may be characterized as a model-based, wizard-driven development environment. Re-entrant wizards are used to guide the construction of many artifacts of the SOA Suite, including adapters and transformation.

JDeveloper has a consistent view that the code is also the model, so that graphical views are always in synchronization with the underlying code. It is possible to exercise some functionality of SOA Suite using the Eclipse platform, but to get full value out of the SOA Suite it is really necessary to use JDeveloper. The Eclipse platform does, however, provide the basis for the Service Bus designer, the Workspace Studio. There are some aspects of development that may be supported in both tools, but are easier in one than the other.

Other components

We have now touched on all the major components of the SOA Suite. There are, however, a few items that are either of a more limited interest or are outside the SOA Suite, but closely related to it.

Service repository and registry

Oracle has a service repository and registry product that is integrated with the SOA Suite but separate from it. The repository acts as a central repository for all SOA artifacts and can be used to support both developers and deployers in tracking dependencies between components both deployed and in development. The repository can publish SOA artifacts such as service definitions and locations to the service registry. The Oracle Service registry may be used to categorize and index services created. Users may then browse the registry to locate services. The service registry may also be used as a runtime location service for service endpoints.

BPA Suite

The Oracle BPA Suite is targeted at business process analysts who want a powerful repository-based tool to model their business processes. The BPA Suite is not an easy product to learn, and like all modeling tools, there is a price to pay for the descriptive power available. The fact of interest to SOA Suite developers is the ability for the BPA Suite and SOA Suite to exchange process models. Processes created in the BPA Suite may be exported to the SOA Suite for concrete implementation. Simulation of processes in the BPA Suite may be used as a useful guide for process improvement.

Links between the BPA Suite and the SOA Suite are growing stronger over time, and this provides a valuable bridge between business analysts and IT architects.

The BPM Suite

The Business Process Management Suite is focused on modeling and execution of business processes. As mentioned, it includes BPEL process manager to provide strong system-centric support for business processes, but the primary focus of the Suite is on modeling and executing processes in the BPM designer and BPM server. BPM server and BPEL process manager are converging on a single shared service implementation.

Portals and WebCenter

The SOA Suite has no real end-user interface outside the human workflow service. Frontends may be built using JDeveloper directly or they may be crafted as part of Oracle Portal, Oracle WebCenter, or another Portal or frontend builder. A number of portlets are provided to expose views of SOA Suite to end users through the portal. These are principally related to human workflow, but also include some views onto the BPEL process status. Portals can also take advantage of WSDL interfaces to provide a user interface onto services exposed by the SOA Suite.

Enterprise manager SOA management pack

Oracle's preferred management framework is Oracle Enterprise Manager. This is provided as a base set of functionality with a large number of management packs, which provide additional functionality. The SOA management pack extends Enterprise Manager to provide monitoring and management of artifacts within the SOA Suite.

Summary

As we have seen, there are a lot of components to the SOA Suite, and even though Oracle has done a lot to provide consistent usage patterns, there is still a lot to learn about each component. The rest of this book takes a solution-oriented approach to the SOA Suite rather than a component approach. We will examine the individual components in the context of the role they serve and how they are used to enable service-oriented architecture.

2

Writing your First Composite

In this chapter, we are going to provide a hands-on introduction to the core components of the Oracle SOA Suite, namely, the **Oracle BPEL Process Manager** (or **BPEL PM**), **Mediator**, and the **Oracle Service Bus** (or **OSB**). We will do this by implementing an **Echo** service, which is a trivial service that takes a single string as input and then returns the same string as its output.

We will first use JDeveloper to implement and deploy this as a BPEL process in an SCA Assembly. While doing this, we will take the opportunity to give you a high-level tour of JDeveloper in order to familiarize you with its overall layout.

Once we have successfully deployed our first BPEL process, we will use the **Enterprise Manager (EM)** console to execute a test instance of our process and examine its audit trail.

Next, we will introduce the Mediator component and use JDeveloper to create a Mediator component that fronts our BPEL process. We will deploy this as a new version of our SCA Assembly.

Finally we will introduce the Service Bus, and look at how we can use its web-based console to build and deploy a proxy service on top of our SCA Assembly. Once deployed, we will use the tooling provided by the Service Bus console to test our end-to-end service.

Installing SOA Suite

Before creating and running your first service, you will need to download and install the SOA Suite. Oracle SOA Suite 11*g* deploys on WebLogic 10*g* R3.

To download the installation guide, go to the support page of Packt Publishing (`www.packtpub.com/support`). From here, follow the instructions to download a zip file containing the code for the book. Included in the zip will be a PDF document named `SoaSuiteInstallationForWeblogic11g.pdf`.

This document details the quickest and easiest way to get the SOA Suite up and running and covers the following:

- Where to download the SOA Suite and any other required components
- How to install and configure the SOA Suite
- How to install and run the oBay application, as well as the other code samples that come with this book

Writing your first BPEL process

Ensure that the Oracle SOA Suite has started (as described in the previously mentioned installation guide) and start JDeveloper. When you start JDeveloper for the first time, it will prompt you for a developer role, as shown in the following screenshot:

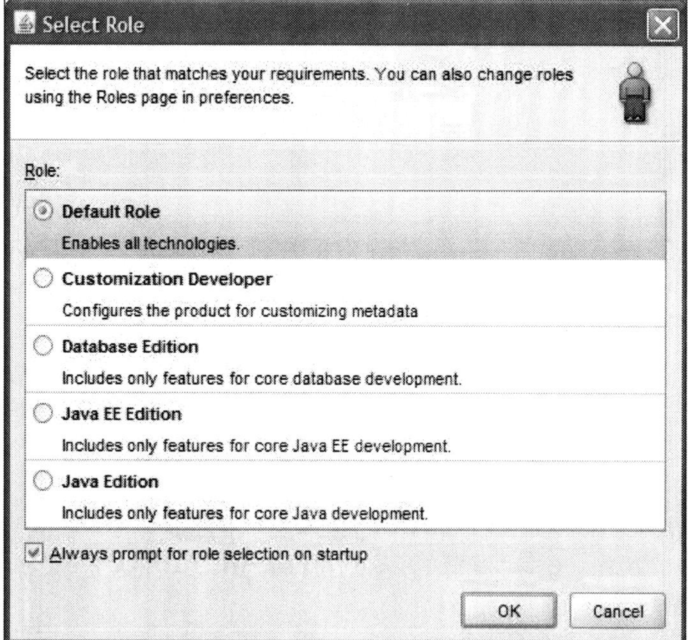

JDeveloper has a number of different developer roles that limit the technology choices available to the developer. Choose the **Default Role** to get access to all JDeveloper functionality. This is needed to access the SOA Suite functionality.

After selecting the role, we are offered a **Tip of the Day** to tell us about a feature of JDeveloper. After dismissing the **Tip of the Day**, we are presented with a blank JDeveloper workspace.

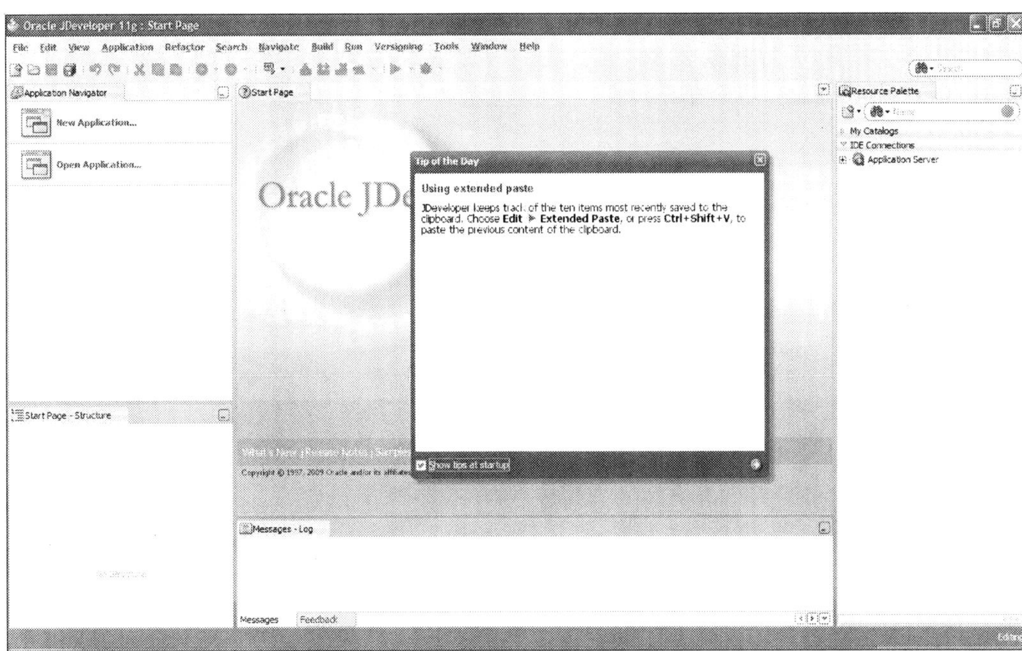

The top-left-hand window is the **Application Navigator**, which lists all the applications that we are working on (it is currently empty as we have not yet defined any). Within JDeveloper, an application is a grouping of one or more related projects. A **Project** is a collection of related components that make up a deployable resource (for example, an SCA Assembly, Java application, web service, and so on).

Within the context of the SOA Suite, each SCA Assembly is defined within its own project, with an application being a collection of related SCA Assemblies.

On the opposite side of the screen to the **Application Navigator** tab is the **Resource Palette,** which contains the **My Catalogs** tab to hold resources for use in composites and the **IDE Connections** tab. If we click on this it will list the types of connections we can define to JDeveloper. A connection allows us to define and manage links to external resources such as databases, application servers, and rules engines.

Once defined, we can expand a connection to inspect the content of an external resource, which can then be used to create or edit components that utilize the resource. For example, you can use a database connection to create and configure a database adapter to expose a database table as a web service.

Connections also allow us to deploy projects from JDeveloper to an external resource. If you haven't done so already, then you will need to define a connection to the application server (as described in the installation guide) because we will need this to deploy our SCA Assemblies from within JDeveloper.

The connection to the application server is used to connect to the management interfaces in the target container. We can use it to browse deployed applications, change the status of deployed composites, or as we will do here, deploy new composites to our container.

The main window within JDeveloper is used to edit the artifact that we are currently working on (for example, BPEL Process, XSLT Transformation, Java code, and so on). The top of this window contains a tab for each resource we have open, allowing you to quickly switch between them.

At the moment, the only artifact that we have opened is the **Start Page**, which provides links to various documents on JDeveloper.

The bottom-left-hand corner contains the **Structure** window. The content of this depends on the resource we are currently working on.

Creating an application

Within JDeveloper, an application is the main container for our work. It consists of a directory where all our application projects will be created.

So, before we can create our `Echo` SCA Assembly, we must create the application to which it will belong. Within the **Applications Navigator** tab in JDeveloper, click on the **New Application...** item.

This will launch the **Create SOA Application** dialog, as shown in the preceding screenshot.

Give the application an appropriate name like **SoaSuiteBook11gChapter2**.

We can specify the top-level directory in which we want to create our applications. By default, JDeveloper will set it to the following:

```
<JDEVELOPER_HOME>\ mywork\<Application Name>
```

Normally, we would specify a directory that's not under `JDEVELOPER_HOME`, as this makes it simpler to upgrade to future releases of JDeveloper.

In addition, you can specify an **Application Template**. For SOA projects, select **SOA Application** template, and click on the **Next** button.

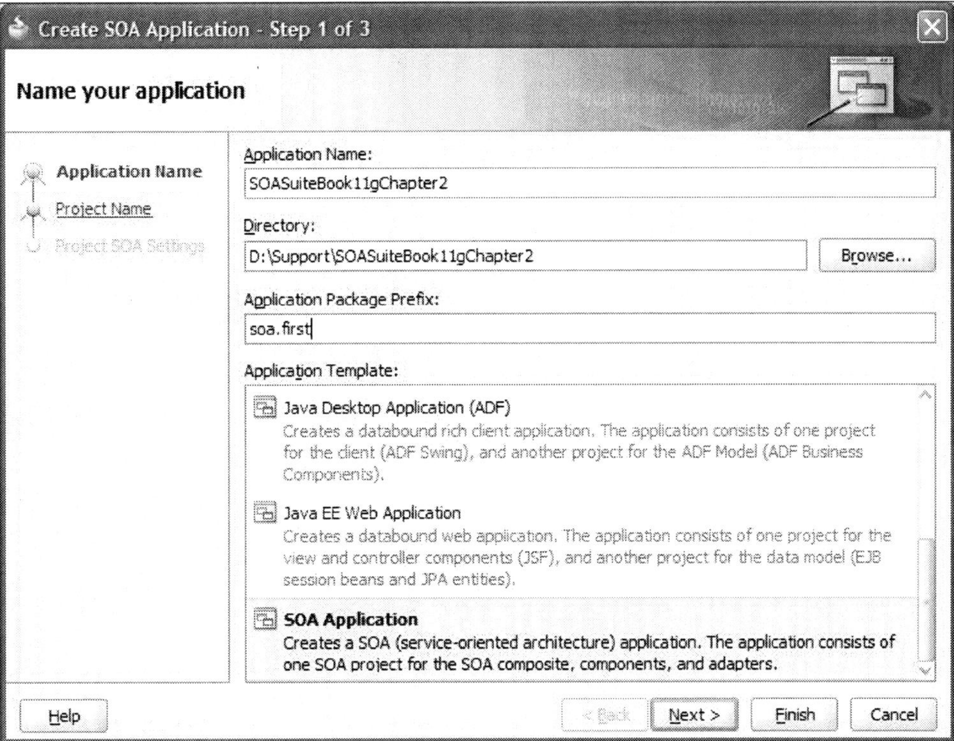

Next, JDeveloper will prompt us for the details of a new SOA project.

Creating an SOA project

We provide a name for our project such as **EchoComposite** and select the technologies we desire to be available in the project. In this case, we leave the default **SOA** technology selected. The project will be created in a directory that, by default, has the same name as the project and is located under the application directory. These settings can be changed.

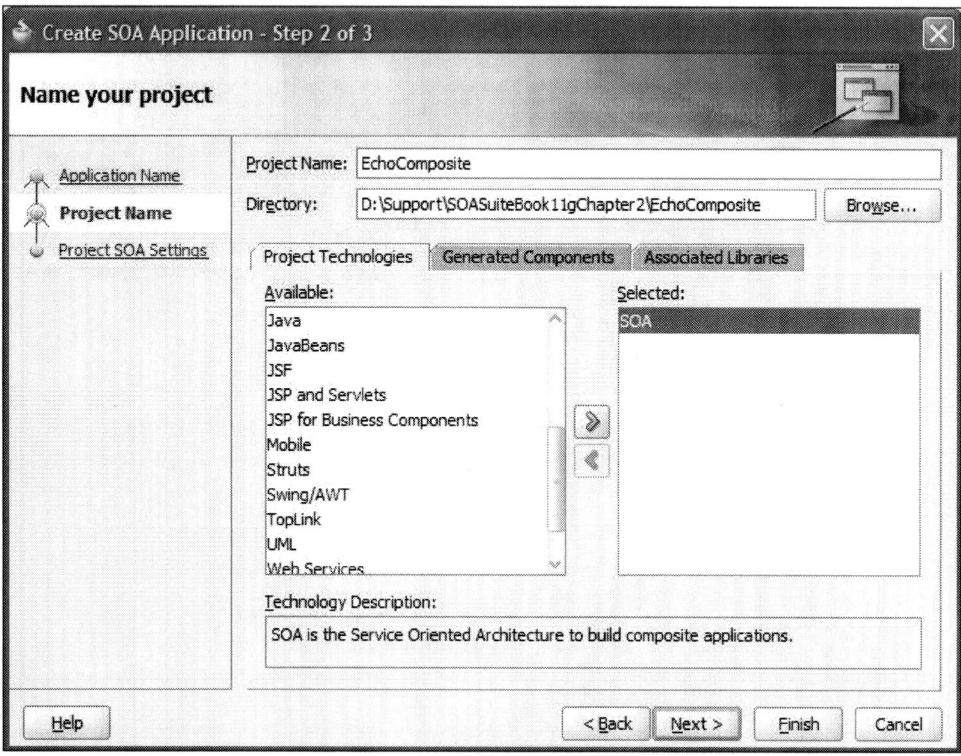

Clicking on **Next** will give us the opportunity to configure our new composite by selecting some initial components. Select **Composite With BPEL** to create a new Assembly with a BPEL process, as shown in the next screenshot:

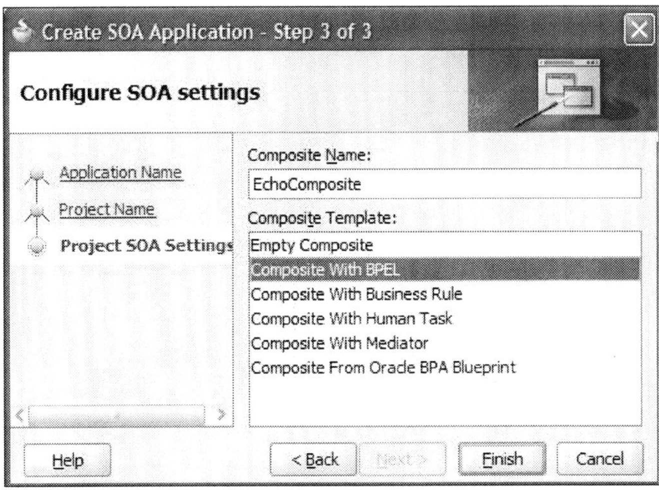

SOA project composite templates

We have a number of different templates available to us. Apart from the **Empty Composite** template, they all populate the composite with an initial component. This may be a BPEL component, a Business Rule component, a Human Task, or a Mediator component. The **Composite From Oracle BPA Blueprint** is used to import a process from the Oracle BPA Suite and generate it as a BPEL component within the composite.

It is possible to create an **Empty Composite** and then add the components directly to the composite, so if you choose the wrong template and start working with it, you can always enhance it by adding more components. Even the **Empty Composite** is not really empty, as it includes all the initial files you need to start building your own composite.

Creating a BPEL process

Clicking **Finish** will launch the **Create BPEL Process** wizard, as shown in the following screenshot:

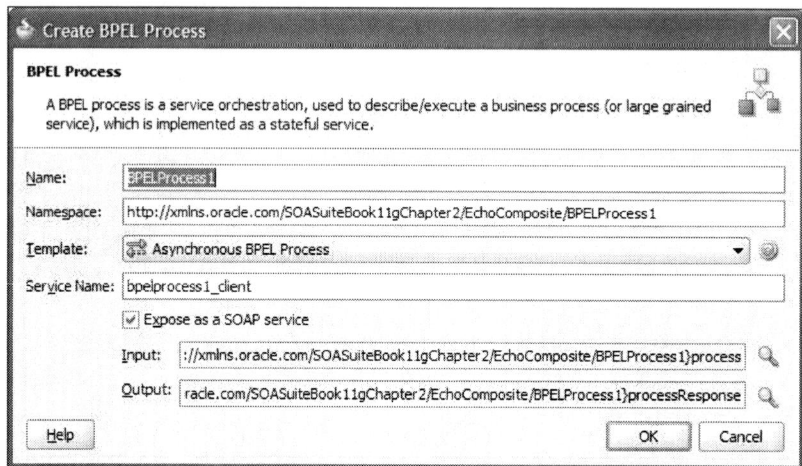

Replace the process with a sensible Name like `EchoProcess` and select a template of the type **Synchronous BPEL Process** and click **OK**. JDeveloper will create a skeleton BPEL Process and a corresponding WSDL that describes the web service implemented by our process. This process will be wrapped in an SCA Assembly.

BPEL process templates cover the different ways in which a client may interact with the process. A **Define Service Later template** is just the process definition and will be used when we want to have complete control over the types of interfaces the process exposes, we can think of this as an empty BPEL process template. An **Asynchronous BPEL Process** template is used when we send a one-way message to a process, and then later on we send a one-way message from the process to the caller. This type of interaction is good for processes that run for a long time.

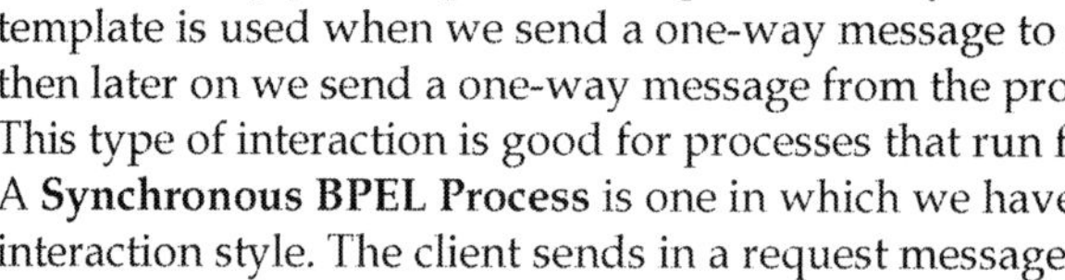

A **Synchronous BPEL Process** is one in which we have a request/reply interaction style. The client sends in a request message and then blocks waiting for the process to provide a reply. This type of interaction is good for processes that need to return an immediate result. A **One Way BPEL Process** simply receives a one-way input message but no reply is expected. This is useful when we initiate some interaction that will initiate a number of other activities. We may also create a BPEL process that implements a specific interface defined in WSDL by using the **Base on a WSDL** template. Finally, we may have a BPEL process that is activated when a specific event is generated by the Event Delivery Network (see *Chapter 8, Using Business Events*) using the **Subscribe to Events** template.

If we look at the process that JDeveloper has created (as shown in the following screenshot), we can see that in the center is the process itself, which contains the activities to be carried out. At the moment, it just contains an initial activity for receiving a request and a corresponding activity for sending a response.

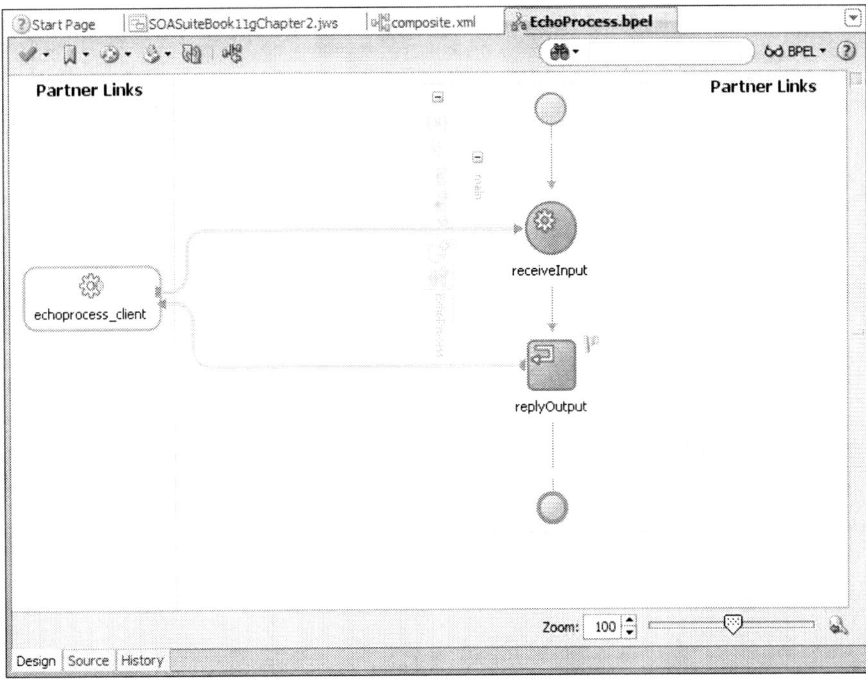

Either side of the process we have a swim lane containing **Partner Links** that represent either the caller of our process, as is the case with the **echoprocess_client** partner links, or services that our BPEL process calls out to. At the moment this is empty as we haven't defined any external references that we use within our BPEL process. Notice also that we don't currently have any content between receiving the call and replying; our process is empty and does nothing.

The **Component Palette** window (to the right of our process window in the preceding screenshot) lists all the **BPEL Activities and Components** that we can use within our process. To use any of these, we have to simply drag-and-drop them onto the appropriate place within our process.

If you click on the **BPEL Services** drop-down, you also have the option of selecting services which we use whenever we need to call out to an external system.

Getting back to our skeleton process, we can see that it consists of two activities; **receiveInput** and **replyOutput**. In addition it has two variables, `inputVariable` and `outputVariable`, which were created as part of our skeleton process.

The first activity is used to receive the initial request from the client invoking our BPEL process; when this request is received it will populate the variable `inputVariable` with the content of the request.

The last activity is used to send a response back to the client, and the content of this response will contain the content of `outputVariable`.

For the purpose of our simple `EchoProcess` we just need to copy the content of the input variable to the output variable.

Assigning values to variables

In BPEL, the `<assign>` activity is used to update the values of variables with new data. The `<assign>` activity typically consists of one or more copy operations. Each copy consists of a target variable, that is, the variable that you wish to assign a value to and a source, which can either be another variable or an XPath expression.

To insert an **Assign** activity, drag one from the **Component Palette** on to our BPEL process at the point just after the **receiveInput** activity, as shown in the following screenshot:

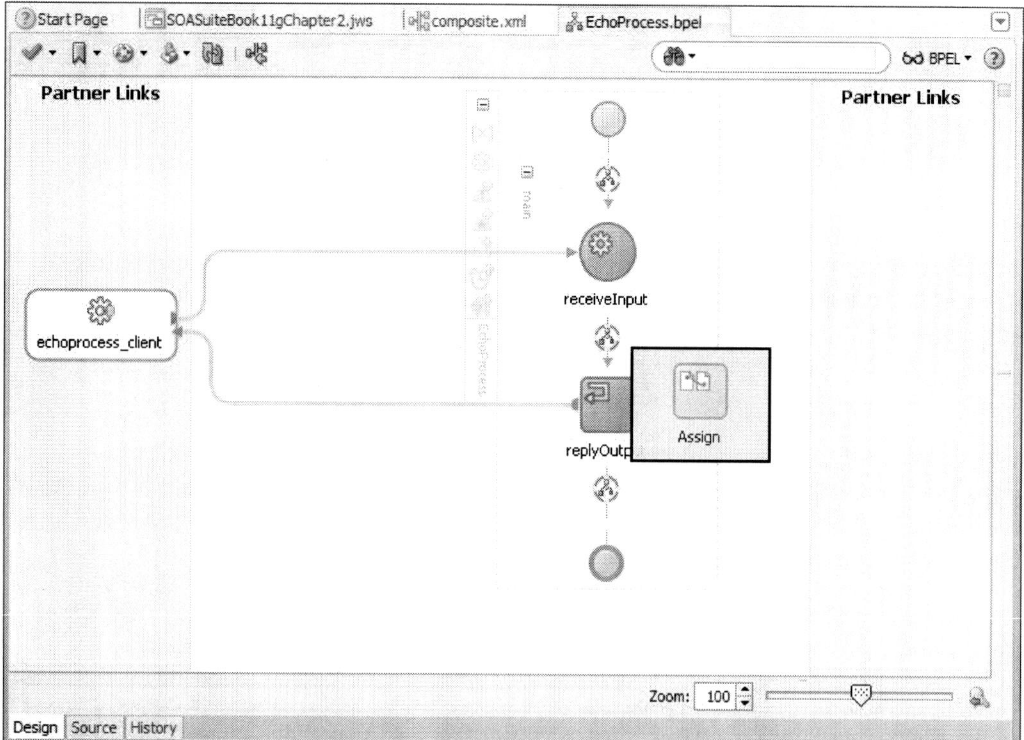

To configure the **Assign** activity, double-click on it to open up its configuration window. Click on the green cross to access a menu and select **Copy Operation...**, as shown in the next screenshot:

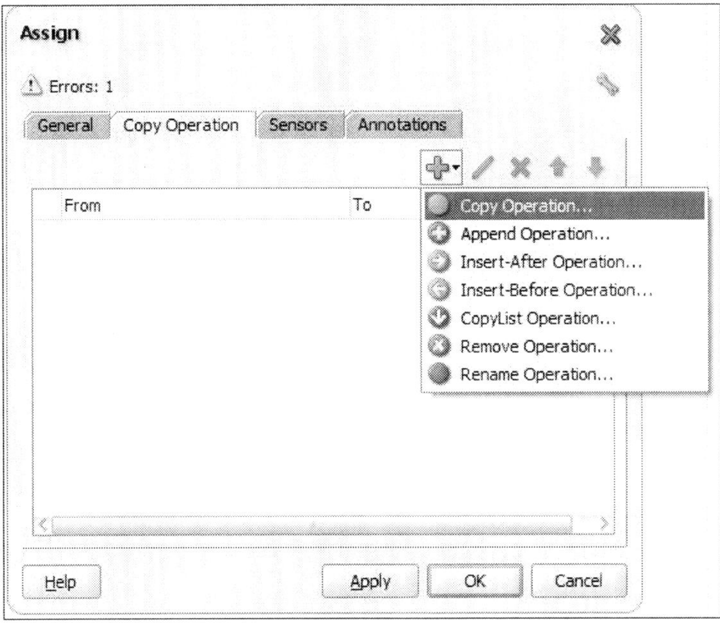

This will present us with the **Create Copy Operation** window, as shown in the following screenshot:

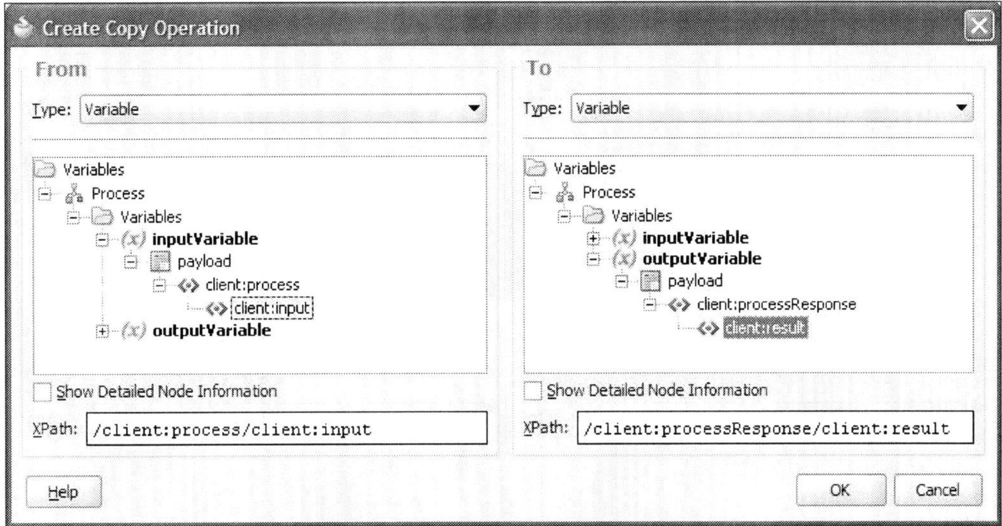

On the left-hand side, we specify the **From** variable, that is, where we want to copy from. For our process, we want to copy the content of our input variable to our output variable. So expand **inputVariable** and select **/client:process/client:input**, as shown in the preceding screenshot.

On the right-hand side, we specify the **To** variable, that is, where we want to copy to. So expand **outputVariable** and select **/client:processResponse/client:result**.

Once you've done this, click **OK** and then **OK** again to close the **Assign** window.

Deploying the process

This completes our process, so click on the **Save All** icon (the fourth icon along, in the top-left-hand corner of JDeveloper) to save our work.

As a BPEL project is made up of multiple files, we typically use **Save All** to ensure that all modifications are updated at the same time.

Our process is now ready to be deployed. Before doing this, make sure the SOA Suite is running and that within JDeveloper we have defined an **Application Server** connection (as described in the installation guide).

To deploy the process, right-click on our **EchoComposite** project and then select **Deploy | EchoComposite | to MyApplicationServerConnection**.

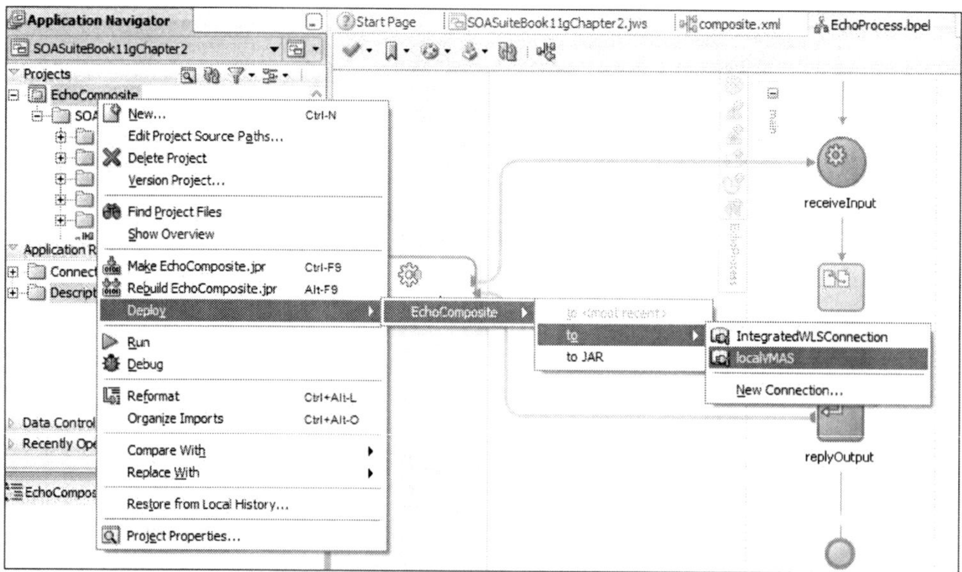

This will bring up the **SOA Deployment Configuration Dialog**. This dialog allows us to specify the target servers onto which we wish to deploy the composite. We may also specify a **Revision ID** for the composite to differentiate it from other deployed versions of the composite. If a revision with the same ID already exists, then it may be replaced by specifying the **Overwrite any existing composites with the same revision ID** option.

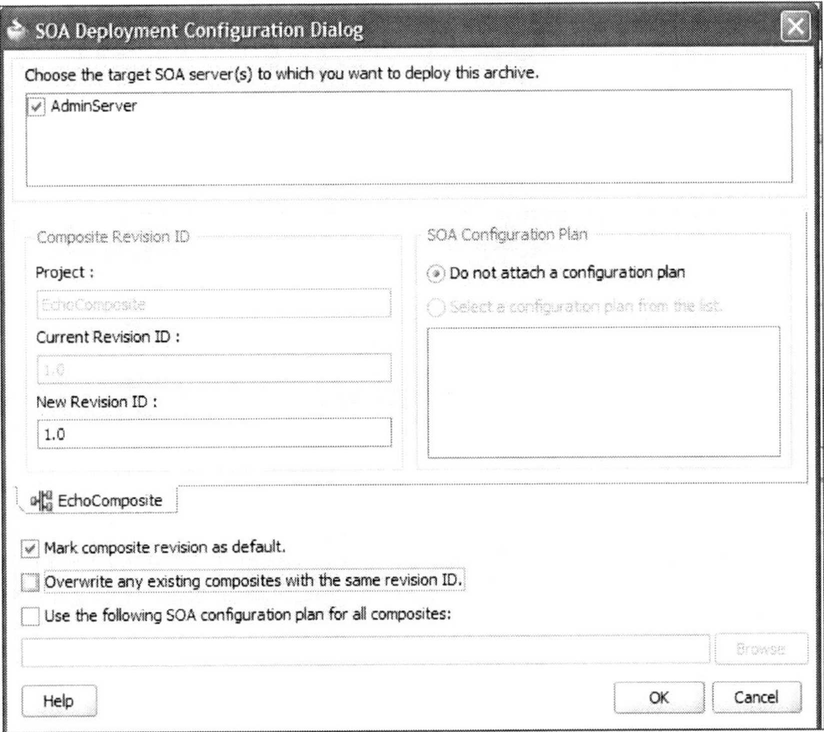

Clicking **OK** will begin the build and deployment of the composite. JDeveloper will open up a window below our process containing five tabs: **Messages**, **Feedback**, **BPEL**, **Deployment**, and **SOA**, to which it outputs the status of the deployment process.

During the build, the SOA tab will indicate if the build was successful, and assuming it was, then an **Authorization Request** window will pop up requesting credentials for the application server.

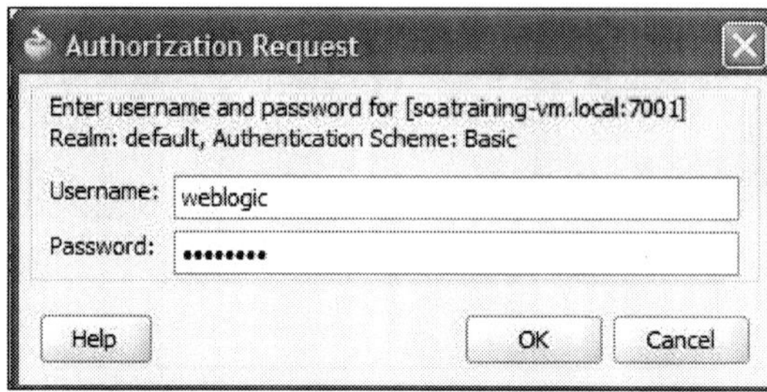

On completion of the build process, the **Deployment** tab should state **Successfully deployed archive** …., as shown in the following screenshot:

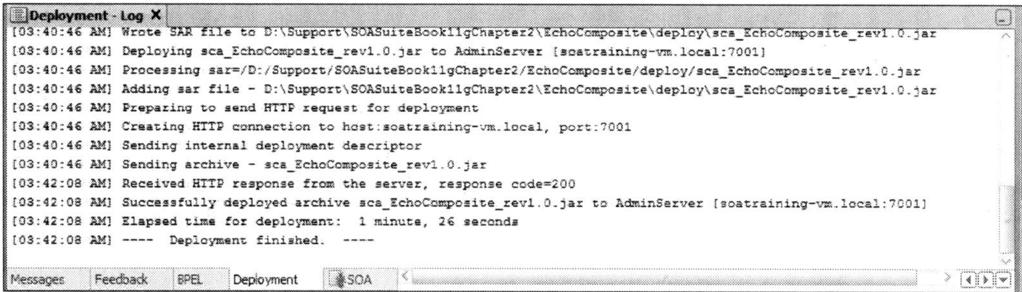

If you don't get this message, then check the log windows for details of the error and fix it accordingly.

Testing the BPEL process

Now that our process has been deployed, the next step is to run it. A simple way to do this is to initiate a test instance using the Enterprise Manager (EM) console, which is the web-based management console for SOA Suite.

To access the EM console, open up a browser and enter the following URL:

```
http://<hostname>:<port>/em
```

This will bring up the login screen for the EM console. Log in as **weblogic**. This will take us to the EM console dashboard, as shown in the following screenshot:

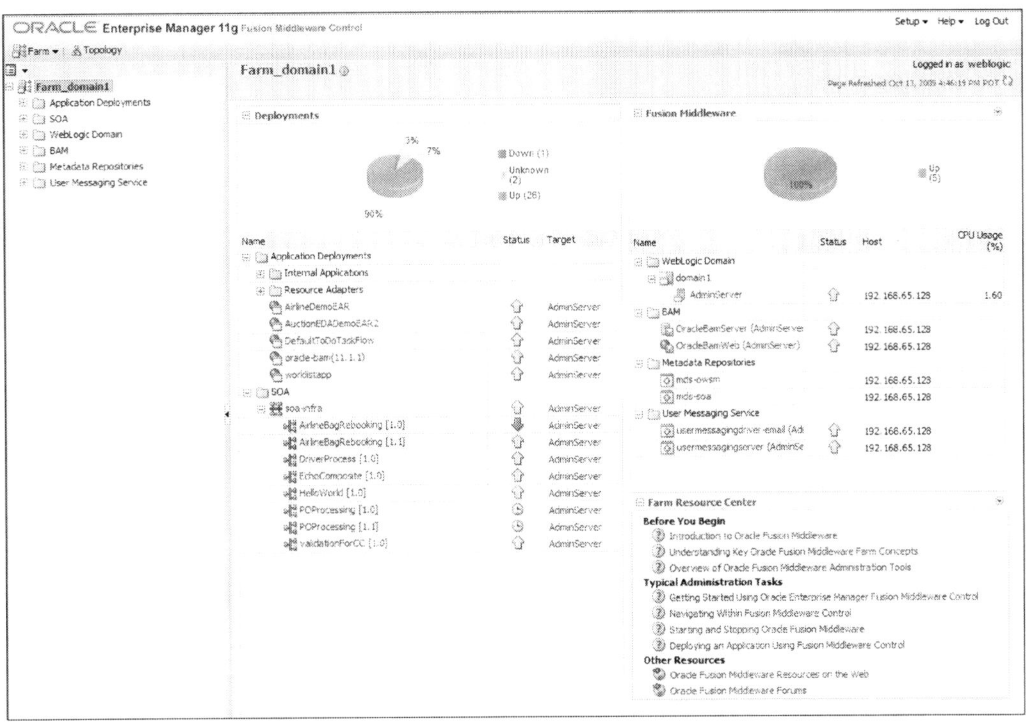

The **Dashboard** provides us with a summary report on the **Fusion Middleware** domain. On the left-hand side we have a list of management areas and on the right we have summaries of application deployments, including our **EchoComposite** under the **SOA** tab.

From here, click on the composite name, that is, **EchoComposite**. This will take us to the **Dashboard** screen for our composite. From here we can see the number of completed and currently executing composite instances.

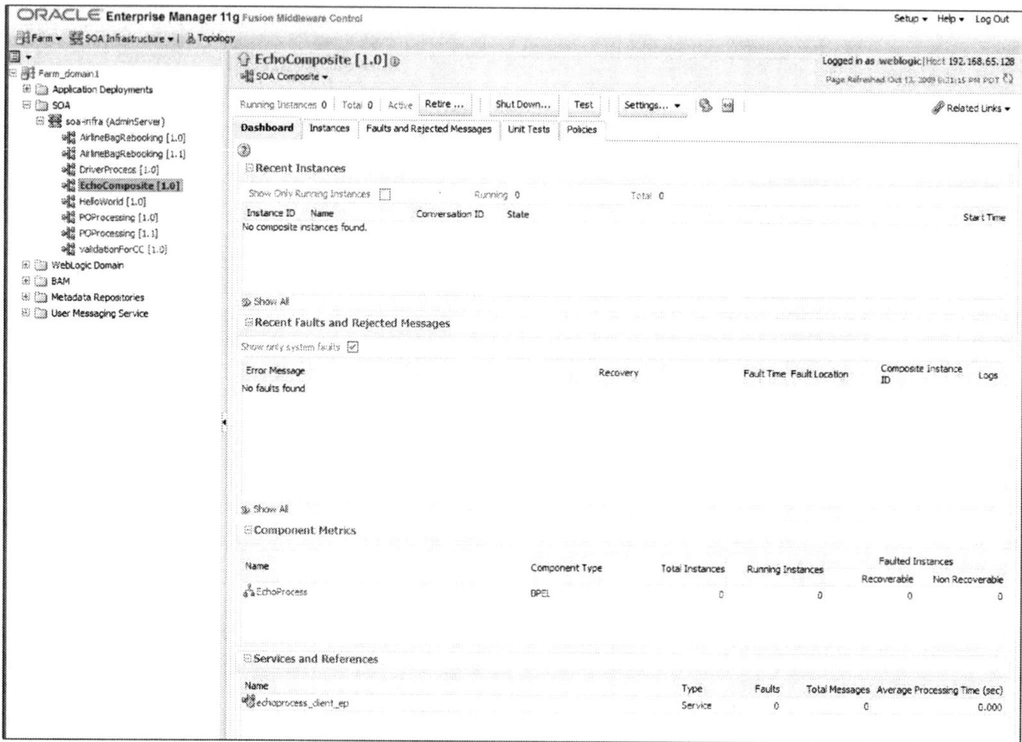

At the top of the **Dashboard** there is a **Test** button that allows us to execute a composite test. Pressing this button brings up the **Test Web Service** page, as shown in the following screenshot:

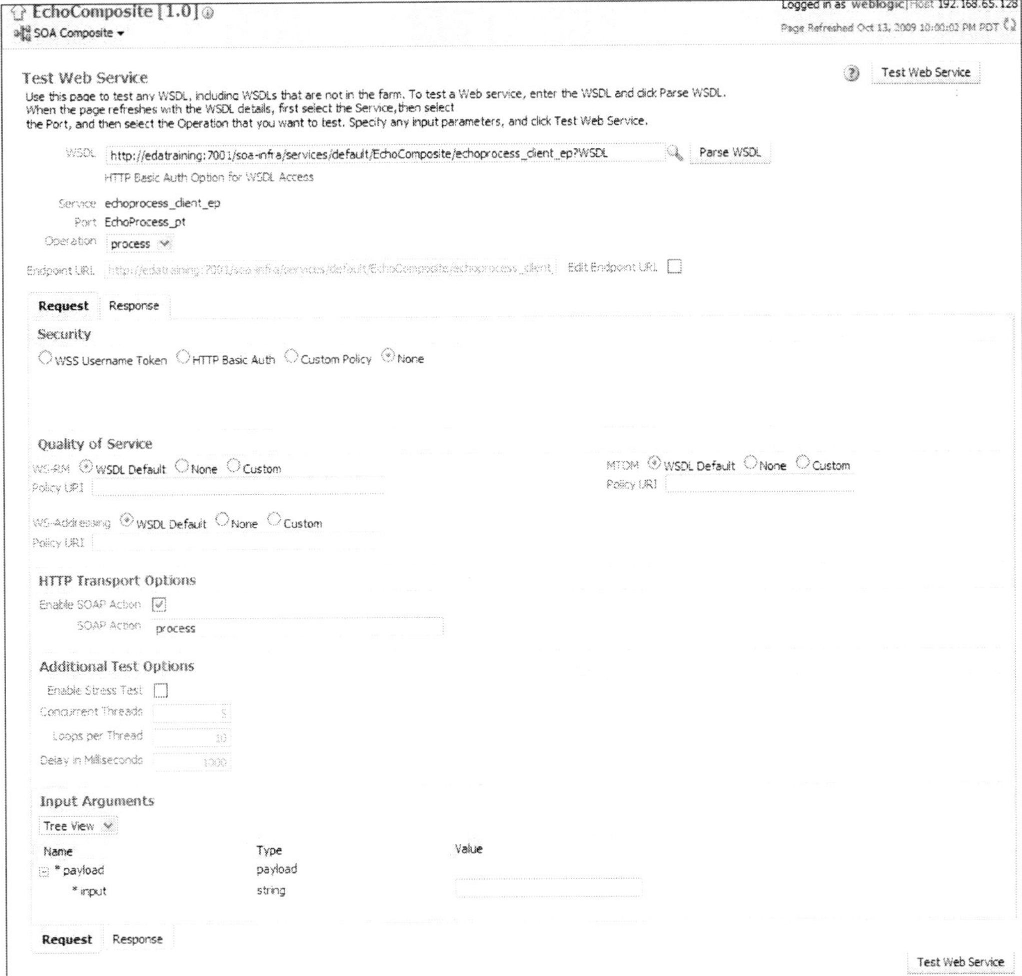

When we created our process, JDeveloper automatically created a WSDL file which contained the single operation (that is, `process`). However, it's quite common to define processes that have multiple operations, as we will see later on in the book.

The **Operation** drop-down list allows us to specify which operation we want to invoke. In our case, it's automatically defaulted to **process**.

When you select the operation to invoke, the console will generate an HTML form with a field for each element in the message payload of the operation (as defined by the WSDL for the process). Here we can enter into each field the value that we want to submit.

For operations with large message payloads it can be simpler to just enter the XML source. If you select the **XML View** drop-down list the console will replace the form with a free text area with a skeleton XML fragment into which we can insert the required values.

To execute a test instance of our composite, enter some text in the **input** field and click **Test Web Service**. This will cause the console to generate a SOAP message and use it to invoke our Echo process.

Upon successful execution of the process, our test page will be updated to show the **result** which displays the response returned by our process. Here we can see that the **result** element contains our original input string, as shown in the following screenshot:

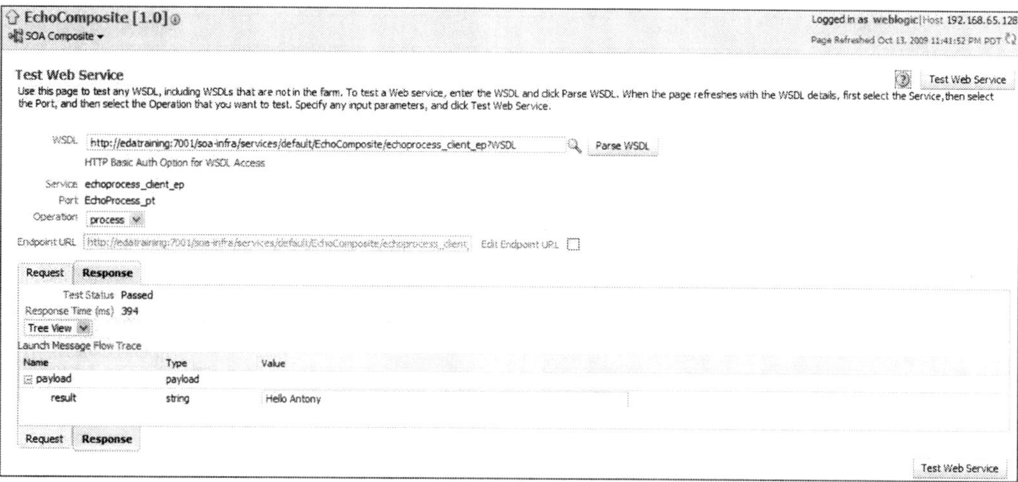

If we expand the **SOA** and **soa-infra** items on the left-hand side of the page, we will arrive back at the dashboard for the **EchoComposite**. Clicking on a completed instance will give us a summary of the composite. From here we can see the components that make up our composite. In this case, the composite consists of a single BPEL process.

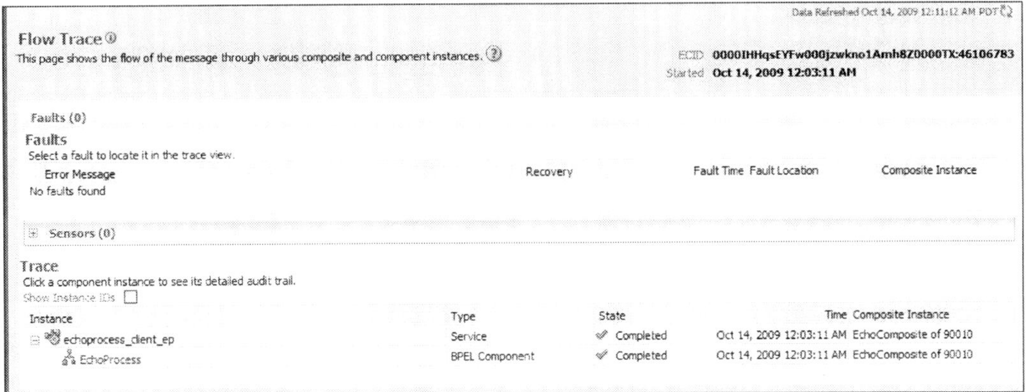

Clicking on the BPEL process takes us to an audit record of the instance. We can expand the tree view to see details of individual operations like the message sent by **replyOutput**.

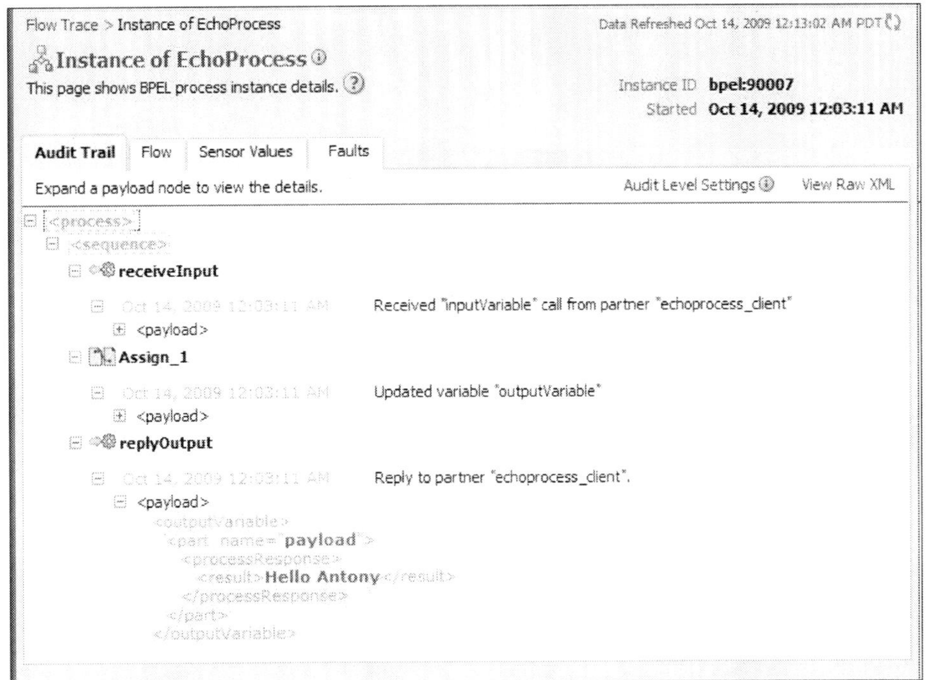

Clicking on the **Flow** tab will display a graphical representation of the activities within the BPEL process.

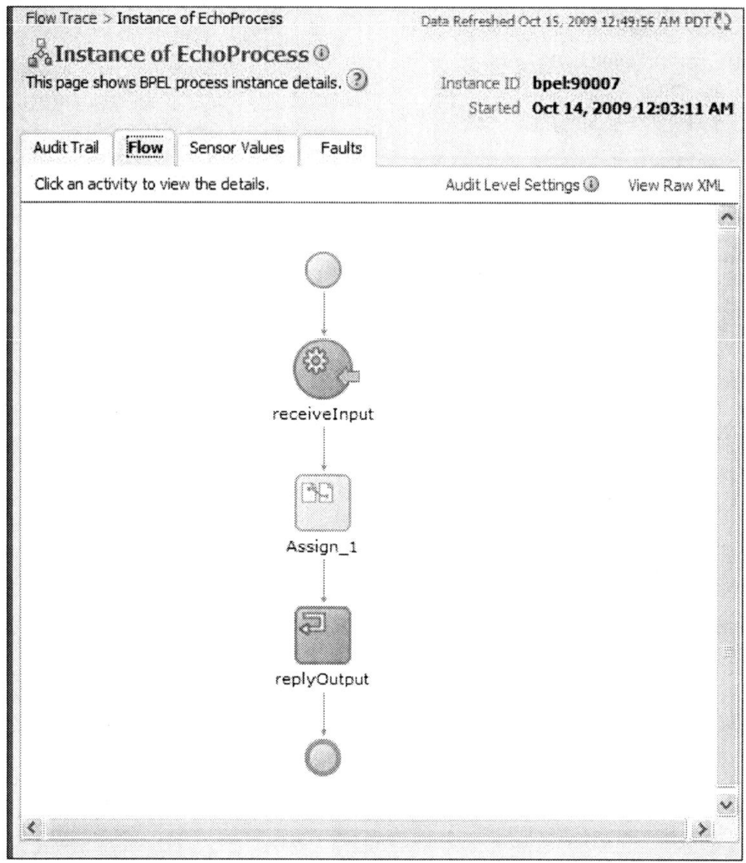

Clicking on any of the activities in the audit trail will pop up a window displaying details of the actions performed by that activity. In the following screenshot, we can see details of the message sent by the **replyOutput** activity:

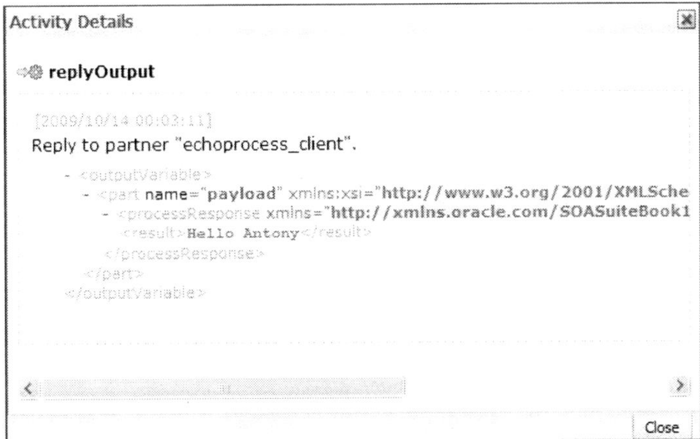

This completes development of our first BPEL process. The next step is to call it via the Mediator. This will give us the option of transforming the input into the format we desire and of routing to different components based on the input content.

Adding a Mediator

By selecting the **composite.xml** tab in JDeveloper, we can see the outline of the Assembly that we have created for the BPEL process. We can add a Mediator to this by dragging it from the **Component Palette**.

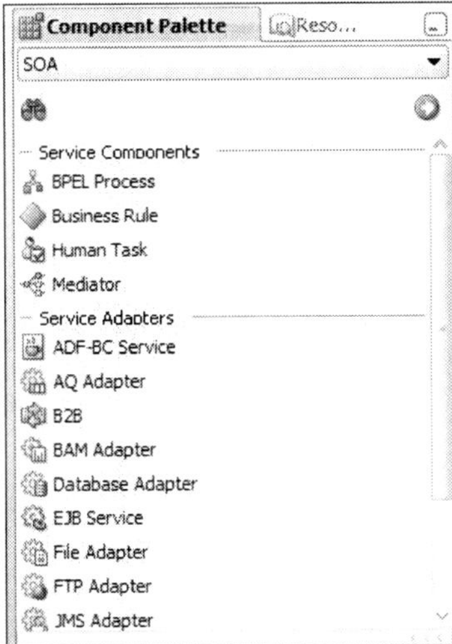

Dragging the **Mediator Component** will cause a dialog to be displayed requesting a **Name** and **Template** for the **Mediator**.

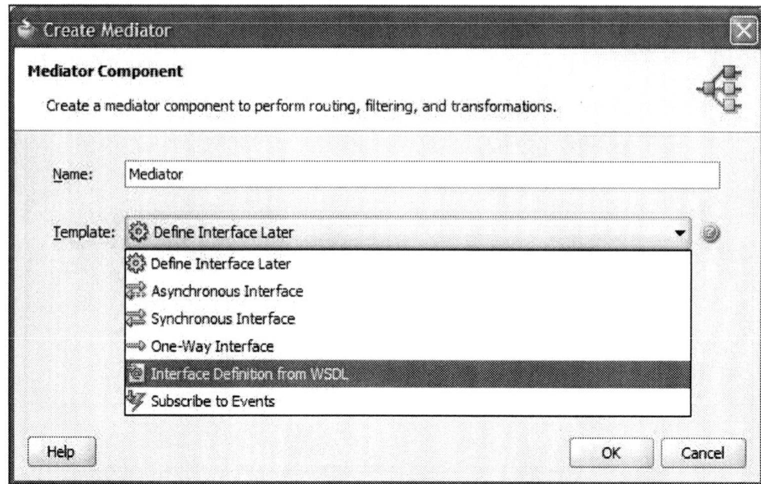

If we select the **Define Interface Later** template, then we can click **OK** to add a Mediator to our Assembly. Defining the interface later will allow us to define the interface by wiring it to a service. Note that the types of interface templates are the same as the ones we saw for our BPEL process.

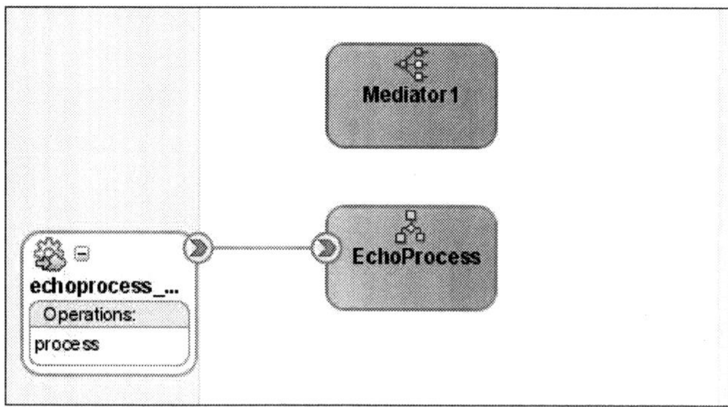

We want to have the Mediator use the same interface as the BPEL process. To rewire the composite to use a Mediator, we first delete the line joining the **EchoProcess** in the **Exposed Services** swimlane to the BPEL process by right-clicking on the line and selecting **Delete**.

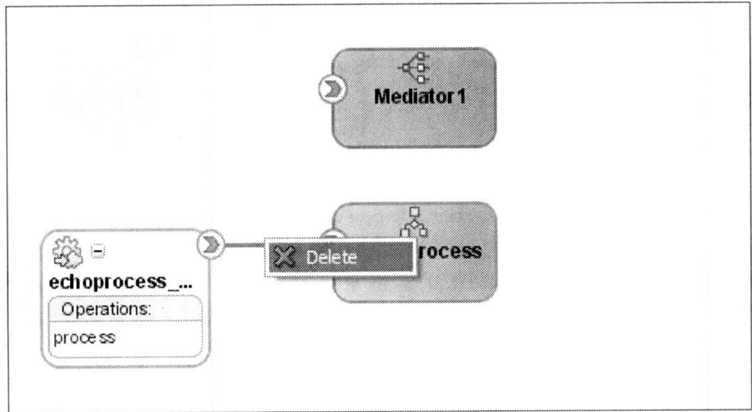

We can now wire the **EchoProcess** service to the input of the Mediator by clicking on the chevron in the top-right corner of the exposed service and dragging it onto the connection point on the left-hand side of the Mediator.

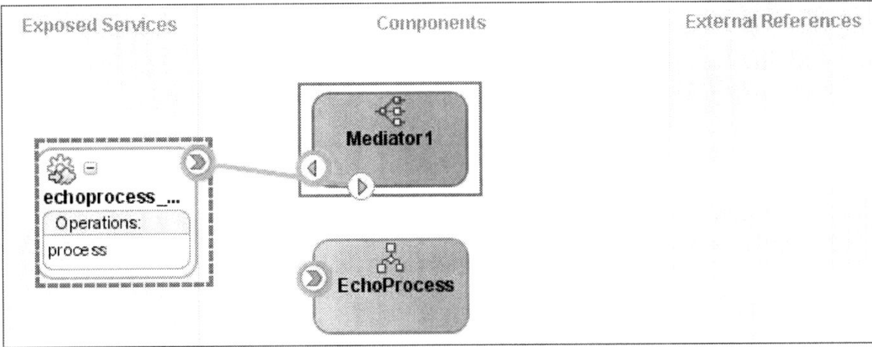

Now wire the Mediator to the BPEL process by dragging the yellow arrow on the Mediator onto the blue chevron on the BPEL process.

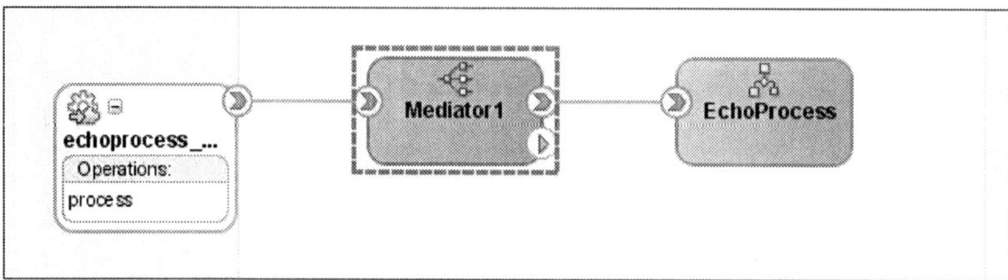

We have now configured the Mediator to accept the same interface as the BPEL process and wired the Mediator to forward all messages onto the BPEL process. The default behavior of the Mediator, if it has no explicit rules, is to route the input request to the outbound request and then route the response, if any, from the target to the client.

We can now deploy and test the Assembly containing the Mediator in the same way that we deployed and tested the Assembly containing the BPEL process.

Using the Service Bus

In preparation for this, we will need the URL for the WSDL of our process. To obtain this, from the EM **Dashboard**, click on the **EchoComposite** Assembly, and then the connector icon to the right of the **Settings** button. This will display a link for the **WSDL location** and **Endpoint**, as shown in the following screenshot:

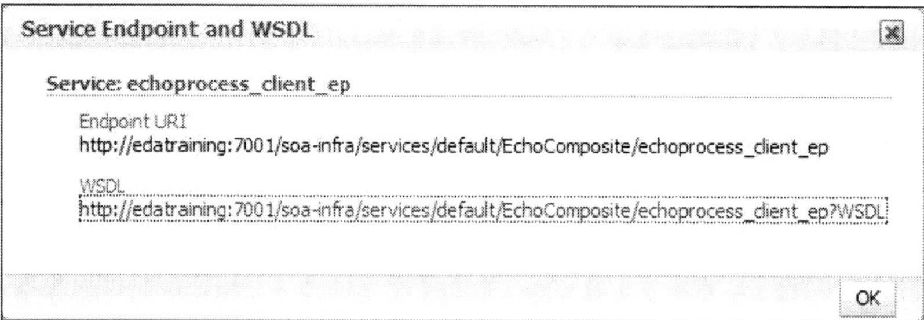

If you click on this link, the EM console will open a window showing details of the WSDL. Make a note of the WSDL location as we will need this in a moment.

Writing our first proxy service

Rather than allowing clients to directly invoke our Echo process, best practice dictates that we provide access to this service via an intermediary or **proxy**, whose role is to route the request to the actual endpoint. This results in a far more loosely-coupled solution, which is the key if we are to realise many of the benefits of SOA.

In this section, we are going to use the **Oracle Service Bus (OSB)** to implement a proxy Echo service, which sits between the client and our echo BPEL process, as illustrated in the following diagram:

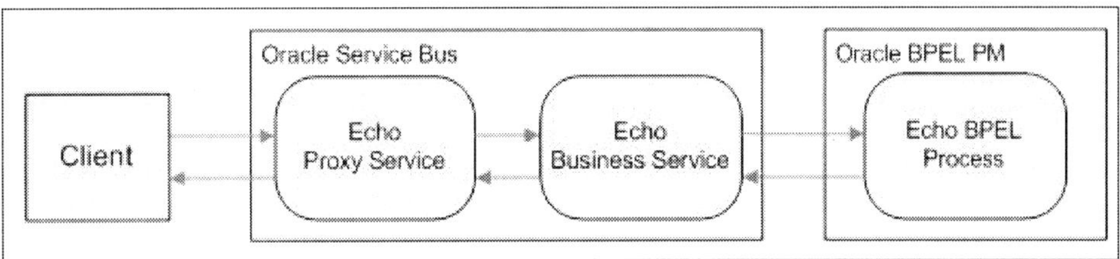

It is useful to examine the preceding scenario to understand how messages are processed by OSB. The Service Bus defines two types of services, a proxy service and a business service.

The proxy service is an intermediary service that sits between the client and the actual end service being invoked (our BPEL process in the preceding example).

On receipt of a request the proxy service may perform a number of actions, such as validating, transforming, or enriching it before routing it to the appropriate business service.

Within the OSB, a business service is a definition of an external service for which OSB is a client. This defines whether OSB can invoke the external service and includes details such as the service interface, transport, security, and so on.

In the preceding example, we have defined an **Echo Proxy Service** that routes messages to the **Echo Business Service**, which then invokes our **Echo BPEL Process**. The response from the **Echo BPEL Process** follows the reverse path with the proxy service returning the final response to the original client.

Writing the Echo proxy service

Ensure that the Oracle Service Bus has started and then open up the Service Bus Console. Either do this from the **Programs** menu in Windows, select **Oracle Weblogic | User Projects | OSB | Oracle Service Bus Admin Console**

Or alternatively, open up a browser, and enter the following URL:

```
http://<hostname>:<port>/sbconsole
```

Where hostname represents the name of the machine on which OSB is running and port represents the port number. So if OSB is running on your local machine using the default port, enter the following URL in your browser:

```
http://localhost:7001/sbconsole
```

This will bring up the login screen for the Service Bus Console, log in as **weblogic**. By default, the OSB Console will display the **Dashboard** view, which provides a summary of the overall health of the system.

Looking at the console, we can see that it is divided into three distinct areas. The **Change Center** in the top-left-hand corner, which we will cover in a moment. Also on the left, below the **Change Center**, is the navigation bar which we use to navigate our way round the console.

The navigation bar is divided into the following sections: **Operations**, **Resource Browser**, **Project Explorer**, **Security Configuration**, and **System Administration**. Clicking on the appropriate section will expand that part of the navigation bar and allow you to access any of its sub-sections and their corresponding menu items.

Clicking on any of the menu items will display the appropriate page within the main window of the console. In the previous diagram we looked at the **Dashboard** view, under **Monitoring**, which is part of the **Operations** section.

Creating a Change Session

Before we can create a new project, or make any configuration changes through the console, we must create a new change session. A **Change Session** allows us to specify a series of changes as a single unit of work. These changes won't come into effect until we activate a session. At any point we can discard our changes, which will cause OSB to roll back those changes and exit our session.

While making changes through a session, other users can also be making changes under separate sessions. If users create changes that conflict with changes in other sessions, then the Service Bus will flag that as a conflict in the **Change Center** and neither user will be able to commit their changes until those conflicts have been resolved.

To create a new change session, click on **Create** in the **Change Center**. This will update the **Change Center** to indicate that we are in a session and the user who owns that session. As we are logged in as weblogic, it will be updated to show **weblogic session**, as shown in the following screenshot:

In addition, you will see that the options available to us in the **Change Center** have changed to **Activate**, **Discard**, and **Exit**.

Creating a project

Before we can create our Echo proxy service, we must create an OSB project in which to place our resources. Typical resources include WSDL, XSD schemas, XSLT, and XQuery as well as Proxy and Business Services.

Resources can be created directly within our top-level project folder, or we can define a folder structure within our project into which we can place our resources.

From within the same OSB domain, you can reference any resource regardless of which project it is included in.

The **Project Explorer** is where we create and manage all of this. Click on the **Project Explorer** section within the navigation bar. This will bring up the **Projects** view, as shown in the following screenshot:

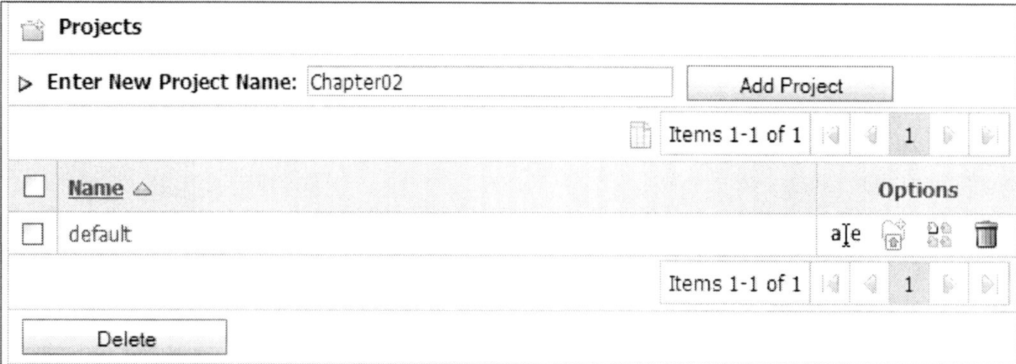

Here we can see a list of all projects defined in OSB, which at this stage just includes the **default** project. From here we can also create a new project. Enter a project name, for example **Chapter02**, as shown in the preceding screenshot, and then click **Add Project**. This will create a new project and update our list of projects to reflect this.

Creating the project folders

Click on the project name will take us to the **Project View**, as shown in the screenshot on the next page.

We can see that this splits into three sections. The first section provides some basic details about the project including any references to or from artifacts in other projects as well as an optional description.

The second section lists any folders within the current project folder and provides the option to create additional folders within the project.

The final section lists any resource contained within this folder and provides the option to create additional resource.

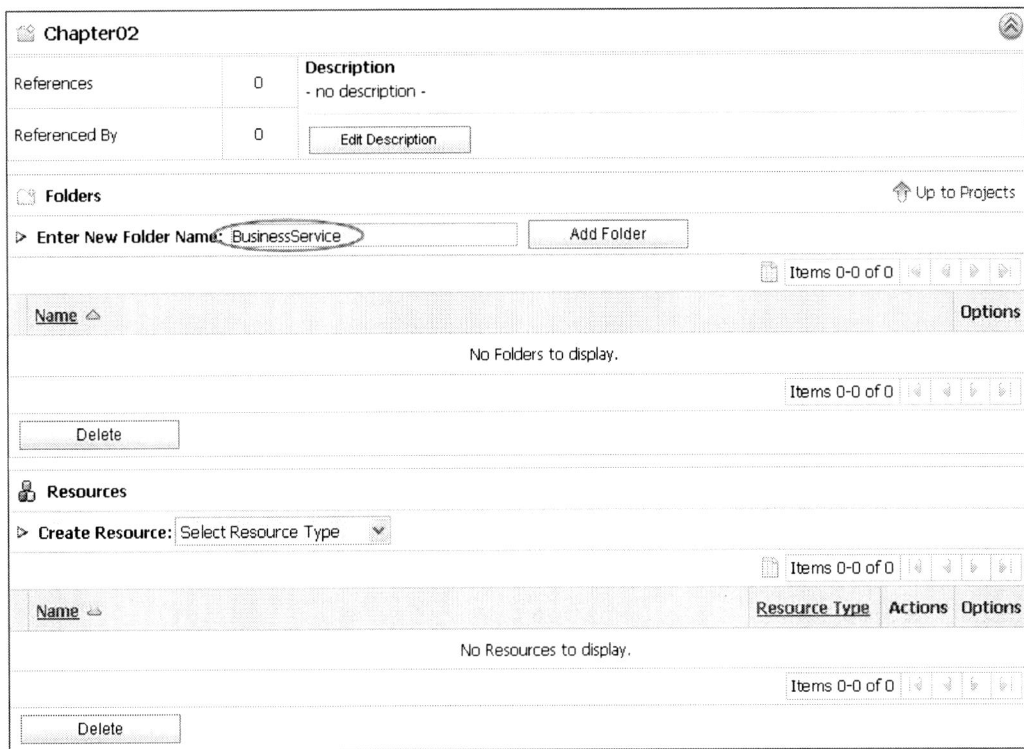

We are going to create the project folders **BusinessService**, **ProxyService**, and **WSDL**, into which we will place our various resources. To create the first of these, in the **Folders** section, enter **BusinessService** as the folder name (circled in the preceding screenshot) and click on **Add Folder**. This will create a new folder and updates the list of folders to reflect this.

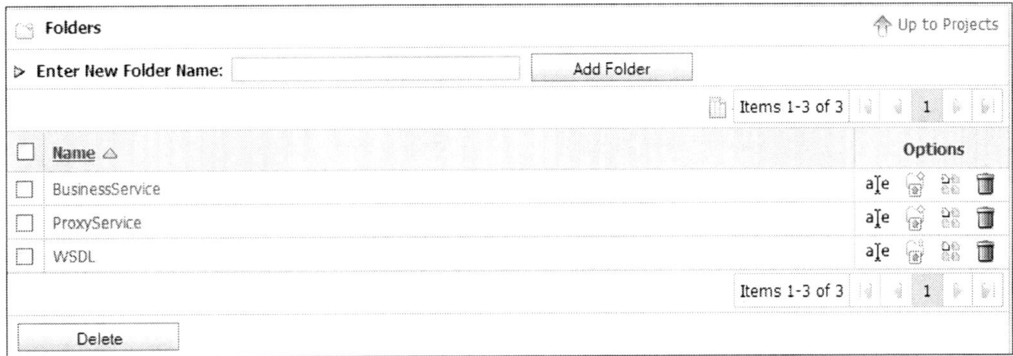

Once created, follow the same process to create the remaining folders; your list of folders will now look as shown in the preceding screenshot.

Creating service WSDL

Before we can create either our proxy or business service, we need to define the WSDL on which the service will be based. For this, we are going to use the WSDL of our `Echo` BPEL process that we created earlier in this chapter.

Before importing the WSDL, we need to ensure that we are in the right folder within our project. To do this, click on the **WSDL** folder in our **Folders** list. On doing this the project view will be updated to show us the content of this folder, which is currently empty. In addition, the project summary section of our project view will be updated to show that we are now within the `WSDL` folder, as circled in the following screenshot:

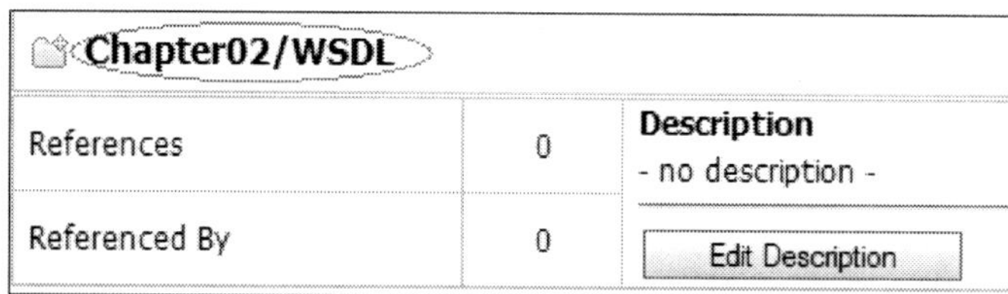

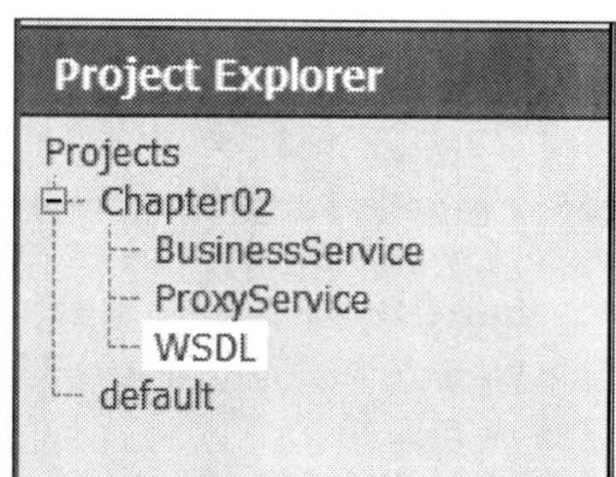

If we look at the **Project Explorer** in the navigation bar, we can see that it has been updated to show our location within the projects structure. By clicking on any project or folder in here, the console will take us to the project view for that location.

Importing a WSDL

To import the Echo WSDL into our project, click on the drop-down list next to **Create Resource** in the **Resources** section, and select **Resources from URL**, as shown in the following screenshot:

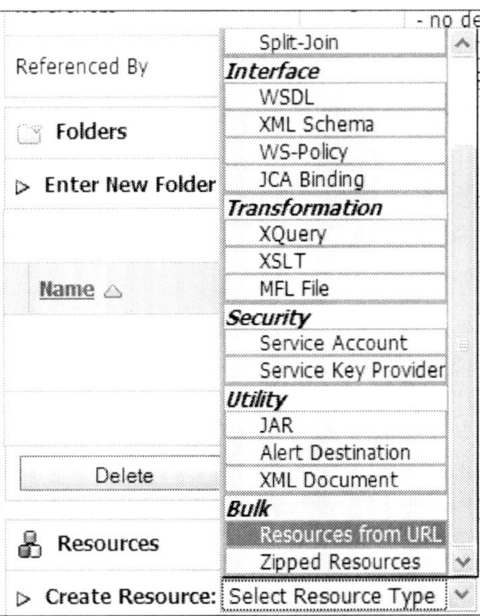

This will bring up the page for loading resources from a URL, which is shown in the following screenshot:

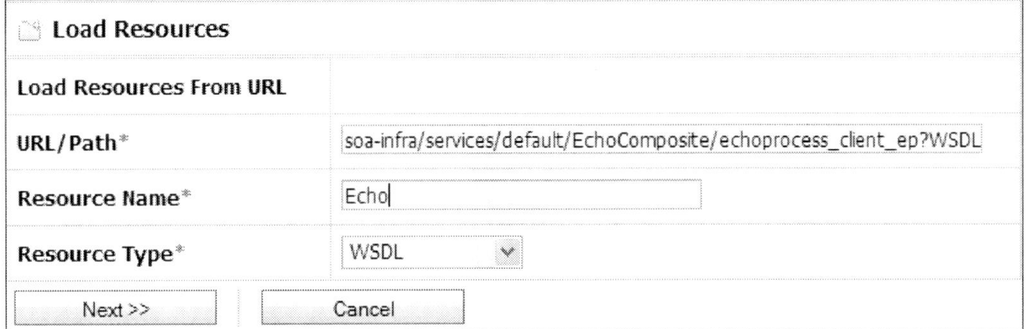

A WSDL can also be imported from the filesystem by selecting the **WSDL** option from the **Create Resource** drop-down list.

In the **URL/Path**, enter the URL for our Echo WSDL. This is the **WSDL** location we made a note of earlier (in the **WSDL** tab for the Echo process in the BPEL console) and should look like the following:

```
http://<hostname>:<port>/orabpel/default/Echo/1.0/Echo?wsdl
```

Enter an appropriate value for the **Resource Name** (for example **Echo**), select a **Resource Type** as **WSDL**, and click on **Next**.

This will bring up the **Load Resources** window, which will list the resources that OSB is ready to import.

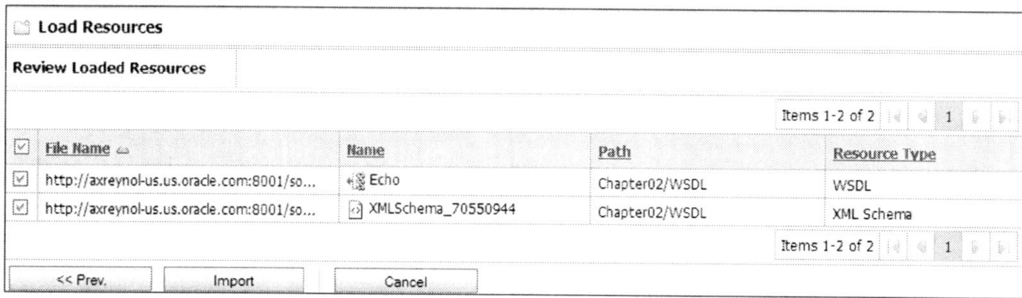

You will notice that in addition to the actual WSDL file, it will also list the **Echo.xsd**. This is because the **Echo.wsdl** contains the following import statement:

```
<wsdl:types>
  <schema>
    <import namespace=
            "http://xmlns.oracle.com/SOASuiteBook11gChapter2_jws
/EchoComposite/EchoProcess"
            schemaLocation=
            "http://axreynol-us.us.oracle.com:8001/soa-infra/services/
default/EchoComposite/echoprocess_client_ep?
XSD=xsd/EchoProcess.xsd"/>
  </schema>
</wsdl:types>
```

This imports the Echo XML schema, which defines the input and output message of our Echo service. This schema was automatically generated by JDeveloper when we created our Echo process. In order to use our WSDL, we will need to import this schema as well. Because of the unusual URL for the XML Schema, the Service Bus generates its own unique name for the schema.

Click **Import**, the OSB console will confirm that the resources have been successfully imported and provide the option to **Load Another** resource, as shown in the following screenshot:

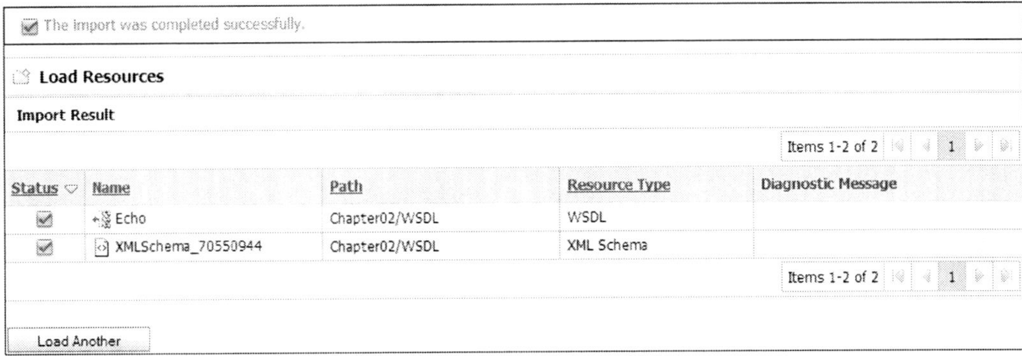

Click on the **WSDL** folder within the project explorer to return to its project view. This will be updated to include our imported resources, as shown in the following screenshot:

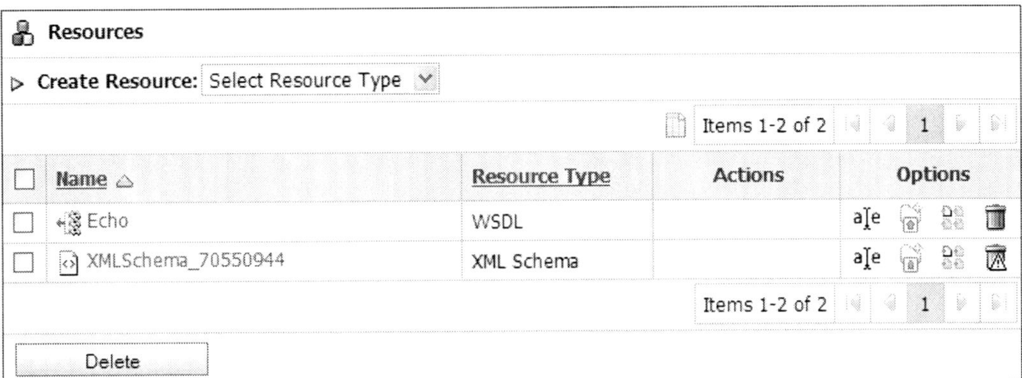

Creating our business service

We are now ready to create our Echo business service. Click on the **Business Service** folder within the **Project Explorer** to go to the project view for this folder.

In the **Resources** section, click on the drop-down list next to **Create Resource** and select **Business Service**. This will bring up the **General Configuration** page for creating a business service, as shown in the following screenshot:

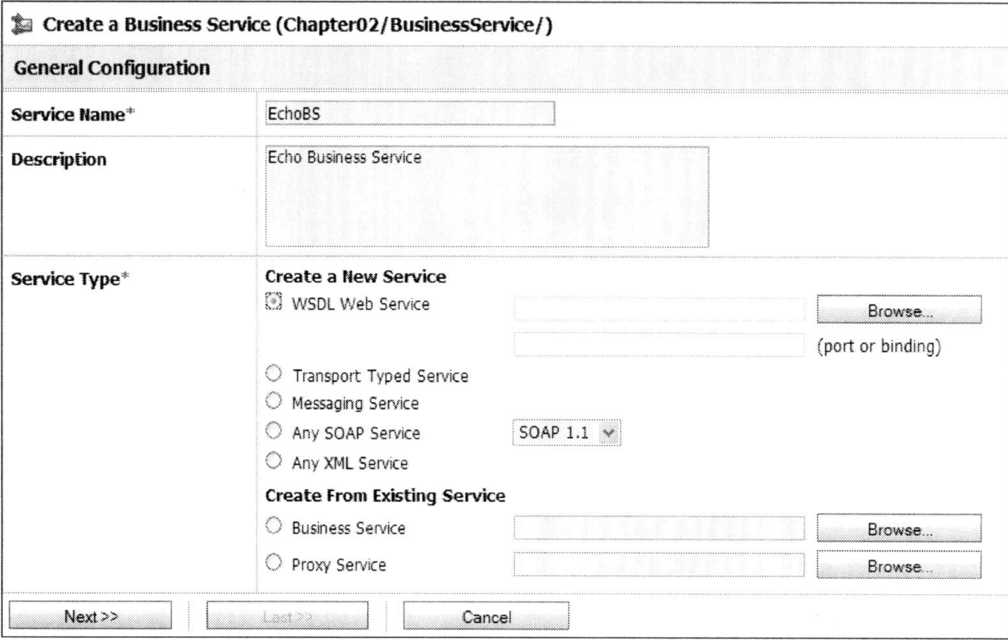

Here we specify the name of our business service (that is, **EchoBS**) and an optional description. Next we need to specify the **Service Type**, as we are creating our service based on a WSDL select **WSDL Web Service**.

Next, click the **Browse** button. This will launch a window from where we can select the WSDL for the **Business Service**, as shown on the next page:

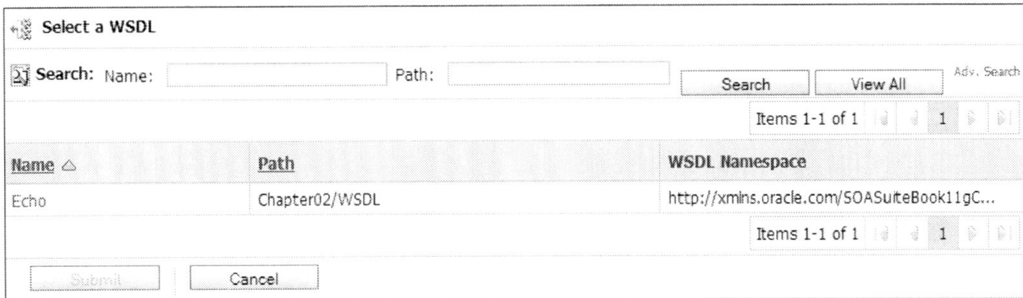

By default, this window will list all WSDL resources that are defined to the Service Bus, though you can restrict the list by defining the search criteria.

In our case, we just have the Echo WSDL, so we click on this. We will now be prompted to select a WSDL definition, as shown in the following screenshot:

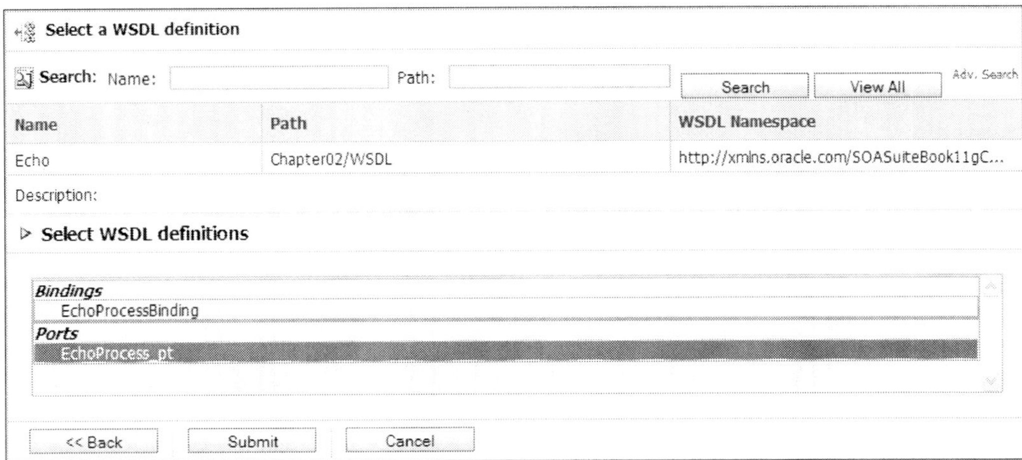

Here we need to select which binding or port definition we wish to use for our Business Service, select **EchoProcess_pt** and click **Submit**. **Bindings** provide an abstract interface and do not specify the physical endpoint, requiring additional configuration later. **Ports** have a physical endpoint and so require no additional configuration.

This will return us to the **General Configuration** screen with the **Service Type** updated to show the details of the selected WSDL and port, as shown in the following screenshot:

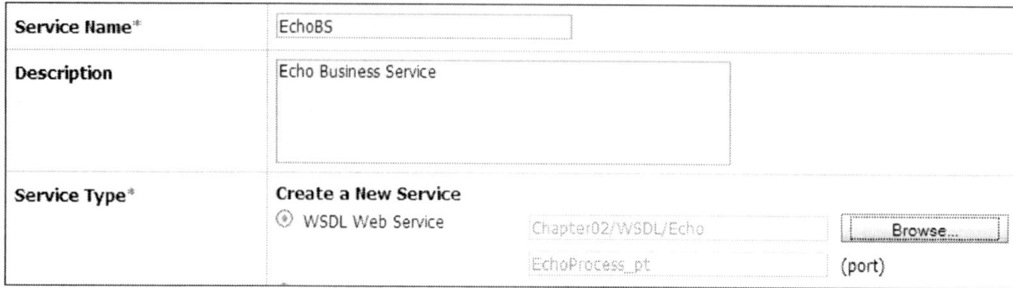

Then, click on **Next**. This will take us to the **Transport Configuration** page, as shown in the following screenshot. Here we need to specify how the business service is to invoke an external service.

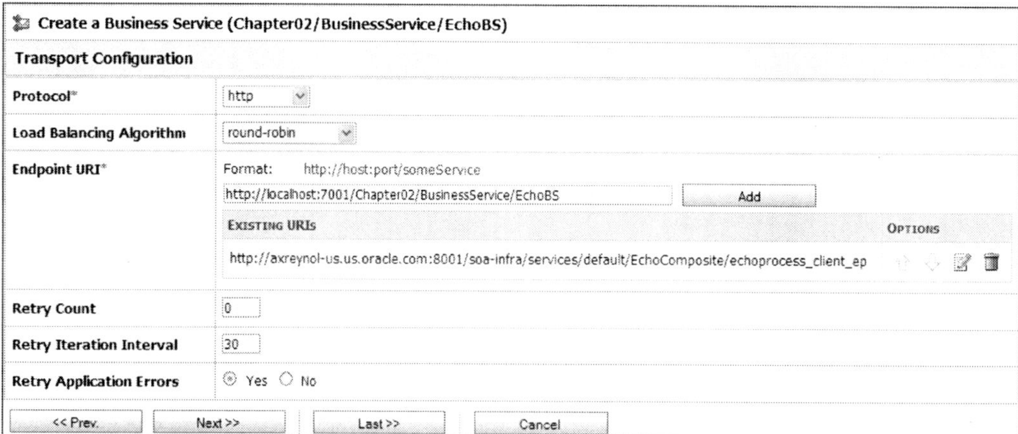

As we based our business service on the **EchoPort** definition, the transport settings are already preconfigured, based on the content of our WSDL file.

If we had based our business service on the **EchoBinding** definition, then the transport configuration would still have been prepopulated except for the **Endpoint URI**, which we would need to add manually.

From here, click on **Last**. This will take us to a summary page of our business service. Click on **Save** to create our business service.

This will return us to the project view on the **Business Service** folder and display the message **The Service EchoBS was created successfully**. If we examine the **Resources** section, we should see that it now contains our newly created business service.

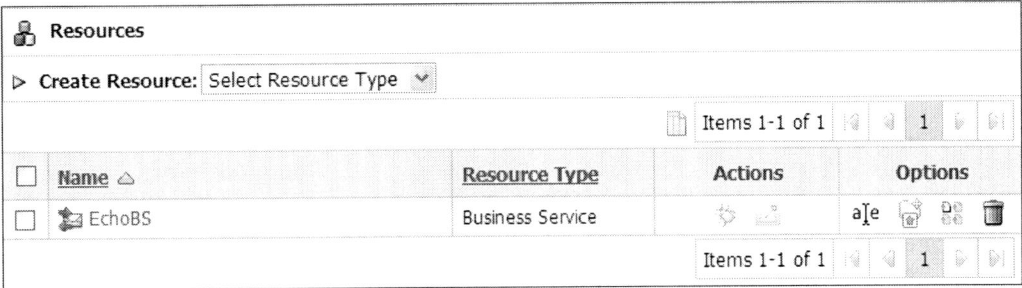

Creating our proxy service

We are now ready to create our Echo proxy service. Click on the **Proxy Service** folder within the **Project Explorer** to go to the project view for this folder.

In the **Resources** section, click on the drop-down list next to **Create Resource** and select **Proxy Service**. This will bring up the **General Configuration** page for creating a proxy service, as shown in the following screenshot:

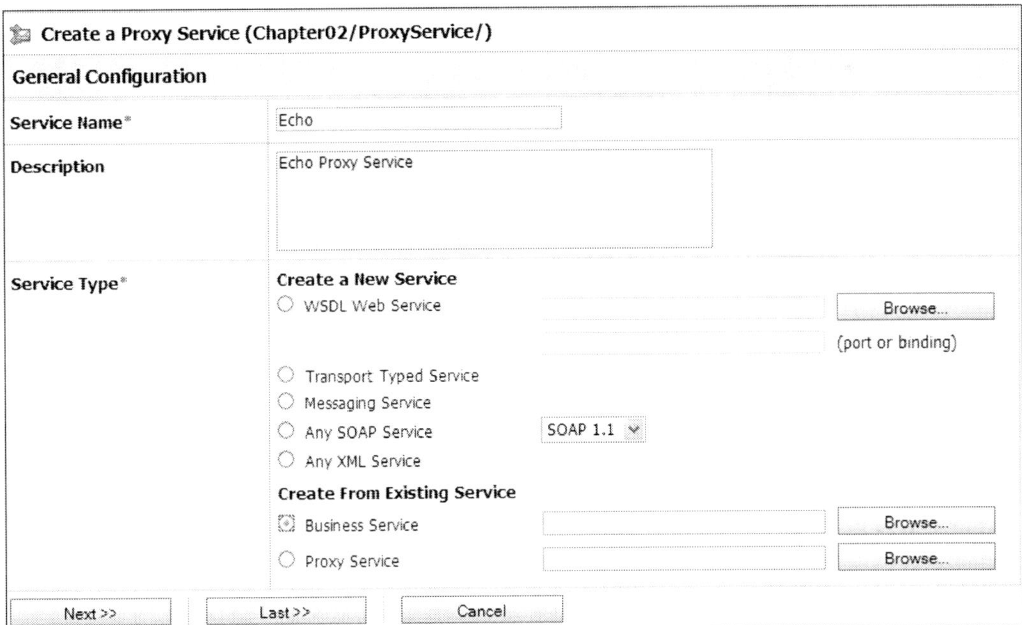

You will notice that this looks very similar to the general configuration screen for a business service. So as before, enter the name of our service (that is, **Echo**) and an optional description.

Next, we need to specify the **Service Type**. We could do this in exactly the same way as we did for our business service and base it on the Echo WSDL. However, this time we are going to base it on our **EchoBS** business service. We will see why in a moment.

For the **Service Type**, select **Business Service**, as shown in the screenshot, and click **Browse...**. This will launch the **Select Business Service** window from where we can search for and select the business service that we want to base our proxy service on.

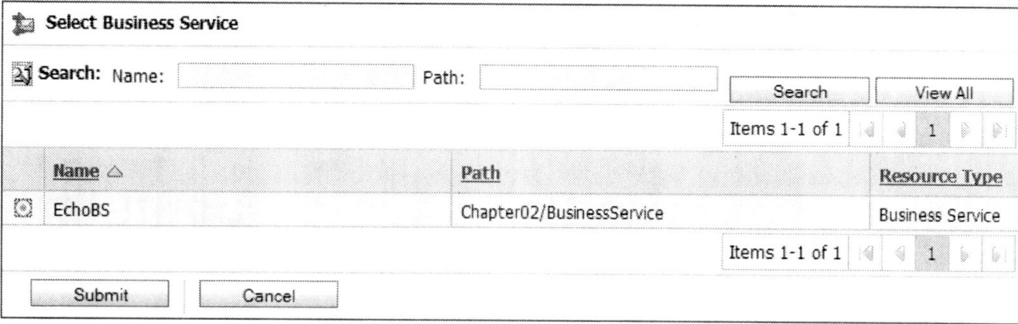

By default, this window will list all the business services defined to the Service Bus, though you can restrict the list by defining the search criteria.

In our case, we just have the **EchoBS**, so select this, and click on **Submit**. This will return us to the **General Configuration** screen with **Service Type** updated, as shown in the following screenshot:

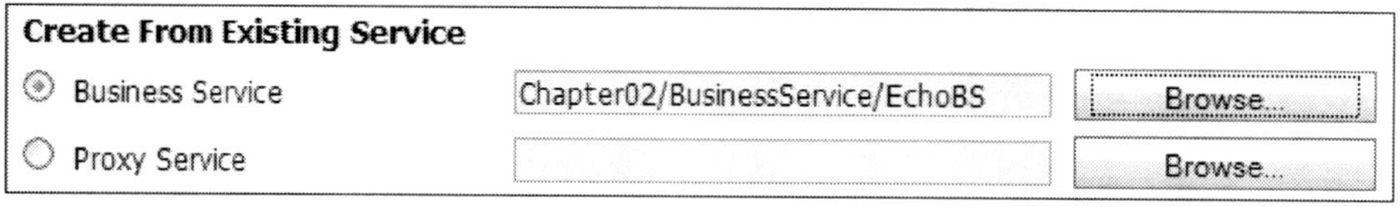

From here, click **Last**. This will take us to a summary page of our proxy service. Click **Save** to create our proxy service.

This will return us to the project view on the **Proxy Service** folder and display the message **The Service Echo was created successfully**.

If we examine the **Resources** section of our project view, we should see that it now contains our newly created proxy service as shown in the following screenshot:

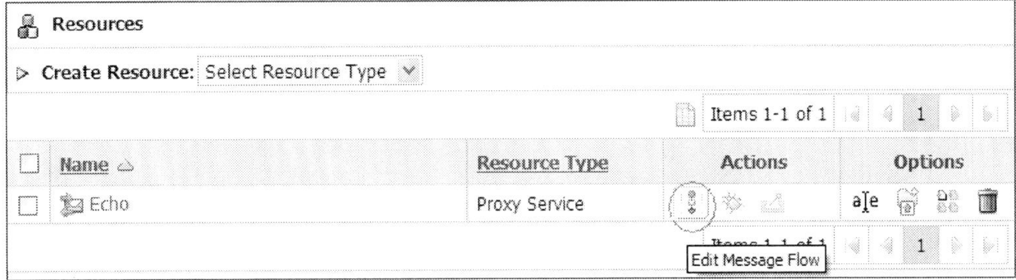

Creating message flow

Once we have created our proxy service, the next step is to specify how it should handle requests. This is defined in the message flow of the proxy service.

The message flow defines the actions that the proxy service should perform when a request is received such as validating the payload, transforming, or enriching it before routing it to the appropriate business service.

Within the resource section of our project view, click on the **Edit Message Flow** icon, as circled in the preceding image. This will take us to the **Edit Message Flow** window, where we can view and edit the message flow of our proxy service, as shown in the following screenshot:

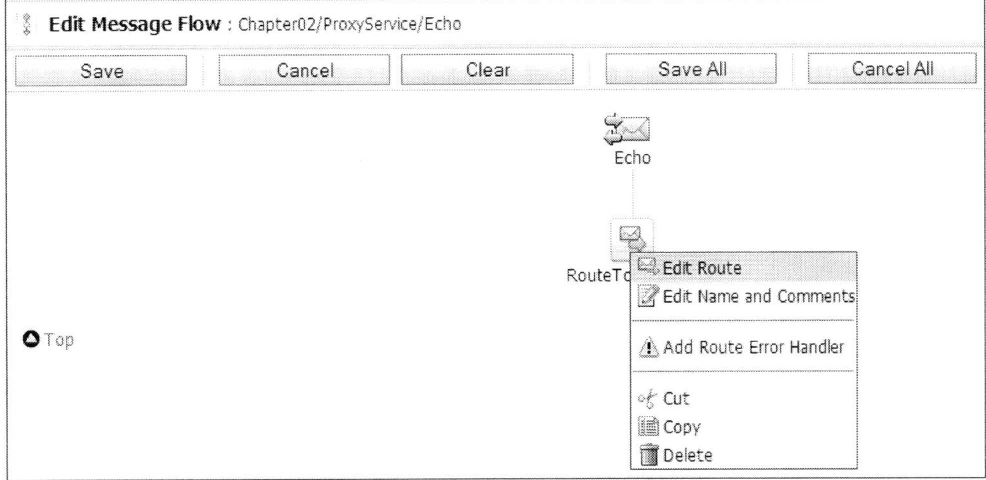

Looking at this, we can see that Echo already invokes the route node **RouteTo_EchoBS**.

Click on this and select **Edit Route** (as shown in the preceding screenshot). This will take us to the **Edit Stage Configuration** window, as shown in the following screenshot:

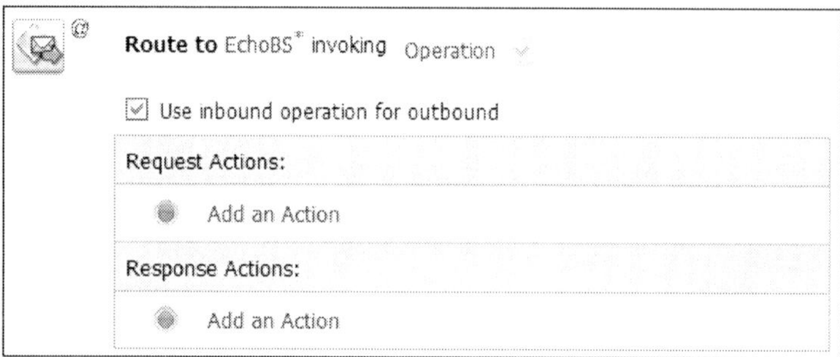

Here we can see that it's already configured to route requests to the **EchoBS** business service.

Normally, when we create a proxy service we have to specify the message flow from scratch. However, when we created our **Echo** proxy service we based it on the **EchoBS** business service (as opposed to a WSDL). Because of this, the Service Bus has automatically configured the message flow to route requests to **EchoBS**.

As a result, our message flow is already predefined for us, so click **Cancel**, and then **Cancel** again to return to our project view.

Activating the Echo proxy service

We now have a completed proxy service; all that remains is to commit our work. Within the **Change Center** click **Activate**.

This will bring up the **Activate Session**, as shown in the following screenshot:

Activate Session

Session Name	weblogic
User	weblogic
Description	Create Echo Proxy Service

Submit

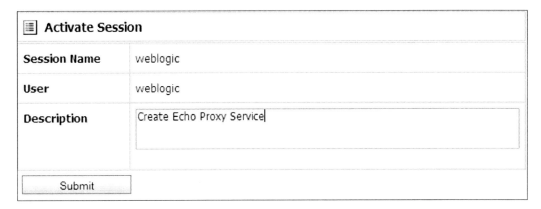

Before activating a session, it's good practice to give a description of the changes that we've made, just in case we need to roll them back later. So enter an appropriate description and then click on **Submit**, as shown in the preceding screenshot:

Assuming everything is okay, this will activate our changes, and the console will be updated to list our configuration changes, as shown in the following screenshot:

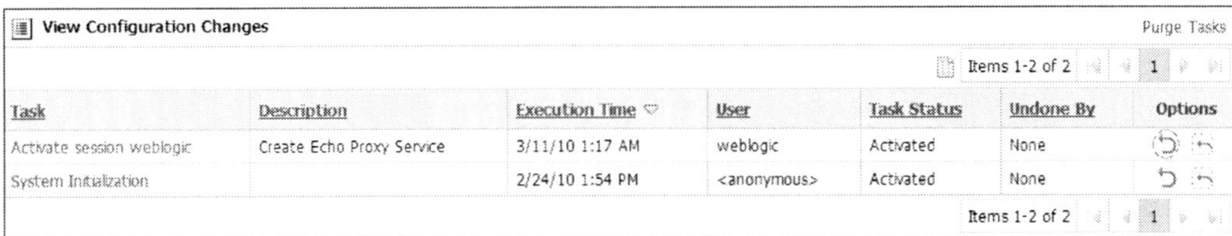

View Configuration Changes — Purge Tasks

Items 1-2 of 2 — 1

Task	Description	Execution Time	User	Task Status	Undone By	Options
Activate session weblogic	Create Echo Proxy Service	3/11/10 1:17 AM	weblogic	Activated	None	
System Initialization		2/24/10 1:54 PM	<anonymous>	Activated	None	

Items 1-2 of 2 — 1

If you make a mistake and want to undo the changes you have activated, then you can click on the undo icon (circled in the preceding screenshot), and if you change your mind, you can revert the undo.

OSB allows you to undo any of your previous sessions as long as it doesn't result in an error in the runtime configuration of the Service Bus.

Testing our proxy service

All that's left is to test our proxy service. A simple way to do this is to initiate a test instance using the Service Bus test console.

To do this, we need to navigate back to the definition of our proxy service, rather than do this via the **Project Explorer**. We will use the **Resource Browser**. This provides a way to view all resources based on their type.

Click on the **Resource Browser** section within the navigation bar. By default, it will list all proxy services defined to the Service Bus, as shown in the following screenshot:

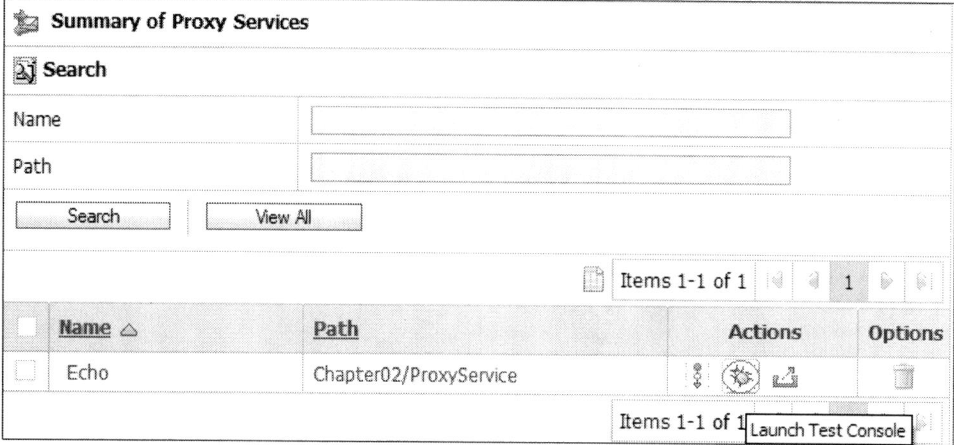

We can then filter this list further by specifying the appropriate search criteria.

Click on the **Launch Test Console** icon for the Echo proxy service (circled in the preceding screenshot). This will launch the test console shown on the next page.

The **Available Operations** drop-down list allows us to specify which operation we want to invoke. In our case, it's automatically defaulted to **process**.

By default, the options **Direct Call** and **Include Tracing** are selected within the **Test Configuration** section; keep these selected as they enable us to trace the state of a message as it passes through the proxy service.

The **Request Document** section allows us to specify the **SOAP Header** and the **Payload** for our service. By default, these will contain a skeleton XML fragment based on the WSDL definition of the selected operation with default values for each field.

To execute a test instance of our service, modify the text in the `<echo:input>` element, as we have in the following screen shot, and click **Execute**. This will cause the console to generate a request message and use it to invoke our Echo proxy service.

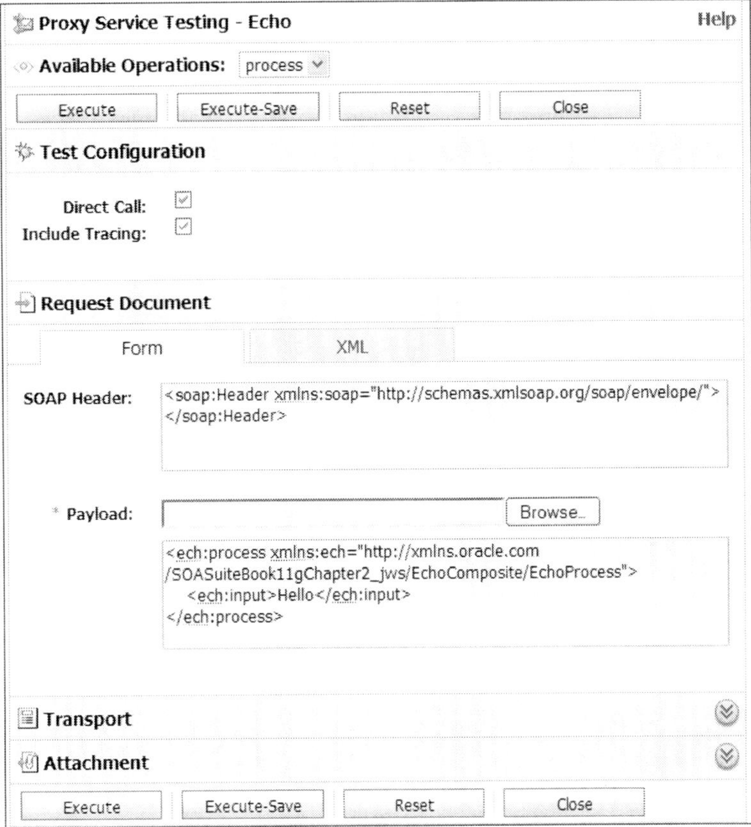

Upon successful execution of the proxy, the test console will be updated to show the response returned. Here we can see that the `result` element contains our original initial input string, as shown in the following screenshot:

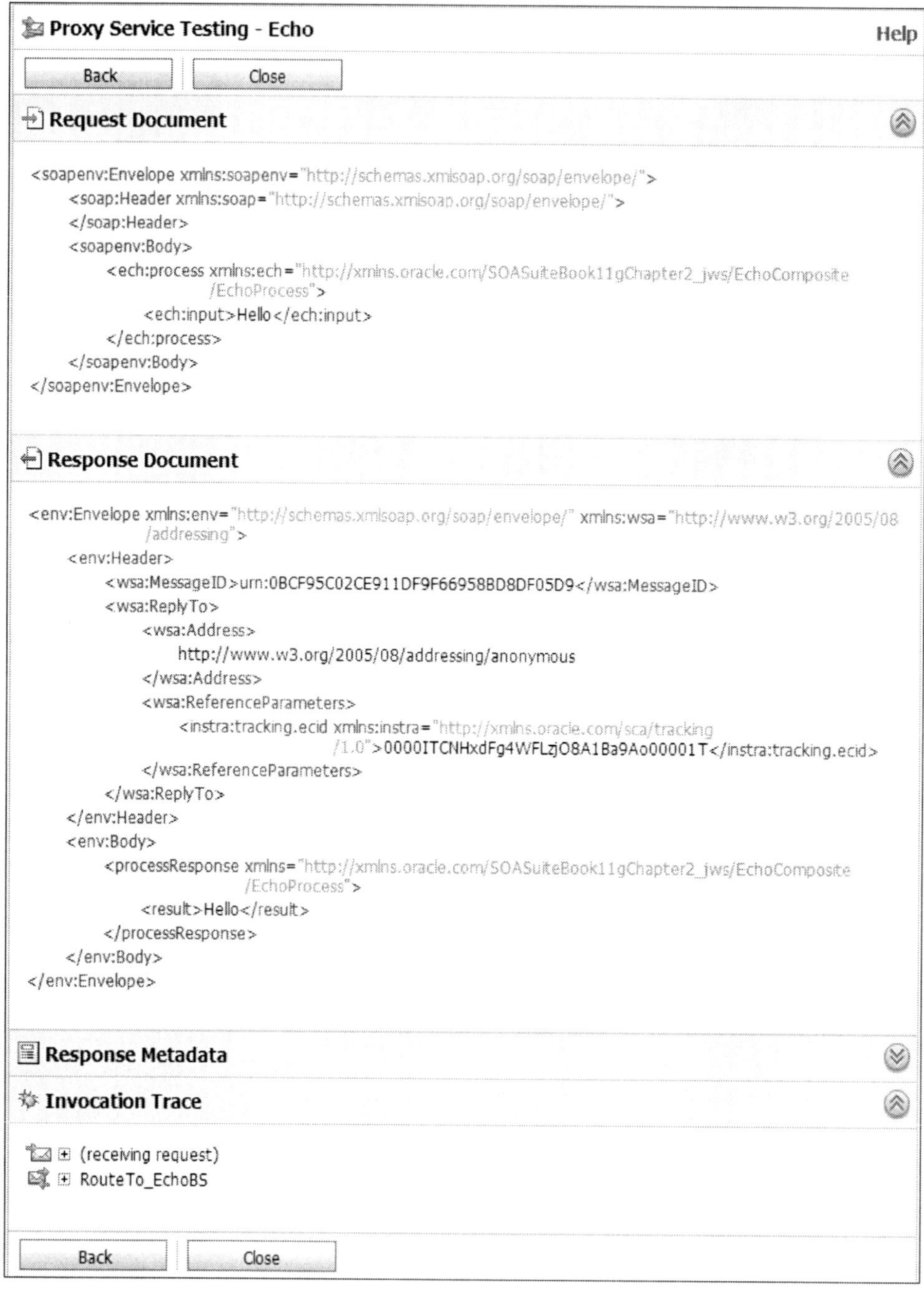

We can examine the state of our message as it passed through the proxy service by expanding the **Invocation Trace**, as we have in the following screenshot:

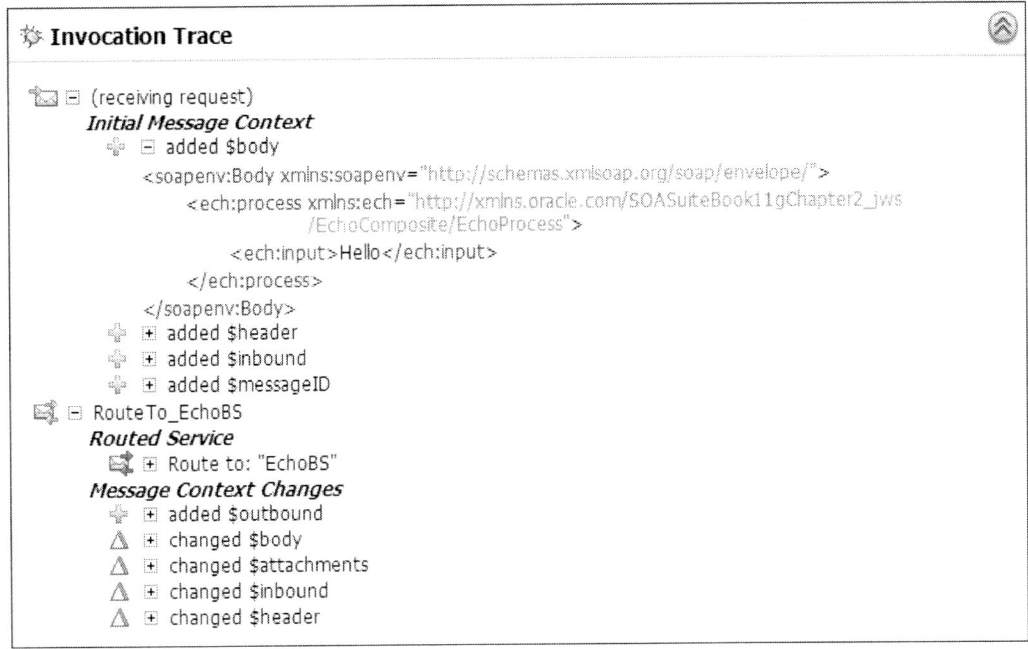

In addition, if you log back into the EM console, you should be able to see the Assembly instance that was invoked by the Service Bus.

Summary

In this section, we have implemented our first SCA Assembly and then built our first proxy service on top of it. While this example is about as trivial as it can get, it has provided us with an initial introduction to both the design time and runtime components of Oracle BPEL PM and Oracle Service Bus.

In the next few chapters we will go into more detail on each of these components as well as look at how we can use adapters to service enable existing systems.

3

Service-enabling Existing Systems

The heart of service-oriented architecture (SOA) is the creation of processes and applications from existing services. The question arises, where do these services come from? Within an SOA solution, some services will need to be written from scratch, but most of the functions required should already exist in some form within the IT assets of the organization. Existing applications within the enterprise already provide many services that just require exposing to an SOA infrastructure. In this chapter, we will examine some ways to create services from existing applications. We refer to this process as service-enabling existing systems. After discussing some of the different types of systems, we will look at the specific functionality provided in the Oracle SOA Suite that makes it easy to convert file and database interfaces into services.

Types of systems

IT systems come in all sorts of shapes and forms; some have existing web service interfaces which can be consumed directly by an SOA infrastructure, others have completely proprietary interfaces, and others expose functionality through some well understood but non web service-based interfaces. In terms of service-enabling a system, it is useful to classify it by the type of interface it exposes.

Within the SOA Suite, components called adapters provide a mapping between non-web service interfaces and the rest of the SOA Suite. These adapters allow the SOA Suite to treat non-web service interfaces as though they have a web service interface.

Web service interfaces

If an application exposes a web service interface, meaning a SOAP service described by a **Web Service Description Language** (**WSDL**) document, then it may be consumed directly. Such web services can directly be included as part of a composite application or business process.

The latest versions of many applications expose web services, for example **SAP**, **Siebel**, **Peoplesoft**, and **E-Business Suite applications** provide access to at least some of their functionality through web services.

Technology interfaces

Many applications, such as SAP and Oracle E-Business Suite, currently expose only part of their functionality or no functionality through web service interfaces, but they can still participate in service-oriented architecture. Many applications have adopted an interface that is to some extent based on a standard technology.

Examples of standard technology interfaces include the following:

- Files
- Database tables and stored procedures
- Message queues

While these interfaces may be based on a standard technology, they do not provide a standard data model, and generally, there must be a mapping between the raw technology interface and the more structured web service style interface that we would like.

The following table shows how these interfaces are supported through technology adapters provided with the SOA Suite.

Technology	Adapter	Notes
Files	File	Reads and writes files mounted directly on the machine. This can be physically attached disks or network mounted devices (for example, Windows shared drives or NFS drives).
	FTP	Reads and writes files mounted on an FTP server.
Database	Database	Reads and writes database tables and invokes stored procedures.

Technology	Adapter	Notes
Message queues	JMS	Reads and posts messages to **Java Messaging Service (JMS)** queues and topics.
	AQ	Reads and posts messages to **Oracle AQ (Advanced Queuing)** queues.
	MQ	Reads and posts messages to **IBM MQ (Message Queue) Series queues**.
Java	EJB	Read and writes to EJBs.
TCP/IP	Socket	Reads and writes to raw socket interfaces.

In addition to the eight technology adapters listed previously, there are other technology adapters available, such as a CICS adapter to connect to IBM mainframes and an adapter to connect to systems running Oracle's Tuxedo transaction processing system. There are many other technology adapters that may be purchased to work with the SOA Suite.

The installed adapters are shown in the **Component Palette** of JDeveloper in the **Service Adapters** section when **SOA** is selected, as shown in the following screenshot:

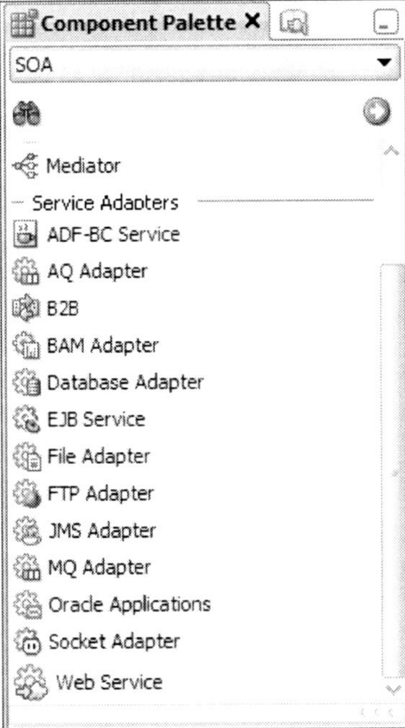

Application interfaces

The technology adapters leave the task of mapping interfaces and their associated data structures into XML in the hands of the service-enabler. When using an application adapter, such as those for the Oracle E-Business Suite or SAP, the grouping of interfaces and mapping them into XML is already done for you by the adapter developer. These application adapters make life easier for the service-enabler by hiding underlying data formats and transport protocols.

Unfortunately, the topic of application adapters is too large an area to delve into in this book, but you should always check if an application-specific adapter already exists for the system that you want to service-enable. This is because application adapters will be easier to use than the technology adapters.

There are hundreds of third-party adapters that may be purchased to provide SOA Suite with access to functionality within packaged applications.

Java Connector Architecture

Within the SOA Suite, adapters are implemented and accessed using a Java technology known as **Java Connector Architecture (JCA)**. JCA provides a standard packaging and discovery method for adapter functionality. Most of the time, SOA Suite developers will be unaware of JCA because JDeveloper generates a JCA binding as part of a WSDL interface and automatically deploys them with the SCA Assembly. In the current release, JCA adapters must be deployed separately to a WebLogic server for use by the Oracle Service Bus.

Creating services from files

A common mechanism for communicating with an existing application is through a file. Many applications will write their output to a file, expecting it to be picked up and processed by other applications. By using the file adapter, we can create a service representation that makes the file producing application appear as an SOA-enabled service that invokes other services. Similarly, other applications can be configured to take input by reading files. A file adapter allows us to make the production of the file appear as an SOA invocation, but under the covers, the invocation actually creates a file.

File communication is either inbound (this means that a file has been created by an application and must be read) or outbound (this means that a file must be written to provide input to an application). The files that are written and read by existing applications may be in a variety of formats including XML, separator delimited files, or fixed format files.

A payroll use case

Consider a company that has a payroll application that produces a file detailing payments. This file must be transformed into a file format that is accepted by the company's bank and then delivered to the bank via FTP. The company wants to use SOA technologies to perform this transfer because it allows them to perform additional validations or enrichment of the data before sending it to the bank. In addition, they want to store the details of what was sent in a database for audit purposes. In this scenario, a file adapter could be used to take the data from the file, an FTP adapter to deliver it to the bank, and a database adapter could post it into the tables required for audit purposes.

Reading a payroll file

Let's look at how we would read from a payroll file. Normally, we will poll to check for the arrival of a file, although it is also possible to read a file without polling. The key points to be considered beforehand are:

- How often should we poll for the file?
- Do we need to read the contents of the file?
- Do we need to move it to a different location?
- What do we do with the file when we have read or moved it?
    - Should we delete it?
    - Should we move it to an archive directory?
- How large is the file and its records?
- Does the file have one record or many?

We will consider all these factors as we interact with the File Adapter Wizard.

Starting the wizard

We begin by dragging the file adapter from the component palette in JDeveloper onto either a BPEL process or an SCA Assembly (refer to *Chapter 2, Writing your First Composite* for more information on building a composite).

This causes the File **Adapter Configuration Wizard** to start.

Naming the service

Clicking on **Next** allows us to choose a name for the service that we are creating and optionally a description. We will use the service name **PayrollinputFileService**. Any name can be used, as long as it has some meaning to the developers. It is a good idea to have a consistent naming convention, for example, identifying the business role (PayrollInput), the technology (File), and the fact that this is a service (**PayrollinputFileService**).

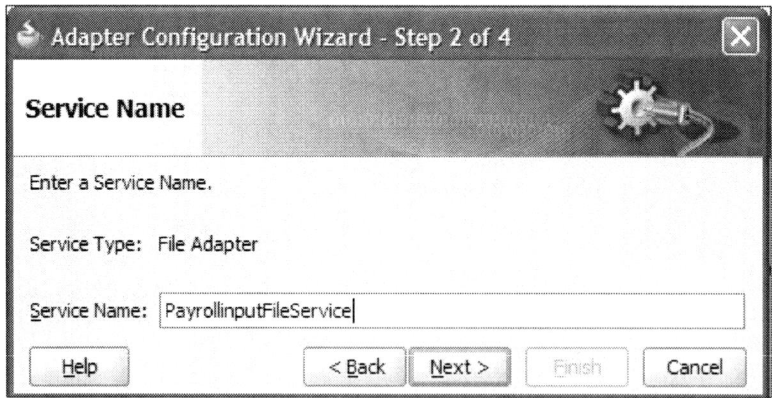

Identifying the operation

Clicking on **Next** allows us to either import an existing WSDL definition for our service or create a new service definition. We would **import an existing WSDL** to reuse an existing adapter configuration that had been created previously. Choosing **Define from operation and schema (specified later)** allows us to create a new definition.

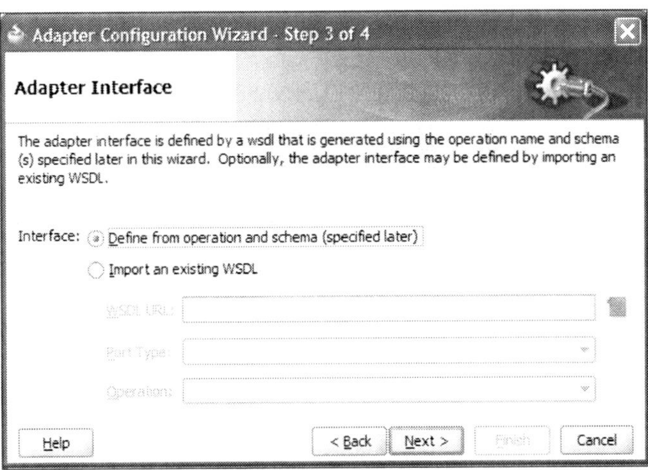

If we choose to create a new definition, then we start by specifying how we map the files onto a service. It is here that we decide whether we are reading or writing the file. When reading a file, we decide if we wish to generate an event when it is available (a normal Read File operation that requires an inbound operation to receive the message) or if we want to read it only when requested (a Synchronous Read File operation that requires an outbound operation).

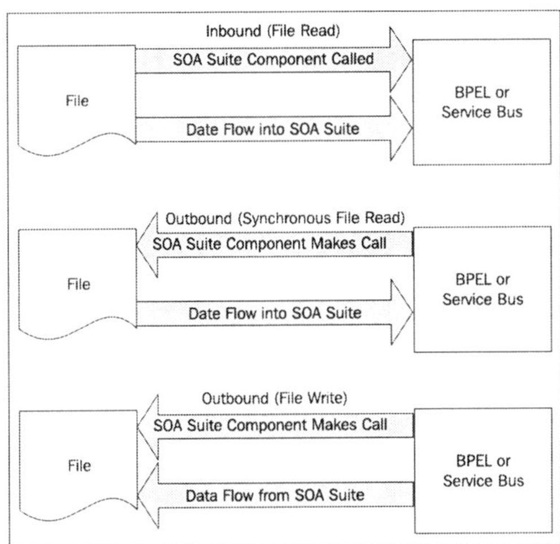

Who calls who?

We usually think of a service as something that we call and then get a result from. However, in reality, services in a service-oriented architecture will often initiate events. These events may be delivered to a BPEL process which is waiting for an event, or routed to another service through the Service Bus, Mediator, or even initiate a whole new SCA Assembly. Under the covers, an adapter might need to poll to detect an event, but the service will always be able to generate an event. With a service, we either call it to get a result or it generates an event that calls some other service or process.

The file adapter wizard exposes four types of operation, as outlined in the following table. We will explore the read operation to generate events as a file is created.

Operation Type	Direction	Description
Read File	Inbound call from service	Reads the file and generates one or more calls into BPEL, Mediator, or Service Bus when a file appears.
Write File	Outbound call to service with no response	Writes a file, with one or more calls from BPEL, Mediator, or the Service Bus, causing records to be written to a file.
Synchronous Read File	Outbound call to service returning file contents	BPEL, Mediator, or Service Bus requests a file to be read, returning nothing if the file doesn't exist.
List Files	Outbound call to service returning a list of files in a directory	Provides a means for listing the files in a directory.

Why ignore the contents of the file?

The file adapter has an option named **Do not read file content**. This is used when the file is just a signal for some event. *Do not use this feature for the scenario where a file is written and then marked as available by another file being written.* This is explicitly handled elsewhere in the file adapter. Instead, the feature can be used as a signal of some event that has no relevant data other than the fact that something has happened. Although the file itself is not readable, certain metadata is made available as part of the message sent.

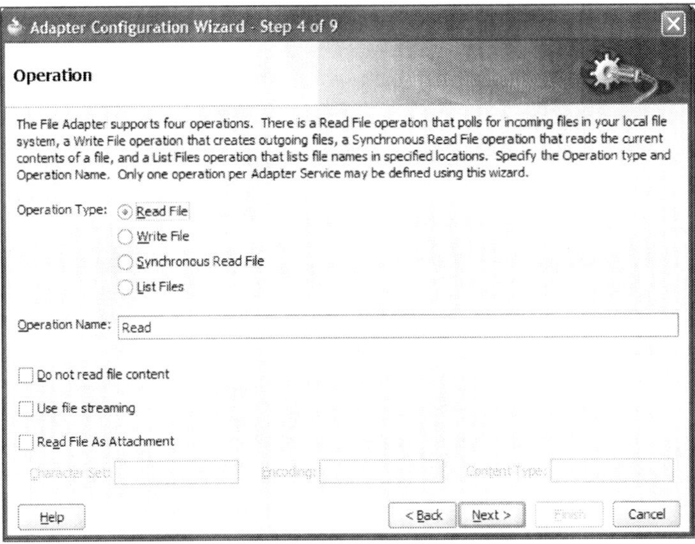

Defining the file location

Clicking on **Next** allows us to configure the location of the file. Locations can be specified as either physical (mapped directly onto the filesystem) or logical (an indirection to the real location). The **Directory for Incoming Files** specifies where the adapter should look to find new files. If the file should appear in a subdirectory of the one specified, then the **Process files recursively** box should be checked.

The key question now is what to do with the file when it appears. One option is to keep a copy of the file in an archive directory. This is achieved by checking the **Archive processed files** attribute and providing a location for the file archive. In addition to archiving the file, we need to decide if we want to delete the original file. This is indicated by the **Delete files after successful retrieval** checkbox.

Logical versus Physical locations

The file adapter allows us to have logical (**Logical Name**) or physical locations (**Physical Path**) for files. Physical locations are easier for developers as we embed the exact file location into the assembly with no more work required. However, this only works if the file locations are the same in the development, test and production environments, particularly unlikely if development is done on Windows but production is on Linux. Hence for production systems, it is best to use logical locations that must be mapped onto physical locations when deployed. *Chapter 19, Packaging and Deploying* shows how this mapping may be different for each environment.

Selecting specific files

Having defined the location where files are found, we can now move on to the next step in the wizard. Here we describe what the filenames look like. We can describe filenames using either wildcards (using '*' to represent a sequence of 0 or more characters) or using Java regular expressions, as described in the documentation for the `java.util.regex.Pattern` class. Usually wildcards will be good enough. For example, if we want to select all files that start with "PR" and end with ".txt", then we would use the wildcard string "PR*.txt" or the regular expression "PR.*\.txt". As you can see, it is generally easier to use wildcards rather than regular expressions. We can also specify a pattern to identify which files should not be processed.

The final part of this screen in the adapter wizard asks if the file contains a single message or many messages. This is confusing because when the screen refers to messages, it really means records.

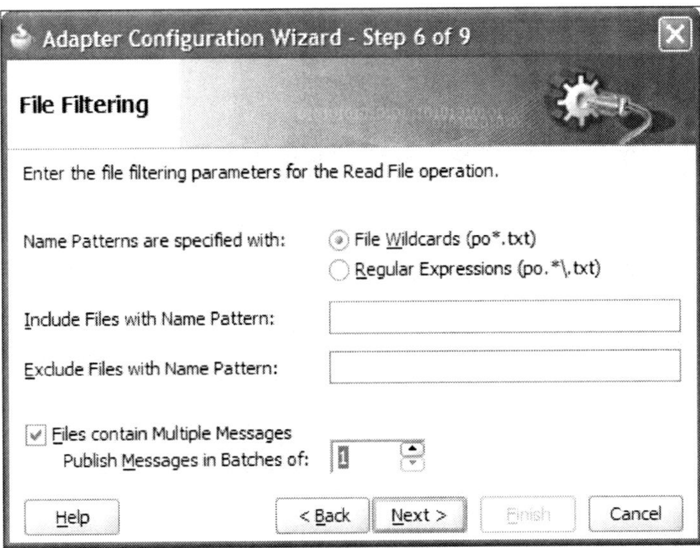

XML files

It is worth remembering that a well formed XML document can only have a single root element, and hence an XML input file will normally have only a single input record. In the case of very large XML files, it is possible to have the file adapter batch the file up into multiple messages, in which case the root element is replicated in each message, and the second level elements are treated as records. This behavior is requested by setting the streaming option.

By default, a message will contain a single record from the file. Records will be defined in the next step of the wizard. If the file causes a BPEL process to be started, then a 1000 record file would result in 1000 BPEL processes being initiated. To improve efficiency, records can be batched, and the **Publish Messages in Batches of** attribute controls the maximum number of records in a message.

Message batching

It is common for an incoming file to contain many records. These records, when processed, can impact system performance and memory requirements. Hence it is important to align the use of the records with their likely impact on system resources.

Detecting that the file is available

The next step in the wizard allows us to configure the frequency of polling for the inbound file. There are two parameters that can be configured here–the **Polling Frequency** and the **Minimum File Age**.

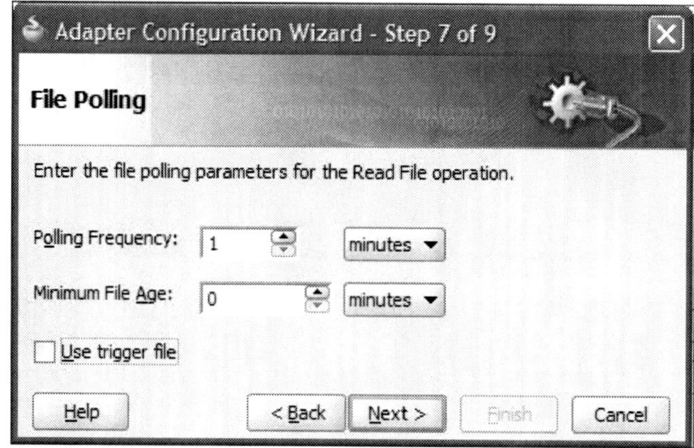

The **Polling Frequency** just means the time delay between checking to see if a file is available for processing. The adapter will check once per interval to see if the file exists. Setting this too low can consume needless CPU resources, setting it too high can make the system appear unresponsive. 'Too high' and 'too low' are very subjective and will depend on your individual requirements. For example, the polling interval for a file that is expected to be written twice a day may be set to three hours, while the interval for a file that is expected to be written every hour may be set to 15 minutes.

Minimum File Age specifies how old a file must be before it is processed by the adapter. This setting allows a file to be completely written before it is read. For example, a large file may take five minutes to write out from the original application. If the file is read three minutes after it has been created, then it is possible for the adapter to run out of records to read and assume the file has been processed, when in reality, the application is still writing to the file. Setting a minimum age to ten minutes would avoid this problem by giving the application at least ten minutes to write the file.

As an alternative to polling for a file directly, we may use a trigger file to indicate that a file is available. Some systems write large files to disk and then indicate that they are available by writing a trigger file. This avoids the problems with reading an incomplete file we identified in the previous paragraph, without the delay in processing the file that a minimum age field may cause.

Message format

The penultimate step in the file adapter is to set up the format of records or messages in the file. This is one of the most critical steps, as this defines the format of messages generated by a file.

Messages may be opaque, meaning that they are passed around as black boxes. This may be appropriate with a Microsoft Word file, for example, that must merely be transported from point A to point B without being examined. This is indicated by the **Native format translation is not required (Schema is Opaque)** checkbox.

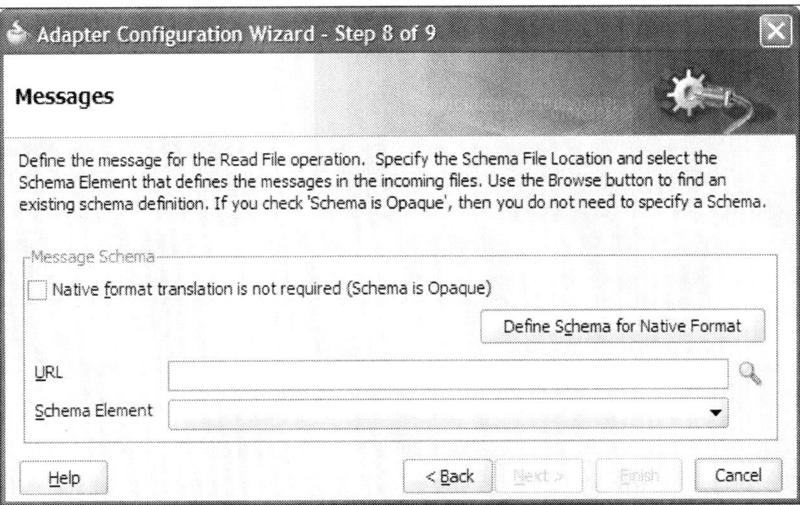

If the document is already in an XML format, then we can just specify a schema and an expected root element and the job is done. Normally the file is in some non-XML format that must be mapped onto an XML Schema generated through the native format builder wizard, which is invoked through the **Define Schema for Native Format** button.

Defining a native format schema

Invoking the **Native Format Builder** wizard brings up an initial start screen that leads on to the first step in the wizard, choosing the type of format, as shown in the following screenshot:

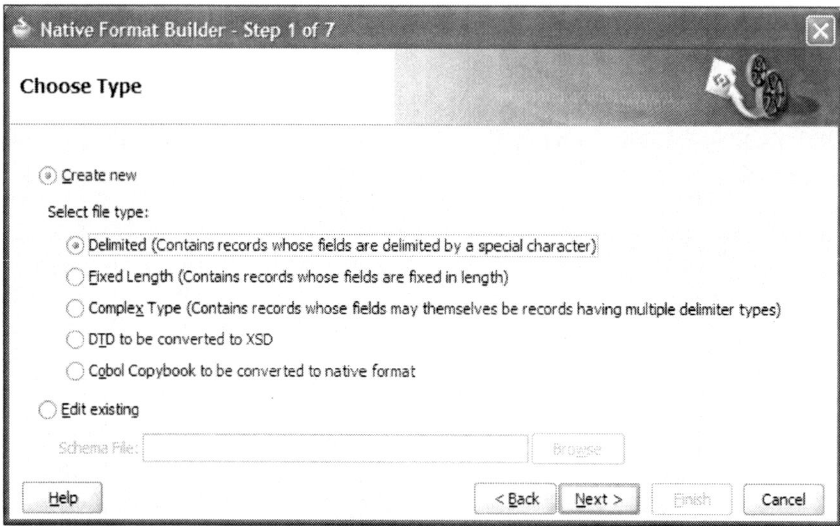

This allows us to identify the overall record structure. If we have an existing schema document that describes the record structure, then we can point to that. Usually, we will need to determine the type of structure of the file ourselves. The choices available are:

- **Delimited**: These are files such as **CSV** files (**Comma Separated Values**), records with spaces, or '+' signs for separators.
- **Fixed Length**: These are files whose records consist of fixed length fields. Be careful not to confuse these with space-separated files, as if a value does not fill the entire field, it will usually be padded with spaces.
- **Complex Type**: These files may include nested records like a master detail type structure.
- **DTD to be converted to XSD**: These are XML Data Type Definition XML files that will be mapped onto an XML Schema description of the file content.
- **Cobol Copybook to be converted to native format**: These are files that have usually been produced by a COBOL system, often originating from a mainframe.

We will look at a delimited file, as it is one of the most common formats.

Although we are using the separator file type, the steps involved are basically the same for most file types including the fixed length field format, which is also extremely common.

Using a sample file

To make it easier to describe the format of the incoming file, the wizard asks us to specify a file to use as a sample. If necessary, we can skip rows in the file and determine the number of records to read. Obviously, reading a very large number of records may take a while, and if all the variability on the file is in the first ten records, then there is no point in wasting time reading any more sample records. We may also choose to restrict the number of rows processed at runtime.

Setting the character set needs to be done carefully, particularly in international environments where non-ASCII character sets may be common.

After selecting a sample file, the wizard will display an initial view of the file with a guess at the field separators.

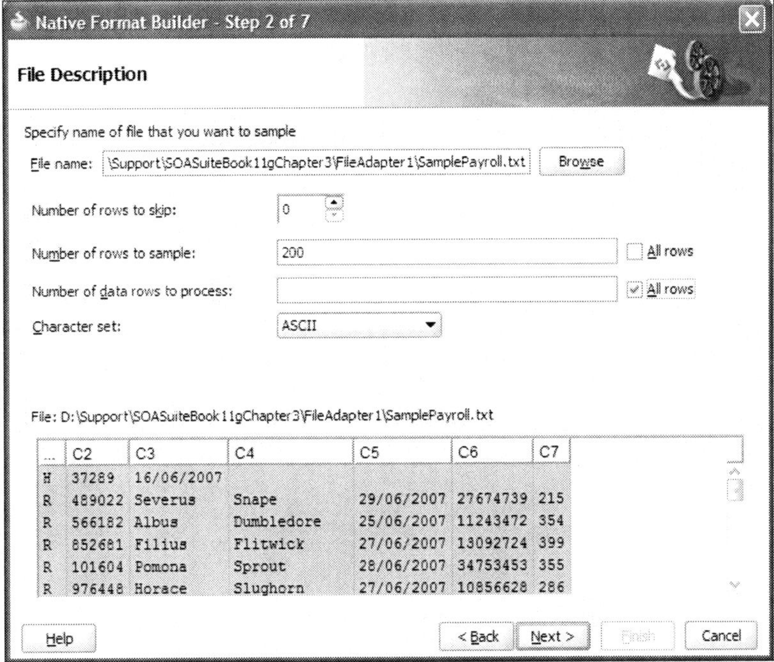

Record structure

The next step of the wizard allows us to describe how the records appear in the file.

The first option **File contains only one record** allows us to process the file as a single message. This can be useful when the file has multiple records, all of the same format, which we want to read as a single message. Use of this option disables batching.

The next option of **File contains multiple record instances** allows batching to take place. Records are either of the same type or of different types. They can only be marked of different types if they can be distinguished, based on the first field in the record. In other words, in order to choose the **Multiple records are of different types**, the first field in all the records must be a record type identifier. In the example shown in the preceding screenshot, the first field is either an **H** for Header records or an **R** for Records.

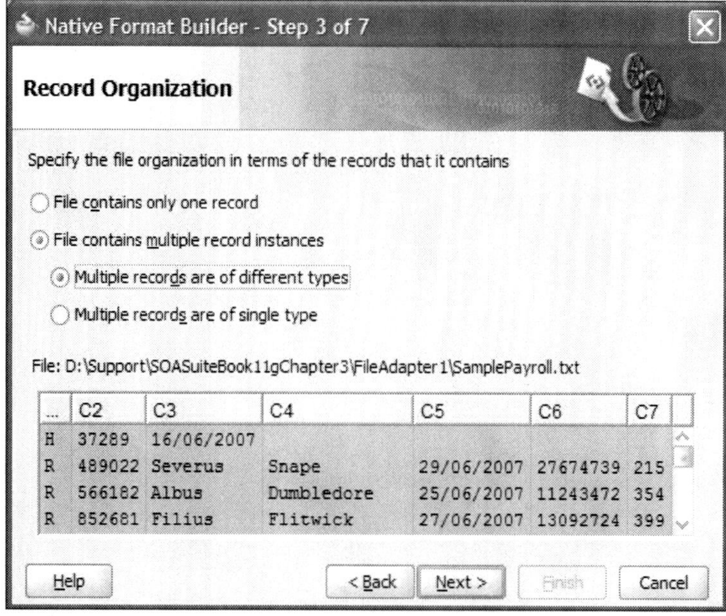

Choosing a root element

The next step allows us to define the target namespace and root element of the schema that we are generating.

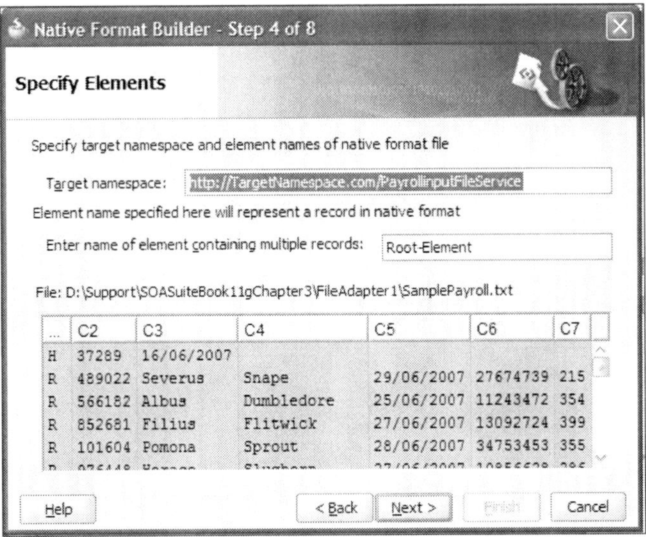

Don't forget that when using the **Native Format Builder** wizard, we are just creating an XML Schema document that describes the native (non-XML) format data. Most of the time this schema is transparent to us. However, at times the XML constructs have to emerge, for example, when identifying a name for a root element. The file is described using an XML Schema extension known as NXSD.

As we can see the root element is mandatory. This root element acts as a wrapper for the records in a message. If message batching is set to 1, then each wrapper will have a single sub-element, namely, the record. If the message is set to greater than 1, then each wrapper will have at least one and possibly more sub-elements, each sub-element being a record. There can never be more sub-elements than the batch size.

Message delimiters

Having described the overall structure of the file, we can now drill down into the individual fields. To do this, we first specify the message delimiters.

In addition to field delimiters, we can also specify a record delimiter. Usually record delimiters are new lines. If fields are also wrapped in quotation marks, then these can be stripped off by specifying the **Optionally enclosed by** character.

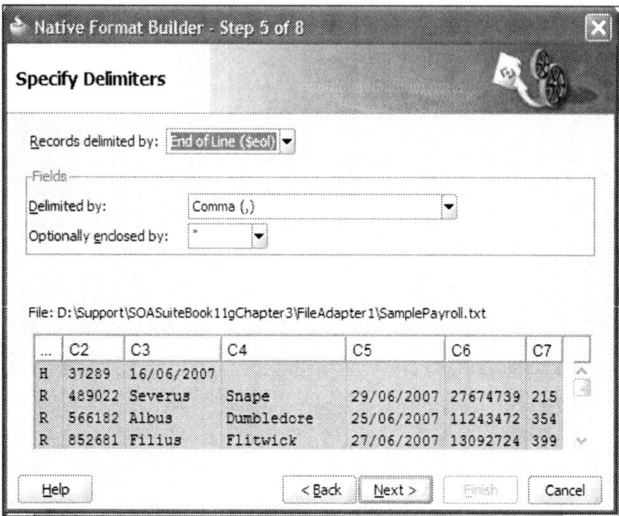

Record type names

The wizard will identify the types of records based on the first field in each record, as shown in the preceding screenshot. It is possible to ignore record types by selecting them and clicking **Delete**. If this is done by mistake, then it is possible to add them back by using the **Add** button. Only fields that exist in the sample data can be added in the wizard.

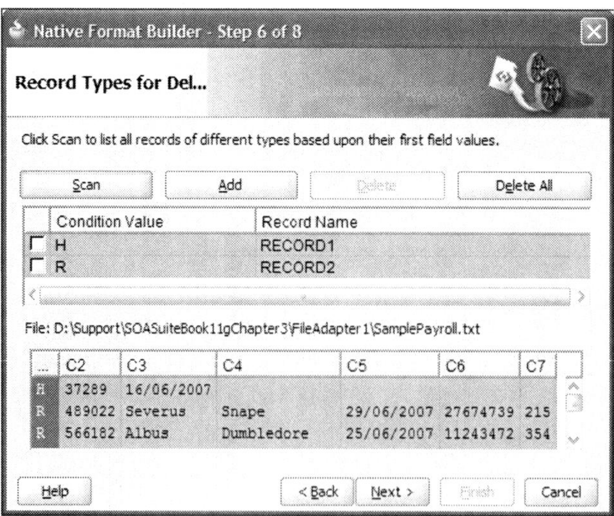

Note that if we want to reset the record types screen, then the **Scan** button will rescan the sample file and look for all the different record types it contains.

The **Record Name** field can be set by double-clicking it and providing a suitable record name. This record name is the XML element name that encapsulates the record content.

Field properties

Now that we have identified record and field boundaries, we can drill down into the records and define the data types and names of individual fields. This is done for each record type in turn. We can select which records to define by selecting them from the **Record Name** drop-down box or by pressing the **Next Record Type** button.

It is important to be as liberal as possible when defining field data types because any mismatches will cause errors that will need to be handled. Being liberal in our record definitions will allow us to validate the messages, as described in *Chapter 13, Building Validation into Services*, without raising system errors.

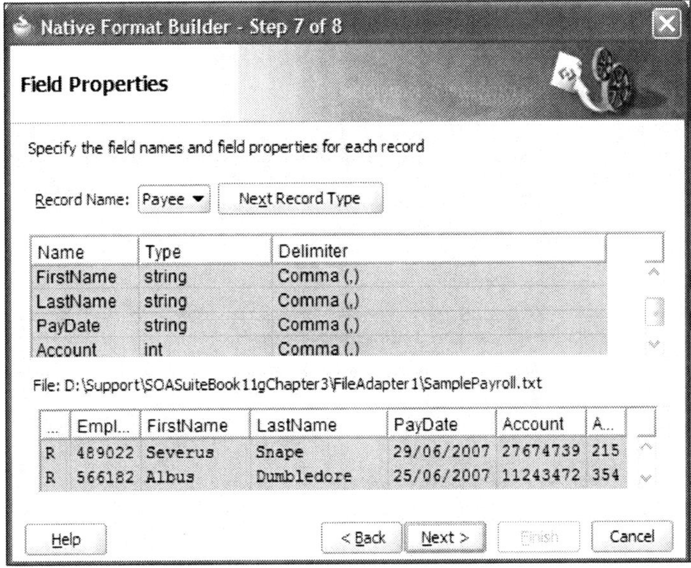

The **Name** column represents the element name of this field. The wizard will attempt to guess the type of the field, but it is important to always check this because the sample data you are using may not include all possibilities. A common error is identifying numbers to be tagged as integers, when they should really be strings—accept integer types only when they are likely to have arithmetic operations performed on them.

Verifying the result

We have now completed our mapping and can verify what has been done by looking at the generated XML Schema file. Note that the generated schema uses some Oracle extensions to enable a non-XML formatted file to be represented as XML. In particular the `NXSD` namespace prefix is used to identify field separators and record terminators.

The XML Schema generated can be edited manually. This is useful to support nested records (records inside other records) like those that may be found in a file containing order records with nested detail records (an order record contains multiple line item detail records). In this case, it is useful to use the wizard to generate a schema with order records and detail records at the same level. The schema can then be modified by hand to make the detail records children of the order records.

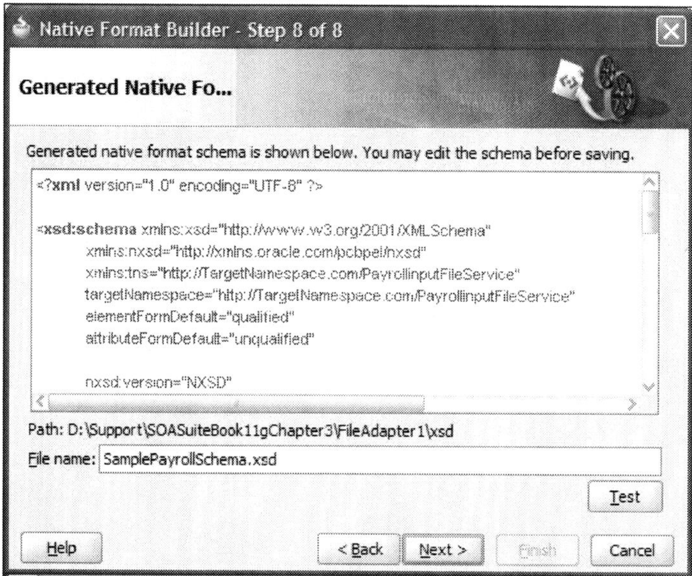

Clicking the **Test** button brings up a simple test screen that allows us to apply our newly generated schema to the input document and examine the resulting XML.

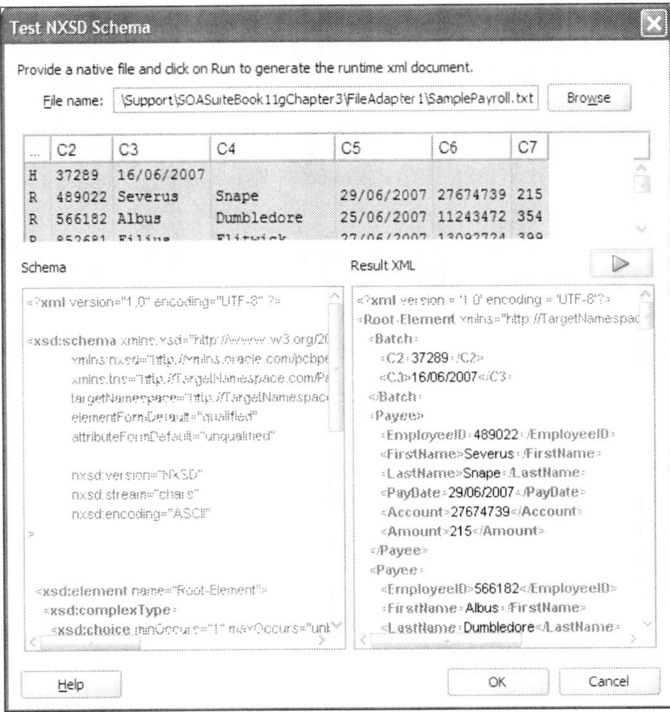

Clicking **Next** and then **Finish** will cause the generated schema file to be saved.

Finishing the wizards

Until now, no work has been saved, except for the XML Schema mapping the file content onto an XML structure. The rest of the adapter settings are not saved, and the endpoint is not set up until the **Finish** button is clicked on the completion screen, as shown in the following screenshot. Note that the file generated is a **Web Service Description Language** (**WSDL**) file with a JCA binding.

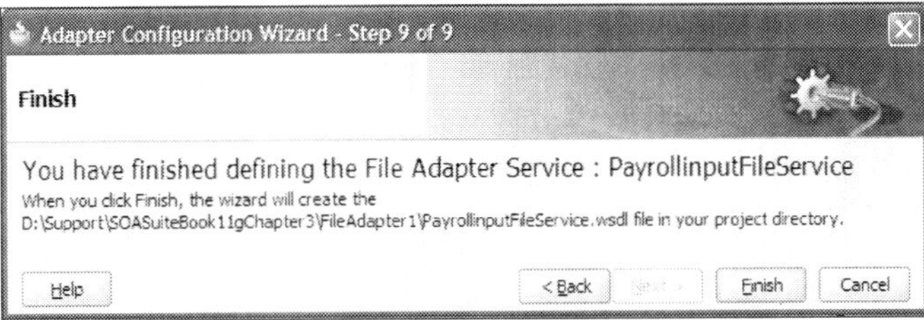

Throttling the file and FTP adapter

The file and FTP adapters can consume a lot of resources when processing large files (thousands of records) because they keep sending messages with batches of records until the file is processed, while not waiting for the records to be processed. This behavior can be altered by forcing them to wait until a message is processed before sending another message. This is done by making the following changes to the WSDL generated by the wizard. This changes the one-way read operation into a two-way read operation that will not complete until a reply is generated by our code in BPEL or the Service Bus.

Creating a dummy message type

Add a new message definition to the WSDL like the one in the following code snippet:

```
<message name="Dummy_msg">
    <part xmlns:xsd="http://www.w3.org/2001/XMLSchema"
          name="Dummy" type="xsd:string"/>
</message>
```

Adding an output message to the read operation

In the `<portType>`, add an `<output>` element to the read `<operation>` element.

```
<portType name="Read_ptt">
  <operation name="Read">
    <input message="tns:PayrollList_msg"/>
    <output message="tns:Dummy_msg"/>
  </operation>
</portType>
```

In the `<jca:operation>` element, add an empty `<output/>` element.

Using the modified interface

The adapter will now have a two way interface and will need to receive a reply to a message before it sends the next batch of records, thus throttling the throughput. Note that no data needs to be sent in the reply message. This will limit the number of active operations to the number of threads assigned to the file adapter.

Writing a payroll file

We can now use the FTP adapter to write the payroll file to a remote filesystem. This requires us to create another adapter within our BPEL process, Mediator, or Service Bus. Setting up the FTP adapter to write to a remote filesystem is very similar to reading files with the file adapter.

Selecting the FTP connection

The first difference is that when using the FTP adapter instead of the File adapter, we have to specify an FTP connection to use in the underlying application server. This connection is set up in the application server running the adapter. For example, when using the WebLogic Application Server, the WebLogic Console can be used. The JNDI location of the connection factory is the location that must be provided to the wizard. The JNDI location must be configured in the application server using the administrative tools provided by the application server. Refer to your application server documentation for details on how to do this, as it varies between applications servers.

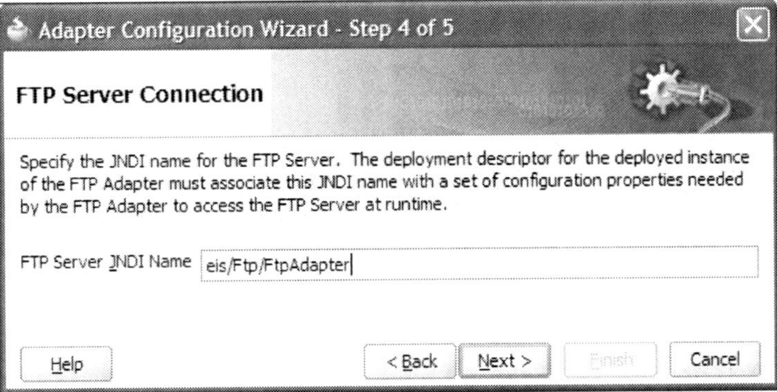

Choosing the operation

When we choose the type of operation, we again notice that the screen is different from the file adapter, having an additional **File Type** category. This relates to the **Ascii** and **Binary** settings of an FTP session. ASCII causes the FTP transfer to adapt to changes in character encoding between the two systems, for example, converting between EBCDIC and ASCII or altering line feeds between systems. When using text files, it is generally a good idea to select the ASCII format. When sending binary files, it is vital that the binary file type is used to avoid any unfortunate and unwanted transformations.

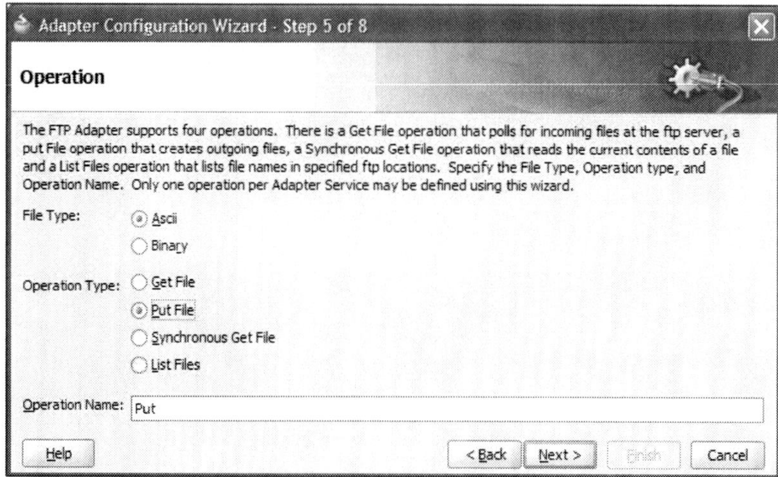

Selecting the file destination

Choosing where the file is created is the same for both the FTP and the file adapter. Again, there is a choice of physical or logical paths. The file naming convention allows us some control over the name of the output file. In addition to the %**SEQ**% symbol that inserts a unique sequence number, it is also possible to insert a date or date time string into the filename. Note that in the current release, you cannot have both a date time string and a sequence string in the file naming convention.

[When using a date time string as part of the filename, files with the same date time string will overwrite each other. If this is the case, then consider using a sequence number instead.]

When producing an output file, we can either keep appending to a single file by selecting the **Append to existing file** checkbox, which will keep growing without limit, or we can create new files, which will be dependent on attributes of the data being written. This is the normal way of working for non-XML files, and a new output file will be generated when one or more records are written to the adapter.

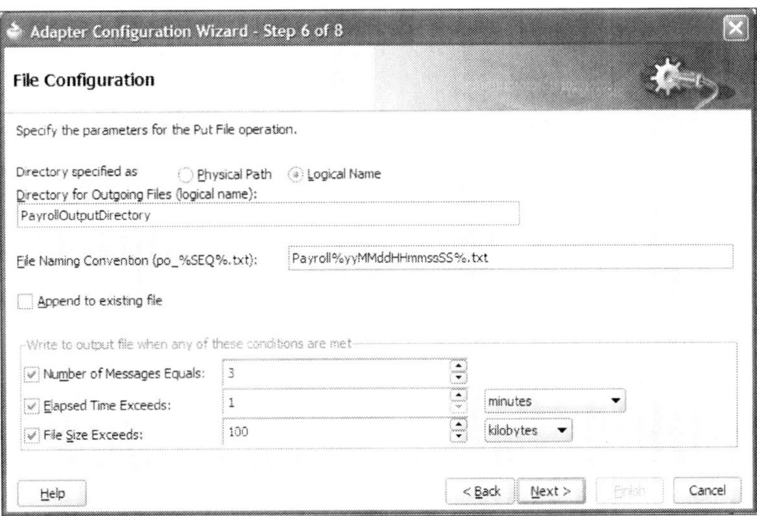

The criteria for deciding to write to a new file are as follows:

- **Number of Messages Equals**: This criterion forces the file to be written when the given number of messages is reached. This can be thought of as batching the output so that we reduce the number of files created.
- **Elapsed Time Exceeds**: This criterion puts a time limit on how long the adapter will keep the file open. This places an upper time limit on creating an output file.
- **File Size Exceeds**: This criterion allows us to limit the file sizes. As soon as a message causes the file to exceed the given size, no further message will be appended to this file.

These criteria can all be applied together, and as soon as one of them is satisfied, a new file will be created.

Writing XML files

When writing XML files, care should be taken to have only a single message per file, or else there will be multiple XML root elements in the document that will make it an invalid XML document.

Completing the FTP file writer service

The next step in the wizard is to define the actual record formats. This is exactly the same as when creating an input file. If we don't have an existing XML Schema for the output file, then we can use the wizard to create one if we have a sample file to use.

Finally, remember to run through the wizard to the end, and click **Finish** rather than **Cancel** or our entire configuration will be lost.

Moving, copying, and deleting files

Sometimes we will just want an adapter to move, copy, or delete a file without reading it. We will use the ability of the file adapter to move a file (refer to *Chapter 16, Message Interaction Patterns*, to set up a scheduler service within the SOA Suite).

The following steps will configure an outbound file or FTP adapter to move, copy, or delete a file without reading it.

Generating an adapter

Use the file or FTP adapter wizard to generate an outbound adapter with a file synchronous read or FTP synchronous get operation. You may also use a write or put operation. The data location should use physical directories, and the content should be marked as opaque, so that there is no need to understand the content of the file. Once this has been done, we will modify the WSDL generated to add additional operations.

Modifying the port type

First, we edit the WSDL file itself, which we call `<AdapterServiceName>.wsdl`. Modify the port type of the adapter to include the additional operations required, as shown in the following code snippet. Use the same message type as the operation generated by the wizard.

```
<portType name="Write_ptt">
  <operation name="Write">
    <input message="tns:Write_msg"/>
    </operation>
  <operation name="Move">
      <input message="tns:Write_msg"/>
    </operation>
</portType>
```

Note that the following operation names are supported:

- Move
- Copy
- Delete

Modifying the binding

We now edit the bindings which are contained in a separate file to the WSDL called `<AdapterServiceName>_<file/ftp>.jca`. Bindings describe how the service description maps onto the physical service implementation. For now, we will just modify the binding to add the additional operations needed and map them to the appropriate implementation, as shown in the following code snippet:

```
<endpoint-interaction portType="Write_ptt" operation="Write">
  <interaction-spec className="oracle.tip.adapter.file.outbound.
FileInteractionSpec">
    <property name="PhysicalDirectory" value="/user/oracle"/>
    <property name="FileNamingConvention" value="fred.txt"/>
    <property name="Append" value="false"/>
  </interaction-spec>
</endpoint-interaction>
<endpoint-interaction portType="Write_ptt" operation="Move">
  <interaction-spec className="oracle.tip.adapter.file.outbound.
FileIoInteractionSpec">
    <property name="Type" value="MOVE"/>
    <property name="SourcePhysicalDirectory" value="/usr/oracle"/>
    <property name="SourceFileName" value="fred.txt"/>
    <property name="TargetPhysicalDirectory" value="/usr/payroll"/>
    <property name="TargetFileName" value="Payroll.txt"/>
  </interaction-spec>
</endpoint-interaction>
```

Note that the following types are supported for use with the equivalent operation names. Observe that operation names are mixed case and types are uppercase:

- `MOVE`
- `COPY`
- `DELETE`

The `interaction-spec` is used to define the types of operations supported by this particular binding. It references a Java class that provides the functionality and may have properties associated with it to configure its behavior. When using the FTP adapter for move, copy, and delete operations, the `InteractionSpec` property in the `<AdapterServiceName>_ftp.jca` file must be changed to `oracle.tip.adapter.ftp.outbound.FTPIoInteractionSpec`.

Configuring file locations through additional header properties

In order to allow runtime configuration of the source and destination locations, it is necessary to pass the source and destination information as properties of the call to the adapter.

For example, when using a BPEL invoke activity, we would pass the properties, as shown in the following code snippet:

```
<invoke name="Invoke_Move" inputVariable="Invoke_Move_InputVariable"
        partnerLink="MoveFileService" portType="ns1:Write_ptt"
        operation="Move">
  <bpelx:inputProperty name="jca.file.SourceDirectory"
                       variable="srcDir"/>
  <bpelx:inputProperty name="jca.file.SourceFileName"
                       variable="srcFile"/>
  <bpelx:inputProperty name="jca.file.TargetDirectory"
                       variable="dstDir"/>
  <bpelx:inputProperty name="jca.file.TargetFileName"
                       variable="dstFile"/>
</invoke>
```

These properties will override the default values in the `.jca` file and can be used to dynamically select at runtime the locations to be used for the move, copy, or delete operation. The properties may be edited in the source tab of the BPEL document, the `.bpel` file, or they may be created and modified through the **Properties** tab of the **Invoke** dialog in the BPEL visual editor.

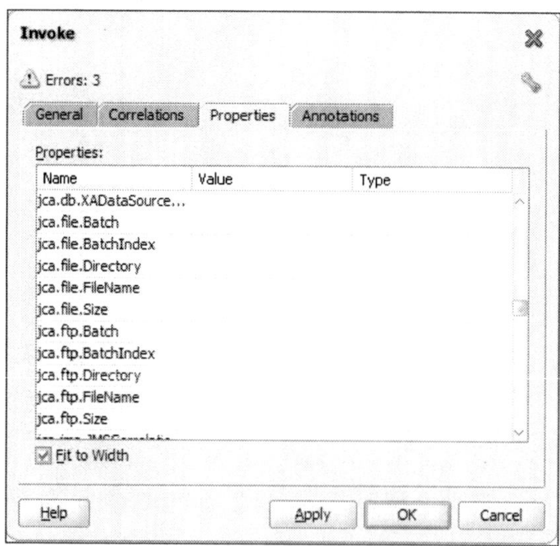

With these modifications, the move, copy, or delete operations will appear as additional operations on the service that can be invoked from the service bus or within BPEL.

Adapter headers

In addition to the data associated with the service being provided by the adapter, sometimes referred to as the payload of the service, it is also possible to configure or obtain information about the operation of an adapter through header messages. Header messages are passed as properties to the adapter. We demonstrated this in the previous section when setting the header properties for the `Move` operation of the file adapter.

The properties passed are of the following two formats:

```
<property name="AdapterSpecificPropertyName" value="data"/>
<property name="AdapterSpecificPropertyName" variable="varName"/>
```

The former style allows the passing of literal values through the header. The latter allows the property to be set from a string variable.

Testing the file adapters

We can test the adapters by using them within a BPEL process or a Mediator like the one shown in the following screenshot. Building a BPEL process is covered in *Chapter 5, Building Composite Services and Business Processes*. This uses the two services we that have just described and links them with a copy operation that transforms data from one format to the other.

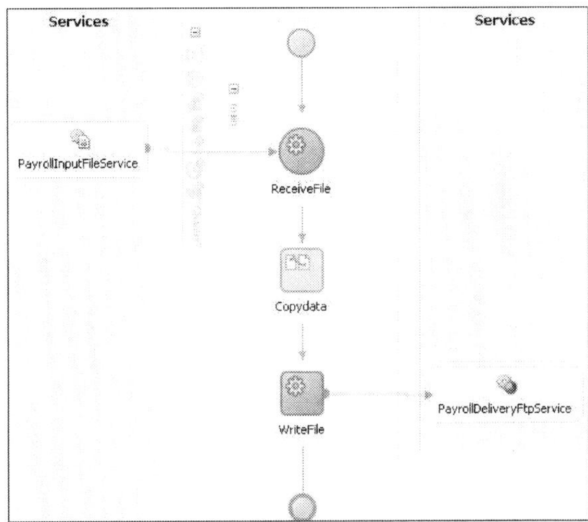

Creating services from databases

Along with files, databases are one of the most common ways of interacting with existing applications and providing them with a service interface. In this section we will investigate how to write recordrs into the database using the database adapter.

Writing to a database

Before we configure a database adapter, we first need to create a new database connection within JDeveloper. This is done by creating a **Database Connection** from the **New Gallery**.

Choosing a database connection brings up the database connection wizard, which allows us to enter the connection details of our database.

Selecting the database schema

With an established database connection, we can now create a service based on a database table. We will create a service that updates the database with the payroll details. The model for the database tables is shown in the following screenshot:

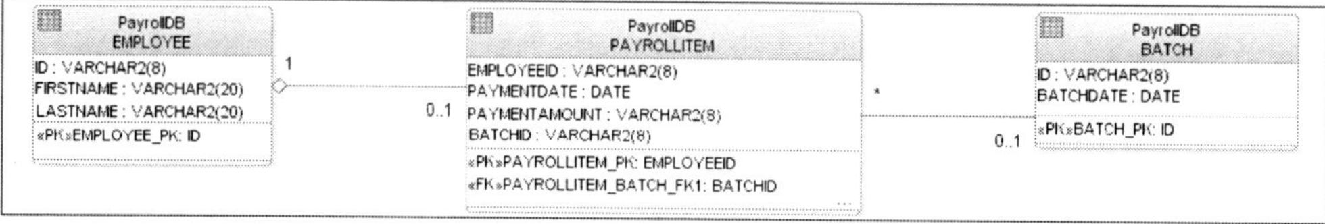

Now that we have our database connection, we can run the Database Adapter Wizard by dragging the database adapter icon from the tool palette onto a BPEL process or an SCA Assembly. This starts the Database Adapter Wizard, and after giving the service a name, we come to the **Service Connection** screen. This is shown as follows:

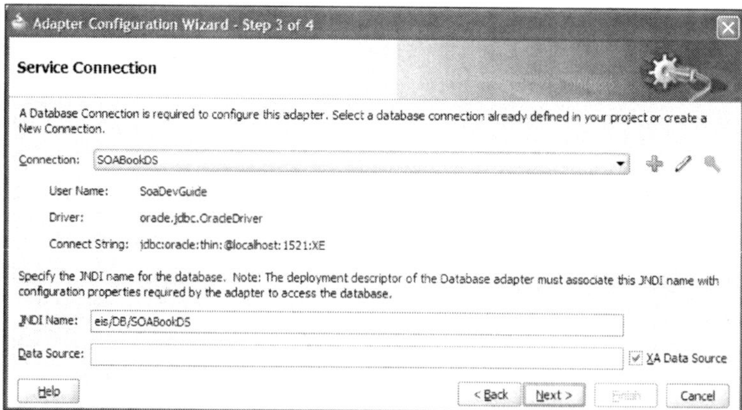

This allows us to choose a local connection in JDeveloper to use and also to select the JNDI location in the runtime environment of the database connection. Note that this JNDI connection must be configured as part of the database adapter in the default application in a similar way to the configuration of the FTP adapter.

How connections are resolved by the database adapter

When the adapter tries to connect to the database, it first tries to use the JNDI name provided, which should map to a JCA connection factory in the application server. If this name does not exist, then the adapter will use the database connection details from the JDeveloper database connection that was used in the wizard. This behavior is very convenient for development environments because it means that you can deploy and test the adapters in development without having to configure the JCA connection factories. However, best practice is to always configure the JCA adapter in the target environment to avoid unexpected connection failures.

Identifying the operation type

The database adapter has many ways in which it can interact with the database to provide a service interface.

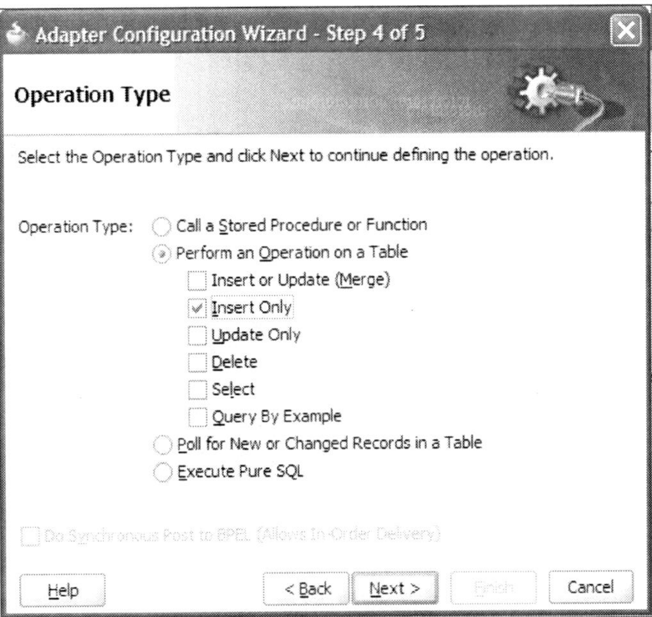

The **Operation Type** splits into two groups, calls into the database and events generated from the database. Calls into the database cover the following operations:

- The stored procedure or function call to execute a specific piece of code in the database. This could either update the database or retrieve information, but in either case, it is a synchronous call into the database.
- Perform an insert, update, delete, or select operation on the database. Again, this is done synchronously as a call into the database.
- Poll for new or changed records in a database table. This is done as a call into the SCA Assembly or BPEL.
- Execute custom SQL. This again runs the SQL synchronously against the database.

Polling for new or changed records is the only way for the database adapter to generate messages to be consumed in a BPEL process or an SCA Assembly. If we wish the adapter to wait for BPEL or the SCA Assembly to process the message, then we can use the **Do Synchronous Post to BPEL** checkbox. For this exercise, we will select insert / update for the operation.

Identifying tables to be operated on

The next step in the wizard asks which table is the root table or the beginning of the query. To select this, we first click the **Import Tables...** button to bring up the **Import Tables** dialog.

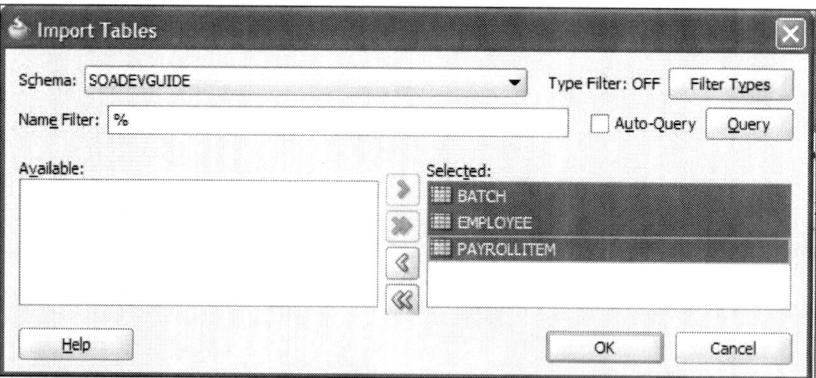

Once we have imported the tables we need, we then select the **PAYROLLITEM** table as the root table. We do this because each record will create a new **PAYROLLITEM** entry. All operations through the database adapter must be done with a root table. Any other table must be referenceable from this root table.

Identifying the relationship between tables

As we have more than one table involved in this operation, we need to decide which table relationship we want to use. In this case, we want to tie a payroll item back to a single employee, so we select the one-to-one relationship.

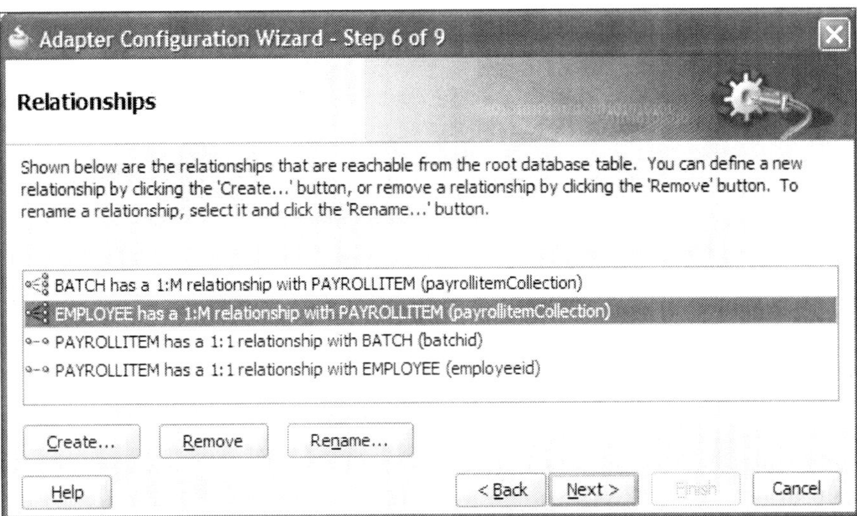

We can now finish the creation of the database adapter and hook it up with the file adapter we created earlier to allow us to read records from a file and place them in a database.

In our example, the adapter was able to work out relationships between tables by analysis of the foreign keys. If foreign key relationships do not exist, then the **Create** button may be used to inform the adapter of relationships that exist between tables.

Under the covers

Under the covers, a lot has happened. An offline copy of the relevant database schema has been created so that the design time is not reliant on being permanently connected to a database. The actual mapping of a database onto an XML document has also occurred. This is done using **Oracle TopLink** to create the mapping and a lot of the functions of the wizard are implemented using TopLink. The mapping can be further refined using the features of TopLink.

Using keys

Always identify the Primary Key for any table used by the database adapter. This can be done by applying a Primary Key constraint in the database, or if no such key has been created, then TopLink will prompt you to create one. If you have to create one in TopLink, then make sure it is really a Primary Key. TopLink optimizes its use of the database by maintaining an identity for each row in a table with a Primary Key. It only reads the Primary Key on select statements and then checks to see which records it needs to read in from the database. This reduces the amount of work mapping fields that have already been mapped because a record appears multiple times in the selection. If you don't identify a Primary Key correctly, then TopLink may incorrectly identify different records as being the same record and only load the data for the first such record encountered. So if you seem to be getting a lot of identical records in response to a query that should have separate records, then check your Primary Key definitions.

Summary

In this chapter, we have looked at how to use the file and database adapters to turn file and database interfaces into services that can be consumed by the rest of the SOA Suite. Note that when using the adapters, the schemas are automatically generated and changing the way the adapter works may mean a change in the schema. Therefore, in the next chapter, we will look at how to isolate our applications from the actual adapter service details.

4

Loosely-coupling Services

In the previous chapter, we explored how we can take functionality in our existing applications and expose them as services. When we do this, we often find that the service interface we create is tightly coupled to the underlying implementation. We can make our architecture more robust by reducing this coupling. By defining our interface around our architecture, rather than around our existing application interfaces, we can reduce coupling. We can also reduce coupling by using a routing service to avoid physical location dependencies. In this chapter, we will explore how service virtualization through the Mediator and the Service Bus of the Oracle SOA Suite can be used to deliver more loosely-coupled services. Loose coupling reduces the impact of change on our systems, allowing us to deploy new functions more rapidly into the market. Loose coupling also reduces the maintenance costs associated with our deployments.

Coupling

Coupling is a measure of how dependent one service is upon another. The more closely one service depends on another service, the more tightly coupled they are. There have been a number of efforts to formalize metrics for coupling, and they all revolve around the same basic items:

- Number of input data items: Basically, the number of input parameters of the service.
- Number of output data items: The output data of the service.
- Dependencies on other services: The number of services called by this service.
- Dependencies of other services on this service: The number of services that invoke this service.
- Use of shared global data: The number of shared data items used by this service. This may include database tables or shared files.
- Temporal dependencies: Dependencies on other services being available at specific times.

Let us examine how each of these measures may be applied to our service interface. The principles below are relevant to all services, but widely re-used services have a special need for all of the items.

Number of input data items

A service should only accept as input the data items required to perform the service being requested. Additional information should not be passed into the service because this creates unnecessary dependencies on the input formats. This economy of input allows the service to focus just on the function it is intended to provide and does not require it to understand unnecessary data formats. The best way to isolate the service from changes in data formats that it does not use is to make the service unaware of those data formats.

For example, a credit rating service should only require sufficient information to identify the individual being rated. Additional information, such as the amount of credit being requested or the type of goods or services for which a loan is required, is not necessary for the credit rating service to perform its job.

Services should accept only the data required to perform their function and nothing more.

When talking about reducing the number of data items input or output from a service, we are talking about the service implementation, not a logical service interface that may be implemented using a canonical data model. The canonical data model may have additional attributes not required by a particular service, but these should not be part of the physical service interface. Adding attributes to "make a service more universal" only serves to make it harder to maintain.

Number of output data items

In the same way that a service should not accept inputs that are unnecessary for the function it performs, a service should not return data that is related only to its internal operation. Exposing such data as part of the response data will create dependencies on the internal implementation of the service that are not necessary.

Sometimes, a service needs to maintain its state between requests. State implies that state information must be maintained at least in the client of the service, so that it can identify the state required by the service when making further requests. However, the state information in the client is often just an index into the state information held in the service. We will return to this subject later in the chapter.

Services should not return public data that relates to their own internal processing.

Dependencies on other services

Generally, re-use of other services to create a new composite service is a good thing. However, having dependencies on other services does increase the degree of coupling because there is a risk that changes in those services may impact the composite service, and consequently, any services with dependencies on the composite service. We can reduce the risk that this poses by limiting our use of functionality in other services to just that required by the composite.

Services should reduce the functionality required of other services to the minimum required for their own functionality.

For example, a dispatching service may decide to validate the address it receives. If this functionality is not specified as being required, because, let's say, all addresses are validated elsewhere, then the dispatching service has an unnecessary dependency that may cause problems in the future.

Dependencies of other services on this service

Having a widely used service is great for re-use, but the greater the number of services that make use of this service, the greater impact a change in this service will have on other services. Extra care must be taken with widely re-used services to ensure that their interfaces are as stable as possible. This stability can be provided by following the guidelines in this section.

Widely re-used services should focus their interface on just the functionality needed by clients and avoid exposing any unnecessary functions or data.

Use of shared global data

Shared global data in the service context is often through dependencies on a shared resource such as data in a database. Such use of shared data structures is subversive to good design because it does not appear in the service definitions and so the owners of the shared data may be unaware of the dependency. Effectively, this is an extra interface into the service. If this is not documented, then the service is very vulnerable to the shared data structure being changed unknowingly. Even if the shared data structure is well documented, any changes required must still be synchronized across all users of the shared data.

Avoid the use of shared global data in services unless it is absolutely necessary. If it is absolutely necessary, then the dependency needs to be clearly documented in all users of the shared data. A service's data should only be manipulated through its defined interface. Consider creating a wrapper service around the shared data.

Temporal dependencies

Not all service requests require an immediate response. Often a service can be requested, and the response may be returned later. This is a common model in message-based systems and allows for individual services to be unavailable without impacting other services. Use of queuing systems allows temporal or time decoupling of services, so that two communicating services do not have to be available at the same instant in time. The queue allows messages to be delivered when the service is available rather than when the service is requested.

Use asynchronous message interfaces to reduce dependencies of one service on the availability of another.

Reducing coupling in stateful services

A stateful service maintains context for a given client between invocations. When using stateful services, we always need to return some kind of state information to the client. To avoid unnecessary coupling, this state information should always be opaque. By opaque, we mean that it should have no meaning to the client other than as a reference that must be returned to the service when requesting follow on operations. For example, a numeric session ID has no meaning to the client and may be used by the service as an index into a table stored either in memory or in a database table. We will examine how this may be accomplished later in this section.

A common use of state information in a service is to preserve the position in a search that returns more results than can reasonably be returned in a single response. Another use of state information might be to perform correlation between services that have multiple interactions, such as between a bidding service and a bidding client.

Whatever the reason may be, the first task, when confronted with the need for state in a service, is to investigate the ways to remove the state requirement. If there is definitely a need for state to be maintained, then there are two approaches that the service can follow.

- Externalize all state and return it to the client.
- Maintain state within the service and return a reference to the client.

In the first case, it is necessary to package up the required state information and return it to the client. Because the client should be unaware of the format of this data, it must be returned as an opaque type. This is best done as an `<any>` element in the schema for returning the response to the client. An `<any>` element may be used to hold any type of data, from simple strings through to complex structured types.

For example, if a listing service returns only 20 items at a time, then it must pass back sufficient information to enable it to retrieve the next 20 items in the query.

In the following XML Schema example, we have the XML data definitions to support two operations on a listing service:

- `searchItems`
- `nextItems`

The `searchItems` operation will take a `searchItemsRequest` element for input and return a `searchItemsResponse` element. The `searchItemsResponse` has within it a `searchState` element. This element is a sequence that has an unlimited number of arbitrary elements. This can be used by the service to store sufficient state to allow it to deliver the next 20 items in the response. It is important to realize that this state does not have to be understood by the client of the service. The client of the service just has to copy the `searchState` element to the `continueSearchItemsRequest` element to retrieve the next set of 20 results.

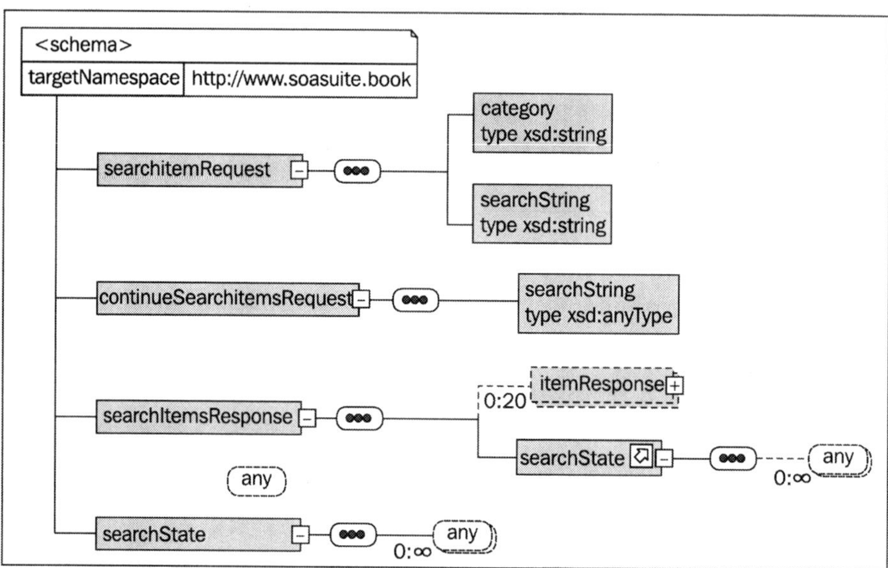

The preceding approach has the advantage that the service may still be stateless, although it gives the appearance of being stateful. The sample schema below could be used to allow the service to resume the search where it left off without the need for any internal state information in the service. By storing the state information (the original request and the index of the next item to be returned) within the response, the service can retrieve the next set of items without having to maintain any state within itself. Obviously, the service for purposes of efficiency could maintain some internal state, such as a database cursor, for a period of time, but this is not necessary.

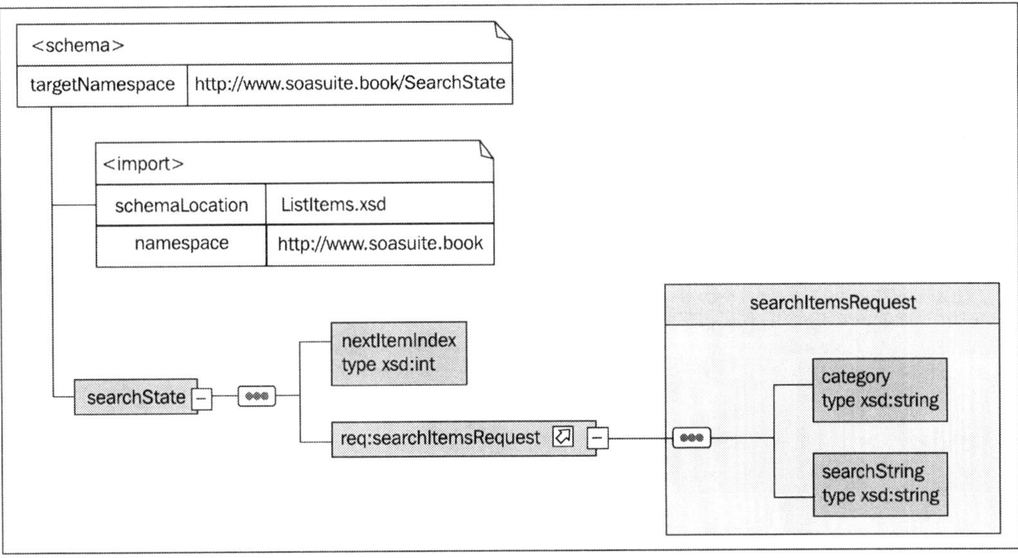

An alternative approach to state management is to keep the state information within the service itself. This still requires some state information to be returned to the client, but only a reference to the internal state information is required. In this case, there are a couple of options for dealing with this reference.

One is to take state management outside of the request/response messages and make it part of the wider service contract, either through the use of WS-Correlation or an HTTP cookie for example. This approach has the advantage that the service can generally take advantage of state management functions of the platform, such as support for Java services, to use the HTTP session state.

Use of WS-Correlation

It is possible to use a standard correlation mechanism such as WS-Correlation. This is used within SOA Suite by BPEL to correlate process instances with requests. If this approach is used, however, it precludes the use of the externalized state approach discussed earlier. This makes it harder to swap out your service implementation with one that externalizes all its state information. In addition to requiring your service to always internalize state management, no matter how it is implemented, your clients must now support WS-Correlation.

The alternative is to continue to keep the state management in the request/response messages and deal with it within the service. This keeps the client unaware of how the state is managed because the interface is exactly the same for a service that maintains internal state and a service that externalizes all states. A sample schema for this is shown below. Note that unlike the previous schema, there is only a service-specific reference to its own internal state. The service is responsible for maintaining all the required information internally and using the externalized reference to locate this state information.

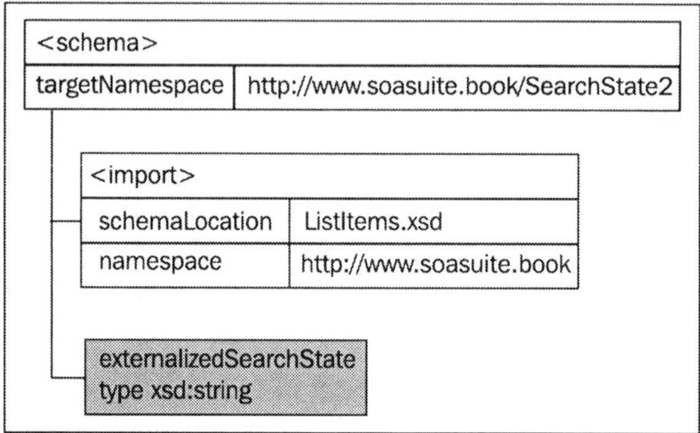

The **Oracle Service Bus (OSB)** in SOA Suite enables us to hide a services native state management and expose it as an abstract state management that is less tightly coupled to the way state is physically handled by the service.

Some web service implementations allow for stateful web services, with state managed in a variety of proprietary fashions.

We want to use native state management when we internalize session state because it is easier to manage. The container will do the work for us using mechanisms native to the container. However, this means the client has to be aware that we are using native state management because the client must make use of these mechanisms. We want the client to be unaware of whether the service uses native state management, its own custom state lookup mechanism, or externalizes all session state into the messages flowing between the client and the service. The latter two can look the same to the client and hence make it possible to switch services with different approaches. However, the native state management explicitly requires the client to be aware of how state is managed.

To avoid this coupling, we can use the OSB or Mediator to wrap the native state management services, as shown in the following diagram. The client passes a session state element of unknown contents back to the service façade, which is provided by the OSB or Mediator. The OSB or Mediator then removes the session state element and maps it onto the native state management used by the service, such as placing the value into a session cookie. Thus we have the benefits of using native state management without the need for coupling the client to a particular implementation of the service. For example, a service may use cookies to manage session state, and by having the OSB or Mediator move the cookie value to a field in the message, we avoid clients of the service having to deal with the specifics of the services state management.

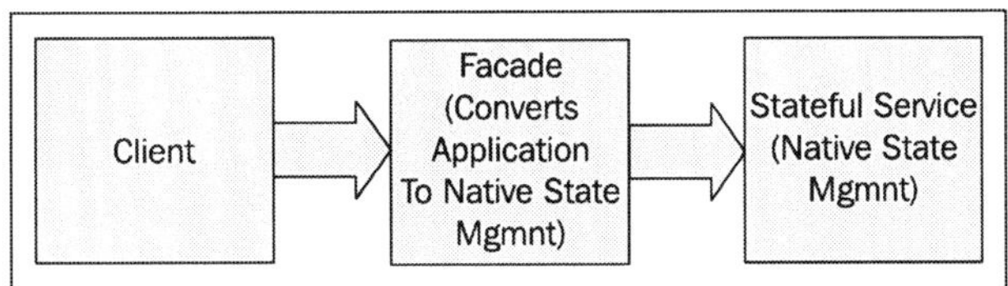

Service abstraction tools in SOA Suite

Earlier versions of the SOA Suite had the Oracle Enterprise Service Bus. This component has become the Mediator in 11*g*. In *Chapter 2, Writing your First Composite,* we introduced the Mediator component of an SCA Assembly. This provides basic routing and transformation abilities. The SOA Suite also includes the Oracle Service Bus. The Oracle Service Bus can also be used for routing and transformation but provides a much richer environment than the Mediator for service abstraction. At first glance, it is not clear whether to use the Oracle Service Bus or the Mediator to perform service abstraction. In this section, we will examine the pros and cons of using each and give some guidance on when to use one and when to use the other.

Do you have a choice?

The Oracle Service Bus currently only runs on the WebLogic platform. The rest of the SOA Suite has been designed to run on multiple platforms such as WebSphere and JBoss. If you need to run on these other platforms then, until OSB becomes multi-platform, you have no choice but to use the Mediator.

When to use the Mediator

Because the Mediator runs within an SCA Assembly, it has the most efficient bindings to other SCA Assembly components, specifically the BPEL engine. This lets us focus on using the Mediator to provide service virtualization services within SCA assemblies. The Mediator enables the virtualization of inputs and outputs within an SCA Assembly. This leads us to four key uses of the Mediator within SCA.

- Routing between components in an SCA Assembly
- Validation of incoming messages into an SCA Assembly
- Transformation of data from one format to another within an SCA Assembly
- Filtering to allow selection of components to invoke based on message content

The Mediator is an integral part of SCA Assemblies and should be used to adapt SCA Assembly formats to the canonical message formats, which we will talk about later in this chapter.

When to use Oracle Service Bus

The Oracle Service Bus runs in a separate JVM to the other SOA Suite components and so there is a cost associated with invoking SOA Suite components in terms of additional inter-process communication and hence time. However, the OSB has some very powerful capabilities that make it well suited to be the enterprise strength Service Bus for a more general enterprise-wide virtualisation role. As it is separate from the other components, it is easy to deploy separately and use as an independent Service Bus.

The Service Bus can be used to virtualize external services, where external may mean outside the company but also includes non-SCA services. OSB makes it very easy for operators to modify service endpoint details at runtime, making it very flexible in managing change.

The Service Bus goes beyond routing and transformation by providing the ability to throttle services, restricting the number of invocations they receive. This can be valuable in enforcing client contracts and ensuring that services are not swamped by more requests than they can handle.

What should I use to virtualize my services?

Service virtualization within an SCA Assembly is the job of the Mediator. The Mediator should be used to ensure that the SCA Assembly always presents a canonical interface to clients and services. Service virtualization of non-SCA components should be done with the Oracle Service Bus. Oracle Service Bus may also be used to transparently enforce throughput restriction on services.

Oracle Service Bus design tools

The Oracle Service Bus can be configured either using the Oracle Workshop for WebLogic or the Oracle Service Bus Console.

Oracle Workshop for WebLogic

Oracle Workshop for WebLogic provides tools for creating all the artifacts needed by the Oracle Service Bus. Based on Eclipse, it provides a rich design environment for building service routings and transformations for deployment to the Service Bus. In future releases, it is expected that all the Service Bus functionality in the Workshop for WebLogic will be provided in JDeveloper. The current versions of JDeveloper do not have support for Oracle Service Bus. Note that there is some duplication functionality between JDeveloper and Workshop for WebLogic. In some cases, such as WSDL generation, the functionality provided in the Workshop for WebLogic is superior to that provided by JDeveloper. In other cases, such as XSLT generation, the functionality provided by JDeveloper is superior.

Oracle Service Bus Console

In *Chapter 2, Writing your First Composite*,we introduced the Oracle Service Bus console and used it to build a proxy service that invoked an SCA Assembly.

Service Bus overview

In this section, we will introduce the key features of the Oracle Service Bus and show how they can be used to support service virtualization.

Service Bus message flow

It is useful to examine how messages are processed by the Service Bus. Messages normally target an endpoint in the Service Bus known as a proxy service. Once received by the proxy service the message is processed through a series of input pipeline stages. These pipeline stages may enrich the data by calling out to other web services, or they may transform the message as well as providing logging and message validation. Finally, the message reaches a routing step where it is routed to a service known as a business service. The response, if any, from the service is then sent through the output pipeline stages, which may also enrich the response or transform it before returning a response to the invoker.

Note that there may be no pipeline stages and the router may make a choice between multiple endpoints. Finally, note that the business service is a reference to the target service, which may be hosted within the Service Bus or as a standalone service. The proxy service may be thought of as the external service interface and associated transforms required to make use of the actual business service.

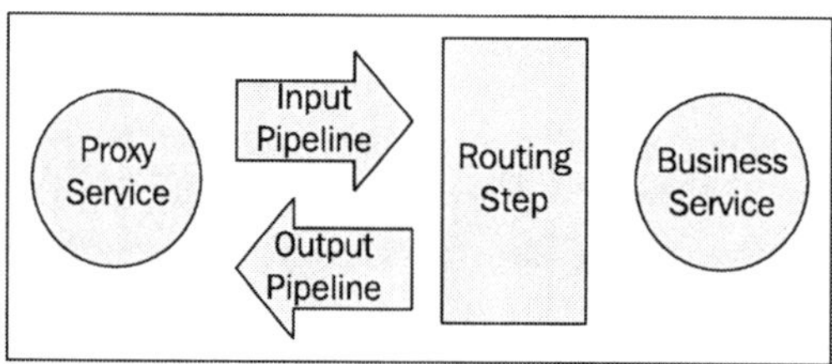

The proxy service should be the canonical interface to our service (see later in the chapter for an explanation of canonical interfaces). The Business Service is the physical implementation interface. The pipelines and routing step transform the request to and from canonical form.

Virtualizing service endpoints

To begin our exploration of the Oracle Service Bus, let us start by looking at how we can use it to virtualize service endpoints. By virtualizing a service endpoint, we mean that we can move the location of the service without affecting any of the services' dependants.

Moving service location

To virtualize the address of our service, we use the business service in the Service Bus. We covered creating a business service in *Chapter 2, Writing your First Composite*. Note that we are not limited to services described by WSDL. In addition to already defined business and proxy services, we can base our service on XML or messaging systems. The easiest to use is the WSDL web service.

Endpoint address considerations

When specifying endpoints in the Service Bus, it is generally not a good idea to use localhost or 127.0.0.1. Because the Service Bus definitions may be deployed across multiple nodes, there is no guarantee that business service will be co-located with the Service Bus on every node the Service Bus is deployed upon. Therefore, it is best to ensure that all endpoint addresses use virtual hostnames. Machines that are referenced by a virtual hostname should have that hostname in the local hosts file pointing to the loopback address (`127.0.0.1`) to benefit from machine affinity.

When we selected the WSDL we wanted to use in *Chapter 2, Writing your First Composite*, we were taken to another dialog that introspects the WSDL, identifies any ports or bindings, and asks us for which one we wish to use. Bindings are mappings of the WSDL service onto a physical transport mechanism such as SOAP over HTTP. Ports are the mapping of the binding onto a physical endpoint such as a specific server.

Note that if we choose a port, we do not have to provide physical endpoint details later in the definition of the business service, although we may choose to do so. If we choose a binding because it doesn't include a physical endpoint address, we have to provide the physical endpoint details explicitly.

If we have chosen a binding, we can skip the physical endpoint details. If, however, we chose a port or we wish to change the physical service endpoint or add additional physical service endpoints, then we hit the **Next>>** button to allow us to configure the physical endpoints of the service.

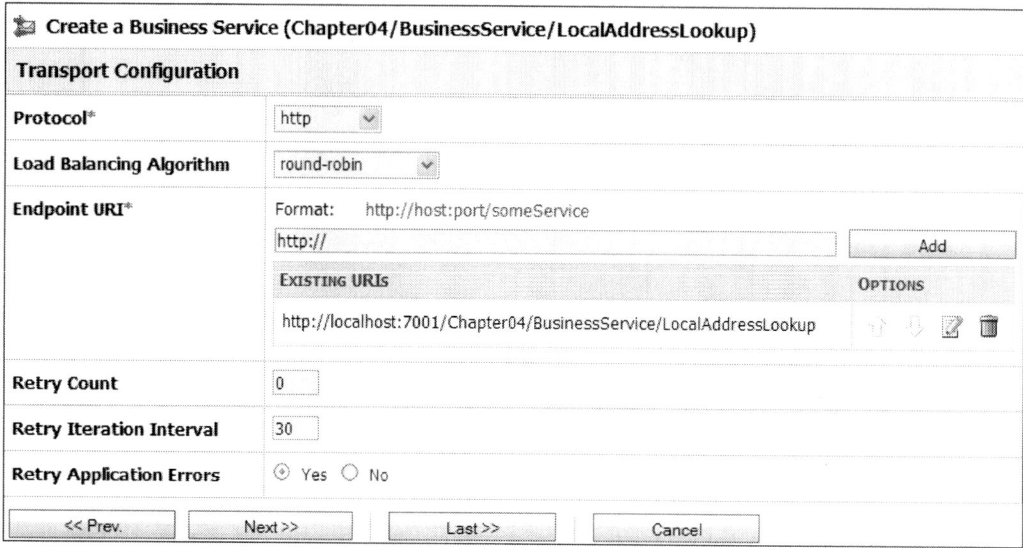

This dialog allows us to do several important things:

- Modify the **Protocol** to support a variety of transports.
- Choose a **Load Balancing Algorithm**. If there is more than one endpoint URI, then the Service Bus will load balance across them according to this algorithm.
- Change, add, or remove **Endpoint URIs** or physical targets.
- Specify retry logic, specifically the **Retry Count**, the **Retry Iteration Interval**, and whether or not to **Retry Application Errors** (errors generated by the service called, not the transport).

Note that the Service Bus gives us the ability to change, add, and remove physical endpoint URIs as well as change the protocol used at runtime. This allows us to change the target services without impacting any clients of the service, providing us with virtualization of our service location.

Using Adapters in Service Bus

The Service Bus can also use adapter definitions created in JDeveloper. To use an adapter from JDeveloper, we cannot directly import the WSDL, we need to import the artifacts in the following order:

1. The XSD generated by the adapter using **Select Resource Type** | **Interface** | **XML Schema**
2. The WSDL generated by the adapter using **Select Resource Type** | **Interface** | **WSDL**
3. The JCA file generated by the adapter using **Select Resource Type** | **Interface** | **JCA Binding**

The WSDL can then be used as a business service. Make sure that references in the JCA file are configured in the WebLogic Server.

The proxy service provides the interface and adaption to our business service, typically joining them by a routing step, as we did in *Chapter 2, Writing your First Composite*. There are other types of actions besides routing flows. Clicking on **Add an Action** allows us to choose the type of **Communication** we want to add. **Flow Control** allows us to add **If .. Then ...** logic to our routing decision. However, in most cases, the **Communication** items will provide all the flexibility we need in our routing decisions. This gives us three types of routing to apply:

1. **Dynamic Routing** allows us to route to the result of an XQuery. This is useful if the endpoint address is part of the input message.
2. **Routing** allows us to select a single static endpoint.
3. **Routing Table** allows us to use an XQuery to route between several endpoints. This is useful when we want to route to different services, based on a particular attribute of the input message.

For simple service endpoint virtualization, we only require the **Routing** option.

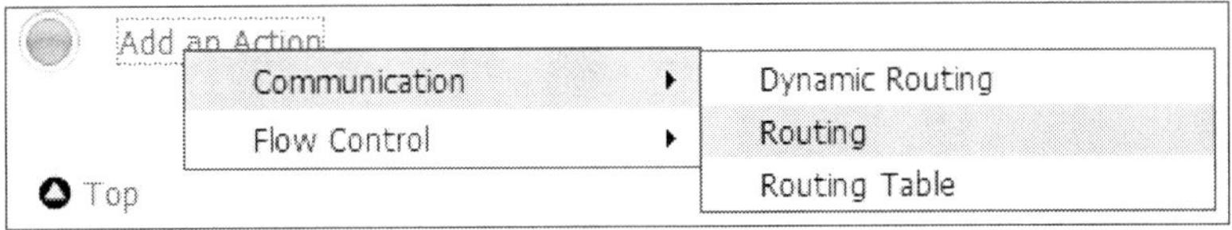

Having selected a target endpoint, usually a business service, we can then configure how we use that endpoint. In the case of simple location virtualization, the proxy service and the business service endpoints are the same, and so we can just pass on the input message directly to the business service. Later on, we will look at how to transform data to allow virtualization of the service interface.

Selecting a service to call

We can further virtualize our endpoint by routing different requests to different services, based upon the values of the input message. For example, we may use one address lookup service for addresses in our own country and another service for all other addresses. In this case, we would use the routing table option on the add action to provide a list of possible service destinations.

The routing table enables us to have a number of different destinations, and the message will be routed based on the value of an expression. When using a routing table, all the services must be selected based on the same expression; the comparison operators may vary, but the actual value being tested against will always be the same. If this is not the case, then it may be better to use "if ... then ... else" routing. The routing table may be thought of as a "switch statement", and as with all switch statements, it is a good practice to add a default case.

In the routing table, we can create additional cases, each of which will have a test associated with it. Note that we can also add the default case.

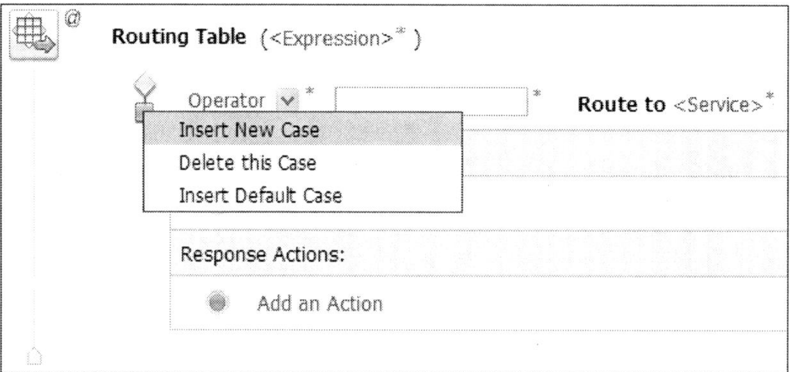

We need to specify the expression to be used for testing against. Clicking on the **<Expression>** link takes us to the **XQuery /XSLT Expression Editor**. By selecting the **Variable Structures** tab and selecting a new structure, we can find the input body of the message, which lets us select the field we wish to use as the comparison expression in our routing table.

When selecting in the tab on the left of the screen, the appropriate XPath expression should appear in the **Property Inspector** window. We can the click on the **XQuery Text** area of the screen prior to clicking on the **Copy Property** to transfer the property XPath expression from the property inspector to the XQuery Text area. We then complete our selection of the expression by clicking on the **Save** button.

In the example, we are going to route our service based on the country of the address. In addition to the data in the body of the message, we could also route based on other information from the request. Alternatively, by using a message pipeline, we could base our lookup on data external to the request.

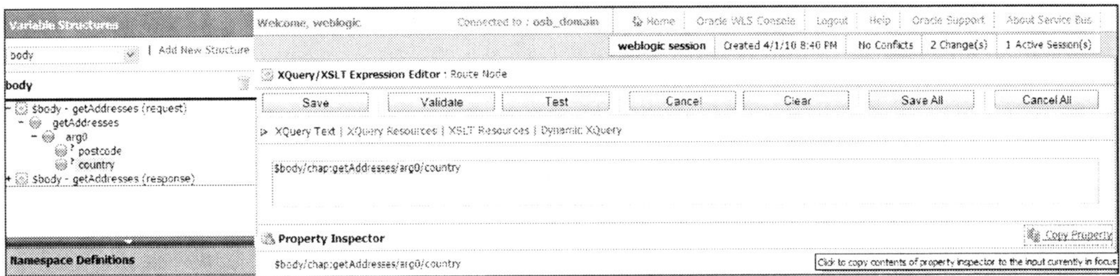

Once we have created an expression to use as the basis of comparison for routing, then we select an operator and a value to use for the actual routing comparison. In the following example, if the country value from the expression matches the string **uk** (include the quotes), then the **LocalAddressLookup** service will be invoked. Any other value will cause the default service to be invoked, as yet undefined in the following example:

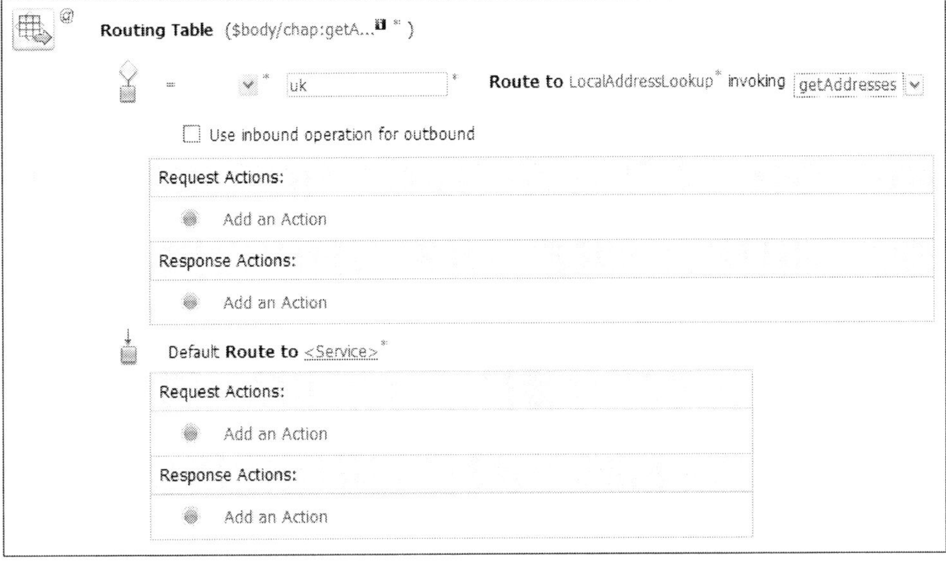

Once the routing has been defined, then it can be saved, as shown in *Chapter 2, Writing your First Composite*.

Note that we have shown a very simple routing example. The Service Bus is capable of doing much more sophisticated routing decisions. A common pattern is to use a pipeline to enrich the inbound data and then route based on the inbound data. For example, a pricing proxy service may use the inbound pipeline to look up the status of a customer, adding that status to the data available as part of the request. The routing service could then route high value customers to one service and low value customers to another service, based on the looked up status. In this case, the routing is based on a derived value rather than on a value already available in the message.

In summary, a request can be routed to different references, based on the content of the request message. This allows messages to be routed based on geography or pecuniary value for example. This routing, because it takes place in the composite, is transparent to clients of the composite and so aids us in reducing coupling in the system.

Virtualizing service interfaces

We have looked at how to virtualize a service endpoint. Now let's look at how we can further virtualize the service by abstracting its interface into a common format, known as canonical form. This will provide us further flexibility by allowing us to change the implementation of the service with one that has a different interface but performs the same function. The native format is the way the data format service actually uses, the canonical format is an idealized format that we wish to develop against.

Physical versus logical interfaces

Best practice for integration projects was to have a canonical form for all messages exchanged between systems. The canonical form was a common format for all messages. If a system wanted to send a message, then it first needed to transform it to the canonical form before it could be forwarded to the receiving system, which would then transform it from the canonical form to its own representation. This same good practice is still valid in a service-oriented world and the Service Bus is the mechanism SOA Suite provides for us to do this.

Canonical data and canonical interface

The canonical data formats should represent the idealized data format for the data entities in the system. The canonical interfaces should be the idealized service interfaces. Generally, it is a bad idea to use existing service data formats or service interfaces as the canonical form. There is a lot of work being done in various industry-specific bodies to define standardized canonical forms for entities that are exchanged between corporations.

The benefits of a canonical form are as follows:

- Transformations are only necessary to and from canonical form, reducing the number of different transformations required to be created
- Decouples format of data from services, allowing a service to be replaced by one providing the same function but a different format of data

This is illustrated graphically by a system where two different clients make requests for one of the four services, all providing the same function but different implementations. Without the canonical form, we would need a transformation of data between the client format and the server format inbound and again outbound. For four services, this yields eight transformations, and for two clients, this doubles to sixteen transformations.

Using the canonical format gives us two transformations for each client, inbound and outbound to the canonical form. With two clients, this gives us four transformations. To this, we add the server transformations to and from the canonical form, of which there are two per server, giving us eight transformations. This gives us a total of twelve transformations that must be coded up rather than sixteen if we were using native-to-native transformation.

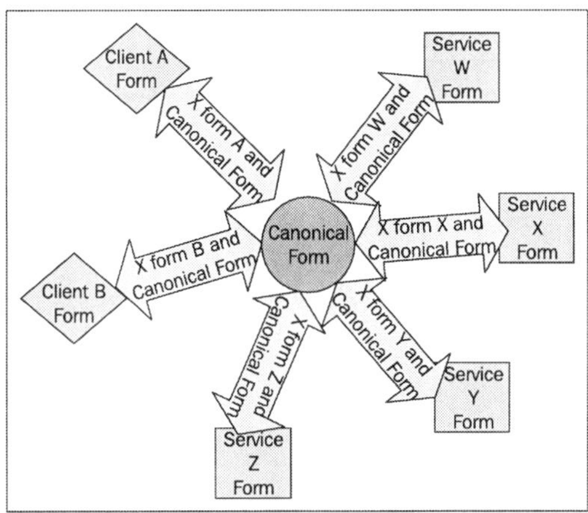

The benefits of the canonical form are most clearly seen when we deploy a new client. Without the canonical form, we would need to develop eight transformations to allow the client to work with the four different possible service implementations. With the canonical form, we only need two transformations, to and from the canonical form.

Let's look at how we implement the canonical form in Oracle Service Bus.

Mapping service interfaces

In order to take advantage of the canonical form in our service interfaces, we must have an abstract service interface that provides the functionality we need without being specific to any particular service implementation. Once we have this, we can then use it as the canonical service form.

We set up the initial project in the same way we did in the previous section on virtualizing service endpoints. The proxy should provide the canonical interface, while the business service provides the native service interface. Because the proxy and business services are not the same interface, we need to do some more work in the route configuration.

We need to map the canonical form of the address list interface onto the native service form of the interface. In the example, we are mapping our canonical interface to the interface provided by a web-based address solution from the Harte-Hanks Global Address (`http://www.qudox.com`). To do this, we create a new Service Bus project and add the Harte-Hanks WSDL (`http://webservices.globaladdress.net/globaladdress.asmx?WSDL`). We use this to define the business service. We also add the canonical interface WSDL that we have defined and create a new proxy with this interface. We then need to map the proxy service onto the Harte-Hanks service by editing the message flow associated with the proxy, as we did in the previous section.

Our mapping needs to do two things as follows:

- Map the method name on the interface to the correct method in the business service
- Map the parameters in the canonical request onto the parameters needed in the business service request

For each method on the canonical interface, we must map it onto a method in the physical interface. We do this by selecting the appropriate method from the business service operation drop-down box. We need to do this because the methods provided in the external service do not match the method names in our canonical service. In the following example, we have mapped onto the **SearchAddress** method.

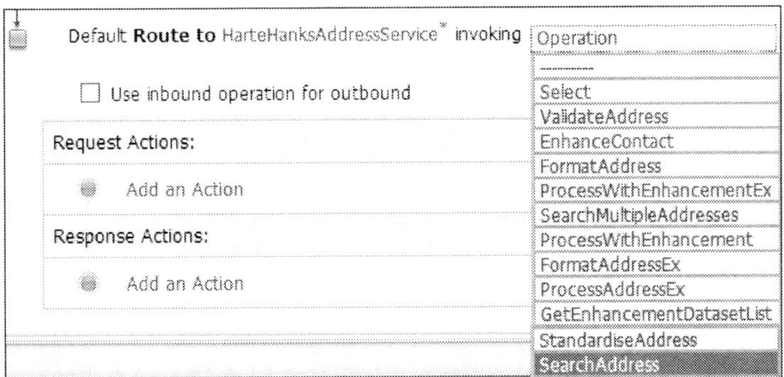

Having selected an operation, we now need to transform the input data from the format provided by the canonical interface into the format required by the external service. We need to map the request and response messages if it is a two-way method or just the request message for one-way method. The actual mapping may be done either by XQuery or XSLT. In our example, we will use the XSLT transform.

To perform the transformation, we add a **Messaging Processing** action to our message flow, which in this case is a **Replace** operation. The variable body always holds the message in the Service Bus flow. This receives the message through the proxy interface and is also used to deliver the message to the business service interface. This behavior differs from BPEL and most programming languages, where we typically have separate variables for the input and output messages. We need to transform this message from the proxy input canonical format to the business service native output format.

Be aware that there are really two flows associated with the proxy service. The request flow is used to receive the inbound message and perform any processing before invoking the target business service. The response flow takes the response from the business service and performs any necessary processing before replying to the invoker of the proxy service.

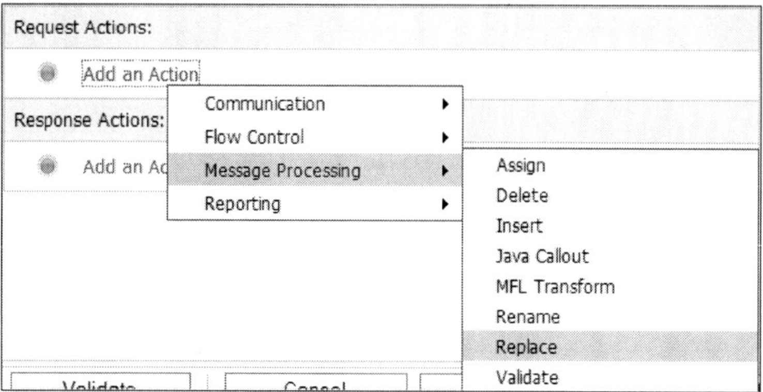

On selecting replace, we can fill in the details in the **Request Actions** dialog. The message is held in the body variable, and so we can fill this (body) in as the target variable name. We then need to select which part of the body we want to replace.

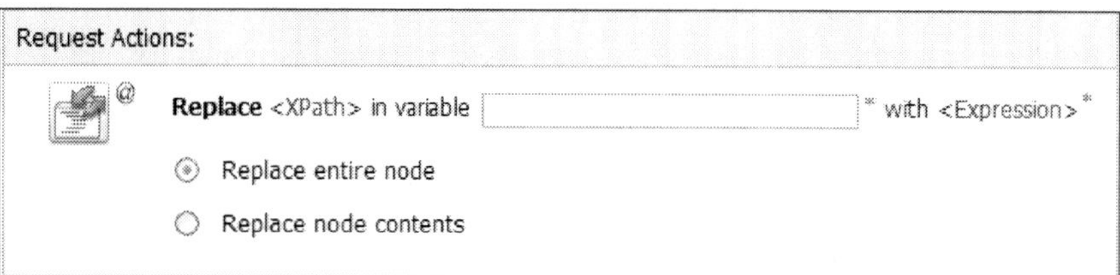

Clicking on the **XPath** link brings up the **XPath Expression Editor**, where we can enter the portion of the target variable that we wish to replace. In this case, we wish to replace all the elements so we enter **./***, which selects the top level element and all elements beneath it. Clicking on the **Save** button causes the expression to be saved in the **Replace Action** dialog.

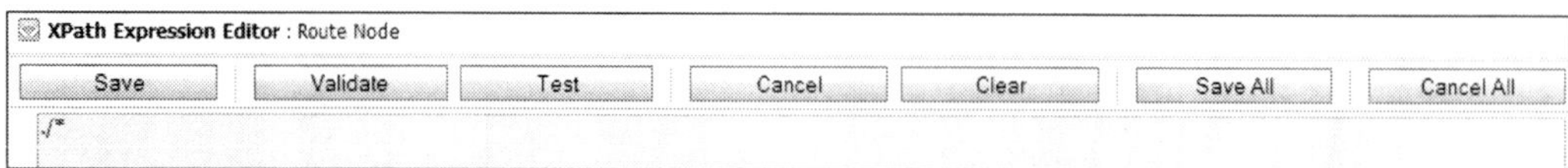

Having identified the portion of the message we wish to replace (all of it) , we now need to specify what we will replace it with. In this case, we wish to transform the whole input message, so we click on the **Expression** link and select the **XSLT Resources** tab. Clicking on the **Browse** button enables us to choose a previously registered XSLT transformation file. After selecting the file, we need to identify the input to the transformation. In this case, the input message is in the body variable, and so we select all the elements in the body by using the expression **$body/***. We then save our transformation expression.

Having provided the source data, the target, and the transformation, we can then save and repeat the whole process for the response message (in this case, converting from native to canonical form).

XQuery Text | XQuery Resources | ▷ XSLT Resources | Dynamic XQuery

1. Select an XSLT resource to execute

XSLT :	AddressLookup/Transforms/GetAddressCanonicalToService [Browse...]

2. Bind Input

Input Document	Binding
Input Document:	$body/*

3. Bind Variables

Variable Name	Binding
	No variables have been found.

We can use JDeveloper to build an XSLT transform and then upload it into the Service Bus. A future release will add support for XQuery in JDeveloper, similar to that provided in Oracle Workshop for WebLogic. XSLT is an XML language that describes how to transform one XML document into another. Fortunately, most XSLT can be created using the graphical mapping tool in JDeveloper, and so SOA Suite developers don't have to be experts in XSLT, although it is very useful to know how it works. Note that in our transform, we may need to enhance the message with additional information, for example, all the Global Address methods require a username and password to be provided to allow accounting of the requests to take place. This information has no place in the canonical request format, but must be added in the transform. A sample transform that does just this is shown in the following screenshot:

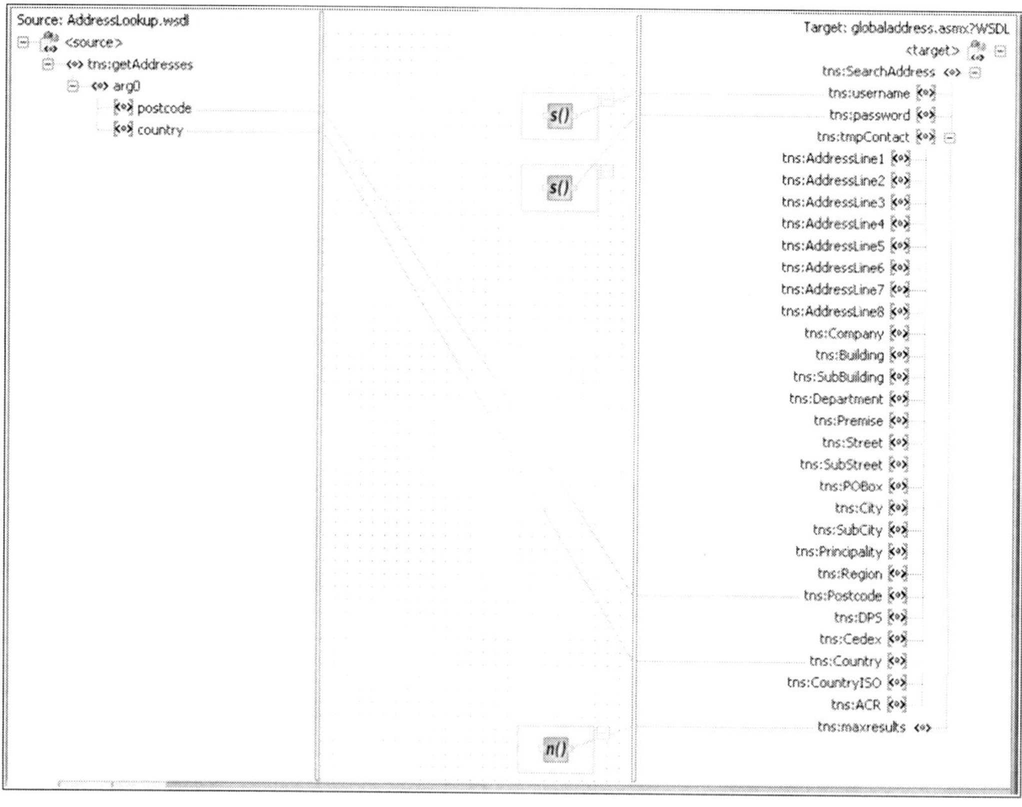

Note that we use XPath string functions to set the username and password fields. It would be better to set these from the properties or an external file, as we would usually want to use them in a number of calls to the physical service. XPath functions are capable of allowing access to composite properties. We actually only need to set five fields in the request, namely, a country, postcode, username, password, and the maximum number of results to return. All the other fields are not necessary for the service we are using and so are hidden from end users because they do not appear in the canonical form of the service.

Applying canonical form in the Service Bus

When we think about the canonical form and routing, we have several different operations that may need to be performed.

- Conversion to/from the native business service form from/to the canonical proxy form
- Conversion to/from the native client form from/to the canonical proxy form
- Routing between multiple native services, each potentially with its own message format

The following diagram represents these different potential interactions as distinct proxy implementations in the service. To reduce coupling and make maintenance easier, each native service has a corresponding canonical proxy service. This isolates the rest of the system from the actual native formats. This is shown below in the **Local-Harte-Hanks-Proxy** and **Local-LocalAddress-Proxy** services that transform the native service to/from the canonical form. This approach allows us to change the native address lookup implementations without impacting anything other than the Local-*-Proxy service.

The **Canonical-Address-Proxy** has the job of hiding the fact that the address lookup service is actually provided by a number of different service providers, each with their own message formats. By providing this service, we can easily add additional address providers without impacting the clients of the address lookup service.

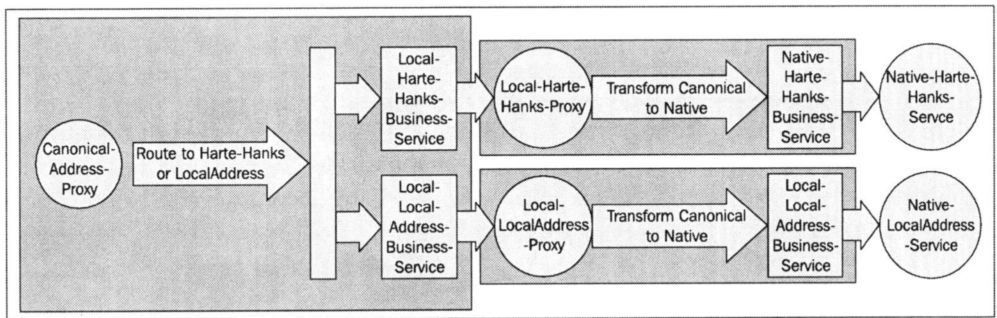

In addition to the services shown in the diagram, we may have clients that are not written to use the canonical address lookup. In this case, we need to provide a proxy that transforms the native input request to/from the canonical form. This allows us to be isolated from the requirements of the clients of the service. If a client requires its own interface to the address lookup service, we can easily provide that through a proxy without the need to impact the rest of the system, again reducing coupling.

An important optimization

The previous approach provides a very robust way of isolating service consumers and service requestors from the native formats and locations of their partners. However, there must be a concern about the overhead of all these additional proxy services and also about the possibility of a client accessing a native service directly. To avoid these problems, the Service Bus provides a **local** transport mechanism that can be specified as part of the binding of the proxy service. The local transport provides two things for us:

- It makes services only consumable by other services in the Service Bus, they cannot be accessed externally
- It provides a highly optimized messaging transport between proxy services, providing in-memory speed to avoid unnecessary overhead in service hand-offs between proxy services

These optimizations mean that it is very efficient to use the canonical form, and so the Service Bus not only allows us great flexibility in how we decouple our services from each other, but it also provides a very efficient mechanism for us to implement that decoupling. Note, though, that there is a cost involved in performing XSLT or XQuery transformations. This cost may be viewed as the price of loose coupling.

Using the Mediator for virtualization

As discussed earlier, we can also use the Mediator for virtualization within an SCA Assembly. The Mediator should be used to ensure that interface into and out of SCA Assemblies use canonical form. We can also use XSL transforms in Mediator in a similar fashion to Service Bus to provide mappings between one data format and another.

To do this, we would select the canonical format WSDL as the input to our composite and wire this to the Mediator in the same way as we did in *Chapter 2, Writing your First Composite*. We can then double-click on the Mediator to open it and add a transformation to convert the messages to and from the canonical form.

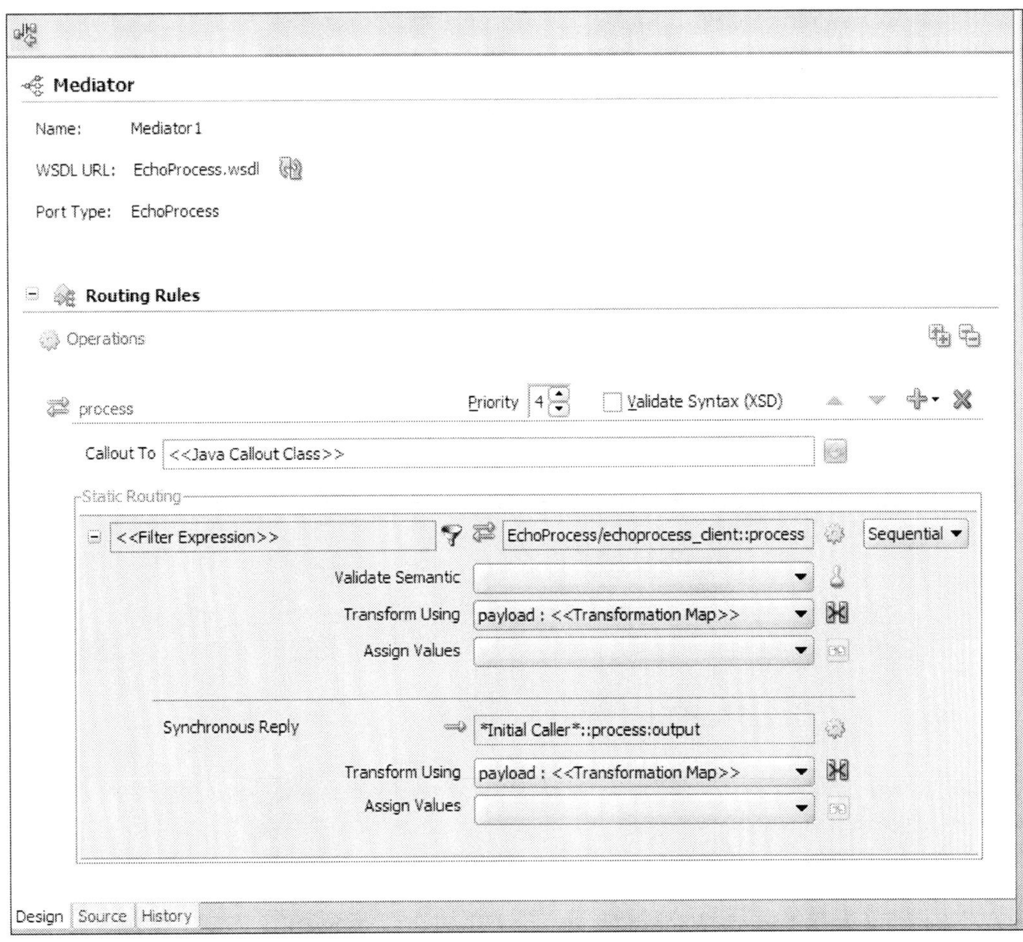

If necessary, we may need to expand the routing rule to show the details. For the input message, we have the option of filtering the message, meaning that we can choose what to call, based on the contents of the input message. If no filter expression is provided, then all messages will be delivered to a single target.

The **Validate Semantic** field allows us to check that the input message is of the correct format. This requires a schematron file and is covered in *Chapter 13, Building Validation into Services.*

The **Assign Values** field allows us to set values using either the input message or message properties. This is particularly useful when using adapters, as some of the data required may be provided in adapter headers such as the input filename. This may also be used to set adapter header properties, if invoking an adapter.

The **Transform Using** field allows us to select an XSL stylesheet to transform the input (in this case, the canonical format) to the internal format. Clicking the icon brings up the **Request Transformation Map** dialog:

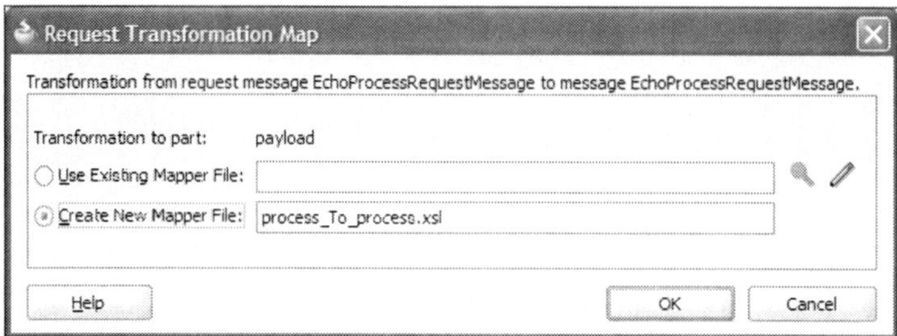

Here we can either select an existing XSL or create a new one based on the input and output formats.

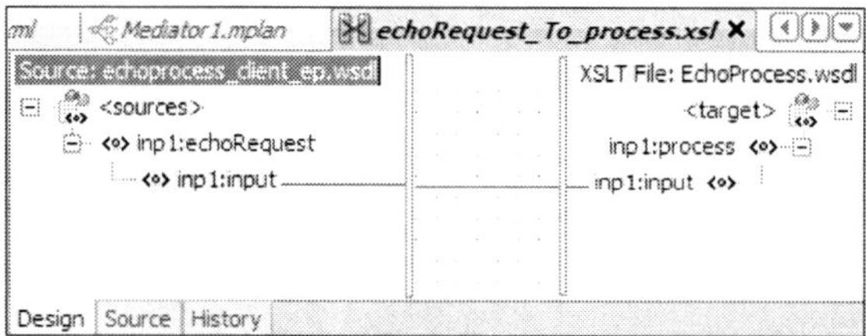

The XSL editor provides a graphical drag-and-drop mechanism for creating XSL stylesheets. Alternatively, it is possible to select the **Source** tab and input XSL commands directly. Note that many XSL commands are not supported by the graphical editor, and so it is best to do as much as possible in the graphical editor before switching to the source mode.

Summary

In this chapter, we have explored how we can use the Oracle Service Bus and the Mediator in the SOA Suite to reduce the degree of coupling. By reducing coupling, or the dependencies between services, our architectures become more resilient to change. In particular, we looked at how to use the Service Bus to reduce coupling by abstracting endpoint interface locations and formats. Crucial to this is the concept of canonical or common data formats that reduce the amount of data transformation that is required, particularly in bringing new services into our architecture. Finally, we considered how this abstraction can go as far as hiding the fact that we are using multiple services' concurrently by allowing us to make routing decisions at runtime.

All these features are there to help us build service-oriented architectures that are resilient to change and can easily absorb new functionality and services.

5

Using BPEL to Build Composite Services and Business Processes

In the previous two chapters, we saw how we can service-enable functionality embedded within existing systems. The next challenge is how to assemble these services to build "composite" applications or business processes. This is the role of the **Web Service Business Process Execution Language** (**WS BPEL**) or **Business Process Execution Language** (**BPEL**), as it's commonly referred to.

BPEL is a rich XML-based language for describing the assembly of a set of existing web services into either a composite service or a business process. Once deployed, a BPEL process itself is actually invoked as a web service.

Thus, anything that can call a web service, can also call a BPEL process, including of course, other BPEL processes. This allows you to take a nested approach to writing BPEL processes, giving you a lot of flexibility.

In this chapter, we first introduce the basic structure of a BPEL process, its key constructs, and the difference between a synchronous and asynchronous service.

We then demonstrate through the building and refinement of two example BPEL processes (one synchronous the other asynchronous), how to use BPEL to invoke external web services (including other BPEL processes), and to build composite services. During this process, we also take the opportunity to introduce the reader to many of the key BPEL activities in more detail.

Basic structure of a BPEL process

The following image shows the core structure of a BPEL process, and how it interacts with components external to it: either web services that the BPEL process invokes (**Service A** and **Service B** in this case) or external clients that invoke the BPEL process as a web service.

From this, we can see that the BPEL process divides into two distinct parts: the partner links (with associated WSDL files, which describe the interactions between the BPEL process and the outside world) and the core **BPEL Process** itself, which describes the process to be executed at runtime.

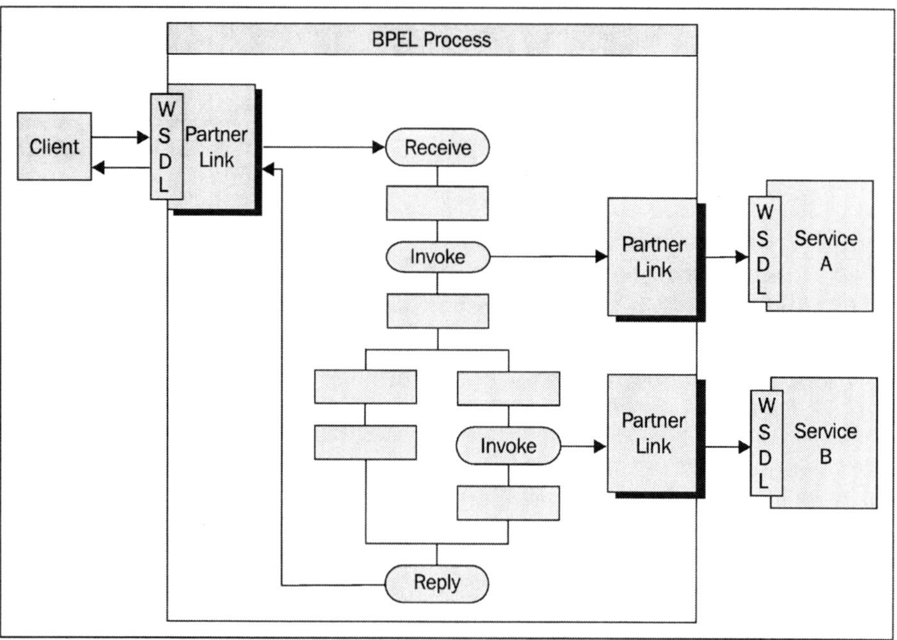

Core BPEL process

The core BPEL process consists of a number of steps or activities as they are called in BPEL.

These consist of simple activities, including:

- **Assign:** Used to manipulate variables.
- **Transform:** A specialized assign activity that uses XSLT to map data from a source format to a target format.

- **Wait:** Used to pause the process for a period of time.
- **Empty:** Does nothing. It is used in branches of your process where syntactically an activity is required, but you don't want to perform an activity.

Structured activities that control the flow through the process, these include:

- **While**: For implementing loops
- **Switch:** Construct for implementing conditional branches
- **Flow:** For implementing branches that execute in parallel
- **FlowN:** For implementing a dynamic number of parallel branches

And messaging activities (for example, **Receive**, **Invoke**, **Reply**, and **Pick**)

The activities within a BPEL process can be subdivided into logical groups of activities, using the **Scope** activity. Along with providing a useful way to structure and organize your process, it also lets you define attributes such as variables, fault handlers, and compensation handlers that just apply to the scope.

Variables

Each BPEL process also defines variables, which are used to hold the state of the process as well as messages that are sent and received by the process. They can be defined at the process level, in which case, they are considered global and visible to all parts of the process, or can be declared within a scope, in which case they are only visible to activities contained within that scope (and scopes nested within the scope to which the variable belongs).

Variables can be one of the following types:

- **Simple type**: Can hold any simple data type defined by XML Schema (for example, string, integer, Boolean, and float)
- **WSDL message type**: Used to hold the content of a WSDL message sent to or received from partners
- **Element**: Can hold either a complex or simple XML Schema element defined in either a WSDL file or a separate XML Schema

Variables are manipulated using the `<assign>` activity, which can be used to copy data from one variable to another, as well as create new data using XPath expressions or XSLT.

For variables that are WSDL messages or complex elements, we can work with it at the subcomponent level by specifying the part of the variable we would like to work with using an XPath expression.

Partner links

All interaction between a process and other parties (or partners) is via web services, as defined by their corresponding WSDL files. Even though each service is fully described by its WSDL, it fails to define the relationship between the process and the partner, that is, who the consumer of a service is and who the provider is. At first glance, the relationship may seem implicit. However, this is not always the case, so BPEL uses partner links to explicitly define this relationship.

Partner links are defined using the `<partnerLinkType>`, which is an extension to WSDL (defined by the BPEL standard). Whenever you refer to a web service whose WSDL doesn't contain a `<partnerLinkType>`, JDeveloper will automatically ask you whether you want it to create one for you. Assuming your answer is yes, it will create this as a separate WSDL document, which then imports the original WSDL.

Messaging activities

BPEL defines three messaging activities `<receive>`, `<reply>`, and `<invoke>`; how you use these depends on whether the message interaction is either synchronous or asynchronous and whether the BPEL process is either a consumer or provider of the service.

Synchronous messaging

With synchronous messaging the caller will block until it has received a reply (or times out), that is, the BPEL process will wait for a reply before moving on to the next activity.

As we can see in the following, **Process A** uses the `<invoke>` activity to call a synchronous web service (**Process B** in this case), once it has sent the initial request, it blocks and waits for a corresponding reply from **Process B**.

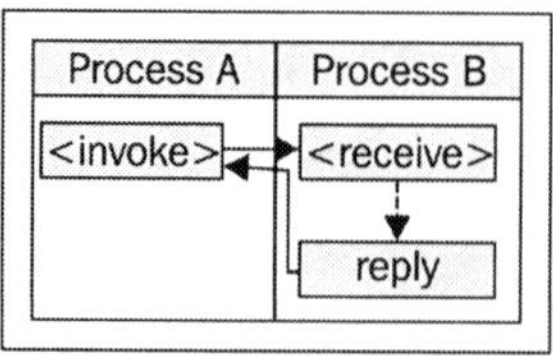

Process B uses the `<receive>` activity to receive the request. Once it has processed the request, it uses the `<reply>` activity to send a response back to **Process A**.

Theoretically, **Process B** could take as long as it wants before sending a reply, but typically **Process A** will only wait for a short time (for example, 30 seconds) before it times out the `<invoke>` operation under the assumption that something has gone wrong. Thus, if **Process B** is going to take a substantial period of time before replying, then you should model the exchange as an Asynchronous Send-Receive (refer to the following section).

Asynchronous messaging

With asynchronous messaging, the key difference is that once the caller has sent the request, the send operation will return immediately, and the BPEL process may then continue with additional activities until it is ready to receive the reply. At this point, the process will block until it receives the reply (which may already be there).

If we look at the following screenshot, you will notice that just like the synchronous request **Process A** uses the `<invoke>` activity to call an asynchronous web service. However, the difference is that it doesn't block waiting for a response, rather it continues processing until it is ready to process the response. It then receives this using the `<receive>` activity.

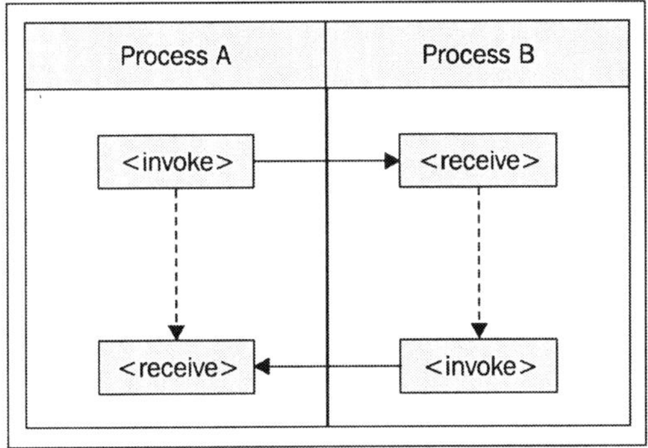

Conversely, **Process B** uses a `<receive>` activity to receive the initial request and an `<invoke>` activity to send back the corresponding response.

While at a logical level, there is little difference between synchronous and asynchronous messaging (especially if there are no activities between the `<invoke>` and `<receive>` activity in **Process A**), at a technical level there is a key difference.

This is because with asynchronous messaging, we have two `<invoke>`, `<receive>` pairs, each corresponding to a separate web service operation. One is for the request and the other is for the reply.

From a decision perspective, a key driver as to which to choose is the length of time it takes for **Process B** to service the request, as asynchronous messaging supports far longer processing times. In general, once the time it takes for **Process B** to return a response goes above 30 seconds, you should consider switching to asynchronous messaging.

> With potentially many instances of **Process A** and **Process B** running at the same time, BPEL needs to ensure that each reply is matched (or correlated) to the appropriate request. By default, BPEL uses WS-Addressing to achieve this. We look at this in more detail in *Chapter 16, Message Interaction Patterns*.

One way messaging

A variation of asynchronous messaging is one way messaging (also known as fire and forget). This involves a single message being sent from the calling process, with no response being returned.

If we look at the following screenshot, you will notice that just like the asynchronous request, **Process A** uses the `<invoke>` activity to send a message to **Process B**.

Once **Process A** has sent the message, it continues processing until it completes, that is, it never stops to wait for a response from **Process B**. Similarly, **Process B**, upon receipt of the message, continues processing until it has completed and never sends any response back to **Process A**.

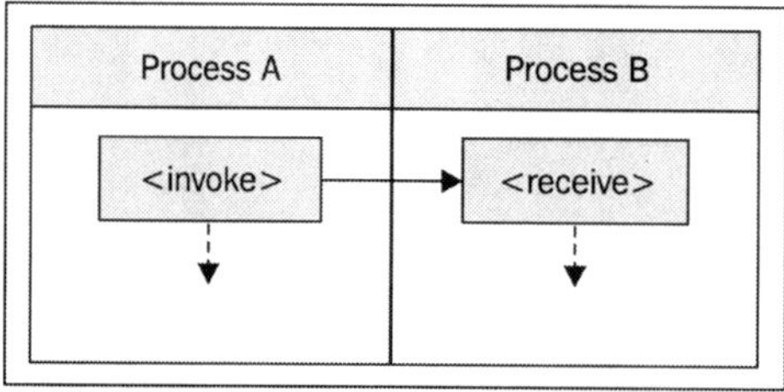

A simple composite service

Despite the fact that BPEL is intended primarily for writing long running processes, it also provides an excellent way to build a composite service, that is, a service that is assembled from other services.

Let's take a simple example: say I have a service that gives me the stock quote for a specified company, and that I also have a service that gives me the exchange rate between two currencies. I can use BPEL to combine these two services and provide a service that gives the stock quote for a company in the currency of my choice.

So let's create our stock quote service, we will create a simple synchronous BPEL process which takes two parameters, the stock ticker and the required currency. This will then call two external services.

Creating our StockQuote service

Before we begin, we will create an application (named **Chapter05**), which we will use for all our samples in this chapter. To do this, follow the same process we used to create our first application in *Chapter 2, Writing your First Composite*. When prompted to create a project, create an **Empty Composite** named **StockService**.

Next, drag a BPEL process from the SOA Component Palette onto our **StockService** composite. This will launch the **Create BPEL Process** wizard, specify a name of **StockQuote**, and select a **Synchronous BPEL Process**. However, at this stage do not click **OK**.

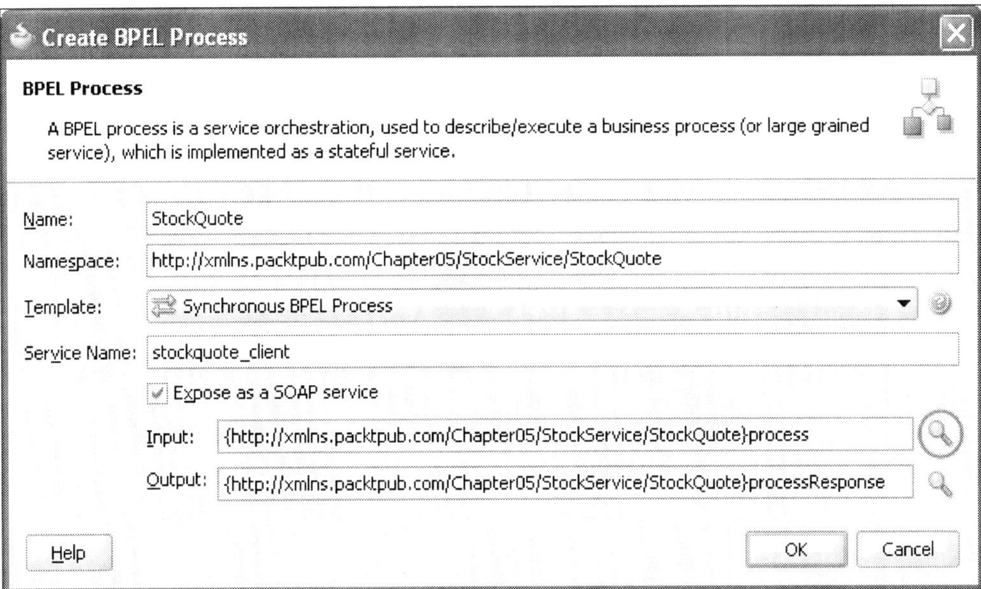

You may remember when we created our Echo service back in *Chapter 2, Writing your First Composite*, JDeveloper automatically created a simple WSDL file for our service, with a single input and output field. For our StockQuote service, we need to pass in multiple fields (that is, Stock Ticker and Currency). So, to define the input and output messages for our BPEL process, we are going to make use of a predefined schema `StockService.xsd`, as shown in the following code snippet (for brevity, only the parts which are relevant to this example are shown. However, the complete schema is provided in the downloadable samples file for the book).

```
<?xml version="1.0" encoding="windows-1252"?>
<xsd:schema xmlns:xsd="http://www.w3.org/2001/XMLSchema"
            xmlns="http://xmlns.packtpub.com/StockService"
            targetNamespace="http://xmlns.packtpub.com/StockService"
            elementFormDefault="qualified">

   <xsd:element name="getQuote"          type=" tGetQuote"/>
   <xsd:element name="getQuoteResponse" type=" tGetQuoteResponse"/>

   <xsd:complexType name="tGetQuote">
         <xsd:sequence>
               <xsd:element name="stockSymbol" type="xsd:string"/>
               <xsd:element name="currency" type="xsd:string"/>
         </xsd:sequence>
   </xsd:complexType>

   <xsd:complexType name="tGetQuoteResponse">
         <xsd:sequence>
               <xsd:element name="stockSymbol" type="xsd:string"/>
               <xsd:element name="currency" type="xsd:string"/>
               <xsd:element name="amount" type="xsd:decimal"/>
         </xsd:sequence>
   </xsd:complexType>

   ...

</xsd:schema>
```

Importing StockService schema

To override the default input schema element generated by JDeveloper, click on **Browse Input Elements ...** (the magnifying glass circled in the previous screenshot). This will bring up the **Type Chooser** , as shown in the following screenshot, which allows you to browse all schemas imported by the composite and select an element from them.

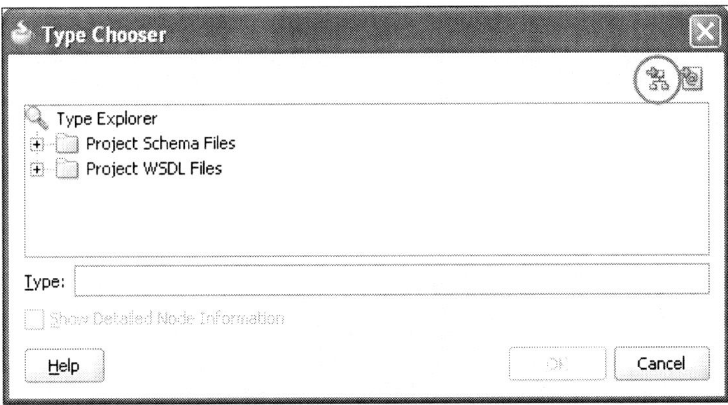

In our case, we have yet to import any schemas, so click on **Import Schema File ...** (circled in the previous screenshot). This will launch the **Import Schema File** window. Click on the magnifying glass to launch the SOA Resource Browser (in **File System** mode), which will allow us to search our filesystem for an appropriate schema.

Find the **StockService.xsd** located in the samples folder for Chapter 5 and select this. Ensure that the option to **Copy to Project** is selected and click **OK**; JDeveloper will then bring up the **Localize Files** window. Keep the default options and click **OK**. This will cause JDeveloper to create a local copy of our XML Schema and any dependant files (of which there are none in this example) within our project.

JDeveloper will now open the schema browser dialog, containing the imported StockService schema. Browse this and select the **getQuote** element, as shown in the following screenshot:

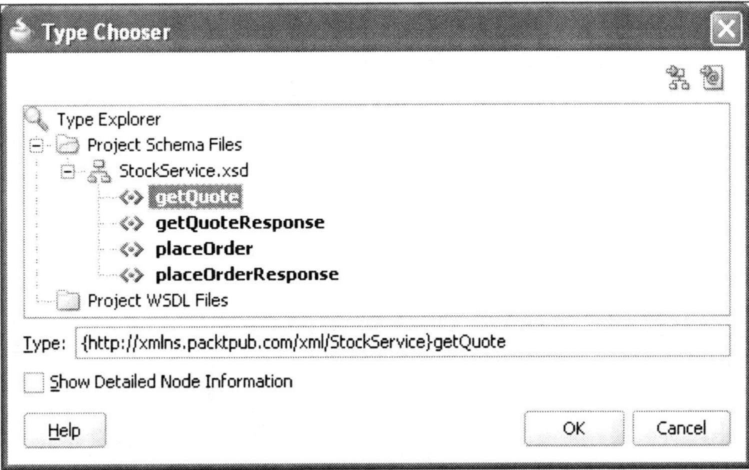

Repeat this step for the output schema element, but select the **getQuoteResponse** element. Click **OK** and this will create our **StockQuote** process within our composite, as shown in the following screenshot:

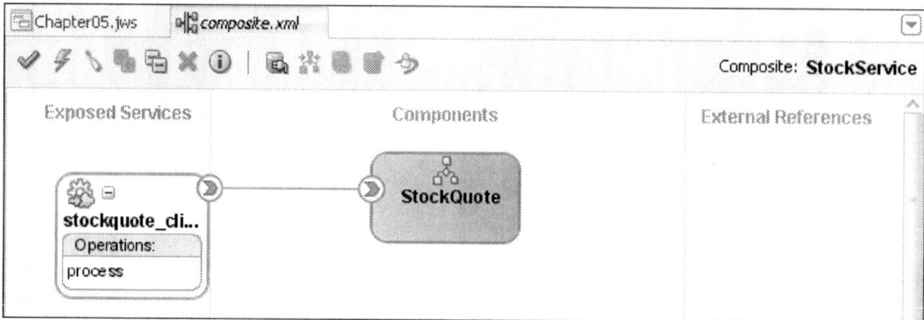

Within the composite, double-click the **StockQuote** process to open it in the BPEL editor. You will see that, by default, JDeveloper has created a skeleton BPEL process, which contains an initial `<receive>` activity to receive the stock quote request, followed by a `<reply>` activity to send back the result (as we discussed in the earlier section - *Synchronous Messaging*). In addition, it will have created two variables; `inputVariable`, which contains the initial stockquote request, and `outputVariable`, in which we will place the result to return to the requestor.

> If you look in the **Projects** section of the **Application Navigator**, you will see that it contains the file `StockQuote.wsdl`. This contains the WSDL description (including partner link extensions) for our process. If you examine this, you will see that we have a single operation; `process`, which is used to call the BPEL process.

Calling the external web services

The next step is to call our external web services. For our stock quote service, we are going to use Xignite's quotes web service, which delivers delayed equity price quotes from all U.S. stock exchanges (**NYSE**, **NASDAQ**, **AMEX**, **NASDAQ OTC Bulletin Board**, and **Pink Sheets**).

> Before you can use this service, you will need to register with Xignite. To do this, or for more information on this and other services provided by Xignite, go to `www.xignite.com`.

To call a web service in BPEL, we first need to create a partner link (as discussed at the start of this chapter). So from the **Component Palette**, expand the **BPEL Services** section and drag a **Partner Link (Web Service / Adapter)** component into the **Partner Link** swim lane in your BPEL process. This will pop up the following screen:

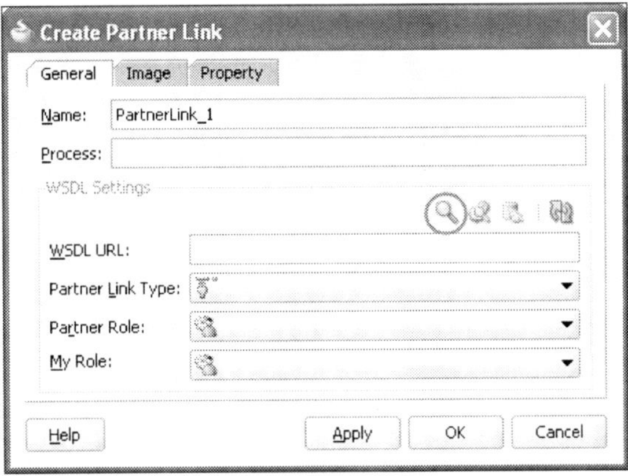

First enter a name for the partner link, for example, **XigniteQuotes**. Next we need to specify the WSDL file for the partner link. JDeveloper provides the following ways to do this:

- **SOA Resource Lookup**: Allows us to browse the filesystem for WSDL files or any connected application server for deployed services
- **SOA Service Explorer**: Allows us to browse other services that are defined within the composite (for example, other BPEL processes, Mediator, or external services)
- **Define Service**: This enables us to define adapter services (refer to *Chapter 3, Service-enabling Existing Systems*) directly within the context of a BPEL process
- **WSDL URL**: Directly enter the URL for the WSDL file into the corresponding field

For our reference, we have a local copy of the WSDL for Xignite's quotes service, called `XigniteQuotes.wsdl`, which is included with the samples for Chapter 5. Click on the **SOA Resource Lookup ...** icon (circled in the preceding screenshot), then browse to and select this file (select **Yes** if prompted to create a local copy of the file).

JDeveloper will parse the WSDL, and assuming it is successful, it will pop up a window saying that there are no partner link types defined in the current WSDL and ask if you want to create partner links for the file. Click **Yes**. JDeveloper will then create one **Partner Link Type** for each port type defined in the WSDL. In cases where we have multiple partner link types, we will need to specify which one to use within our process. To do this, click on the drop-down list next to **Partner Link Type** and select the appropriate one. In our case, we have selected **XigniteQuotesSoap_PL**, as shown in the following screenshot:

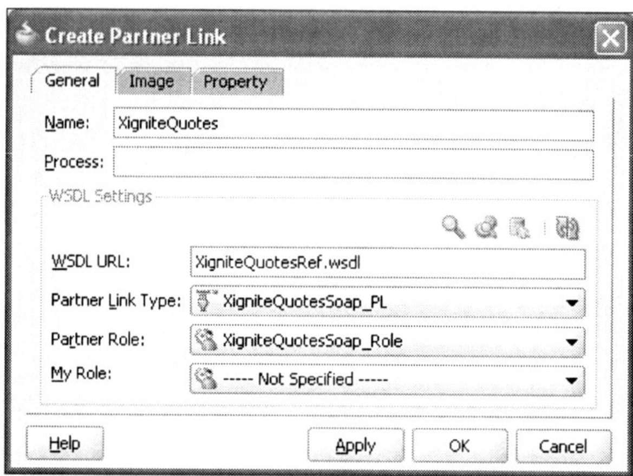

Finally, we need to specify the **Partner Role** and **My Role**. When invoking a synchronous service, there will only be a **single** role defined in the WSDL, which represents the provider of the service. So specify this for the **Partner Role** and leave **My Role** as **----- Not Specified -----**.

> Best practice would dictate that rather than calling the stock quote service directly from within BPEL, we would invoke it via the Oracle Service Bus. This is an area we look at more closely in *Chapter 10, oBay Introduction* when we define our blueprint for SOA.

If you look at the composite view, you will see that **XigniteQuotes** is defined as an **External Reference** and is wired to our BPEL process.

Calling the web service

Once we have defined a partner link for the web service, the next step is to call it. As this is a synchronous service, we will need to use an `<invoke>` activity to call it, as we described earlier in this chapter.

On the **Component Palette**, ensure that the **BPEL Activities and Components** section is expanded. Then from it, drag an **Invoke** activity on to your BPEL process.

Next, place your mouse over the arrow next to the **Invoke** activity. Click and hold your mouse button, drag the arrow over your partner link, and then release, as shown in the following screenshot:

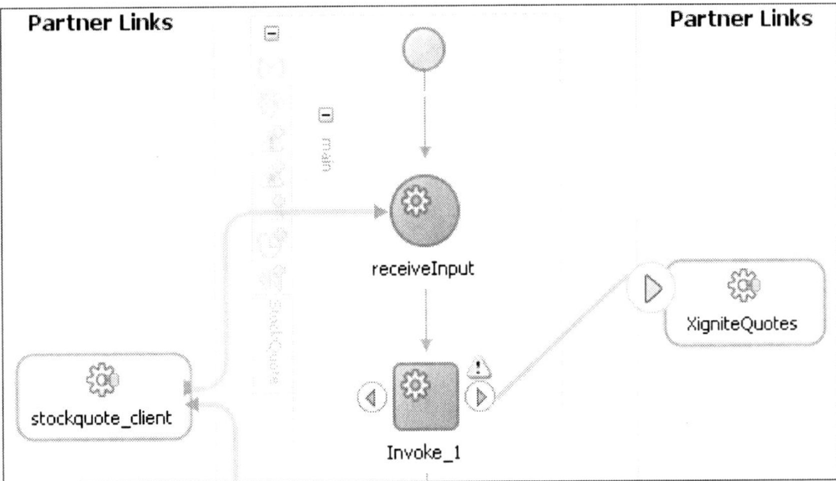

This will then pop up the **Edit Invoke** activity window, as shown in the following screenshot:

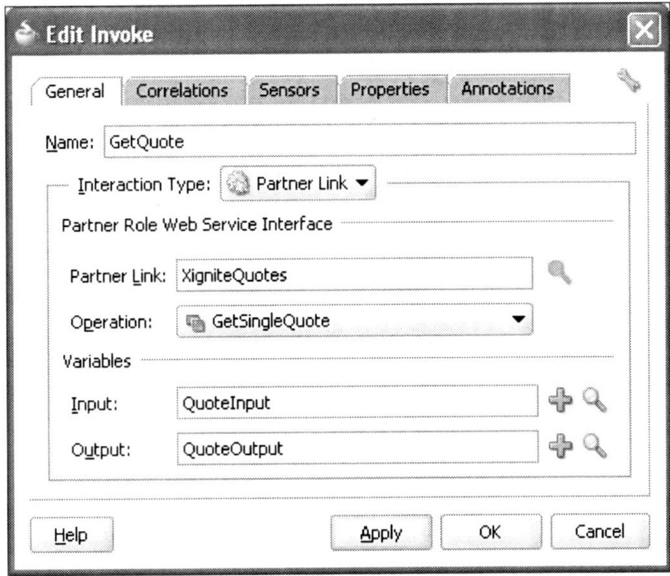

We need to specify a number of values to configure the **Invoke** activity, namely:

- **Name**: This is the name we want to assign to the **Invoke** activity, and can be any value. So just assign a meaningful value such as **GetQuote**.
- **Partner Link**: This is the **Partner Link** whose service we want to invoke; it should already be set to use **XigniteQuotes**, as we have already linked this activity to that **Partner Link**. An alternate approach would be to click on the corresponding spotlight icon, which would allow us to select from any **Partner Link** already defined to the process.
- **Operation**: Once we've specified a **Partner Link**, we need to specify which of its operations we wish to invoke. This presents us with a drop-down list, listing all the operations that are available, for our purpose, select **GetSingleQuote**.
- **Input:** Here we must specify the variable that contains the data to be passed to the web service that's being invoked. It is important that the variable is of type **Message**, and that it is of the same message type expected by the **Operation** (that is, as defined in the WSDL file for the web service).

  The simplest way to ensure this is by getting JDeveloper to create the variable for you. To do this, click on the green plus sign to the right of the input variable field. This will bring up the **Create Variable** window, as shown in the following screenshot. You will notice that JDeveloper creates a default name for the variable (based on the name you gave the invoke operation and the operation that you are calling). You can override this with something more meaningful (for example, **QuoteInput**).
- **Output**: Finally, we must specify the variable into which the value returned by the web service will be placed. As with the input variable, this should be of the type **Message** and corresponds to the output message defined in the WSDL file for the selected operation. Again, the simplest way to ensure this is to get JDeveloper to create the variable for you.

Once you've specified values for all these fields, as illustrated in the preceding screenshot, click **OK**.

Assigning values to variables

In our previous step, we created the variable **QuoteInput**, which we pass to our invocation of **GetSingleQuote**. However, we have yet to initialize the variable or assign any value to it.

To do this, BPEL provides the `<assign>` activity, which is used to update the values of variables with new data. The `<assign>` activity typically consists of one or more copy operations. Each copy consists of a target variable, that is, the variable that you wish to assign a value to and a source (this can either be another variable or an XPath expression).

For our purposes, we want to assign the stock symbol passed into our BPEL process to our **QuoteInput** variable.

To do this, drag an **Assign** activity from the **Component Palette** on to your BPEL process at the point just before our **Invoke** activity. Then double-click on it to open up the **Assign** configuration window. Click on the green plus sign and select **Copy Operation…**.

This will present us with the **Create Copy Operation** window, as shown in the following screenshot:

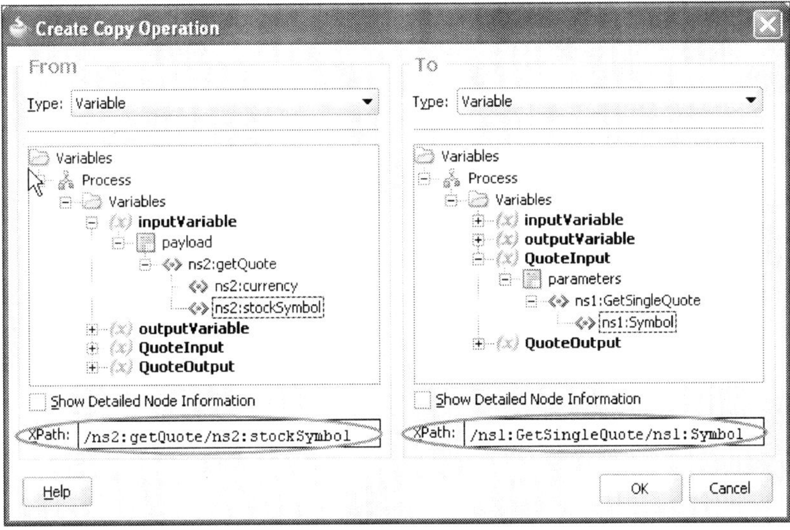

On the left-hand side, we specify the **From** variable (that is, the source). Here we want to specify the stock symbol passed in as part of the input variable to the BPEL process. So expand the **inputVariable** tree, and select **/ns2:getQuote/ns2:stockSymbol**.

For the target, expand **QuoteInput** and select **/ns1:GetSingleQuote/ns1:Symbol**.

You will notice that for both the source and target, JDeveloper has created the equivalent **XPath** expression (circled in the preceding screenshot).

> The source and target can either be a simple type (for example, `xsd:int`, `xsd:date`, or `xsd:string`), as in the preceding example. Or a complex type (for example, `ns2:getQuote`), but make sure the source and target are either of the same type, or at least compatible.

Testing the process

At this stage, even though the process isn't complete, we can still save, deploy, and run our composite. Do this in the same way as previously covered in *Chapter 2, Writing your First Composite*. When you run the composite from the console you will notice that it doesn't return anything (as we haven't specified this yet). But if you look at the audit trail, you should successfully see the **GetSingleQuote** operation being invoked. Assuming this is the case, we know we have implemented that part of the process correctly.

Calling the exchange rate web service

The next step of the process is to determine the exchange rate between the requested currency and the US dollar (the currency used by the `GetSingleQuote` operation). For this, we are going to use the currency convertor service provided by **webserviceX.NET**.

For more information on this and other services provided by webserviceX.NET, go to `www.webservicex.net`.

This service provides a single operation `ConversionRate`, which gets the conversion rate from one currency to another. The WSDL file for this service can be found at the following URL:

```
http://www.webservicex.net/CurrencyConvertor.asmx?wsdl
```

For convenience, we have included a local copy of the WSDL for webserviceX.NET's currency convertor service, called `CurrencyConvertor.wsdl`. It's included with the samples of *Chapter 5*.

To invoke the `ConversionRate` operation, we will follow the same basic steps that we did in the previous section to invoke the `GetSingleQuote` operation. For brevity, we won't repeat them here, but will allow the reader to do this.

To follow the examples, name the input variable for the exchange rate web service **ExchangeRateInput** and the output variable **ExchangeRateOutput**.

Assigning constant values to variables

The operation **ConversionRate** takes two input values as follows:

- **FromCurrency**: This should be set to **'USD'**
- **ToCurrency:** This should be set to the currency field contained within the `inputVariable` for the BPEL process.

To set the **FromCurrency**, create another copy operation. However, for the **From** value, select **Expression** as the **Type** (circled in the following screenshot).

This will replace the variable browser with a free format textbox. Here you can specify any value, within quotes, that you wish to assign to your target variable. For our purposes, enter **'USD'**, as shown in the following screenshot:

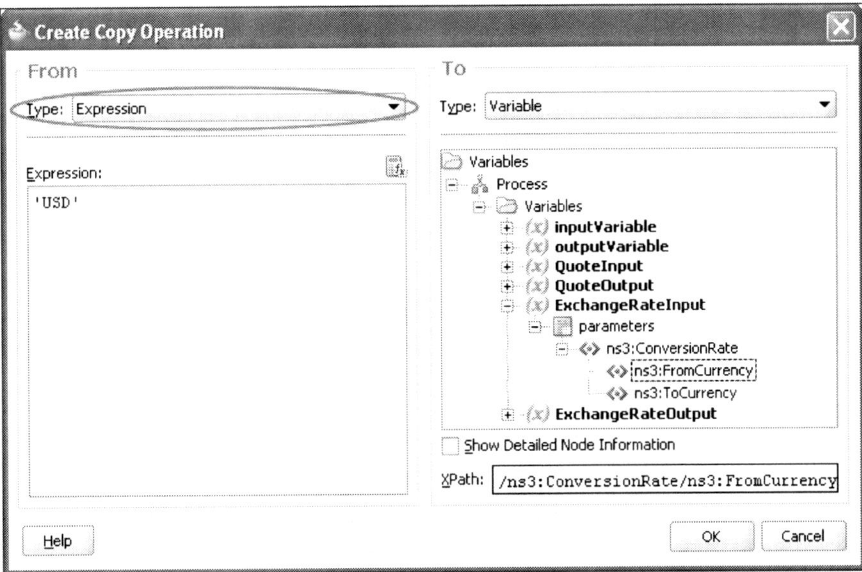

To set the value of **ToCurrency**, create another copy operation and copy in the value of the **currency** field contained within the **inputVariable**.

At this stage again, save, deploy, and run the composite to validate that we are calling the exchange rate service correctly.

Using the expression builder

The final part of the process is to combine the exchange rate returned by one service with the stock price returned by the other, in order to determine the stock price in the requested currency and return that to the caller of the composite.

To do this, we will again use an `<assign>` activity. So drag another `<assign>` activity onto the process, just after our second invoke activity. Now in our previous use of the `<assign>` activity, we have just used it to copy a value from one variable to another.

Here, it is slightly different, in that we want to combine multiple values into a single value, and to do that, we will need to write the appropriate piece of **XPath**. Create a copy operation as before, but for the source type, select **Expression** from the drop-down list, as shown in the following screenshot:

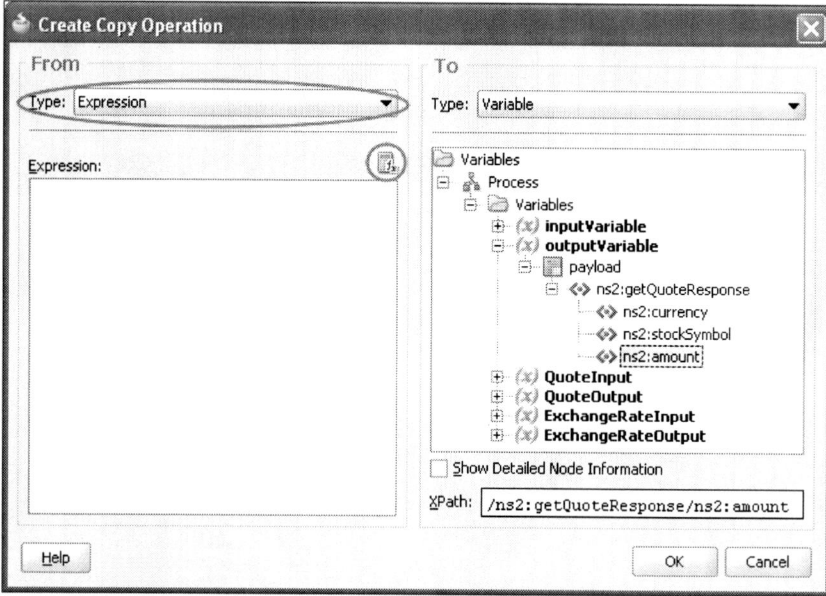

Now, if you want, you can type in the XPath expression manually (into the **Expression** area), but it's far easier and less error prone to use the **Expression Builder**. To do this, click on the XPath expression builder icon; the calculator icon, which is circled in the preceding screenshot, will pop up the **Expression Builder** (shown below):

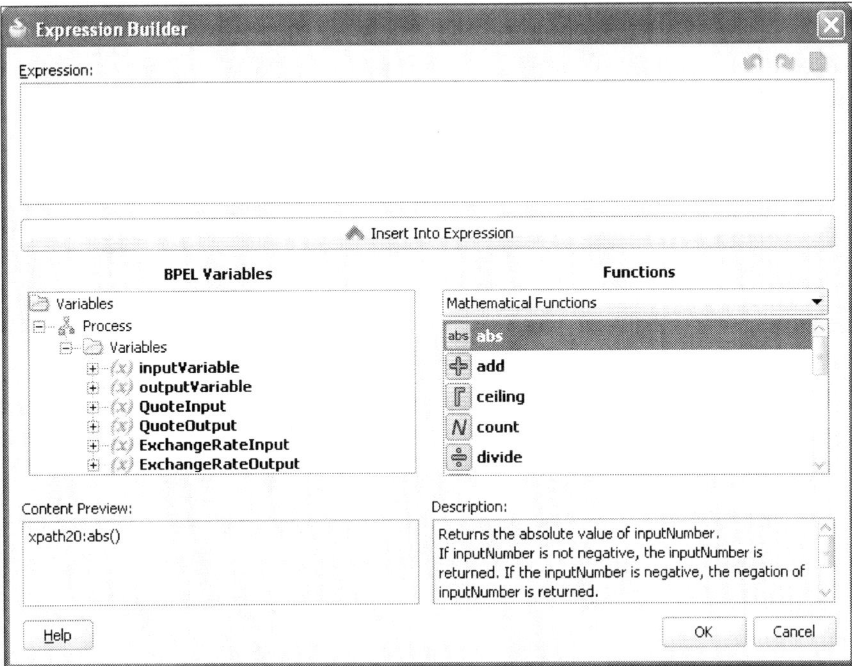

The **Expression Builder** provides a graphical tool for writing XPath expressions, which are executed as part of the copy operation. It consists of the following areas:

- **Expression**: The top textbox contains the XPath expression that you are working on. You can either type data directly in here, or use the **Expression Builder** to insert XPath fragments to build up the XPath required.
- **BPEL variables**: This part of the **Expression Builder** lets you browse the variables defined within your BPEL process. Once you've located the variable that you wish to use, click on the **Insert Into Expression** button, and this will insert the appropriate code fragment into the XPath expression.

> The code fragment is inserted at the point within the expression where the cursor is currently positioned.

- **Functions**: This shows you all the different types of XPath functions that are available to build up your XPath expression. To make it easier to locate the required function, they are grouped into categories such as **String Functions**, **Mathematical Functions**, and so on.

  The drop-down list lets you select the category that you are interested in (for example, **Mathematical Functions**, as illustrated in the preceding screenshot), and then the window below that lists all the functions available to that group.

  To use a particular function, select the required function, and click **Insert Into Expression**. This will insert the appropriate XPath fragment into the XPath Expression (again at the point that the cursor is currently positioned).
- **Content Preview**: This box displays a preview of the content that would be inserted into the XPath Expression if you clicked the **Insert Into Expression** button. For example, if you had currently selected a particular BPEL variable, it would show you the XPath to access that variable.
- **Description**: If you've currently selected a function, this box provides a brief description of the function, as well as the expected usage and number of parameters.

So let's use this to build our XPath expression. The expression we want to build is a relatively simple one, namely, the stock price returned by the stock quote service multiplied by the exchange rate returned by the exchange rate service.

To build our XPath expression, carry out the following steps:

First, within the **BPEL Variables** area, in the variable **QuoteOutput**, locate the element **ns1:GetSingleQuoteResult | ns1:Last**, as shown in the following screenshot:

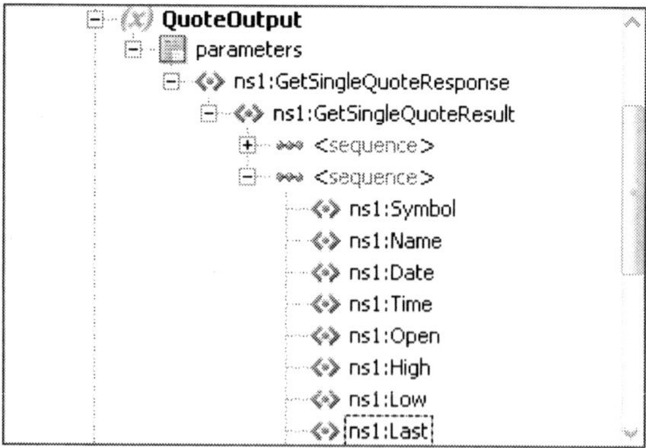

Then click **Insert Into Expression** to insert this into the XPath expression.

Next, within the **Functions** area, select the **Mathematical Functions** category, and select the **multiply** function (notice the description in the **Description** box, as shown in the following screenshot), and insert this into the XPath expression:

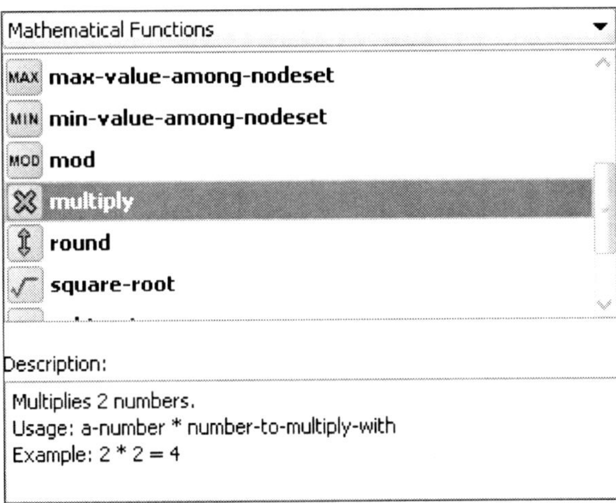

Finally, back in the **BPEL Variables** area, locate the element **ConversionRateResult** within the variable **ExchangeRateOutput**, and insert that into the XPath expression.

You should now have an XPath expression similar to the one illustrated below, once you are happy with it, click **OK**.

```
bpws:getVariableData('QuoteOutput','parameters','/ns1:GetSingleQuoteResponse
/ns1:GetSingleQuoteResult/ns1:Last') * bpws:getVariableData('ExchangeRateOutput'
,'parameters','/ns3:ConversionRateResponse/ns3:ConversionRateResult')
```

Finally make sure you specify the target part of the copy operation, which should be the **amount** element within the **outputVariable**.

In order to complete the `<assign>` activity, you will need to create two more copy operations to copy the `Currency` and `StockSymbol` specified in the `inputVariable` into the equivalent values in the `outputVariable`.

Once done, your BPEL process should be complete. So deploy and run the composite.

Asynchronous service

Following our StockQuote service, another service would be a stock order service, which would enable us to buy or sell a particular stock. For this service, a client would need to specify the stock, whether they wanted to buy or sell, the quantity, and the price.

It makes sense to make this an asynchronous service, as once the order has been placed, it may take seconds, minutes, hours, or even days for the order to be matched.

Now, I'm not aware of any trade services that are free to try (probably for a good reason!). However, there is no reason why we can't simulate one. To do this, we will write a simple asynchronous process.

Drag another BPEL process on to our **StockService** composite and give it the name **StockOrder**, but specify that it is an asynchronous BPEL process.

As with the **StockQuote** process, we also want to specify predefined elements for its input and output. The elements we are going to use are `placeOrder` for the input and `placeOrderResponse` for the output, the definitions for which are shown in the following code snippet:

```
<xsd:element name="placeOrder"         type="tPlaceOrder"/>
<xsd:element name="placeOrderResponse" type="tPlaceOrderResponse"/>

<xsd:complexType name="tPlaceOrder">
  <xsd:sequence>
    <xsd:element name="currency"    type="xsd:string"/>
    <xsd:element name="stockSymbol" type="xsd:string"/>
    <xsd:element name="buySell"     type="xsd:string"/>
    <xsd:element name="quantity"    type="xsd:integer"/>
    <xsd:element name="bidPrice"    type="xsd:decimal"/>
  </xsd:sequence>
</xsd:complexType>

<xsd:complexType name="tPlaceOrderResponse">
  <xsd:sequence>
```

```
      <xsd:element name="currency"    type="xsd:string"/>
      <xsd:element name="stockSymbol" type="xsd:string"/>
      <xsd:element name="buySell"     type="xsd:string"/>
      <xsd:element name="quantity"    type="xsd:integer"/>
      <xsd:element name="actualPrice" type="xsd:decimal"/>
    </xsd:sequence>
  </xsd:complexType>
```

These are also defined in the `StockService.xsd` that we previously imported into the `StockService` composite. So, for each field, we click on the magnifying glass to bring up the type chooser and select the appropriate element definitions. Then click **OK** to create the process. This will create a second BPEL process within our composite, so double-click on this to open it.

You will see that, by default, JDeveloper has created a skeleton asynchronous BPEL process, which contains an initial `<receive>` activity to receive the stock order request. But this time it's followed by an `<invoke>` activity to send the result back (as opposed to a `<reply>` activity used by the synchronous process).

If you look at the WSDL for the process, you will see that it defines two operations: `process` to call the process, and `processResponse`, which will be called by the process to send back the result. Thus the client that calls the `process` operation will need to provide the `processResponse` callback in order to receive the result (this is something we will look at in more detail in *Chapter 15, Message Interaction Patterns*.

Now, for the purpose of our simulation, we will assume that the `StockOrder` request is successful and the `actualPrice` achieved is always the bid price. So to do this, create an assign operation that copies all the original input values to their corresponding output values. Deploy the composite, and run it from the console.

When you click the **Test Web Service** button for the `StockService` composite, you will now be presented with two options: **stockorder_client_ep** and **stockquote_client_ep**. These correspond to each of the exposed services we have defined in our composite. Ensure you select **stockorder_client_ep**, which is wired to our `StockOrder` process.

This time, you will notice that no result is returned (as it's being processed asynchronously); rather it displays a message to indicate that the service was invoked successfully, as shown in the following screenshot:

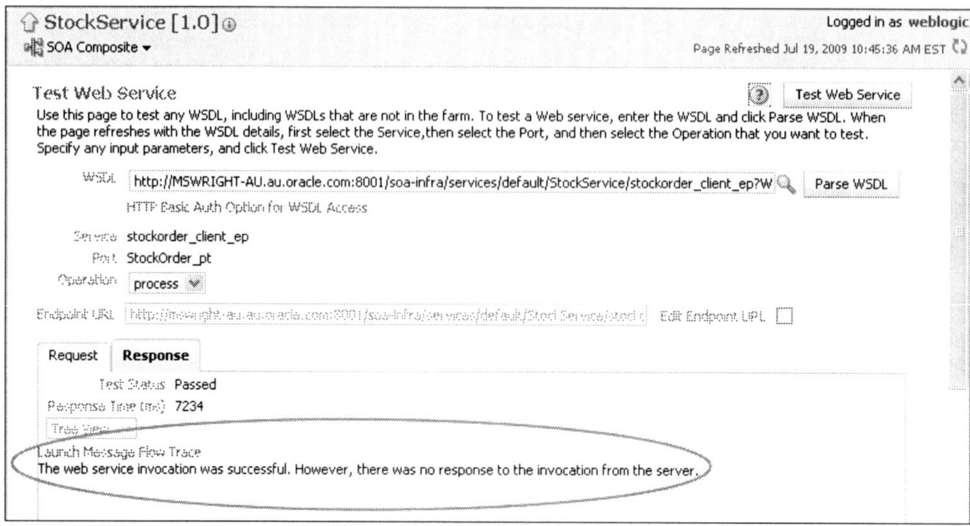

Click on **Launch Message Flow Trace** to bring up the trace for the composite, and then select **StockOrder** to bring up the audit trail for the process. Switch to the flow view, and expand the **callbackClient** activity at the end of the trace. This will pop up a window showing the details of the response sent by our process, as shown in the following screenshot:

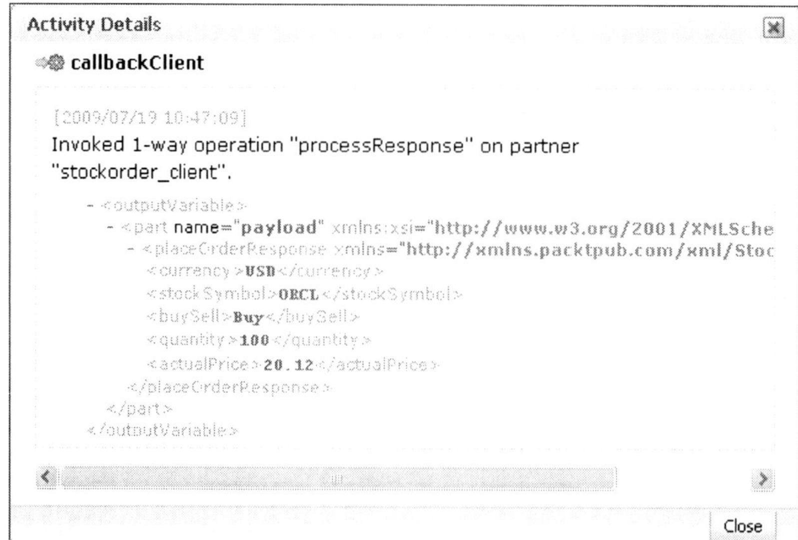

Using the wait activity

Now you've probably spotted the most obvious flaw with this simulation, in that the process returns a response almost immediately, which negates the whole point of making it asynchronous.

To make it more realistic, we will use the `<wait>` activity to wait for a period of time. To do this drag the `<wait>` activity from the Component Palette onto your BPEL process just before the `<assign>` activity, and then double-click on it to open the **Wait** activity window, as shown below.

The `<wait>` activity allows you to specify that the process wait for a specified duration of time or until a specified deadline. In either case, you specify a fixed value or choose to specify an XPath expression to evaluate the value at runtime.

If you specify **Expression**, and then click the calculator icon to the right of it, this will launch the **Expression Builder** that we introduced earlier in the chapter. The result of the expression must evaluate to a valid value of `xsd:duration` for periods and `xsd:dateTime` for deadlines. The format of `xsd:duration` is `PnYnMnDTnHnMnS`, for example. `P1M` would be a duration of 1 month and `P10DT1H25M` would be 10 days, 1 hour and 25 minutes.

For deadlines, the expression should evaluate to a valid value of `xsd:date`.

The structure of `xsd:dateTime` is `YYYY-MM-DDThh:mm:ss+hh:mm`, where the `+hh:mm` is optional and is the time period offset from UTC (or GMT, if you prefer). Obviously, the offset can be negative or positive.

For example, `2010-01-19T17:37:47-05:00` is the time 17:37:47 on January 19th 2010, 5 hours behind UTC (that is, Eastern Standard Time in the US).

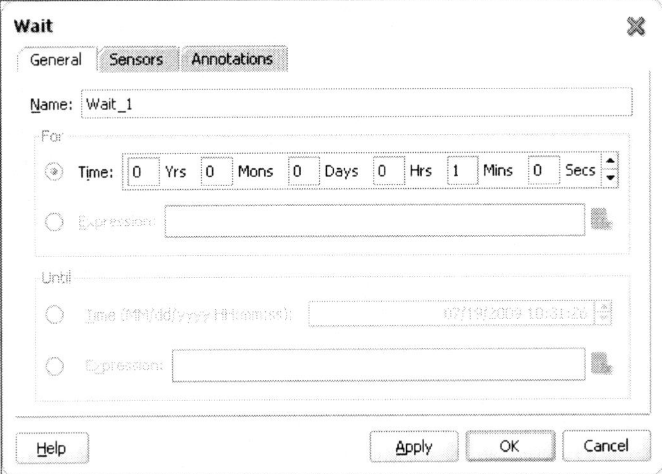

For our purposes, we just need to wait for a relatively short period of time, so set it to wait for one minute.

Now save, deploy, and run the composite. If you now look at the audit trail of the process, you will see that it has paused on the `<wait>` activity (which will be highlighted in orange).

Improving the stock trade service

We have a very trivial trade service, which always results in a successful trade after one minute. Let's see if we can make it a bit more "realistic".

We will modify the process to call the **stockQuote** service and compare the actual price against the requested price. If the quote we get back matches or is better than the price specified, then we will return a successful trade (at the quoted price). Otherwise we will wait a minute and loop back round and try again.

Creating the while loop

The bulk of this process will now be contained within a while loop, so from the **Process Activities** list of the **Component Palette**, drag a **While** activity into the process.

Click on the plus symbol to expand the **While** activity. It will now display an area where you can drop a sequence of one or more activities that will be executed every time the process iterates through the loop.

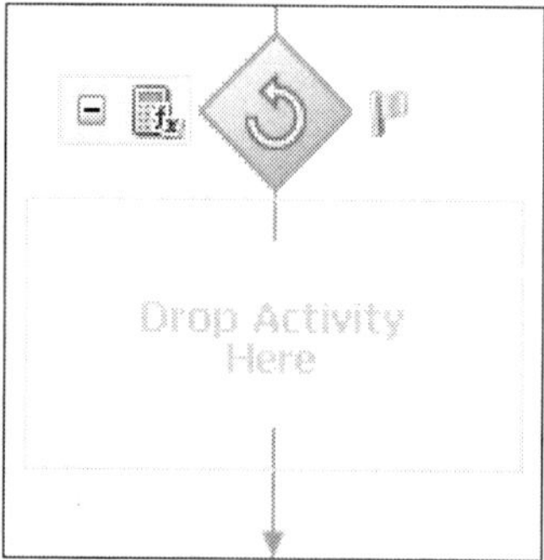

We want to iterate through the loop until the trade has been fulfilled, so let's create a variable of type `xsd:Boolean` called **tradeFulfilled** and use an `<assign>` statement before the while loop to set its value to false.

The first step is to create a variable of type `xsd:Boolean`. Until now, we've used JDeveloper to automatically create the variables we've required, typically as part of the process of defining an **Invoke** activity. However, that's not an option here.

If you look at the diagram of your BPEL process, you will see that it is surrounded by a light grey dashed box, and on the top left-hand side there are a number of icons. If you click on the top one of these **(x)**, as shown in the following screenshot, this will open a window that lists all the variables defined in the process:

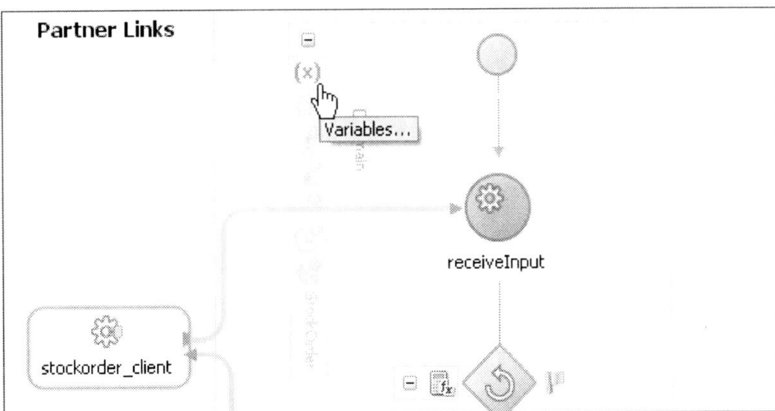

At this stage, it will list just the default `inputVariable` and `outputVariable`, which were automatically created with the process. Click on the green plus button. This will bring up the **Create Variable** window, as shown in the following screenshot:

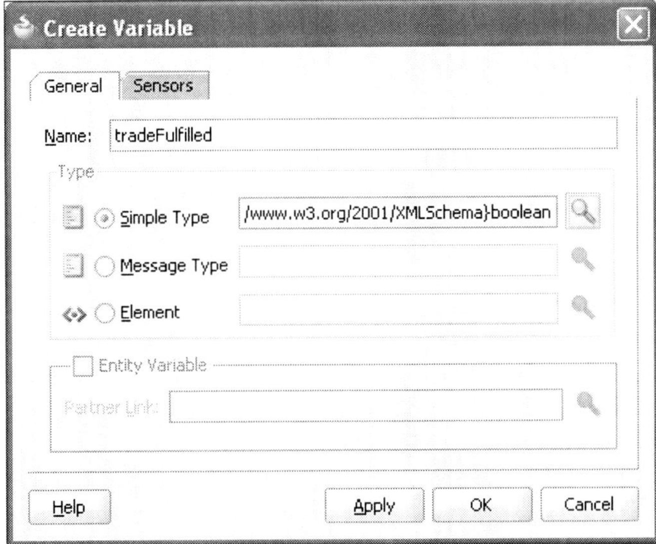

Here we simply specify the **Name** of the variable (for example, **tradeFulfilled**) and its **Type**. In our case, we want an `xsd:Boolean`, so select **Simple Type** and click the magnifying glass to the right of it.

This will bring up the **Type Chooser**, which will list all the simple built-in data types defined by XML Schema. Select **Boolean** and click **OK**.

We need to initialize the variable to false, so drag an `<assign>` statement on to your process just before the while loop. Use the function `false()`, under the category **Logical Functions**, to achieve this.

Next, we need to set the condition on the while loop, so that it will execute only while `tradeFulfilled` equals false. Double-click on the while loop. This will open the **While** activity window, as shown in the following screenshot:

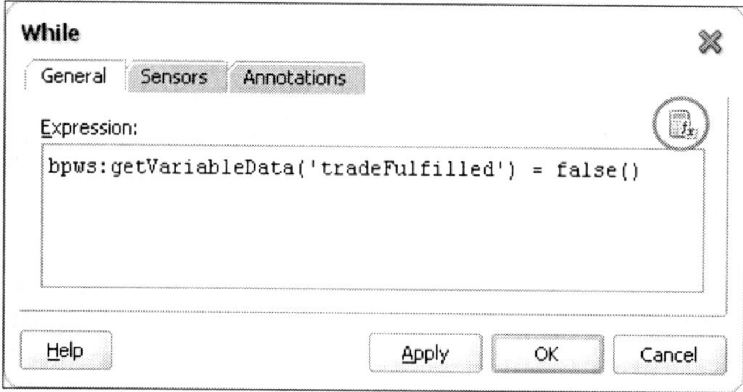

We must now specify an XPath expression, which will evaluate to either true or false. If you click on the expression builder icon, which is circled in the preceding screenshot, this will launch the **Expression Builder**. Use this to build the following expression:

```
bpws:getVariableData('tradeFullfilled') = false()
```

Once we are happy with this, click **OK**.

Checking the price

The first activity we need to perform within the while loop is to get a quote for the stock that we are trading. For this, we will need to invoke the stock quote process we created earlier. As both of these processes are in the same composite, the simplest way to do this is to wire them together.

Switch to the composite view in JDeveloper, next place your mouse over the yellow arrow on the **StockOrder** process (the one to **add a new Reference**). Click and hold your mouse button, then drag the arrow onto the blue arrow on the **StockQuote** process (the one that represents the **Service Interface**), then release, as shown in the following screenshot:

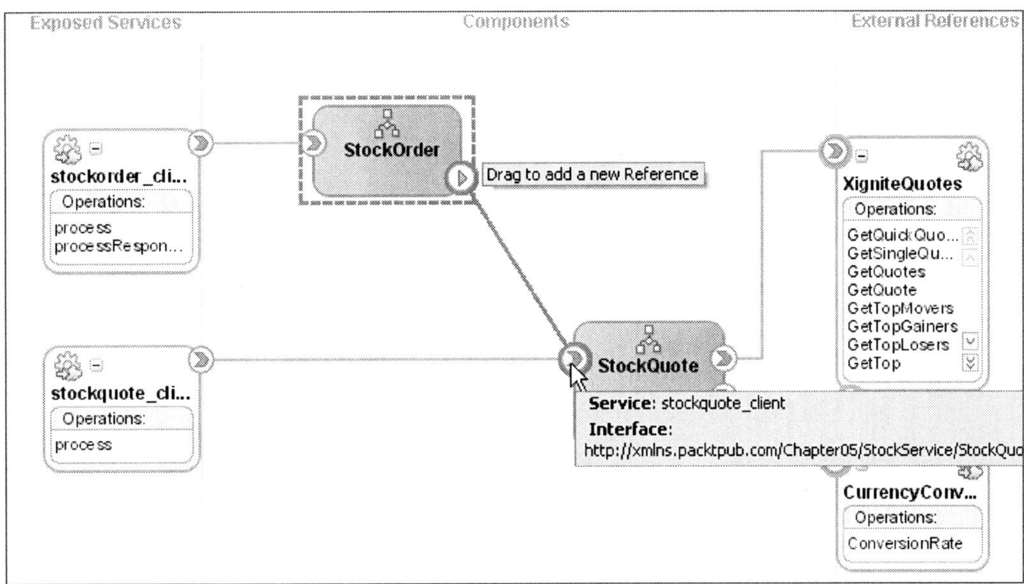

This will wire these two processes together and create a corresponding partner link in the **StockOrder** process. From here, implement the required steps to invoke the **process** operation of the **StockQuote** process, making sure that they are included within the while loop.

Using the switch activity

Remember our requirement is that we return success if the price matches or is better than the one specified in the order. Obviously, whether the price is better depends on whether we are selling or buying. If we are selling we need the price to be equal to or greater than the asking price; whereas if we are buying, we need the price to be equal to or less than the asking price.

So for this, we will introduce the `<switch>` activity. Drag a `<switch>` activity from the **Process Activities** list of the **Component Palette** on to your process after the invoke activity for the **StockQuote** service. Next, click on the plus symbol to expand the `<switch>` activity. By default, it will have two branches illustrated as follows:

The first branch contains a <case> condition, with a corresponding area where you can drop a sequence of one or more activities that will be executed if the condition evaluates to true.

The second branch contains an <otherwise> subactivity, with a corresponding area for activities. The activities in this branch will only be executed if all case conditions evaluate to false.

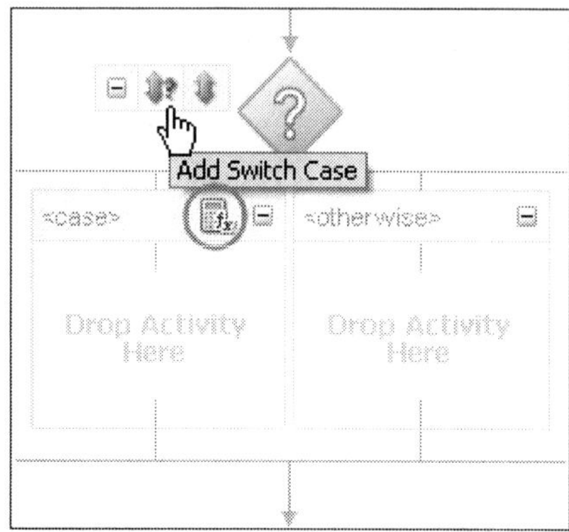

We want to cater to two separate tests (one for buying the other for selling), so click on the **Add Switch Case** arrow (highlighted in the preceding screenshot) to add another <case> branch.

Next, we need to define the test condition for each <case>. To do this, click on the corresponding **Expression Builder** icon to launch the expression builder (circled in the preceding screenshot). For the first one, use the expression builder to create the following:

```
bpws:getVariableData ( 'inputVariable','payload',
                      '/ns1:PlaceOrder/ns1:BuySell') = 'Buy' and
bpws:getVariableData ( 'inputVariable', 'payload',
                      '/ns1:PlaceOrder/ns1:BidPrice') >=
bpws:getVariableData ( 'stockQuoteOutput', 'payload',
                      '/ns1:getQuoteResponse/ns1:Amount')
```

For the second branch, use the expression builder to define the following:

```
bpws:getVariableData ( 'inputVariable','payload',
                       '/ns1:PlaceOrder/ns1:BuySell') = 'Sell' and
bpws:getVariableData ( 'inputVariable', 'payload',
                       '/ns1:PlaceOrder/ns1:BidPrice') <=
bpws:getVariableData ( 'stockQuoteOutput', 'payload',
                       '/ns1:getQuoteResponse/ns1:Amount')
```

Once we've defined the condition for each case, we just need to create a single `<assign>` activity in each branch. This needs to set all the values in the `outputVariable` to the corresponding values in the `inputVariable`, except for the `ActualPrice` element, which we should set to the value returned by the StockQuote process. Finally, we also need to set `tradeFullfilled` to true, so that we exit the while loop.

The simplest way to do this is by dragging the original `<assign>` we created in the first version of this process onto the first branch and then modify it as appropriate. Then create a similar `<assign>` activity in the second branch.

You've probably noticed that you could actually combine the two tests into a single test. However, we took this approach to illustrate how you can add multiple branches to a switch.

If we don't have a match, then we have to wait a minute and then circle back round the while loop and try again. As we've already defined a `<wait>` activity, simply drag this from its current position within the process into the activity area for the `<otherwise>` activity.

That completes the process, so try deploying it and running it from the console.

The other obvious thing is that this process could potentially run forever if we don't get a stock quote in our favor. One way to solve this would be to put the while activity in a scope and then set a timeout period on the scope so that it would only run for so long.

Summary

In this chapter, we've gone beyond individual services and looked at how we can use BPEL to quickly assemble these services into composite services. By using this same approach, we can also implement end-to-end business processes or complete composite applications (something we will do in the second section of this book).

You may have also noticed that although BPEL provides a rich set of constructs for describing the assembly of a set of existing services, it doesn't try to reinvent the wheel where functionality is already provided by existing SOA standards. Rather, it has been designed to fit naturally with and leverage the existing XML and web services specifications such as XML Schema, XPath, XSLT, and of course, WSDL, and SOAP.

This chapter should have given you a solid introduction to the basic structure of a BPEL process, its key constructs, and the difference between a synchronous and asynchronous service. Building the examples will help to reinforce this as well as give you an excellent grasp of how to use JDeveloper to build BPEL processes.

Even though this chapter will have given you a good introduction to BPEL, we haven't yet looked at much of its advanced functionality such as its ability to handle long running processes, its fault and exception management, and how it uses compensation to undo events in the case of failures. These are areas we will cover in more detail in later chapters of the book.

6

Adding in Human Workflow

Many business processes require an element of human activity. Common tasks include approving an expense item or purchase order. But even fully automated processes can require human involvement, especially when things go wrong.

In this chapter, we will introduce you to the various parts of the human workflow component of the Oracle SOA Suite and take you through a practical example to create and run your first "simple" workflow. Once we've done that, we will examine how to carry out other basic workflow activities such as how to:

- Dynamically assign a task to a user or group based on the content of the task
- Cancel or change a workflow task while it's still in process
- Enable the workflow user to request additional details about a task
- Reassign, delegate, or escalate a task, either manually or through the use of user-defined business rules

Workflow overview

The following diagram illustrates the three, typical participants in any workflow:

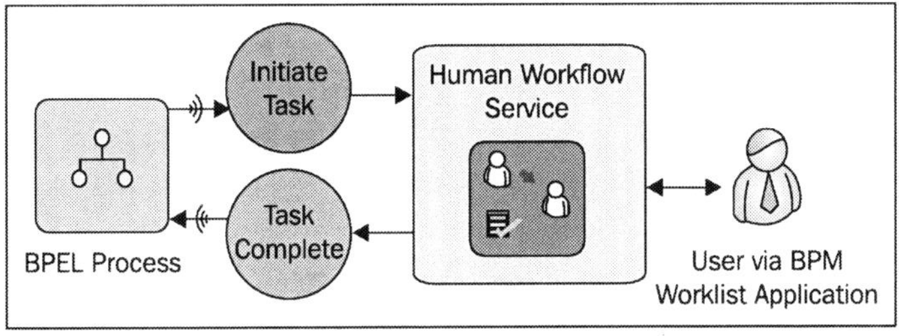

On the left-hand side we have the BPEL process, which creates the task and submits it to the human workflow service. Once it has initiated the task, the process itself will pause until the completed task is returned.

On the right-hand side we have the user who carries out the task. Tasks can either be directly assigned to a user or to a group to which the user belongs; in this case they need to claim the task before they can work on it. When working on a task, a user typically does this via the **BPM Worklist Application**, which is a web-based application included as part of the SOA Suite.

Sitting between the BPEL process and the worklist application is the human workflow service. It is responsible for routing the task to the appropriate user or group, managing the lifecycle of a task until it completes, and returning the result to the initiator (that is, the BPEL process in the preceding diagram).

The human workflow services have a full set of WSDL and Java APIs that allow us to build our own custom equivalent of the BPM worklist application. This is an area we examine in *Chapter 17, Workflow Patterns*.

The human workflow service utilizes an external identity store for details of users, their privileges, and which groups they belong to. In a production deployment, you would typically configure the identity store to be an LDAP repository such as **Oracle Internet Directory** or **Active Directory**.

For the sake of simplicity, the workflow examples within this book make use of the sample user community provided by Oracle. To install this community, go to `http://www.oracle.com/technology/sample_code/products/hwf/index.html` and download the file **workflow-001-DemoCommunitySeedApp**. Unzip this file and follow the instructions in `README.txt`.

Leave approval workflow

For our first workflow, we will create a very simple BPEL process that takes a leave request and creates a simple approval task for the individual's manager, who can then either approve or reject the request.

The first step is to create a composite containing a simple asynchronous leave approval BPEL process. The input and output schema elements for the process are defined in `LeaveRequest.xsd`, as shown in the following code snippet (note that the schema is also provided in the samples folder for Chapter 6):

```
<?xml version="1.0" encoding="windows-1252"?>
<xsd:schema xmlns:xsd="http://www.w3.org/2001/XMLSchema"
           xmlns="http://schemas.packtpub.com/LeaveRequest"
           targetNamespace="http://schemas.packtpub.com/LeaveRequest"
           elementFormDefault="qualified" >
  <xsd:element name="leaveRequest" type="tLeaveRequest"/>
  <xsd:complexType name="tLeaveRequest">
    <xsd:sequence>
      <xsd:element name="employeeId" type="xsd:string"/>
      <xsd:element name="fullName" type="xsd:string" />
      <xsd:element name="startDate" type="xsd:date" />
      <xsd:element name="endDate" type="xsd:date" />
      <xsd:element name="leaveType" type="xsd:string" />
      <xsd:element name="leaveReason" type="xsd:string"/>
      <xsd:element name="requestStatus" type="xsd:string"/>
    </xsd:sequence>
  </xsd:complexType>
</xsd:schema>
```

Make sure you import this file as part of the process of creating the BPEL process and set the input and output schema elements to **LeaveRequest**.

Defining the human task

Once you've created your composite, drag a **Human Task Component** from the SOA **Component Palette** onto it. This will pop up the following screen:

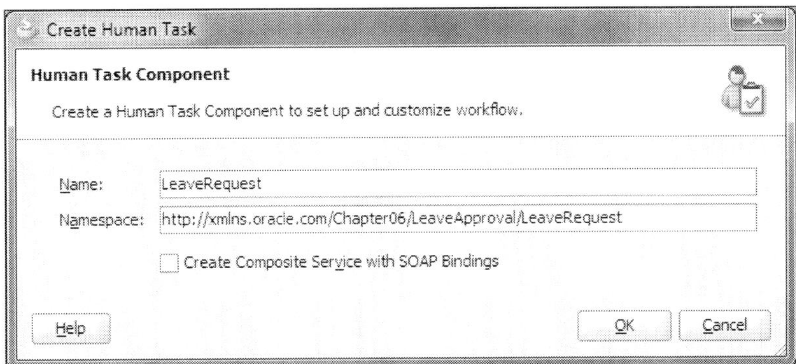

Give the task a meaningful name (for example, **LeaveRequest**) and click **OK**. This will add a **Human Task** with the corresponding name to our composite, as shown in the following screenshot:

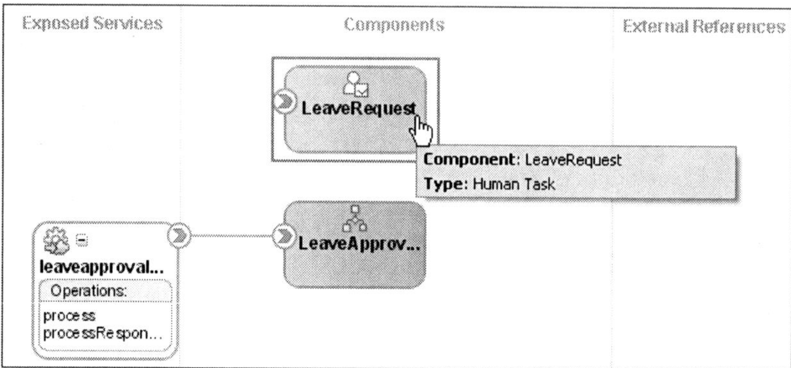

Double-click on the **LeaveRequest task** tab. This will open up the task definition form as a new tab within JDeveloper (as shown in the following screenshot) where we can configure our task:

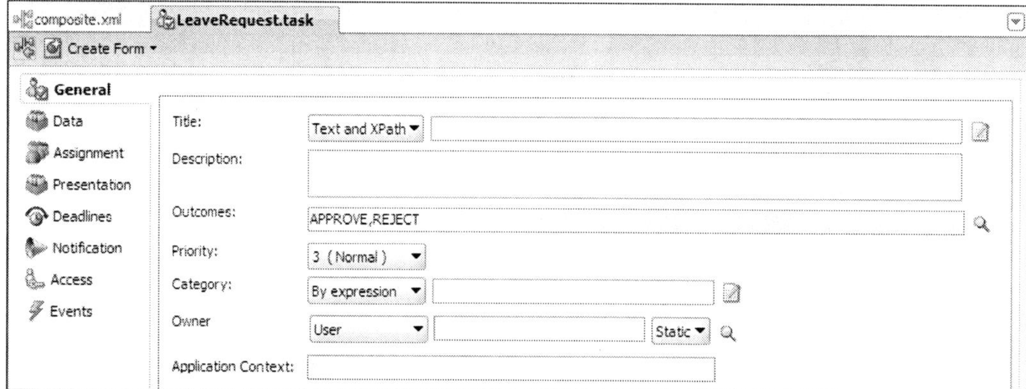

By default, JDeveloper displays the **General** subtab where we define the basic details about the task.

> For readers familiar with Oracle SOA Suite 10gR3, you will notice the task definition form looks a lot simpler. This is because it's been restructured to organize the task configuration parameters into categories, each accessed by a corresponding tab (rather than display them all on the same form as was previously the case).

The key things we need to define for the task are its **Title**, what the possible **Outcomes** are (that is, leave request approved or rejected), the **Parameters** (or payload) of the task, and who to route or assign it to.

On the **General** tab, give the task a **Title**, such as **Approval Required for Leave Request**. Note that this is what a user will see in their work queue if they are allocated the task. For the time being we can leave the other values (**Description**, **Outcomes**, **Priority**, **Category**, and **Owner**) with their default values.

Specifying task parameters

Next, we need to define the task data, that is, the content of the task that we want the approver to base their decision upon. For this, we can specify one or more parameters; each parameter can be a standard XML type such as string, integer, or boolean. In addition, we can use any type or element defined in one of our imported XML schemas.

For our purposes, we simply want to pass in the leave request received by the BPEL process. To do this, select the **Data** tab, click on the plus symbol (circled in the following screenshot), and select **Add other payload**:

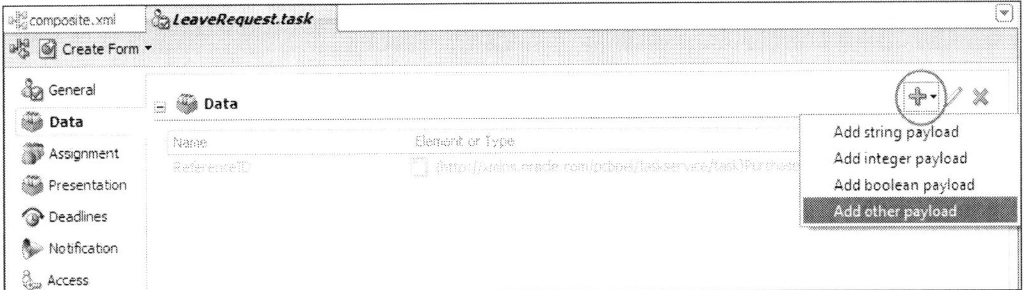

This will launch the **Add Task Parameter** window:

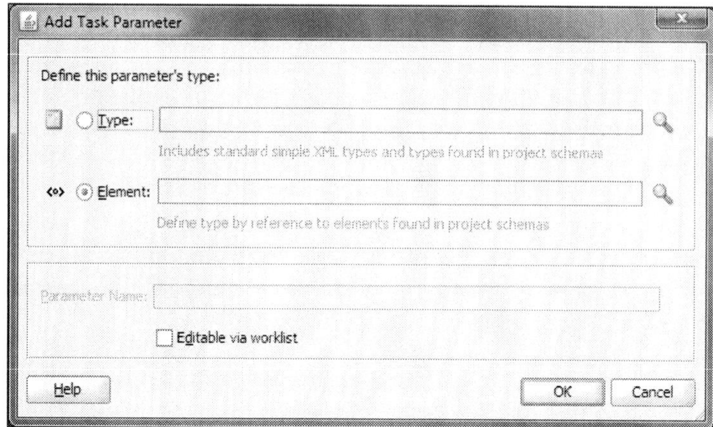

Ensure that **Element** is selected as the parameter type and then click on the corresponding search icon to bring up the standard type chooser. From here, just browse the `LeaveRequest` schema file that we imported at the start, and select the **LeaveRequest** element.

If we check **Editable via worklist**, anyone who has write access to the task payload will be able to update the content of this parameter. In our case, we will leave it unchecked.

Click **OK**. We should now have a **LeaveRequest** parameter defined for our task.

Specifying task assignment and routing policy

Finally, we need to specify who is going to approve the task. We do this by creating an **Assignment and Routing Policy**. An assignment and routing policy consists of one or more stages that can be executed sequentially or in parallel (or any combination thereof), with each stage consisting of one or more participant types that in turn can also be sequential or in parallel (or any combination thereof). A participant type can be:

- **Single**: Used to specify a single user or group to assign the task to
- **Serial**: Used when a set of users must work in sequence, for example, when a task has to proceed through several layers of a management chain
- **Parallel**: Used when a set of users must work in parallel, a common usage for this is when a group of participants need to vote on an outcome
- **FYI**: Used to send a notification to a user or group

For our purposes we need a single stage containing one participant of type **Single** approver (we will examine the other types in more detail in *Chapter 17, Workflow Patterns*). Select the **Assignment** tab. You will see that, by default, our task consists of a single stage named **Stage1**, as shown in the following screenshot:

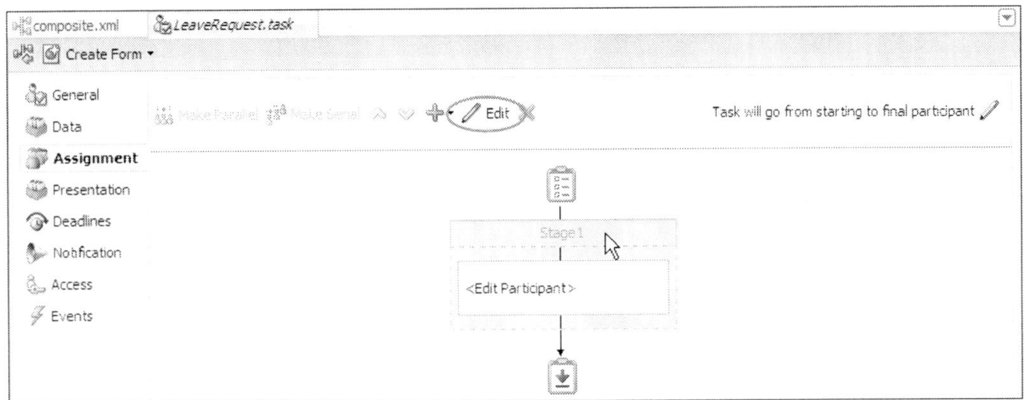

First, we will give our stage a more meaningful name. To do this, select the stage by clicking on its name. The stage will turn gray to indicate that it has been selected, as shown in the preceding screenshot. Then select **Edit** (circled in the preceding screenshot). This will bring up the **Edit** window. Give it an appropriate name, and click **OK**.

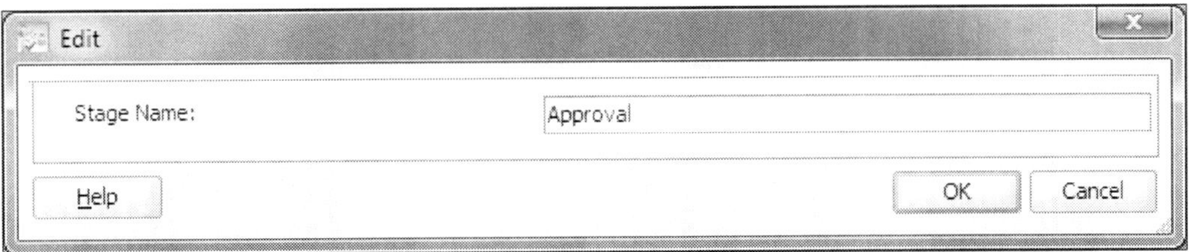

Next, we need to add a participant of type **Single** to our **Approval** stage. First, select the **<Edit Participant>** section of our stage by clicking on it. It will turn gray to indicate that it has been selected, as shown in the following screenshot:

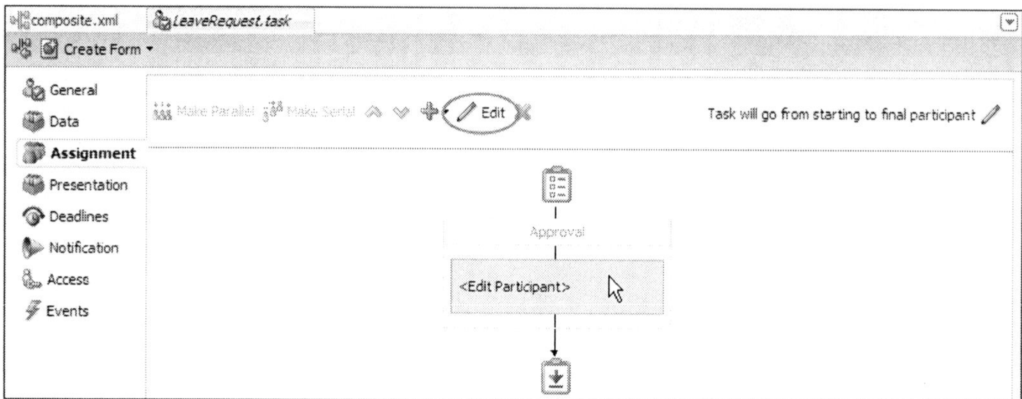

Select **Edit** (circled in the preceding screenshot). This will launch the **Add Participant Type** window.

You will notice that the menu icons in the **Assignment** tab are context-sensitive, based on whether you have selected one or more stages or participants.

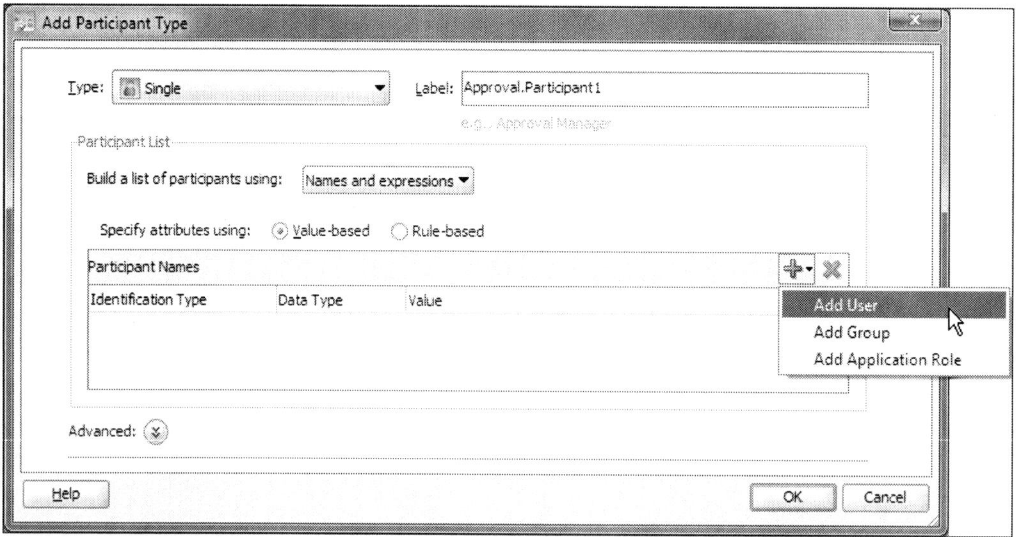

By default, a participant type of **Single** approver is selected, which is fine for our purpose. Labels are used to provide a meaningful description of the routing rules and are also useful if we specify multiple participants for a stage. So for our purpose, just enter a meaningful value (for example, **Manager Approval**).

We now need to specify the **list** of participants that the task is going to be assigned to. Each participant can either be a specific user, group, or application role (and we can have any combination of these in our list).

For our purpose, we are going to assume that the CEO of the company is required to approve every holiday, so we will always assign it to **cdickens**. This is probably not ideal! But we will revisit this later in the chapter to look at how we can make it more realistic.

Click on the plus symbol, and select **Add User**, as shown in the preceding screenshot. This will add a participant of type **User** to our participant list, as shown in the following screenshot. We can either directly enter the name of a user into the **Value** field or click the browse icon (**...**) to bring up the identity lookup dialog. This allows you to search and browse the users and groups defined in the identity service.

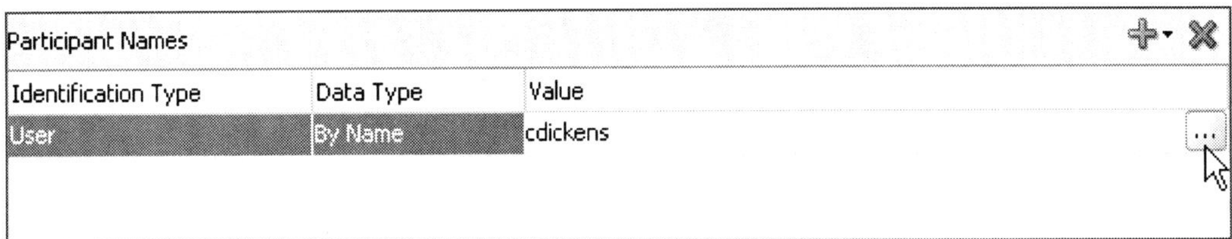

Once you've specified the participant details, click **OK**; this will take us back to the task definition window, which will have been updated with our routing policy. Select **Save** on JDeveloper to make sure you save the task definition.

Invoking our human task from BPEL

So far, we have defined our human task. The next step is to incorporate it into our **LeaveApproval** BPEL process. To do this, drag a **Human Task** activity from the BPEL component palette onto our process, as shown in the following screenshot:

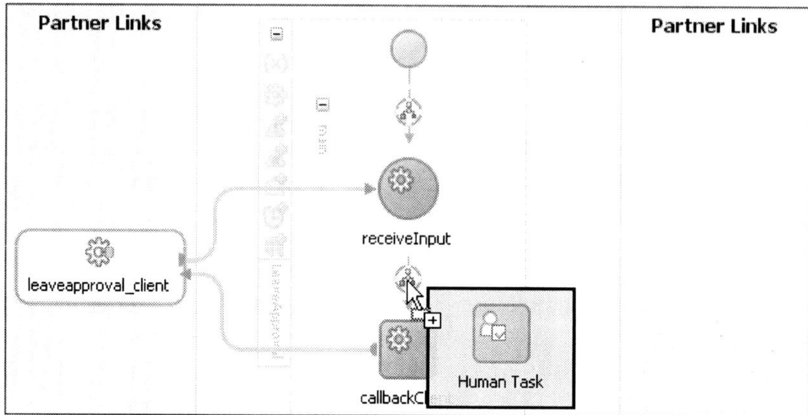

JDeveloper will prompt us to specify the **Task Definition** to use for this activity; from the drop-down list, select **LeaveRequest**. This will present us with the **Human Task** activity window from where we can configure the task within the context of our BPEL process:

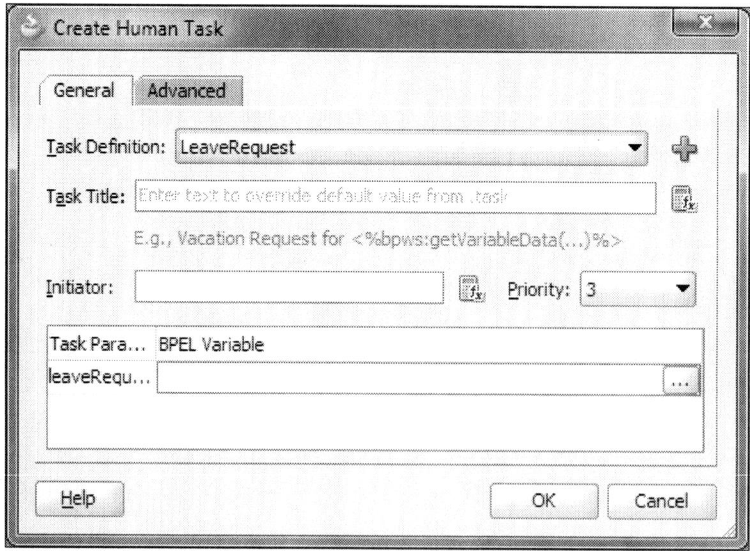

The first value we need to specify is the **Task Title**. This is optional, since if we don't specify a value, it will use the task title we specified earlier as part of the task definition. We want to make the task title a bit friendlier, so first type in (without the quotes):

```
Leave Request for
```

Then click on the calculator icon to the right of the **Task Title** field. This will launch the now familiar **Expression Builder**. Here, from the **inputVariable**, just select the element:

```
ns1:LeaveRequest/ns1:fullName
```

This expression will be appended to the end of our title text embedded between `<% %>` to give the following:

```
Leave Request for <%bpws:getVariableData('inputVariable', 'payload',
'/ns1:LeaveRequest/ns1:fullName')%>
```

At runtime, the BPEL process will evaluate the expression between `<% %>` and substitute the result. For now, we won't specify a task initiator as this is optional, and we will leave the **Priority** set to **3**.

The final thing to specify is the value of each of the **Task Parameters** defined to the task. Click on the browse icon (**...**) for the **LeaveRequest** parameter, and this will bring up the **Task Parameters** window, which allows you to browse the variables defined to the BPEL process. Select the **LeaveRequest** element passed in as part of the `inputVariable` for the BPEL process.

This completes the configuration of the task, so click **OK**. This will return us to the BPEL process, which will now contain our human task activity, followed by an additional switch. If you expand the switch, you will see it contains a **Case** for each of our task outcomes (**APPROVE** or **REJECT**), where we can specify the appropriate next step in our process. For the purpose of this example, we don't need to do anything. However, in a real system we might update the HR system with details of the leave, if it was approved.

Your composite is now complete, so deploy it to the server in the normal way.

Creating the user interface to process the task

So far, we have defined the task that needs to be carried out and plugged it into a simple BPEL process. What we need to do next is implement the part of the user interface that allows someone to view the details of our specific task and then either approve or reject the leave request.

Out-of-the-box, SOA Suite provides the worklist application with all the main workflow user interface screens and a framework in which to plug your task-specific interface component. This can be developed from scratch if you want, using ADF, but the simplest way is to get JDeveloper to generate an ADF form based on the task definition.

To do this, go back to the task definition form, click on **Create Form**, and select **Auto-Generate Task Form**, as shown in the following screenshot:

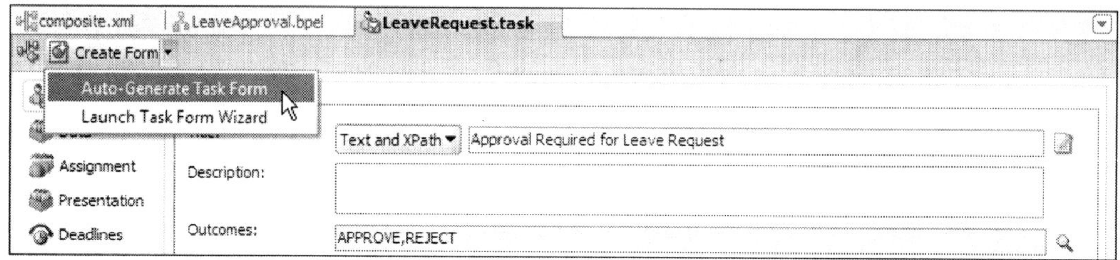

This will launch the **Create Project** window, prompting us to specify the name of the project in which to create our form. Specify an appropriate name, such as **LeaveRequestForm**, and click **OK**.

This will generate an ADF form plus all the supporting components; JDeveloper will automatically open the form, which can then be customized as required.

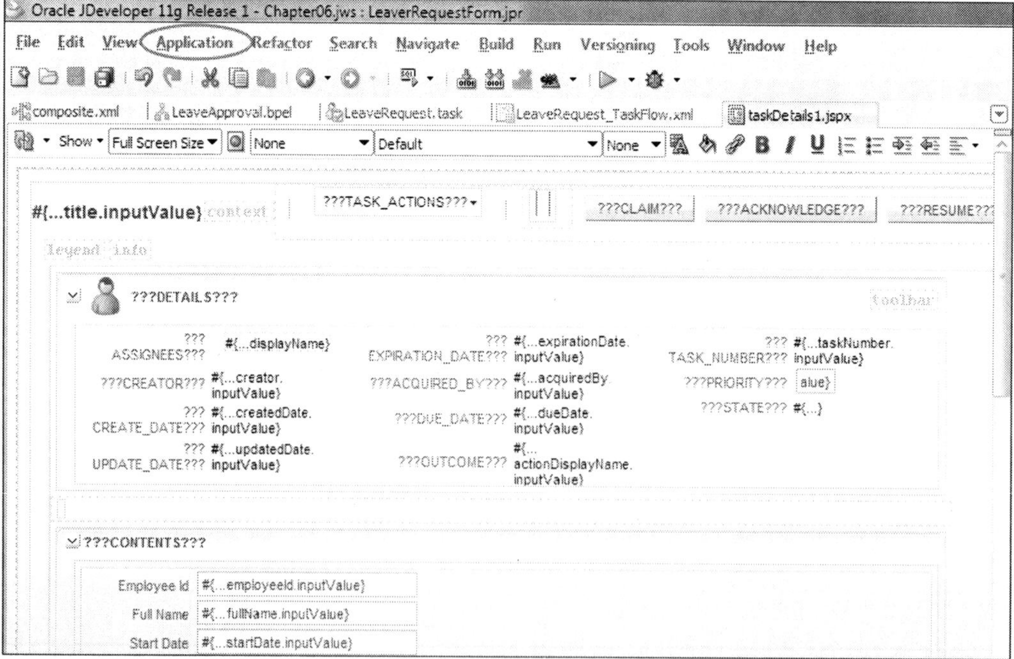

To deploy the form, click on the **Application** menu (circled in the preceding screenshot) and select **Deploy | LeaveRequestForm.** This will launch the **Deployment** dialog. Select **Deploy to Application Server**, and click on **Next**. On the **Select Server** page, uncheck the option **Deploy to all server instances in the domain** and click on **Next**. On the **Server Instances** page, select the SOA server instance, click on **Next**, and then click **Finish**.

Running the workflow process

Log into the SOA console and launch the composite, ensuring that you specify a valid employee ID (such as **jcooper**). This will invoke the BPEL process, which in turn will create the `LeaveRequest` task.

If you browse the audit trail for the composite, you will see it paused at the **LeaveRequest** activity, as shown in the following screenshot:

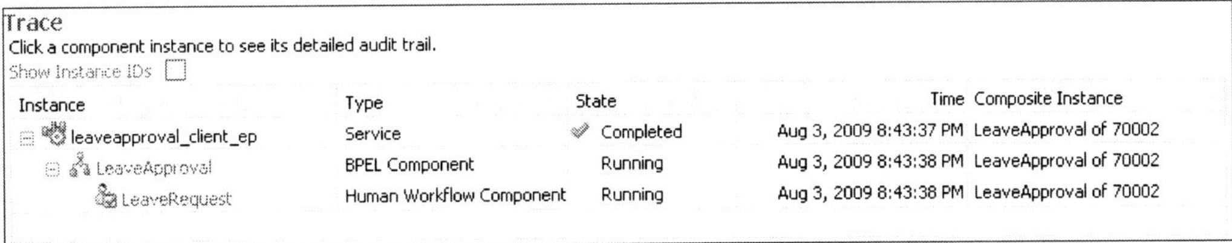

Click on the **LeaveRequest** activity, and this will bring up the **Activity Audit Trail** for the workflow task, showing that it is assigned to **cdickens**, as shown in the following screenshot:

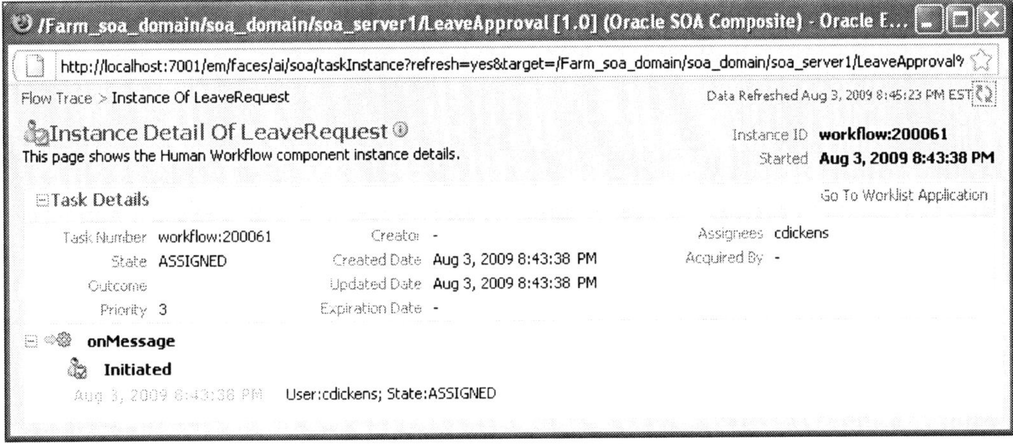

At the moment, the composite will wait forever, until the task is either approved or rejected. To do that, we need to log into the BPM worklist application to process the task.

Processing tasks with the worklist application

To launch the worklist application, open up a browser and enter the following URL:

```
http://<hostname>:<port>/integration/worklistapp
```

This will bring up the login screen for the BPM worklist application; log in as **cdickens** (password **welcome1**). This will bring you into the **My Tasks** tab, which provides access to our various tasks and work queues. By default, it displays our inbox, which lists all the tasks currently allocated to us (or any groups that we belong to). We can then filter this based on assignee and task status.

The application also provides a number of other views that enable us to quickly identify high priority tasks, tasks due soon or new tasks. In addition, we can also define our own views.

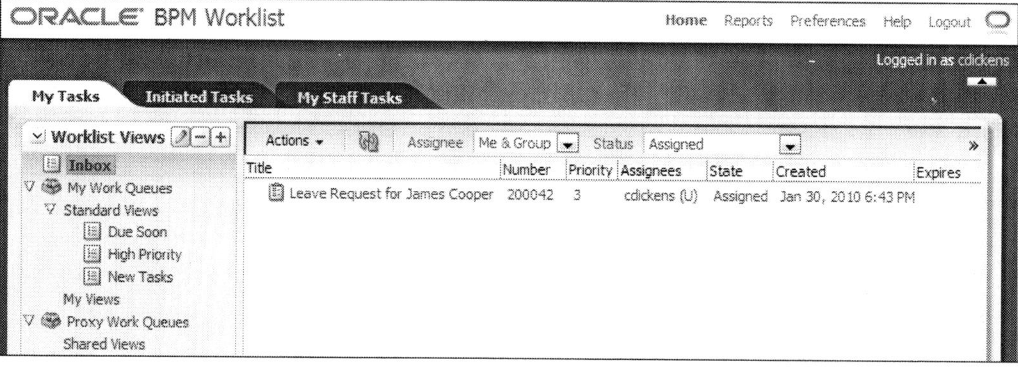

Here, you should see the LeaveRequest task created by our process. Click on the task and it will display details of the task in the bottom pane of the page, like the one shown in the following screenshot:

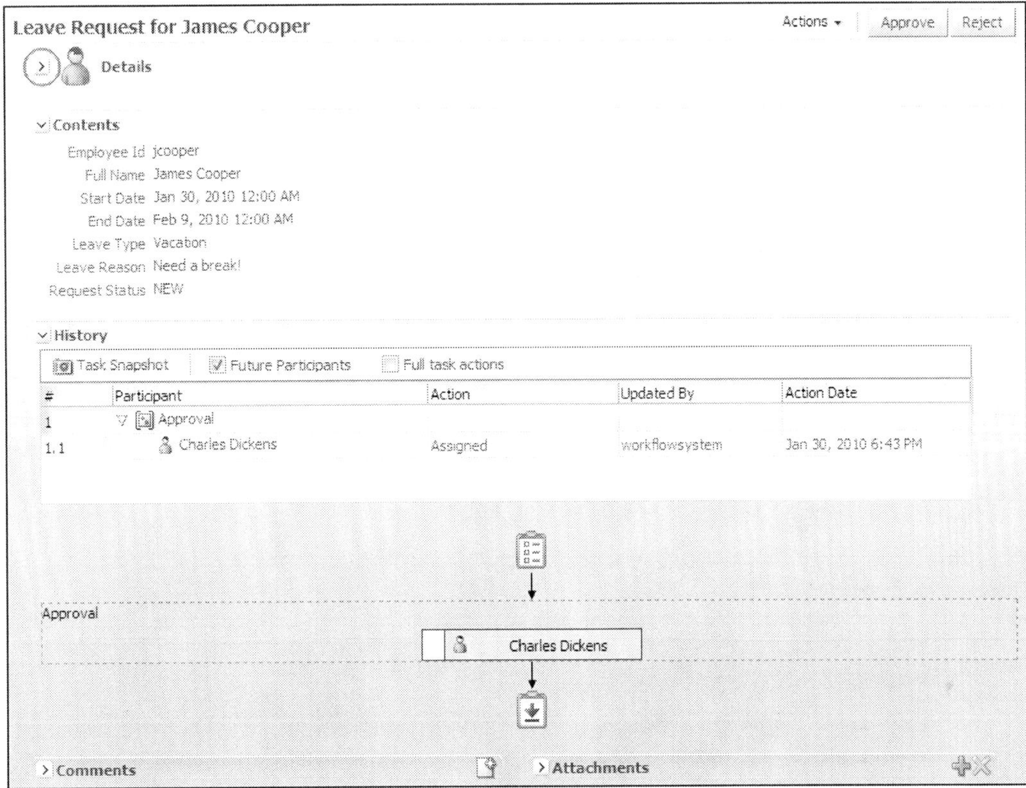

If we study this, we can see it is made up of the following five areas:

- **Actions**: Contains the actions that can be performed on a task. This is split into two parts. The first is a drop-down list that lists standard actions available for tasks such as Escalate and Suspend, which we will examine later. The second is a set of buttons that correspond to each of the outcomes defined in the task definition (that is, **Approve** or **Reject**).
- **Details:** Contains the standard header information about the task, a summary of which was displayed for each task in our work queue. In the preceding screenshot this is minimized. To expand it, click on the **>** sign (circled in the preceding screenshot).
- **Contents**: This contains the task specific payload, in our case, details of the leave request. This may be editable, depending on how we configure the task.

- **History**: Provides a history (in tabular and pictorial form) of when the task was created, who it's been assigned to, and so on. This is useful as it provides a complete audit trail of the task. Note this is also available in the SOA console.
- **Comments, Attachments**: Here we can add comments or attach documents to the task. This can be especially useful when a task is exchanged between multiple participants.

For our purpose, we just want to approve or reject the task, so just click the appropriate button. This will complete the task and remove it from our work queue.

However, change the search filter for the task list to show tasks with a completed status and you will see that the task is still there. If you select the task, it will display its details in the task pane, where you can view the content of the task but no longer perform any actions as it is now complete.

Go back to the SOA console and look at the audit trail for the process, you will see that it is completed.

Improving the workflow

At this point, we have a simple workflow up and running. However, we have the following issues with it:

- At the moment, all requests go to the CEO, but it would be better if requests went to the applicant's manager.
- Also, what happens if the requester makes a mistake with his/her request, or changes their mind? How do we let the original requester amend or cancel their request?
- What if the approver needs additional information about a task, is there a simple way to enable that?

Dynamic task assignment

There are two approaches here. One is to assign the task to a specific group, which may contain one or more individuals. A classic example would be to assign a support request to the customer support group.

The other is to dynamically specify the user to assign to a task at runtime, based on the value of some parameter, which is roughly what we want to do. Actually, we want to look up the manager of the employee requesting the task and assign it to them.

If we go back to the **Human Task Definition** form (refer to *Defining the human task section*), and double-click on the **Manager Approval** step in the routing policy we defined, this will reopen the **Edit Participant Type** form. For the **Data Type**, specify that you want to select the participant **By Expression**, and then click on the browse icon for the **Value** field (circled in the following screenshot):

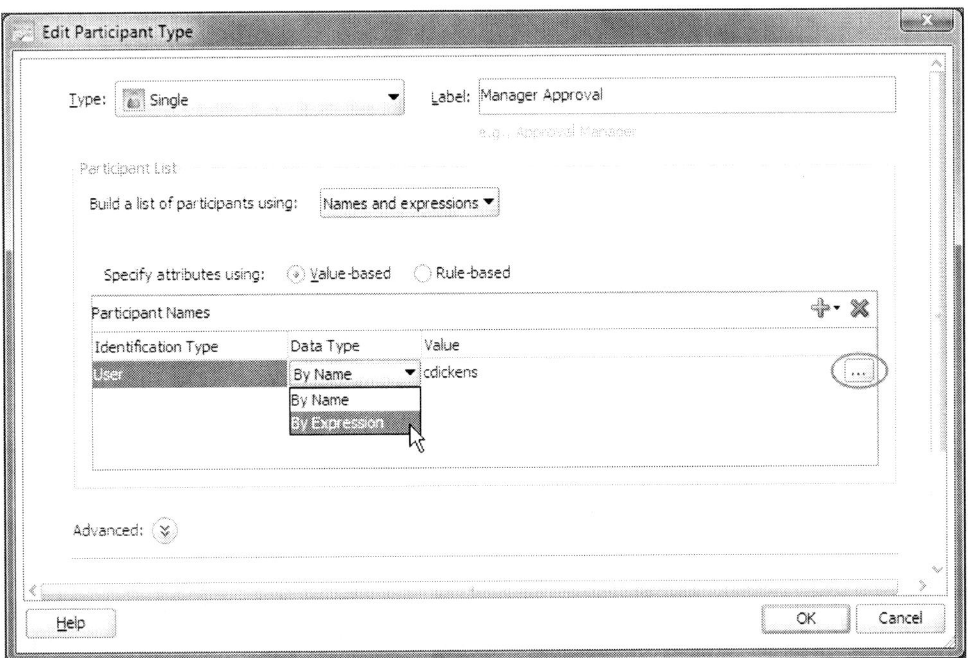

This will open up the **Expression Builder** , which was introduced in *Chapter 5, Using BPEL to Build Composite Services and Business Processess*. However, the key thing to notice here is that we only have access to the content of the task we are working on (not the full content of the BPEL process).

We need to create an expression that evaluates to the user ID of the employee's manager. Fortunately, one of the services that come with workflow is the identity service, which provides us with a simple way of querying the underlying identity layer to find out details about a user. In our case, we can use the **getManager** function to get the ID of the manager.

So within the **Expression Builder**, select the **Identity Service Functions**, and from here, select the **getManager** function and insert it into the expression. We now need to pass it the employee ID of whoever is requesting the leave. Expand the task payload; you will find it contains the content of the leave request. Select the **employeeId** and insert that as the parameter, as shown in the following screenshot:

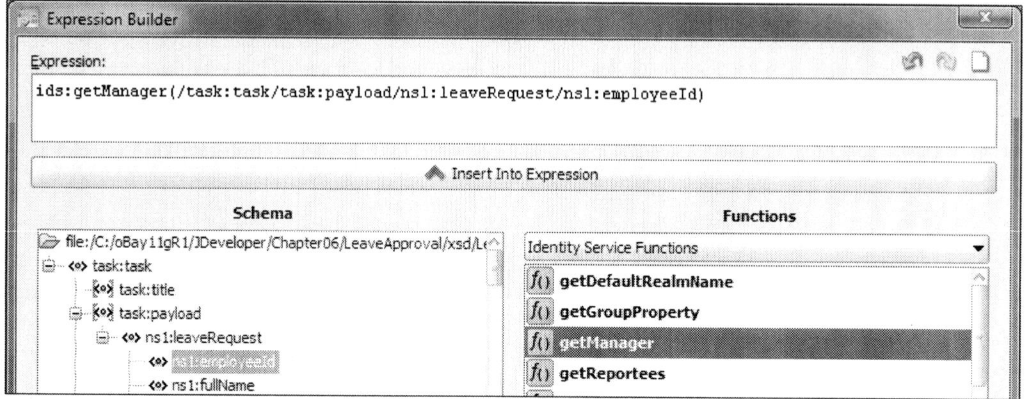

You can now save the task, redeploy it, and run the process. Assuming you specify that the request is for **jcooper**, you will need to log in as **jstein** to approve the task.

Assigning tasks to multiple users or groups

So far, we have only looked at scenarios where we assign a task to a single user. However, workflow enables you to either assign a task to multiple users, or to one or more groups (or a combination of the two).

In this case, every user who is a member of the group or has the task assigned to them will be able to see the task on their queue. However, before anyone can work on the task, they must first claim it. Once claimed, other users will still be able to see the task, but only the user who has claimed the task will be able to perform any operations on it.

Although group assignments are more likely to be static, you can also specify them dynamically in the same way we have for the user.

Cancelling or modifying a task

Another common requirement is to cancel or modify a task before it has completed the workflow. If we take our example, suppose that having submitted the leave request we changed our mind. Ideally we would like to be able to withdraw the task or modify it before someone goes to the effort of approving it.

Withdrawing a task

You may remember that when we first added the task to the BPEL process we had a field where we could specify a task initiator that we previously left blank. Well, if you specify a task initiator they are effectively the **creator** of the task and have the ability to withdraw the task.

To specify the task initiator, go back to your BPEL process and double-click on the **Human Task**. This will reopen the Human Task Configuration window (see *Initializing the Workflow Parameter* section), click the icon to the right of the initiator field, and this will launch the **Expression Builder**. Use this to specify the **employeeId** as the task initiator.

Now save the process, redeploy it, and run the process. Again, specify that the request is for **jcooper**, then log into the worklist application as **jstein**. You should notice that the task creator is **jcooper**. Don't approve the task, rather log out and log back into the worklist application as **jcooper**.

This will take you into the **My Tasks** tab, which is probably empty, but if you click the **Initiated Tasks** tab, then this will list all the tasks that you have initiated. If you look at the task, you will see that you can perform a single action on the task, which is to withdraw it.

Modifying a task

When we defined the task parameters on the task definition form, we had the option to specify if the parameters are **Editable via Worklist**, and at the time we didn't select this option. If this option is selected, then anyone who the task is assigned to has the ability to modify the task payload, including the task owner and initiator.

Difference between task owner and initiator

Now you may have noticed while specifying the various task details that as well as being able to specify the task initiator, we can also specify the task owner. At this point, you may be asking what is the difference between these two roles?

The simple answer is the **task owner** has more administrative privileges when it comes to a task. The **task initiator** is the person who creates a particular instance of a task. Say, in our example, **jcooper** and **jstein** both request leave. In this case, they are both initiators and can each withdraw the task they requested (but not each other's).

On the other hand, the task owner may be the holiday administrator. They are responsible for administering **all** leave requests. This enables them to perform operations on behalf of any of the assigned task participants; additionally they can also reassign or escalate tasks.

The task owner can either be specified as part of the task definition, or on the **Advanced** tab of the BPEL **Human Task Configuration** window.

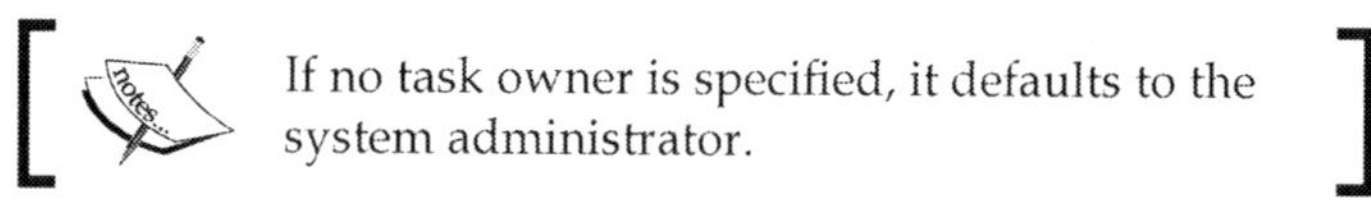

If no task owner is specified, it defaults to the system administrator.

When the task owner logs into the worklist application they will see an additional tab, **Administration Tasks**, which will list all the tasks for which they are the task owner.

Requesting additional information about a task

Once assigned a task, sometimes you need additional information about it, before you can complete it. In our example, the manager may need more information about the reason for the leave request.

If a task initiator has been specified, then on the **Task details** form we have the option of selecting **Request Information**. If we select this option we are presented with the **Request More Information** form, where we can select who we want more information from, and enter details of the information required (which will be added as a comment to the task).

This will then assign the task to the initiator. The task will then appear on the task creators work queue, with a state of **Info Requested**. The task creator can either update the details of the task (if allowed) or add their own comment to provide the additional information. Once done, they can choose the action **Submit Information**, and the task will be reassigned back to whoever requested the additional information.

This feature is automatically enabled when the task is opened. You can disable this feature if you want by overriding the default access settings for **Actions** in the **Access** tab of the task configuration form.

We can request additional information, not just from the person who created the task, but anyone else who has already worked on the task or anyone else that we need further information from.

Managing the assignment of tasks

There is often a requirement to reassign tasks; maybe the task approver is about to go on leave themselves. Before they go, they may want to reassign all uncompleted tasks so they can be dealt with by someone else while they are away.

Alternatively, the individual may have already gone on leave (or be indisposed for some other reason) with a series of tasks already on their queue, which their manager may need to reassign to someone else.

Depending on a user's privileges and whether they are a manager, the worklist application provides a number of methods for either reassigning, delegating, or escalating tasks. We will examine these in detail below.

Reassigning reportee tasks

If a user has any direct reports, then the worklist application will treat them as a manager. This will give them additional privileges to work on tasks that are either assigned to any of their direct reports or groups that they own.

Within the work list application, managers have the additional tab, **My Staff Tasks**. If they select this, it will list all tasks currently assigned to any of their reports.

The list can be further filtered by selecting **Advanced Search** and specifying an appropriate query. For example, you could just show tasks assigned to a particular user or high priority tasks about to expire.

The manager has two basic options when it comes to staff tasks, they can either work on the task directly themselves, where they can carry out the same sets of actions as the assignee. Alternatively, they can choose to reassign the task to another of their direct reports or to any of the groups that they own.

To see how we do this, log in as **wfaulk** (**jstein**'s manager), and click on **My Staff Tasks**. Select the task(s) you want to reassign; then from the **Actions** drop-down list, select **Reassign**. This will open the **Reassign Task** window, as shown in the following screenshot:

Here we have the option to either **Reassign** or **Delegate** the task. Stick with the **Reassign** option for the time being, as we will look at delegation shortly.

The remainder of the screen allows us to search for the users and or groups that we want to reassign the task to. You can choose to search just **Users** or **Groups**. In addition, you can further filter the list on the ID of the user or group, as well as the first name or last name of the user.

When specifying the search criteria, you can use a * to match any character. For example, the pattern **st*** will bring back the list of users whose user ID, first, or last name begin with **st**.

You will also notice that if you select a user, the **Details** panel will display basic information about the user, including their **Manager**, **Reportees**, and any **Roles** they have.

Use the arrows to move users/groups that you wish to reassign the task to from the search results box to the **Selected** box, and then click **OK**.

Reassigning your own task

In addition to reassigning staff tasks, **any user** can reassign their own tasks. To do this, they simply open the task from their task list as normal and select the **Reassign** option from the **Action** drop-down list. This will bring up the **Reassign Task** form that we just looked at.

An important point here is that the same restrictions on who a user can assign a task to apply regardless of whether it's the user's own task or a task belonging to one of their reportees.

Thus, users who have no direct reports will not be able to reassign their task to any other user. However, if they are a group owner, they will still have the ability to reassign the task to the group.

If a user has the role "BPMWorkflowReassign", then they are allowed to reassign a task to anyone.

Delegating tasks

The other option we have when reassigning a task is to delegate it. This is very similar to reassigning a task, but with a number of key differences as follows:

- You can only delegate a task to a single user
- You cannot delegate a task to a group
- You can delegate a task to anyone regardless of where they are in the organizational hierarchy

When you delegate a task it is assigned to a new user, but it also remains on your work queue so that either you or the delegated user can work on the task.

Escalating tasks

There will often be cases where a user needs to escalate the task. To do this, they simply select the task from their task list as normal and choose **Escalate** from the **Action** drop-down list. This will reassign the task to the user's manager.

Tasks can also be automatically escalated, usually if not handled within a specified period of time. This is specified in **Expiration and Escalation Policy**, which forms part of the task definition.

Using rules to automatically manage tasks

Even though it's possible to manually reassign tasks, this can be inefficient and time-consuming. An alternative approach is to automate this using workflow rules.

You can either define a rule to be applied to a particular task type (for example our leave request) or to all tasks. In addition, you can also specify when a rule is active, which can be during vacation periods, for a specified time period, or active all the time (which is the default).

You can specify various filter criteria that are applied to the task attributes (for example, priority, initiator, acquired by) to further restrict which tasks the rule applies to.

Once you've specified the matching criteria for a rule, you can then specify whether you want to reassign or delegate the task. Essentially, the same criteria applies to whomever you are allowed to reassign a task to (if you were to do it manually, as covered in the previous section, with the added caveat that you can only reassign a task to a single user or group).

For rules defined for a particular task type, we have the option of being able to automatically set the task outcome. In the case of our leave request task, we can write a rule to automatically approve all leave requests that are one day in duration.

The final option is to take no action, which may seem a bit strange. However, this serves a couple of useful purposes. Often you only want a rule to be active at certain periods of time. One way to do this is to just specify a date range. An alternative is to use this to turn the rule on and off, as required over time.

The other use comes in when you define multiple rules. Rules are evaluated in order against a task until a rule is found that matches a particular task.

For example, to create a rule that reassigned all tasks, except say an expense approval task, you would do the following. Define two rules, a generic rule to reassign any task and a specific rule that matched the expense approval task that did nothing. We would then order the rules so that the expense approval rule triggered first. This way, the generic rule to reassign a task would be triggered for all tasks except the expense approval task.

Setting up a sample rule

For example, let's say Robert Stevenson (user ID **rsteven**) is John Steinbeck's deputy, and we want to create a rule that reassigns all leave requests assigned to **jstein** to **rsteven** except for any leave request made by **rsteven**.

To do this, you log onto the worklist application as **jstein**, and click on the **Preferences** link on the top-right-hand corner of the worklist title bar. This will bring you into the **My Rules** tab, where a user can configure various rules for managing the assignment of tasks. By default it displays the users currently defined **Vacation Period** (which in this case is disabled).

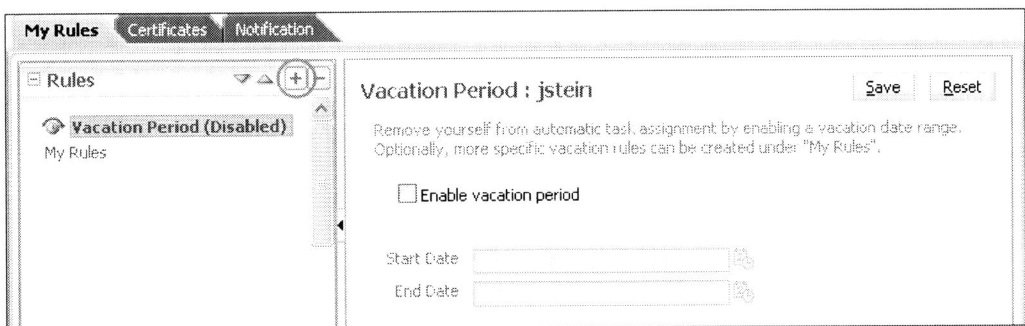

Select the **My Rules** folder (below **Vacation Period (Disabled)**), and click on the plus icon (circled in the preceding screenshot). This will display the template for defining a new rule.

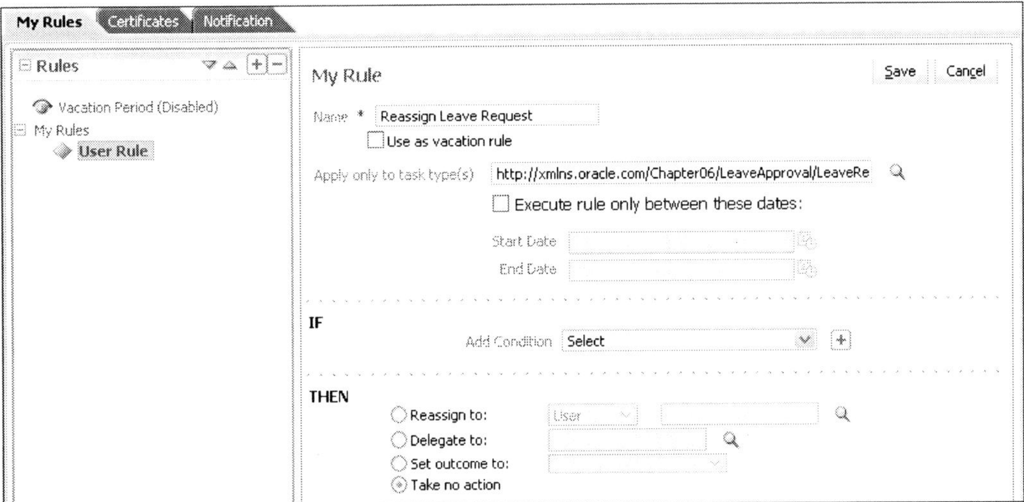

Enter a suitable name for the rule, but leave the checkbox **Use as vacation rule** unchecked. If we were to check this, then the rule would only be active during the user's vacation period.

Next we want to specify which tasks the rule should apply to. Click on the search icon to the right and this will pop up the **Task Type Browser**, where we can search for the required task type. Select the **LeaveRequest** task for the process **default/LeaveApproval/1.0**.

We will not specify a time period for the rule, as we want it to be active all the time. We now need to specify the conditions that apply to the rule and the appropriate action to take. First let's add the condition to prevent the rule reassigning leave requests made by **rsteven**.

From the **Add Condition** drop-down list, select the task attribute to which we want to apply the rule, which is, in our case, the **Creator** (that is, the task initiator), and then click the plus icon (circled in the following screenshot):

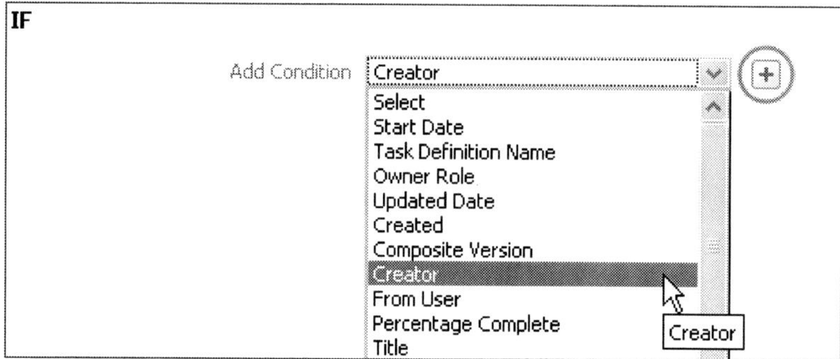

This will insert a condition line for testing the **Creator** attribute into our rule, as shown in the following screenshot:

In the drop-down list, select the test to be applied to the attribute. So in our case, we select **isn't** and finally specify the user (**rsteven**). You can either directly enter the user ID or click the magnifying glass icon to search for the user with the user search facility we introduced earlier.

Finally, specify the task action, which is to reassign the task to **rsteven**. Your rule description should now look like the one shown in the following screenshot:

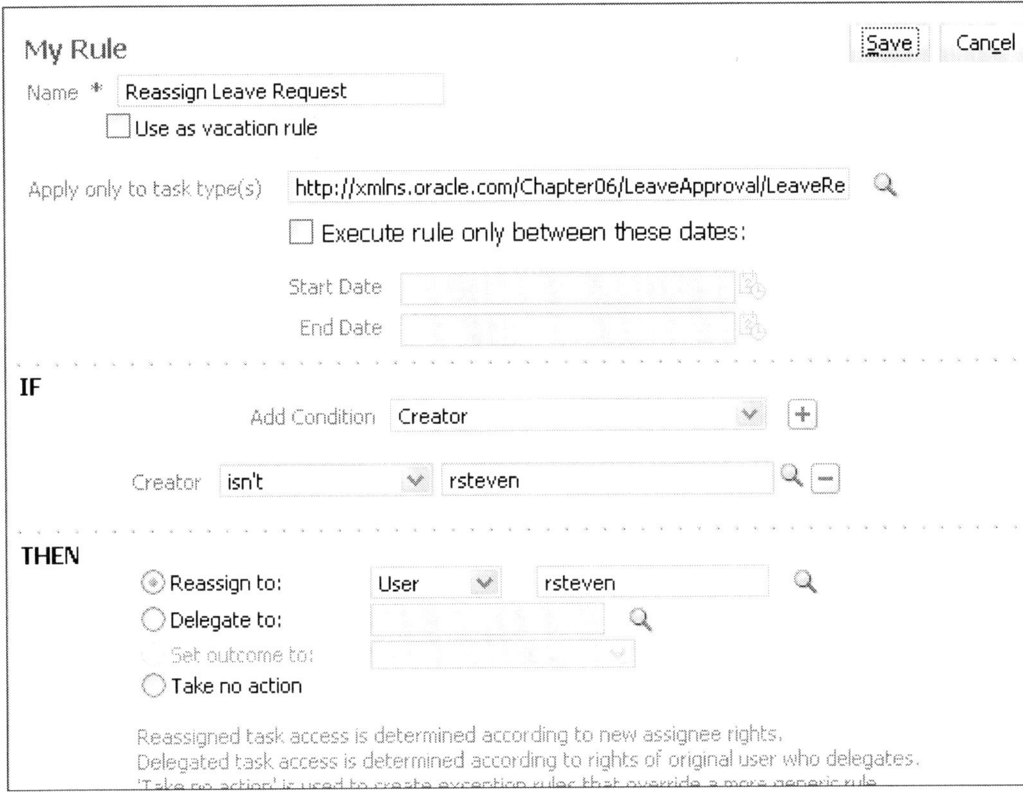

Finally, click on **Save** to create the rule. Once you have created the rule, try creating two leave requests, one for **jcooper** and another for **rsteven**. You should see that only the request created for **jcooper** is reassigned to **rsteven**.

Log in as **rsteven**, and select the leave request that has been reassigned to that user. If you examine the full task history, you will see that it shows which rule was triggered to cause the task to be reassigned.

> A user can also specify rule conditions against the content of the task payload through the use of flex fields, as well as define rules for any groups that they own. We will examine flex fields in *Chapter 17, Workflow Patterns*.

Summary

Human workflow is a key requirement for many projects. In this chapter, we saw how easy it is to insert a human task into a BPEL process, as well as implement the corresponding user interface to process the task.

We also looked at how business users can use the BPM worklist application to process their tasks as well as manage routing them, including reassigning, delegating, and escalating tasks. We also looked at how business users could automate most of the task management by defining business rules to automatically delegate, reassign, or complete a task.

7
Using Business Rules to Define Decision Points

At runtime, there may be many potential paths through a BPEL process, controlled by conditional statements such as `switch` or `while` activities. Typically, the business rules that govern which path to take at any given point are written as XPath expressions embedded within the appropriate activity.

Although this is an acceptable approach, we often find that while the process itself may be relatively static, the business rules embedded within the activities may change on a more frequent basis. This will require us to update the BPEL process and redeploy it, even though the process flow itself hasn't changed.

In addition, by embedding the rule directly within the decision point, we often end up having to reimplement the same rule every time it is used, either within the same process or across multiple processes. Apart from being inefficient, this can lead to inconsistent implementations of the rules, as well as requiring us to update the rules in multiple places every time it changes.

The **Oracle Business Rules** engine that comes as part of the SOA Suite provides a declarative mechanism for defining business rules externally to our application. This not only ensures that each rule is used in a consistent fashion, but in addition, it makes it simpler and quicker to modify. We only have to modify a rule once and can do this with almost immediate effect, thus increasing the agility of our solution.

For those of you familiar with 10gR3, you will notice that JDeveloper comes with a new rules editor which is a lot more intuitive and simpler to use than the old browser-based editor. In addition, 11gR1 introduces **decision tables**, which provide a spreadsheet-like format for defining rules. While still very much a developer-oriented tool, these improvements make the tool a lot friendlier for business analysts, allowing them to better understand the rules that have been written as well as make simple changes.

In this chapter, we will introduce the new rules editor and look at how we can use it to define a decisions service to automate the approval of leave requests. Then, once we've done this, we'll see how to invoke the rule from the leave approval BPEL process. We will first implement these as a standard set of rules and then examine how we can simplify these rules by using a decision table.

Business rule concepts

Before we implement our first rule, let's briefly introduce the key components which make up a business rule. These are:

- **Facts**: Represent the data or business objects that rules are applied to.
- **Rules**: A rule consists of two parts, namely, an `IF` part that consists of one or more tests to be applied to a fact(s), and a `THEN` part that lists the actions to be carried out, should the test evaluate to true.
- **Rule Set**: As the name implies, it is just a set of one or more related rules that are designed to work together.
- **Dictionary**: A dictionary is the container of all components that make up a business rule. It holds all the Facts, Rule Sets, and Rules for a business rule.

In addition, a dictionary may also contain decision tables, functions, variables, and constraints. We will introduce these in more detail later in this chapter.

To execute a business rule, you assert (submit) one or more facts to the rules engine. It will apply the rules to the facts, that is, each fact will be tested against the `IF` part of the rule, and if it evaluates to `true`, then it will perform the specified actions for that fact. This may result in the creation of new facts or the modification of existing facts (which may result in further rule evaluation).

XML facts

The rule engine supports four types of facts: **Java Facts**, **XML Facts**, **RL Facts**, and **ADF Facts**. The type of fact that you want to use typically depends on the context in which you will be using the rules engine.

For example, if you are calling the rule engine from Java, then you would work with Java Facts as this provides a more integrated way of combining the two components. As we are using the rule engine within a composite, it makes sense to use XML facts.

The rule editor uses XML schemas to generate JAXB 2.0 classes, which are then imported to implement the corresponding XML facts. Using JAXB, particularly when used in conjunction with BPEL, places a number of constraints on how we define our XML schemas, including:

- Within BPEL, you can only define variables based on globally defined **elements**. Thus all input and output facts passed to the decision service must be defined as global elements within our XML schemas.
- When defining the input and output facts for any `complexType` (for example, `tLeaveRequest`), there can only be one global element of that type (for example, `leaveRequest`).
- The element naming convention for JAXB means that elements or types with underscores in their names can cause compilation errors.

Decision services

To invoke a business rule within a composite, we need to go through a number of steps. First, we must create a session with the rules engine, then we can assert one or more facts, before executing the ruleset and finally we can retrieve the results.

We do this via a decision service (or function). This is essentially a web-service wrapper around a rules dictionary, which takes care of managing the session with the rules engine as well as governing which ruleset we wish to apply.

The wrapper allows a composite to assert one or more facts, execute a ruleset(s) against the asserted facts, retrieve the results, and then reset the session. This can be done within a single invocation of an operation or over multiple operations.

Leave approval business rule

For our first rule, we are going to build on our leave request example from the previous chapter, *Adding in Human Workflow*. If you remember, we implemented a simple process requiring every leave request to go to an individual's manager for approval. However, what we would like is a rule that automatically approves a request as long as it meets certain company guidelines.

To begin with, we will write a simple rule to automatically approve a leave request that is of the type `Vacation` and only for one day's duration. This is a pretty trivial example, but once we've done this, we will look at how to extend this rule to handle more complex examples.

Creating a decision service

Within JDeveloper, open up your **LeaveApproval** application from the previous chapter (or alternately open the sample provided with the book). Open up the **composite.xml** file for the application and then from the **Component Palette**, drag-and-drop a **Business Rule** onto the composite, as shown in the following screenshot:

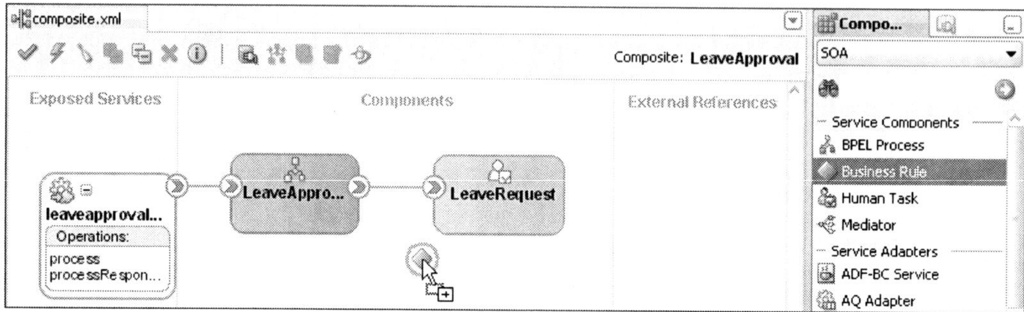

This will launch the **Create Business Rules** dialog, as shown in the following screenshot:

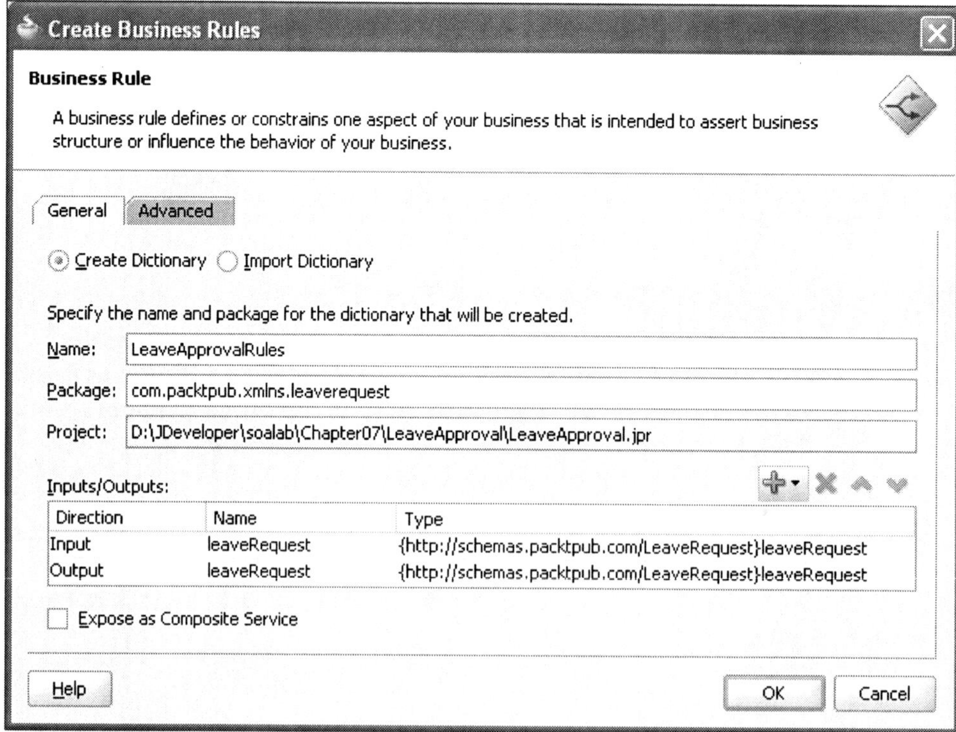

The first step is to give our dictionary a name, such as **LeaveApprovalRules,** and a corresponding **Package** name.

In addition, we need to specify the **Input** and **Output** facts that we will pass to our decision service. For our purpose, we will pass in a single leave request. The rule engine will then apply the rules that we define and update the status of the leave request to either **Approved** or **Manual** (to indicate the request needs to be manually approved).

So we need to define a single input fact and output fact, both of type **leaveRequest**. To do this, click on the **plus** symbol (marked in the preceding screenshot), and select **Input**.

This will bring up the standard **Type Chooser** window; browse the **LeaveRequest. xsd** and select **leaveRequest**. Do the same again to specify an **Output** fact.

When creating facts based on an XML schema, the rules editor will generate corresponding JAXB Java classes and place them in the specified **Package**. It is a good practice to specify a different package name for every XML schema to prevent conflicting class definitions.

Next, click the **Advanced** tab. Here we can see that JDeveloper has given the default name **LeaveApprovalRules_DecisionService_1** to our decision service. Give it a more meaningful name such as **LeaveApprovalDecisonService**.

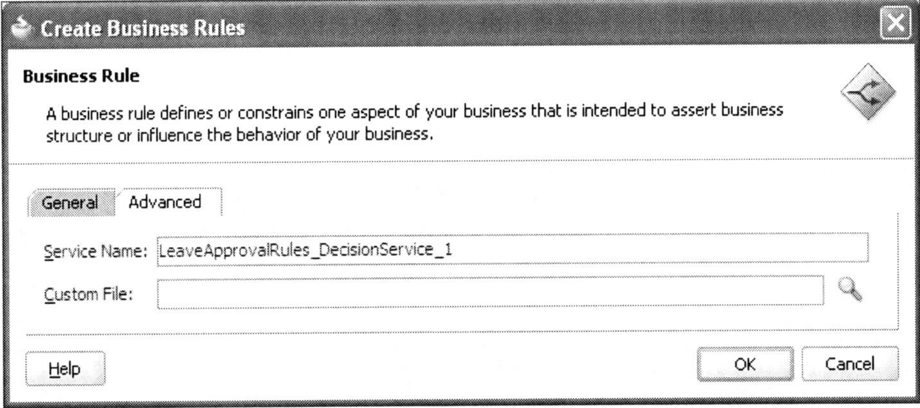

Now click **OK**. JDeveloper will inform you that it is creating the business rule dictionary for **LeaveApprovalRules**. Once completed, your composite should now look as shown in the following screenshot:

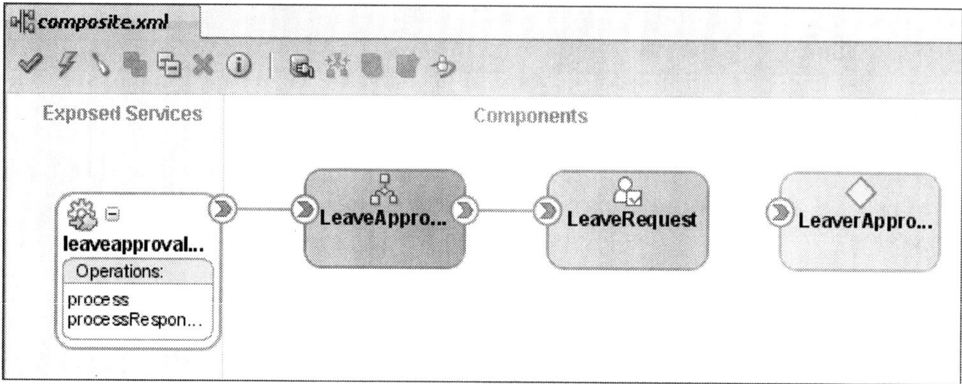

We are now ready to implement our business rules. Double-click on the **LeaveApprovalRules** component, and this will launch the rules editor, which is shown in the next screenshot.

Implementing our business rules

The rules editor allows you to view/edit the various components which make up your business rules. To select a particular component, such as **Facts**, **Functions**, **Globals**, and so on, just click on the corresponding tab down the left-hand side.

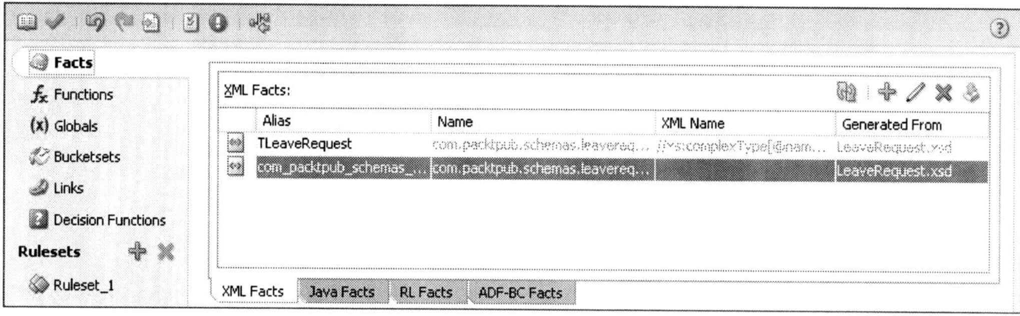

You will see that, by default, JDeveloper has created a skeleton rules dictionary-based on the inputs we just specified.

Select the **Facts** tab (as shown in the preceding screenshot). You will see that it contains two XML facts (**TLeaveRequest** and **com.packtpub.schemas.leaverequest.ObjectFactory**), which are based on the inputs/outputs we defined earlier as well as a set of standard Java facts, which are automatically included within a rules dictionary.

Next, select the **Decision Functions** tab. You will see that it contains a single decision function **LeaveApprovalDecisonService** (that is, the name we specified on the **Advanced** tab when creating our business rule).

We will introduce some of the other tabs later in this chapter, but for the time being, we will start by defining our first rule. By default, the rules editor will have created a single ruleset with the name **Ruleset_1**. Click on the **Ruleset_1** tab to open up the ruleset within the editor.

Expand the ruleset to show its details by clicking on the plus symbol (circled in the following screenshot). We can see that the ruleset has three properties: **Name**, **Description**, and **Effective Date**.

The **Effective Date** enables us to specify a period in time for which the ruleset will be applied, allowing you to define multiple versions of the same ruleset. For example, a current ruleset and a future version that we wish to come into effect at a defined time in the future.

Rename the ruleset to something more meaningful, for example, **Employee Leave Approval Policy**; add a description if you want and ensure that **Effective Date** is set to **Always Valid**.

Adding a rule to our ruleset

To add a rule, click the green plus symbol on the top-right-hand corner, and select **Create Rule**, as shown in the following screenshot (alternatively click on the **Create Rule** button, circled in the following screenshot).

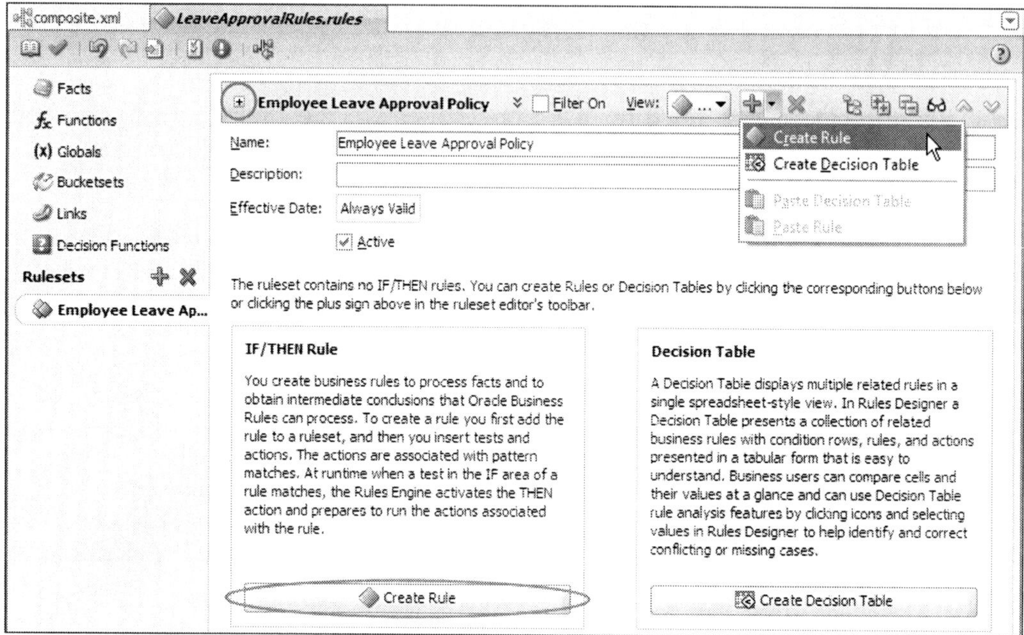

This will add a rule to our ruleset with the default name **Rule_1**, as shown in the following screenshot. Here, we can see that a rule consists of two parts, an **IF** part, which consists of one or more tests to be applied to a fact or facts, and a **THEN** part, which specifies the actions to be carried out, should the test evaluate to true.

To give the rule a more meaningful name, simply click on the name and enter a new name (for example, **One Day Vacation**). By clicking on the **<enter description>** element, you can also add a description for the rule.

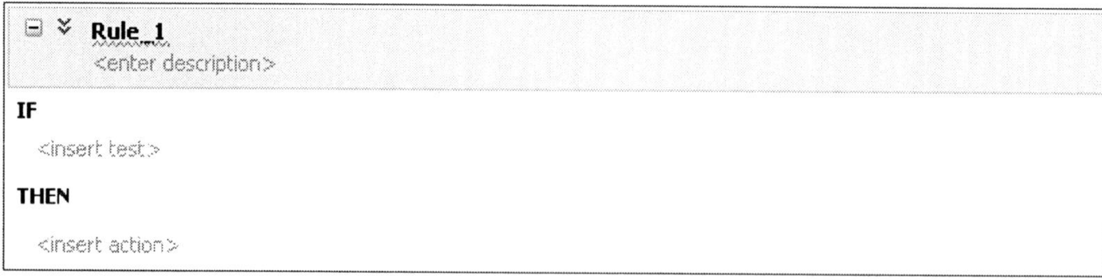

Creating the IF clause

For our leave approval rule, we need to define **two** tests, one to check that the request is only for a day in duration, which we can do by checking that the start date equals the end date, and the second to check that the request is of type **Vacation**.

To define the first test, click on **<insert test>**. This will add the line **<operand> = = <operand>** under the **IF** statement where we can define the test condition.

One Day Vacation
Approve leave request if its for a one day vacation.
IF
<operand> == <operand>
<insert test>
THEN
<insert action>

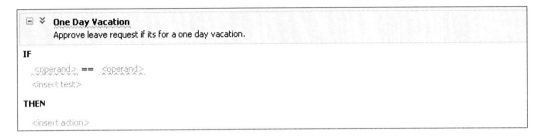

Click on the first **<operand>**. This will display a drop-down list listing the valid facts and their attributes that we can test. From here, we can select the value to be tested, for example, **TLeaveRequest.startDate** in our case.

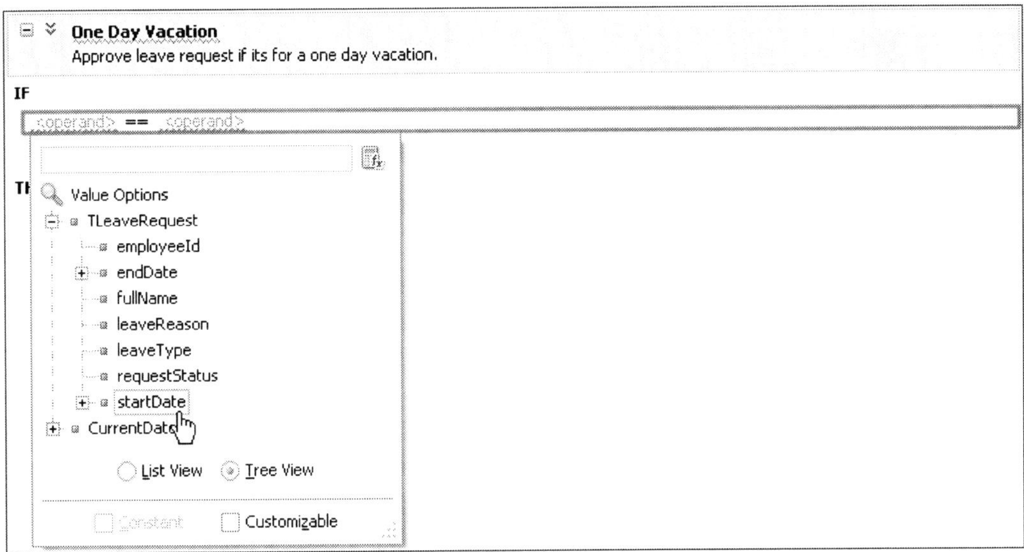

Next from the **operator** drop-down list, select the test to be applied to the first operand (== in our case). We can either choose to compare it to a specified value or a second **Operand**. For our purpose, we want to check that the **request.startDate** equals the **request.endDate**, so click on the operand and select this from the drop-down list.

To create our second test, we follow pretty much the same process. This time we want to test that the operand **leaveRequest.leaveType** is equal to the value **Vacation**, so select the right-hand operator and type this in directly:

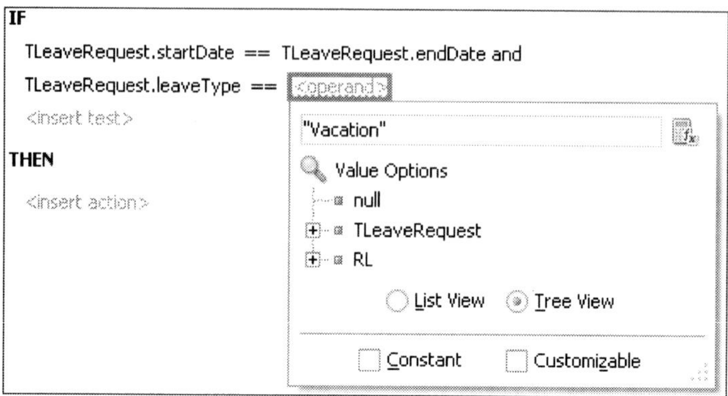

Note, the rule editor has automatically inserted an **and** clause between our two tests. If you click on this, you have the option of changing this to an **or** clause.

Creating the Then clause

Now that we have defined our test, we need to define the action to take if the test evaluates to true. Click on **<insert action>**. This will display a drop-down list where you need to specify the **Action Type** you wish to carry out.

The rule editor allows us to choose from the following action types:

- **assert new**: We use this to create and assert a new fact, for example, a new **LeaveRequest**. Once asserted, the new fact will be evaluated by the rules engine against the ruleset.
- **modify**: We can use this to either assign a value to a variable or a fact attribute; in our case we want to assign a status of **Approved** to the **requestStatus** property.
- **retract**: This enables you to retract any of the facts matched in the pattern (for example, **TLeaveRequest**) so that it will no longer be evaluated as part of the ruleset.
- **call**: This allows you to call a function to perform one or more actions.

The actions **assert new** and **retract** are important when we are dealing with rulesets that deal with multiple interdependent facts, as this allows us to control which facts are being evaluated by the rule engine at any particular time. Here, we are only dealing with a single fact, so we don't examine these constructs in this chapter, leaving them to *Chapter 18, Using Business Rules to Implement Services*.

For our purposes, we want to update the status of our leave, so select **modify**. Our rule should now look as shown in the following screenshot:

One Day Vacation
Approve leave request if its for a one day vacation.

IF
TLeaveRequest.startDate == TLeaveRequest.endDate and
TLeaveRequest.leaveType == "Vacation"
<insert test>

THEN
modify <target>
<insert action>

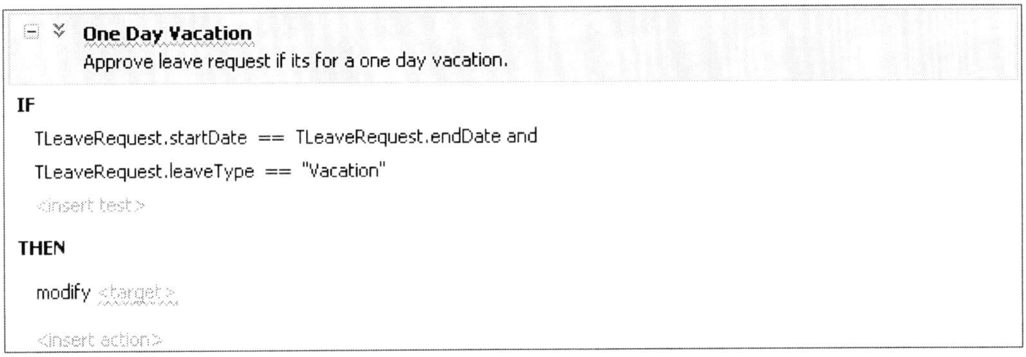

The next step is to specify the fact to be modified. Click on the **<target>** element and you will be presented with a list of facts that are within scope. In our case, this will only be the **TLeaveRequest** that has just been matched by the `IF` clause, so select this. Our rule will now appear, as shown in the following screenshot:

THEN
modify TLeaveRequest (<add property>)
<insert action>

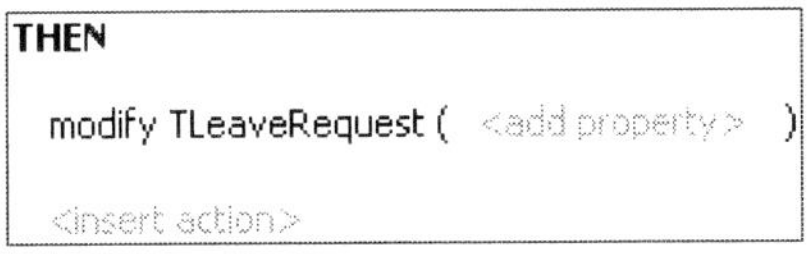

We now need to specify the properties we wish to modify, click on **<add property>** to open the **Properties** dialog. This will display a list of all the facts properties, allowing us to modify them as appropriate.

Select the **Value** cell for **requestStatus**. From here, you can directly enter a value, select a value from the drop-down list, or launch the expression builder. For our purposes, just enter the string **Approved**, as shown in the following screenshot, and then click **Close**.

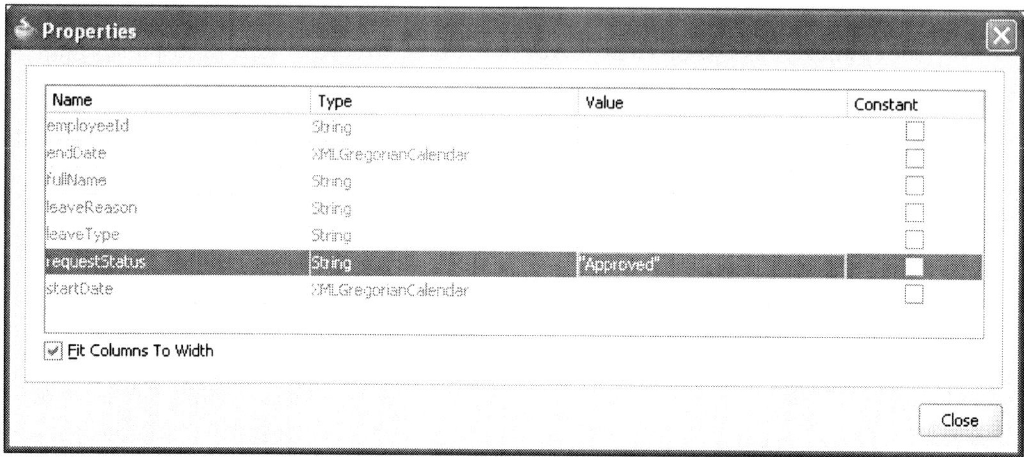

We don't need to specify values for any of the other properties, as the rules engine will only update those properties where a new value has been specified.

This completes the definition of our first rule. The next step is to wire it into our BPEL process.

```
One Day Vacation
Approve leave request if its for a one day vacation.
IF
  TLeaveRequest.startDate == TLeaveRequest.endDate and
  TLeaveRequest.leaveType == "Vacation"
  <insert test>
THEN
  modify TLeaveRequest ( <add property> requestStatus : "Approved" )
  <insert action>
```

Calling a business rule from BPEL

Save the rule, and then switch back to our composite and double-click the **LeaveRequest** BPEL process to edit it. Drag a **Business Rule** from the **BPEL Activities and Components** palette into your BPEL process (before the Human Task activity). This will open the **Business Rule** dialog (as shown in the following screenshot):

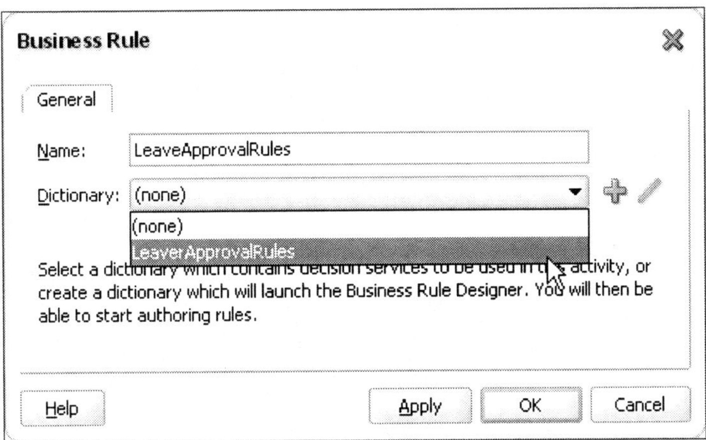

First, we need to specify a name for the Business Rule activity within our BPEL process, so give it a meaningful name such as **LeaveApprovalRules**.

Next we need to specify the Business Rule **Dictionary** that we wish to use. If we click on the drop-down list, it will list all the dictionaries within our composite application, which in our case is **LeaveApprovalRules** that we have just defined.

Select this and the rule dialog will be updated (as shown in the following screenshot) to enable us to specify additional information about how we want to invoke the rule. First, we need to select the decision service that we want to invoke from BPEL. Our rule only contains a single decision service, **LeaveApprovalDecisionService**, so select it.

Once we've specified the service, we need to specify how we want to invoke the decision service. We specify this through the **Operation** attribute. Here we have two options:

- Execute function and reset the session
- Execute function

If we choose the option **Execute function** and thus don't reset the session, if we were then to call the decision service several times within the same instance of our BPEL process, each new invocation would reuse the same session and would also evaluate facts asserted in any previous invocation. For our purposes, we just need to assert a single fact and run the ruleset, so accept the default value of **Execute function and reset the session** (we will look at other modes of operation in more detail in *Chapter 18, Using Business Rules to Implement Services*).

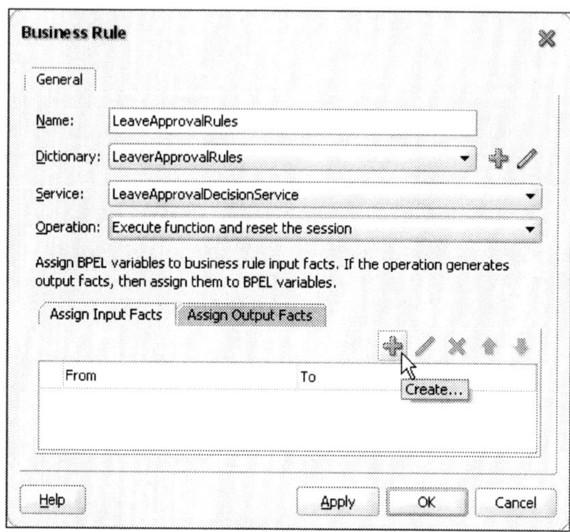

Assigning facts

The final step to invoke our business rules is to assign BPEL variables to the input and output facts. Click on the green plus symbol (as shown in the preceding screenshot), and this will launch the **Decision Fact Map** window, as shown in the following screenshot:

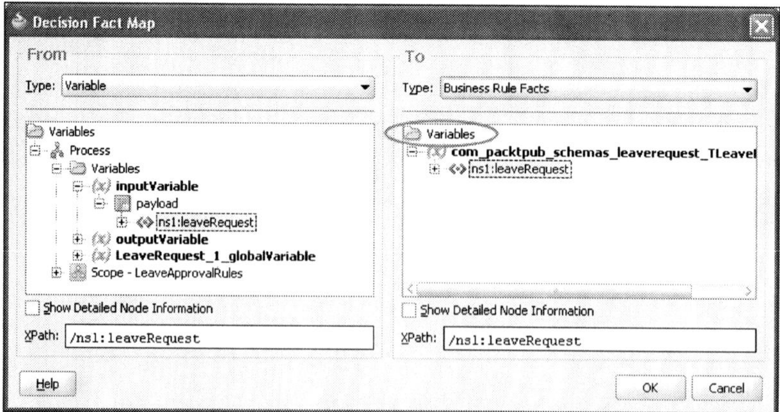

At first glance, this looks like the standard **Create Copy Operation** window that we use when carrying out assigns within BPEL (which in reality is exactly what it is).

The key difference is that we are using this to assign values to the input facts to be submitted to the rules engines, so the **Type** on the **To** side of the copy operation is a **Business Rule Facts**.

The reverse is true for an output fact, where we use this dialog to map the output from the decision service back into a corresponding BPEL variable.

For our purpose, we just want to map the initial `LeaveRequest` in the process `inputVariable` into the corresponding fact, as shown in the preceding screenshot. Then we will map the output fact, which will contain our updated `LeaveRequest` back into our `inputVariable`.

When JDeveloper opens the **Decision Fact Map** window, the **Variables** folder for the **Business Rules Facts** (circled in the preceding screenshot) is closed and it appears that there are no input facts. You must double-click on this to open it and expose the facts.

We have now wired the rule invocation into our BPEL process, before finally running our process; we need to modify our process to only invoke the workflow if the leave request hasn't been automatically approved.

To do this, just drag a switch onto your process, and then drag your workflow task into the first branch in the switch and define a test to check that the `LeaveRequest` hasn't been approved. You are now ready to deploy and run your modified process.

Using functions

Our current rule only approves vacations of one day in duration, requiring all other leave requests to be manually approved. Ideally, we would like to approve holidays of varying duration as long as sufficient notice has been given, for example:

- Approve vacations of one day in duration with a start date that's two weeks or more in the future
- Approve if for 2-3 days and more than 30 days in the future
- Approve if 5 days or less and more than 60 days in the future
- Approve if 10 days or less and more than 120 days in the future

To write these rules, we will need to calculate the duration of the leave period, as well as calculate how long it is before the start date. Out of the box, the rule engine provides the **Duration** extension methods, which allow us to calculate the number of days between two dates, but doesn't allow us to exclude weekends.

So we will need to write our own logic to calculate these values. Rather than embedding this logic directly in each rule, best practice dictates that we place this logic into a separate function. This not only ensures that we have a single version of the logic to implement but minimizes the size of our rules, thus making them simpler and easier to maintain. For our purposes, we will create the following functions:

- **startsIn**: Which returns the number of days before the specified start date
- **leaveDuration**: Which returns the number of days from the start date to the end date, excluding weekends

Creating a function

To create our first function, within the rule editor, click on the **Functions** tab. This will list all the functions currently defined to our ruleset. To create a new function, click on the green plus icon, as shown in the following screenshot:

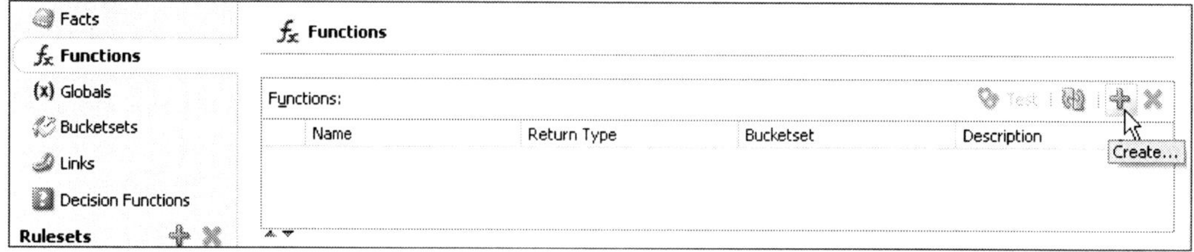

This will add a new function with a default name (for example, **Function_1**) to our list. Click on the function name to select it and update it to **startsIn**. From the drop-down list, select the **Return Type** of the function, which is **int** in our case.

Next, we need to specify the arguments we wish to pass to our function. Click on the green plus sign, as shown in the following screenshot, and this will add an argument to our list. Here we can specify the argument name (for example, **startDate**), and from the drop-down list, the argument **Type**, which should be **XMLGregorianCalendar** (when creating XML facts, the JAXB processor maps the type `xsd:date` to `javax.xml.datatype.XMLGregorianCalendar`).

The list of valid types is made up of the basic types (for example, `int`, `double`, `char`, and so on), plus the XML facts (excluding object factories) and the Java Facts (excluding the Rules Extension Method) defined in our rules dictionary.

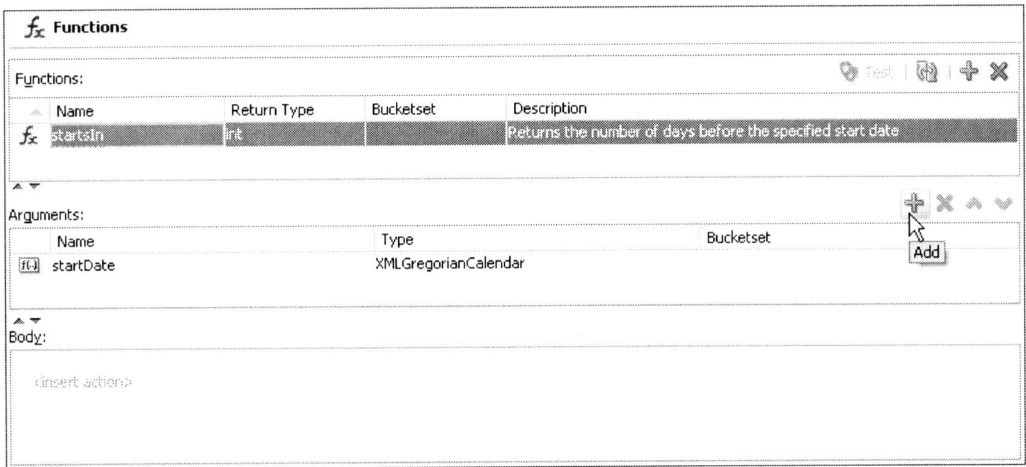

The final step is to implement the business logic of our function, which consists of one or more actions. We enter these actions in the **Body** section of the function. The first action we need to create is one that creates a local variable of type calendar, which holds the current date.

To do this, click on **<insert action>** within the **Body** section of our function. The rule editor will display a drop-down list that lists all the available actions.

For our purpose, we want to create a new variable and assign a value to it, so select the **assign new** action, as shown in the preceding screenshot. This will insert a *template* for the **assign new** action into our function body (as shown in the following screenshot). We then configure the action by clicking on each part within the template and defining it as appropriate.

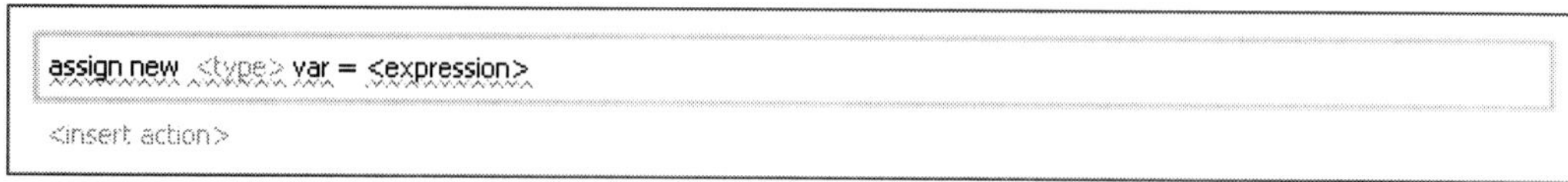

The first part we need to define is the type of variable we wish to create. Click on the **<type>** element within our `<assign>` statement, and the rule editor displays a drop-down list displaying all the available types. For our purposes, select **Calendar**.

Next, click on **var**. This will prompt us to enter the name of the variable that we want to create. Specify **today**, and hit *enter*.

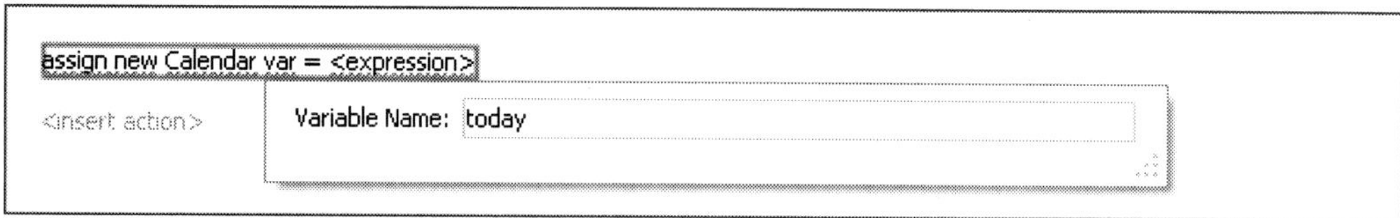

Finally, we need to specify the value we want to initialize our variable with. Click on the **<expression>** element. The rule editor will display a drop-down box listing all the valid values we can assign to our variable, as shown in the following screenshot:

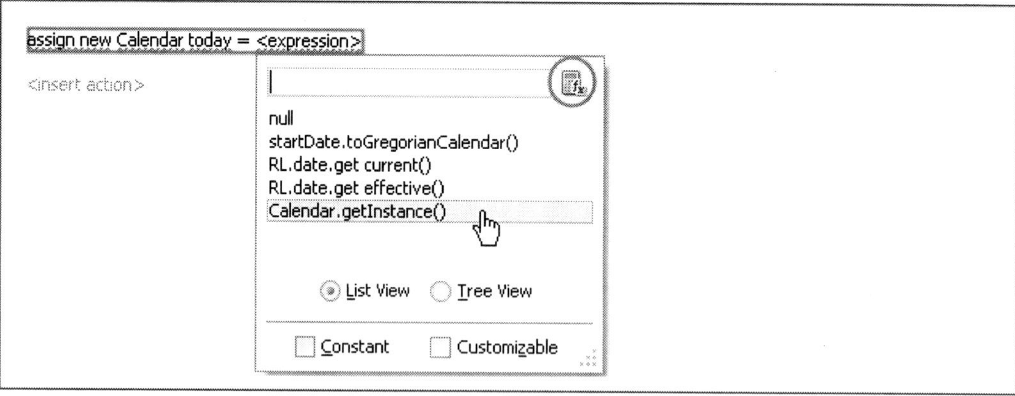

Select **Calendar.getInstance()**, which will initialize our variable to hold the current date.

For our second action, we want to calculate the number of days before the specified start date and place the result into the variable **duration**. To calculate this, we will make use of the **Duration** extension method provided with the rules engine.

We will do this by defining another **assign new** action in a similar way to the previous action. The key difference is how we specify the **<expression>**. This time, instead of selecting a value from the drop-down list, click on the **Expression Builder** icon (circled in the preceding screenshot) to launch the **Expression Builder** for the rules editor.

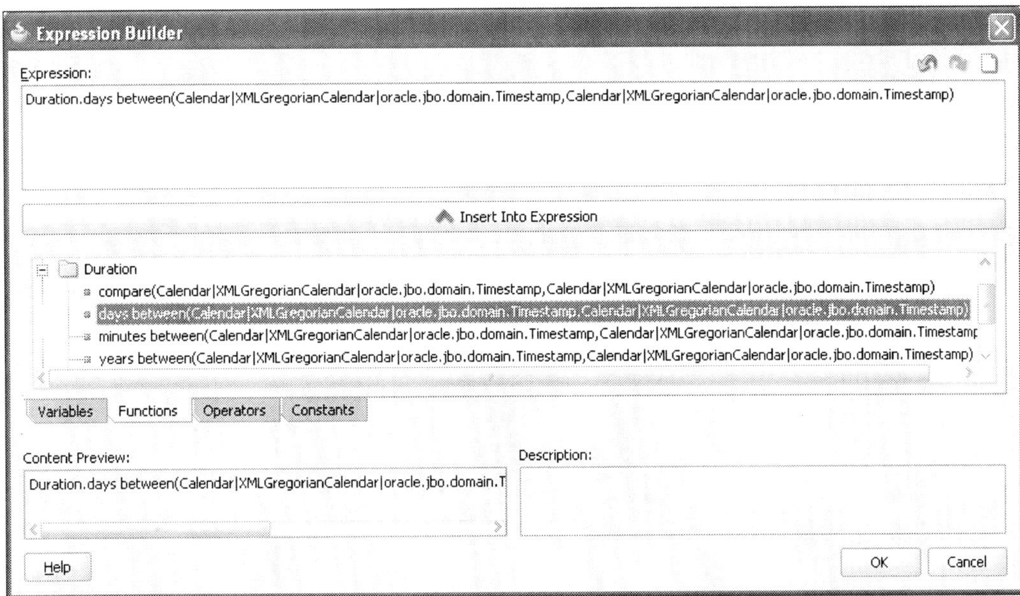

The **Expression Builder** provides a graphical tool for writing rule expressions and is accessed from various parts of the rule editor. It consists of the following areas:

- **Expression**: The top textbox contains the rule expression that you are working on. You can either type data directly in here or use the **Expression Builder** to insert code fragments to build up the expression required.
- **Variables, Functions, Operators, Constants**: This part of the **Expression Builder** lets you browse the various components that you can insert into your expression. Once you've located the component that you wish to use, click the **Insert Into Expression** button, and this will insert the appropriate code fragment into the expression.

The code fragment is inserted at the point within the expression that the cursor is currently positioned.

- **Content Preview**: This box displays a preview of the content that would be inserted into the expression if you clicked the **Insert Into Expression** button.

So let's use this to build our rules expression. The expression we want to build is a relatively simple one, namely:

```
Duration.days between(today,startDate) + 1
```

To build our expression, carry out the following steps. First, within the **Functions** tab, locate the function **Duration.days between** and insert this into the expression (as shown in the previous screenshot).

Next, within the **Variables** tab, locate the variable **today**. Then within the expression, highlight the first argument of the function (as shown in the following screenshot), and click **Insert Into Expression**.

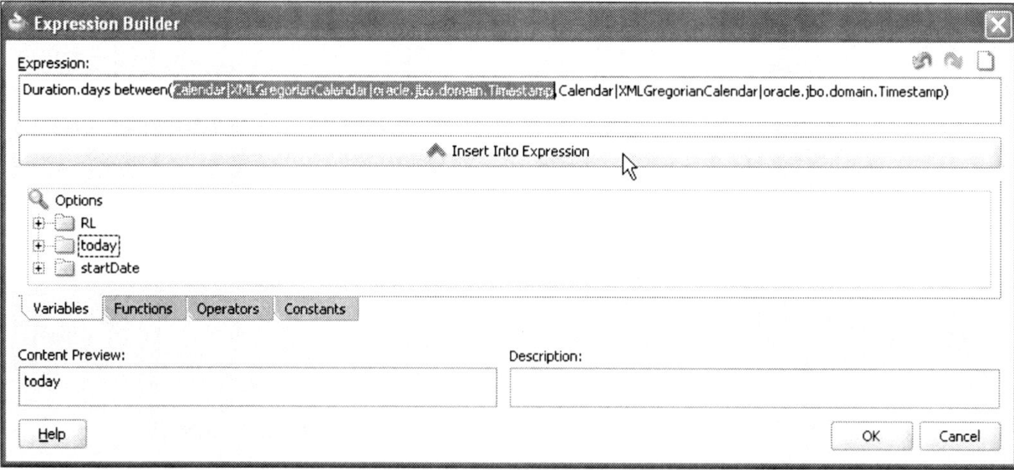

This will update the value of the first argument to contain **today**; repeat this to update the second argument to contain **startDate**. Next, manually enter **+1** to the end of the expression to complete it and click **OK**.

Finally add a third action to return the **duration**. The completed body of our function looks as shown in the following screenshot:

```
assign new Calendar today = Calendar.getInstance()

assign new int duration = Duration.days between(today,startDate) + 1

return duration
```

To implement our `leaveDuration` function, we follow the same approach (for details of this, see the code samples included with the book).

Testing a function

JDeveloper provides a test option that allows us to run a function in JDeveloper without the need to deploy it first. However, it will only allow us to run functions with no input parameters and returns a type of **boolean**.

In order to test our **startsIn** function, we need to write a wrapper function (for example, **testStartsIn**) which creates the required input parameters for our function, invokes it, and then prints out the result. So the body of our test function will look as shown in the following screenshot:

```
assign new XMLGregorianCalendar startDate = XMLDate.from string("2009-08-21")

call print( message : "Starts in: " + startsIn(startDate) + " days" )

return true
```

To run this, with the **Functions** tab, select the **testStartsIn** function, and click the **Test** button, as shown in the following screenshot:

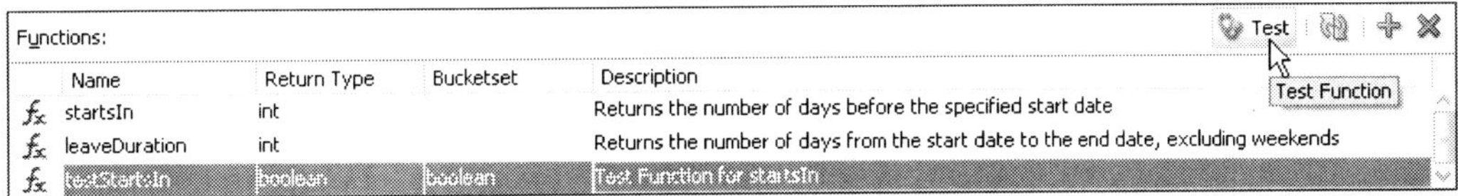

Functions:
Test
Test Function
Name
Return Type
Bucketset
Description
startsIn
int
Returns the number of days before the specified start date
leaveDuration
int
Returns the number of days from the start date to the end date, excluding weekends
testStartsIn
boolean
boolean
Test Function for startsIn

If there are any validation errors within our rules dictionary, then the **Test** button will be disabled.

This will execute the function and open a window displaying the result of the function and any output as shown in the following screenshot:

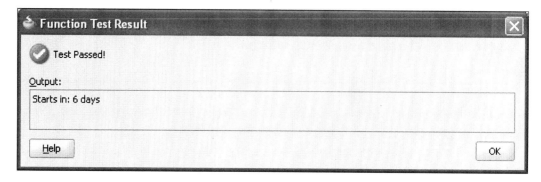

Testing decision service functions

We can also use this approach to test our decision service. The body for this `test` function appears as shown in the following screenshot:

```
call RL.watch.all( )

assign new TLeaveRequest leaveRequest = new TLeaveRequest()

assign leaveRequest.startDate = XMLDate.from string("2010-01-15")

assign leaveRequest.endDate = XMLDate.from string("2010-01-15")

assign leaveRequest.leaveType = "Vacation"

assign new List resultList = LeaveApprovalDecisionService(leaveRequest)

assign leaveRequest = (TLeaveRequest) resultList.get(0)

call print( message : "Status: " + leaveRequest.requestStatus )

return true
```

A couple of interesting points to note about this: the statement **call RL.watch.all()** will cause the function to output details about how the facts are being processed and which rules are being activated. This is something we cover in more detail in *Chapter 18, Using Business Rules to Implement Services*.

The other point to note is that the decision service return type is a result **List**, so we need to extract our fact from this list and cast it to the appropriate fact type in order to examine its content. We do this with the statement:

```
assign leaveRequest = (TLeaveRequest) resultList.get(0)
```

Invoking a function from within a rule

The final step is to invoke the functions as required from our ruleset. Before writing the additional rules for a vacation of less than 3, 5, and 10 days respectively, we will update our existing rule to use these new functions.

Go back to the **One Day Vacation** rule, and select the first test (so it has an orange box around it). Right-click and select **Delete Test** from the drop-down list, as shown in the following screenshot:

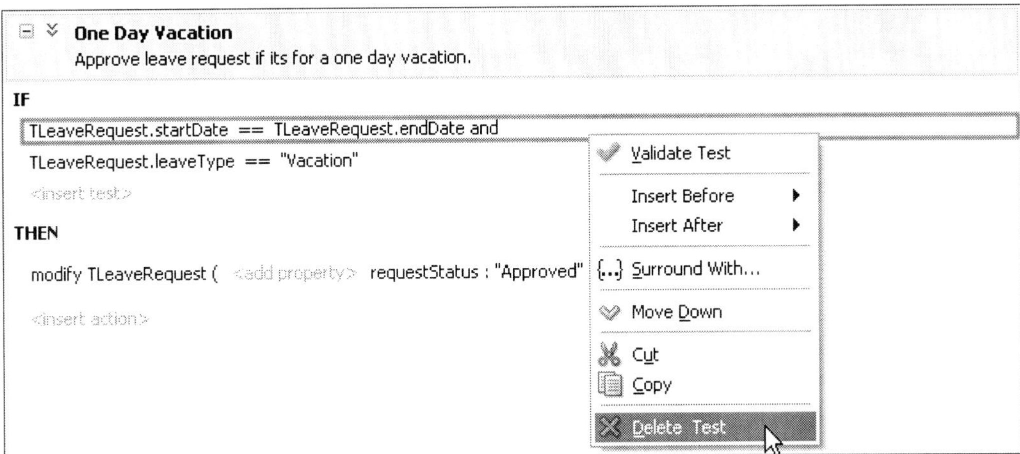

Next, click on **<insert test>** to add a new test to our **IF** clause. Click on the left operand. This time, instead of selecting an item from the drop-down list, click on the calculator icon to launch the **Expression Builder** and use it to build the expression:

```
startsIn(TLeaveRequest.startDate)
```

Set the value of the operator to **>=**. Finally, enter the value of **14** for the second operand. Follow the same approach to add another test to check that the leave duration is only one day. Our updated rule should now looks as shown in the following screenshot:

```
One Day Vacation
Approve leave request if its for a one day vacation.
IF
  TLeaveRequest.leaveType == "Vacation" and
  startsIn(TLeaveRequest.startDate) >= 14 and
  leaveDuration(TLeaveRequest.startDate, TLeaveRequest.endDate) == 1
THEN
  modify TLeaveRequest ( <add property> requestStatus : "Approved" )
```

Once we have completed our test pattern, we can click validate just to check that its syntax is correct. Having completed this test, we can define similar approval rules for vacations of 3, 5, and 10 days respectively.

When completed, save your dictionary and rerun the leave approval process; you should now see that the vacations that match our leave approval rules are automatically approved.

Using decision tables

Our updated ruleset consists of four rules that are very repetitive in nature. It would make more sense to specify the rule just once and then parameterize it in a tabular fashion. This is effectively what decision tables allow you to do.

Before creating your decision table, you will need to delete the rules we have just defined, otherwise we will end up with two versions of the same rules within our ruleset.

Defining a bucket set

When creating a decision table, you are often required to specify a list of values or a range of values that apply to a particular rule. For example, in the case of our vacation approval rule, we will need to specify the following ranges of leave duration values that we are interested in:

- 1 day
- 2-3 days
- 4-5 days
- 6-10 days

We define these in a bucketset. To do this, select the **Bucketsets** tab in the rule editor, then click on the green plus symbol and select **List of Ranges** from the drop-down list, as shown in the following screenshot:

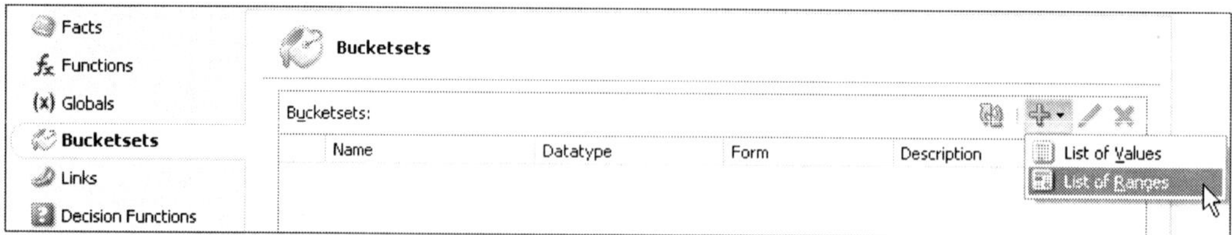

This will create a new bucketset called **Buckset_1**. Click on the name and change it to something more meaningful such as **LeaveDuration**. By default, the bucketset will have a **Datatype** of **int**, which is fine for our purposes.

Click on the pencil icon. This will launch the **Edit Bucketset - LeaveDuration** window, as shown in the following screenshot:

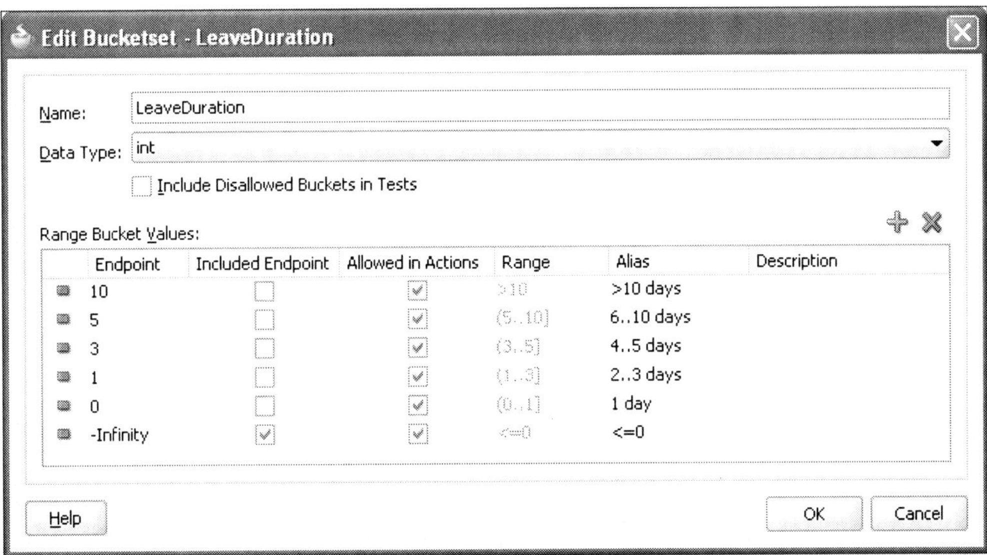

A bucketset, as its name implies, consists of one or more buckets, each corresponding to a range of values. For each bucket, you specify its **Endpoint** and whether the endpoint is included within the bucket. The range of values covered by a bucket is from the endpoint of the bucket to the endpoint of the next bucket.

You can also choose whether to include the specified endpoint in its corresponding bucket. If you don't, then the endpoint will be included in the preceding bucket.

For example, in the preceding screenshot, the second bucket (with the endpoint of **5**) covers the integer values from **6** (as the endpoint **5** isn't included in the bucket) to **10** (the end point of the next bucket).

It is good practice to specify a meaningful alias for each bucket, as when you reference a bucket in a decision table, you do so using its alias. If you don't specify an alias, then it will default to the description in the **Range**.

In preparation for defining our decision table, we have defined two bucketsets: **LeaveDuration**, as shown in the preceding screenshot, and **StartsIn**.

Creating a decision table

To create a decision table, select the **Employee Leave Approval** ruleset tab. Click on the green plus icon and select **Create Decision Table**, as shown in the following screenshot:

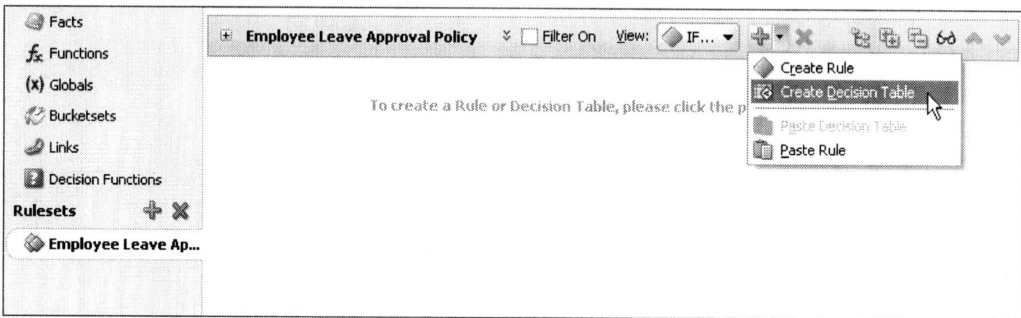

This will add an empty decision table to our ruleset, as shown in the following screenshot:

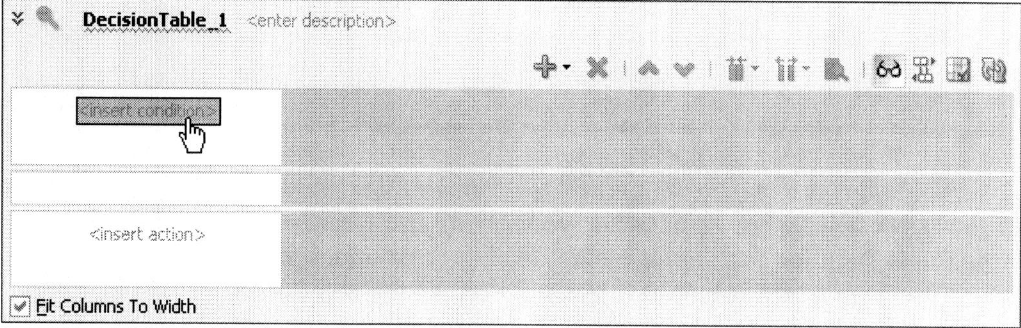

The decision table consists of three areas: the first is for defining our tests (or conditions), the second is for conflict resolution (for resolving overlapping rules within our decision table), and the final area is for defining our actions.

Click on **<insert condition>**. This will add an empty condition with the name **C1** to our ruleset. At the same time, the rule editor will also add an additional column to our decision table. This represents our first rule and is given the name **R1**. To specify the condition that we want to test, double-click on **C1**. This will bring up a drop-down list (similar to the one used to define an operand within the test part of a rule), as shown in the following screenshot:

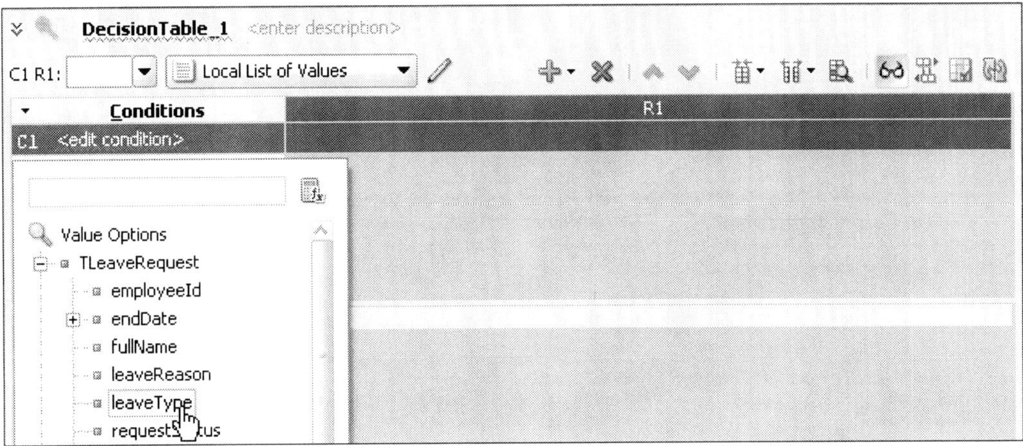

As with our original rule, the first condition we want to test is the type of leave request, so select **TLeaveRequest.leaveType** from the drop-down list.

For our first rule, we want to check that the leave request is of type **Vacation**, so click on the appropriate cell (the intersection of **C1** and **R1**). The rule editor will present us with a drop-down listing our options. In this case, directly enter **Vacation**, as shown in the following screenshot:

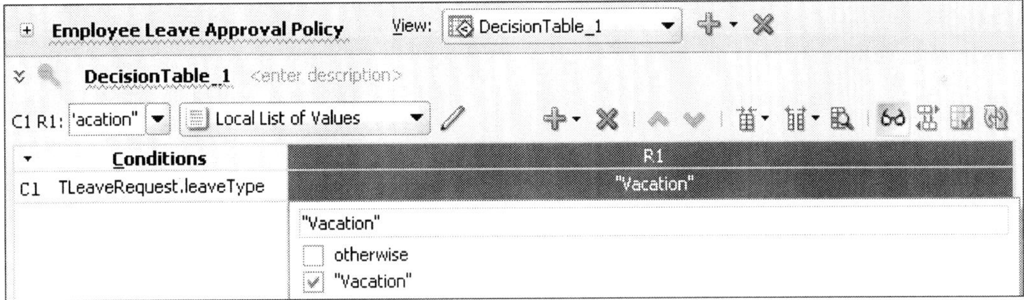

The next step is to add a second condition to test the leave duration. To do this, click on the green plus icon and select **Conditions**. This will add another condition row to our decision table. Click on **<edit condition>** and use the expression builder to define the following:

```
leaveDuration(TLeaveRequest.startDate, TLeaveRequest.endDate)
```

For each rule, we need to test the result of this function against the appropriate value in our **LeaveDuration** bucketset. Before we can do this, we must first associate the condition with that bucketset. To do this, ensure that the condition cell is selected and then click on the drop-down list above it and select **LeaveDuration**, as shown in the following screenshot:

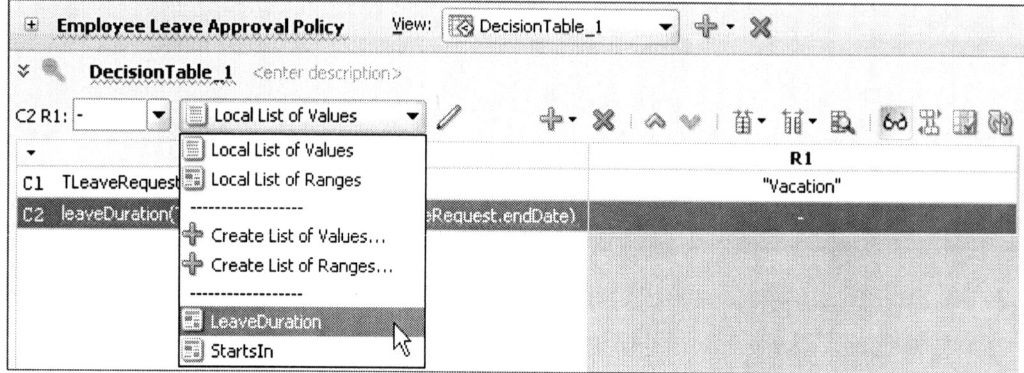

The next step is to check that the leave duration is one day, so click on the appropriate cell (the intersection of **C2** and **R1**). The rule editor will present us with a drop-down listing our options, which will be the list of buckets in the **LeaveDuration** bucketset. From here, select the option **1 day**.

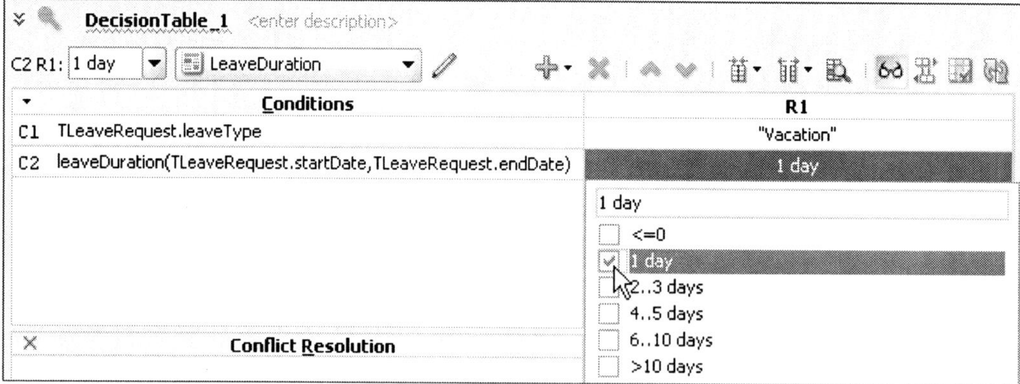

Add three more rules to our decision table (to add a rule, click on the green plus icon and select **Rule**). For **R2**, specify a leave duration of **2..3 days**, for **R3 4..5 days**, and **R4 6..10 days**.

For each of these rules, we want to check that the leave type is **Vacation**. Rather than specifying this individually for each rule (which we could do), we can merge these into a single cell and specify the test just once. To do this, select each cell (hold down the **Ctrl** key while you do this) and then right-click. From the drop-down list, select **Merge Selected Cells**.

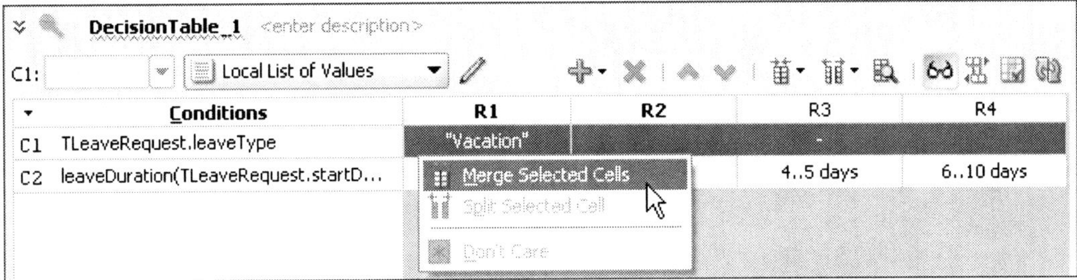

Next, we need to add the final condition as follows:

```
startsIn(TLeaveRequest.startDate)
```

To check whether sufficient notice has been given to automatically approve the vacation request, add this in the normal way and associate the condition with the **StartsIn** bucketset.

For our first rule, we want to approve the leave request if it starts in 14 or more days time, so select **ALL** the appropriate buckets from our bucketset (as shown in the following screenshot). Complete the test for rules **R2**, **R3**, and **R4**.

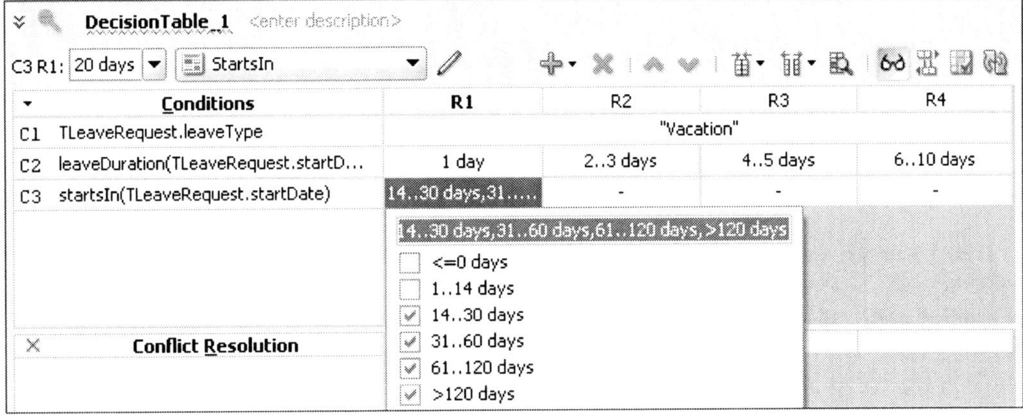

The final step is to specify the action we want to take for each of our rules. Click on **<insert action>**. This will display a drop-down list where you need to specify the **Action Type** you wish to carry out. Select **Modify**. This will insert a modify action into our decision table; double-click on this to open the **Action Editor** (as shown in the following screenshot):

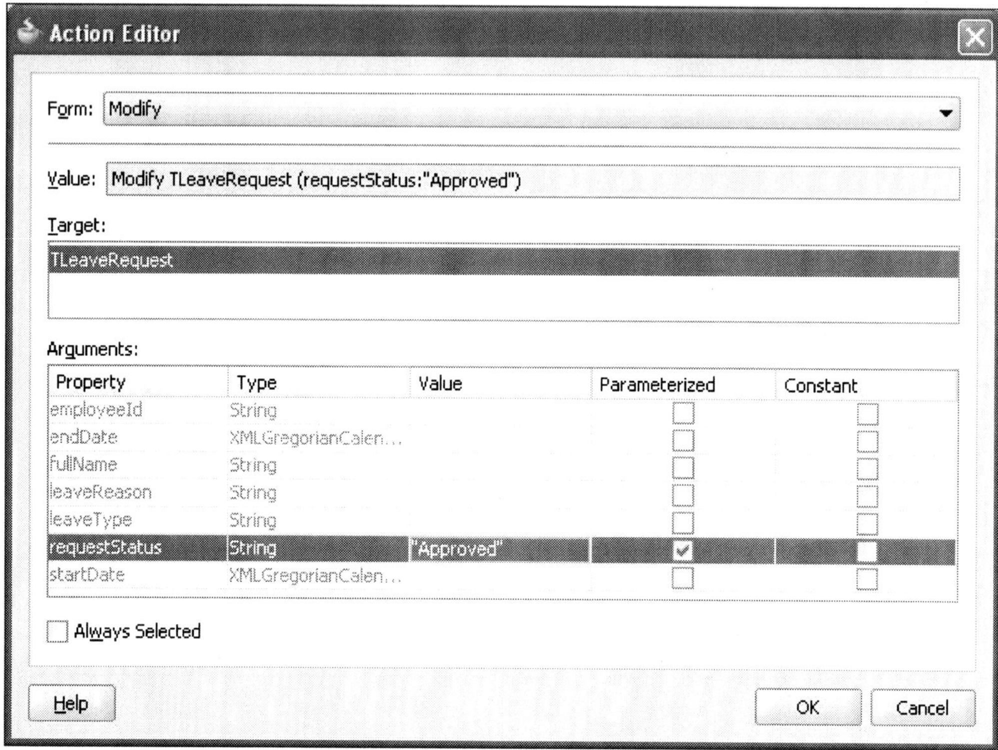

The **Form** option allows us to select from the drop-down list which action we want to perform. For the **Modify** action, we first need to specify the fact we wish to update, so select **TLeaveRequest** in the **Target** section.

The **Arguments** section will then be populated to list all the properties for the selected fact. Select **requestStatus** and enter a value of **Approved**. Also select the cell to be parameterized. If you don't specify this, then it forces every rule within our decision table to use the same value.

Finally, ensure that the checkbox **Always Selected** is unchecked (we will see why in a moment) and click **OK**. This will return us to our decision table, as shown in the following screenshot:

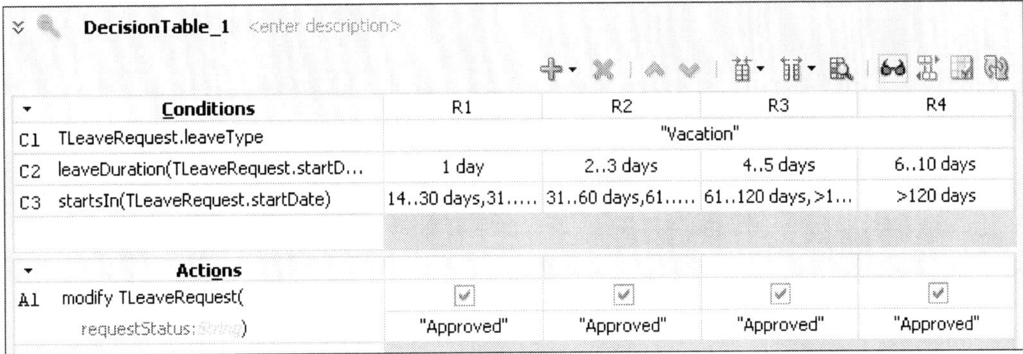

At this point, the action will contain an identical configuration for each rule, which we can then modify as appropriate.

Each rule has an associated checkbox for the action, which, by default, is unchecked. This specifies whether that action should be taken for that rule. In our case, we want each rule to update the request status, so ensure that the checkbox is selected for every rule (as shown in the preceding screenshot).

> If you had checked the **Always Selected** checkbox in the **Action Editor**, then the action would be selected for each rule and would also be read-only to prevent you from modifying it.

The action will also contain a row for every property that we are modifying, which, in our example, is just one (**requestStatus**). As we selected this property to be parameterized, we could override the specified value for each individual rule.

Conflict resolution

This almost completes our decision table. However, we will add one more rule to handle any other scenario that isn't covered by our current ruleset. Add one more rule, but don't specify any values for any of the conditions, so the rule will apply to everything. In the actions section, specify a value of **Manual** to indicate that the request requires manual approval.

Upon doing this, the rule editor will add a row to the conflicts section of the decision table, as shown in the following screenshot:

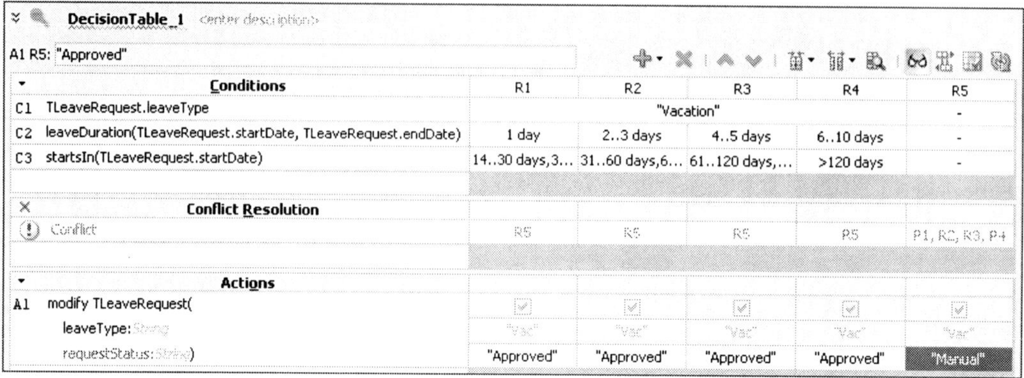

This is indicating that **R5** is in conflict with **R1**, **R2**, **R3**, and **R4**, that is, that they both apply to the same scenario. Double-click on the conflict warning for **R1**, and this will launch the **Conflict Resolution** window, as shown in the following screenshot:

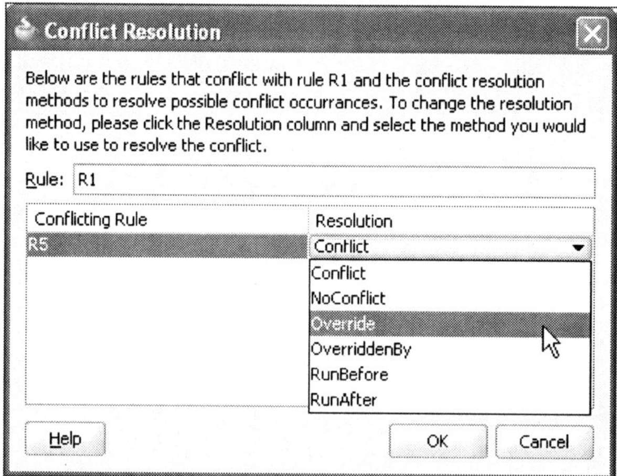

Here, we can specify how we wish to handle the conflict. Click on the drop-down list and select **Override** to specify that **R1** takes precedence over **R5**. Do the same for rules **R2**, **R3**, and **R4**. The decision table will be updated to show no conflicts and that rules **R1** to **R4** override **R5**.

This completes our decision table, so save the rules dictionary and redeploy the leave approval composite to test it.

Summary

Business rules are a key component of any application. Traditionally, these rules are buried deep within the code of an application, making them very difficult to change.

Yet, in a typical application, it is the business rules that change most frequently, by separating these out as a specialized service, it allows us to change these rules without having to modify the overall application.

In this chapter, we have looked at how we can use the Oracle Business Rules engine to implement such rules, and how we can invoke these from within BPEL as a decision service.

It's worth noting that you are not restricted to calling these rules from just BPEL, as the rules engine comes with a Java API that allows it to be easily invoked from any Java application, or alternatively, you can expose the rules as web services, which can then be invoked from any web service client.

Finally, while in this chapter, we have only looked at very simple rules. The Oracle Business Rules engine implements the industry standard Rete Algorithm, making it ideal for evaluating a large number of interdependent rules and facts. We examine some of these capabilities in more detail in *Chapter 18, Using Business Rules to Implement Services*.

8

Using Business Events

In the previous chapters, we focused on routing messages to the correct destination and managing process flow. All of this requires knowledge of the dependencies, and for most business processes and service integrations, this is required to ensure that everything works reliably. However, even with transformation and service abstraction, there are still dependencies between services. In this chapter, we will look at the tools available in SOA Suite for completely decoupling providers of messages from consumers of messages. This is useful if we wish to add new attributes that do not require responses to be returned, for example, adding fraud detection services or usage auditing services. In these cases, we just want message producers to publish events, and allow new services to receive these events by subscribing to them without impacting the publisher. This is the function of the **Event Delivery Network** (EDN) in the SOA Suite and is the focus of this chapter.

How EDN differs from traditional messaging

Message Oriented Middleware (**MOM**) uses queuing technologies to isolate producers from consumers. The classic MOM product was **IBM MQ Series**, but other products in this space include **Tibco Rendezvous** and **Oracle AQ**. Messages may be delivered point to point (a single service consumes the message) or one-to-many (multiple services may consume the same message). The **Java Messaging Service** (**JMS**) provides an abstraction over messaging systems and supports both one-to-one interactions through queues and one-to-many interactions through topics. When using JMS to subscribe to an event, a developer must know the format of data associated with the event and the message channel (topic or queue) on which to listen to receive the event. This message channel must be configured for each event and filters might be added to restrict the messages delivered. The **Event Delivery Network** (EDN) takes the view that the publishers and subscribers of a message, known as an event, only need to know the subject matter, the event name, and the event data format. All the delivery details can be hidden under the covers. EDN uses JMS to deliver events from subscribers to publishers, but the configuration of JMS queues and topics and any associated filters is hidden from users of the EDN service.

The following table highlights the differences between traditional MOM and EDN. As can be seen, the focus of EDN is to make it very easy for event producers to publish an event that can then be received by an arbitrary number of event subscribers. EDN developers only need to be aware of the events themselves, as all the underlying delivery mechanisms are taken care of within the EDN.

Interaction Pattern	Messaging Support	Configuration	EDN Notes
Request/Reply	Separate JMS queues are used for Request and Response messages. JMS Message Headers are used to correlate requests with responses.	Request and response queues must be configured with appropriate connection factories and message store.	EDN does not support request/reply. It is not possible to target the receiver of an event. Event subscribers are not visible to event producers and so cannot be directly targeted. Similarly, event producers are not visible to event subscribers and so it is not possible to send direct replies just to the originator of the event.
One way guaranteed delivery	Single JMS queue with a single subscriber	Queue must be configured with appropriate connection factory and message store	EDN does not support guaranteed one way delivery of events. An event producer has no way of knowing how many subscribers will receive the message or if any subscribers will receive the message.
One-to-many message delivery	Single JMS topic with zero or more subscribers	Topic must be configured with appropriate connection factory and message store.	EDN supports exactly this message interaction pattern without the need to configure any JMS artifacts. EDN uses JMS but this is hidden from the developer.

A sample use case

Consider an auction process. The basic auction process accepts new items for auction from a seller service, accepts bids from a bidder service, and identifies the winning bid in an auction service. All these operations require co-ordination between the services involved.

There may be concerns about the proprietary of some bids, but the time taken to validate the bid and ensure that it is legitimate may be viewed as too lengthy and instead it may be desired to have a background process to validate bids, so we do not slow down the normal bid taking process.

This is an extension to the business functionality that does not require a conversation between the bid process and the validation service. In fact, a conversation may slow down the auction process and increase the time taken to accept and confirm bids and winners. This is an excellent use case for the EDN because of the following features:

- No conversation is required between the event consumer (bid legitimacy process) and the event producer (auction process).
- The event consumer can be added to the system without any changes to the event producer. As long as the auction process is publishing bid events, adding the bid validator will not impact the auction process.
- Additional producers may be added to the system without impacting existing producers and/or consumers. For example, different auction systems may raise the same event.
- Additional consumers may also be added independently of either existing producers and/or consumers. For example, an automated bidding service may make use of this event later without impacting the existing services.

Event Delivery Network essentials

The EDN is a very simple but very powerful concept, and we will now explain the basic principles associated with it.

Events

An event is the message that will be published and consumed on the Event Delivery Network. Events consist of three parts:

1. A namespace that identifies the general area that the event is associated with and helps to avoid clashes between event names
2. A name that identifies the type of event within a namespace
3. A data type that defines the data associated with the event

Namespaces of events behave in the same way as namespaces in XML and identify the solution area of the events and avoid clashes between events with the same name that belong to different solution areas. For example, a namespace would differentiate an event called NewOrder in a military command and control system from an event called NewOrder in a logistics system.

Events are defined using an XML-based language called the **Event Description Language** (**EDL**).

We can model business events from within JDeveloper by clicking on the event icon on the top-left-hand corner of the composite editor as shown in the following screenshot.

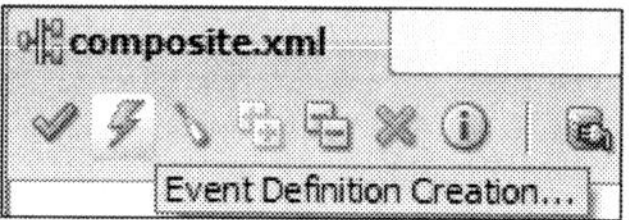

This brings up the **Create Event Definition File** dialog to allow us to create a new EDL file to contain our event definitions.

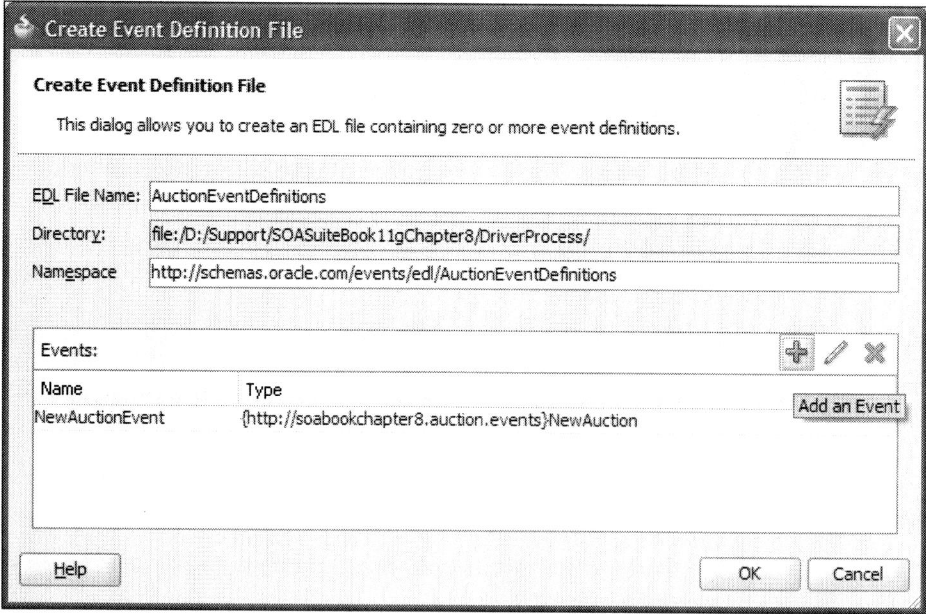

After defining the **EDL File Name**, the **Directory** it resides in, and the **Namespace** of the EDL file, we can add events to it by clicking on the green plus symbol. This takes us to the **Add an Event** dialog, where we can choose the XML **Element** that represents the data content of the event and give the event a **Name**.

Event elements and data types should always be defined in an XML schema file, which is separate from other SOA XML artifacts such as message schemas. This is because the events may be used across many areas, and they should not have dependencies on other SOA artifacts.

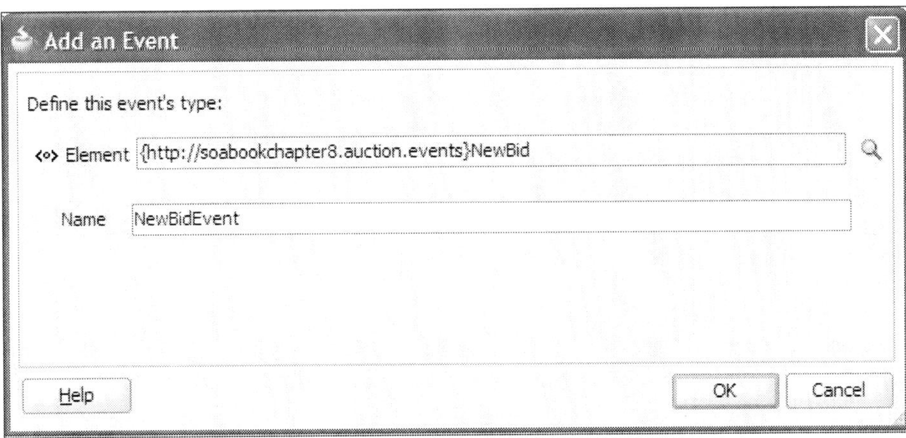

After completing the definition of our EDL file, it is displayed in JDeveloper, where we can continue to add or remove events.

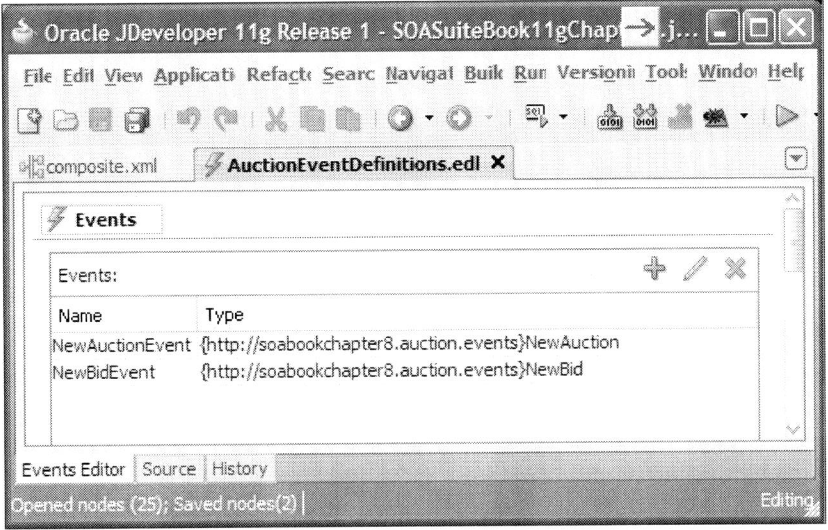

The EDL file itself is a very simple format, shown as follows:

```
<?xml version="1.0" encoding="UTF-8" standalone="yes"?>
<definitions xmlns=http://schemas.oracle.com/events/edl
  targetNamespace="AuctionEventDefinitions">
    <schema-import namespace="auction.events"
      location="xsd/AuctionEvents.xsd"/>
        <event-definition name="NewAuctionEvent">
        <content xmlns:ns0=" auction.events"
          element="ns0:NewAuction"/>
        </event-definition>
        <event-definition name="NewBidEvent">
          <content xmlns:ns0=" auction.events" element="ns0:NewBid"/>
        </event-definition>
</definitions>
```

The `targetNamespace` attribute of the `<definitions>` element defines the namespace for the events. XML-type definitions are imported using `<schema-import>`, and `<event-definition>` is used to define events and their associated element.

Event publishers

Events are created by event publishers. An event publisher may be a Mediator or BPEL component in an SCA Assembly or it may be a custom Java application. The event publisher raises the event by creating an XML element and passing it to the Event Delivery Network. Once passed to the EDN, the publisher is unaware of how many subscribers consume the event or even if the event is consumed by any subscriber. This provides a degree of isolation between the publisher and subscribers. The EDN is responsible for keeping track of who is subscribing and ensuring that they receive the new event.

Publishing an event using the Mediator component

When using a Mediator to publish an event, we usually want to publish the event in parallel with other processing that the Mediator is doing. Typically, we want the Mediator to take the request from some service call and publish the event.

In the following example, we have a Mediator **NewAuctionMediator** that routes to a dummy service implemented by a Mediator **ServiceMediator** that uses Echo functionality to provide a synchronous response to its caller. We will raise a **NewAuction** event as part of the inbound processing in the Mediator. Note that although the Mediator will route a reply to the specific caller of the composite, the event will be routed to all subscribers of that event type.

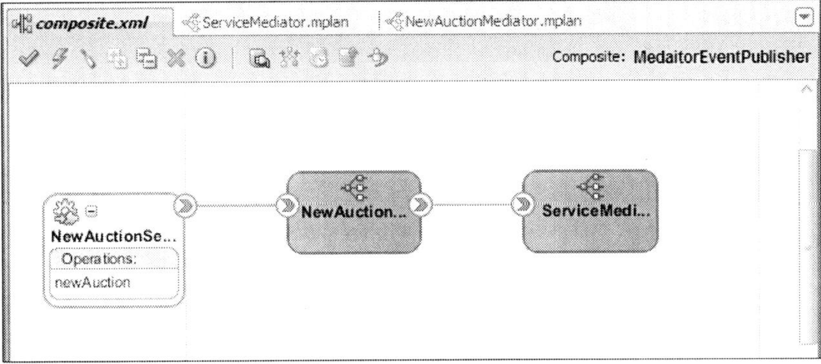

We can raise an event based on the input request in the following fashion.

We open the routing Mediator component, in this case, **NewAuctionMediator**, and add a new sequential static routing rule. When the **Target Type** dialog comes up, select the **Event** button to generate an event.

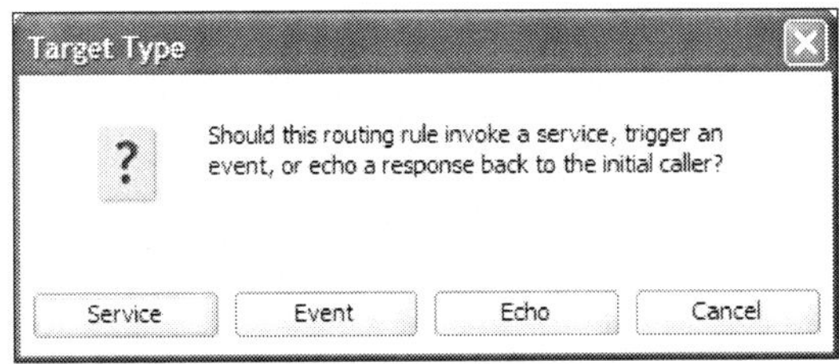

In the **Event Chooser** dialog, we can choose the **Event Definition File** that contains our event. We can either browse for an existing EDL file using the magnifying glass icon or we can create a new EDL file by using the thunderbolt icon. Once an EDL file has been chosen, we can then select the specific event that we wish to produce.

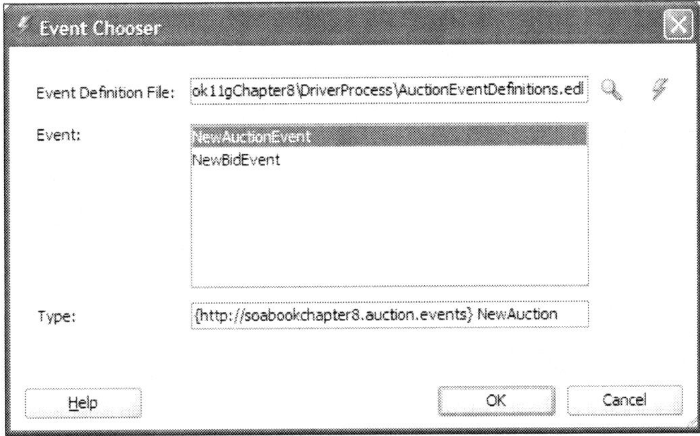

If we choose an existing EDL file that is not in our project, JDeveloper will assume that we want to copy the EDL file and its associated XML schemas into the project. On the **Localize Files** dialog, we have the choice of keeping existing directory relationships between files or flattening any existing directory structure.

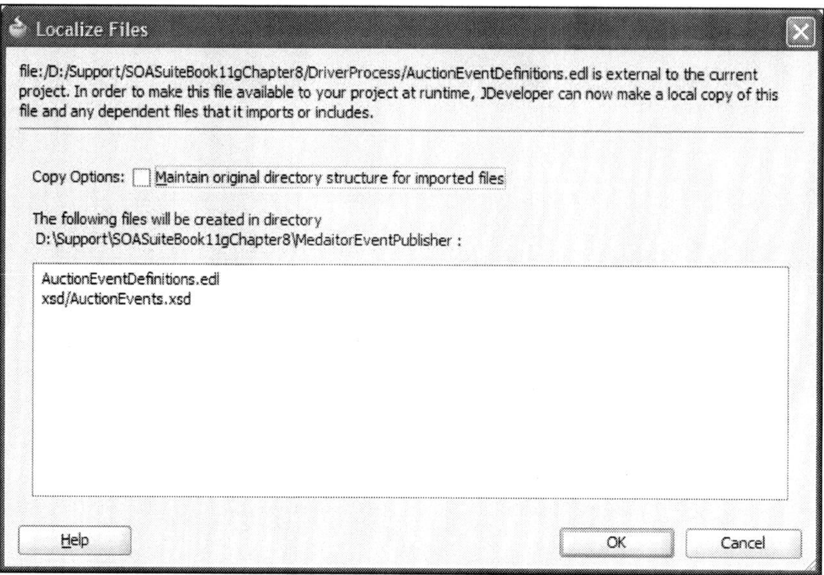

Once the event is selected, we then just need to add a transformation to transform the input of the request to the event format.

Publishing an event using BPEL

We can also publish events using BPEL. Using the previous example, we may decide that rather than just publishing a **NewAuction** event that contains the input data used to create the auction, we also wish to include the auction identifier generated by the response to the new auction request. This is best achieved using the BPEL event publisher.

Using the previous example, we insert a BPEL process between the service requestor, in this case, **NewAuctionMediator**, and the service provider, in this case **ServiceProvider**. We use the **Base on a WSDL** template to create the process and select the WSDL of the target service as our WSDL, in this case the WSDL for **ServiceMediator**. We then rewire the composite so that the target service is now invoked by our new BPEL process, and the original client of the service is now a client of the BPEL process, as shown in the following diagram:

We then edit the BPEL process to invoke the original target service. Because we have used the target service WSDL for the WSDL of the BPEL process, we can use the input and output variables of the process as parameters to invoke the target service. With this done, we are ready to publish the event as part of our BPEL process.

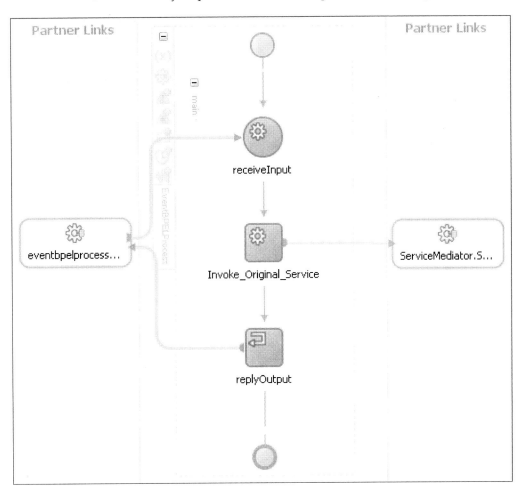

We publish an event from within BPEL by using an invoke and setting the **Interaction Type** to be **Event** rather than the more usual **Partner Link**.

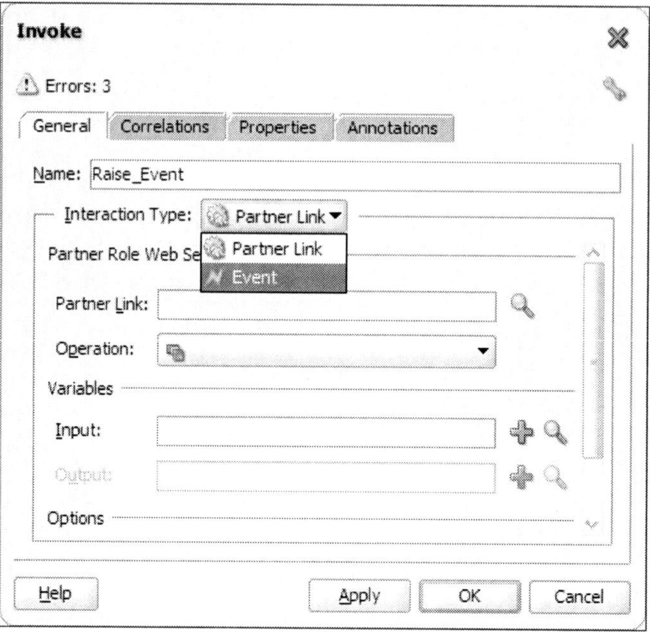

This allows us to select an event and a variable to hold the data for that event. The event itself is chosen from the **Event Chooser** dialog, which was introduced in the previous section. We then need to add an assign statement to initialize the variable used to populate the event. The fact that this invoke is actually raising an event is identified by the lightning symbol on the **Invoke**.

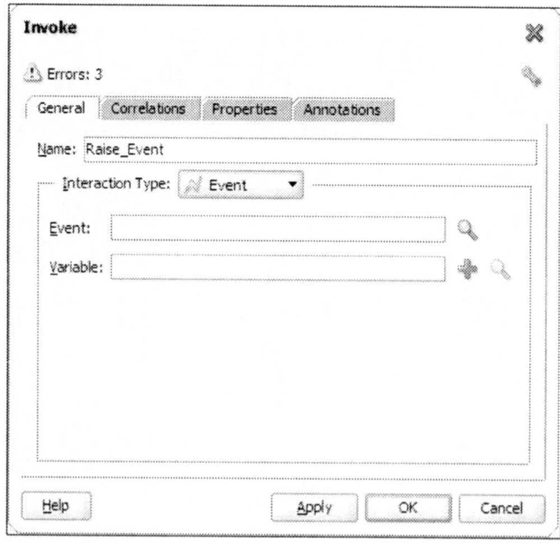

Note that when we raise an event, there is no indication provided as to how to route or deliver the event. In the next section, we will look at how events are consumed.

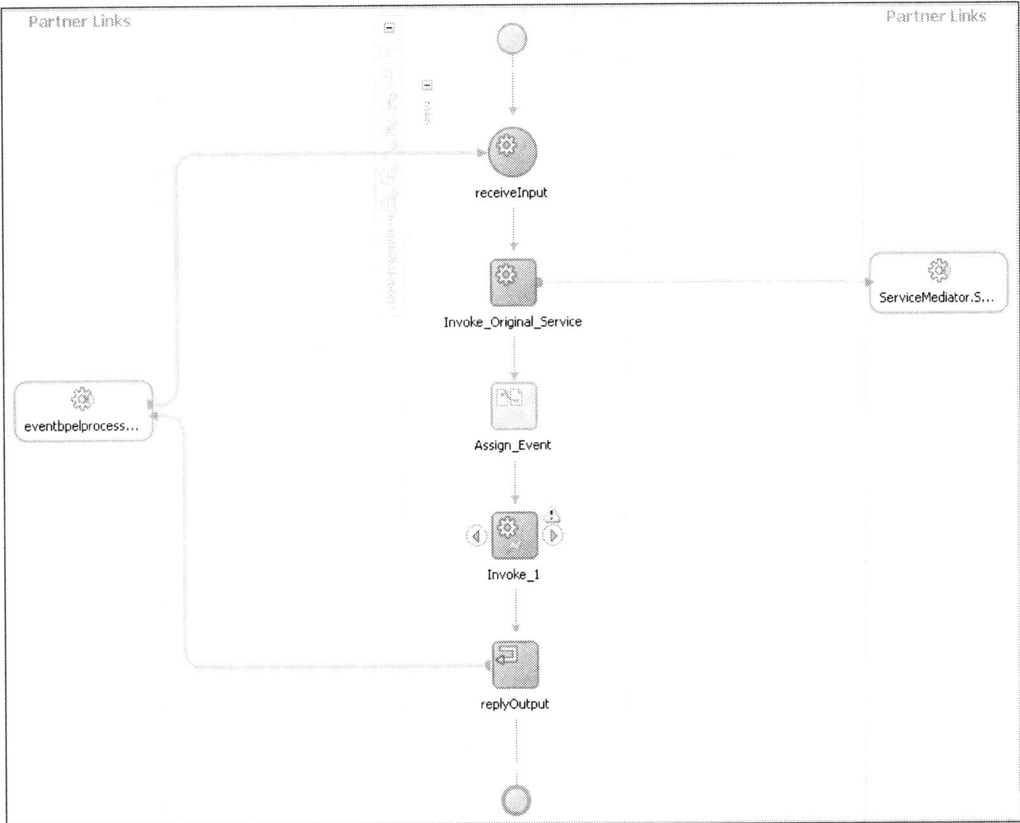

Publishing an event using Java

We can also publish and consume events using Java. In this section, we will look at how Java code can be used to publish an event.

To publish an event, we need to go through the following steps:

1. Create the event
2. Connect to the Event Delivery Network
3. Publish the event on the connection

Creating the event

We create the event in Java by using the `oracle.integration.platform.blocks.event.BusinessEventBuilder` class. An instance of this class is created by a static factory method called `newInstance`. We need to provide a qualified name (QName that includes the namespace and the entity name) and a body for the event through setter methods on the `builder` class. Once these have been set, we can call `createEvent` to generate an instance of a `BusinessEvent`.

```
BusinessEventBuilder builder = BusinessEventBuilder.newInstance();
QName name = new QName(
    "http://schemas.oracle.com/events/edl/AuctionEventDefinitions",
    "NewAuctionEvent");
builder.setEventName(name);
XMLElement content = …
builder.setBody(content);
BusinessEvent event = builder.createEvent();
```

The event name is a combination of the event schema, acting as an XML namespace, and the event name. The content is the XML element containing the event content.

Once we have a `BusinessEvent`, we need a connection to the Event Delivery Network in order to publish the event.

Creating the event connection

The event connection can be created using either a JMS queue connection to the Event Delivery Network or an Oracle AQ connection. The latter requires the use of a data source and is the approach we will show. We obtain an `oracle.fabric.blocks.event.BusinessEventConnection` from a `BusinessEventConnectionFactory`. We will use the AQ version of this connection factory, which is provided by the `oracle.integration.platform.blocks.event.saq. SAQRemoteBusinessEventConnectionFactory class`.

```
DataSource ds = …
  BusinessEventConnectionFactory factory = new
    SAQRemoteBusinessEventConnectionFactory(ds, ds, null);
  BusinessEventConnection conn =
    factory.createBusinessEventConnection();
```

We use the connection factory to create a connection to Event Delivery Network. The data source we provide must be configured to connect to the SOA infrastructure schema in the database, which by default is called `<PREFIX>_SOAInfra`.

Publishing the event

Now that we have an EDN connection, we can publish our event on it by calling `publishEvent`:

```
conn.publishEvent(event, EVENT_PRIORITY);
```

This publishes our event on our previously created connection. The event priority is usually set to 3, but it is not used in this release.

Event subscribers

Events are consumed by event subscribers. In a similar fashion to event publishers, event subscribers may be BPEL processes or Mediators. When subscribing to an event, the subscriber can filter the events. Subscribers subscribe to a specific event within an event namespace. They can limit the instances of an event that they receive by applying a filter. Only events for which the filter evaluates to true are delivered to the event subscriber. Event filters are XPath expressions.

Consuming an event using Mediator

To consume an event, we can add an event subscriber to a Mediator. We do this by clicking on the green plus sign next to the **Event Subscriptions** label under **Routing Rules**.

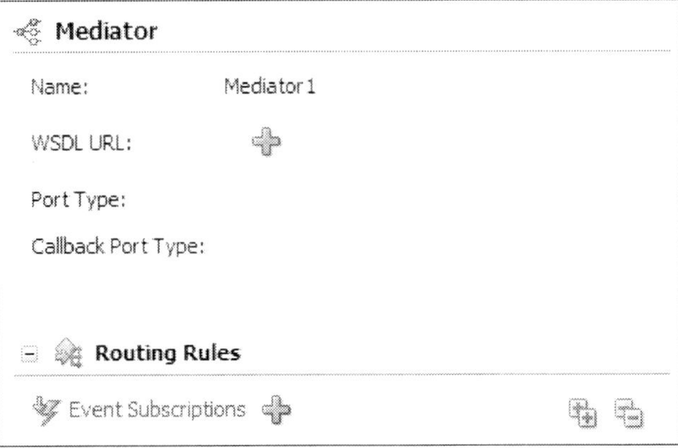

This brings us to the **Subscribed Events** dialog where, by clicking on the green plus sign, we add a new event subscription using the **Event Chooser** dialog introduced in the section on publishing an event.

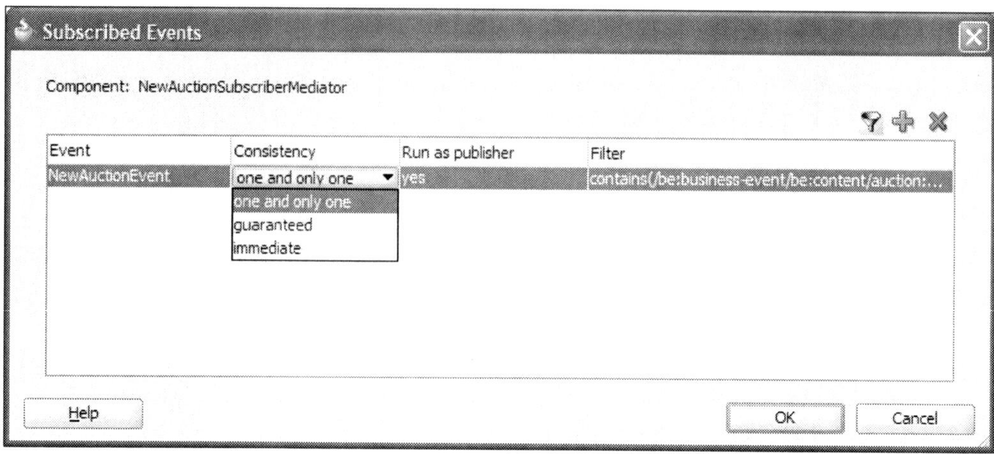

Having chosen an event, we can determine how the event is to be delivered using the **Consistency** option. Transactions are discussed later in *Chapter 15, Advanced SOA Suite Architecture*. The consistency options are:

- Exactly once by selecting the **one and only one** option. This makes the event delivery transaction part of the Mediator transaction. If the Mediator transaction completes successfully, then the event will also be marked as read, otherwise it will be rolled back and thus appear not to have been delivered. Transaction boundaries are explained in more detail in *Chapter 15, Advanced SOA Suite Architecture*
- At least once by selecting **guaranteed**. This keeps the Mediator transaction separate from the delivery transaction. The event will be delivered to the subscriber, but any errors in the Mediator may cause that event to be lost to that subscriber.
- **immediate** makes the delivery transaction part of the event publishing transaction. This option should be avoided as it couples the subscriber and the publisher.

Avoid using the **immediate** delivery option as it tightly couples the publisher to a subscriber that it should be unaware of. The Java API for this is marked as deprecated, and it is likely that this option will disappear in the future.

The **Run as publisher** option allows the Mediator to run in the same security context as the event publisher. This allows the subscriber component to perform any actions that the publisher could perform.

The **Filter** option brings up the **Expression Builder** dialog when clicked on. This allows us to construct an XPath expression to limit the delivered event to only those for which the XPath expression resolves to true.

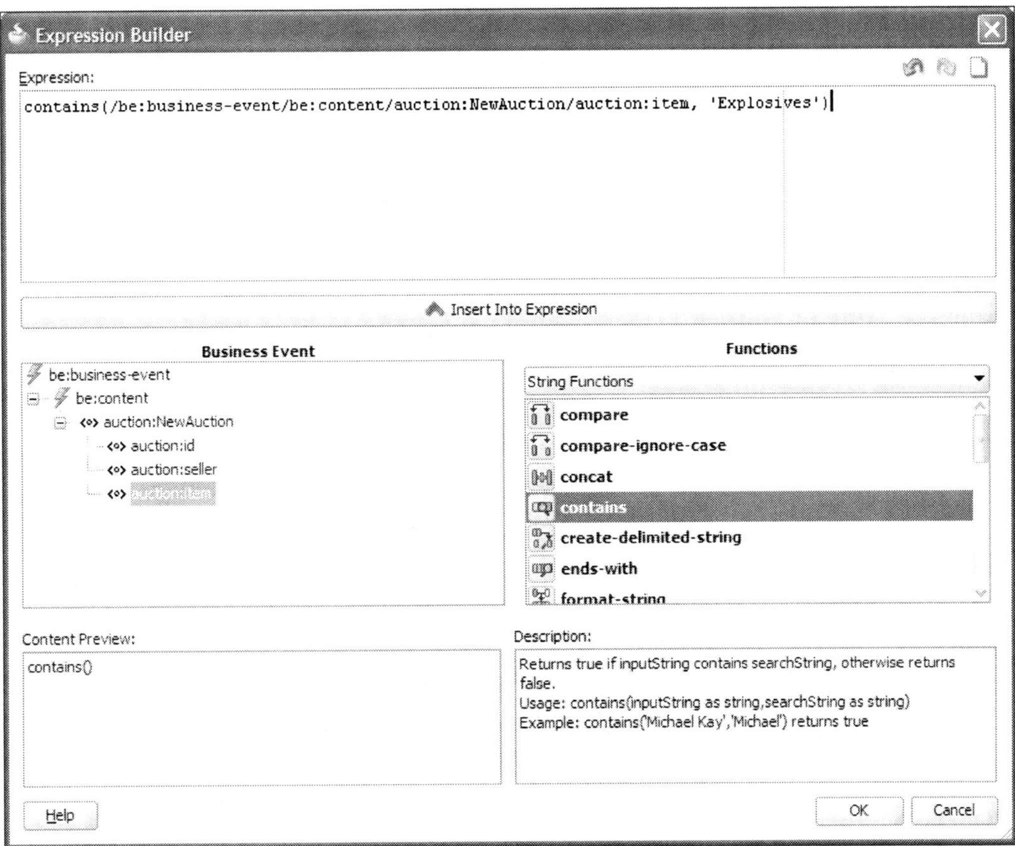

A component in a composite that has subscribed to an event has a lightning bolt on its service side to identify it within a composite.

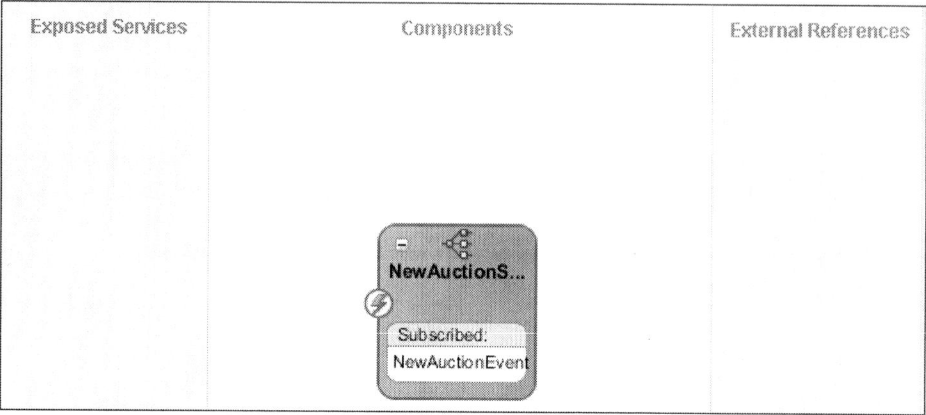

Consuming an event using BPEL

To subscribe to an event using BPEL, we can create a BPEL process using the **Subscribe to Events** template. This allows us to add the events to which we wish to subscribe to in a similar fashion to having the Mediator subscribe to events by using the **Event Chooser** dialog and adding quality of service options and filters.

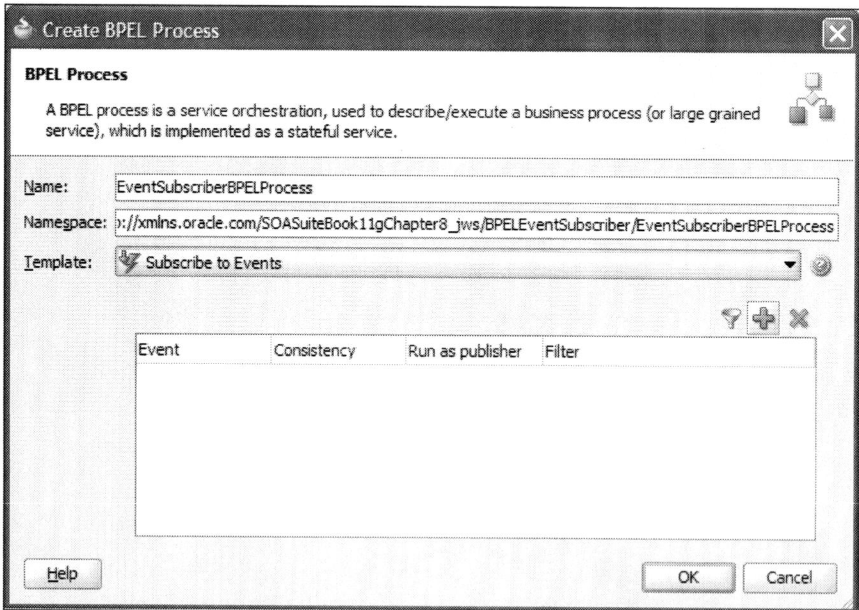

This creates a BPEL process with a single receive activity that identifies itself as subscribing to an event by the lightening icon on the receive.

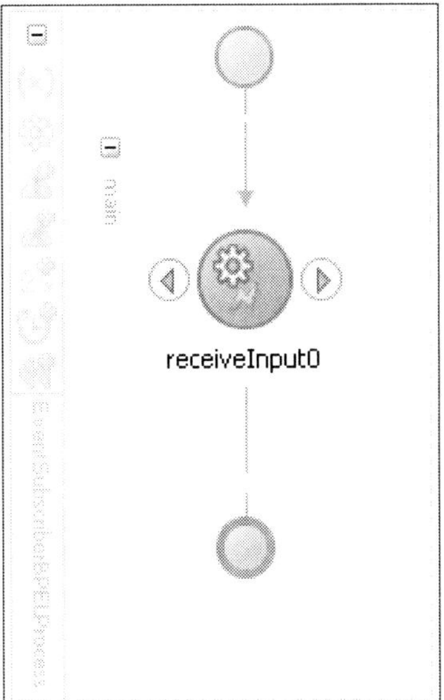

Events may also be subscribed to by adding a BPEL **Receive** activity to the process and choosing an **Interaction Type** of **Event**.

EDN publishing patterns with SOA Suite

The table in this section summarizes the different ways in which events may be published within the SOA Suite depending on the requirement.

Requirement	Pattern
Publish an event on receipt of a message	A Mediator can achieve this by implementing the target service interface and passing the message through the target while adding a publish event item in sequence.
Publish an event on a synchronous message response	A BPEL process can achieve this by implementing the target service interface and passing the message through the target and passing the response back to the caller. Either before or after the return to the caller, the process can publish an event item using data from the response.
Publish an event on a synchronous message request and reply	A BPEL process can achieve this by implementing the target service interface and passing the message through the target and passing the response back to the caller. Either before or after the return to the caller, the process can publish an event item using data from the request and the response.
Publish an event on an asynchronous response	A BPEL process can achieve this by implementing the async interface, and before or after passing the message from the target back to the caller, it can publish an event item using data from the response.
Publish an event on an asynchronous message request and reply	A BPEL process can achieve this by implementing the target service interface and the callback interface and passing the message through the target and passing the callback back to the caller. Either before or after the callback to the caller, the process can publish an event item using data from the request and the response.
Publish an event on an event	A Mediator can achieve this by subscribing to an event and then publishing an event.

We will now look at how each of these patterns may be implemented.

Publishing an event on receipt of a message

If we receive a message, either a one way or a request/reply interaction, we can use the Mediator to publish an event based on the content of the inbound message by using a static routing rule to raise the event before or after forwarding the request to a target service, as shown in the following screenshot:

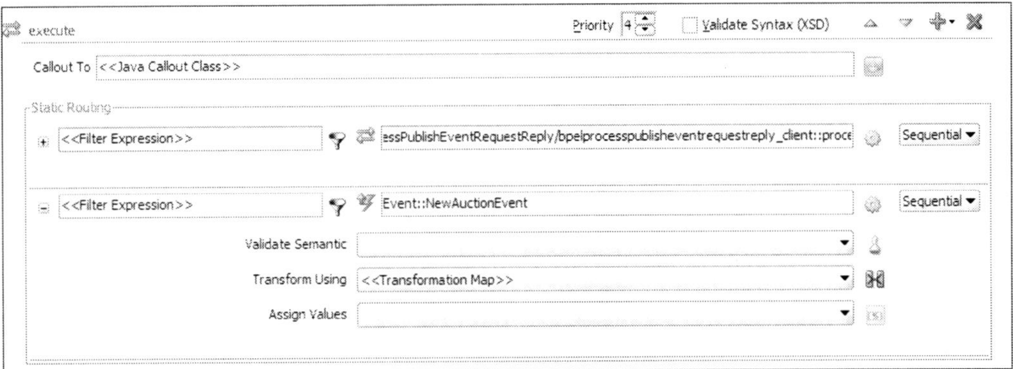

Publishing an event on a synchronous message response

If we wish to raise an event based on the response to a request/reply interaction, then we need to use a BPEL process to invoke the target service and then raise the event based on the content of the response, as shown in the following screenshot:

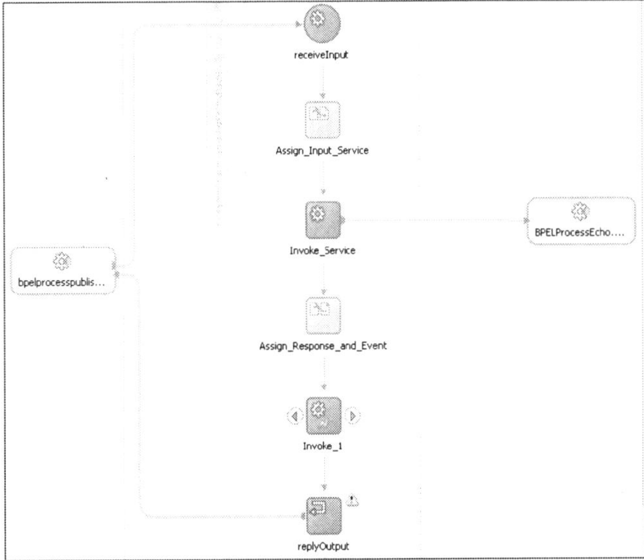

Publishing an event on a synchronous message request and reply

When an event needs to be raised, based on the content of both the request and reply parts of a synchronous interaction, a BPEL process can be used to do this. The pattern is essentially the same as the previous pattern, except that in the `<assign>` to the event variable, we include data from both the request message and the reply message.

Publishing an event on an asynchronous response

When an event needs to be raised based on the content of an asynchronous response, we can use a BPEL process to do this. We invoke the target service and get the reply. Then, either before or after sending the reply back to the initiator of the service interaction, we can raise the event, as shown in the following screenshot:

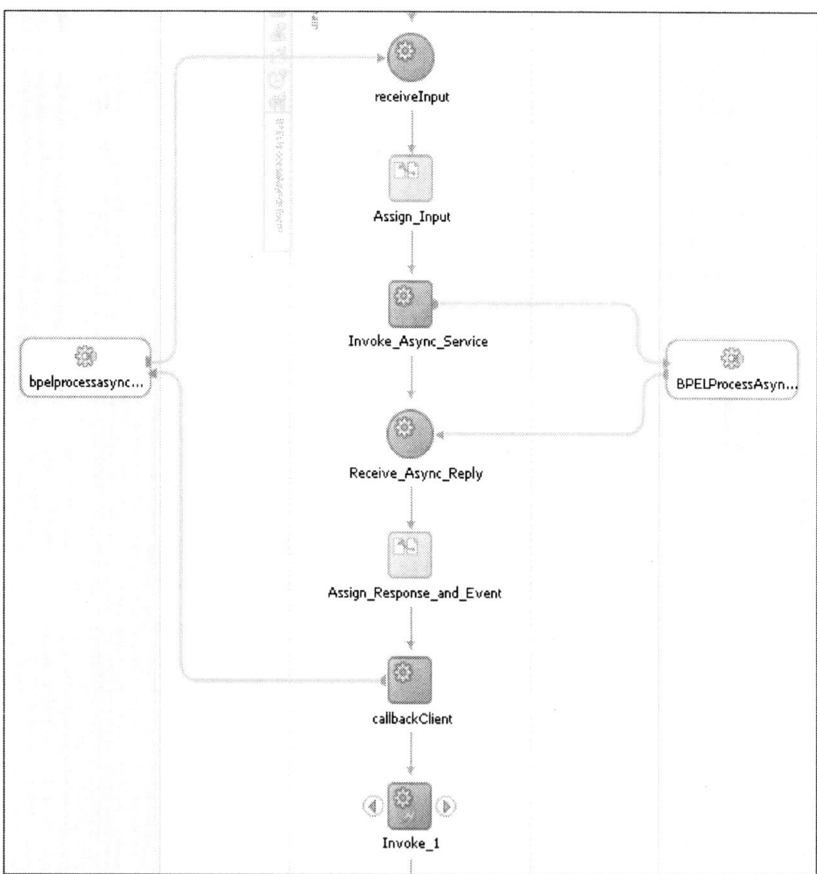

Publishing an event on an asynchronous message request and reply

When an event needs to be raised based on the content of both the request and reply parts of an asynchronous interaction, a BPEL process can be used to do this. The pattern is essentially the same as the previous pattern, except that in the `<assign>` to the event variable, we include data from both the request message and the reply message.

Publishing an event on an event

We can use a Mediator to raise an event based on an incoming event. We may want to do this to map events from one namespace to another or to manage backwards compatibility between different versions of an event without having to change subscribers or publishers. The Mediator can simply raise the outgoing event based on the incoming event by using a sequential routing rule, as shown in the following screenshot:

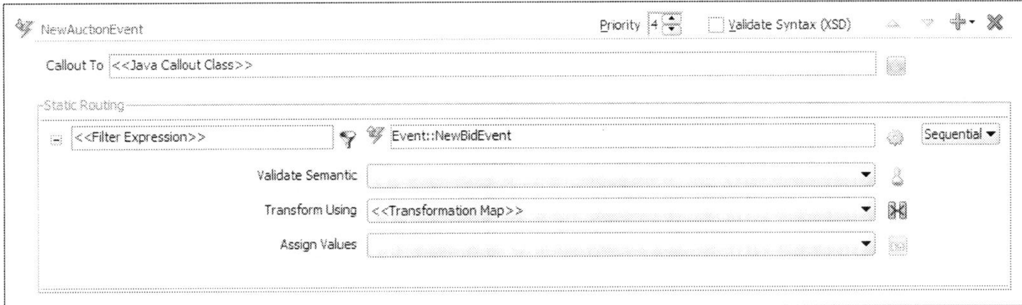

Monitoring event processing in Enterprise Manager

We can monitor what is happening with events from within Enterprise Manager. We can also create new events from the EM console.

We can track what is happening with events by using the **Business Events** menu item of the **soa_infra** tree node. This brings up the **Business Events** screen.

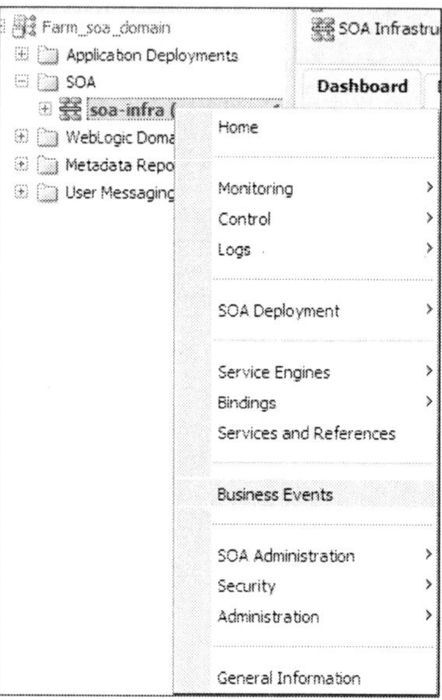

On the **Events** tab of this screen, we can see the list of events registered with the server and the number of subscriptions and failed deliveries for each event. We can also create database event subscriptions from this screen by selecting an event and clicking on the **Subscribe...** link.

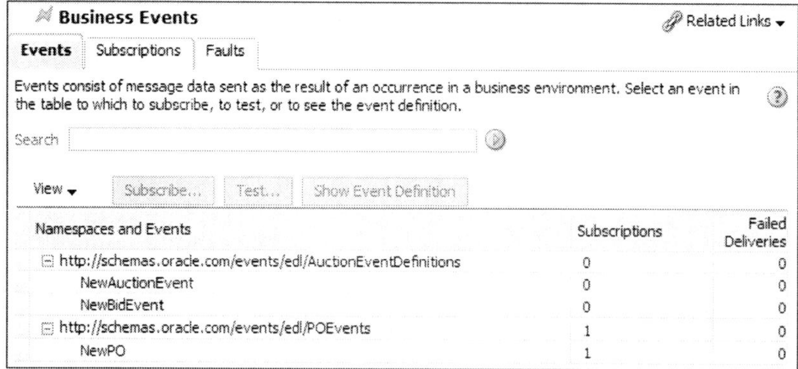

Selecting an event and clicking the **Test...** button allows us to publish a new event. No assistance is provided with the format of the event, which should be laid out as shown in the following example:

```
<business-event
  xmlns:ns1=http://soa.suite.book/events/edl/AuctionEvents
  xmlns="http://oracle.com/fabric/businessEvent">
    <name>ns1:NewAuction</name>
      <id>e4196227-806c-4680-a6b4-6f8df931b3f3</id>
        <content>
          <NewAuction xmlns="http://soa.suite.book/AuctionEvents">
            <seller>Antony</seller>
              <item>Used Running Shoes</item>
                <id>12345</id>
          </NewAuction>
        </content>
</business-event>
```

Note that the event content inside the `<content>` tab is the data associated with our new event. The `<business-event>` identifies the namespace of the event, and under this, the `<name>` element identifies the specific event.

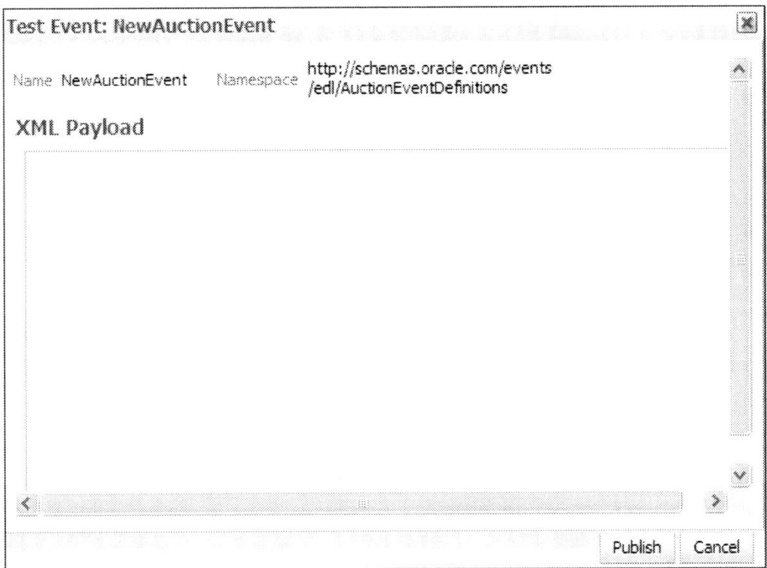

The **Subscriptions** tab gives us more information about subscriptions, identifying the composite and component within the composite that are subscribing to a particular event. We can also see the transaction consistency level and any filter that is being applied.

Subscriptions can either be linked to a stored procedure in the database, database subscriptions, or they can be subscriptions within components in a composite.

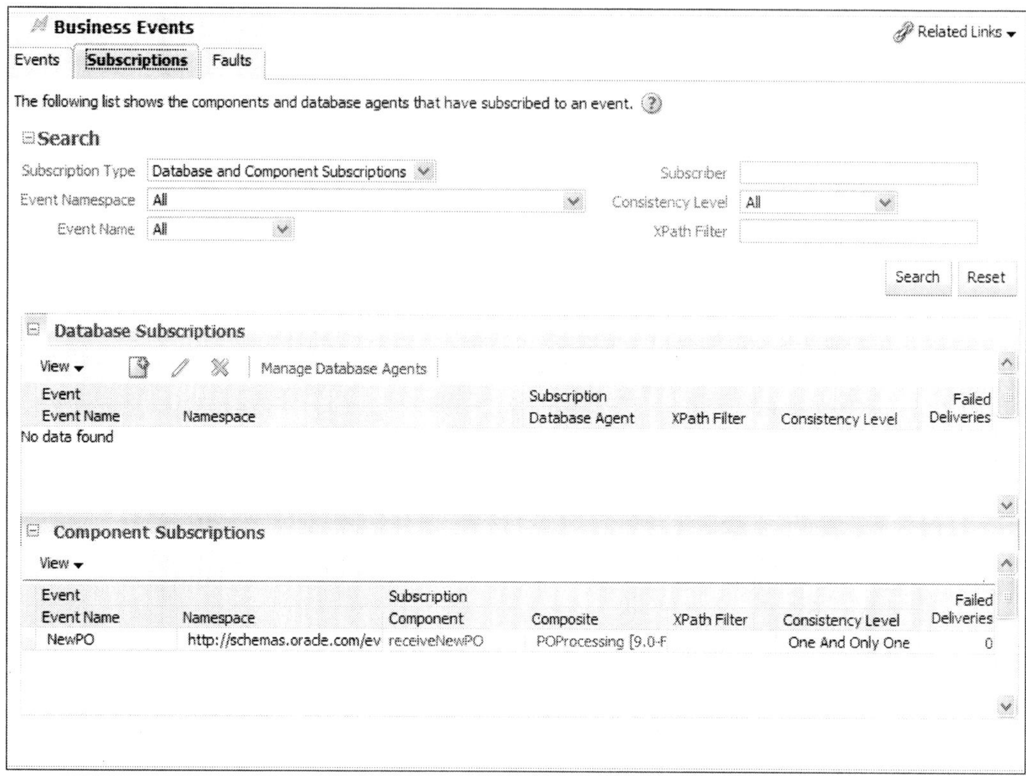

The **Faults** tab allows us to see the details of any faults generated by subscriptions when trying to receive an event.

Summary

In this chapter, we have explored how EDN differs from traditional MOM systems and also how it is used to allow seamless extension of business functionality without requiring any modification of business processes and services. We have looked at the different ways in which Mediator and BPEL may be used to publish events and taken a brief overview of the event monitoring abilities of Enterprise Manager.

9
Building Real-time Dashboards

The key objective driving service-oriented architecture is to move the IT organization closer to the business. Creation of services and their assembly into composite applications and processes is how IT can become more responsive to business. However, it is the provision of real-time business information via dashboards that really gives business the confidence that IT can add value. In this chapter, we will examine how to use **Business Activity Monitoring** (**BAM**) to provide real-time dashboards that give the business an insight into what is currently happening with their processes, not what happened yesterday or last week.

How BAM differs from traditional business intelligence

The Oracle SOA Suite stores the state of all processes in a database in documented schemas so why do we need yet another reporting tool to provide insight into our processes and services? In other words, how does BAM differ from traditional BI? In traditional BI, reports are generated and delivered either on a scheduled basis or in response to a user request. Any changes to the information will not be reflected until the next scheduled run or until a user requests the report to be rerun. BAM is an event-driven reporting tool that generates alerts and reports in real-time, based on a continuously changing data stream, some of whose data may not be in the database. For example, BAM may gather data from the currently executing state of BPEL processes to track how many orders are at each step of the order process. As events occur in services and processes, they are captured by BAM, transformed to business-friendly reports and views, and delivered and updated in real-time. Where necessary, these updated reports are delivered to users. This delivery to users can take several forms. The best known is the dashboard on user desktops that will automatically update without any need for the user to refresh the screen. There are also other means to deliver reports to the end user, including sending them via text message or e-mail.

Traditional reporting tools such as **Oracle Reports** and **Oracle Discoverer**, as well as Oracle's latest **Business Intelligence Suite**, can be used to provide some real-time reporting needs, but they do not provide the event-driven reporting that gives the business a continuously updating view of the current business situation.

Event-Driven Architecture (**EDA**) is about building business solutions around responsiveness to events. Events may be simple triggers such as a stock out event or they may be more complex triggers such as the calculations to realize that a stock out will occur in three days. An event-driven architecture will often take a number of simple events and then combine them through a complex event-processing sequence to generate complex events that could not have been raised without aggregation of several simpler events.

Oracle BAM scenarios

Oracle business activity monitoring is typically used to monitor two distinct types of real-time data. Firstly, it may be used to monitor the overall state of processes in the business. For example, it may be used to track how many auctions are currently running, how many have bids on them, and how many have been completed in the last 24 hours (or other time periods). Secondly, it may be used to track in real-time **Key Performance Indicators**, or **KPIs**. For example, it may be used to provide a real-time updating dashboard to a seller to show the current total value of all the sellers' auctions and to track this against an expected target.

In the first case, we are interested how business processes are progressing and are using BAM to identify bottlenecks and failure points within those processes. Bottlenecks can be identified by processes spending too much time in given steps in the process. Currently, BAM requires us to identify key points in a process and capture data at those key points. There is no direct linkage back to the process models in the current release of SOA Suite or Oracle's Business Process Analyst tool. BAM allows us to compute the time taken between two points in a process, such as the time between order placement and shipping, and provides real-time feedback on those times. Similarly, BAM can be used to track the percentage drop-out rate between steps in a sales process, allowing the business to take the appropriate action. For example, it can do this by tracking the number of shopping carts created, then by tracking the number of carts that continue to get a shipping cost, and finally by tracking the number of carts that result in an order being placed. For example, the business can use this real-time information to assess the impact of a free shipping offer.

In the second case, our interest is on some aggregate number, such as our total liabilities, should we win all the auctions we are bidding on. This requires us to aggregate results from many events, possibly performing some kind of calculation on them to provide us with a single KPI that gives an indication to the business of how things are going. BAM allows us to continuously update this number in real-time on a dashboard, without the need for continued polling. It also allows us to trigger alerts, perhaps through e-mail or SMS, or to notify an individual when a threshold is breached.

In both cases, reports delivered can be customized based on the individual receiving the report.

BAM architecture

It may seem odd to have a section on architecture in the middle of a chapter about how to effectively use BAM, but the key to successfully utilizing BAM is an understanding of how the different tiers relate to each other.

Logical view

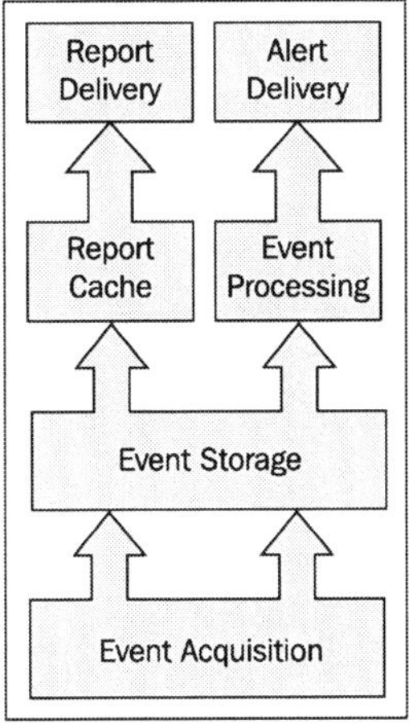

The preceding diagram represents a logical view of how BAM operates. Events are acquired from one or more sources through event acquisition and then normalized, correlated, and stored in event storage (generally a memory area in BAM that is backed up to the disk). The report cache generates reports based on events in storage and then delivers those reports, together with real-time updates through the report delivery layer. Event processing is also performed on events in storage, and when defined conditions are met, alerts will be delivered through the alert delivery service.

Physical view

To understand the physical view of the architecture of BAM better, we have divided this section into four parts.

Acquire

This logical view maps onto the physical BAM components, as shown in the following diagram. Data acquisition in the SOA Suite is primarily handled by a **BAM Adapter**. BAM can also receive events from **JMS** message queues. BAM exposes a web service interface to allow any web service-capable application to act as an event source. Finally, there is an **Oracle Data Integrator** (**ODI**) knowledge module that can be used to feed BAM. BAM has the ability to query data in databases (useful for historical comparison and reference data) but does not detect changes in that data. For complex data formats, such as master details record relationships or for other data sources, using the **ODI Knowledge Module** in conjunction with Oracle Data Integrator is recommended by Oracle.

As an alternative to using ODI, it is possible to use adapters to acquire data from multiple sources and feed it into BAM through SCA Assemblies or OSB. This is more work for the developer, but it avoids an investment in ODI if it is not used elsewhere in the business.

For high volume, real-time data capture, Oracle provides a **Complex Event Processing Engine** (**CEP**) that can batch events before forwarding them to BAM. This reduces the number of calls into BAM, allowing it to scale better.

Finally, it is possible to send messages straight from applications into BAM using a JMS queue or direct web service call. This, however, tightly couples the application and BAM and generally requires reworking the application to support BAM. Using the middleware approaches, which were shown earlier, allows us to avoid this coupling.

At the data capture level, we need to think of the data items that we can provide to feed the reports and alerts that we desire to generate. We must also consider the sources of that data and the best way to load it into BAM. If all the data we require passes through the composite engine, then we can use the BAM adapter within SOA Suite to capture our BAM data. If there is some data that is not visible through the composites, then we need to consider the other mechanisms discussed earlier, such as using ODI, creating new composites to capture the data, or directly wiring the sources of the data to BAM.

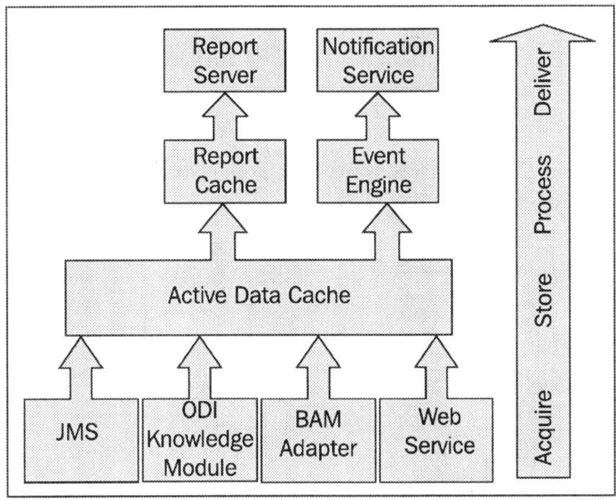

Store

Once the data is captured, it is stored in a normalized form in memory in a component called the **Active Data Cache** (**ADC**). This storage facility has the ability to do simple correlation based on fields within the data, and multiple data items received from the acquisition layer may update just a single object in the data cache. For example, the state of a given BPEL process instance may be represented by a single object in the ADC and all updates to that process state will just update that single data item, rather than creating multiple data items. The ADC contents are also stored in the BAM data store to avoid losing data across restarts and to avoid running out of memory.

Process

Reports are run-based on user demand. Once a report is run, it will update the user's screen on a real-time basis. Where multiple users are accessing the same report, only one instance of the report is maintained by the report server. As events are captured and stored in real-time, the report engine will continuously monitor them for any changes that need to be made to the reports that are currently active. When changes are detected that impact active reports, the appropriate report will be updated in memory and the updates are sent to the user's screen.

In addition to the event processing required to correctly insert and update items in the ADC, there is also a requirement to monitor items in the ADC for events that require some sort of action to be taken. This is the job of the event processor. This will monitor data in the ADC to see if registered thresholds on values have been exceeded or if certain timeouts have expired. The event processor will often need to perform calculations across multiple data items to do this.

This monitoring of events in the event processor is accomplished through BAM rules, which are used to trigger BAM alerts. A BAM rule may be to monitor the percentage of aborted sales processes in the last 30 minutes and to raise an alert when the percentage exceeds a threshold value.

Deliver

Delivery of reports takes place in two ways. First, users can view reports on their desktop by selecting views within BAM. These reports are delivered as HTML pages within a browser and are updated whenever the underlying data used in the report changes. The other approach is that reports are sent out as a result of alerts being raised by the Event Processing Engine. In this latter case, the report may be delivered by e-mail, SMS, or voice messaging using the notifications service. A final option available for these alerts is to invoke a web service to take some sort of automated action.

Closing the Loop

While monitoring what is happening is all very laudable, it is only beneficial if we actually do something about what we are monitoring. BAM not only provides the real-time monitoring ability very well, but it also provides the facility to invoke other services to respond to undesirable events such as stock outs. The ability to invoke external services is crucial to the concept of a closed loop control environment where, as a result of monitoring, we are able to reach back into the processes and either alter their execution or start new ones. For example, when a stock out or low stock event is raised, rather than just notifying a manager about the stock out, the message centre could invoke a web service requesting a supplier to send more stock to replenish inventory. Placing this kind of feedback mechanism in BAM allows us trigger events across multiple applications and locations in a way that may not be possible within a single application or process, because they do not have sufficient visibility. For example, in response to a stock out, we may be monitoring stock levels in independent systems, and based on stock levels elsewhere, may redirect stock from one location to another rather than requesting our supplier to provide more stock. By invoking web services, we avoid the need for manual intervention in responding to these alerts.

Another way of accessing BAM reports is through Application Development Framework (ADF is Oracle's UI development framework) BAM data controls. These controls can be used on ADF pages to provide custom applications and portals with access to BAM data. These controls will update in real-time on a user desktop in the same way as reports retrieved directly from BAM.

Steps in using BAM

The following steps are used in creating BAM reports:

1. Decide what reports are desired
2. Decide what data is required to provide those reports
3. Define suitable data objects
4. Capture events to populate the data objects
5. Create reports from the data objects

The first two steps are paper-based exercises to define the requirements. The remaining steps are the creation of suitable artifacts in BAM to support the desired business reports, defined in step 1.

User interface

Development in Oracle BAM is done through a web-based user interface.

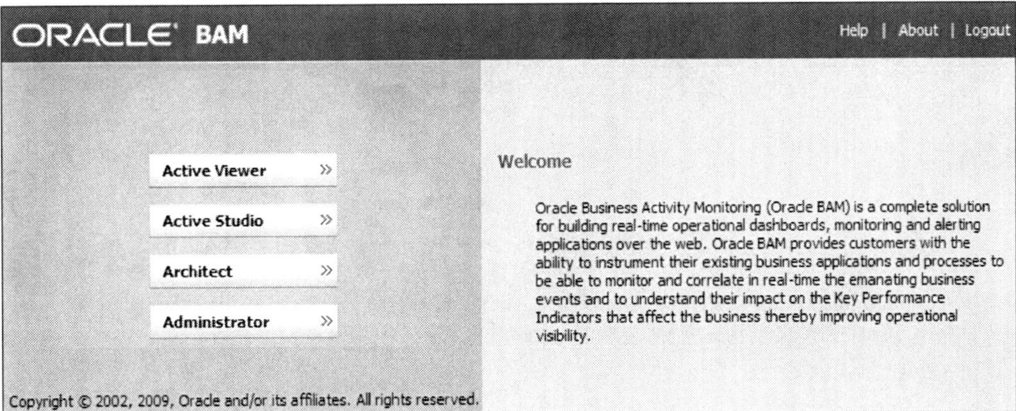

This user interface gives access to four different applications that allow you to interact with different parts of BAM:

- **Active Viewer**: For giving access to reports, this relates to the deliver stage for user-requested reports.
- **Active Studio:** For building reports, this relates to the 'process' stage for creating reports.
- **Architect:** For setting up both inbound and outbound events. Data elements are defined here, as are data sources. Alerts are also configured here. This covers setting up acquire and store stages as well as the deliver stage for alerts.
- **Administrator**: For managing users and roles as well as defining the types of message sources.

We will not examine the applications individually, but we will take a task-focused look at how to use them as a part of providing some specific reports.

Monitoring process state

Now that we have examined how BAM is constructed, let us use this knowledge to construct some simple dashboards that track the state of a business process. We will create a simple version of an auction process. The process is shown as follows:

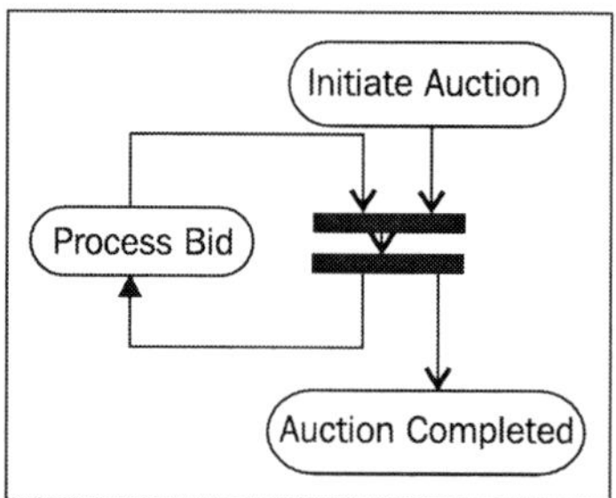

An auction is started, then bids are placed until the time runs out, at which point, the auction is completed. This is modeled in BPEL. This process has three distinct states. They are as follows:

1. Started
2. Bid received
3. Completed

Defining reports and data required

We are interested in the number of auctions in each state as well as the total value of auctions in progress. This leads us to the following reporting requirements:

- Display current number of auctions in each state
- Display value of all auctions in each state
- Allow filtering of reports by bidder and seller
- Allow filtering of reports by auction end date

These reports will require the following data:

- Auction identifier, so that we can correlate status changes back to a particular auction
- Auction state, so that we can track the number of auctions in each state
- Current highest bid, so that we can calculate the worth of all auctions
- Current highest bidder, so that we can filter reports by a particular bidder
- Seller, so that we can filter reports by a particular seller
- Auction end date, so that we can filter auctions by completion date

Having completed our analysis, we can proceed to define our data objects, capture events, and build our reports.

We will follow a middle-out approach to building our dashboard. We will take the following steps:

1. Define our data within the Active Data Cache
2. Create sensors in BPEL and map to data in the ADC
3. Create suitable reports
4. Run the reports

Defining data objects

Data in BAM is stored in data objects. Individual data objects contain the information that is reported in BAM dashboards and may be updated by multiple events. Generally, BAM will report against aggregations of objects, but there is also the ability for reports to drill down into individual data objects.

Before defining our data objects, let's group them into an auction folder so that they are easy to find. To do this, we use the **BAM Architect** application, and select **Data Objects**, which gives us the following screenshot:

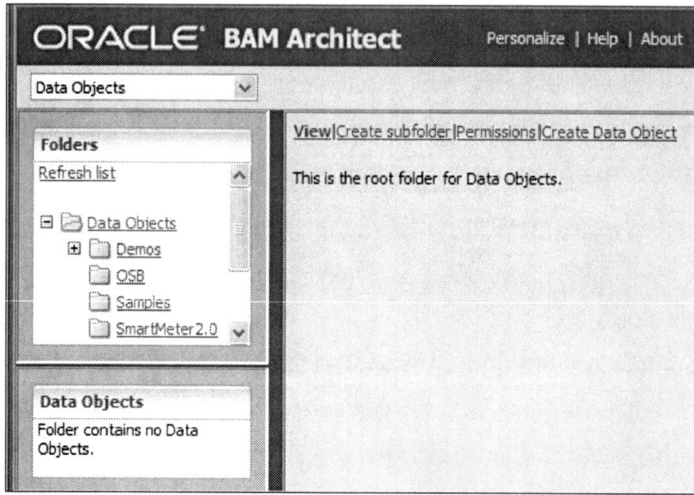

We select **Create subfolder** to create the folder and give it a name (**Auction**).

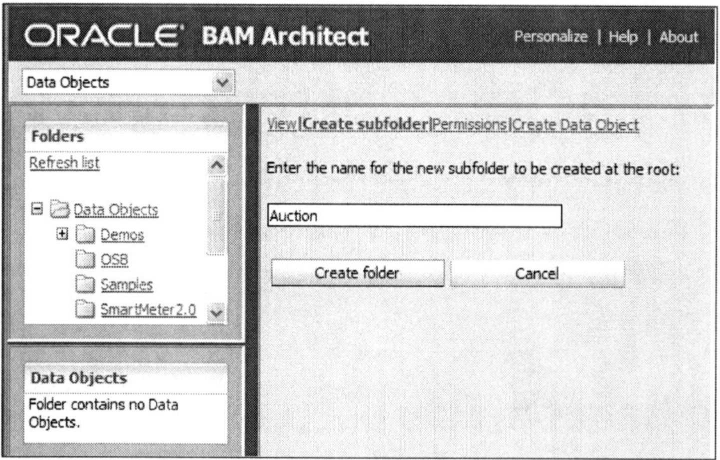

We then click on **Create folder** to actually create the folder, and we get a confirmation message to tell us that it has been created. Notice that once created, the folder also appears in the **Folders** window on the left-hand side of the screen.

Now that we have our folder, we can create a data object. Again, we select **Data Objects** from the drop-down list. To define the data objects that are to be stored in our Active Data Cache, we open the **Auction** folder, if it is not already open, and select **Create Data Object**. If we don't select the **Auction** folder, then we pick it later when filling in the details of the data object.

We need to give our object a unique name within the folder and optionally provide it with a tip text that helps explain what the object does when the mouse is moved over it in object listings. Having named our object, we can now create the data fields by selecting **Add a field**. When adding fields, we need to provide a name and type as well as indicating if they must contain data; the default **Nullable** does not require a field to be populated. We may also optionally indicate if a field should be publically available for display and whether it should have any tool tip text.

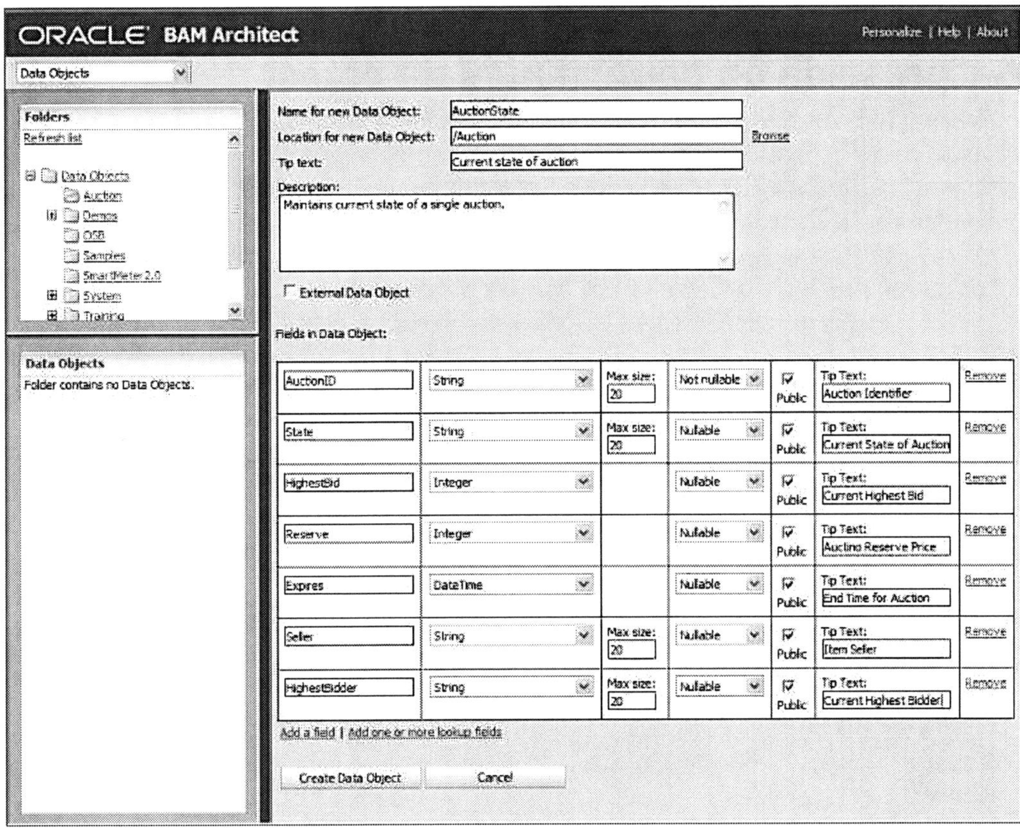

Once all the data fields have been defined, we can click **Create Data Object** to actually create the object as we have defined it. We are then presented with a confirmation screen that the object has been created.

Grouping data into hierarchies

When creating a data object, it is possible to specify "Dimensions" for the object. A dimension is based on one or more fields within the object. A given field can only participate in one dimension. This gives the ability to automatically group the object by the fields in the given dimension. If multiple fields are selected for a single dimension, then they can be layered into a hierarchy; for example, to allow analysis by country, region, and city. In this case, all three elements would be selected into a single dimension, perhaps called geography. Within geography, a hierarchy could be set up with country at the top, region next, and finally city at the bottom, allowing drill down to occur in views. Just as a data object can have multiple dimensions, a dimension can also have multiple hierarchies.

A digression on populating data object fields

In the previous discussion, we mentioned the **Nullable** attribute that can be attached to fields. This is very important as we do not expect to populate all or even most of the fields in a data object one at a time. Failing to initialize a field will generate an error unless it is **Nullable**. Do not confuse data objects with the low-level events that are used to populate them. Data objects in BAM do not have a one-to-one correspondence with the low-level events that populate them. In our auction example, there will be just one auction object for every auction. However, there will be at least two, and usually more, messages for every auction; one message for the auction starting, another for the auction completing, and additional messages for each bid received. These messages will all populate, or in some cases overwrite, different parts of the auction data object. The table shows how the three messages populate different parts of the data object.

Message	Auction ID	State	Highest Bid	Reserve	Expires	Seller	Highest Bidder
Auction Started	Inserted	Inserted	Inserted	Inserted	Inserted	Inserted	
Bid Received		Updated	Updated				Updated
Auction Finished		Updated					

Instrumenting BPEL and SCA

Having defined the data we wish to capture in BAM, we now need to make our auction process generate appropriate events. We can instrument BPEL and SCA by making explicit calls to a BAM adapter as we would to any other adapter. Within BPEL, we may also take advantage of the sensor framework to raise BAM events from within an activity.

Sensors versus explicit calls

Explicit calls are available within both SCA and BPEL. Within BPEL, they make it more obvious where the BAM events are being generated. BPEL sensors, however, provide the ability to generate events at a finer grained level than explicit calls. For example, a BAM sensor in a BPEL activity could be set to fire not just on activation and completion (which could be captured by an explicit call just before and after the event), but also on events that are harder to catch with an explicit invoke, such as faults and compensation. Finally, sensors can fire on retry events that are impossible to capture in any other way. BAM sensors do not use partner links or references, but refer to the adapter JNDI location directly.

Sensors are not part of the normal BPEL executable flow. They can be thought of as event generators. They are attached to almost any kind of activity in BPEL, including partner link operations (invoke, receive, reply) and assigns. They can also be attached to variables and will fire whenever the variable is modified.

Invoking the BAM adapter as a regular service

When using the BAM adapter, we first need to configure an adapter instance.

Creating a BAM adapter

Let us start by creating a new BAM adapter. We begin by creating a new **BAM Connection** from the **Connection** section of the **New Gallery** (**File | New**, and then select **Connection** under **General**).

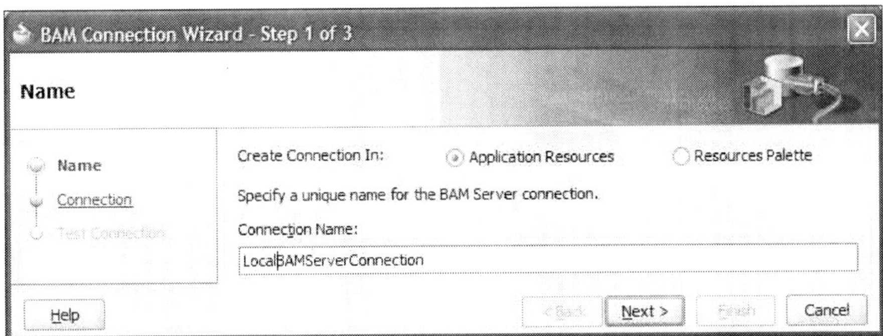

We provide a name for the connection and identify if we wish it to be local to this application or available to all applications. We then define the connection characteristics of hostnames and port numbers for the Active Data Cache (**BAM Server Host**) and web applications (**Web Server**). Generally, these will be the same hostname and port number. We also provide a username and password for the BAM server. Finally, we can test our connection to ensure that it works.

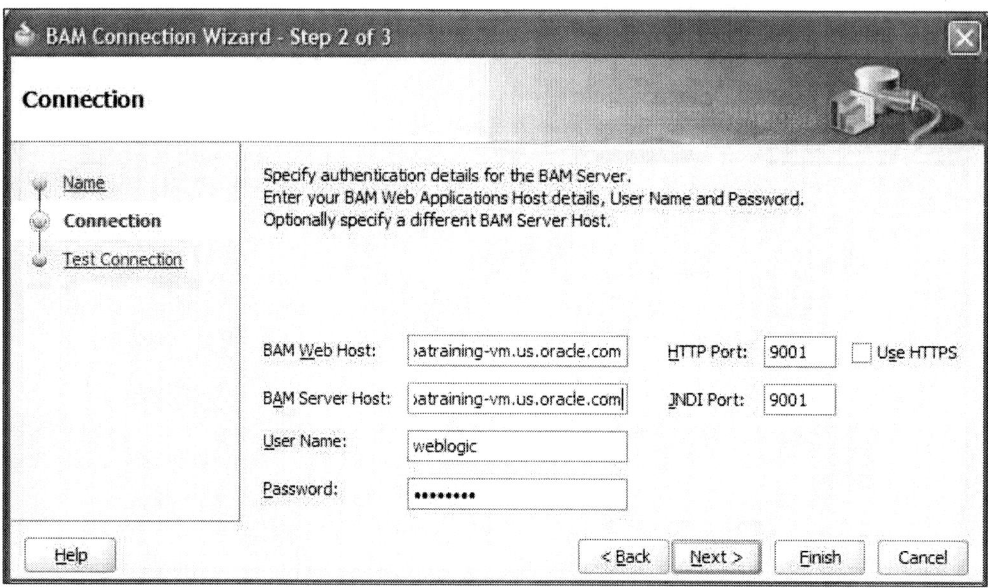

Having created our connection, we can now create a BAM partner link for use in BPEL or SCA. We do this in the same way as we create any other adapter-based link. We can drag a **BAM Adapter** from the **Service Adapters** section of the **Component Palette** onto either the **External References** section of an SCA or the **Partner Links** section of a BPEL process. This will launch the **Adapter Configuration Wizard**. After providing a name for our service, we are asked to select a **BAM Data Object** and determine the **Operation** to perform on the object. We must also provide an **Operation Name** and determine the batching behavior.

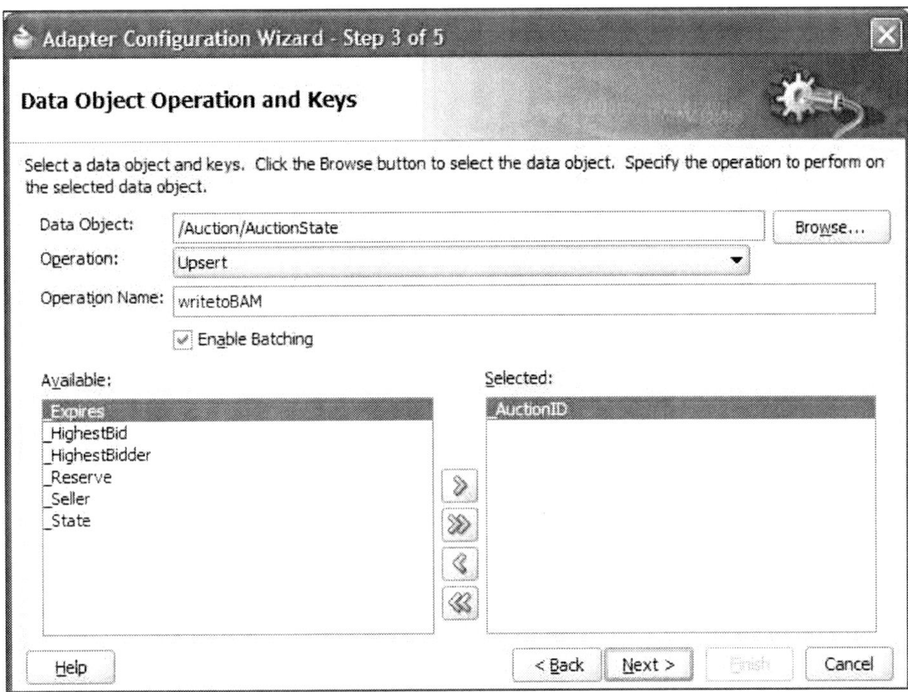

The **Data Object** may be selected directly from the BAM server by using the **Browse...** button to pop up the **BAM Data Object Chooser** dialog box, which allows selection of the correct data object.

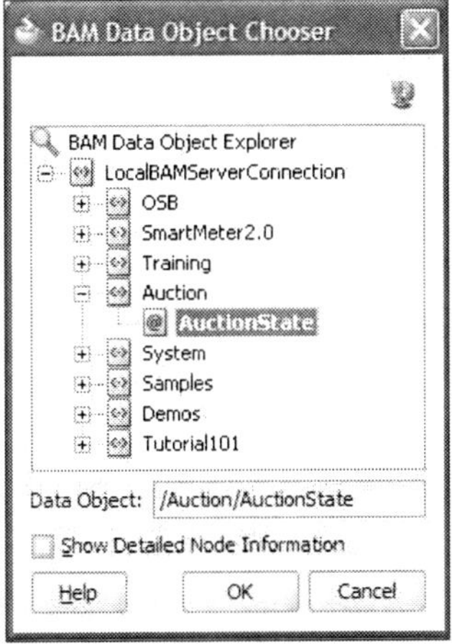

Depending on the operation, we may need to provide a key to locate the correct data object instance. **Update**, **Upsert**, and **Delete** all require a key, only **Insert** does not.

Upsert the universal update mechanism

When using upsert, if the key already exists then that object is updated. If the object does not exist, then it is inserted. This enables upsert to cover both insert and update operations and is generally the most useful operation to perform on BAM objects, as it requires only one BAM adapter instance to provide two different operations.

Having identified the update characteristics of our adapter, we now must map it onto a resource in the underlying application server by providing the JNDI location of the BAM connection. Once this is completed, we can complete the wizard and finish creating our BAM adapter.

Invoking the BAM adapter

Invoking the BAM adapter is the same as invoking any other adapter from BPEL or the Mediator. The BAM adapter provides an interface to allow a collection of data objects to be submitted at the same time, each field in the data object is represented by an XML element in the interface to the adapter. XSLT or copy operations may be used to populate the fields of the input variable.

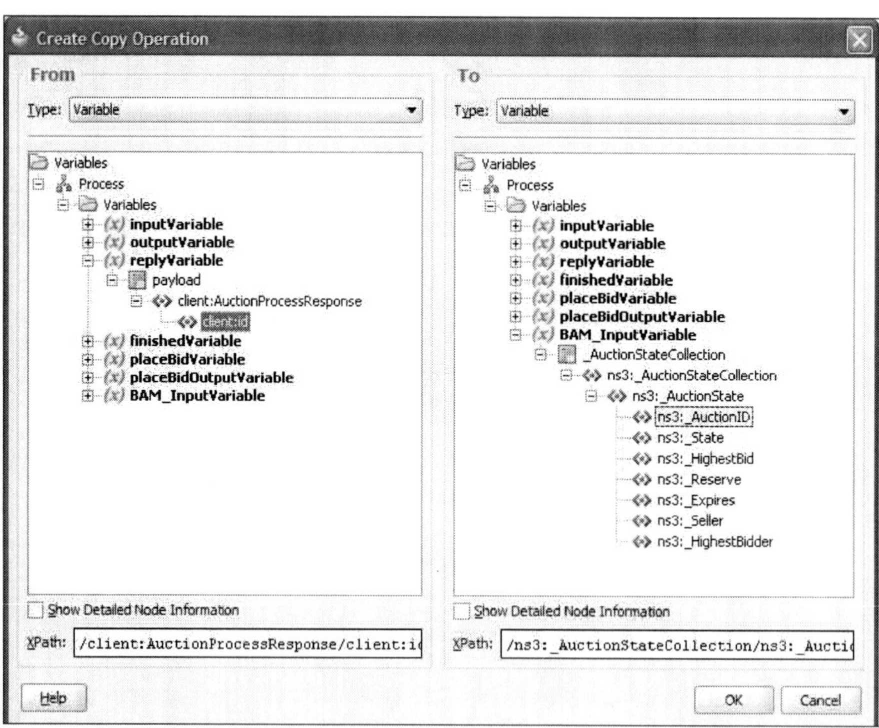

Invoking the BAM adapter through BPEL sensors

In this section, we will examine how to use BPEL sensors to invoke the BAM adapter.

Within JDeveloper, there are several modes in which we can view the BPEL process. On the right-hand side of the title bar for the BPEL editor, there is a drop-down list that allows us to select the viewing and editing mode.

The drop-down list shows us the three modes available:

- **BPEL**: Lets us edit and view the BPEL activities
- **Monitor:** Lets us edit and view sensor annotations to the BPEL process
- **BPA**: Is only used with the Oracle BPA suite.

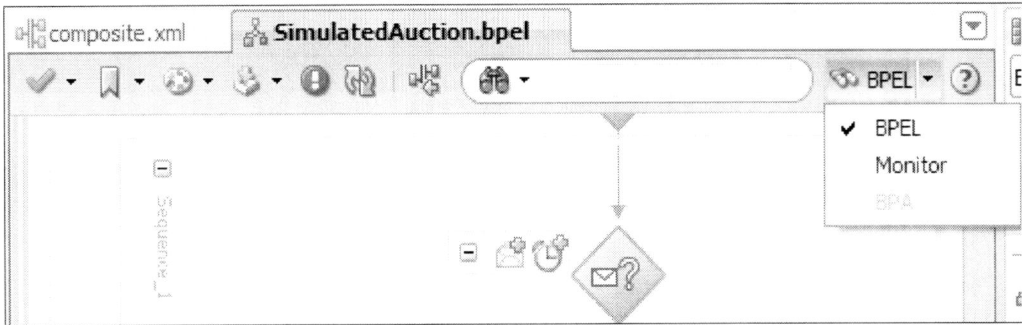

After choosing **Monitor,** we can right-click on a BPEL activity to start creating the sensor. This brings up a pop-up menu from which we can select the **Create | Sensor** item. Note that there are also options to create other monitoring items.

- **Counter:** Creates a count of the number of times an activity has been reached
- **Business Indicator:** Evaluates an XPath expression when an activity has been reached
- **Interval:** Calculates the elapsed time between two activities

- **Sensor**: Creates a BAM sensor

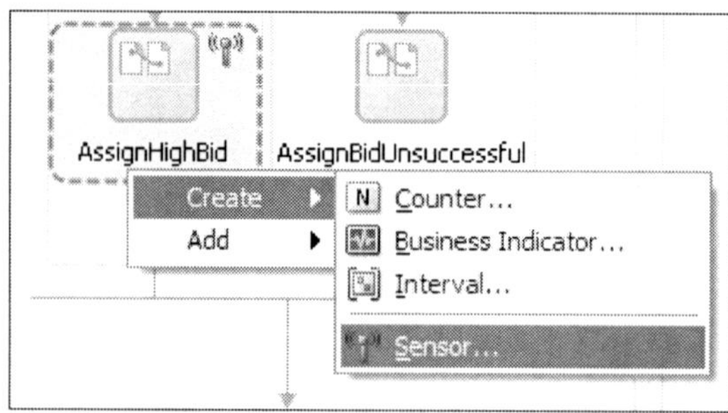

When creating a new sensor we need to provide it with a name and indicate when it should fire. The options are as follows:

- **Activation**: When the activity is started
- **Completion**: When the activity is completed
- **Fault**: When the activity raises a fault
- **Compensation**: When compensation is invoked on a surrounding scope
- **Retry**: When the activity is retried, such as retrying an invoke
- **All**: All of the above

We must also provide a variable that contains the data we want to be part of the sensor-generated event. This variable must be an element variable, not a simple type or a message type.

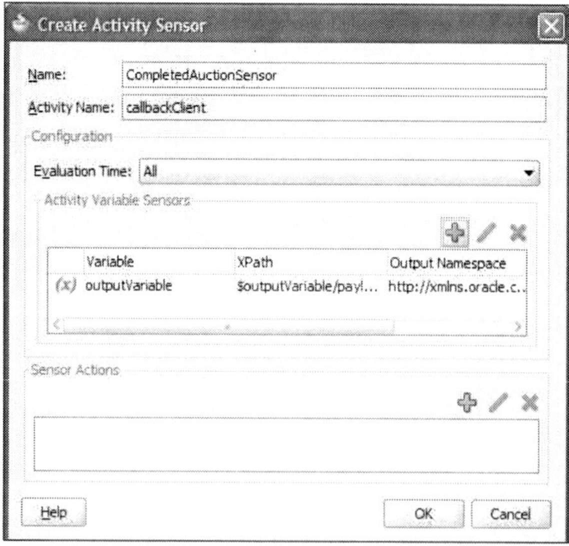

Sensors can have a number of sensor actions associated with them. Sensor actions can be thought of as the targets for the sensor event. One option is to send the events into the BPEL repository, which is useful for testing purposes. Another option is to send them to BAM. Other options revolve around JMS Queues and Topics.

Unfortunately, we cannot add a BAM sensor from the **Create Activity Sensor** dialog. They can only be created by using the structure pane for the BPEL process. To do this, we navigate to **Sensor Actions** in the structure pane, right-click, and select **Bam Sensor Action**. This brings up the **Create Sensor Action** dialog.

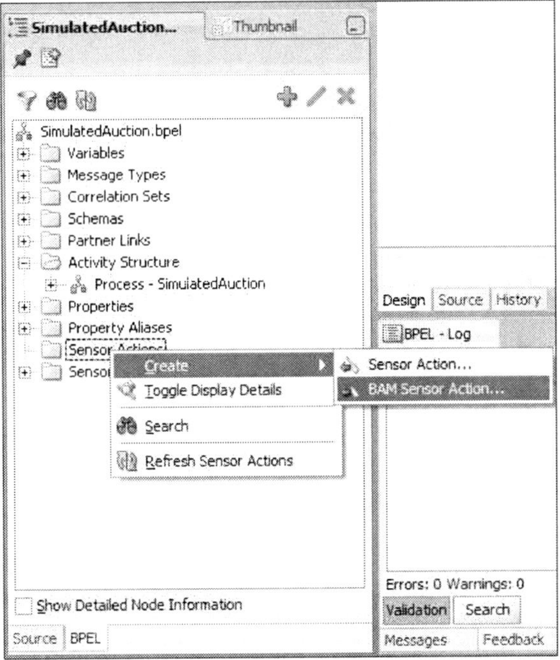

We provide a name for the sensor action and then select an eligible sensor from the drop-down list. There is a one-to-one relationship between BAM sensor sections and sensors. This is not the case for other types of sensors. The reason for the one-to-one relationship is that BAM sensor actions transform the variable associated with the action into the relevant fields for the BAM data object. This is done through an XSLT transform.

Having selected our sensor, we then click the torch next to the **Data Object** so that we can choose the BAM data object that we will map the sensor variable onto.

Having selected the BAM data object, we need to select the operation to be performed on the data object. The drop-down list gives us four options:

- **Insert**
- **Update**
- **Delete**
- **Upsert**

The **Insert** operation creates a new instance of the BAM data object. This may result in multiple data objects having the same field values.

The **Insert** operation does not use a key as it always creates a new data object. The remaining three operations require a key because they may operate on an existing data object. The key must uniquely identify a data object and may consist of one or more data object fields.

The **Update** operation will update an existing data object, overwriting some or all of the fields, as desired. If the object cannot be found from the key, then no data is updated in the ADC.

The **Delete** operation will remove a data object from the ADC. If the key does not identify an object, then no object will be deleted.

The **Upsert** operation behaves as an update operation if the key does identify an existing data object in the ADC. If the key does not identify an existing object in the ADC, then it behaves as an **Insert** operation.

Generally, we use the **Insert** operation when we know we are creating an object for the first time, and we use the **Update** operation when we know that the object already exists. We use the **Upsert** operation when we are unsure if an object exists.

For example, we may use an **Insert** operation to create an instance of a process status object and then use an update to change the status value of the object as the process progresses. When tracking process state, it is a good idea to use the process instance identifier as a key field in the data object.

Having chosen our operation, an **Insert** operation for example, we then need to map the fields in the sensor variable defined in BPEL to the BAM data object. We do this by creating a new XSLT transformation by clicking the green cross next to the **Map File** field.

Within the XSLT transformation editor, we can map the BPEL variable to the BAM data object. In addition to the variable itself, there is a host of other information available to us in the BPEL variable source document. This can be categorized as follows:

- Header Information
    - This relates to the process instance and the specific sensor that is firing
- Payload
    - This contains not only the sensor variable contents but also information about the activity and any fault associated with it

Useful data includes the instance ID of the process and also the time the sensor fired as well as the elapsed times for actions. Once we have wired up the variable data, we can save the transform file.

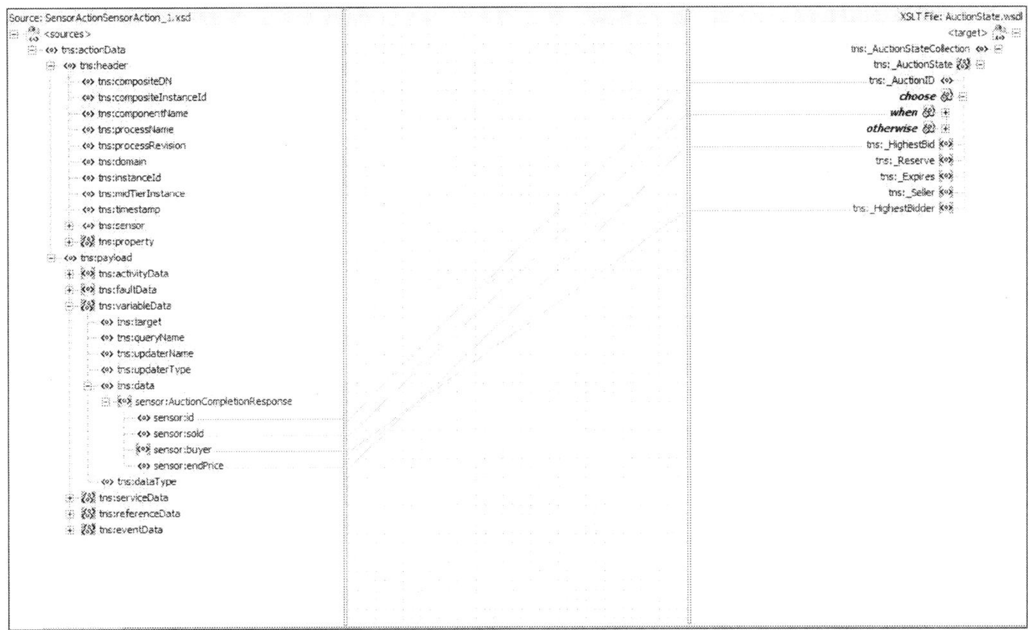

When we have finished creating the sensor action, we can deploy it to the BPEL server and events will be fired to populate the BAM active data cache.

Testing the events

After creating our BAM sensors, we can test them by executing a process in BPEL and ensuring that the events appear in the Active Data Cache. We can find the actual event data by selecting the object in BAM architect and then clicking **Contents**, which will then list the actual data object instances.

Creating a simple dashboard

Now that our sensors are in place and working, we can use the BAM Active Studio application to create a report based on the sensor information. To help organize our reports, it is possible to create folders to hold reports in a similar fashion to the way we created folders to hold data objects.

Let us create a report that shows the status of auctions in the system and also shows the value of all auctions currently open. We will start by creating the report itself. The report is just a holder for views, and we create it by selecting the **Create A New Report** button.

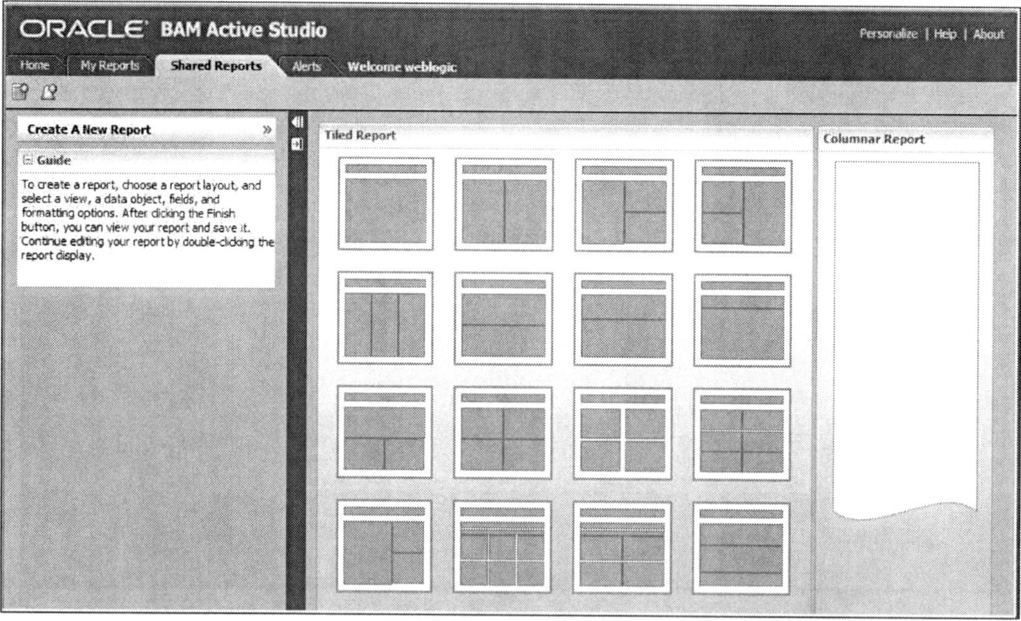

We can select a report that has the right number of panes for the number of views we want. Note that it is possible to change the number of panes on the report, so if we get it wrong, it does not matter. For now, we will choose a simple split-screen report with two panes, one above the other.

We can provide a title for a report by editing the title section directly. Having updated the title, we can then proceed to create the views.

Monitoring process status

For our first view, let us monitor how many auctions are at particular states. We are interested in a count of the number of auctions with a given state value. This would be well represented with a histogram style chart, so we select a 3D bar chart from the view pane.

A wizard appears at the bottom of the screen, which gives us the opportunity to select a data object to be used as the basis of the view. We navigate to the **Auction** folder and select the **AuctionState** object. Note that it is possible to have multiple data objects in a view, but additional data objects are added later.

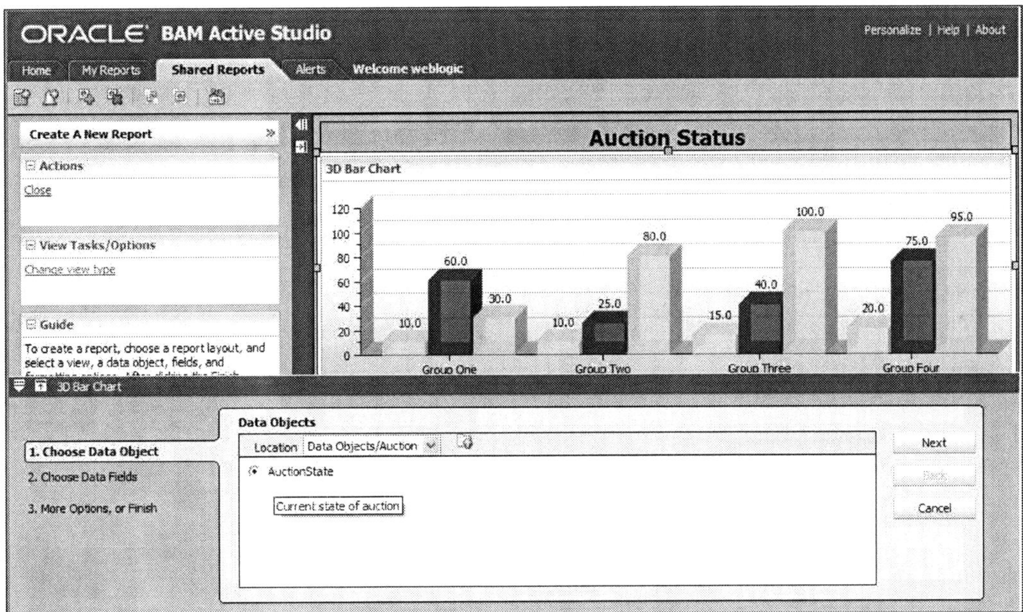

Having selected the data object, we select the fields from the data object that we will need in order to present the current state an auction is in. We choose the state field as a value we want to use in our report by selecting it from the **Chart Values** column. We can choose to group the data by particular fields, in this case, the state of the auction. By default, date and string fields can be grouped, but by selecting **Include Value Fields**, it is possible to group by any field by selecting it in the **Group By** column. By selecting a summary function (**Count**) for our state field, we can count the number of auctions in a given state.

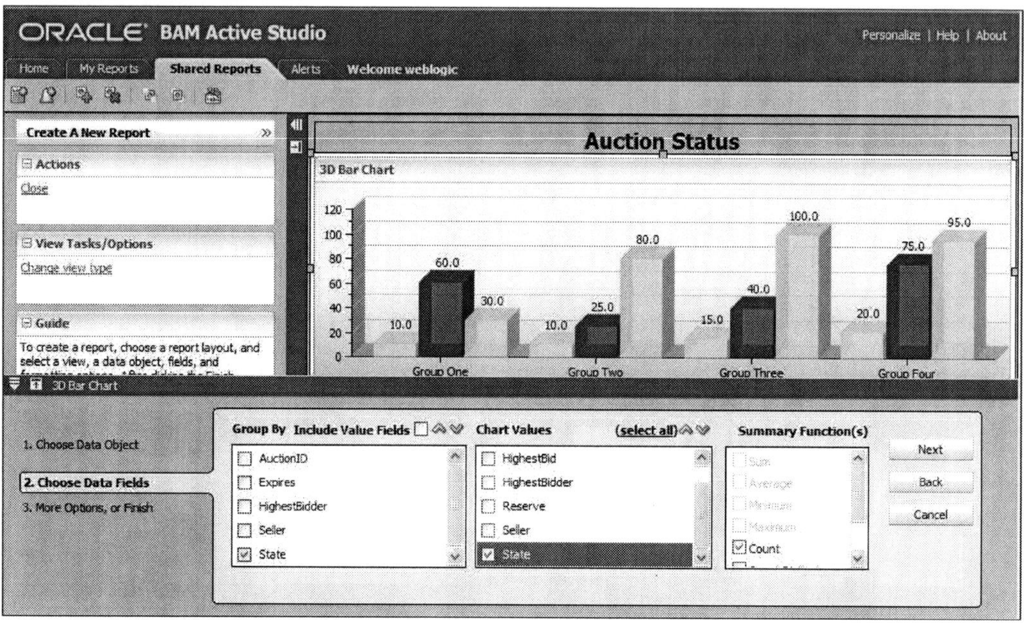

Finally, the wizard gives us the opportunity to further modify the view by:

- Creating a filter to restrict the range of data objects included in the view
- Adding additional calculated fields to the view
- Adding additional data objects to the view to be displayed alongside the existing data object
- Changing the visual properties of the view

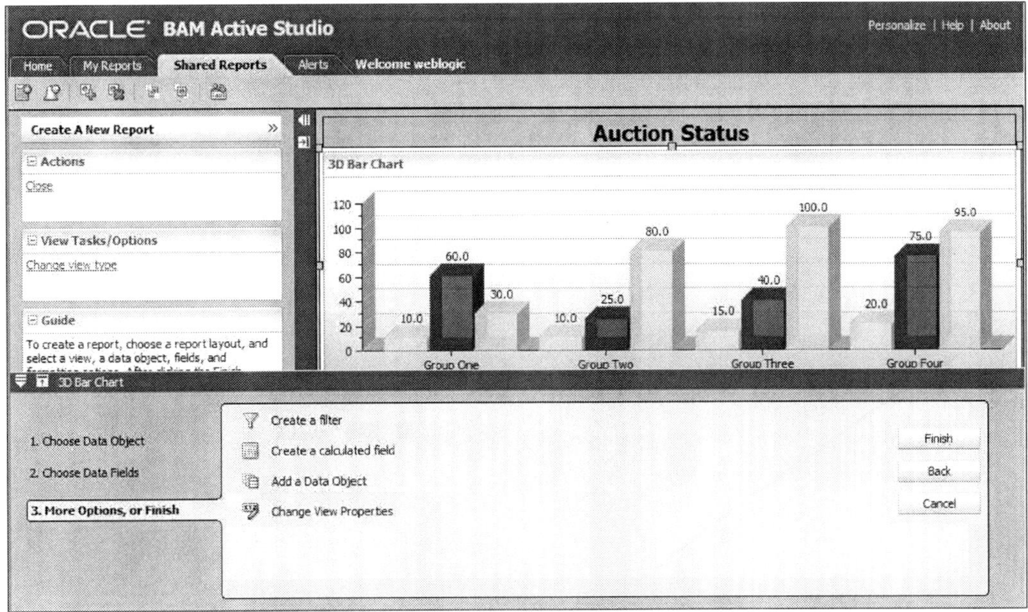

We will create a filter to restrict the display to those processes that are either currently running or have completed in the last seven days. To do this, after selecting the filter link, add a new entry to the filter.

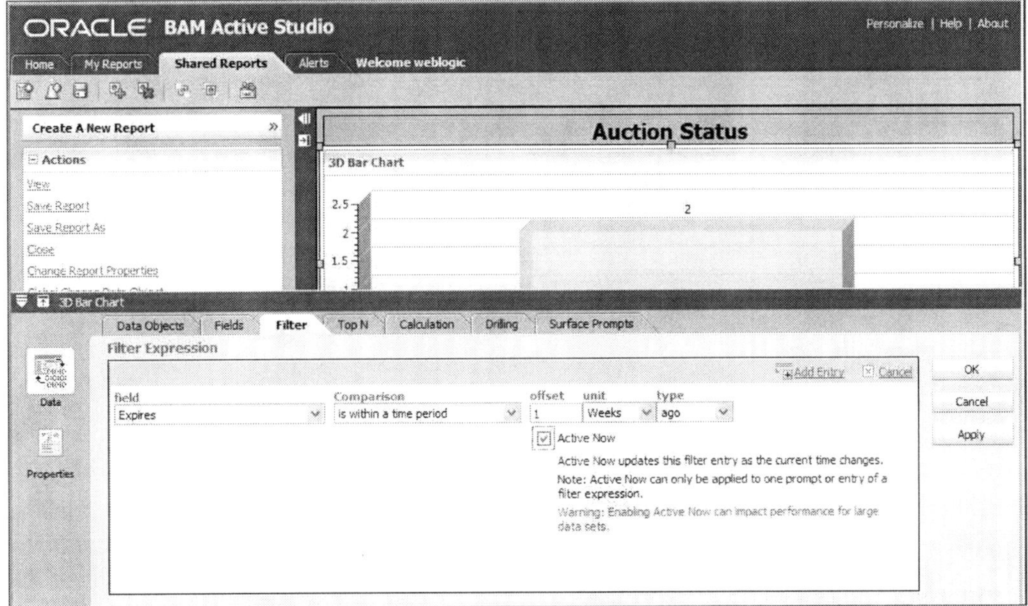

We can now select a date field (**Expires**) and select that we want to include any data object whose **Expires** field **is within a time period** of one week ago. This will prevent us from having an ever increasing number of completed processes. When the filter expression is completed, we click **Update Entry** to add the entry to the filter.

> **Update Entry link**
>
> Always remember to click the **Update Entry** or **Add Entry** link after making changes in your filter expressions. Only after clicking this can you select **OK** to complete your changes, otherwise your changes will be lost.

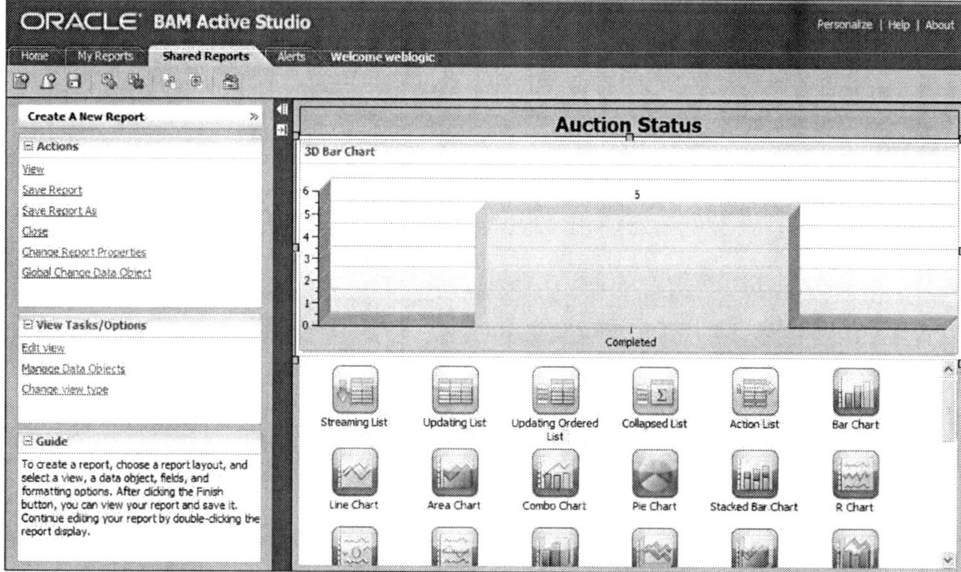

When we have clicked **Update Entry**, we can review the filter and select **Apply**. This will update the underlying view and we can verify that the data is as we expect it to look.

Monitoring KPIs

In the previous section, we looked at monitoring the state of a process. In this section, we will use BAM to give a real-time view of our KPIs. For example, we may be interested in monitoring the current value of all open auctions. This can be done by creating a view, for example, using a dial gauge. The gauge will give us a measure of a value in the context of acceptable and unacceptable bounds. Creating the view is done in a similar fashion as done previously, and again, we may make use of filters to restrict the range of data objects that are included in the view.

When we have completed the views in our report and saved the report, we may view the report through the active viewer application and watch the values change in real-time.

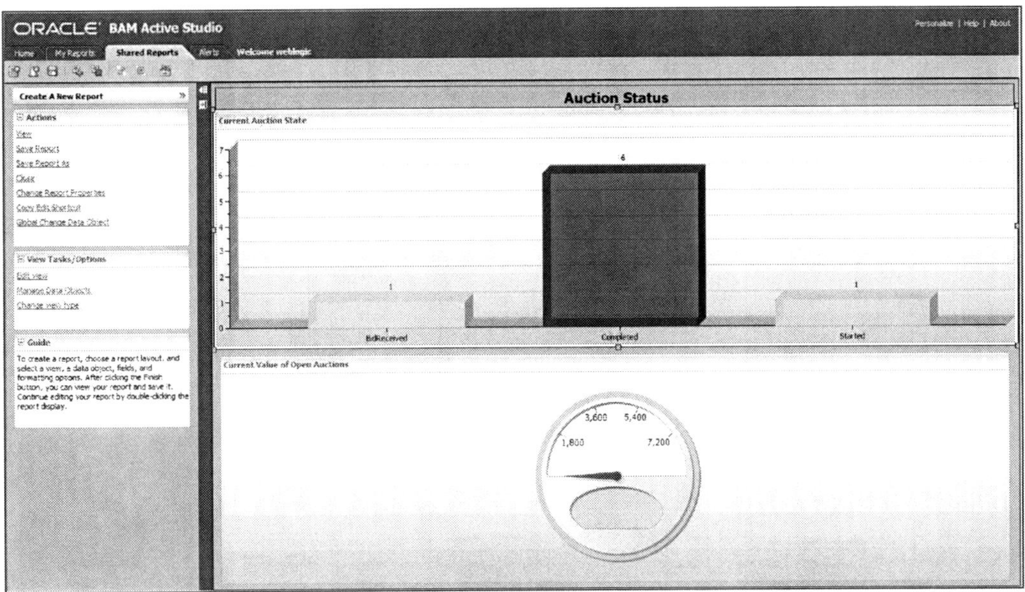

Note that we can drill down into the reports to gain additional information. This only gives a list of individual data objects with the same values displayed as on the top level view. To gain more control over drill down, it is necessary to use the **Drilling** tab in the view editor to specify the drill-down parameters.

Summary

In this chapter, we have explored how business activity monitoring differs from and is complementary to more traditional business intelligence solutions such as Oracle Reports and Business Objects. We have explored how BAM can allow the business to monitor the state of business targets and Key Performance Indicators, such as the current most popular products in a retail environment or the current time taken to serve customers in a service environment. We also looked at how BAM can be used to allow the business to monitor the current state of processes, both in aggregate and also drilling down to individual process instances.

Part 2

Putting it All Together

oBay Introduction

Designing the Service Contract

Building Entity Services Using Service Data Objects (SDOs)

Building Validation into Services

Error Handling

Advanced SOA Suite Architecture

Message Interaction Patterns

Workflow Patterns

Using Business Rules to Implement Services

10
oBay Introduction

By now, you should have a good initial understanding of all the key components that make up the Oracle SOA Suite. Typically we find that once someone has an initial grasp of the various components, one of the next questions we get is:

> "*What is the best way to combine/use all of these different components to implement a real world SOA solution?*"

Answering this question is very much the focus of this section. To do this, we have built a complete, albeit, relatively small SOA solution designed for an online auction site for a fictional company called **oBay** (the o stands for Oracle).

Each chapter in this section tackles specific areas that need to be considered when developing an SOA-based solution, such as the design of the service contract, validation, error handling, message interaction patterns, and so on. To highlight and demonstrate key design considerations, each chapter uses examples based on key parts of the oBay application to illustrate what it is talking about.

This chapter introduces oBay and details the overall business requirements of the online auction site. Before looking at the overall design of the oBay application, we take a step back and consider some of the key goals of a SOA-based approach, such as interoperability, reusability, and agility, and what we mean by that.

Next, we present you with our outline of a typical SOA Architecture, and in particular, pay attention to how we might want to layer our services, as well as highlight some of the key design considerations behind this. Only when we have our blueprint for SOA do we apply it to the business requirements of oBay and present you with its overall architecture.

oBay requirements

oBay is a new start-up company that provides a web-based auction site for users to buy and sell items online.

User registration

Before someone can either sell or bid on items, they must first register as a user on oBay. When registering, a user will be required to provide the following information:

- Name (First Name and Last Name)
- Date of Birth
- Address (Line 1, Line 2, City, State, Zip, Country)
- E-mail Address
- User ID and Password
- Credit Card (Card Type, Number, Expiry Date)

They will also be required to accept oBay's standard terms and conditions. As part of the registration process, the system will perform the following checks:

- That the User ID is not already in use
- That the user is at least 18 years of age
- The e-mail address will be validated by sending the user a confirmation e-mail to the supplied address, with a link for them to activate their account
- The Credit Card details provided are valid

User login

Once a user has successfully registered and activated their account, they can log into oBay. This will take them to their home page, from where they can choose to start selling or bidding on items.

Selling items

When a user goes to their seller's page, it will list all the items they have put up for auction. By default, it will be filtered to show just those items where the auction is still in progress, or the sale has yet to complete (for example, still awaiting payment or shipping).

The user can further refine this filter in a number of ways, for example, to show all listings in a particular state (such as awaiting payment) or all listings regardless of state. The filter can be further qualified by specifying a time period, for example, just show me all listings for the last day, week, month, 90 days, 180 days, or year.

From here, they can choose to view the details of any of these items, as well as update the status of an item where the sale is still in process (for example, Payment Received, Shipped, and so on) In addition, the user may choose to list a new item or view the status of their account.

List a new item

Once a user has successfully registered with oBay, they are ready to start selling. The first step is to create a listing for the item that they want to sell. To do this, the user will need to enter the following details about the item:

- Category and subcategory (from a pre-defined list of values)
- Title and description
- Condition (new or used)
- Confirm accepted payment methods (for example, check, cash, credit card, or bank transfer)
- Starting price, plus an optional reserve price
- Auction duration, which can be 1, 3, 7, or 10 days
- An optional start time; if not specified, this defaults to an immediate start
- Postage description and cost

Once submitted, the system will perform a number of validations on the listing, including:

- Values are specified for all mandatory fields
- The starting price is positive and less than the reserve price (if specified)
- The reserve price is above a pre-determined amount (for example, $50)
- The start time, if specified, is in the future

The final part of the validation is to check whether the item being listed meets the criteria for what constitutes an acceptable item, for example, the item isn't one that is prohibited by law. Ideally, the system is required to do an initial automated check on the listing to identify potentially suspect items. If an item is flagged as suspect, then a task will need to be created for an oBay administrator to check whether the item is suitable for sale.

Whether an item is acceptable is not always black and white. The solution will need to allow for questionable items to be submitted to a panel who will vote on whether to accept it or not (assuming there is a majority vote, the item will be deemed acceptable).

For valid non-questionable items, the system will calculate the listing fee and return this to the user, who can then confirm whether they wish to proceed with the listing or not. Upon confirmation, the item will be listed immediately, unless a start time has been specified, in which case the item will be held in a queue until the specified start time.

Listing fees are calculated according to the starting price (or **reserve price**, if specified), as shown in the following table:

Starting or reserve price	Listing fee
$0.01 - $0.99	$0.15
$1.00 - $4.99	$0.25
$5.00 - $14.99	$0.40
$15.00 - $29.99	$0.75
$30.00 - $99.99	$1.50
$100.00 or more	$2.00

If the item is suspect, the user will be informed that the listing requires manual vetting before it can be approved for listing. Upon completion of the manual vetting, the user will be informed of the result by e-mail. If the item has been approved, the user will be informed of the listing fee and can then choose whether to proceed with the listing.

Completing the sale

The auction will end automatically after the specified duration. The user with the highest bid (subject to it meeting the reserve price, if specified) will be declared the winner. Once completed, the listing will proceed through the following steps to complete the sale:

1. **Specify Shipping Details**: The winning bidder will be notified by e-mail and requested to provide details of where the item is to be delivered to as well as any preferences for postage. An e-mail will be sent to the seller containing the shipping details.
2. **Invoice Buyer**: The seller will invoice the buyer for the winning amount, plus postage. An e-mail will be sent to the buyer, containing details of the invoice.

3. **Make Payment**: The buyer will then be required to pay the seller via a method accepted by the seller (note this is done outsite of oBay). Once done, the buyer will update the status of the item to indicate that they have made the payment. An e-mail will be sent to the seller to inform them that the payment has been made.
4. **Confirm Receipt of Payment**: The seller on receipt of the payment will update the status of the item accordingly. An e-mail will be sent to the buyer to inform them that the seller has received the payment.
5. **Ship Item**: After receiving the payment the seller will pack and ship the item to the buyer, again they will update the status of the item to indicate that it has been shipped. An e-mail will be sent to the buyer to inform them that the item has been dispatched.
6. **Receive Item**: Upon receipt of the item, the buyer will record the fact that they have received the item. An e-mail will be sent to the seller to inform them that it has been received.

Upon successful completion of the sale, a seller's fee, based on the final price as set out in the following table, will be charged to the seller's account.

Sale price	Seller's fee
$0.01 - $50.00	5% of the sale price
$50.01 - $1000.00	$1.00 plus 3% of the sale price
$1000.00 or more	$16.00 plus 1.5% of the sale price

If there are no bids or the reserve price isn't met, the auction will just finish without a winner, in this case, a seller's fee will not be charged to the seller's account.

View account

Whenever a user lists an item, they will be charged a listing fee. Upon successful sale of an item, they will be charged a seller's fee, based on the actual sale price. Each of these charges will be billed against the user's oBay account, and then on a monthly basis, oBay will automatically charge the user's credit card for the outstanding amount.

Buying items

When a user goes to his buyer's page, it will list all the items on which they have placed a bid. By default, it will be filtered to show just those items where the auction is still in progress, but they will be able to view items on which they have bid, but lost.

From here, the user can choose to view the details of the item, as well as place a bid if the auction is still in progress.

In addition, it will show those items that they have successfully won. By default, it will only show those items where the sale is still in progress (for example, still awaiting payment or shipping). The user can further refine this by listing all items in a particular state (for example, awaiting payment) or all items regardless of state.

The filter can be further qualified by specifying a time period, for example, just show me all listings for the last week, month, 90 days, 180 days, or year.

From here they can choose to view the details of any of these items, as well as perform outstanding tasks on open items (for example, specify shipping details, confirm receipt of item, and so on). In addition, the user may choose to search for a new item on which to bid.

Search for items

The first step in bidding for an item is to find something that you're interested in. oBay will provide buyers with the ability to search for items listed on oBay. The user will be able to search on a combination of category, subcategory, title, and condition.

The search will return all items that match the criteria, which will display 10 items at a time.

Bidding on items

Once a user has found an item of interest, they can view all its details, including existing bids. They can then choose whether to place a bid.

oBay uses an auction format, which lets a user bid the maximum amount they currently want to go up to. However, their bid will only be increased by a sufficient amount required to beat the current winning bid.

When the first bid is placed, it must be at least equal to the starting price set by the seller. However, regardless of the amount actually bid, the current winning bid will be equal to the starting price of the item.

After this, any future bids must be at least equal to the current winning bid plus one bidding increment, where the bidding increment is determined by the amount of the current winning bid, as shown in the following table:

Current winning bid	Bidding increment
$0.00 to $1.00	$0.05
$1.01 to $5.00	$0.25
$5.01 to $10.00	$0.50
$10.01 to $50.00	$2.50
$50.01 to $100.00	$5.00
$100.01 to $500.00	$25.00
and so on	

When a new bid is placed, oBay determines the winning bid by comparing the **maximum amount** of the current winning bid with the new bid; whichever is highest is determined to be the winner. However, the amount of the winning bid is determined by adding one bidding increment to the maximum amount of the losing bid.

If the calculated winning bid is greater than the maximum bid of the winning bid, then the winning bid is set equal to the maximum bid. In the event of a tie, then whoever placed the bid first is deemed to have the winning bid, and the winning bid is set to their maximum bid amount.

At first glance, this might sound quite complicated, so let's take an example to clarify. If the minimum amount set by the seller is $1.00, then the winning bid would be worked out as follows:

- If bidder A places a bid of $7.00, then they would currently have a winning bid of $1.00
- If bidder B then bids $3.00, bidder A would still have the winning bid, but it would now be $3.25 (bidder B's maximum bid plus one bidding increment)
- If bidder B then bids $6.99, bidder A would still have the winning bid, but now it would be $7.00

If it had gone up by a full bidding increment, it would now be $7.49, but the maximum bid of bidder A is $7.00.

- Finally, if bidder B bids $10.00, then they would now be the winning bidder, with a winning bid of $7.50

Upon placing a bid, the user will be informed if they have been successful or not as well as about the amount of the current winning bid. If successful, then the previous highest bidder will be e-mailed to inform them that they have been outbid.

On completion of the auction, the winning bidder will be notified by e-mail and requested to provide shipping details and any preferences on postage. Once provided, they will subsequently receive an invoice from the seller, confirming the amount to pay (that is, the winning price plus shipping and packing costs) and instructions on how to pay it.

Once paid, the buyer should notify the seller that they have made the payment. Once the seller has received the payments, they will then ship the item to the buyer. Upon receipt of the item, the buyer should then record that they have received the item.

Defining our blueprint for SOA

Before we leap in and start building our service-oriented solution, let's take a moment to understand why we would want to do this. After all, we could build this application using a standard web-based architecture with tools such as Java or .NET.

We will use this section to remind ourselves of the goals we are trying to achieve, as well as discuss the basic concepts of SOA. We then look at how we can bring this together to define a blueprint for a typical SOA Architecture, which we can use to architect our oBay application.

Architecture goals

The core goals of SOA can typically be summarized as:

- **Improved interoperability**: A major cost of any project is the effort required to integrate an application with existing applications, both inside and outside the enterprise.

  The use of standards-based communication frameworks (for example, web services); a standard representation for the exchange of data and common design standards can greatly simplify the integration between disparate systems, greatly reducing the cost of cross-application integration.
- **Improved reuse**: Designing and building services to be intrinsically reusable enables you to not just meet initial requirements, but also leverage them in future applications. Similarly, you can service-enable existing systems, and this enables you to further leverage existing investments.

This not only saves you the time and effort of rebuilding similar functionality, but can also help consolidate your IT estate; now you only need to implement a piece of functionality once, as opposed to having similar functionality buried in multiple systems. This can help reduce the cost of administering and maintaining your existing systems.

- **Improved agility**: One of the key design principles behind SOA is that systems are no longer built to last, but rather built to change.

  The following SOA principles not only allows you to more rapidly implement new solutions through re-using existing functionality, but also enable you to reduce the time it takes to modify and adapt existing SOA-based solutions in response to ever-changing business requirements.

Using SOA standards and technologies will take you part of the way towards achieving some of these goals, but as the A in SOA indicates, a key component of this is architecture.

Typical SOA Architecture

So far, we've been throwing around the term SOA without really spending much time looking at what a service is. At least, what a well designed service looks like, or how we should go about assembling them into an overall solution, that is, the architecture of our application.

The simple reality is that services come in all shapes and sizes, each of which has some bearing on how you design, build, and use them within your overall architecture. So it makes sense to further define the different types of services that we will need, how they should be used, how they should be organized into different layers, and so on.

Taking this approach enables us to ensure services are designed, built, and used in a consistent fashion, improving the overall interoperability and reusability of a service as well as ensuring the overall implementation is architected in such a way to address key non-functional requirements such as performance, fault tolerance, and security, as well as providing a solution that addresses our other goal of agility.

Now before we do this, we should add a **health warning** that there is no single definition as to how you should compose your SOA Architecture, but there are many opinions. It is also a pretty big topic in its own right, so you could quite easily dedicate an entire book to this subject alone.

So we offer this as an introductory opinion on how you might want to design your overall SOA Architecture. Feel free to agree or disagree with parts of it as you see fit. However, we would stress that you need to go through the process of defining your architectural approach to SOA and that you continue the process of refining it over time, based on the experience and requirements of your organization.

With that caveat out of the way, the following diagram illustrates one way of organizing our services into distinct layers within our overall architecture:

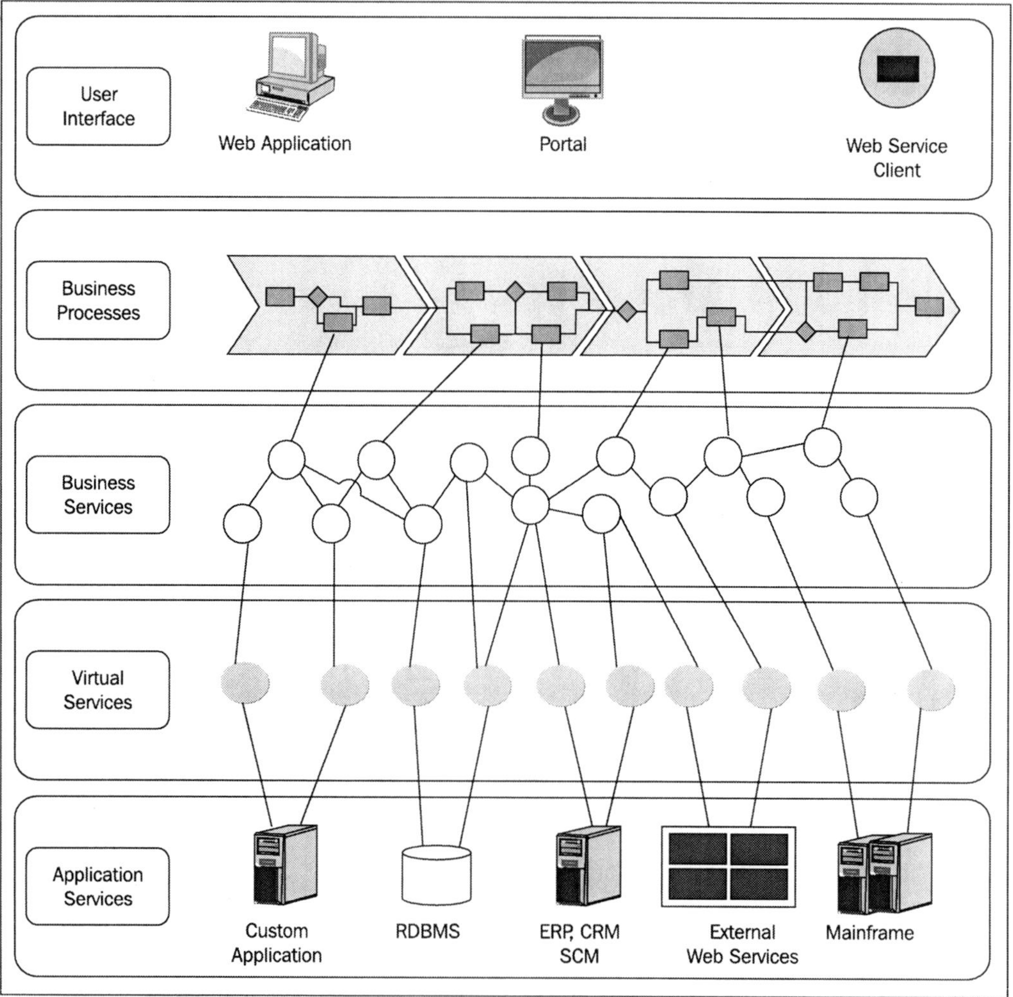

We can see that this breaks into five layers. It should also be apparent that all layers, except the top layer, actually provide a set of services to the layer above and typically do this by building on the layer beneath it.

Like most architecture diagrams, this is over simplified. For example, it implies here that the **User Interface** layer will always have to go via the business processes layer to access a business service. In many circumstances, to mandate this as an architectural requirement would be over-burdensome, and as a result, impair our key goals of re-usability and agility.

While we've labeled the top layer **User Interface**, it could potentially be any consumer of our services, who sits outside our domain of control, whether internal or external to our organization. Let's examine these layers one-by-one, starting at the bottom and working our way up.

Application services layer

When we look at the various layers within a service-oriented architecture, each layer typically builds on the previous layer. However, at some point we need to hit the bottom. This is the layer we have termed the '**Application Services** layer'. This layer is typically where the core service is actually implemented, or if you like, where the "real" work happens.

We refer to it as the **Application Service** layer, as most services are typically provided by existing applications. These could be packaged applications, such as Oracle E-Business Suite, Siebel, PeopleSoft, SAP, or custom applications developed in-house using technologies, such as Java, C#, Oracle Forms, PL/SQL, and so on.

Many modern day applications are web service-enabled, meaning that they provide web services out-of-the-box. For those that aren't, adapters can be used to service enable them (as we discussed in *Chapter 3, Service-enabling Existing Systems*).

The key here is that from our perspective, this is the lowest level of granularity that we can go down to, and also the actual control we have over the interface of services, at this level, is limited or non-existent. This tends to be the case regardless of whether or not we have control of the application that provides the service, as the actual interface provided is often a reflection of the underlying application.

It's for this reason (that is, lack of control over the service interface) that we also include in this category native web services provided by other third parties, for example, services provided by partners, suppliers, customers, and so on, as well as **Software as a Service** (**SaaS**).

Virtual services layer

This is a relatively thin layer that provides a façade on top of the **Application Services** layer. The key driver here is to achieve our goal of decoupling the services provided by the underlying applications (over which we have varying degrees of control) from any consumers of that service.

The simplest way to illustrate the **criticality** of this layer is to demonstrate the potential impacts of trying to bypass it, which, during the pressure of a development life cycle, can be easily done (and often is).

A typical scenario is where a developer or an architect will argue that it's only used in one place, and it's unlikely to change for a long time anyway, or we need to do it this way for performance reasons, and so on. And often, it is the case that the FIRST time you use something, it is only being used in one place. The trouble is that before long, you may find it being used in many places (and often you don't always know where).

Then change happens. It may initially be a simple change, for example it may be just moving the application to a bigger box (as the amount of requests it is now processing has increased), or the actual application itself may be changing. Maybe it's being upgraded to a new version, or maybe it's being replaced with a completely new application.

Either way the WSDL for the service is likely to change, requiring every caller of that service to be modified, tested, and redeployed, and of course, this needs to be coordinated across all users of that service.

This becomes more complicated when you have multiple changes in the same time frame. You could very quickly end up with hundreds or thousands of changes to implement and coordinate. Suddenly, change becomes very complicated and our systems far from agile.

As we mentioned earlier, the job of this layer is to provide a **virtual services** layer to decouple consumers of services from the underlying application and thus minimize the impact of change. It achieves this in two ways:

- First, it provides a virtual endpoint for the client to call. Upon receipt of a request, it then routes it to the underlying application service.
- Secondly, it allows us to define an abstract description of the service, that is, the operations provided by the service and its corresponding input and output messages, so that these are no longer dictated by the underlying application. This layer is then responsible for transforming an incoming input message from the format of our service contract to the one expected by the application service and vice versa for any response.

Business services layer

As the name suggests, this is a fairly generic term used to describe encapsulated business logic that is made available through a designed service contract. The keyword here is **designed**, particularly when it comes to exchanging data models, as each service will typically share a common data model defined in one or more XML schemas. This is often referred to as the canonical model and is something we will look at in a lot more detail in *Chapter 11, Designing the Service Contract*.

One of the implications of this is that a virtual service, as discussed in the previous layer, is in reality a specialized type of business service, and as we will see in a moment, a business process is also a specialized type of business service. However, each of these has a specific role and tends to gravitate towards a specific layer.

This still leaves us with a rather large category for all our remaining services, so from a design perspective, it makes sense to break these down further into specific subcategories.

There are many ways and many opinions on how exactly business services should be categorized. From a personal standpoint, we believe that there are two key perspectives to consider. The first is to look at the **type of functionality** contained within the service, as this will guide how we may wish to implement the service.

The second is to consider who is going to call or **consume the service**, in particular where they sit within our layered architecture, as this will often drive other considerations such as granularity, security, and so on.

Functional type

Our first category is the type of functionality provided by a service. We've split this into three groups: Entity, Functional, and Task-based service. Let's examine each of these in more detail:

- **Entity services**: Also known as data services, emulate business objects within an enterprise; for example User, Account, and Item are all entities within oBay. Entity services often represent data entities held in a relational database and provide the corresponding lifecycle (that is, create, read, update, and delete) and query operations.

  Entity services can often be used within multiple contexts, making them excellent candidates for reuse. To further promote this, it is considered a good practice to minimize any business specific logic (such as validation) that you place within the service.

  One of the drawbacks here is that you wouldn't want to expose an entity service directly to the presentation layer or any external third-party service; rather you would use it within a task-based service or business process.

- **Functional services**: Are used to implement raw business logic, for example, business rules, pricing algorithms, and so on. It is quite common to embed rules directly within task-based (or even entity) services, often leading to the same rule being implemented in multiple locations and not always consistently.

  By separating out this logic as a standalone service, you not only ensure that it's used in a consistent fashion, but also make it simpler to modify (that is, you only have to do it once), thus increasing the agility of your solution.

  Functional services typically don't use entity services (except maybe to look-up reference values used by the algorithm); if you have a functional service that does, then in reality, you have a task-based service with functional logic embedded within it.

  In many cases this may be fine. However, it will limit how reusable the service is and could result in the same functionality being reimplemented in other task-based services.

- **Task-based services**: They are modeled to carry out a specific set of related activities, often within the context of a business process. By their nature, they will often act across one or more entity services, and may also make use of other task-based or functional services.

  For example, if we look at the operation `placeBid`, this would very much form part of a task-based `Auction` service, as it supports the task of placing a bid. However, it is likely to use an entity service (that is, `Bid`) to store the received bid in the underlying database, and it may use a functional service (that is, `AuctionEngine`) to calculate the result of placing the bid.

Service consumer

A key design point that needs to be considered is who will be consuming our business services? It could be other business services, business processes, or an external consumer such as the user interface layer, partners, or other parts of the organization, though a service could potentially be called by all types of consumers. Knowing who will call a service will impact on areas such as service granularity, validation, and security.

Granularity is a key consideration in service design. Current industry wisdom tends to encourage the use of more coarse-grained services, but it's important to understand why when considering the granularity of an individual service.

Granularity is essentially the number of operations we need to call on a service in order to achieve the desired result. The more fine-grained a service is, the more operations you will typically need to call, the coarse-grained the less.

The key driver for coarse-grained services is the performance impact of going across a network. Thus if you can achieve the desired result by calling a coarse-grained service, as opposed to calling say four fine-grained services, then it is likely to be approximately four times faster, as the actual processing time of the service is likely to be insignificant in comparison to the cost of going across the network.

However, using coarse-grained services can come at a price. If you combine multiple functions into a single operation it may becomes less useable, as requestors may be required to provide additional data to use the service or the service could result in unwanted side effects. Conversely, if done well, coarse-grained services can simplify the service interface, thus making it more reusable.

Additionally, coarse-grained services may impose redundant processing on the server-side which could adversely impact performance. For example, it may cause the service to make unnecessary reads to a database or make calls to additional services across the network, each with resultant implications for overall performance.

The other consideration is that if a service is calling another service within the same environment (for example, it is deployed on the same instance of the 11*g* service infrastructure), then the call is likely to be optimized and not require a network hop.

Understanding where the service consumer lives in relation to the service is a key design consideration. So when deciding on service granularity, it's worth bearing the following guidelines in mind:

- For business services that are only going to be consumed by either business processes or other business services (for example, entity services and functional services), then you can afford to use finer-grained services.
- If a service is to be used outside the domain of control, then coarse-grained services are more appropriate, though you should consider the downstream performance implications of any redundant processing.
- When providing coarse-grained services, if there are potential impacts on either performance or reuse then consider providing a number of redundant fine-grained services in addition to the coarse-grained services. Effectively by de-normalizing the service contract, it gives the consumer the ability to choose the appropriate service.

In addition, depending on the nature of the service consumer, you may need to place other requirements on a service, such as:

- **Security**: As with all IT systems, security is key, but more so if you start using SOA to expose your systems via web services to external third-party consumers.
- **Management**: Many third-party consumers will want to agree to some sort of service level agreement, and you need to ensure you have sufficient infrastructure in place to manage your services appropriately.
- **Support**: When exposing services to third-parties, you need to consider how they are going build systems that use them, that is, what level of documentation are you going to provide, who do they call when something goes wrong, and so on
- **Change Management**: When services change, how are you going to manage that? Depending on who the consumer is, you may be able to coordinate any upgrades with them. However, that won't always be the case.
- **Validation**: The less control we have over the implementation of the consumer of a service, the less the number of assumptions we can make about the quality of the data our service will receive, and the more validation will be required.

Typically, service management and security is not something you build into individual services. Rather, it tends to be provided by the underlying infrastructure in which you host the service (something we will look at in more detail in *Chapter 21, Defining Security and Management Policies*).

Support is more of an organizational issue, as is change management to a certain extent. However, design of the service contract is the key to making change more manageable and something we look at in detail in *Chapter 11, Designing the Service Contract*. Finally, validation is an important consideration in design, and something we look at in more detail in *Chapter 13, Building Validation into Services*.

Business process

As we've already mentioned, you could argue that a business process is no more than just a specialized business service, especially when viewed through the eyes of the service consumer. However, it has a number of key differences that make it worth considering as a separate layer in its own right.

Before we look at why, let's take a step back. Look at the traditional application architecture, which splits up an application into its presentation layer, business logic, and database layer. Within that business logic, it is the business process that is more likely to change.

A business process is more likely to span multiple systems, which has led to the proliferation of point-to-point integration solutions, aimed at tying those bits of process together into an end-to-end business process. This can further obfuscate the business process, making it more resistant to change.

Abstracting out a business process into a separate layer gives us a number of advantages. Firstly, rather than having the process logic buried across multiple applications, we can now define a single end-to-end process with a far higher level of visibility and clarity than would normally be achievable. This makes it far simpler to monitor the end-to-end process, as well as modify it in the future.

It also simplifies our underlying business services, as by extracting the business process specific logic from them, they naturally become more generic, and therefore more reusable.

Another byproduct is that as processes are long running in nature, whether for minutes, hours, days, months, or even years, they are inherently stateful. Thus, the need for other services to manage state is often removed, again simplifying them as well as making them more reusable.

It is currently deemed the best practice to make services stateless, as stateless architectures are typically more scalable (or at least easier to scale) than stateful ones. In addition, stateless services tend to be simpler to build and use, making them more reusable.

While to a certain extent this is true, you could argue that up until recently, many of the WS-* standards and corresponding vendor tools have not had the required completeness of functionality to support stateful services. This is now starting to change, so going forward there is likely to be more of a mix of stateless and stateful services within SOA.

User interface layer

As the top layer within our architecture, this is the layer that consumes the services provided by the business processes and business services layers. We have labeled this the user interface layer, mainly because we are using our SOA Architecture as the blueprint for building a composite application, and this is the layer where the GUI (either web-based or thick client) would sit.

For the purposes of this book we will not spend much time looking at this layer, as it falls outside the boundary of what is provided by the Oracle SOA Suite. However, for the purposes of delivering a fully-working application, we have provided a simple web-based user interface developed using JDeveloper.

The reality, however, is that many users of the SOA Suite continue to develop the GUI component of an application using their technology of choice, as in most cases, it dovetails very nicely with an SOA-based approach.

Many user interfaces are based on variations of the **Model-View-Controller** (**MVC**) design pattern. The Model represents the business logic and data of an application and defines a set of operations that can be performed against it.

The View is the user interface (for example, web page). It presents information from the Model to the user, and then captures actions taken by the user against the view. The Controller maps actions performed on the View (for example, pressing a **Submit** button) to operations on the Model (for example, placing a bid). After the Model is updated, the View is refreshed, and the user can perform more actions.

This approach fits extremely well within the context of SOA, where the Model is effectively provided by the business process and business service layers. The View and Controller can then be implemented using your GUI framework of choice (for example, Oracle ADF, Spring, or Struts). The Controller would then provide the integration between the two, invoking the appropriate operations on the underlying services.

One additional layer

Although we have focused on the user interface being the top layer within our architecture, the reality is that these services could be consumed by applications built by other parts of the organization or those of our partners or customers.

If these consumers are using the same architecture as us, then they would view our services in the same way as we are viewing external web services within the application services layer of our architecture.

This implies the need to have an additional virtual services layer in our model, between the user interface and business process layer. We could rely on the consumer of our services to build this layer, but it actually makes a lot of sense for us to provide it.

Remember the goal of our original virtual services layer was to decouple our composite application from the underlying services provided by the application services layer, so that we can insulate ourselves from changes to the underlying applications.

Here it is the opposite. We want to decouple the services we are providing from the consumers of those services, as this gives us greater flexibility to change our services without being constrained by the consumer of our services.

This layer also provides a suitable point of control for managing access to our services. Enabling us to define, enforce, and monitor polices for security and service level agreements. With this additional layer, our SOA Architecture now looks as follows:

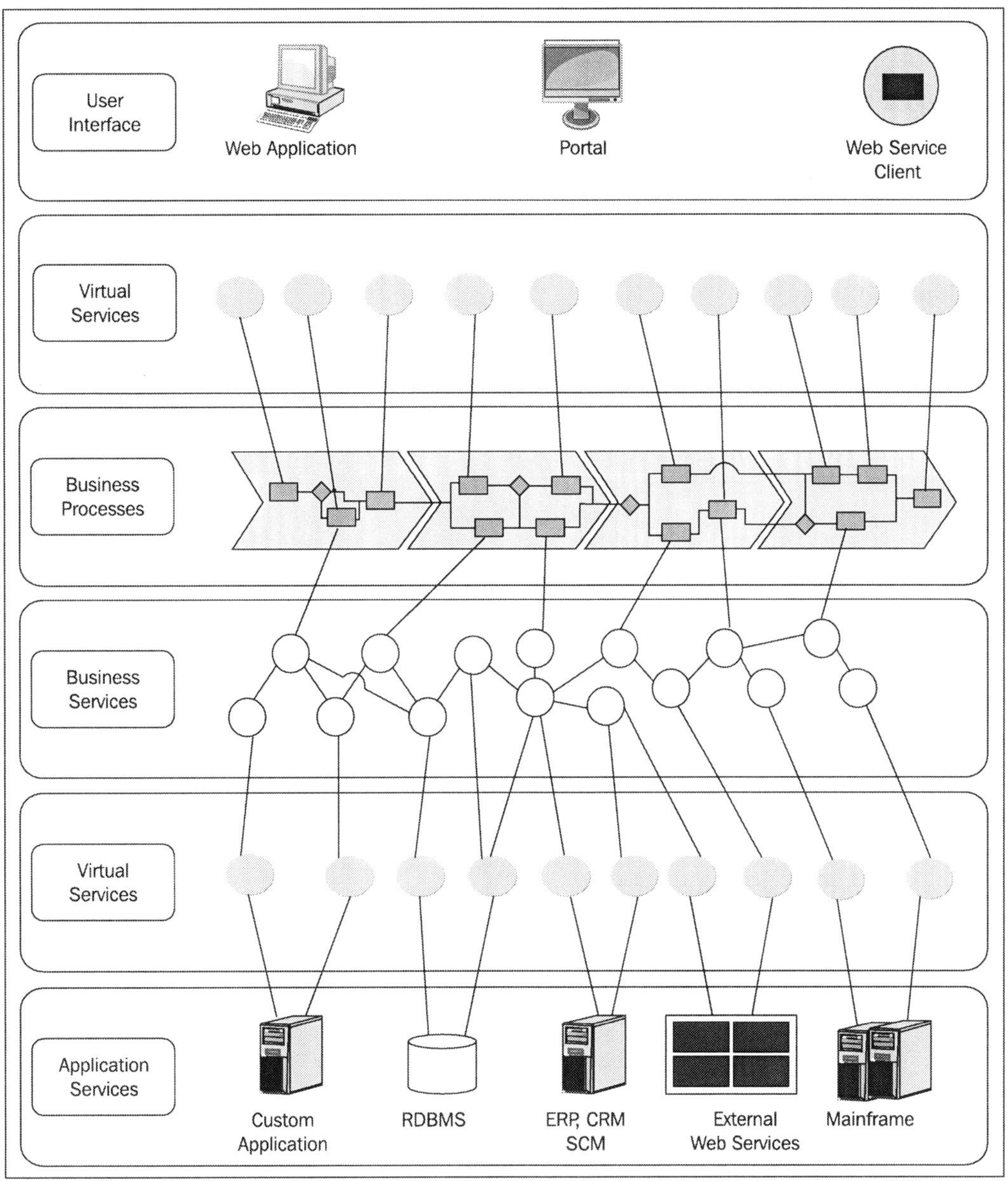

Where the SOA Suite fits

You may have noticed that we have deliberately stayed clear of saying which parts of the Oracle SOA Suite are used for which areas within our architecture, and there is a good reason for this. Firstly, we wanted to produce a meaningful architecture that clearly demonstrated the key objectives and considerations of each layer, rather than just a piece of marketecture.

Secondly, it's not a simple one-to-one mapping, as within most layers, we have multiple options available when it comes to implementation.

The first step is to map our architecture to the SOA Suite, which is to determine which layers should be implemented as SOA composites and deployed to the 11*g* Service Infrastructure and which layers should be implemented as proxy services on the Oracle Service Bus.

> Oracle Service Bus has the concepts of proxy service and business service. Within our terminology, a proxy service maps to a virtual service. However, an OSB business service maps to what we have termed an application service.
>
> We realized this could be confusing and did consider changing our terminology to match. However, we have tried to base our architecture on accepted industry practice and terminology. So, we believed it was better to keep this terminology rather than modify it to fit with the naming of specific products.

There are, as always, a number of ways to do this. However, we will start with a *simplistic* view of what are regarded as best practices, and then layer on some additional considerations. The following diagram depicts one way of partitioning our services across these two components:

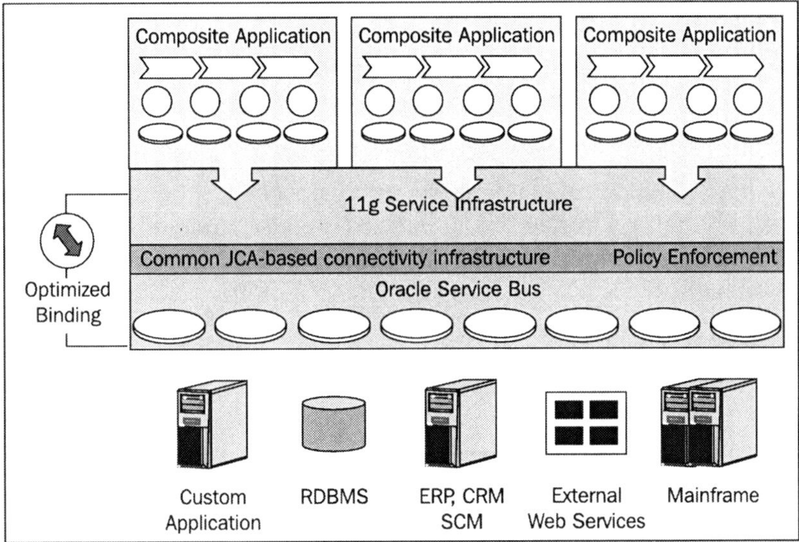

The diagram illustrates the deployment of multiple composite applications on to the 11*g* service infrastructure, with each composite application composed of multiple composites. In other words, a composite application is a collection of composites that have been designed and implemented as part of the same solution (for example, oBay).

From this, we can see that each composite application is made up of a combination of virtual services, business services, and business processes.

The diagram also depicts a number of virtual services deployed to the Oracle Service Bus. These virtual services implement the internal and external virtual service layer. An obvious question that this prompts is when to implement a virtual service in a composite, and when to implement it using the OSB.

It's worth recalling that the function of the virtual services layer is **NOT** about implementing a new service, but rather we are providing a layer of abstraction over an existing service. In other words, the focus of this layer is all about decoupling the service consumer from the service provider.

This, of course, is the primary objective of the Oracle Service Bus, so should be the default technology for implementing this layer. The reality is that it's not that simple and there are a number of scenarios where it makes sense to implement these (using a Mediator) within a composite, which we will highlight over the following pages.

Composite application

As we have already mentioned, a composite application is made up of a number of composites, with each composite providing a service that could potentially sit in any layers of our architecture.

A composite itself is made up of one or more types of components (for example, BPEL process, Mediator, Human Task). Each of these components has an affinity to various layers within our architecture. The following is a *guide* to which components can be used where:

- **Application services layer**: This layer is pretty straightforward in that if the application doesn't provide inbuilt support for web services, it is the case of using the appropriate Service Adapter to hook into the underlying application.
- **Virtual services layer**: Within a **composite**, a Mediator should be your default starting point for this layer, as it has been designed to address the specific challenges tackled by this layer of our architecture.
- **Business services layer**: BPEL is typically used for task-based services, as it provides a rich language for building composite services, with Human Workflow being used for manual tasks.

  Business Rules provide an excellent tool for implementing functional services, as well as the validation within task-based services.

  For entity services, we can use ADF business components. While it is not part of the SOA Suite, it is tightly integrated within the 11*g* service infrastructure.
- **Business Processes Layer**: This layer, as you've no doubt already realized, is the natural domain for BPEL. However, Business Rules also play an important role in allowing you to externalize the logic behind decision points within your process.

Business Activity Monitoring is then used to instrument your composite and any other relevant services, in order to provide you with a holistic view across your application.

Composite granularity

A key consideration when designing a composite application is the appropriate level of granularity when partitioning it into multiple composites.

For example, it is quite feasible to build a single composite that spans all layers of our architecture (excluding the service consumer layer). While this may work, the issue that we have is that we would need to modify and re-deploy the whole composite whenever a change occurs at any level within our composite.

The other extreme would be to deploy every component as a standalone composite in its own right. This is similar to what we had to do in 10gR3. However, this will lead to an overly fragmented solution, which will be more complex to test, integrate, deploy, and maintain. So the key question is what is the right level of granularity of a composite?

When identifying services, we typically advocate a top-down process-driven approach, which will help us to identify our **core** business processes and services, for which we can define our service contract (as covered in the next chapter add).

We use this as our starting point for our level of granularity, with each business process or service being implemented as a single composite (using the appropriate components).

Once we start to design a composite, we will typically identify other business processes or services that are required by the composite. At this point, we need to decide whether the child service needs to be split out as a separate service, and therefore be implemented as a composite in its own right.

Key considerations when making this decision are reusability, lifecycle, and operational management of the composite.

Performance isn't really a consideration, assuming all composites are deployed on the same service infrastructure, as there is no real difference in the overhead of invoking a component within the same composite as opposed to invoking it with a separate composite.

From an audit and tractability perspective, there is little difference, since Enterprise Manager is sophisticated enough to join audit trails across components that span multiple composites.

Composite reusability

The first consideration is whether the child service needs to be reused by other composites (independently of the parent composite), either now or in the future. If the answer is yes, then typically we want to split it out as a separate composite.

This isn't always as obvious as it may seem, as it is quite easy to take the approach that every component could potentially be a reusable service and end up with all the issues of an overly-fragmented solution.

The other consideration is that although it is technically simple enough to deploy a child service as its own composite, the reality is that contextually it is coupled to the parent service, that is, it is designed based on the requirements of the parent composite.

To make it truly reusable, you will be required to break this coupling and design the child service to be reusable, which takes extra time and effort. If it is a genuine reusable service, then this investment may be justified. However, just because a service could be reusable doesn't mean it should.

Finally, we need to consider the timing. It may be prudent for an initial implementation not to split up the child components. But if we decided at a later point in time that we needed to reuse a component of a composite (typically when we understand the requirements better from a reuse perspective), then we could always choose to split up the component then.

Composite lifecycle

Another consideration is whether the lifecycle of the child composite is likely to be different from that of the parent composite, particularly if the composite is stateful (for example, a long running business process).

If the child service is likely to change either more frequently or at different times from the parent composite, then by splitting it up, we can simplify the process of managing change.

For example, consider that we have a long running business process that invokes a child business process. If deployed as a single composite, then whenever the child process changes, we will need to redeploy a new version of the parent and child process. As part of this, we need to deal with the issue of what do with the running instances of the previous versions of the parent process.

However, if each process is deployed as a separate composite, then whenever the child process changes, we will only need to deploy a new version of the child process. If managed correctly, we can have the parent process automatically pick up the new version of the child process.

Composite security and management policies

The majority of security and management policies are applied at the composite level (refer to *Chapter 21, Defining Security and Management Policies* for details).

If you need to apply any of these policies to specific components, then you may need to split that component up as a separate composite.

In addition, the Enterprise Management pack for SOA provides additional support for runtime management with tooling for monitoring and managing areas such as service availability, service level agreements, and key performance indicators. At the time of writing, the Management Pack for SOA suite 11gR1 has yet to be released. However, it is likely that much of the management capability will be provided at the composite level.

Basic composite design pattern

When implementing composites, we recommend a contract-first approach (as detailed in *Chapter 11, Designing the Service Contract*). Once we have defined the contract, we can then use that as the starting point for implementing our composite.

With this approach, the default design pattern that we recommend is to use a Mediator as the entry point for a composite, as shown in the following diagram:

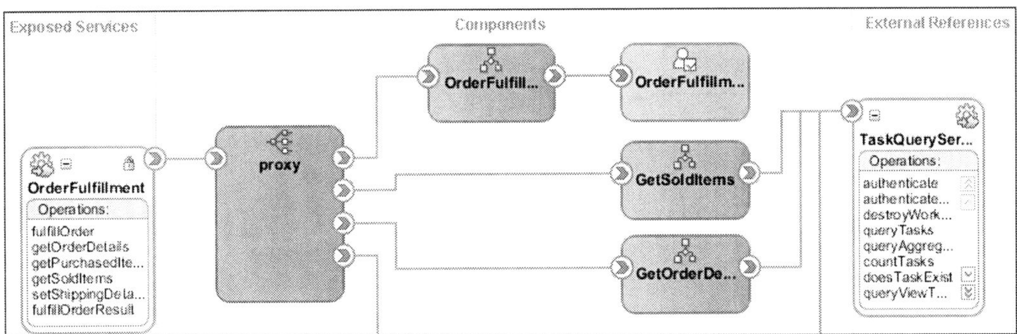

With this pattern, the Mediator implements the abstract WSDL for our services and acts as a proxy responsible for routing requests from the service consumer to the appropriate components within the composite. As the service contract is based on the canonical model, then the Mediator should not be required to perform any level of transformation. This provides a very light way to control the entry point to our composite.

This allows us to present a single consolidated WSDL contract to the consumer (something that we couldn't easily do in 10gR3, where each BPEL process required its own WSDL). In addition, there are a number of other advantages, including having a single point at which to:

- Define security and management policies
- Validate the XML syntax of any incoming request
- Perform additional validation using schematron
- Abstract the structure of the composite, allowing us to change its implementation without changing its interface

Where to implement virtual services

We stated earlier that our default technology of choice for implementing both virtual service layers within our architecture should be the Oracle Service Bus, but why?

From a functional perspective, you can view the Mediator as a *light-weight* Service Bus. Certainly, OSB gives you a number of significant advantages, including:

- Performance
- Service throttling
- Service pooling
- Service caching
- Flexibility

Given this, are there any reasons why we might choose to use the Mediator instead?

The obvious one is that we might choose not to deploy the Oracle Service Bus in order to simplify our overall architecture. If this is your first SOA implementation, or you only have a small scale deployment, then this approach may be perfectly valid.

But assuming that OSB is part of your architecture, are there any scenarios where you might use the Mediator? The answer is of course yes. We will examine some of them later.

Mediator as a proxy for a composite

In the composite design pattern that we have just outlined, we are already using the Mediator. So it may seem strange to be asking this question.

However, in this scenario, it is not being used to implement a virtual services layer. Instead, it's acting as a proxy within our composite. This may seem pedantic, but recall that the composite could potentially be deployed to any layer within our architecture.

Mediator as a proxy for an external reference

The reverse of the previous pattern is to use the Mediator as a proxy for any external service invoked by a composite. However, unless we are implementing a virtual service (which we will cover in a moment), there is little need for this pattern.

Firstly, if we are following our architecture, then any service we are calling from a business process or service already implements our canonical model, thus no transformation or enrichment of the date is required.

If we want to route the operation based on the content of the message, then this should also be done in the virtual layer.

If we need to modify the endpoint that a composite invokes, then this is defined in an external reference (regardless of whether we go via a Mediator or not).

So all that we are left with is validation. When you consider that it is the composite that is responsible for creating the data, you would hope that in most cases, we could be confident that we were creating our own valid data (in cases where we were not, then this, of course, is a valid pattern).

Using a composite as a virtual service

With the above in mind, the real question we should have asked is:

> *Are there any scenarios where we would use a composite (based on a Mediator) to implement a virtual service?*

Recall that a composite application is a collection of related composites, that is, they have been designed and implemented as part of the same solution.

With this in mind, a scenario that we usually want to avoid is where we have a composite calling another composite (in the same application) via the Service Bus. This is because it will typically add an additional layer of complexity, as well as the overhead of *marshalling* and *un-marshalling* a message between the SOA infrastructure, which in the case of a simple synchronous call, would need to happen four times.

> The first time for the hop from the calling composite in the service infrastructure to the Service Bus, the second for the hop from the Service Bus back to the invoked composite on the service infrastructure and then another two hops to return the response.

A typical scenario where this could occur is where we have a composite business service which needs to invoke some logic on an external system via a technology adapter (such as the database, file, or FTP adapter).

One way to implement this would be to build a simple composite that references the external system via the appropriate adapter. We could then plug this into the Oracle Service Bus (as a business service) and then use a proxy service to expose this as a virtual service, which could then be invoked by our composite business service.

This (in the absence of any other requirements) is clearly an overly complicated solution and a classic example of when we would use a Mediator in the same composite as the adapter to expose it as an internal virtual service.

An alternative would be to connect to an external system via an adapter deployed to the Oracle Service Bus (as opposed to the Service Infrastructure in the previous scenario).

This would be the approach when integrating with an enterprise application such as Oracle E-Business Suite, Siebel, or SAP, since these are likely to be invoked from composite applications and thus need to be considered as a composite apps in their own right.

Service invocation between composite applications

The boundaries between where one composite application finishes and another begins is not always clear. Take the previous scenario; we could be using the database adapter to connect to a custom application that we may need to include within multiple composite applications (say Application A and Application B).

In this scenario, we could say that the virtual services we have exposed are part of composite Application A or composite Application B or a composite application in its own right. With any of these outcomes, we have the issue of how we want to handle inter-composite application communication, when deployed on the same Service Infrastructure.

In this scenario, we have three basic approaches:

- Centralized topology(that is, go via the Service Bus)
- Peer-to-peer topology(that is, go direct via the service infrastructure)
- Hybrid approach

Centralized approach

With this approach, whenever a composite application needs to invoke a service provided by another composite application, it would do so via an external virtual service implemented as a proxy service on the Service Bus.

This is essentially the model that we have advocated from the start, as it allows us to completely de-couple our service consumer from our service provider. In addition to the advantages we covered earlier, mandating that all external services are accessed via the OSB gives us a number of other benefits.

From a service development lifecycle perspective, having this very clear line of delineation between composite apps makes it simpler to communicate and enforce our overall SOA Architecture, thus simplifying our governance requirements.

From an operational perspective, it allows us to use the Oracle Service Bus as a centralized point of control for managing, monitoring, and securing our services.

Peer-to-peer topology

With this topology, we are allowing composite applications deployed on the same Service Infrastructure to communicate directly with each other, without the need to go via the Service Bus. In this scenario, we would need to implement the external virtual services layer using a **Mediator**.

With this approach, all invocations happen over the service infrastructure, which has a number of advantages, including the following:

- All invocations are optimized, resulting in improved performance
- Transactions can be propagated between composite applications
- Complete audit trails across composite applications

The disadvantage of this approach is that without a well-defined governance process, you can quickly lose the overall visibility and control of your architecture.

For example, how do you stop a developer from implementing a composite in one application that bypasses the external virtual services layer of another application, calling a business service directly?

Note, we may still need to implement a set of external virtual services in the OSB layer, for the purpose of controlling the invocation of the composite by consumers that aren't deployed directly on the service infrastructure, adding additional complexity to our solution.

Hybrid approach

With this approach, the default is to follow the centralized approach and mandate that communication between composite applications go via the Service Bus, but direct composite application to composite application communication is allowed under certain circumstances.

The key to this approach is that the default is to use the centralized approach, but provide a mechanism through your governance process for peer-to-peer communication where there is a justified reason, for example, improved performance.

oBay high-level architecture

Now that we have our blueprint for SOA, let us apply it to the business requirements of oBay. By doing this, we come up with the following high-level architecture:

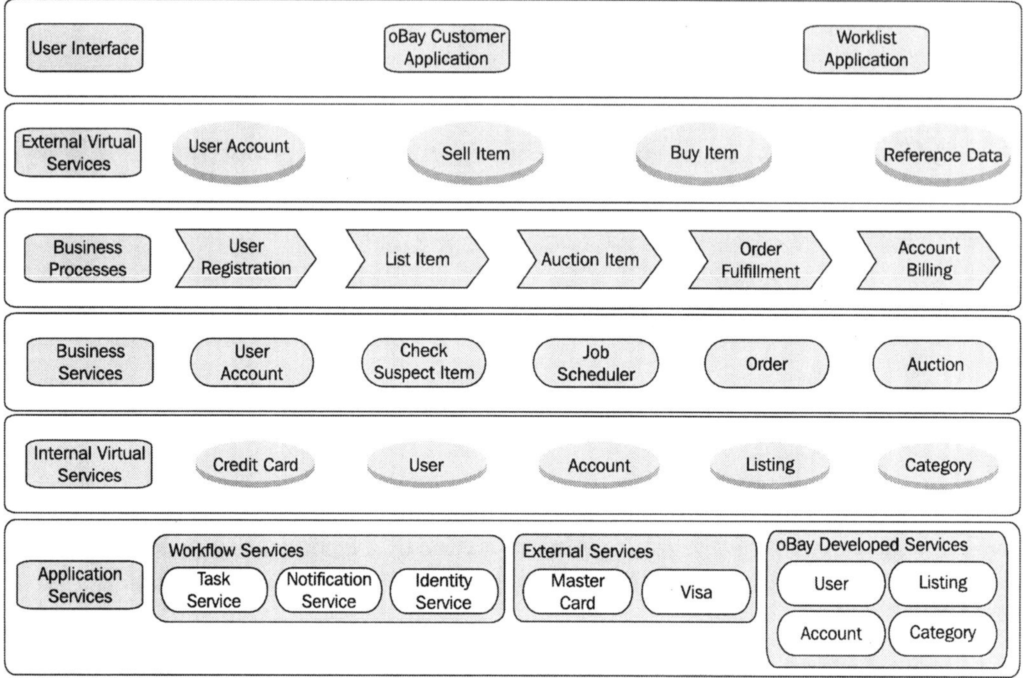

We won't go into this in detail at this point (as we do that in the remainder of this section), but it's worth looking at each layer and highlighting a few significant features.

oBay application services

As you will see from the previous diagram, we have broken out our **Application Services** into three categories, namely, **oBay Developed Services**, **External Services**, and **Workflow Services**. Each of these raises some interesting points, which we examine further later.

Workflow services

The **Task**, **Identity**, and **Notification** services are a subset of the services provided out of the box by the Oracle SOA Suite. As we typically access these services via the **Human Task** activity within a composite, it is easy to overlook their very existence.

The workflow services have documented APIs, so they can be invoked just like any other web service. We take advantage of these APIs to build the order management business service and look at how to do this as part of *Chapter 17, Workflow Patterns*.

External web services

oBay makes use of a number of "simulated" real world web services, which are invoked via OSB. A key consideration when using external web services is what happens if they fail. We look at this as part of *Chapter 14, Error Handling*.

oBay developed services

As oBay is a start-up, it has rather limited inhouse applications, so we are going to build most of these services from scratch. The great thing about SOA is that we can actually build these application services using whichever technology is appropriate, for example, Java or PL/SQL.

One option is to use Oracle ADF business components, which can be used to implement Service Data Objects, a new feature in 11gR1. We cover this in detail in *Chapter 12, Building Entity Services using Service Data Objects (SDOs)*.

oBay internal virtual services

All of our oBay developed application services have a straight one-to-one mapping with a corresponding virtual service. This is quite common when developing the underlying application services as part of the overall implementation.

When exposing functionality from existing systems, this won't always be the case. For example, you may have multiple systems performing the same function. In this scenario, multiple application services would map to a single virtual service, which would be responsible for routing requests to the appropriate system. This is the case for our external services, where we have multiple services for address and credit card services.

oBay business services

At first glance, this looks pretty unremarkable. However, there are a few areas worth further scrutiny. Many of the task-based services, such as `UserManagement`, are built using one or more entity services and do little more than layer validation on top. We examine this approach in *Chapter 13, Building Validation into Services*.

A number of the task-based services (for example, `Order`) are manual in nature and therefore, predominately built using the Workflow Service provided by the SOA Suite. In *Chapter 17, Workflow Patterns*, we look at why we have split them up as separate business services, rather than embed them directly within the core business processes.

Finally, the auction engine is an interesting example of a functional service. One way to implement this would be to write it using a standard programming language such as Java or C#. However, an alternative is to use Business Rules; we look at this in *Chapter 18, Using Business Rules to Implement Services* and examine some of the advantages and disadvantages to this approach.

oBay business processes

Effectively within oBay, there are two **key** business processes, namely, registering a customer and the end-to-end process of listing an item and selling it through auction, the second of which we've split up into three subprocesses (for the purpose of reusability and agility, should oBay change or extend its core business model at any point in the future).

It is also worth examining the `Account Billing` process. All our other processes are initiated to handle a specific request (for example, register a user, list an item for auction), while this is a scheduled process, which we will run nightly to settle the account of all users with outstanding monies. We examine how we do this in *Chapter 16, Message Interaction Patterns*.

oBay user interface

Here we've defined two user interfaces; one is for oBay customers, and we've built it using JDeveloper. The other is for oBay employees who need to perform human workflow tasks. Both sets of users will be performing human workflow tasks, one via the out of the box worklist application, the other through our own hand-cranked GUI. We will look at how to do this in *Chapter 17, Workflow Patterns*.

Summary

In this chapter, we've provided you with a detailed introduction to the business requirements of oBay—our fictional online auction site, as well as presenting you with the architecture for our composite application.

Before we developed our solution, we took you through the process of defining our high level SOA blueprint, outlining some of the objectives and considerations you should take into account when developing an SOA-based architecture. Along the way we've also thrown up a number of questions or issues that need to be addressed, as well as highlighting particular areas of interest in our overall design.

In the remainder of this section, each chapter will focus on addressing a particular subset of those issues raised, using various parts of the oBay application to illustrate each answer. So that, by the end of this section, we will have tackled all the matters that we've raised including the key question:

> "*What is the best way to combine/use all of these different components to implement a real world SOA solution?*"

As you are, no doubt, already gathering from this chapter, there isn't a single simple answer, but rather you have many choices, each with their own set of advantages and disadvantages. By the end of this section, you should at least be in a position to understand those choices better and which ones are more applicable to you and that of your own development.

11
Designing the Service Contract

Service contracts provide the glue that enables us to assemble disparate pieces of software or services into complete, composite applications. If we are to build a sustainable solution, that is, one that will achieve our goals of improved agility, reuse, and interoperability, then a careful design of the service contract is crucial.

The contract of a web service is made up of the following technical components:

- **WSDL Definition**: Defines the various operations which constitute a service, their input and output parameters, and the protocols (bindings) it supports.
- **XML Schema Definition** (**XSD**): Either embedded within the WSDL definition or referenced as a standalone component, this defines the XML elements and types which constitute the input and output parameters.
- **WS-Policy Definition**: An optional component that describes the service's security constraints, quality of service, and so on.

Additionally, the service contract may be supported by a number of non-technical documents, which define areas such as service-level agreements, support, and so on.

From a contract design perspective, we are primarily interested in defining the XML Schema and the WSDL definition of the service. This chapter gives guidance on best practices in the design of these components as well as providing strategies for managing change, when it occurs. We leave the discussion on defining security and management policies to *Chapter 21, Defining Security and Management Policies*.

Using XML Schema to define business objects

Each business service acts upon one or more business objects. Within SOA, the data that makes up these objects is represented as XML, with the structure of the XML being defined by one or more XML Schemas. Thus the definition of these schemas forms a key part in defining the overall service contract.

To better facilitate the exchange of data between services, as well as achieve better interoperability and reusability, it is a good practice to define a common data model, often referred to as the "canonical data model", which is used by all services.

As well as defining the structure of data exchanged between components, XML is also used in all components of the SOA Suite. For example, it defines the structure of variables in BPEL and provides the vocabulary for writing business rules and transforming data via XSLT. So it is important that our XML model is well thought out and designed.

Modeling data in XML

When designing your XML data model, a typical starting point is to base it on an existing data model, such as a database schema, UML model, or EDI document.

While this is a perfectly legitimate way to identify your data elements, the crucial point in this approach is how you make the transition from your existing model to an XML model. Very often, the structure of the existing model is directly replicated in the XML model, resulting in poor design.

Data decomposition

In order to produce an effective model for XML, it's worth taking a step back to examine the core components that make up an XML document. Consider the following XML fragment:

```
<order>
  <orderNo>123456</orderNo>
   <shipTo>
      <name>
         <title>Mr</title>
         <firstName>James</firstName>
         <lastName>Elliot</lastName>
      </name>
      <address>
```

```
            <addressLine1>7 Pine Drive</addressLine1>
            <addressLine2></addressLine2>
            <city>Eltham<city>
            <state>VIC</state>
            <zip>3088</zip>
            <country>Australia</country>
        </address>
    </shipTo>
</order>
```

If we pull out the raw data from this, we would end up with:

```
123456 Mr, James, Elliot, 7 Pine Drive, , Eltham, VIC, 3088.
Australia.
```

By doing this, we have greatly reduced our understanding of the data. XML, through the use of tags, gives meaning to the data, with each tag describing the content of the data it contains. Now this may seem an obvious point, but too often, by failing to sufficiently decompose our data model, we are doing exactly this, albeit within an XML wrapper. For example, another way of modeling the previous piece of XML is as follows:

```
<order>
    <orderNo>123456</orderNo>
    <shipTo>
        <name>Mr James Elliot</name>
        <address>7 Pine Drive, Eltham, VIC, 3088, Australia</address>
    </shipTo>
</order>
```

With this approach, we have again reduced our understanding of the data. So you should always look to decompose your data to the appropriate level of granularity. If in doubt go for the more granular model, as it's a lot simpler to convert data held in a granular model to a less granular model than the other way round.

Data hierarchy

Another key component of our data model is the relationship between the different elements of data, which is defined by the composition or hierarchy of the data. If from our example fragment we take the element `<city>Eltham<city>`, on its own it does not signify much, as we have provided insufficient context to the data.

However, in the context of `<order><shipTo><address><city>`, we have a far clearer understanding of the data.

A common mistake is to use a flat structure, and then name the elements to compensate for this, for example, changing the name to `<order_shipTo_address_city>`. While this provides more context than just `<city>`, it introduces a whole set of other problems, including:

- It makes your XML far harder to read, as well as more bloated.
- The relationships are no longer visible to your XML parser. This makes XPath manipulation, XSLT mappings, and so on a lot more complex and onerous.
- It reduces the opportunity for reuse; for example, each address element will have to be redefined for every single context in which it is used. This is likely to lead to inconsistent definitions as well as make changes harder to manage.

If you see elements named in this fashion, for example, `<a_b_c>`, `<a_b_d>`, it's a pretty good clue that the schema has been poorly designed.

Data semantics

Another key to our data model is the semantics of our data. Looking at the preceding example, it is obvious what the `<state>` element contains, but the exact format of that data is not as obvious; that is, it could be Victoria, VIC, Vic, 0, and so on.

While different target systems will have different requirements, it is important that a set of semantics are agreed upon for the canonical model, so that these differences can be isolated in the Virtual Services layer.

While semantics can be enforced within our XML Schema through the use of facets such as `enumeration`, `length`, `pattern`, and so on, this is not always the best approach. This is an area we examine in more detail in *Chapter 13, Building Validation into Services*.

Using attributes for metadata

A common debate is when to model XML data using elements and when to use attributes, or whether attributes should be used at all.

Elements are more flexible than attributes, particularly when it comes to writing extensible schemas, as you can always add additional elements (or attributes) to an element. However, once an attribute has been defined, it can't be extended any further.

One approach is to use attributes for metadata and elements for data. For example, on some of our query-based operations (for example. `getSellerItems`, `getBuyerItems`) we have defined two attributes, `startRow` and `endRow`, which are used to control which portion of the result set is returned by the query.

Schema guidelines

It's important to have a clear set of guidelines for schema design. This not only warrants that the best practice is followed, it also ensures that schemas are created consistently, making them more reusable, easier to combine, simpler to understand, and easier to maintain.

Element naming

Consistent naming of elements within an XML Schema will ensure that schemas are easier to understand, and reduce the likelihood of error due to names being spelt differently within a different context.

Name length

While there is no theoretical limit on the length of an element or attribute name, you should try and limit them to a manageable length. Overly long names can reduce the readability of a document as well as make them overly bloated, which, in extreme cases, could have performance implications.

We tend to try and limit names to a maximum of 15 characters; now this may not always be possible, but there are a number of simple strategies.

Compound names

For element and attribute names that are made up of multiple words, we follow the practice of capitalizing the first letter of each word (often called camel case). For example, we would write the name 'shipping address' as `shippingAddress`.

Another approach is to use a separator, that is, a hyphen or an underscore between words. Personally, we don't find this as readable as well as resulting in marginally longer names. Whichever approach you use, you should ensure that you do so consistently.

For types (for example, `complexType` and `simpleType`), we follow the same convention but prefix the name with a '`t`' in order to easily distinguish it from elements and attributes.

> An alternative convention is for type names to have the word `Type`' at the end. However, we are not as keen on this convention as it can lead to type names finishing in `TypeType`. For example we have the element `auctionType`; using this convention; its type name would be `auctionTypeType`.

Naming standards

We also recommend the use of a defined dictionary for commonly used words, abbreviations, and so on to ensure that they are used in a consistent fashion. Areas that should be considered include:

- **Synonyms**: For names that have multiple potential options, for example, Order and Purchase Order, the dictionary should define the standard term to be used.
- **Abbreviations**: For words that are used commonly, it makes sense to define a standard abbreviation. For example, we may use `address` on its own, but when combined with another word (for example, shipping), we use its abbreviation to get `shippingAddr`.
- **Context Based Names**: When a name is used in context, don't repeat the context in the name itself. For example, rather than using `addressLine1` inside an `address` element, we would use `line1`.

> In some cases, this is not always pragmatic, particularly if it reduces clarity in the meaning of the element. For example, if within the context of name, you have the element `family`, then this is not as clear as using `familyName`. So a degree of common sense should be used.

- **Generic Names**: As far as possible, use generic names. For example, avoid using specific company or product names, as this will result in more reusable models and also reduce the likelihood of change.

A sample of the oBay dictionary is shown in the following table:

Standard term	Abbreviation	Synonyms
address	addr	
amount	amt	cost, price, fee
description	desc	
end	end	finish, stop
id	id	number, identifier
item	item	product
max	max	ceiling, maximum, top
min	min	least, lowest, minimum
order	ord	purchase order
start	start	effective, begin
status	status	state
user	usr	client, customer

Namespace considerations

Namespaces are one of the biggest areas of confusion with XML Schemas, yet in reality, they are very straightforward. The purpose of a namespace is just to provide a unique name for an element, type, or attribute, thus allowing us to define components with the same name.

For example, the element `Glass`, will have a different definition to a company that sells windows as opposed to one that runs a bar. The namespace allows us to uniquely identify each definition, so that we can use both definitions within the same instance of an XML document, as well as understand the context in which each element is being used.

If you're familiar with Java, then a namespace is a bit like a package name, that is, you can have multiple classes with the same name, but each one would be defined in a separate package.

One feature of namespaces is that they have a degree of flexibility in how you apply them, which then impacts how you construct and interpret an instance of an XML document. This is often a cause of confusion, especially when they are used inconsistently across multiple schemas.

So it's critical that you define a standard approach to namespaces before defining your canonical model.

Always specify a target namespace

Unless you are defining a chameleon schema (seen later in the chapter) always specify a target namespace.

Default namespace

When defining a schema, you have the option of defining a default namespace. If you do, we would recommend setting the default namespace to be equal to the target namespace. The advantage of this approach is that you only prefix elements, types, and attributes that are defined externally to the schema (that is, anything that is not prefixed is defined locally).

An alternative approach is not to use a default namespace, so that all elements require a prefix. This can often be clearer when combining many schemas from multiple namespaces, especially if you have similarly named elements.

Qualified or unqualified element names

When constructing an XML instance based on an XML Schema, we have the option as the schema designer to decide whether each element should be qualified, that is, have a prefix that identifies the namespace of where the element is defined, or have no prefix, that is, it is unqualified and the origin of the namespace is hidden within the instance.

The approach you take is often a question of style. However, each has its own advantages and disadvantages, particularly when you create XML instances that are defined across multiple namespaces. Take the schema definition for the element `<address>`, as shown in the following code snippet:

```
<xsd:schema xmlns:xsd="http://www.w3.org/2001/XMLSchema"
            xmlns="http://rubiconred.com/obay/xsd/common"
            targetNamespace="http://rubiconred.com/obay/xsd/common"
            elementFormDefault="qualified or unqualified">

    <xsd:element name="address" type="tAddress"/>
    <xsd:complexType name="tAddress">
        <xsd:sequence>
            <xsd:element name="addressLine1" type="xsd:string"/>
            <xsd:element name="addressLine2" type="xsd:string"/>
            <xsd:element name="city" type="xsd:string"/>
            <xsd:element name="state" type="xsd:string"/>
            <xsd:element name="zip" type="xsd:string"/>
            <xsd:element name="country" type="xsd:string"/>
        </xsd:sequence>
    </xsd:complexType>
</xsd:schema>
```

If we chose **unqualified** elements, then an instance of this schema would look as shown in the following code snippet:

```
<cmn:address xmlns:cmn="http://rubiconred.com/obay/xsd/common">
   <addressLine1>7 Pine Drive</addressLine1>
   <addressLine2></addressLine2>
   <city>Eltham<city>
   <state>VIC</state>
   <zip>3088</zip>
   <country>Australia</country>
</cmn:address>
```

However, if we chose to use **qualified** elements, our XML instance would now appear as shown in the following code snippet:

```
<cmn:address xmlns:cmn="http://rubiconred.com/obay/xsd/common">
   <cmn:addressLine1>7 Pine Drive</cmn:addressLine1>
   <cmn:addressLine2></cmn:addressLine2>
   <cmn:city>Eltham<cmn:city>
   <cmn:state>VIC</cmn:state>
   <cmn:zip>3088</cmn:zip>
   <cmn:country>Australia</cmn:country>
</cmn:address>
```

With unqualified namespaces, the XML instance loses most of its namespace declarations and prefixes, resulting in a slimmed down and simpler XML instance that hides the complexities of how the overall schema is assembled.

The advantage of using qualified namespaces is that you can quickly see what namespace an element belongs to. As well as removing any ambiguity, it provides the context in which an element is defined, giving a clearer understanding of its meaning.

Whichever approach you use, it's important to be consistent, as mixing qualified and unqualified schemas will produce instance documents where some elements have a namespace prefix and others don't. This makes it a lot harder to manually create or validate an instance document, as the author needs to understand all the subtleties of the schemas involved, making this approach more error-prone.

Another consideration over which approach to use is whether you are using local or global element declarations, as unqualified namespaces only apply to local elements. Having a mixture of global elements and local unqualified elements in your schema definition will again produce instance documents where some elements have a namespace prefix and others don't, with the same issues mentioned earlier.

A final consideration is whether you are using default namespaces. If you are then you should use qualified names, as unqualified names and default namespaces don't mix.

As we recommend, using both global elements (see later for the reason why) and default namespaces, we would also recommend using qualified namespaces.

Qualified or unqualified attributes

Like elements, XML Schema allows us to choose whether an attribute is qualified or not. Unless an attribute is global (that is, declared a child of `schema` and thus can be used in multiple elements), there is no point in qualifying it.

The simplest way to achieve this is to not specify the `form` and `attributeFormDefault` attributes. This will result in globally declared attributes being prefixed with a namespace and locally declared attributes will have unqualified names.

Namespace naming conventions

We also recommend defining a namespace naming convention, as this will provide greater clarity as well as simplify the overall governance of assets. In the case of oBay, our namespaces use the following convention:

```
http://<domain>/<sub-domain>/<namespace-type>/<subject_area>
```

Here, `obay` is a sub-domain within `rubiconred.com`. The `<namespace-type>` defines the type of component (for example, schema, service, and so on) to which the namespace applies.

So within our canonical model, we have defined several namespaces, including:

```
http://rubiconred.com/obay/xsd/account
http://rubiconred.com/obay/xsd/auction
http://rubiconred.com/obay/xsd/common
```

As part of your naming standards, you should also define standard namespace prefixes for each namespace in your canonical model.

Global versus local

A component (element, simple type, or complex type) is considered global if it's defined as a child of the schema element. If defined within another component, it's considered local. Consider the following fragment of XML:

```
<shipTo>
    <name>
        <title>Mr</title>
        <firstName>James</firstName>
        <lastName>Elliot</lastName>
    </name>
    <address>
        <addressLine1>7 Pine Drive</addressLine1>
        <addressLine2></addressLine2>
        <city>Eltham<city>
        <state>VIC</state>
        <zip>3088</zip>
        <country>Australia</country>
    </address>
</shipTo>
```

One way of implementing its corresponding schema would be to design it to mirror the XML, for example:

```
<xsd:element name="shipTo">
    <xsd:complexType>
        <xsd:sequence>
            <xsd:element name="name">
                <xsd:complexType>
                    <xsd:sequence>
                        <xsd:element name="title"     type="xsd:string"/>
                        <xsd:element name="firstName" type="xsd:string"/>
                        <xsd:element name="lastName"  type="xsd:string"/>
                    </xsd:sequence>
                </xsd:complexType>
            </xsd:element>
            <xsd:element name="address">
                <xsd:complexType>
                    <xsd:sequence>
                        <xsd:element name="line1"     type="xsd:string"/>
                        <xsd:element name="line2"     type="xsd:string"/>
                        <xsd:element name="city"      type="xsd:string"/>
                        <xsd:element name="state"     type="xsd:string"/>
                        <xsd:element name="zip"       type="xsd:string"/>
                        <xsd:element name="country"   type="xsd:string"/>
                    </xsd:sequence>
                </xsd:complexType>
            </xsd:element>
        </xsd:sequence>
    </xsd:complexType>
</xsd:element>
```

Using this approach, only the `shipTo` element is declared globally and thus is reusable; no other elements or types either within this schema or another schema can make use of the elements or types declared inside the `shipTo` element.

Another way of defining the schema would be as shown in the following code snippet:

```
<xsd:element name="shipTo">
    <xsd:complexType>
        <xsd:sequence>
            <xsd:element ref="name"/>
            <xsd:element ref="address/>
        </xsd:sequence>
    </xsd:complexType>
```

```
</xsd:element>

<xsd:element name="name">
   <xsd:complexType>
      <xsd:sequence>
         <xsd:element name="title"     type="xsd:string"/>
         <xsd:element name="firstName" type="xsd:string"/>
         <xsd:element name="lastName"  type="xsd:string"/>
      </xsd:sequence>
   </xsd:complexType>
</xsd:element>

<xsd:element name="address">
   <xsd:complexType>
      <xsd:sequence>
         <xsd:element name="line1"     type="xsd:string"/>
         <xsd:element name="line2"     type="xsd:string"/>
         <xsd:element name="city"      type="xsd:string"/>
         <xsd:element name="state"     type="xsd:string"/>
         <xsd:element name="zip"       type="xsd:string"/>
         <xsd:element name="country"   type="xsd:string"/>
      </xsd:sequence>
   </xsd:complexType>
</xsd:element>
```

With this approach `shipTo`, `name`, and `address` are globally declared. Therefore, the elements `name` and `address` are also reusable now.

You could always go a step further and separately define all the simple types such as title, first name, and so on as global elements.

The temptation may be to define elements you wish to reuse within your schema as global and have the rest as local definitions. However, you should consider the following point:

- Any element you may wish to use as a parameter for a web service operation must be globally defined
- BPEL variables can only be declared for global elements, not local elements

As at the point of schema definition, it's not always easy to determine where an element may need to be reused. We would recommend always declaring your components as global.

Elements versus types

A common dilemma is whether to use elements or types to define global components. Types tend to be more flexible, in that once you've defined the type, it can be reused to define multiple elements of the same type.

Also, once you have defined a type, you can easily use it to define an element. In the following example, we have remodeled the above schema to separately define the types and then use them to define the elements. As a result, we have slightly fewer lines of XML as well as a more flexible model:

```
<xsd:element name="shipTo" type="tShipTo">
<xsd:complexType name="tShipTo">
   <xsd:sequence>
      <xsd:element ref="name"/>
      <xsd:element ref="address/>
   </xsd:sequence>
</xsd:complexType>

<xsd:element name="name" type="tName">

<xsd:complexType name="tName">
   <xsd:sequence>
      <xsd:element name="title"     type="xsd:string"/>
      <xsd:element name="firstName" type="xsd:string"/>
      <xsd:element name="lastName"  type="xsd:string"/>
   </xsd:sequence>
</xsd:complexType>

<xsd:element name="address" type="tAddress">

<xsd:complexType name="tAddress">
   <xsd:sequence>
      <xsd:element name="line1"     type="xsd:string"/>
      <xsd:element name="line2"     type="xsd:string"/>
      <xsd:element name="city"      type="xsd:string"/>
      <xsd:element name="state"     type="xsd:string"/>
      <xsd:element name="zip"       type="xsd:string"/>
      <xsd:element name="country"   type="xsd:string"/>
   </xsd:sequence>
</xsd:complexType>
```

With BPEL 1.1, you can only create variables based on global elements, NOT global types.

When reusing components from other namespaces, refer to the **element** that is defined against the type (as highlighted previously), rather than using the type directly. Otherwise, the namespace of the top element will take on the namespace of the schema that is reusing the type.

Finally, we recommend that you use different names for elements and complex types. Although the XML Schema specification allows for an element and a type to have the same name, this can cause issues for some tools. So for our purposes, we prefix all types with a lower case "`t`" to indicate that it's a type.

Partitioning the canonical model

When building your first SOA application, it's very easy to fall into the trap of defining a single schema that meets the specific needs of your current set of services. However, as each project develops its own schema, it will often redesign its own version of common elements. This not only reduces the opportunity for reuse, but makes interoperability between applications more complicated as well as increases the maintenance burden.

The other common pitfall is to design a single, all encompassing schema that defines all your business objects within an organization. There are two issues with this approach. First, you could end up "boiling the ocean", that is, you set out to define every single business object with the organization and the project never starts because it's waiting for the model to be completed.

Even if you take a more iterative approach, only defining what's required upfront and extending this schema as new applications come on line, you very quickly end up with the situation where every application will become dependent on this single schema. Change often becomes very protracted, as a simple change could potentially impact many applications. The end result is a strict change control being required, often resulting in protracted time frames for changes to be implemented, which is not exactly an agile solution.

The approach, of course, lies somewhere in the middle, and that is to partition your data model into a set of reusable modules, where each module is based on a logical domain. For example, in oBay, we have defined the following schemas:

- `Account.xsd`: Defines every business object specific to a financial account, that is, a record of all debit and credit activities related to a specific user
- `Auction.xsd`: Defines all business objects specific to an auction
- `Order.xsd`: Defines all business objects specific to order fulfillment, that is, from the placement of an order through to its final shipment and delivery
- `User.xsd`: Defines all business objects specific to a user
- `Common.xsd`: This schema is used to define common objects, such as name, address, credit card, which are used by multiple domains, but have no obvious owner

Once we have partitioned our data model, we need to decide on our strategy for namespaces. There are a number of potential approaches, which we cover below.

Single namespace

With this approach, we have a single target namespace which is used by all schema definitions. We typically have a single master document which uses the `xsd:include` element to combine the various schema documents into a single schema.

This approach is illustrated below, where we have a master "oBay" schema that includes all of our other schemas:

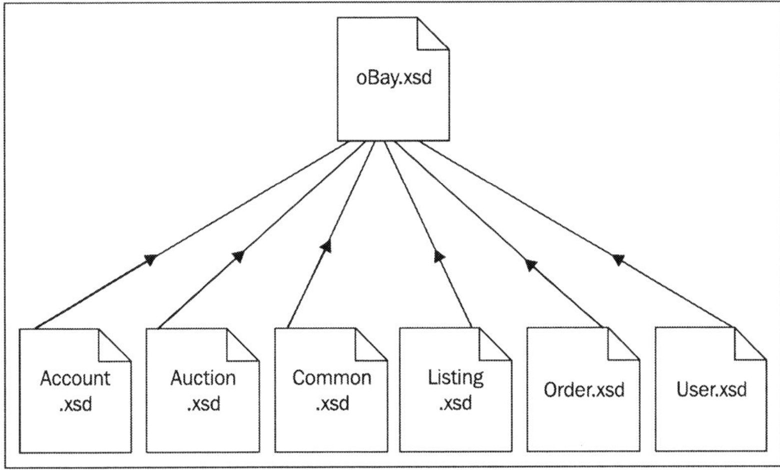

The advantage of this approach is that it keeps it simple, as we only have a single namespace and corresponding prefix to worry about.

The disadvantage is that we have taken a single schema and just broken it up into multiple manageable files. But apart from this, we still have all the other disadvantages that we outlined previously when creating a single master model.

The major disadvantage is that if we change any single document, we change the entire model. This would result in a new version of the entire model, and thus for us, potentially having to update every single service implemented to date.

Multiple namespaces

The other approach, of course, is to define a namespace for each individual domain; each schema can then reference a definition in other schema's by making use of the `xsd:import` element. This is the approach we have taken for oBay and is illustrated as follows:

With this approach, we have no master schema, thus services only need to import the parts of the canonical model which are relevant to them. Whilst with the single namespace approach, you will typically end up being required to import the entire schema.

Another advantage of this approach is that it allows different groups to be responsible for each namespace, and for each namespace to evolve to a certain extent, independent of others.

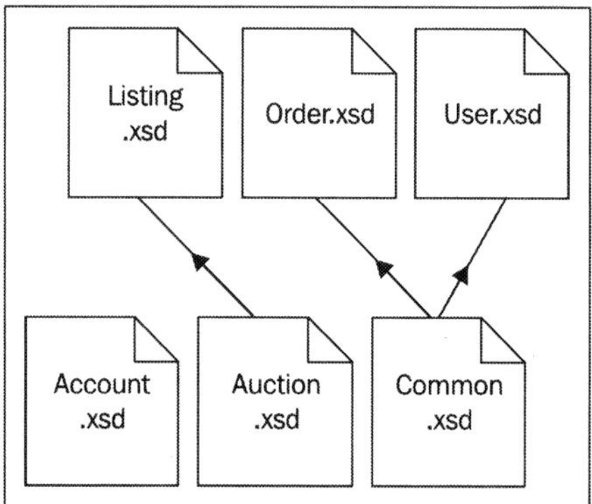

The drawback to this approach is that instance documents become more complex, as they will need to reference multiple namespaces. To prevent this from becoming a problem, it's important to partition your data model into sensible domains and also resist the urge to over partition it and end up with too many namespaces.

Separate common objects into their own namespaces

Common objects, which are used across multiple namespaces, should be created in their own namespace. For example, the address element is used across all domains. If we were to create it in the order namespace, we would be forcing all our other schemas to import the order schema, which would unnecessarily complicate our XML instances. The issue would become more acute if common object definitions were sprinkled across multiple namespaces.

Using WSDL to define business services

A service, as defined by a WSDL document, is made up of two parts. Firstly, there is the abstract part, which defines the individual operations that make up a service, the messages that define the parameters for the operations, and the types which define our XML data types used by our messages.

The second part of the WSDL document defines the binding, that is, how to physically encode the messages on the wire (for example, SOAP), the transport protocol on the wire (for example, HTTP), and also the physical location or endpoint of the service (for example, its URL).

Ideally, we should only be concerned with designing the abstract part of the WSDL document, as the runtime binding should be more of a deployment detail. However, the reality is that the style of binding has implications for how we design the abstract components if we want to ensure interoperability between service providers and consumers.

By far, the most common binding for a web service is SOAP over HTTP. However, this comes in a number of different varieties, as we can specify whether the invocation method adopts a Remote Procedure Call (RPC) style or a document style binding (that is, a more message-oriented approach). We also have a choice as to whether the SOAP message is encoded or literal. This gives us four basic combinations, that is, RPC/encoded, RPC/literal, Document/encoded, and Document/literal.

It is generally accepted that for the purposes of interoperability, Document/literal is the best practice. However, the Document/literal style has some drawbacks.

Firstly, not all Document/literal services are WS-I compliant, as WS-I recommends that the SOAP body contains only a single child element within the SOAP body. However, Document/literal allows you to define WSDL messages containing multiple parts, where each part is manifested as a child element within the SOAP body.

Another minor issue with document/literal is that it doesn't contain the operation name in the SOAP message, which can make dispatching of messages difficult in some scenarios and can also make debugging complicated when monitoring SOAP traffic, particularly when multiple operations contain the same parameters.

Use Document (literal) wrapped

Document Wrapped is a particular style or use of Document/literal that addresses these issues. With this approach, the request and response parameters for an operation are 'wrapped' within a single request and response element.

The request wrapper must have the same name as the corresponding operation, while the name of the response wrapper is derived by appending 'Response' to the operation name.

This ensures that the SOAP body only contains a single nested element whose name matches that of the operation.

These wrapping elements must be defined as elements, not complex types. While WSDL allows either, the use of `complexTypes` is not WS-I compliant.

This approach ensures that you have WS-I compliant messages.

> A document wrapped web service looks very similar to a RPC/literal style, as they both produce a SOAP message containing a single nested element matching the name of the operation within the `soap:Body`.

Building your abstract WSDL document

Once we have standardized on the document wrapped pattern, we can define the abstract part of our WSDL contract at this stage, without having to worry about the actual binding.

WSDL namespace

As with our schema definitions, we need to define a namespace for our business service. Here we would recommend defining a different namespace for each service. This should also be different from the namespaces used within your canonical model.

Defining the 'wrapper' elements

In the 10gR3 release of SOA Suite, we used to advocate defining the wrapper elements within the WSDL document of the web service, as separating those out into a standalone schema provided little value.

With 11gR1, we recommend a **different** approach—to define the wrapper elements in a separate schema in their own namespace, which we then import into our WSDL document. This allows us to reuse these wrapper elements within our composite.

Recall the basic composite design pattern that we introduced in the previous chapter, where we use a Mediator as the entry point for a composite, as shown in the following screenshot:

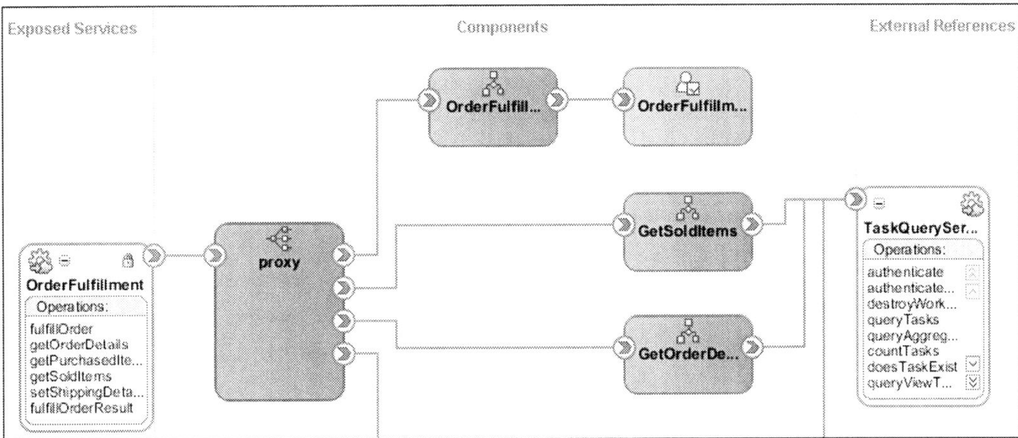

With this pattern, the Mediator implements the abstract WSDL for our service, and acts as a proxy responsible for routing requests from the service consumer to the appropriate components within the composite.

Each of these components, in turn, implements one or more of the operations defined in our abstract WSDL. By separating out the wrapper elements into a separate schema, we can reuse these when defining the WSDL for each of these components.

This ensures that within our composite, we have a single consistent definition of our message types. This makes it simpler to manage change as well as ensuring our proxy is not required to perform any transformations.

Whichever approach you follow, resist the temptation to define your wrapper elements within your canonical model, as doing so will pollute your model as well as make changes harder to manage.

Defining a schema for our wrapper elements

When defining an XML Schema for our wrapper elements, we need to import the relevant parts of our canonical model, and for each imported schema, define its namespace and corresponding prefix.

For example, we have defined our wrapper elements for the `OrderFulfillment` service in the schema `OrderFulfillmentEBM.xsd`. This imports the `Order.xsd` schema, defined in the namespace '`http://rubiconred.com/obay/xsd/order`', as highlighted in the following code:

```
<xsd:schema xmlns:xsd="http://www.w3.org/2001/XMLSchema"
targetNamespace="http://rubiconred.com/obay/ebm/OrderFulfillment"
   xmlns="http://rubiconred.com/obay/ebm/OrderFulfillment"
   xmlns:ord="http://rubiconred.com/obay/xsd/order"
   elementFormDefault="qualified">

   <xsd:import namespace="http://rubiconred.com/obay/xsd/order"
               schemaLocation="Order_v1_0.xsd" />

    <!-- Wrapper Elements Defined Here -->

</xsd:schema >
```

Next, we can define our wrapper elements, so for the `setShippingInstruction` operation within the `OrderFulfillment` service, we have defined the following:

```
<xsd:element name="setShippingInstruction"
             type="tSetShippingInstruction"/>

<xsd:element name="setShippingInstructionResponse"
            type="tSetShippingInstructionResponse"/>

<xsd:complexType name="tSetShippingInstruction">
   <xsd:sequence>
       <xsd:element ref="ord:orderNo"/>
       <xsd:element ref="ord:shippingDetail" />
  </xsd:sequence>
</xsd:complexType>

<xsd:complexType name="tSetShippingInstructionResponse">
  <xsd:sequence>
       <xsd:element ref="ord:order"/>
  </xsd:sequence>
</xsd:complexType>
```

Importing our wrapper elements

The next step is to import the schema containing the wrapper elements into our WSDL; we do this by using an `import` statement within the `types` section of our WSDL, as shown in the following code snippet:

```
<types>
  <xsd:schema elementFormDefault="qualified">
    <xsd:import schemaLocation="OrderFulfilmentEBM_v1_0.xsd"
        namespace="http://rubiconred.com/obay/ebm/OrderFulfilment"/>
    ...
  </xsd:schema>
<types>
```

Before we can refer to the wrapper elements contained within this schema, we must also declare its namespace and corresponding prefix within the `definitions` element of the WSDL, as highlighted in the following code snippet:

```
<definitions name="OrderFulfillment"
    targetNamespace="http://rubiconred.com/obay/svc/OrderFulfillment"
    xmlns:tns="http://rubiconred.com/obay/svc/OrderFulfillment"
    xmlns:ebm="http://rubiconred.com/obay/ebm/OrderFulfillment"
    xmlns="http://schemas.xmlsoap.org/wsdl/"
    xmlns:xsd="http://www.w3.org/2001/XMLSchema">
```

Defining the 'message' elements

Once we have defined and imported our wrapper elements, it's pretty straightforward to define our message elements. We should have one message element per wrapper element. From a naming perspective, we use the same name for the message element as we did for our wrapper elements. So for our `setShippingInstruction` operation, we have defined the following message elements:

```
<message name="setShippingInstruction">
   <part name="payload" element="ebm:setShippingInstruction"/>
</message>

<message name="setShippingInstructionResponse">
  <part name="payload" element="ebm:setShippingInstructionResponse"/>
</message>
```

Defining the 'PortType' Element

The final component of an abstract WSDL document is to define the `portType` and its corresponding operations. For our `OrderFulfillment` service, we have defined the following:

```
<portType name="orderFulfilment">
    <operation name="setShippingInstruction">
        <input message="tns:setShippingInstruction"/>
        <output message="tns:setShippingInstructionResponse"/>
    </operation>
    <operation name="submitInvoice">
        <input message="tns:submitInvoice"/>
        <output message="tns:submitInvoiceResponse"/>
    </operation>
    ...
</portType>
```

Note that for the sake of brevity, we have only listed two operations; for the full set, please refer to `OrderFulfilment.wsdl` contained within the sample application.

Using XML Schema and the WSDL within SOA Suite

Once we have defined the abstract WSDL and corresponding XML Schemas, we are ready to implement the services they define within the SOA Suite. These services will typically be implemented as composites or proxy services within the Service Bus.

As we've seen in earlier chapters, the simplest way to use a predefined schema within a composite is to import the schema from the filesystem into our SOA project.

When we do this, JDeveloper does two things. First, it will add a copy of the schema file to our SOA project. Second, it will add an import statement into the WSDL of the service component (for example, BPEL, Mediator) that is referring to it, for example:

```
<types>
    <schema xmlns="http://www.w3.org/2001/XMLSchema">
        <import  namespace="http://rubiconred.com/obay/xsd/order"
                 schemaLocation="Order_v1_0.xsd" />
    </schema>
</types>
```

Here, schemaLocation is a relative URL that refers to the imported file. In many scenarios, this is fine. However, if you have several processes, each referring to their own local copy of the same XML Schema, which is likely to be the case with our canonical model. Then when you need to change the schema, you will be required to update every copy.

One way is to just have a master copy of your XML Schema and use build scripts to update each of the copies every time you create a build. However, this isn't ideal. A better approach is to have a single copy of the schema that is referenced by all composites.

Sharing XML Schemas across composites

The SOA infrastructure incorporates a **Metadata Service (MDS)**, which allows you to share common artifacts such as XML Schemas across SOA composites. MDS supports two types of repository:

- **File-based repository**: This is quicker and easier to set up, so it is typically used as the design-time MDS by JDeveloper.
- **Database repository**: This is installed as part of the SOA infrastructure. This is used at runtime, but can also be used by JDeveloper as the MDS at design-time.

By default, a file-based repository is installed with JDeveloper and sits under the directory structure:

```
<JDeveloper Home>/jdeveloper/integration/seed
```

This already contains the subdirectory soa, which is reserved for and contains artifacts used by the SOA infrastructure. For artifacts that we wish to share across our applications in JDeveloper, we should create the subdirectory apps (under the seed directory). This is critical as when we deploy the artifacts to the SOA infrastructure, they will be placed in the apps namespace.

For oBay, we have created the following file structure under apps:

```
com/rubiconred/obay/xsd/Account_v1_0.xsd
com/rubiconred/obay/xsd/Auction_v1_0.xsd
com/rubiconred/obay/xsd/Base_v1_0.xsd
com/rubiconred/obay/xsd/Common_v1_0.xsd
com/rubiconred/obay/xsd/Item_v1_0.xsd
com/rubiconred/obay/xsd/Listing_v1_0.xsd
com/rubiconred/obay/xsd/Order_v1_0.xsd
com/rubiconred/obay/xsd/User_v1_0.xsd
```

We have defined the path based on the namespace for each of the XML Schemas as this makes it simple to locate the schema within the resource browser.

Defining an MDS connection

Before we can reference these from within JDeveloper, we need to define a connection to the file-based MDS. Within JDeveloper, from the **File** menu, select **New** to launch the **Gallery**. Under **Categories**, select **General | Connections**, and then select **SOA_MDS Connection** from the **Items** list. This will launch the **MDS Connection Wizard**, as shown in the following screenshot:

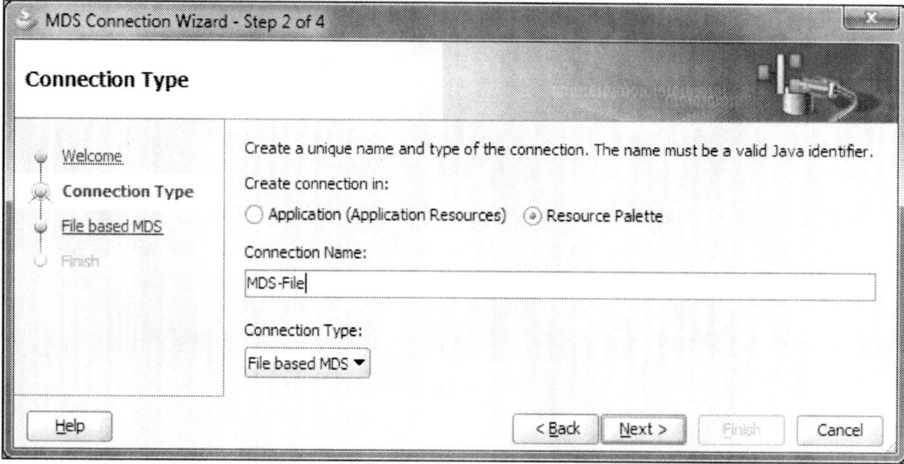

Create the connection in the **Resource Palette**, give it an appropriate name, specify a **Connection Type** of **MDS-File**, and then click on **Next**.

We then need to specify the MDS root folder on our local filesystem. This will be the directory that contains the `apps` directory, namely:

```
<JDeveloper Home>\jdeveloper\integration\seed
```

Once specified, click **Next**, and then click **Finish**.

Alternatively, we could create a **DB based MDS** connection against the MDS database repository installed as part of the SOA infrastructure. In this case, we would need to specify the database connectivity information for the SOA MDS schema (which we defined when we installed the SOA Suite).

Importing schemas from MDS

We import schemas from MDS in a similar fashion to how we import them from the local filesystem. The key here is that when we launch the **SOA Resource Browser**, we select **Resource Palette** from the drop-down menu (as shown in the following screenshot).

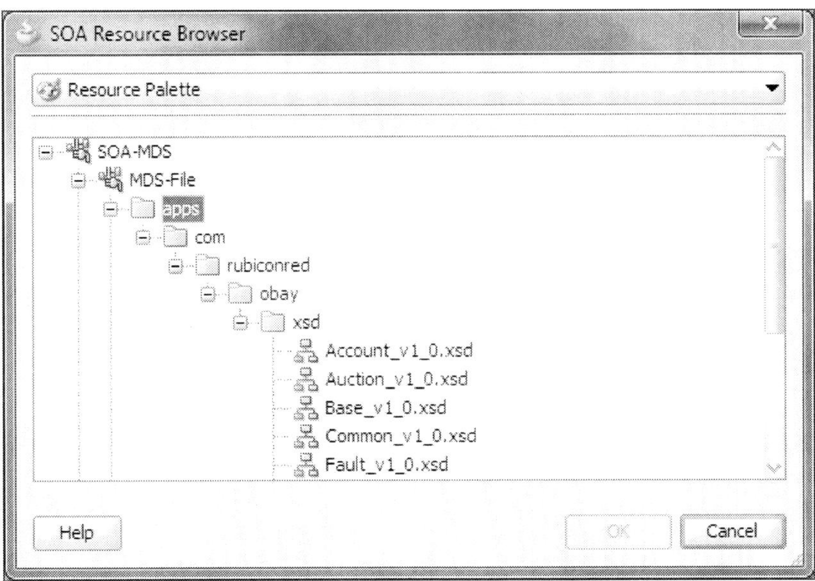

Select the schema that you wish to import, and click **OK**. This will take you back to the **Import Schema File** window. Make sure you deselect **Copy to Project** (as circled in the following screenshot):

When we import a schema in this fashion, JDeveloper will import it as an **Inline Schema**, meaning it doesn't actually make a copy of the schema; rather it just adds an import statement into the WSDL for the service component where the `schemaLocation` attribute is set to the specified URL.

For schemas referenced by the MDS, the `schemaLocation` attribute takes the following format:

```
oramds:/apps/<schema name>
```

While `oramds` indicates that it is located in the MDS, `apps` indicates that it is in the application namespace and `<schema name>` is the full path name of the schema in the deployed archive. So in the preceding example, it would be:

```
schemaLocation="oramds:/apps/com/rubiconred/obay/xsd/Common_v1_0.xsd"
```

The schema location doesn't specify the physical location of the schema; rather it is relative to the MDS (which is specific to the environment in which the composite is deployed). This makes the WSDL more portable, as we don't have to modify the schema location for each environment that it's deployed to (as we did with SOA Suite 10.1.3).

Manually importing schemas

Instead of using the **SOA Resource Browser** to import the schema, it may seem simpler (particularly if we have to import multiple schemas) to manually edit the WSDL file to contain the appropriate import statements.

However, there is one nuance that we need to be aware of, that is, we need to define in the application properties how it should resolve the location of metadata in the `apps` namespace. The reason we didn't have to worry about this earlier is that when we imported the schema via the resource browser, JDeveloper automatically updated the application properties for us.

Within the **Application Resources** view for our SOA application, you will notice that it contains the file **adf:config.xml**, as shown in the following screenshot:

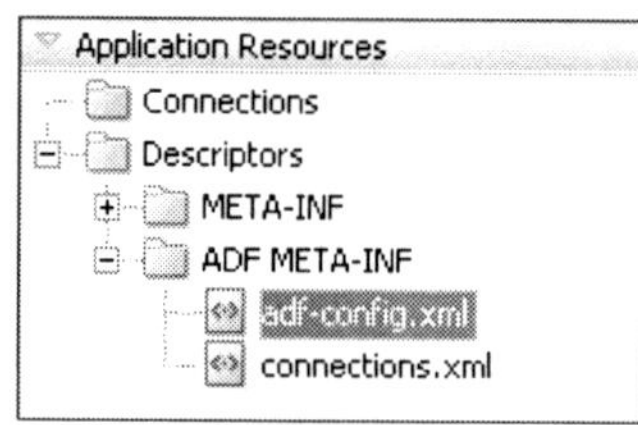

Double-click on this to open it, switch to the source view, and scroll down to the `metadata-namespaces` section, as shown in the following code snippet:

```
<persistence-config>
  <metadata-namespaces>
    <namespace metadata-store-usage="mstore-usage_1"
               path="/soa/shared"/>
    <namespace metadata-store-usage="mstore-usage_2"
               path="/apps/com"/>
  </metadata-namespaces>
  <metadata-store-usages>
    <metadata-store-usage id="mstore-usage_1">
      <metadata-store class-name
        ="oracle.mds.persistence.stores.file.FileMetadataStore">

        <property value="${oracle.home}/integration"
                  name="metadata-path"/>
        <property value="seed" name="partition-name"/>
      </metadata-store>
    </metadata-store-usage>
    <metadata-store-usage id="mstore-usage_2">
      <metadata-store class-name
        ="oracle.mds.persistence.stores.file.FileMetadataStore">

        <property value="${oracle.home}/integration"
                  name="metadata-path"/>
        <property value="seed" name="partition-name"/>
      </metadata-store>
    </metadata-store-usage>
  </metadata-store-usages>
</persistence-config>
```

By default, this contains a single `namespace` entry and a corresponding `metadata-store-usage` entry. However, for those applications where we have imported a resource from MDS, it will contain a second entry (highlighted earlier), which defines the MDS repository to the application. If we manually edit the WSDL files to import a schema (something we will do in a moment), then we will need to manually edit this file.

If you examine the definition of `mstore-usage_2`, you will see that it's the same as the default definition `mstore-usage_1` and so is redundant. This is because we choose to use the file-based repository installed with JDeveloper.

Thus the only change we need to make to the default `adf:config.xml` file is to add a second namespace entry that references the default metadata store and defines the `apps` path, as shown in the following code snippet:

```
<persistence-config>
  <metadata-namespaces>
    <namespace metadata-store-usage="mstore-usage_1"
               path="/soa/shared"/>
    <namespace metadata-store-usage="mstore-usage_1"
               path="/apps/com"/>
  </metadata-namespaces>
  <metadata-store-usages>
    <metadata-store-usage id="mstore-usage_1">
      <metadata-store class-name
        ="oracle.mds.persistence.stores.file.FileMetadataStore">

        <property value="${oracle.home}/integration"
                  name="metadata-path"/>
        <property value="seed" name="partition-name"/>
      </metadata-store>
    </metadata-store-usage>
  </metadata-store-usages>
</persistence-config>
```

Note that for those scenarios where we are using the DB-based MDS of the SOA infrastructure, we would need to keep the `mstore-usage_2 entry` and configure it appropriately, for example:

```
<metadata-store-usage id="mstore-usage_2">
  <metadata-store class-name=
    "oracle.mds.persistence.stores.db.DBMetadataStore">

    <property value="DEV_MDS" name="jdbc-userid"/>
    <property value="welcome1" name="jdbc-password"/>
    <property value="jdbc:oracle:thin:@localhost:1521:XE"
                    name="jdbc-url"/>
    <property value="soa-infra" name="partition-name"/>
  </metadata-store>
</metadata-store-usage>
```

Deploying schemas to the SOA infrastructure

Before we can deploy a composite that references artifacts held in MDS, we must deploy those artifacts to the MDS on the SOA infrastructure. To do this, we need to create a `JAR` file containing the shared artifacts and then deploy it as part of an SOA Bundle.

Creating a JAR file within JDeveloper

To create this JAR file within JDeveloper, create a **Generic Application** (for example, **obayMetadata**) and when prompted to, create a project and give it an appropriate name (for example, `mdslib`). In the application navigator, right-click the **mdslib** project and select **Project Properties**. This will launch the **Project Properties** window, select **Deployment** from the navigational tree, as shown in the following screenshot:

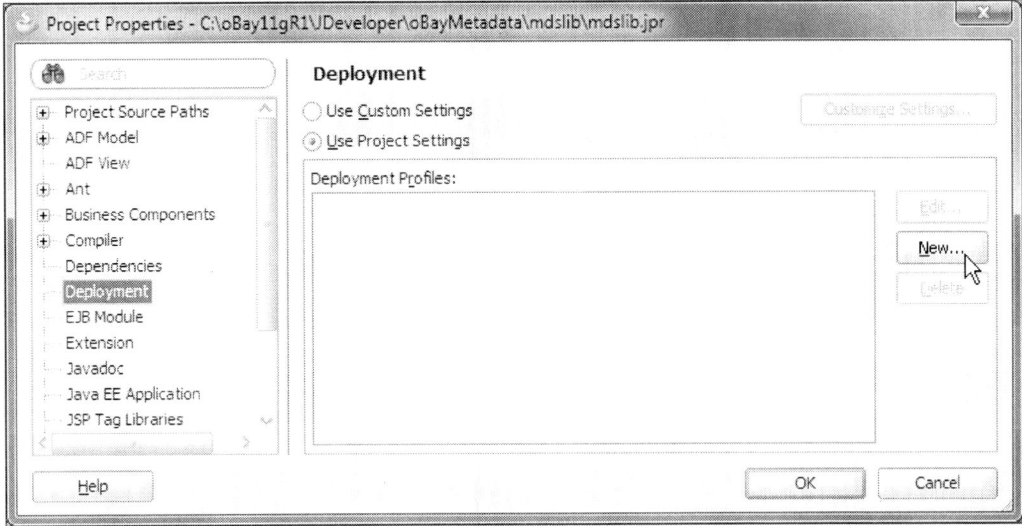

Click **New...**, this will launch the **Create Deployment Profile** dialog. Specify an archive type of **JAR File**, specify an appropriate name (for example, **mdslib**), and click **OK**. This will launch the **Edit JAR Deployment Profile Properties** window, where we can specify what goes in the JAR file.

We only want to include the actual XML Schemas in the JAR file, so deselect **Include Manifest File**, then select **File Groups** | **Project Output** | **Contributors** from the navigational tree, and deselect **Project Output Directory** and **Project Dependencies**.

Now we can specify the actual schemas we wish to add to the JAR file. Click on **Add**. This will launch the **Add Contributor** window. Click on the magnifying glass and browse to the **apps** directory that we previously created and click **OK**. Next select **File Groups | Project Output | Filters**, and check that only the files we want are included within the JAR file.

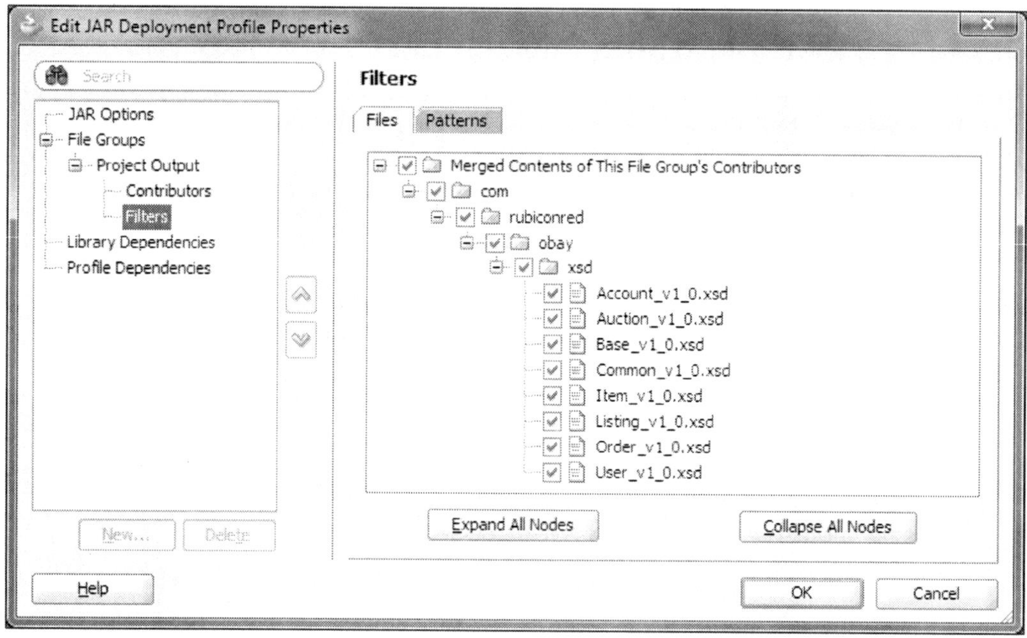

Click **OK** to confirm the content of the JAR file, and then click **OK** one more time to complete the deployment profile, finally, from the main menu select **Save All**.

Creating an SOA Bundle for a JAR file

In order to deploy our JAR file to the metadata repository, we need to place it within an SOA Bundle (see *Chapter 19, Packaging and Deployment* for more details on what an SOA Bundle is) and deploy that to our SOA infrastructure.

To create an **SOA Bundle**, from the **Application Menu** select **Application Properties**, which will launch the corresponding window. From the navigational tree, select **Deployment**, and then click **New**. This will launch the **Create Deployment Profile** window, as shown in the following screenshot:

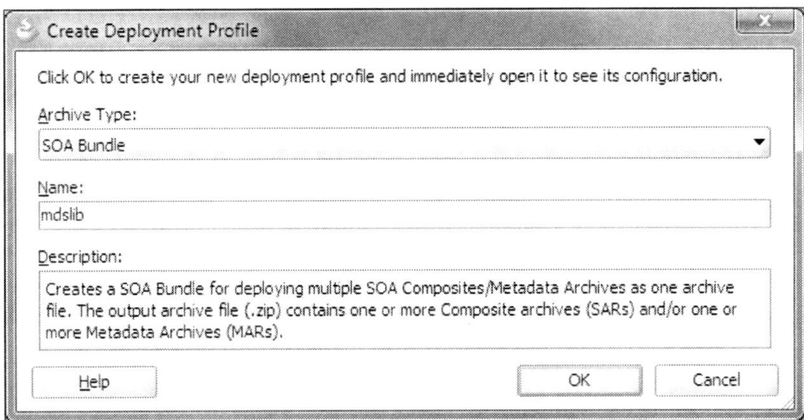

Specify an archive type of **SOA Bundle** and an appropriate name and then click **OK**. This will launch the **SOA Bundle Deployment Profile Properties** window; select **Dependencies** from the navigational tree, and ensure that **mdslib** is selected.

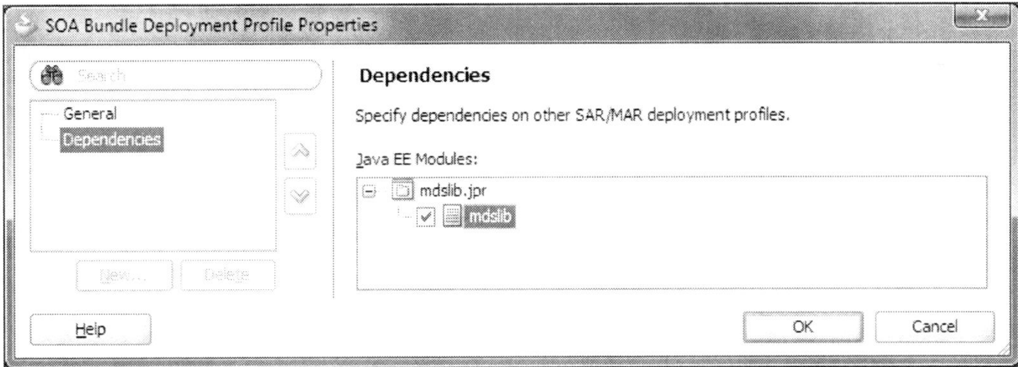

Click **OK** twice and then select **Save All** from the toolbar. We are now ready to deploy our XML Schemas to the metadata repository. In order to do this, from the **Application Menu**, select **Deploy | SOA Bundle Name**. This will launch the **Deployment Action** dialog. Select **Deploy to Application Server** and follow the standard steps to deploy it to your target SOA infrastructure server(s).

The schemas will then be made available to SOA Composites deployed on the same SOA infrastructure.

Importing the WSDL document into a composite

As discussed in the previous chapter, when creating a composite, it is a good practice to use a Mediator as a proxy for the composite, which implements the abstract WSDL contract that we have designed.

Essentially, there are two approaches to this. The first is to create a Mediator in the normal way, using the appropriate template—synchronous, asynchronous, or one-way. When you do this, JDeveloper will create a basic WSDL file for the process. You can then modify this WSDL (using the WSDL editor in JDeveloper) to conform to the abstract WSDL that you have already defined.

The alternative is to import the abstract WSDL document into the Mediator itself. With this approach, you create your Mediator using the template for an **Interface Definition from WSDL**, as shown in the following screenshot:

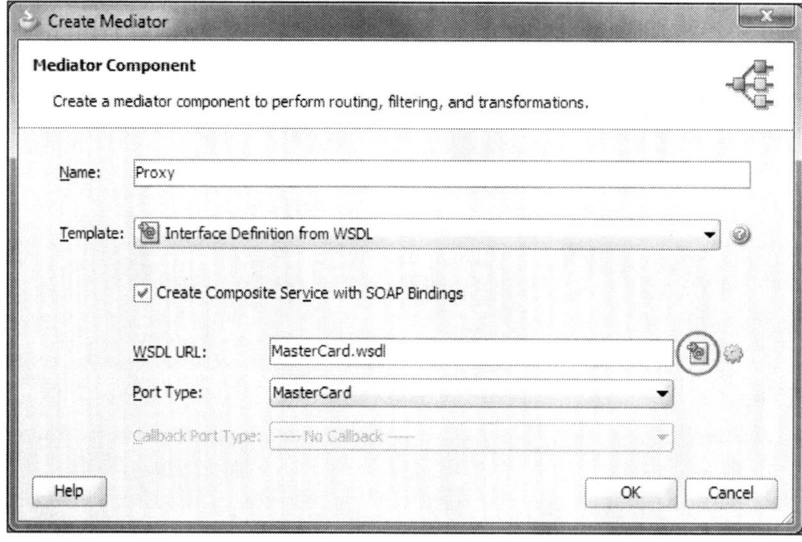

Ensure that **Create Composite Service with SOAP Bindings** is selected. Then click on **Find existing WSDLs** (circled in the preceding screenshot) and select the WSDL we want to import from the local filesystem. Ensure that the appropriate Port Type is selected and click **OK**.

This will add an empty Mediator component to our composite and expose it as an external service.

Note that if the WSDL references any external resources defined in the MDS, we must first define the MDS repository to the applications; otherwise we will get an exception when we try to create the Mediator.

The simplest way to achieve this, when we first create a new SOA application, is to create the project using the template for an **Empty Composite**. We can then update the `adf:config.xml` file, as described earlier. Finally, we can add a Mediator to the composite and create it based on our predefined WSDL.

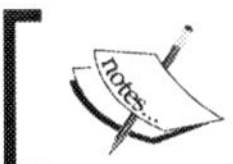

We can also create a BPEL process based on our abstract WSDL by following the same approach.

Sharing XML Schemas in the Service Bus

As with composites, it is possible within the Service Bus to create multiple projects each with their own local copy of the schema. However, as before, it's considered best practice to only have a single copy of each schema.

This is easily achieved by having a single project that defines your schemas, which is then shared across other projects. In order to be consistent with the SOA infrastructure, we have defined the project `mds`, and under this, created an identical folder structure into which we have imported our schemas.

For example, to mirror how we have deployed the order schema to MDS, we have created the folder structure `com/rubiconred/obay/xsd` within the `mds` project, into which we have imported the `Order_v1_0.xsd` schema.

Importing the WSDL document into the Service Bus

Before we create a proxy service that implements our abstract WSDL, we need to define the bindings for the service, which in our case will be Document/literal. We can either modify the WSDL file to include the bindings before we import it, or add in the bindings after we have imported the WSDL into the Service Bus.

Defining the SOAP bindings for our service and each of its corresponding operations is pretty straightforward, as we have already settled on Document/literal for this.

For example, the bindings for our `orderFulfillment` service are as follows:

```
<binding xmlns:soap="http://schemas.xmlsoap.org/wsdl/soap/"
         name="orderFulfillmentBinding"
         type="tns:orderFulfillment">
    <soap:binding style="document"
                  transport="http://schemas.xmlsoap.org/soap/http"/>
    <operation name=" setShippingInstruction">
        <soap:operation style="document"
                        soapAction="setShippingInstruction"/>
        <input>
           <soap:body use="literal"/>
        </input>
        <output>
            <soap:body use="literal"/>
        </output>
    </operation>
    <operation name="submitInvoice">
        <soap:operation style="document" soapAction="submitInvoice"/>
        <input>
           <soap:body use="literal"/>
        </input>
        <output>
            <soap:body use="literal"/>
        </output>
    </operation>
    ...
</binding>
```

When we import our WSDL, if it imports any schemas, then the Service Bus will present us with a warning message, similar to the one shown in the following screenshot, indicating that there were validation errors with the WSDL:

The WSDL "orderFullfilment" was successfully created with validation errors.
View the WSDL/Conflicts to see detailed diagnostic messages.

If you look at the list of resources in the browser, it will also have an **X** next to the WSDL we just imported.

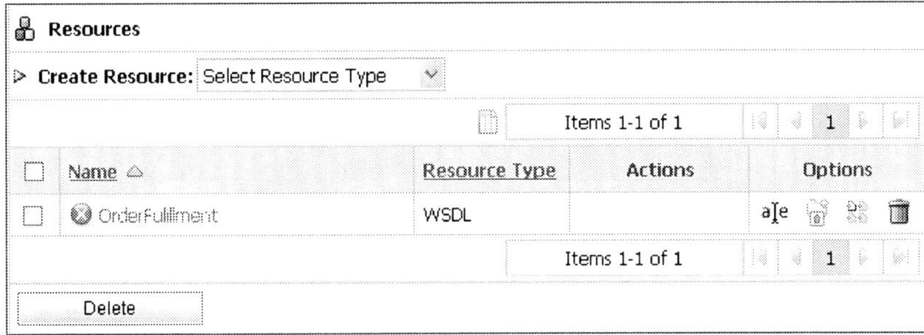

If you click on the WSDL name to edit it, the Service Bus will display the WSDL details with the error **One of the WSDL dependencies is invalid**.

This is because if a WSDL references any external resources (that is, the order schema in this case), we must first import that resource into the Service Bus and then update the WSDL reference to point to the imported resource.

To do this, click on the button **Edit References**. The Service Bus will display a window listing all the references included in the WSDL, with a section listing all the schema references, as shown in the following screenshot:

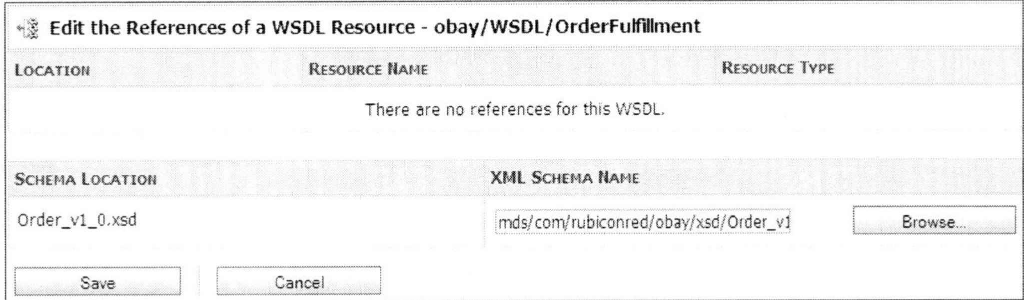

Clicking on the **Browse...** button will launch a window from where you can select the corresponding XML Schema that the WSDL is referring to, as shown in the following screenshot:

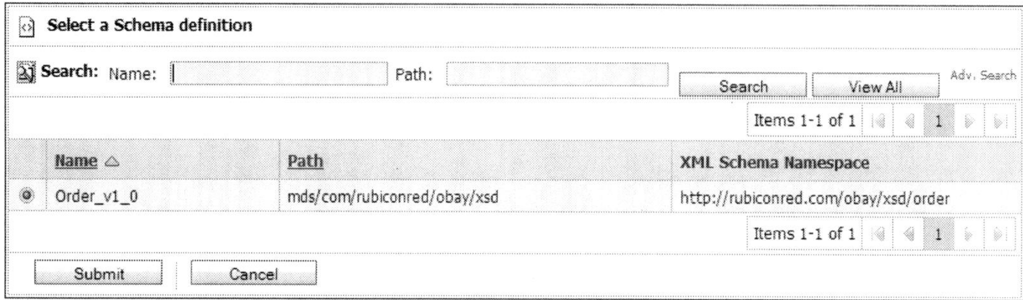

By default, the window will list all the schemas defined to the Service Bus, though you can restrict the list by defining the search criteria. In the case of our `orderFulfilment` service, just select the schema `Order_v1_0.xsd`, and click on **Submit**.

This will take you back to the **Edit References** screen and click **Save**. This will take you back to the **View/Edit WSDL** screen, which should display the confirmation **The References for the WSDL "orderFulfillment" were successfully updated**.

Your WSDL can now be used to define a proxy service in the normal way.

If you import a schema into the Service Bus, which references other schemas, then you will need to go through a similar process to define all its dependencies.

Strategies for managing change

One of the key design principles behind SOA is that systems should be designed and built to accommodate future changes in response to ever-changing business requirements.

So far, we have looked at how to design and build the initial system, so that when change does occur, it can be isolated through the use of service contracts to particular parts of the overall system.

While allowing us to restrict the impact of change, it doesn't completely mitigate all the complexities, especially when you consider that the consumer and provider of a service may be in completely separate organizations.

Major and minor versions

When we upgrade the version of a service, for example, from version 1 to version 2, then from the consumer's perspective, there are two possible outcomes. Either the version 1 consumer can continue to successfully use version 2 of the service, in which case the service is said to be backward compatible or the change will break the existing contract.

To be explicit, a service is said to be backward compatible if **ALL** messages that would have been successfully processed by version 1 of the service, will be successfully processed by version 2 of the service.

It is a good practice to assign a version number to each service, which indicates the level of backward compatibility. A typical approach is to assign a major and minor version of the format `<major>`, `<minor>` (for example, 1.0, 1.1, 2.0, and so on), where:

- A minor change signifies a change that is backward compatible with previous versions of the service that share the same major number. These types of changes typically contain small new features, bug fixes, and so on.
- A major change signifies a change that is incompatible with a previous deployment of the service. Major changes typically indicate significant new features or major revisions to the existing services.

You also have the concept of forward compatibility, whereby the consumer is upgraded to use a future version of the service, before the actual provider of the service is upgraded.

If we examine the anatomy of a web service, it is essentially made up of three components, namely, its WSDL contract, referenced data types from our canonical model, and the actual implementation of the service.

From a versioning standpoint, we need to consider how a change to any of these components is reflected in the version of the overall service.

Service implementation versioning

This may seem a strange topic to cover. After all, surely one of the key concepts of SOA is to isolate change. For example, if I change the implementation of a service, but the consumer sees no change to the contract, then has it really changed at all?

Initially, the answer may seem obvious. However, if we revisit our earlier definition of backward compatible, we can see some issues:

> *A service is said to be backwards compatible if* **ALL** *messages that would have been successfully processed by version 1 of the service, will be successfully processed by version 2 of the service.*

Under this definition, if we add some extra validation to version 2 of the service (for example, we check that a date is in the future). This would mean some messages valid under the original version are no longer valid. The same sort of scenario could again occur if we were to fix a bug (or even introduce one).

Another more surreptitious change is one whereby we change the processing of the data, so that ALL messages are still processed successfully, but the result is different. For example, if we had a service which returned the price of an item, but instead of returning the price in dollars and cents, it now returned the price in cents.

With each of these scenarios, there is no hard and fast rule. However, when you implement these types of changes, you need to consider whether it requires the release of a new version of a service and whether that should be a minor or major version.

Another way of handling this type of change is not to modify the version of the service, but rather provide a means of notifying the consumer that there has been a change to the service. One mechanism for managing this is through the Oracle Enterprise Repository.

Schema versioning

When we modify a schema, we follow the same core principles for major and minor versions that we outlined earlier: a minor change to a schema indicates that an instance document, which was created against a previous version of the schema, is still valid against the new version of the schema, as long as the schemas share the same major version number. Minor changes include:

- The definition of new elements, attributes, and types
- Adding optional attributes and elements to existing elements and types
- Making existing mandatory attributes and elements optional
- Convert an element into a choice group
- Making simple types less restrictive

Changing schema location

Encode the schema version in the filename of the schema; for example, we have named our auction schema `Auction_v1_0.xsd`. Whenever we import a schema, either in another schema or within a WSDL document, the `schemaLocation` attribute will contain the version of the schema being used.

- This has two advantages, we can immediately see what version of a schema a web service is based on, simply by looking at what files we are importing within the WSDL. Additionally, it allows us to have multiple versions of a schema deployed side-by-side allowing each service to upgrade to a newer version of a schema as it suits them.
- When we upgrade a service to use the new version of a schema, then of course we will have a corresponding new version of the service.

Updating schema version attribute

Use the schema version attribute to document the version of the schema. Note that this is purely for documentation, as there is no processing of this attribute by the parser. This ensures that if the schema is renamed so as to remove the encoding of the schema version from the filename, we still know the version of that schema.

Resisting changing the schema namespace

One common practice is to embed the version of the schema within its namespace, and update the namespace for new versions of the schema. However, this has the potential to cause major change to both consumers and providers of a service, so I would strongly recommend that you use this approach with care, if at all.

Firstly, when you change the namespace of a schema, it is no longer backward compatible with previous versions of the schema. So by definition, changing the namespace is a major change in its own right. Therefore, never change the namespace for a minor change.

For major changes, changing the namespace would seem a very valid approach, as apart from being a clear indication to the client that we have introduced a service that is not backward compatible, it will prevent you from successfully calling any of the operations provided by the new version of the service.

However, it is important to understand the magnitude of this change, as it will typically break a number of components on both the client and service provider. For example, all your XPath assignments and XSLT transformations will have to be updated to use the new namespace. Therefore, implementing the change will be more time-consuming.

In some ways, you may want to consider how significant a major change is. For example, the change might impact one operation out of ten. Do you really want your clients to have to reimplement every call to every single operation because one operation (which they might not be using) has changed?

WSDL versioning

When we modify our WSDL contract, we again follow the same core principles for major and minor versions that we outlined previously. From a service perspective, a minor change includes:

- Addition of an operation: This merely extends the WSDL and thus on its own is backwards compatible
- Addition of a new optional parameter within the element wrapper used by an input message
- Making existing mandatory parameters within the element wrapper optional for input messages

While major changes would include:

- Deletion or renaming of an operation
- Changes to the input and output parameters of an operation that don't fall under the category of a minor change, that is, adding a new parameter whether optional or mandatory to the response wrapper

Incorporating changes to the canonical model

If we upgrade our service to use a new minor version of the canonical model, then our initial reaction might be that this only results in a minor change to the service, as our new version will still be able to process all requests from consumers using a service definition, based on an earlier version of the schema.

While this is true, the response generated by our service may no longer be compatible with an earlier version of the schema. So, the consumer may not be able to successfully process the response. In this scenario, you need to create a new major version of the service.

Changes to the physical contract

From a versioning perspective, we don't generally consider changes to either the `<binding>` or `<service>` element. With regards to the `<binding>` element, we find it helpful to consider it as part of the service implementation and thus follow the same guidelines discussed earlier to decide whether it warrants a new version of a service.

While changes to the service end point presented by a composite merely indicates the relocation of a service, as is typically required when moving a composite from development into test and finally into production. As such, this is more of a deployment consideration and is covered in detail in *Chapter 19, Packaging and Deployment*.

Updating the service endpoint

A simple way to record the version of a service is to encode it within its endpoint. The SOA Composite infrastructure does this for you already; for example, whenever you deploy a composite, you specify its version.

For example, when deploying version `1.0` of the `Auction` composite to the SOA infrastructure, its end point will be:

```
http://host:port/soa-infra/services/default/Auction!1.0/proxy_ep
```

With the WSDL for the service being available at the following URL:

```
http://host:port/soa-infra/services/default/Auction!1.0/proxy_
ep?WSDL
```

With the Service Bus, you have even more flexibility over the endpoint of a proxy service, as you can specify this as part of the transport configuration. We recommend following a similar naming strategy to that used by SOA composites in order to maintain consistency.

This has two advantages; first we can immediately see from the URI what version of a service we are looking at. Additionally, it provides a simple mechanism for us to have multiple versions of a service deployed side-by-side, which is important when we consider the lifecycle of a service.

Including version identifiers in the WSDL definition

While the WSDL definition element doesn't provide an explicit version attribute, we can still make use of the WSDL documentation element to hold the version number. For example, to add a version number to the Order Fulfilment WSDL, we can add the `<documentation>` element, as highlighted in the following code snippet:

```
<definitions name="OrderFulfillment"
    targetNamespace="http://rubiconred.com/obay/svc/OrderFulfillment"
    xmlns:tns="http://rubiconred.com/obay/svc/OrderFulfillment
    xmlns="http://schemas.xmlsoap.org/wsdl/"
    xmlns:xsd="http://www.w3.org/2001/XMLSchema"
    xmlns:ord="http://rubiconred.com/obay/xsd/order"
    xmlns:plnk="http://schemas.xmlsoap.org/ws/2003/05/partner-link/">
```

```
        <documentation>Version 1.0</documentation>
    ...
    </definitions>
```

Managing the service lifecycle

When we release a new version of a service, we need to consider how we wish to manage previous releases of that service.

A typical first step is to set the status of the previous version to be deprecated. This indicates to existing users that the service has been updated with a newer version and therefore will be retired at some point in the future.

This tells the existing users that they need to start the process of migrating to the newer version of the service as well as indicating to new users that there is a newer version of the service they should use. The final step is to retire the service. At this point, the service is removed from production, so that it is no longer available for use.

When we make a minor release of the service, as it is backward compatible with the previous version it should be straightforward to migrate to the newer version, as the only change that the consumer will be required to make is to call the service at a new endpoint (and even this may not have changed). In this case, the previous version of the service can be retired relatively quickly.

However, with a major release, changes will have to be made to the consumer before they can move to the new version; in this case, the deprecated service will need to be maintained for a longer period of time and may require even minor releases of its own to fix bugs and so on.

With both of these scenarios, a lot will depend on the number of consumers, and how easy or difficult they are to identify and coordinate changes across, as well as the nature of the change.

> One way to handle change is to create a façade that would map the old interface to the new service interface. This maintains support for existing consumers (without modification), but means that there is only a single instance of the implementation of the service.

A key to simplify this is to also keep service consumers informed of planned future versions of services, as well as those under development, as this will allow them to plan for future releases and thus shorten the required life span of deprecated services.

Summary

Design of the service contract and the underpinning canonical model are fundamental steps in the overall implementation of an SOA-based solution. The keyword here is design, as it's all too easy with the tools we have at our disposal to knock out a model in order that the "real work" of implementation can begin.

In this chapter, we have given you an overview of how to go about structuring your XML canonical model, both in terms of modeling your data in a tree-like structure as well as how to partition it across multiple namespaces.

We've also given some guidance on best practice for the implementation of those schemas, whether you follow ours or define your own. The key is to put in place some standard guidelines in order to ensure consistency, as this will result in schemas which interoperate better and are easier to reuse and maintain.

The canonical model provides the foundation for our service contracts, and with this in place, we have defined the best practice regarding how we define our service contract, paying particular attention to using the Document/literal wrapped pattern in order to conform to WS-Interoperability guidelines.

As stated earlier, a core tenet of SOA is that systems should be designed to accommodate change. With this in mind, we have also examined how we can manage change, both in our schemas and in our actual service contract, and have outlined a versioning approach to support this.

Lastly, we looked at how the SOA Suite supports the running of deprecated services alongside the most recent release in order to enable consumers to upgrade to the newer version of a service in their own time.

12
Building Entity Services Using Service Data Objects (SDOs)

In *Chapter 10, oBay Introduction*, we went through the process of defining our high level SOA blueprint. One of the key layers within this blueprint is the business services layer, which we further categorized into Entity, Functional, and Task-based services.

When it comes to implementing Task-based or Functional services, the SOA Suite provides a number of ways of implementing these (many of which are covered within the pages of this book), depending on the nature of the requirements. In addition, with SOA we have the flexibility of implementing these services pretty much in a language of our choice, a key driver often being the existing skill sets within our organization.

However, when it comes to Entity services, which typically represent data entities held in a relational database, apart from the database adapter, the SOA Suite provides limited functionality for implementing these types of services. Certainly, prior to 11gR1, most SOA Suite implementations would typically build these services in either Java, often as **Enterprise Java Beans** (**EJBs**), or in PL/SQL, which would then be service-enabled.

In this chapter, we are going to look at how we can leverage the **Oracle Application Development Framework** (or **Oracle ADF**) to build entity-based business services. Oracle ADF, as the name suggests, is Oracle's Java development framework for building enterprise applications, including the next generation of Oracle Fusion Applications.

For our purposes, we are only going to use one piece of the overall framework, namely, ADF Business Components. This provides a declarative framework for implementing business services, including Service Data Objects (that is, standards-based Entity services).

For those readers familiar with the SOA Suite 10gR3, this may seem a strange choice, and certainly prior to the 11gR1 release of Oracle Fusion Middleware, there was little synergy between Oracle ADF and the Oracle SOA Suite, with earlier versions of ADF more targeted at providing a Java development framework for Oracle Forms developers.

However, with 11gR1 that has changed, with a number of significant integrations between the respective product stacks, including:

- ADF Business Components are used to implement Service Data Objects
- Service Data Objects can be referenced as entity variables in BPEL
- The Human Worklist application is implemented in ADF
- JDeveloper automatically generates Worklist Task Forms in ADF
- BAM objects can be embedded in ADF user interfaces
- ADF Business Components can publish events to the Event Delivery Network

In this chapter, we will provide a brief introduction to ADF Business Components and how we can use them to implement Service Data Objects. We will then examine how we can reference SDOs within an SOA composite, and in particular how we can use entity variables in a BPEL process to reference an SDO as if it were a local BPEL variable.

Note that there is nothing to stop you from developing your services in Java, EJBs, and PL/SQL, and then exposing them as web services. Indeed, JDeveloper provides excellent tooling for this very purpose.

Service Data Objects

Service Data Objects (**SDO**) originated in 2004 as a joint development between IBM and BEA; since then it has been adopted as a key component of the **Service Component Architecture** (**SCA**) specifications being developed by the **Open Service Oriented Architecture** (**OSOA**) group, of which Oracle is one of the contributors. While this is not an official standards body, the group is working towards formal standardization within OASIS.

The goal of SDO is to provide a standardized and simplified layer through which applications handle data, regardless of the data source (for example, relational databases, XML data sources, web services, and so on).

The architecture of SDO is based on the concept of disconnected data graphs, where a data graph is a collection of Service Data Objects linked together in a tree-like structure. Under this model, a client can retrieve a data graph, make changes to it, and then apply those changes back to the data source.

Rather than connecting directly to the data source, the client goes via a data access service (or entity service), which is responsible for querying the data source(s), building the corresponding data graphs, and synchronizing changes to the data graph with the underlying data source(s).

Oracle 11*g* R1 support for SDO

The 11*g* R1 release of Oracle Fusion Middleware introduces support for the Service Data Objects within a number of areas of the stack. Most notably, within the Oracle Application Development Framework, which provides tooling for the creation of SDOs and their corresponding data access service, and the Oracle SOA Suite which provides out of the box support for integrating with SDOs.

Oracle SOA Suite 11*g* SDO support

Oracle SOA Suite 11*g* provides support for integrating with SDOs in a couple of ways. Firstly, it enables you to define an SDO as an external reference within a composite, just as you would access any other external service. While not that interesting, it does provide you with the advantage that you are invoking the SDO over RMI, with the associated improvements in performance as well as the ability to propagate transactions.

What's more interesting is BPEL's support for direct integration with SDOs, which is provided by a new feature called an entity variable.

Entity variables within a BPEL process appear almost like any other variable defined within the process. The key difference is that the variable is actually bound to a remote SDO. This allows you to work with a remote data as if it were local.
This has a number of advantages, including:

- If you update an entity variable within a BPEL process, then the remote data is automatically updated.
- If the remote data is updated outside the scope of the BPEL process (for example, while the process is paused waiting for a callback), then the next time the BPEL process references any values within that variable, it will receive the updated version.
- Remote data is accessed within the same transactional context as the BPEL process, allowing you to modify data within the BPEL transaction. This can simplify error handling, because if a BPEL process is rolled back, any changes to the remote data will also be rolled back.

Implementing a Service Data Object

For our purposes, we are going to create a ListingSDO based on the following two database tables in the oBay schema:

- **Listing**: Holds details of an item put up for auction on oBay
- **Bid**: Holds details of all bids placed against an item

These tables are installed as part of the oBay schema created during the process of installing the sample oBay application. Please see the oBay installation guide for details.

We will first look at how we can use Oracle ADF to create and deploy our ListingSDO, and then look at how we can use the SDO within our composite application.

Overview of ADF Business Components

Oracle ADF provides a standard-based Java framework for building enterprise applications, and is architected around the Model-View-Controller pattern (discussed in *Chapter 10, oBay Introduction*).

Within this framework, the ADF model layer is used to bind to the underlying components, which implement the business services so that they can be implemented using a variety of technologies, including SOA composites, web services, and Enterprise Java Beans (EJBs). One of the core technologies ADF provides for implementing these business services is **ADF Business Components** (or **ADF-BC**).

ADF-BC provides a database-centric approach to implementing business logic. It is built on a rich, powerful, and extensible framework that handles the mapping of database objects to Java. Within ADF, each Service Data Object is implemented as an ADF Business Component. Each ADF-BC is itself made up of a number of components, the key ones being:

- **Entity object**: An Entity object definition typically corresponds to a single database table, with an instance of an Entity object representing a single row in that database table.
- **Association**: It defines a relationship between two Entity object definitions, which typically corresponds to the relationship between the underlying database tables (for example, Master-Detail).
- **View object**: A View object definition typically defines a SQL query over 1 or more *Entity object definitions*. With an instance of a View object holding the result set of the query, which is a set of *Entity object instances*, each one corresponding to a row in the database that makes up the result of the query.
- **View link**: It defines a relationship (such as master-detail) between the query result sets of two *View object definitions*. A View link definition is often based on an *association*.
- **Application module**: Encapsulates the business logic for an ADF-BC Component. It defines the operations that can be performed on the underlying data model, which it performs against the corresponding *View objects* and *View links*.

While ADF BC is a Java framework, it's quite easy to write an ADF Business Component without having to write a single line of Java. This is because the core components listed earlier are implemented by a set of Java class libraries, which are then configured using XML metadata.

However, it's quite straightforward to extend the business components to use custom classes in order to implement application-specific behavior, though how to do that is beyond the scope of this book.

Creating our ListingSDO application

We are now ready to implement our Listing Business Component, which will form the basis of our ListingSDO. The first step is to create a new application in JDeveloper. JDeveloper provides a number of application templates (for example, Fusion Web Application), which are preconfigured with a project containing the ADF-BC component. However, all of these contain a variety of other projects that we don't need.

We will create our application using the **Generic Application** template, which, in our example, we have named **ListingSDO**. We have created a single project to contain our business component. In step two of the **Create Generic Application** wizard, we will be prompted to define our project. Give the project an appropriate name (for example, **ListingBC**) and select **ADF Business Components** from the list of available technologies, as shown in the following screenshot:

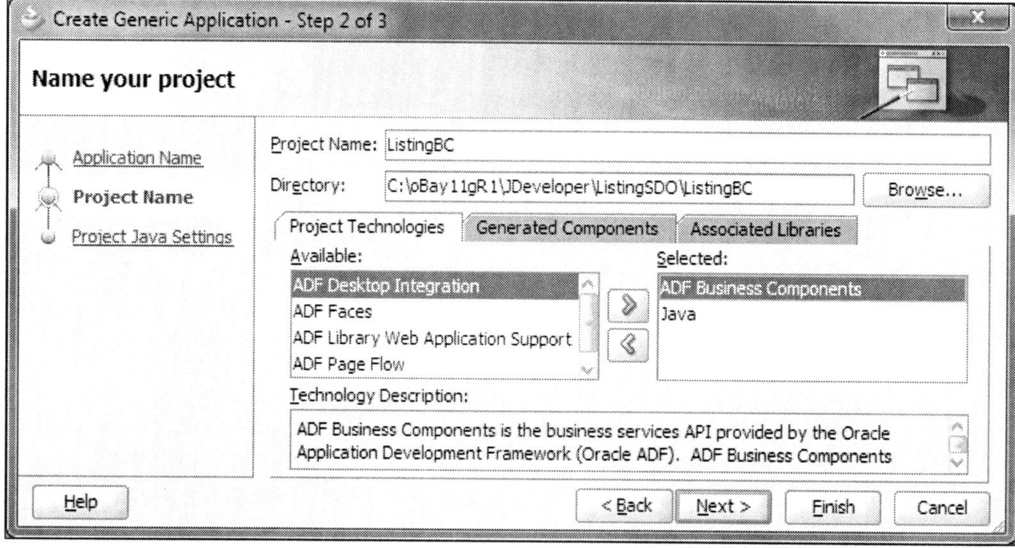

Click **Finish**. This will create our application with an empty project preconfigured for us to create our Listing ADF-BC Component.

Creating our Listing Business Components

We can now create the ADF Business Components for our ListingSDO. For our purposes, we are going to create them based on the **LISTING** and **BID** database tables that are defined as part of the `OBAY` schema.

To do this, right-click on the **ListingBC** project and select **New.** This will launch the **New Gallery**. From here, select the category **ADF Business Components** under the **Business Tier** and select **Business Components from Tables**, as shown in the following screenshot:

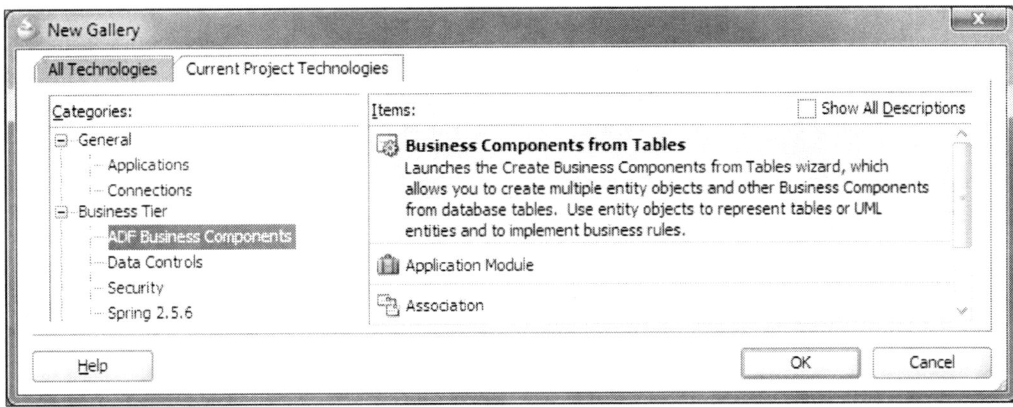

As this is the first ADF Business Component that we have defined for this project, JDeveloper will launch the **Initialize Business Components Project** window (shown below). Here we need to select the database connection for the database schema that we want to base our business components on.

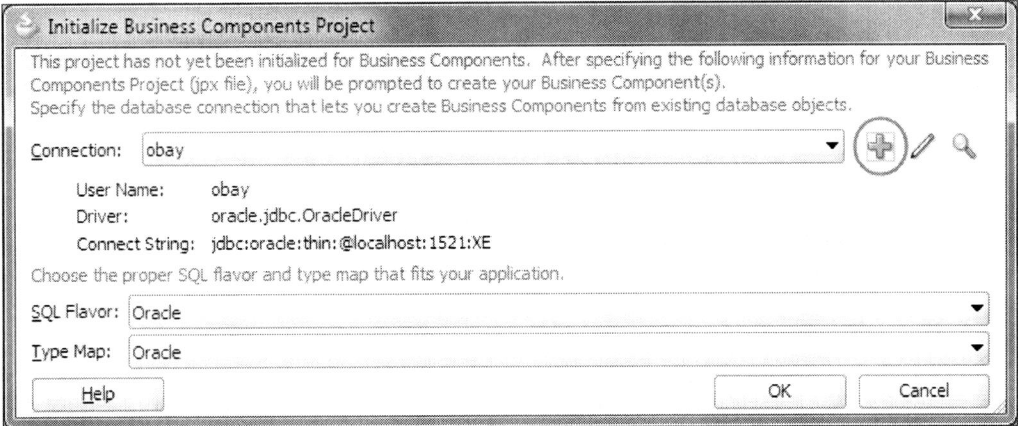

To do this, click on the green plus sign to launch the **Create Database Connection** wizard, and specify the appropriate connection details to connect to the `oBAY` schema.

Later in this chapter, when we deploy our ADF-BC application, we will configure it to use a global data source defined at the application server level. By default, this application will expect the data source to be named as follows:

```
jdbc/<connection name>DS
```

`<connection name>` is the name we specify for our database connection. Once we have specified the database connection, accept the remaining default values and click **OK**.

Defining Entity objects

JDeveloper will now launch the **Create Business Components from Tables** wizard. The first step allows us to specify the database tables we wish to base our **Entity objects** on.

Click on the **Query** button; this will retrieve a list of all the database tables defined in the `oBAY` schema. From here, select **LISTING** and **BID**, as shown in the following screenshot, and click **Next >**.

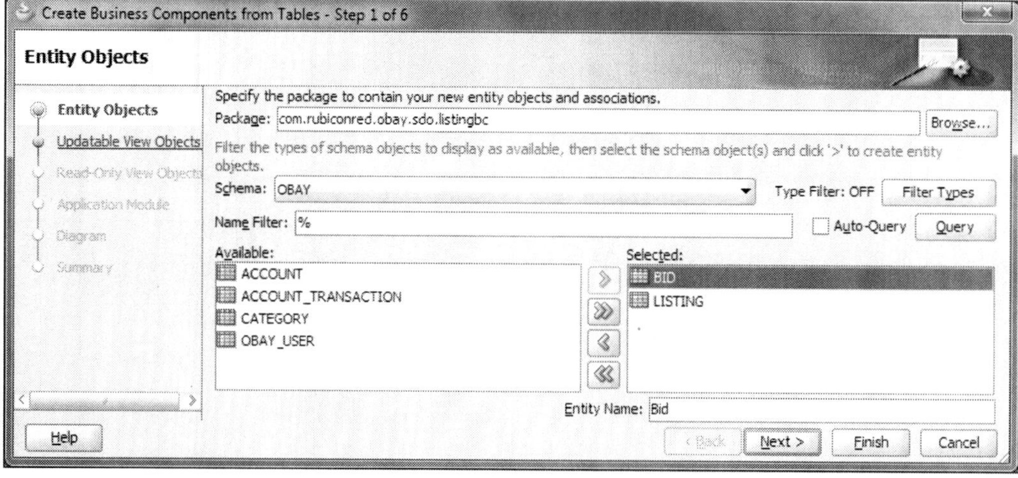

Defining updatable View objects

In the second step, we specify the Entity objects for which we want to create an **Updatable View Object**. As we want to be able to create and update both **LISTING** and **BID** entities through our ListingSDO, we need to create a corresponding View object for each of them. So select both **BidView (Bid)** and **ListingView (Listing)**, as shown in the following screenshot:

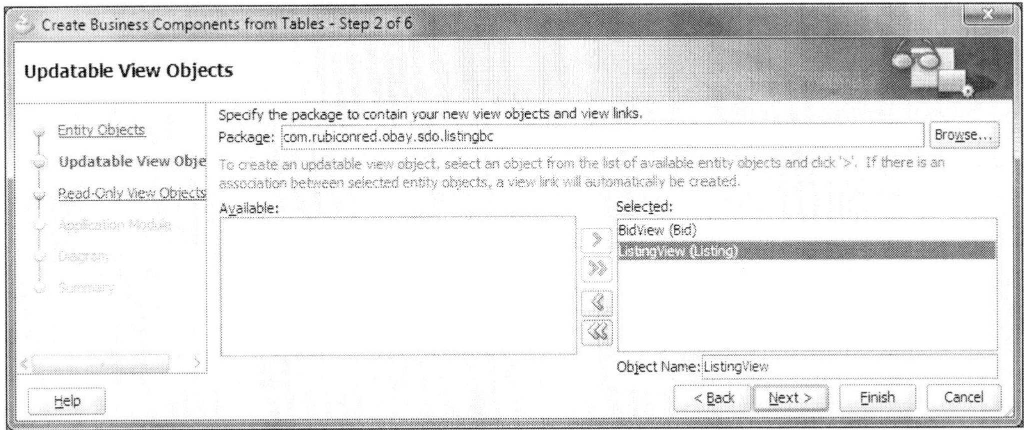

Click on **Next**; this will take us to the **Read-Only View Objects** window. At this point, we do not want to create any read-only views, so click **Next**.

Defining the application module

In the fourth step, we can specify an appropriate name for the **Application Module**. Remember that this will provide the Entity service for our updatable views, so we should name it appropriately, for example, **ListingSDO**.

Click on **Finish**. JDeveloper will now create the various resources that make up our ADF Business Component. If we look at the content of our project, we can see that it now contains a number of components, as shown in the following screenshot:

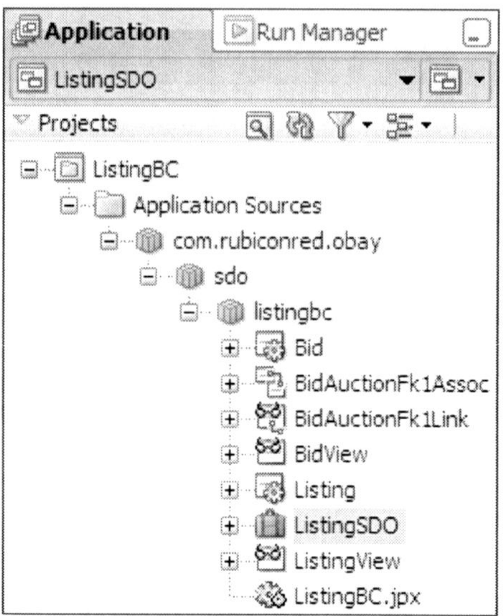

These have all been created in the Java package `com.rubiconred.com.sdo.listingbc`, the default package we specified in **Steps 1** and **2** of the wizard. It's worth taking a moment to understand what all these are:

- **Bid** and **Listing**: These are the Entity objects for the corresponding database tables, with each instance of an Entity object representing a row of data in the underlying database.
- **BidView** and **ListingView**: These are the corresponding updatable View objects, which provide a queryable view over the **Bid** and **Listing** Entity objects.
- **BidAuctionFk1Assoc**: This is an association that defines the master detail relationship between **Bid** and **Listing**.
- **BidAuctionFK1Link**: This is a View link which, in this case, defines the master detail relationship between the query result set of **ListingView** and **BidView**. The View link itself is based on the association **BidAuctionFk1Assoc**.
- **ListingSDO**: This is our application module, which represents our Business Component. This encapsulates all the operations that we can perform on the underlying objects.

Testing the listing ADF-BC in JDeveloper

At this point, we have a working ADF Business Component, which we can run and test in JDeveloper. To do this, right-click on the **ListingSDO** application module and select **Run**.

This will launch the **Oracle Business Component Browser**, a Java application which allows us to run ADF-BC components within JDeveloper. Double-click on any of the views to open a tab giving access to the view. From here, we can create, read, update, and delete data accessed via the view.

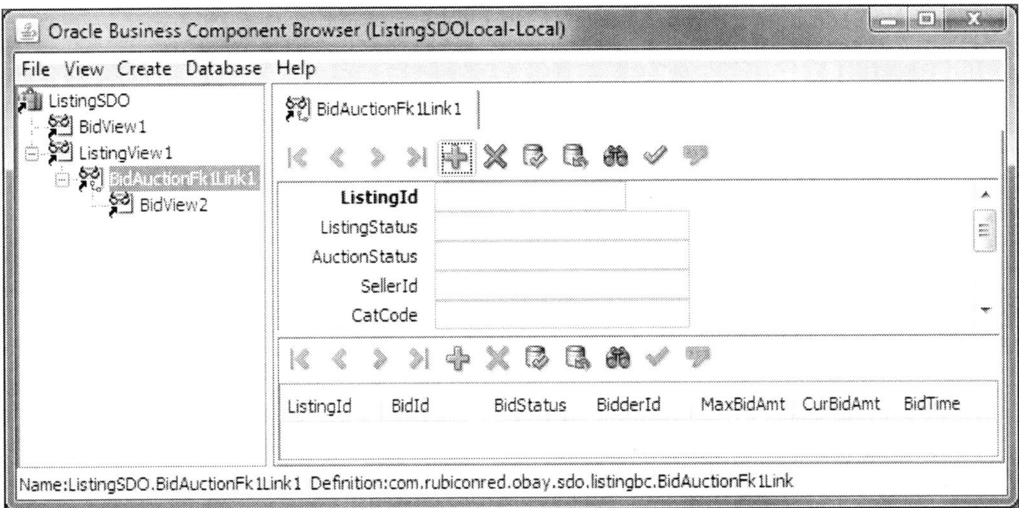

As our Business Components become more sophisticated (for example, adding in additional business logic, validation, and so on), this provides a very simple, yet powerful, way to test them.

Generating the primary key using an Oracle Sequence

As part of the process of creating a new listing, we want to automatically generate the primary key using an Oracle Sequence. Out of the box, ADF doesn't provide a simple way to achieve this. However, it's relatively straightforward to extend the Oracle ADF Framework to provide the required functionality.

An alternative way to do this is to define a `BEFORE INSERT FOR EACH ROW` trigger on the database table, which can assign the value of the primary key, based on an Oracle Sequence.

Creating the ADF extension class for EntityImpl

The first step is to define an extension class to the ADF Framework for `EntityImpl`, the class on which Entity objects are based. For our purposes, we just need to override the `create()` method. Our version (shown as follows) just checks for the presence of the custom property `SequenceId`, which contains the ID of the Oracle Sequence to use. If the property is defined, then we set the value of the attribute to the next value in the specified sequence.

```
package com.rubiconred.obay.adfx;

import oracle.jbo.AttributeDef;
import oracle.jbo.AttributeList;
import oracle.jbo.server.EntityImpl;
import oracle.jbo.server.SequenceImpl;

public class CustomEntityImpl extends EntityImpl
{
  protected void create(AttributeList attributeList)
  {
    super.create(attributeList);

    for (AttributeDef def : getEntityDef().getAttributeDefs())
    {
      String seqId = (String)def.getProperty("SequenceId");
      if (seqId != null)
      {
        SequenceImpl s = new SequenceImpl(seqId, getDBTransaction());
        setAttribute(def.getIndex(), s.getSequenceNumber());
      }
    }
  }
}
```

Updating default ADF base classes

Once we have implemented our class, we have to configure our project to use the extension class. To do this within the **Application Navigator**, right-click on the **ListingBC** project, and select **Project Properties** to launch the corresponding dialog.

Select **Base Classes** under **Business Components** from the navigational tree. Then update the **Entity Object Row** base class to point at our custom class, as shown in the following screenshot:

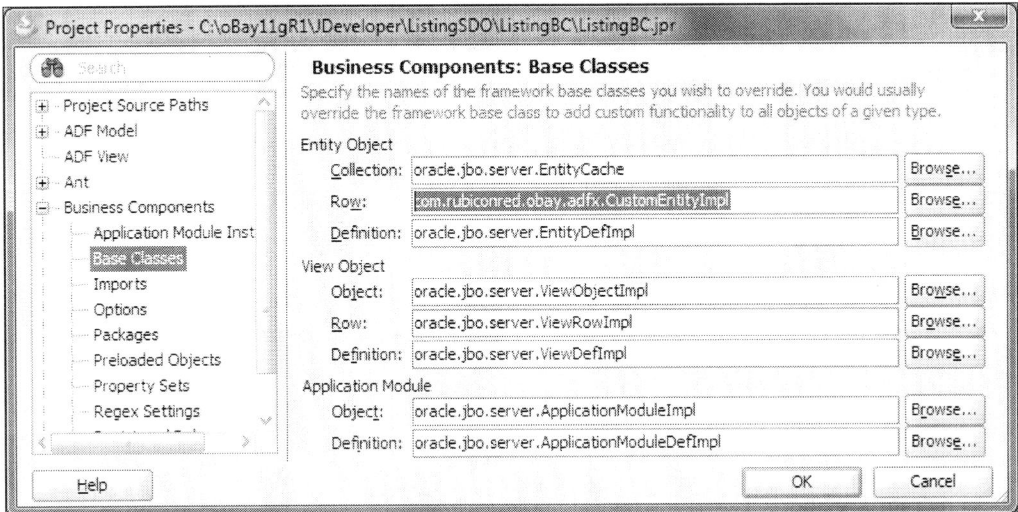

It's recommended as the best practice that before you define any Business Components, you should create a layer of extension classes for all the business components base classes. While initially these might not contain any custom code, it provides a convenient place to insert such code, if required, at a later stage.

Configuring Listing entity to use Oracle Sequence

With our customized extension class in place, the final step is to add a custom property on the **ListingId** attribute of the **Listing** entity to use the Oracle Sequence `LST_ID_SEQ` to generate the primary key.

In the **Application Navigator**, double-click the **Listing** entity. This will open the **Entity** editor, select the **Attributes** tab, and select **ListingId** attribute; next click on the edit icon, which is circled in the following screenshot:

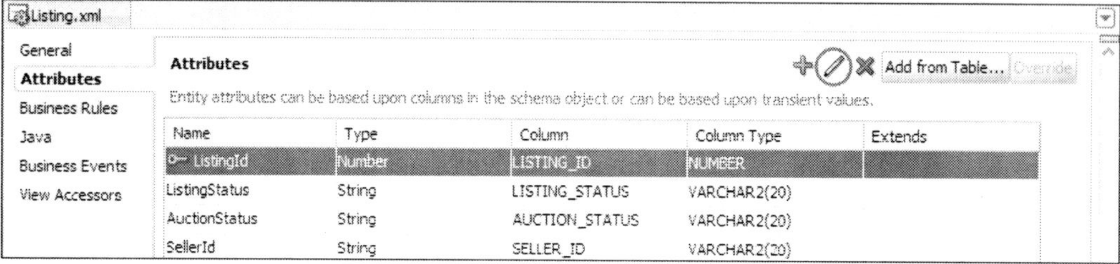

This will launch the **Edit Attribute** window. Select the **Custom Properties** tab. Enter a value of **SequenceName** for the property **Name** (this is the property name we check for in our extension class) and a value of **LST_ID_SEQ** for the property **Value** and click **Add**. This will add a corresponding property, as shown in the following screenshot:

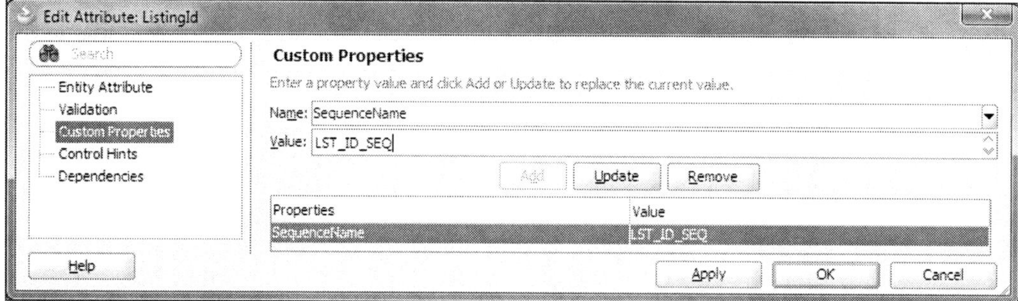

Click **OK** and make sure you save the updates to the project. You can now run and test the **ListingSDO** application with JDeveloper (as described earlier). Within the **Oracle Business Component Browser**, if you open the **ListingView** and click on the plus sign to create a new row, you should see the **ListingId** automatically populated with a unique ID.

Creating the ListingSDO service interface

Now that we have implemented our Business Component, we are ready to service-enable it. In the **Application Navigator**, double-click the **ListingSDO** application module. This will open the **Application Module** editor.

Select the **Service Interface** navigation tab (which, at this stage, isn't populated). Click on the green plus sign in the top-right-hand corner. This will launch the **Create Service Interface** wizard. In step 1 of the wizard, we need to specify the name of the web service (for example, **ListingSDO**) and its **Target Namespace**.

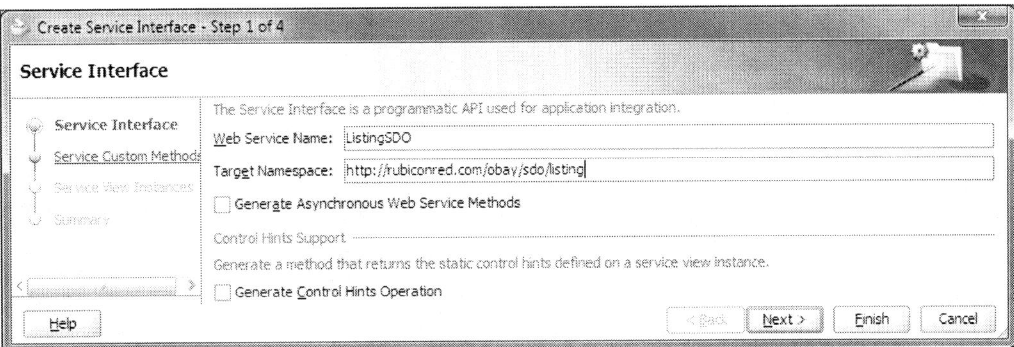

Make a note of the **Web Service Name**, as this will form a part of the URL for the **ListingSDO** WSDL and endpoint.

Click on **Next**. This will take us to step 2 of the wizard, where we can choose to service-enable any custom methods that we have defined against the Business Component. As we haven't defined any, click **Next** to move on to step 3.

Here, we can specify which View objects we wish to service-enable. Add **BidView1** and **ListingView1** to the **Selected** list. Next, we need to specify which operations we want to make available for each view.

Highlight **BidView1**. This will populate the **Basic Operations** tab, which lists all the operations that we can enable for the selected view. Select all of them.

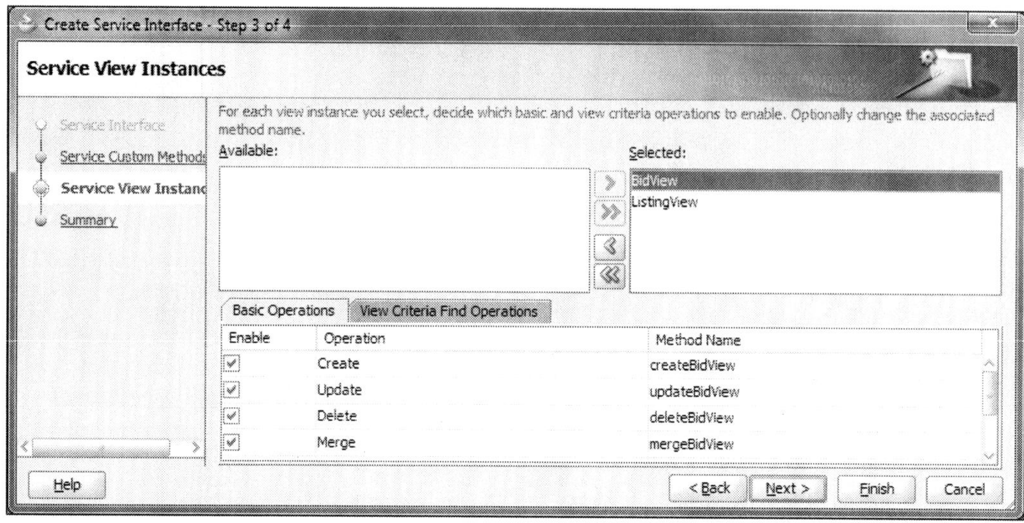

Repeat this step for the **ListingView1** instance. Then click **Finish**. JDeveloper will now generate the required metadata and code to service-enable the Application module.

Enabling master detail updates

By default, if we have a master detail relationship between Entity objects, as is the case between the **Listing** and **Bid** entities, then any service operations that we enable for the master view SDO will not process any information contained in the detail view SDO(s).

> The WSDL interface for any operation, which modifies the entity contained in the master view, still allows us to pass the corresponding detail views. It's just that the operation will quietly ignore them.
>
> For example, if we call the `updateListingView` operation passing in details of the updated `ListingViewSDO`, which, in turn, contains multiple `BidViewSDOs` containing details of updated or new bids, then the operation will just ignore the `BidViewSDOs` and update the `Listing` row in the database.

To enable service operations on the master SDO (for example, `ListingViewSDO`) to also process detail SDOs (for example, `BidViewSDO`), we need to set the property `SERVICE_PROCESS_CHILDREN` to `true` on the Association that links the Master and Detail Entity objects, which is the `BidAuctionFk1Assoc` in the case of the `ListingSDO`.

To do this, in the **Application Navigator** double-click on the **BidAuctionFk1Assoc** Association. This will open the **Association** editor. Ensure that the **General** tab is selected, and then click on the green plus icon to add a custom property (circled in the following screenshot).

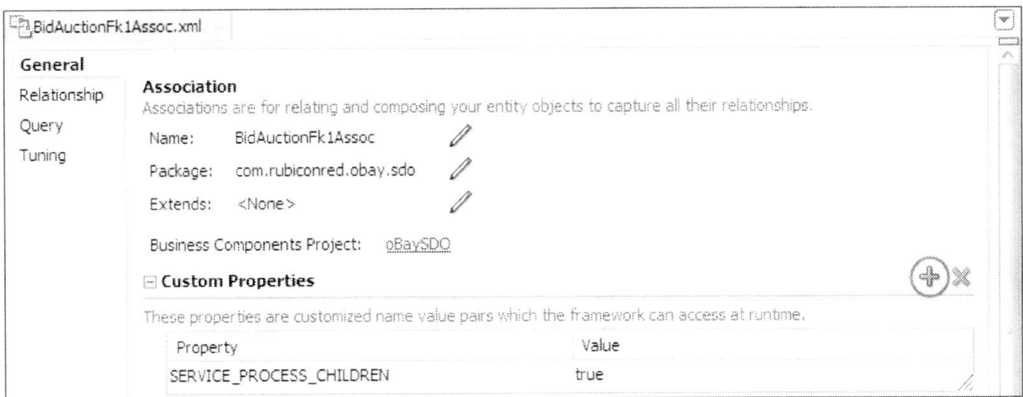

Create the property **SERVICE_PROCESS_CHILDREN** and set its value to **true**.

Deploying the Service Data Object

As we are planning on accessing our SDO directly from our composites, it makes sense to deploy it on the same WebLogic server that is running our SOA Infrastructure (for example, `soa_server1`). Before we can do this, we need to carry out the following configuration tasks:

- Create a service deployment profile
- Configure the web context root of the SDO

Creating a service deployment profile

Right-click the **ListingBC** project and select **Project Properties**. This will launch the **Project Properties** window. Select **Deployment** from the navigational tree, as shown in the following screenshot:

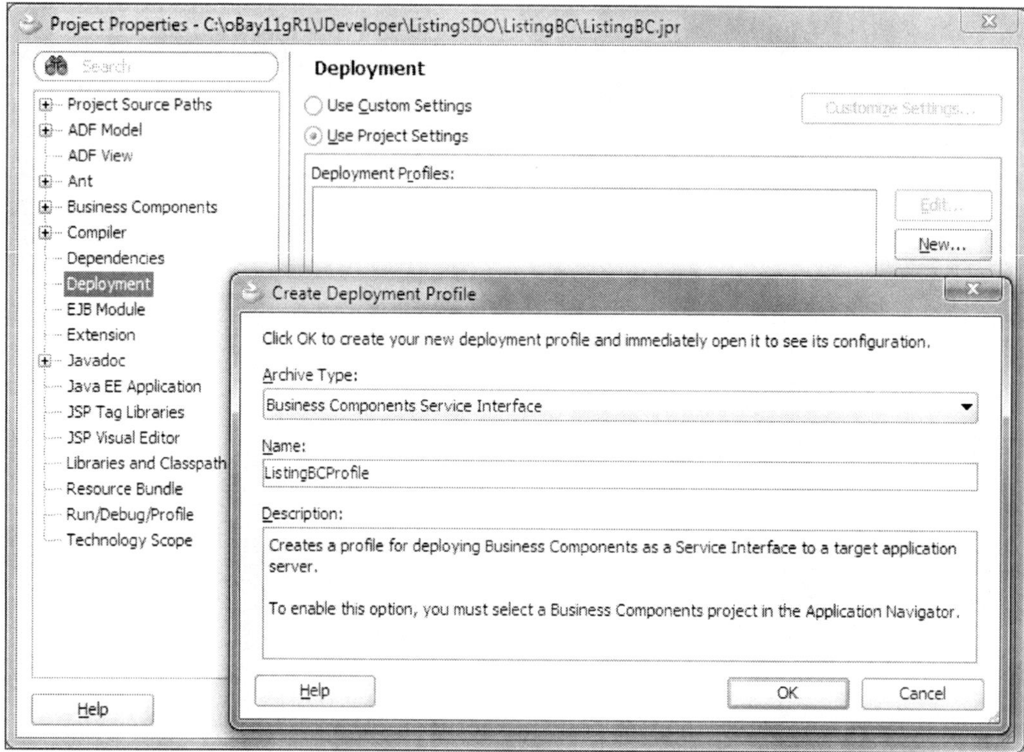

Click **New**, this will launch the **Create Deployment Profile** dialog. Specify an **Archive Type** of **Business Components Service Interface** and specify an appropriate name (for example, **ListingBCProfile**) and click **OK**.

Setting Web Context Root

The Web Context Root forms part of the URL for the endpoint of our deployed Service Data Object. Rather than accepting the default value generated by JDeveloper, it's a good idea to specify a more succinct and meaningful name.

Within the **Project Properties** window, select **Java EE Application** from the navigational tree. Here we can specify an appropriate value for the **Java EE Web Context Root** (for example, `ListingBC`)

It's also a good practice to specify a corresponding value for the **Java EE Web Application Name** (for example, `ListingBC-webapp`).

Once deployed, the WSDL for the Service Data Object is located at:

```
http://<hostname>:<port>/<web context root>/<web service name>?wsdl
```

Here, `hostname` represents the name of the machine on which the SOA server is running and `port` represents the port number. The `web context root` is the value we have just configured, and the `web service name` is the value we specified when creating the service interface.

Registering SDO with SOA infrastructure

At this point we can deploy the SDO and invoke it from a composite via SOAP over HTTP, just as we would for any other web service. However, we also want to bind the SDO to a BPEL entity variable so that we can access it as if it were a local variable within the transactional context of the BPEL process.

When invoking an SDO via a BPEL Entity variable, the BPEL process will require the SDO to participate in its transaction. To do that, we need to invoke the SDO via a protocol such as RMI, which will allow the propagation of the transactional context between the two components.

To enable the SDO to be invoked via RMI, we need to configure an appropriate **ADF Application Lifecycle Listener** to register the SDO as an RMI service. Additionally, we must also configure the SDO to use a JDBC data source, which can participate in a distributed transaction.

Registering the ListingSDO as an RMI service

Within the **Application Resources** section of the **Application Navigator**, expand the **Descriptors** | **META-INF** folder structure and open the `weblogic-application.xml` file.

Select the **Listeners** tab, and click the green plus sign to add a new listener circled; set the **Class** to **oracle.jbo.client.svc.ADFApplicationLifecycleListener**, but don't specify any value for **JAR Path** and **Run-As Principle**.

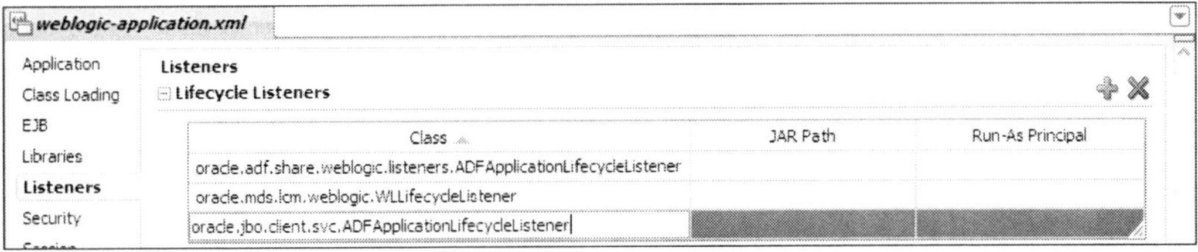

Configuring global JDBC data source

When an ADF application connects to a database, it does this via a JDBC URL or JDBC data source, which can be defined either globally or at the application level.

To enable the SDO to participate as part of the BPEL transaction, we need to deploy the corresponding ADF-BC component configured to use a global JDBC data source, which, in turn, is configured to support distributed transactions.

When we create our ADF-BC project, JDeveloper automatically defines a number of application-level database connections: a couple of JDBC URL connections and an application level JDBC data source. By default, these application-level data connections will be packaged and deployed along with the ADF-BC component, meaning that, at runtime, the ADF application will connect directly to the database using the JDBC URL (ignoring any global JDBC data source defined to the WebLogic server).

To prevent this, right-click on the **ListingSDO** application, select **Application Properties** to open the corresponding window, and select **Deployment** from the navigation tree. Then deselect the option **Auto Generate and Synchronize weblogic-jdbc.xml Descriptors During Deployment**, which is circled in the following screenshot:

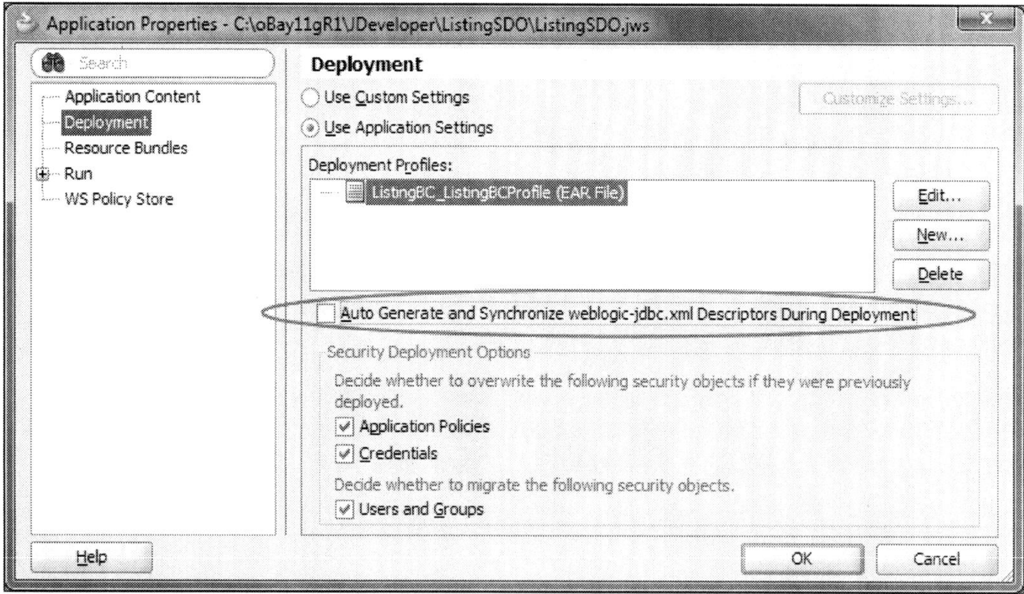

When this option is disabled, the application-specific data sources are no longer packaged and deployed with the application. Instead, the application is configured to use a global data source named as follows:

```
jdbc/<connection name>DS
```

Using the JNDI, look for the following:

```
java:comp/env/jdbc/<connection name>DS
```

Here, `<connection name>` is the name of the database connection we specified when we created our ADF-Business Component.

In our case, we specified a name of **obay**, so all we need to do now is to configure a data source on WebLogic with the name `jdbc/obayDS`. We actually do this as part of the installation process of the oBay application, so please refer to the installation guide for details on how to do this.

You may find that when you disable this option, you are no longer able to run the ListingSDO Application Module in JDeveloper, in which case, you need to re-enable it for the purpose of testing.

Determining the SDO registry key

At runtime, before the SOA infrastructure can invoke the SDO via RMI, it must first look for it using a registry key. The registry key is generated automatically and has the following structure:

```
<ApplicationName>_JBOServiceRegistry
```

Here, `<ApplicationName>` is specified in the EAR deployment profile of the ADF-BC application.

To set the application name, reopen the **Application Properties** window and select **Deployment** from the Navigation Tree (as we did in the previous section). From the deployment profiles, select the EAR File deployment profile (**ListingBC_ListingBCProfile** in the preceding screenshot) and click **Edit**.

This will open the **Edit EAR Deployment Profile Properties** window. Specify an appropriate **Application Name**, for example **ListingSDO**, as circled in the following screenshot:

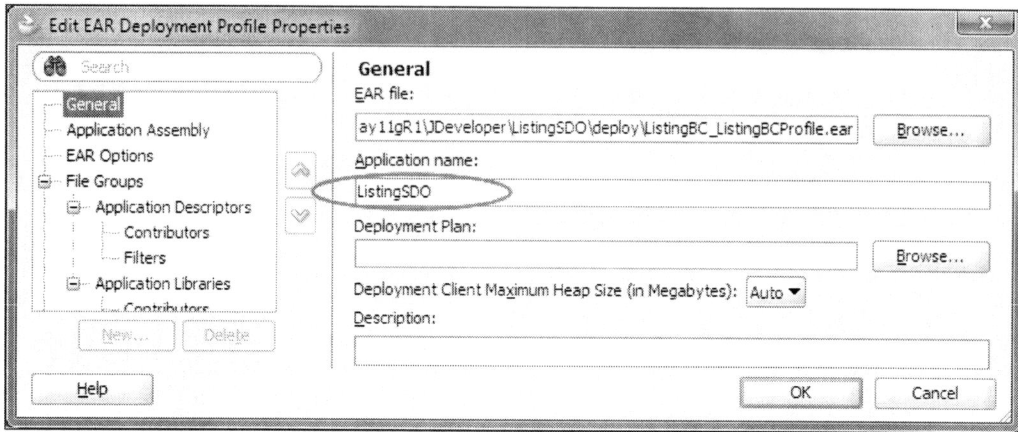

Our Listing Service Data Object is now ready to deploy. Right-click on the **ListingSDO** application and select **Deploy**. Specify `soa_server1` as the application server to deploy it to.

Using the ListingSDO in an SOA composite

We need to use our `ListingSDO` in a number of composites. Firstly, within the **ListItem** composite, we need to create a listing when a new item is submitted, and then as it progresses through the listing process (for example, it is approved), we also need to update the listing status accordingly.

Secondly, within the **AuctionItem** composite we need to record details of bids against the listing as well as update the listing appropriately. For example, we would need to update the value of the current winning bid.

Creating an ADF-BC Service Reference

Before we can reference an SDO within our composite, we must first create an ADF-BC Service Reference.

Open up the **composite.xml** file for the `ListItem` composite, and then from the **Component Palette**, drag-and-drop an **ADF-BC Service** onto the composite. This will launch the **Create ADF-BC Service** window.

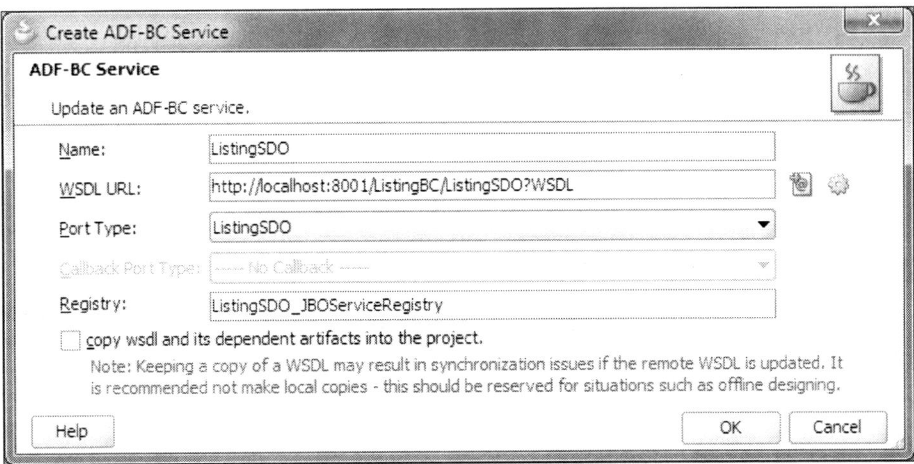

We need to specify the following values:

- **Name**: Specify an appropriate name such as **ListingSDO**.
- **WSDL URL**: This is the URL of the WSDL for the Service Data Object. See the earlier section *Setting Web Context Root* for details on how this is determined.
- **Port Type**: This will default to the appropriate **Port Type** based on the specified WSDL.
- **Callback Port Type**: This will default to the appropriate **Port Type** based on the specified WSDL.
- **Registry**: This is the registry key for the Service Data Object. See the earlier section *Determining the SDO Registry Key* for details on how this is determined.

Once created, use the Composite Editor to wire the **ListingSDO** reference up to our List Item Process. This will create a corresponding partner link within our BPEL process.

Invoking the SDO from BPEL

Within a BPEL process, we interact with a Service Data Object via an **entity variable**, a feature which is new to the 11gR1 release of SOA Suite.

Within a BPEL process, an entity variable appears to be *almost* like any other variable defined to the process in that we can assign values to and from this variable as we would do with any standard variable. The key difference is that the variable is actually bound to a remote SDO, which itself provides an abstraction over the underlying data source.

Thus, when a BPEL process reads data from an entity variable, it is actually reading data from the underlying database. Conversely, when it updates the content of an entity variable, it is actually updating the corresponding content in the database.

Before we can perform operations on an entity variable (for example, assigning values to or from it), we must first bind our entity variable to an SDO. We can either do this using a **Bind Entity** activity, where we specify the primary key of the SDO we wish to bind to, or using the **Create Entity** activity, which is used to insert a new entity (row) into a database table. In this process our entity variable is bound to the newly created SDO.

Creating an entity variable

For our List Item Process, we need to define an **entity variable** for the new listing we wish to create and manage. We create an entity variable in a similar way to a standard variable, but with a couple of key differences.

First, the variable must be of type **Element**, where the element is defined on the corresponding SDO type (**listingViewSDO** in our example). To do this, launch the **Type Chooser** and expand the structure underneath the SDO partner link, as shown in the following screenshot, and select the corresponding SDO element:

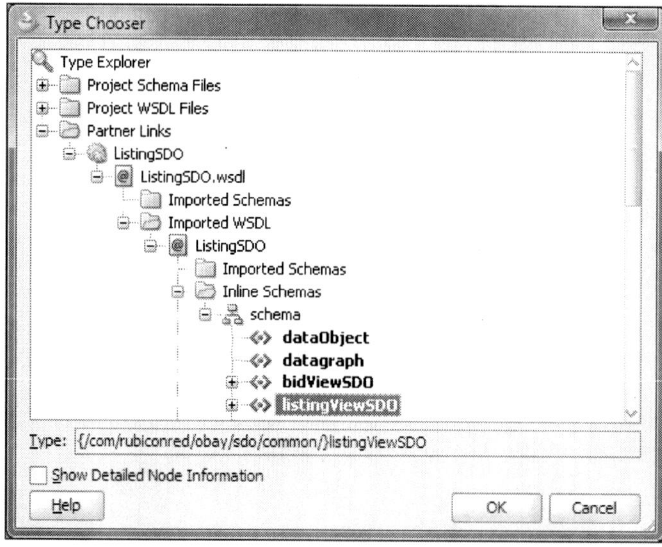

Secondly, we need to select the checkbox **Entity Variable** and connect it to the **Partner Link** of the **ADF-BC Service**, as shown in the following screenshot:

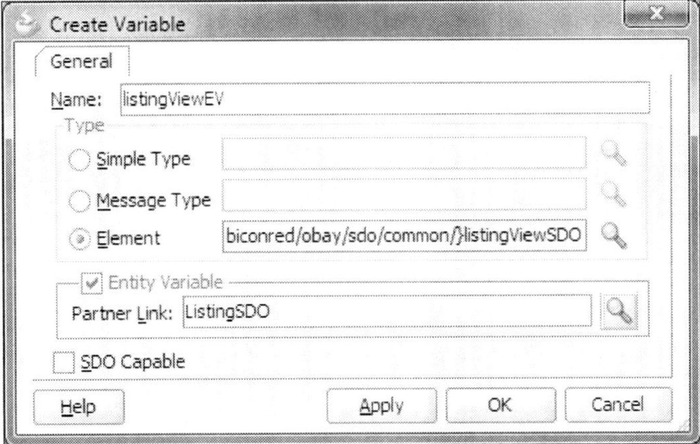

Finally, you may have noticed that when naming our variable, we have appended **EV** to the name (for example, **listingViewEV**) to indicate that this is an entity variable.

The entity variable that we have just created is an **SDO-based** variable, which is different from a standard BPEL variable, that is, XML DOM-based. SDO-based variables are similar to DOM-based variables, but only support a subset of XPath expressions (for example, there is no support for AND, OR, and NOT). Additionally, the BPELX extension functions exhibit slightly modified behavior when working with SDO-based variables.

SDO and DOM-based variables can be interchanged with Oracle BPEL Process Manager taking care of automatically converting back and forth between DOM and SDO forms as required.

Creating a Listing entity

One of the first steps we want to perform in our List Item Process is to insert details of the new item into the Listing table. The traditional way to do this would be to use an **Invoke** activity to call an external service (or the database adapter) to insert a new row into our database table.

But in our case, we are going to use the entity variable that we just defined. To do this, drag a **Create Entity** activity from the component palette on to your BPEL process. This will typically be where we would have previously put the **Invoke** activity. Double-click on it; this will open the **Create Entity** activity window, as shown in the following screenshot:

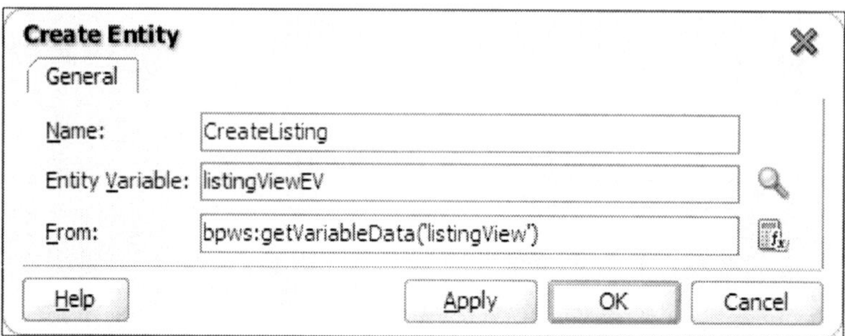

We need to specify a number of values to configure the **Create Entity** activity, namely:

- **Name**: This is the name we want to assign to the **Create Entity** activity, and can be any value. So, just assign a meaningful value such as **CreateListing**.
- **Entity Variable**: This is the entity variable that we want to create, which is the one that we just defined.
- **From**: Here, we must specify the variable which contains the data to be used to initialize the entity variable. For this purpose, we have created a standard variable **listingView**, which is the same type as our entity variable and uses an **Assign** (or **Transform**) activity to populate it.

At this point, you may be asking:

> "*What is the advantage of using an entity variable?*"

After all, if we had used the database adapter to insert a row into the LISTING database we would have had very similar activities within our BPEL process, with the only real difference being that we would have used an **Invoke** activity instead of the **Create Entity** activity.

The answer is that the real difference comes after we have created the entity variable. As we mentioned earlier, in the process of creating our Listing entity, we have bound it to the entity variable within our BPEL process. This means that whenever we update the entity variable, as we do at several points in our Item Listing process, the corresponding record in the underlying database will be updated.

Conversely, if the underlying database record is updated outside our process (for example, by the **AuctionItem** process), then the next time we reference the content of the entity variable, we will receive the updated variable.

Binding to the Listing entity

The **Auction Process** is another example of how we typically want to interact with an SDO via an entity variable.

In this scenario, we want to retrieve details of the Listing against which the auction is being held. As bids are placed, we record details of them against the listing as well as update the listing itself with details of the winning bid.

As with the **ListItem** composite, we need to define an ADF-BC External Service in the **AuctionItem** composite for the **ListingSDO**, and within the **AuctionItem** process, define a corresponding entity variable.

Again, as with the **ListItem**, before we can perform any operations on the entity variable, we must first bind it to an SDO. Previously, we did this using the **Create Entity** activity, but as the SDO in question already exists, we need to use the **Bind Entity** activity.

To do this, drag a **Bind Entity** activity from the **Component Palette** on to your BPEL process. Double-click on it; this will open the **Bind Entity** activity window, as shown in the following screenshot:

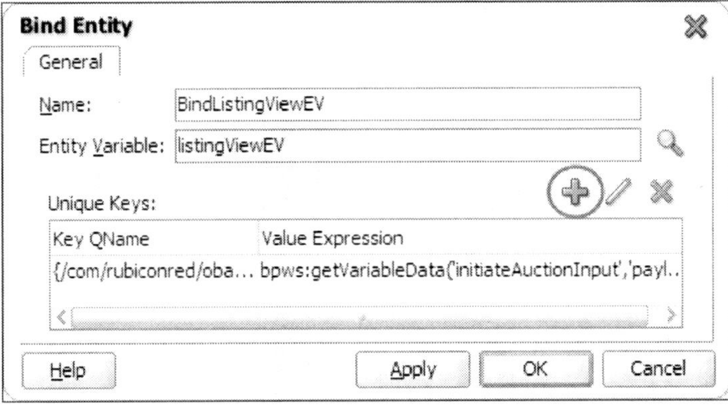

We specify the **Name** and **Entity Variable** as we did for the **Create Entity** activity. The final value we need to specify is the unique key for the Entity object that we wish to bind to.

To specify a key, click on the green plus icon (circled in the previous screenshot). This will launch the **Specify Key** window, as shown in the following screenshot:

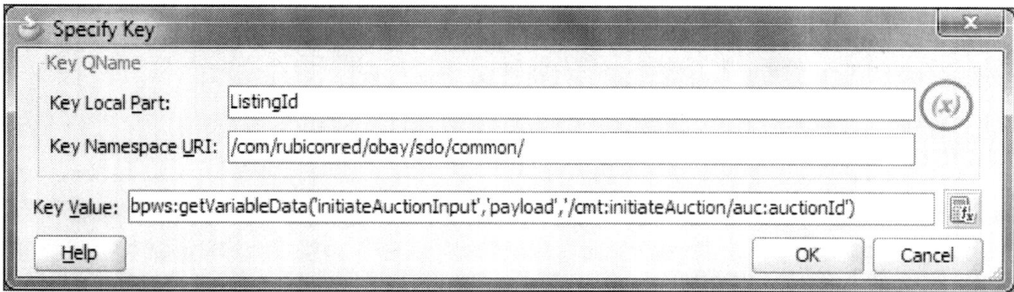

Here we need to specify the actual **Key QName** and its **Key Value**. To specify the key, click on the **Browse Entity Variable** icon (circled in the preceding screenshot) to launch the corresponding window.

Expand the appropriate entity variable, which is **listingViewEV**, and select the element that holds the primary key, that is, **ListingId**.

> If you look at the preceding screenshot, you will see that the **listingViewSDO** contains two **ListingId** entries, the first with an orange icon next to it. This is an annotation, which indicates that **ListingId** is the key for the SDO. However, when selecting the key you still need to select the actual element itself.

Once we have specified the key, we need to specify the **Key Value**, which in our case is the auction ID (as this is the same as the ListingID). To do this, click on the calculator icon to launch the expression builder and specify the appropriate value in the normal way.

Inserting a detail SDO into a master SDO

Once we have bound our entity variable to the underlying SDO, our **Auction Process** can access its content as if it were a local variable and also update it (with those changes being reflected in the underlying database).

However, the interesting part of our scenario is that when the **Auction Process** evaluates a new bid, we want it to insert that bid into the BID table in the underlying database. One way to do this would be to create a **bidViewSDO** entity variable and use the **Create Entity** activity to insert it into the database, just as we did with our listing.

However, you may recall that when we service-enabled our Listing Business Component, we enabled master detail updates. This means that if we add a **bidViewSDO** to our **listingViewEV** entity variable, then it will also insert a bid into our database table.

First, create a standard variable **bidView**. This should be a variable of type **Element**, where the element is the definition of a **bidViewSDO** (as circled in the following screenshot). Then use either an **Assign** or **Transform** activity to populate it appropriately.

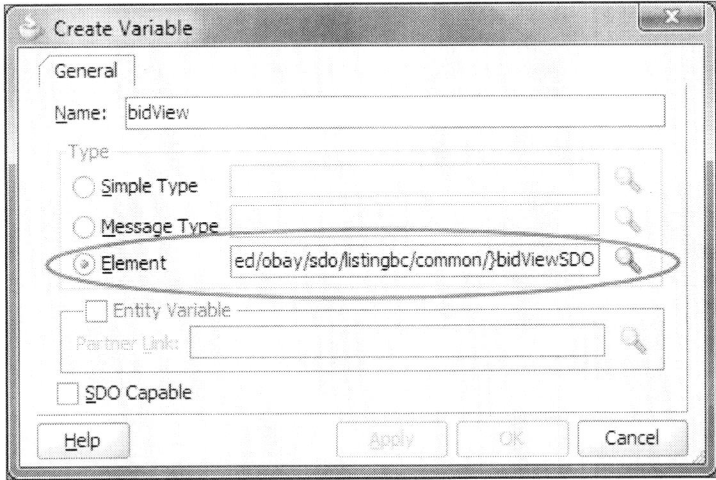

The next stage requires us to insert the **bidView** variable into our **listingViewEV** entity variable. Typically, we would do this using an **Assign** with an **Append Operation**. However, **Append Operation** is not supported by SDO-based variables.

Instead, we are going to use the **Insert-After Operation**. However, again we need to be aware that the behavior of this operation is slightly different for SDO-based variables. As we will see in a moment, this actually simplifies things.

To do this within the **Assign** activity, insert an **Insert-After Operation**, as shown in the following screenshot:

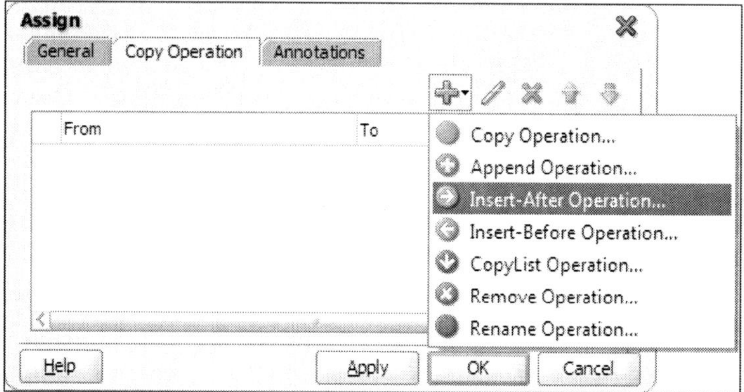

When using **Insert-After Operation** to insert data into an SDO variable, the target must be the variable element into which the source data should be inserted. In our example, this is the **bidView** element of our **listingViewEV**, as shown in the following screenshot:

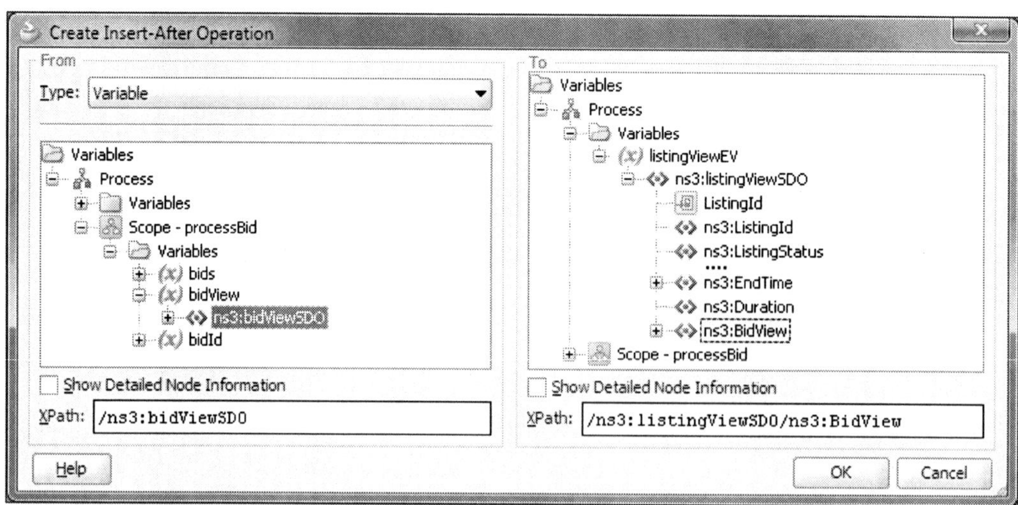

If the target was a DOM-based variable, then the target XPath would be expected to return a reference to one or more nodes, after which the contents of the source variable are inserted. In the event that no nodes are returned, as would be the case if we had no bids recorded against the listing, then a selection exception would be generated.

However, as the target is an SDO-based variable, the behavior is different. In this case, the operation will create a new **bidView** element, copy into it the contents of **bidView**, and insert it into the **listingViewEV** variable at the place specified.

Updating a detail SDO

In addition to inserting new bids into our listing, we need to be able to update existing bids. For example, if the current winning bid is outbid, then we need to update its status accordingly.

For this scenario, we can use a standard **Copy Operation** to update the status of the bid within the entity variable. The trick here is to restrict the target of the **Copy Operation** to the appropriate bid.

The simplest way to achieve this is to create a standard **Copy Operation**, and then modify the **To XPath** expression to contain a **predicate** to select the required `bid`, based on its `bidId`. To do this, we would need to create an expression that looks similar to the following:

```
/listingViewSDO/BidView[BidId=bpws:getVariableData('bidId')]/
Status
```

Here, `bidId` is just an integer-based variable containing the ID of the bid that we want to modify.

Deleting a detail SDO

There may also be scenarios where we need to delete a bid from the entity variable. In such a case, we can do this using an **Assign** with a **Remove Operation** to remove the **bidView SDO** from the **listingViewEV** entity variable.

As is the case when updating a detail SDO, we need to modify the XPath predicate to remove only the required **bidView SDO**.

Deleting a Service Data Object

The **Remove Entity** activity allows us to delete an SDO that is bound to an entity variable, as well as any detail SDOs that are associated with it, a bit like a cascade delete within SQL.

To do this, drag a **Remove Entity** activity from the component pallet on to your BPEL process. Double-click on it; this will open the **Remove Entity** activity window, as shown in the following screenshot:

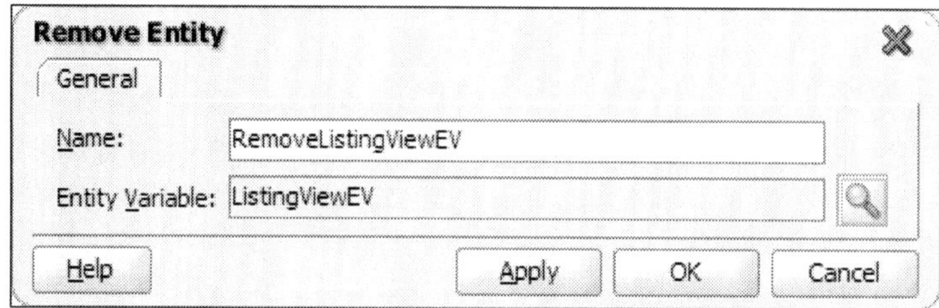

Here, we just need to specify the name of the entity variable that we want to remove. Note that this should be an entity variable that we have already bound to an SDO, either through a **Create Entity** or **Bind Entity** activity.

Exposing the SDO as a business service

The one issue which we have avoided so far is that if we look at the interfaces of our SDO objects, then they are very much driven by the underlying structure of the database tables on which they are based.

If we were to follow the strict interpretation of our SOA blueprint, as laid out in *Chapter 10, oBay Introduction*, you could argue that they belong in the application services layer, and therefore should always be called via a virtual services layer. This, in the preceding examples, is clearly not the case.

There are a couple of ways to counter this point. The first is to simply accept that the ListingSDO, while an entity service, is not intended to be a reusable service in its own right. It is just a component of our Auction and ListItem composite, and thus all components, while not necessarily packaged as part of the same JDeveloper project, will always be deployed together.

However, in other cases it may make sense that the SDO is a reusable service in its own right. In this scenario, it's quite straightforward to use a Mediator to invoke the ADF-BC service, which can then perform the transformation from our canonical model to that of the SDO and vice versa. Then, we can expose it as a completely abstracted Business Service.

The question that then arises is how to invoke the SDO from a BPEL process. Do I invoke the SDO directly via an entity variable or do I invoke the virtual service? Each approach has it merits. We could take a purist approach and mandate that we always go via the virtual services layer as this will provide (or at least initially seems to provide) better interoperability and agility. However, we also need to ensure that we balance this requirement with other non-functional requirements, such as reliability and scalability.

By using entity variables, we are able to take advantage of the "*out of the box*" design and runtime integration between BPEL and ADF BC services.

From a runtime perspective, this can provide improved performance due to optimized invocation of ADF BC components and the BPEL process having a smaller dehydration store footprint (since entity variables aren't stored in the dehydration store).

In addition, the ability to manage database updates directly within the BPEL transaction can help improve the overall reliability of the solution due to the integrity provided by ACID transactions.

From a design-time perspective, the use of distributed transactions has the added benefit of simplifying error handling within the application. In addition, by using entity variables, we have fewer activities within our BPEL process (as we no longer have to explicitly invoke an external service every time we need to update the database). Each of these can reduce the overall complexity of the BPEL process, making it easier to implement and maintain and thus improving its overall agility.

The drawback of this approach is that we reduce the level of interoperability between components (as we have the coding overhead of having to translate between our canonical model and the SDO model). Also, the BPEL process is tightly coupled to the SDO.

As always there is no single answer; rather it will depend on the nature of the requirements and the constraints that we are working under. As a result, we are likely to end up having a blended approach.

Summary

In this chapter, we have introduced you to Service Data Objects, one of the key new features in the 11gR1 release of SOA Suite, and looked at how we can leverage these as entity variables within a BPEL process.

We have also discovered that SDOs are actually implemented outside of the Oracle SOA Suite, using the Oracle Application Development Framework. For many readers, this will be their first exposure to Oracle ADF, so we have also covered how we can build an ADF Business Component from scratch.

Here of course, we have only scratched the surface, so we would recommend further reading in this area in order to fully utilize the power of ADF.

13
Building Validation into Services

Once we have divided our solution into a number of composite components, one of the next questions we are typically faced with is:

> *"Where should I put my validation and how should I implement it?"*

At first glance, this may seem like an obvious question, but once you consider that a composite may be made up of other services, which in turn could be made up of other services and so on; it becomes clear that you could potentially end up implementing the same validation in every level.

Apart from the obvious performance implications, you also have the issue of having to implement and maintain the same validation at multiple points within the solution.

When you get down to an individual composite, you still have to consider, where in the service to place the validation and how best to implement it. Particularly, if you want the flexibility to be able to change the validation within a service without having to re-deploy it.

This chapter guides us on how best to address this question. It examines how we can implement validation within a service using XSD validation, Schematron, and Business Rules as well as within the service itself. With each of these options, it looks at the pros and cons and how they can be combined to provide a flexible validation strategy.

Finally, we look at validation within the context of the overall solution and provide guidelines for deciding which layer within the architecture to place our validation.

Validation within a composite

A composite service exposes one or more operations. These operations provide the entry point for the outside world, so it provides the obvious starting point for implementing validation in our composite. However, we also need to consider the validation requirements of other messages exchanged within our composite as well as messages exchanged with external services, as illustrated in the following diagram:

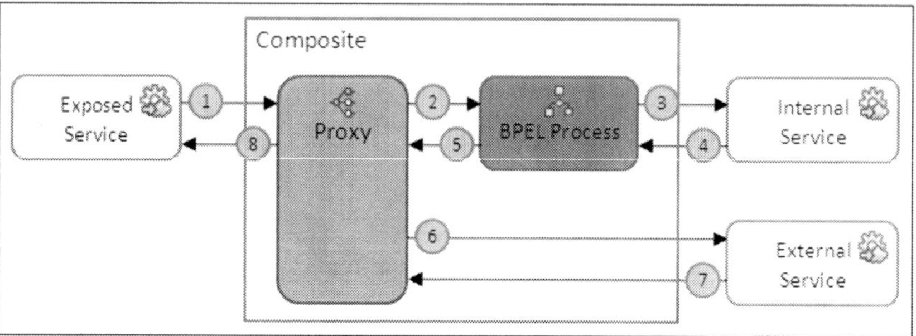

If we look at the preceding diagram, we can see that there are up to eight messages exchanged, each of which imposes its own requirements in terms of validation.

The first message is the one the composite receives through an **Exposed Service**. From a data quality perspective, we are likely to have little or no knowledge of the client invoking the composite, thus we need to validate the content of the incoming message before we process it any further.

The second message (as well as the fifth) represents an internal exchange of messages between components within the same composite. In this case, we should have absolute confidence in the quality of the messages exchanged, so no validation is required here.

The third and fourth messages are exchanged between our composite and what we have labeled as **Internal Service**. What we mean here is that this is another service, which is part of our overall solution (for example, another composite) or at least part of a portfolio of services under our control, and thus, again we should have confidence in the quality of the messages exchanged, so typically validation is not required here.

However, the reality is that the **Internal Service** may be called by a variety of consumers, if not now, then possibly in the future. So the **Internal Service** would typically implement validation against the incoming message in much the same way that our composite would validate message number one.

In cases where the internal service is a human interface (for example, Workflow), then it is quite possible for an error to be introduced in the fourth message, in these cases validation should be applied.

> You could argue that whilst we should have confidence in the quality of messages exchanged between components that we control, that this is somewhat idealistic. At the very least it assumes that adequate care is taken during the implementation and testing of our composites to ensure that they don't actually create invalid messages.
>
> Another factor we need to consider when making the decision about where to apply validation is nothing other than basic risk analysis; in other words what is the probability of an error being introduced at any of these points, and if such an error were to occur what would be the consequence. Again, we need to balance these requirements against our other objectives, such as the performance and agility of the overall solution.
>
> One approach is to initially implement validation for these message exchanges, but only to apply this whilst developing and testing a service, and then disable it once we move the service into production. Assuming we have a rigorous test process, this allows us to have far greater confidence in the quality of the message that we are exchanging and thus reduce the likelihood of an error being introduced.
>
> To assist in this, Enterprise Manager allows you set Payload Validation on a composite, doing this will validate all inbound and out messages (that is, one through eight in the preceding diagram) against their XML Schema(s).

The sixth and seventh messages are exchanged between our composite and what we have labeled as **External Service**. What we mean here is a service which is outside our domain of control. Again, this is from the perspective of (not) being able to guarantee the quality of the data returned, and thus we should validate the data returned in message number seven is validated.

However, best practice dictates that we call an **External Service** via a proxy service implemented on the Oracle Service Bus, in which case, it makes sense to place the validation in the proxy service and only implement it once (as opposed to implementing it in every composite that calls the same external service). As the proxy service may have little knowledge of either the external service or consumer of it, the proxy would typically perform validation against both the request and response message.

The eighth message is the response returned by our composite. Again, we should be confident in the quality of the data returned.

With these assumptions in mind, the key point of validation is any message received through the service interface exposed by the composite (that is, message number one). Assuming we are following the best practice (as covered in *Chapter 10, oBay Introduction*), our composite will contain a Mediator that acts as the entry point to our composite.

The Mediator component provides support for XSD and Schematron validation. Thus this provides the ideal point to implement validation, as it allows us to provide a centralized point within our composite for implementing all validation as well as ensuring that we perform the validation early on within the flow.

We also need to ensure that adequate validation is provided for messages exchanged with the **External Service**, so we will cover how we can implement this using OSB.

Using XML Schema validation

The interface for each service is defined by its WSDL contract, with the core structure of the data being exchanged defined by one or more XML Schemas. So XSD validation provides an excellent way to implement the initial level of validation.

When implementing schema-based validation, we have two basic approaches, that is, to either implement strongly-typed web services or loosely-typed services.

Strongly-typed services

With strongly-typed services, we use XML Schema to very precisely specify the exact structure of each element within our XML instance. For example, if we look at the definition of a credit card within the oBay canonical model, a strongly-typed version may be defined as the following code snippet:

```
<xsd:complexType name="tCreditCard">
    <xsd:sequence>
        <xsd:element name="cardType"           type="tCardType"/>
        <xsd:element name="cardHolderName"     type="tCardHolderName"/>
        <xsd:element name="cardNumber"         type="tCardNumber" />
        <xsd:element name="expiryMonth"        type="tExpiryMonth"/>
        <xsd:element name="expiryYear"         type="tExpiryYear"/>
        <xsd:element name="securityNo"         type="tSecurityNo" />
    </xsd:sequence>
</xsd:complexType>
```

```
<xsd:simpleType name="tCardType">
    <xsd:restriction base="xsd:string">
        <xsd:enumeration value="MasterCard"/>
        <xsd:enumeration value="Visa"/>
    </xsd:restriction>
</xsd:simpleType>

<xsd:simpleType name="tCardHolderName">
    <xsd:restriction base="xsd:string">
        <xsd:maxLength value="32"/>
    </xsd:restriction>
</xsd:simpleType>

<xsd:simpleType name="tCardNumber">
    <xsd:restriction base="xsd:integer">
        <xsd:pattern value="[0-9]{16}"/>
    </xsd:restriction>
</xsd:simpleType>

<xsd:simpleType name="tExpiryMonth">
    <xsd:restriction base="xsd:integer">
        <xsd:minInclusive value="1"/>
        <xsd:maxInclusive value="12"/>
    </xsd:restriction>
</xsd:simpleType>

<xsd:simpleType name="tExpiryYear">
    <xsd:restriction base="xsd:integer">
        <xsd:minInclusive value="2010"/>
        <xsd:maxInclusive value="9999"/>
    </xsd:restriction>
</xsd:simpleType>

<xsd:simpleType name="tSecurityNo">
    <xsd:restriction base="xsd:integer">
        <xsd:pattern value="[0-9]{3}"/>
    </xsd:restriction>
</xsd:simpleType>
```

With this approach, we have very precisely defined the following restrictions:

- Valid card types are either 'MasterCard' or 'Visa'
- Credit card number is a 16 digit integer
- The expiry month must be between 1 and 12
- The expiry year must be a four digit integer with a minimum value of 2010
- The security code is a three digit integer

The advantage with this approach is that we have a far more explicit definition of the interface, thus providing a far more robust and tightly-controlled entry point for our service. From a client perspective, it provides a far clearer understanding of what does or doesn't constitute a valid data structure.

From an implementation perspective, by placing the majority of the validation in the service contract we have removed the need for the underlying service to build in this validation, simplifying the construction of the actual service.

However, the major disadvantage with this approach is that the tighter the constraints, the more resistant to change a service becomes.

For example, if oBay decided to accept American Express as payment, then `CardType` would need to be updated to contain an additional enumeration, `CardNumber` would need to be amended to accept 15-digit numbers, and `SecurityCode` amended to accept 4-digit numbers.

This would require oBay to release a new version of their XML Schema and a corresponding new version of any service that relies on `CreditCard` in any of its operations.

In addition, every year a new version of the canonical model would be required to update `ExpiryYear` as appropriate.

You could also argue that it's perfectly valid to have details of an expired credit card, in which case, you would not want to put this constraint in the canonical data model.

Loosely-typed services

With a loosely-typed approach, we use XML Schema to define the overall structure of the XML instance, that is, which elements may appear in the document, whether they are optional or mandatory, and how often they may occur. But define minimal constraints around the content of each element. Using this approach, our definition of a credit card could be as shown in the following code snippet:

```
<xsd:complexType name="CreditCard">
   <xsd:sequence>
      <xsd:element name="cardType"          type="xsd:string"/>
      <xsd:element name="cardHolderName"    type="xsd:string"/>
      <xsd:element name="cardNumber"        type="xsd:integer"/>
      <xsd:element name="expiryMonth"       type="xsd:integer"/>
      <xsd:element name="expiryYear"        type="xsd:integer"/>
      <xsd:element name="securityNo"        type="xsd:integer"/>
   </xsd:sequence>
</xsd:complexType>
```

This is about as loose a definition as we could provide, though we could have gone one step further and made every element a string.

The major advantage of this approach is that the service is far more conducive to change; following on from our previous example, if oBay decided to accept American Express as payment, then no changes would be required to the schema or service contract.

However, the key disadvantage with this approach is that we have far less control over the data that comes into our service and thus need to rely on the required validation being implemented elsewhere within our service.

What we want to avoid is coding the majority of this validation into the service itself, as this can overcomplicate the implementation of the service, result in the same validation being implemented in multiple services (possibly inconsistently), as well as make change harder to manage, as we would have to update the service code every time the validation rules changed.

Another disadvantage with this approach is that the service contract provides far less guidance to the consumer of the service as to what constitutes valid data, thus additional documentation would be required along with the service to define this.

Combined approach

Rather than using one approach exclusively, the key here is to strike the right balance and use schema validation to provide at least an initial sanity check of the data, that is, that the data is of the correct type (for example, integer, date, and so on) and that the size of the data is within reasonable limits.

For example, with the loosely-coupled schema definition, all our fields could be of any length. Often, this data will, at some point, be persisted in a database. If a service consumer issued a request with elements containing data larger than the underlying data stored, then this could cause the service to fail.

These types of validations can easily be overlooked by developers, yet cause problems which are hard to diagnose at runtime. By ensuring that we perform some level of sanity checking at the service entry point we can prevent these issues from occurring.

This also prevents services being called with significantly oversized payloads, which could have performance implications for the system if allowed to permeate through the application.

For elements which are far less prone to change, we can define tighter constraints around the content of those elements, to remove as much validation as possible from the underlying service implementation.

However, we would still like to extract as much of the validation logic from the underlying service as possible. This not only makes the service simpler to implement, it also makes the service more reusable, as we could potentially provide different validation depending on the context in which it is used. Fortunately, this is where Schematron comes in.

Schema validation within the Mediator

Schema validation of **incoming** messages is configured for each operation implemented by the Mediator. To enable schema validation for an operation, in the Mediator Editor select the option **Validate Syntax (XSD)** as we have for the **activateUser** operation.

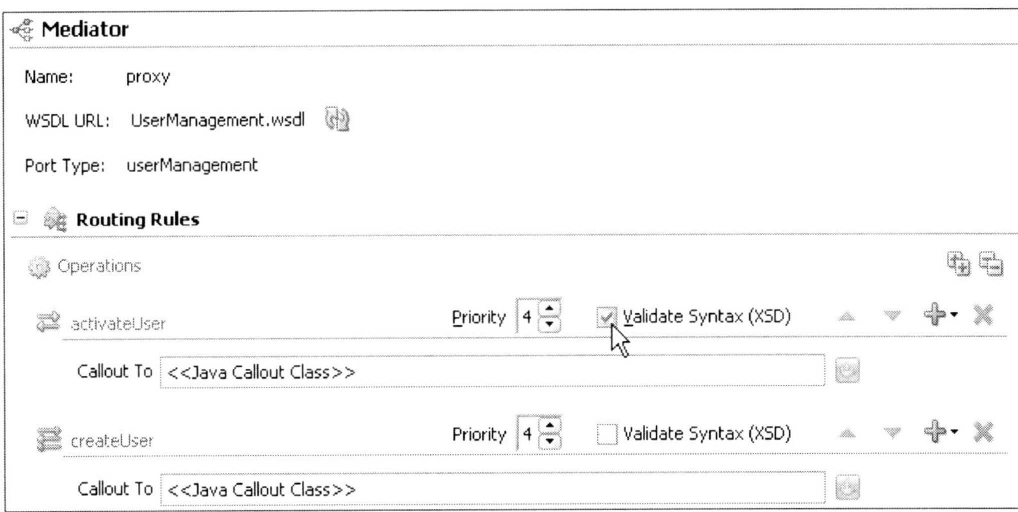

This will cause the Mediator to validate the payload of inbound messages prior to executing the routing rules of the operation. If the payload is invalid, the Mediator will return a fault containing details of the error to the initial caller of the Mediator.

Setting **Validate Syntax(XSD)** will **only** validate the incoming request messages; response messages from synchronous services or callbacks from asynchronous services that have been invoked by the Mediator are **NOT** validated.

If we refer to our earlier examination of messages exchanged, then this is the required behavior. Since, if validation of these messages is required, we would typically classify it as an external service and implement the required validation within the Service Bus. If this is not an option, another approach is to perform the validation within BPEL PM.

Using schema validation within BPEL PM

We have two ways of performing schema validation in BPEL PM. The first is to create an activity within your BPEL process to validate the required XML, and the second is to configure your process to perform schema validation of incoming and outgoing XML documents.

Validation of BPEL variables

BPEL PM provides the extension activity `<bpelx:validate/>` that allows you to specify one or more variables that you wish to validate. To use this, drag a **Validate** activity from the BPEL Activities and Component Palette into your BPEL process, as shown in the following screenshot:

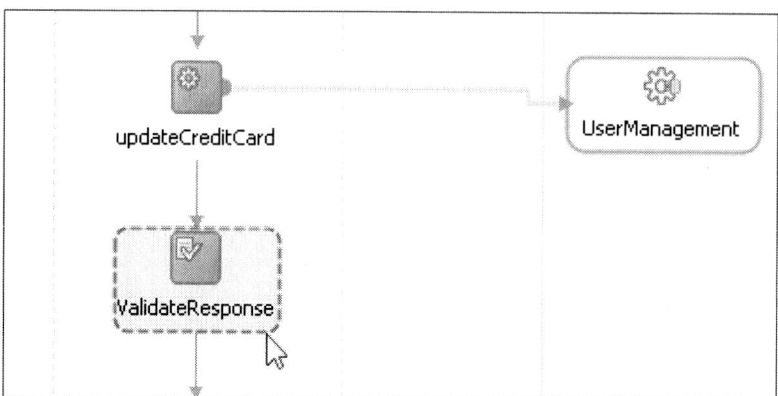

Double-click on this to open the **Validate** configuration window.

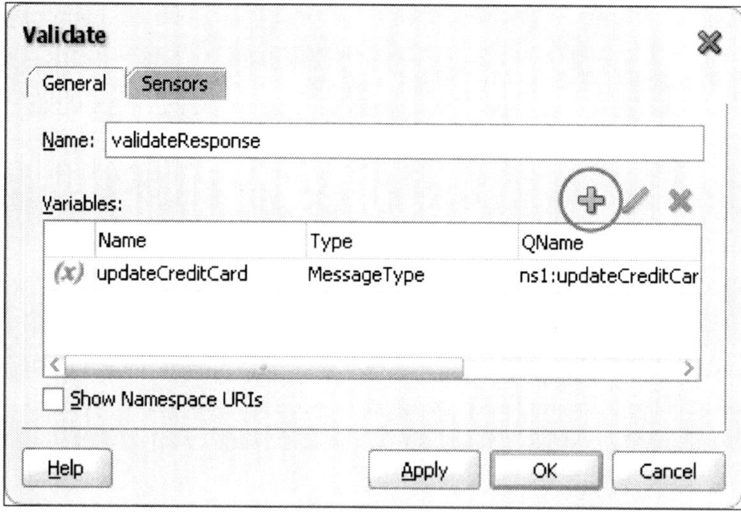

Here, we can specify a name for the activity, for example, **validateResponse**. To specify which variables to validate, click on the plus sign (circled in the preceding screenshot). This will launch the **Variable Chooser** from where we can select the variable we want to validate.

At runtime, in the event of a validation failure, the validate activity throws an `env:Server` fault, containing details of the validation error in the `faultstring`. We can then use a fault handler to catch the fault and handle it appropriately.

We can also embed the **Validate** activity within an **Assign** activity, to do this select the **Validate** checkbox on the **General** tab of the **Assign** activity, as shown in the screenshot below:

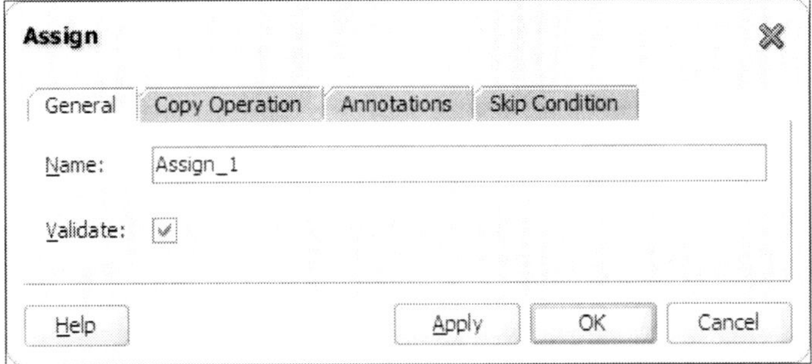

Validation of inbound and outbound documents

An alternative approach is to configure schema validation of incoming and outgoing XML documents for a partner link by setting the **validateXML** property on a partner link to `true` (or `false` to disable it). If the document fails validation, then the corresponding activity (that is, `receive`, `invoke`, or `reply`) will throw an `env:Server` fault.

Within an **Invoke** activity, validation is only performed against the outbound document.

Setting validateXML for a partner link

To specify the **validateXML** property for a partner link, open the partner link within the BPEL process, and select the **Property** tab, as shown in the following screenshot:

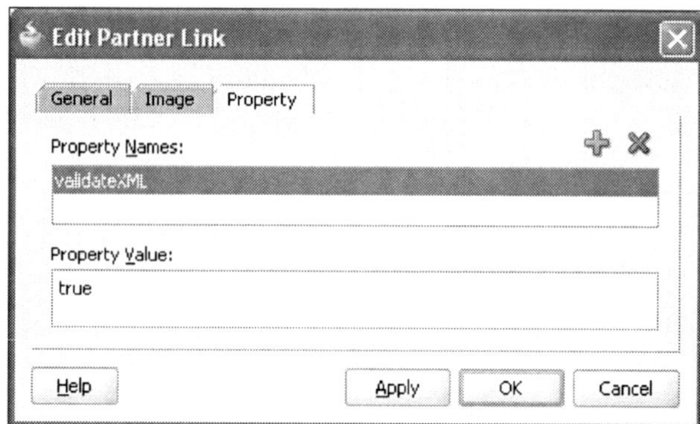

Next click the plus sign. This will pop-up a window with a drop-down list containing properties you can set on the partner link. Select **validateXML**, and then for the **Property Value**, specify **true**.

> In Enterprise Manager, you can also set this property to true for the BPEL Service engine. This will enable schema validation of incoming and outgoing XML documents for all partner links in all composites (unless specifically disabled on a partner link by setting **validateXML** to **false**).
>
> This is usually an unnecessary overhead, but it can be useful for the purpose of testing.

Using schema validation within the Service Bus

Within the Service Bus, schema validation is carried out using a **Validate** action, which is typically invoked during a pipeline stage or route node.

The **Validate** action provides an additional degree of flexibility when compared to the Mediator, in that, rather than validating the entire payload of a document, you can choose to validate just a fragment of the XML document, which you specify using XPath.

Upon completing validation, you can specify that the **Validate** action records the result of the validation, either `true` or `false` in a variable, or that it should throw an exception if the validation fails.

Validation of inbound documents

When processing an inbound document, it is best practice to perform validation as early as practically possible within the flow, as this prevents unnecessary processing of an invalid document.

This typically means creating a validation stage as the first stage within the request pipeline of a pipeline pair.

If we look at the operation `updateCreditCard`, which forms part of the `userManagement` service, a typical XML instance for this operation would appear, as shown in the following code snippet:

```
<soap:Envelope xmlns:soap="http://schemas.xmlsoap.org/soap/envelope">
 <soap:Body xmlns:ebm="http://rubiconred.com/obay/ebm/UserAccount"
            xmlns:usr="http://rubiconred.com/obay/xsd/user"
            xmlns:cmn="http://rubiconred.com/obay/xsd/common">
    <ebm:updateCreditCard>
      <usr:userId>jsmith</usr:userId>
      <cmn:creditCard>
        <cmn:cardType>MasterCard</cmn:cardType>
        <cmn:cardHolderName>John Smith</cmn:cardHolderName>
        <cmn:cardNumber>4570126723982904</cmn:cardNumber>
        <cmn:expiryMonth>10</cmn:expiryMonth>
        <cmn:expiryYear>2010</cmn:expiryYear>
        <cmn:securityNo>528</cmn:securityNo>
      </cmn:creditCard>
    </ebm:updateCreditCard>
  </soap:Body>
</soap:Envelope>
```

If we wanted to add a validation step to check the `creditCard` details, then we would add a validation stage (for example, Validate Credit Card) at the start of the request pipeline.

To add a validation action, click on the validate stage within the request pipeline and select **Edit Stage**. This will bring up the **Edit Stage Configuration** window. Click on **Add an Action | Message Processing | Validate**. This will insert the following validate action into our stage:

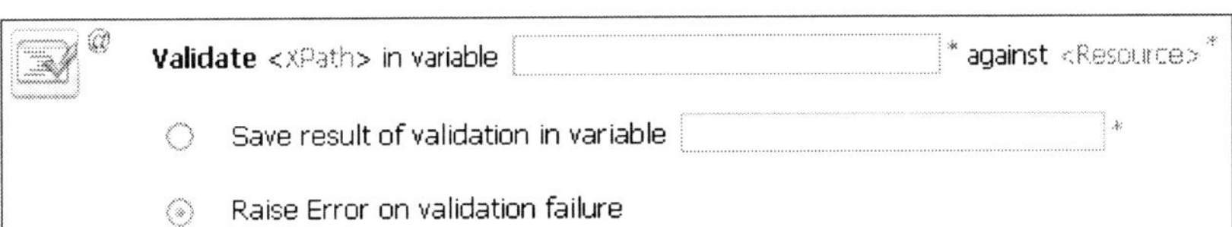

In the **variable** text field, enter the name of the variable that contains the XML fragment we wish to validate, for example, **body** in our example. Next, we need to specify which part of the **body** variable we want to validate. To do this, click the **<XPath>** link to bring up the **XPath Expression Editor** and define the appropriate XPath expression.

In our case, we want to validate the **creditCard** fragment from our **body** variable, so our expression is defined as follows:

```
./tns:updateCreditCardProcessRequest/cmn:creditCard
```

Next, we need to specify which schema element or type we wish to validate against; click on the **<Resource>** link and select **Schema** from the drop-down list. This will display the **Select an XML Schema** window, as shown in the following screenshot:

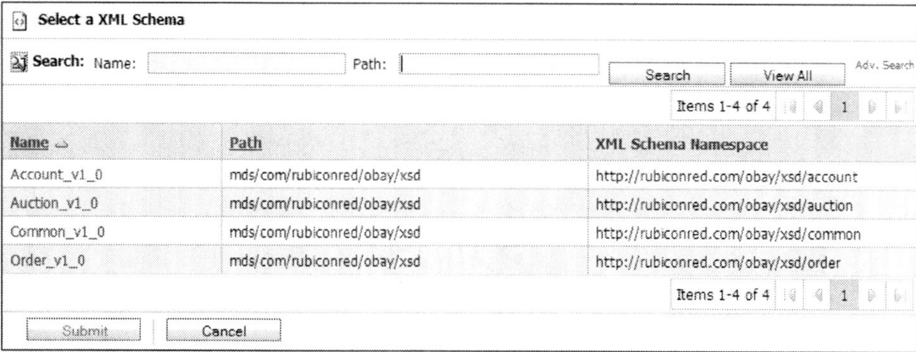

Select the required schema, that is, **common_v1** in our case, and this will launch the **Select a Schema definition** window, as shown in the following screenshot:

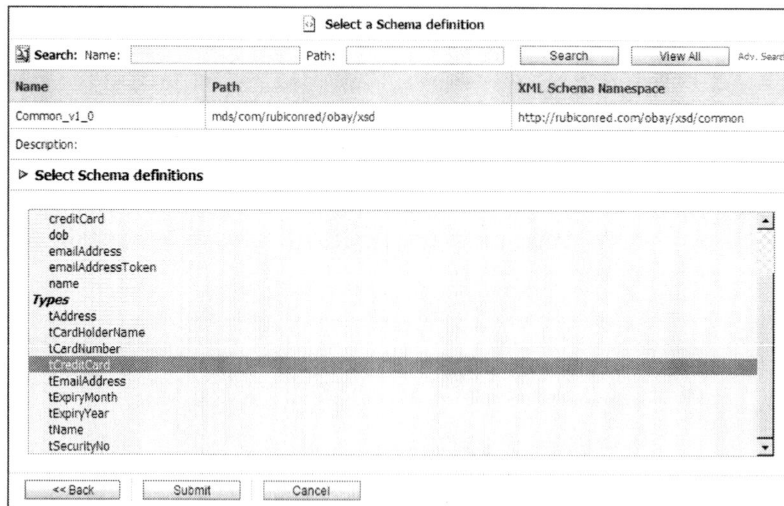

This lists all the types and global elements defined in the XML Schema. From here, we select the element or type we wish to validate our XML fragment against. So for our example, select **tCreditCard** and click on **Submit**.

Our completed validate action will look as shown in the following screenshot:

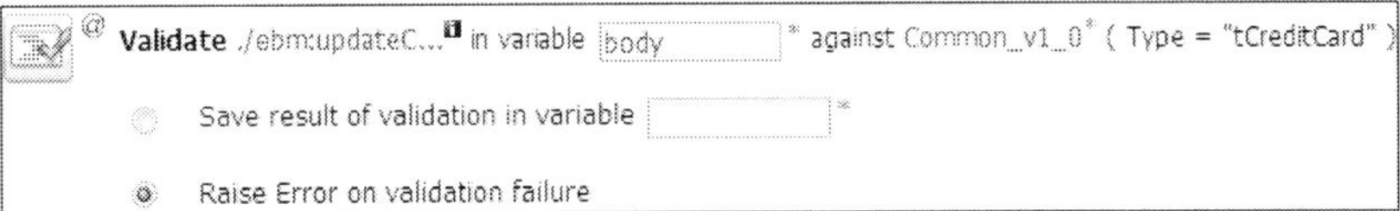

At runtime, if the validation fails, then the validate action will throw an exception. Typically, we would define a **Stage Error Handler** for our validation stage to catch the exception and handle it appropriately; we look at how to do this in *Chapter 14, Error Handling*. If we don't define an error handler, then the Service Bus will return the default validation fault to the caller of the service.

Validation of outbound documents

Within the Service Bus, we can also use the validate action to check any outbound documents. Typically, we would do this just prior to invoking any external service, and we would do this in a similar fashion for inbound documents.

However, strictly speaking, if we have received a valid inbound document and our service has been **correctly** implemented, it shouldn't be generating any invalid XML.

In reality, this is not always the case, so in many scenarios it still makes sense to include this level of validation. Even if we follow this approach strictly, we run the risk of over-validating, something we cover in more detail later.

Using Schematron for validation

Schematron provides another means of validating the message payload of a web service. It takes a markedly different approach from Schema validation in that rather than checking the overall structure of the XML instance, it enables you to specify one or more assertions that we wish to enforce. If all these assertions are met, the document is deemed to be valid.

These assertions are specified using XPath, so it allows us to specify constraints that can't be expressed using XML Schema. For example, following on from the preceding example, we can define the following validations on a credit card.

- If the card type is American Express, then the card number should be 15 digits in length, otherwise it should be 16 digits
- If the card type is American Express, then the security code should be four digits in length, otherwise it should be three digits
- The expiry date, which consists of the `expiryMonth` and `expiryYear` elements, should be in the future

For each assertion, we can also specify meaningful diagnostic messages, which indicate why an assertion hasn't been met (as opposed to schema validation messages, which aren't always so enlightening).

The other advantage of using Schematron is that it enables us to modify the assertions for a document without the need to change the schema.

However, rather than considering Schematron as an alternative approach to XML Schema validation, we see it very much as complementary. Thus, we would use XML Schema to validate the core structure of the XML, but not make those checks too granular. Rather, we will place those checks along with ones that can't be expressed in XML Schema in Schematron.

Overview of Schematron

One of the advantages of Schematron is that being based on XSLT makes it extremely easy to learn. Effectively, it has several key constructs. Once these are understood, you are ready to unleash the full power of the tool.

So before we look at how to use Schematron within the SOA Suite, we will give a quick introduction to Schematron itself. Readers who are familiar with Schematron may still want to skim this section, just to understand some of the idiosyncrasies of how Schematron behaves within the Oracle SOA Suite.

If we look at the operation `updateCreditCard`, which forms part of the `userManagement` service, a typical XML instance for this operation would appear as shown in the following code snippet:

```
<soap:Envelope xmlns:soap="http://schemas.xmlsoap.org/soap/envelope">
 <soap:Body xmlns:ebm="http://rubiconred.com/obay/ebm/UserAccount"
            xmlns:usr="http://rubiconred.com/obay/xsd/user"
            xmlns:cmn="http://rubiconred.com/obay/xsd/common">
   <ebm:updateCreditCard>
     <usr:userId>jsmith</usr:userId>
```

```
        <cmn:creditCard>
          <cmn:cardType>MasterCard</cmn:cardType>
          <cmn:cardHolderName>John Smith</cmn:cardHolderName>
          <cmn:cardNumber>4570126723982904</cmn:cardNumber>
          <cmn:expiryMonth>10</cmn:expiryMonth>
          <cmn:expiryYear>2010</cmn:expiryYear>
          <cmn:securityNo>5285</cmn:securityNo>
        </cmn:creditCard>
      </ebm:updateCreditCard>
    </soap:Body>
  </soap:Envelope>
```

A Schematron that checks that the credit card type is MasterCard or Visa could be written as the following code snippet:

```
<?xml version="1.0" encoding="UTF-8"?>
<schema xmlns="http://www.ascc.net/xml/schematron">
  <ns uri="http://rubiconred.com/obay/ebm/UserAccount" prefix="ebm"/>
  <ns uri="http://rubiconred.com/obay/xsd/cmn" prefix="cmn"/>
  <pattern name="Check Credit Card Type">
    <rule context="/ebm:updateCreditCard/cmn:creditCard">
      <assert test="cmn:cardType='MasterCard' or
                    cmn:cardType='Visa'">
        Credit Card must be MasterCard or Visa
      </assert>
    </rule>
  </pattern>
</schema>
```

From this, we can see that a Schematron is made of four key components: `pattern`, `rule`, `assert`, and `ns` contained within the `schema` element. We'll examine these elements one-by-one, starting with the inner most element and working outwards.

Assertions

The `assert` element, as its name suggests, is used to define the constraints to be enforced within an XML document. In the previous Schematron, we have defined the following `assert` element:

```
<assert test="cmn:cardType = 'MasterCard' or cmn:cardType = 'Visa'">
   Credit Card must be MasterCard or Visa
</assert>
```

We can see that it contains the `test` attribute, which specifies an XPath expression, and it should return a boolean value. If the test expression evaluates to true, then the assertion has been met.

If the test evaluates to false, then the assertion has failed and the document is invalid. When this happens, Schematron will raise an error and the content of the `assert` element (for example, '`Credit Card must be MasterCard or Visa`') is returned as an error message.

Rules

Asserts are defined within a `rule` element; each rule has a `context` attribute, which contains an XPath expression used to specify the nodes within an XML instance to which the rule should be applied.

In effect, it will perform a select on the root node of the service payload, which may result in a node set containing zero, one, or more nodes. Each node returned will then be validated against all asserts defined within the rule.

In the case of the `valCreditCard.sch` Schematron, we have defined the following rule:

```
<rule context="/emb:updateCreditCard/cmn:creditCard">
   ...
</rule>
```

Here we have specified a context of "`/emb:updateCreditCard/cmn:creditCard`". When applied to the payload of our `updateCreditCard` operation, the rule will return just a single node, `cmn:CreditCard`, as shown in the following code snippet to which our single assertion will be applied:

```
<cmn:creditCard>
   <cmn:cardType>MasterCard</cmn:cardType>
   <cmn:cardHolderName>John Smith</cmn:cardHolderName>
   <cmn:expiryMonth>10</cmn:expiryMonth>
   <cmn:expiryYear>2010</cmn:expiryYear>
   <cmn:securityNo>5285</cmn:securityNo>
</cmn:creditCard>
```

In the case where we have multiple assertions defined for a rule, if more than one assertion fails for a particular node, then Schematron will return a diagnostic message for each failed assertion.

Using a relative context

As we have defined an absolute path name for the rule `context`, it can only be applied to the `updateCreditCard` operation. Ideally, we would like to write a Schematron that can be used to validate all occurrences of `creditCard`, regardless of which operation it appears in.

To do this, we need to specify a rule context that will match any occurrence of `creditCard`, regardless of where it appears in the XML payload. We can achieve this by using a relative context, such as "`//cmn:CreditCard`", as shown in the following code snippet:

```
<rule context="//cmn:creditCard">
   ...
</rule>
```

The key here is the `//`, as this tells Schematron to match a pattern which may occur anywhere within the XML instance.

Patterns

Rules are defined with a `pattern` element. Each `pattern` can hold a collection of one or more associated rules. Pattern contains a single attribute name, which contains free format text used to describe the rules contained within it.

In our `valCreditCard.sch` Schematron, we have defined the following pattern:

```
<pattern name="Check Credit Card Type">
   ...
</pattern>
```

When processing an XML instance, Schematron will apply each pattern against the XML instance in pattern order. When checking against a pattern, Schematron will check the XML instance against each rule contained within the pattern in rule order.

Namespaces

Namespaces are declared using the `ns` element. This has two attributes; one is `uri`, which is used to define the namespace URI, and the other is `prefix`, which is used to define the namespace prefix.

For example, in our credit card validation Schematron, we define the namespace `http://rubiconred.com/obay/xsd/cmn` with the following:

```
<ns uri="http:// rubiconred.com/obay/xsd/cmn" prefix="cmn"/>
```

Schema

The root element of a Schematron document is the `schema` element defined within the namespace `http://www.ascc.net/xml/schematron`. In our example, we've made this the default namespace, so we don't have to prefix any of the Schematron elements.

```
<?xml version="1.0" encoding="UTF-8"?>
<schema xmlns="http://www.ascc.net/xml/schematron">
   ...
</schema>
```

Intermediate validation

So far, we have just implemented some basic validation that we could have quite easily performed using XML Schema. However, to give you a feel for the real capability of Schematron, we will also look at some validation requirements that can't be implemented using XSD.

Cross field validation

An area where Schematron excels is cross field validation. For example, if we wanted to check if `cardNumber` is 16 digits long for MasterCard and Visa and 15 digits long for American Express, we could write the following assertion:

```
<rule context="cmn:CreditCard">
  <assert test="((cmn:cardType='MasterCard' or
                  cmn:cardType='Visa') and
                  string-length(cmn:cardNumber) = '16') or
                 (cmn:cardType='American Express' and
                  string-length(cmn:cardNumber) = '15')">
        Invalid Card Number.
  </assert>
</rule>
```

Using XPath predicates in rules

The previous approach, while perfectly valid, could become quite verbose, especially once we start to add additional checks for specific card types, for example, if wanted to check the length of `securityCode` based on `cardType`.

Another approach is to use an XPath predicate within the rules context attribute to narrow down the context to a specific card type. For example, we can specify a set of assertions for credit cards of type **MasterCard** as follows:

```
<rule context="cmn:creditCard[cmn:cardType='MasterCard']">
    <assert test="string-length(cmn:cardNumber) = '16'">
        Mastercard card number must be 16 digits.
    </assert>
    <assert test="string-length(cmn:securityNo) = '3'">
        Security code for Mastercard must be 3 digits.
    </assert>
</rule>
```

Using this approach, we can specify a different rule for each card type, allowing us to maintain assertions for each card type independently from one another as well as simplifying the process of adding new card types.

Using XPath 2.0 functions

In the previous assertion, we are just testing that `cardNumber` is 16 characters in length, but we are not checking that it's an actual integer. We are relying on schema validation for this.

There is nothing wrong with this approach, but what if some cards allowed alphanumeric numbers? In this scenario, we would need to declare `cardNumber` as a string and then carry out specific validation in Schematron to check the format of the element based on `cardType`.

For this, we can use the `matches` function to test whether the content of the element conforms to a particular regular expression. However, this is an XPath 2.0 function, so in order to use this within Schematron, we need to define its namespace. We do this in exactly the same way as we would for any other namespace, that is:

```
<ns uri="http://www.oracle.com/XSL/Transform/java/oracle.tip.pc.
services.functions.Xpath20" prefix="xp20"/>
```

We can then create an assertion that matches the `cardNumber`, like this:

```
<assert test="xp20:matches(cmn:cardNumber, '[0-9]{16}')">
   Mastercard number must be 16 digits.
</assert>
```

Date validation

Using Schematron is also an excellent method of validating dates based on the current time. For example, we need to check that the expiry date for the credit card is not in the past.

To do this, we need to check that the expiry year of the CreditCard is greater than the current year, or that the expiry year of the CreditCard equals the current year, and the current month is less than or equal to the expiry month of the card.

To do this, we could write the following test:

```
cmn:expiryYear > xp20:year-from-dateTime(xp20:current-dateTime()) or
(cmn:expiryYear= xp20:year-from-dateTime(xp20:current-dateTime()) and
 cmn:expiryMonth>=xp20:month-from-dateTime(xp20:current-dateTime()) )
```

Element present

Another requirement is to check whether an element is present or not. We can do this with XML Schema by defining an element as being mandatory. However, whether an element is optional or mandatory may well be based on values in other fields.

For example, if we had made `securityNo` optional within our schema definition, but we wanted to make it mandatory for American Express, we could write the following rule:

```
<rule context="//cmn:creditCard[cmn:cardType='American Express']">
   <assert test="cmn:securityNo">
      Security No must be specified
   </assert>
</rule>
```

Note that this will only check to see if the element is present in the XML instance. It doesn't actually check if it actually contains a value. The simplest way to check this is to use the string-length function, as shown in the following code snippet:

```
<rule context="//cmn:creditCard[cmn:cardType='American Express']">
   <assert test="cmn:securityNo and string-length(cmn:securityNo)>0">
      Security No must be specified
   </assert>
</rule>
```

Using Schematron within the Mediator

Schematron validation of incoming messages is specified at the routing rule level for an operation. This gives us the flexibility to specify a different Schematron for an operation based on where we are routing the request to.

You assign a Schematron to a routing rule by clicking on the Schematron icon, circled in the following screenshot:

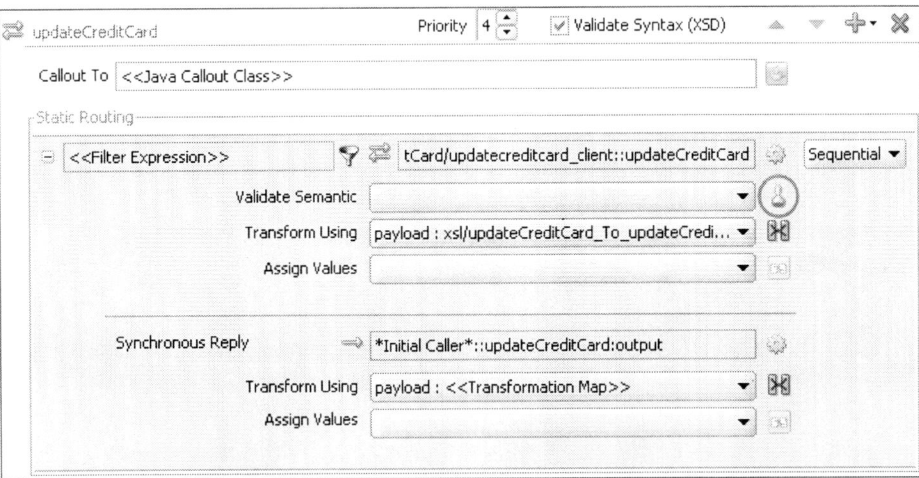

This will bring up the **Validations** window, where you can specify one or more Schematron files for the routing rule, as shown in the following screenshot:

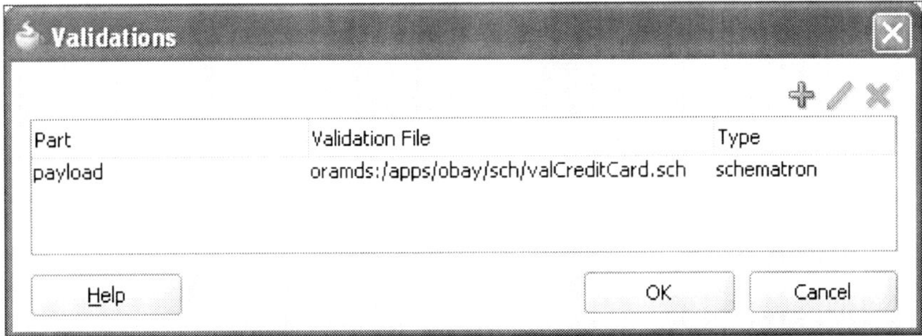

To add a Schematron, click on the plus sign. This will bring up the **Add Validation** window, as shown in the following screenshot:

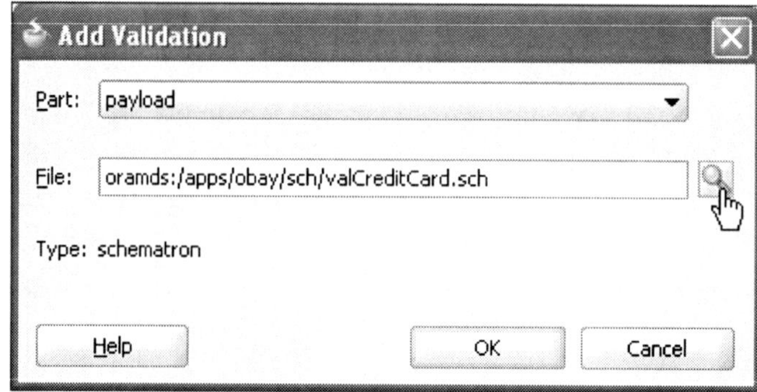

Here you specify the part of the SOAP message to which you want to apply the Schematron.

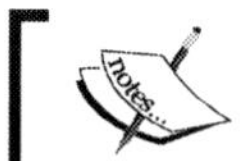

If you are following the document-wrapped pattern laid out in *Chapter 11, Designing the Service Contract,* you will only ever have a single part.

Next, click the search icon. This will launch the standard SOA Resource Browser Window, from where you can browse your filesystem for a local Schematron file and import it into your project. Alternatively, you can specify a Schematron already held in MDS.

You can specify multiple Schematrons for a routing rule. In this case, the Schematrons are compared in the order specified. As soon as a Schematron returns any failed assertions, no more Schematrons are executed.

Using the Metadata Service to hold Schematron files

Rather than importing Schematron files directly into your composite project, which then get deployed with the composite into the runtime environment, you can actually reference a Schematron already deployed to the **Metadata Service** (**MDS**) that we introduced in *Chapter 11, Designing the Service Contract*.

This has a number of distinct advantages. Firstly, you can ensure that all your composites use the same version of a particular Schematron. Secondly, if you need to modify your validation rules, you simply need to update a single copy of your Schematron and redeploy it to the MDS. In addition, any composite which references that Schematron will automatically pick up the modified version, without the need to be redeployed.

Schematron files are deployed to MDS in an identical way to XML Schemas, as covered in *Chapter 11, Designing the Service Contract*.

Returning Schematron errors

In the event that one or more assertions are violated within a Schematron, then an error will be raised by the Mediator and a `Fault`, similar to the one shown in the following code snippet, will be returned to the service consumer.

```
<env:Fault>
  <faultcode>env:Server</faultcode>
  <faultstring>… Schematron validation fails with error
    <ns1:ValidationErrors>
      <error>Security code for Mastercard must be 3 digits.</error>
      <error>Credit Card has expired.</error>
    </ns1:ValidationErrors>
  </faultstring>
  <faultactor/>
  <detail>
    <exception/>
  </detail>
</env:Fault>
```

Using Schematron with the Service Bus

The Service Bus does not support Schematron validation. However, it does provide a Java Callout Action that allows you to invoke a Java method within a message flow.

One approach would be to implement a lightweight Java class that wraps the Schematron classes and exposes a single method, which can then be invoked using a Java Action in the Service Bus.

Putting validation in the underlying service

So far we have looked at using XML Schema and Schematron to put validation either in the service contract or the Mediator layer in order to provide initial validation of a service invocation, before we actually invoke the underlying service. This provides a number of benefits, including:

- Simplifies the development of validation within the actual service, as it can now rely on the fact that it is receiving relatively sensible data.
- Allows us to implement a more generic service, as business-specific validation can be provided at a higher level within the service. This makes the service more reusable, as it can be used in multiple scenarios, each with different validation requirements.
- Makes changes easier to manage, as changes to business rules which impact the overall validation of the service can happen at either the schema or Schematron level, and thus may require no changes to the actual underlying service.
- By placing the validation in a centralized place, which can be reused across multiple services, it enables us to implement the same validation across multiple services in a consistent fashion. This also makes change simpler to manage, as we only have to make the changes once, as opposed to everywhere the validation is required.

However, at some point, we will still be required to put some level of validation in the underlying service itself. For example, take our `updateCreditCard` operation; despite all our checks, we can't be completely sure that the credit card itself is actually a valid card and that the card name, security no, and so on, correspond to the given card number. To validate this, we will still need to call out to an external validation service.

Additionally, we still need to validate that the user ID provided as part of the operation is a valid user within our system.

Using Business Rules for validation

One option for implementing validation checks within your service is to separate them as a Business Rule. This allows us to implement the validation just once and then share it across multiple services; this shares a number of advantages with the approaches already discussed, including:

- Simplifies development of rules, as we only need to implement it once
- Rules are implemented consistently across multiple services
- Easier to maintain as rules only need to be modified once, should a change be required

When implementing a service using BPEL, the use of rules for validation is a pretty natural fit. But natively, rules are implemented in Java, so come with a Java API, making it relatively straightforward to call from any services implemented in Java.

Additionally, you can also expose a ruleset as a web service, either in the standard way you would expose a Java code as a web service or just by wrapping the rule in a decision service embedded within a synchronous BPEL process.

Coding in validation

While providing an extra option for validation, using Business Rules will not be appropriate in every case. In these scenarios, the only remaining option is to implement the validation in code.

However, even when we take this approach, we can still follow the same pattern that we used for Business Rules, namely, to separate the validation from the core service so that it can be used in multiple services. Also consider the option of providing a means to maintain the validation rules without the need to modify the actual code.

Returning validation failures in synchronous services

When putting the validation in the underlying service, apart from carrying out the validation, we also need a mechanism for returning any validation failures to the client, ideally with some meaningful information about why the error occurred.

For synchronous services, the mechanism for achieving this is to return a SOAP Fault to the service caller. A SOAP Fault contains four pieces of information, namely:

1. `faultcode`: This provides a high level indication as to the cause of the fault. SOAP 1.1 defines the following fault codes: `VersionMismatch`, `MustUnderstand`, `Client`, or `Server`. As the fault is because of an error in the message payload, which the client needs to fix, we should return a fault code of type `Client`, unless we are returning a custom fault code.
2. `faultstring`: This should contain a human-readable description of why the fault occurred, that is, the reason for the validation failure.
3. `faultactor`: This provides details of where in the message path the fault occurred. If the failure occurred somewhere other than the final destination of the SOAP message, then this must be present to indicate where. For our purposes, we can leave this blank.
4. `detail`: This is an optional element that can be used to provide further details about why the fault occurred. We only need to provide this if the `faultstring` does not provide sufficient information for the client to handle the error.

Defining faults

Unless returning a basic fault, that is, using a predefined fault code and no structured content within the `soap:detail`, it is a good practice to define the fault as part of the WSDL contract defining your service.

Faults are defined by adding the appropriate `fault` elements to the `operation` declarations. A fault has two attributes: `name`, which corresponds to the fault code returned in the SOAP fault and `message`, which will contain additional information about the fault and is returned within the `soap:detail` element.

For example, to define a fault for the `updateCreditCard` operation, we would just add the following `fault` element to our definition, as shown in the following code snippet:

```
<operation name="updateCreditCard">
   <input message="tns:updateCreditCard "/>
   <output message="tns:updateCreditCardResponse "/>
   <fault name="tns:invalidCreditCard"
          message="tns:invalidCreditCardFault "/>
</operation>
```

There is nothing to stop a service returning a fault which is undeclared in its service contract. However, by declaring the fault, the service consumer has the opportunity to handle the fault in an appropriate manner and by knowing the structure of the fault detail, is able to process it in a more meaningful way.

Custom fault codes

Often it is desirable to define a custom fault, particularly for services which may return a number of faults, as this can simplify fault handling for the service consumer (as they can implement targeted fault handling mechanisms for each type of fault).

SOAP 1.1 allows custom fault codes to be implemented through the use of the dot notation, for example we could define a fault code of `client.invalidCreditCard` in the SOAP namespace (`http://schemas.xmlsoap.org/soap/envelope/`). However, this can result in namespace collision and interoperability issues so is not WS-I Basic Profile-compliant and should be avoided.

Instead, custom fault codes should be defined within their own namespace. For example, we have defined our `invalidCreditCard` fault code to be in the same namespace as the actual `userManagement` service.

While defining custom faults within their own namespace is WS-I Basic Profile-compliant, WS-I Basic Profile still encourages you to use the standard SOAP 1.1 fault codes and use the detail element to provide any extra information.

Validation failures in asynchronous services

If an asynchronous service needs to return a fault to a client, it can't do this in the reply message in the same way that a synchronous service can. This is because an asynchronous service consists of two one-way operations; the first contains the original request the second contains a callback from the service containing the result.

To return a fault, we need to do this within the callback. We have two basic options to choose from. The first is to return the success or otherwise with the content of the standard callback and allow the client to inspect the content to determine whether the service was successfully invoked or not.

The other is to define additional operations on the callback port specifically for the purpose of returning an error message. The latter of these is the preferred approach as it allows the client to implement separate handlers for callbacks indicating errors (in much the same way, we can implement separate fault handlers for each type of fault returned with synchronous services).

In many ways, it's helpful to think of the operation name as being the equivalent of the fault code, and the message payload of the operation can be used to hold the equivalent of the remainder of the fault information (for example, fault string and detail).

For example, one way to define an asynchronous version of our `updateCreditCard` operation is shown in the following code snippet:

```
<portType name="UserAccount">
    <operation name="updateCreditCard">
        <input message="tns:updateCreditCard "/>
    </operation>
</portType>

<portType name="UserAccountCallback">
    <operation name="updateCreditCardCallback">
        <input message=" tns:updateCreditCardCallback "/>
    </operation>

    <operation name="invalidCreditCard">
        <input message="tns:invalidCreditCard"/>
    </operation>
</portType>
```

The final callback operation (highlighted in the preceding code), is the equivalent of the fault defined within our synchronous service.

Layered validation considerations

Within a single composite application, we have a certain amount of control over what validation to put in the schema, Schematron, and the underlying services. This allows us to design and implement these in a coordinated fashion, so that they can work in synergy with one another.

However, once we start assembling services from other composite applications, then the lines of demarcation, and thus which service is responsible for which validation, becomes less clear.

There are a number of potential strategies which can be adopted, but each has its own strengths and weaknesses. We examine some of these below, but in reality, there is not always a simple answer and it really comes down to good design and being aware of the issues.

Dangers of over validation

Probably the "safest" approach is to make each service fully responsible for its own validation, and thus perform whatever validation is required, regardless of what validation is performed by any other service in the chain.

However, this could have potential performance implications. Apart from the obvious overhead of performing the same work several times, it could introduce potential points of contention within the system.

If we take the `updateCreditCard` operation, at some point our application will need to fully validate the card. To do this, it will need to call out to an external web service. If we follow the approach of performing this validation in every service involved in the operation, and the request has to go through N layers of services, then that would require N callouts to the external service with the implied latency of making N callouts. Not to mention that the card company might wonder why this card is being validated so many times!

Another issue with this approach is that the validation may be implemented several times, not always identically, resulting in inconsistent validation that is hard to change. This can be addressed by using shared XML Schema, Schematron, and Business Rules validation.

Dangers of under validation

An alternate approach is to push the responsibility of validation down to the lowest service in the chain on the basis that if an error occurs, it will catch the error which will then be propagated up the chain and returned to the original consumer of the service.

Again, on the surface, this approach seems fine. However, the main issue here is whether we have to undo any work as a result of the error, which we could have avoided if we had caught it earlier. For example, if we have a service A, which is a composite of service B and service C, the call to service B may succeed but if just the call to C fails, we may need to undo any work carried out by service B.

Negative coupling of validation

Another issue that arises with service composition is that a high level component, which calls other components effectively "inherits" the validation of the lower level components.

The strategy we recommend here is that we put the minimal amount of validation in the lower level component and put the more restrictive constraints in the higher level components.

Assuming the service is only designed for internal use, that is, via other components within our control, this approach works well. As we can mandate that any additional validation that is required is applied in a higher level component.

For those components that we need to expose directly to external consumers, we can still follow this approach by implementing a wrapper component with the required validation and then expose this externally.

This approach allows us to develop more generic lower level components, which are easier to reuse while at the same time minimizing over and under validation.

Summary

In this chapter, we've looked at how we can implement validation within an individual service through a combination of XSD validation, Schematron, and Business Rules.

Ideally we should use XSD validation to check the overall sanity of the data, but in order to provide a greater level of flexibility, we then extract the business-specific validation into a separate component such as Schematron. This gives us more flexibility to change the validation for a component without the need to redeploy a new version of it.

In situations where Schematron can't provide the required validation, we've looked at how we can use Business Rules to build this into the underlying service implementation, again giving us the flexibility to change the validation without having to redeploy the service.

Finally, we've looked at some of the issues and potential strategies for validation when combing multiple services, while there are no simple solutions. By at least having an idea of the issues, we are able to take these into account in the design of our overall solution.

14
Error Handling

Handling errors or faults is an important consideration for **service-oriented architecture** (**SOA**) based applications, especially if you consider that a solution is likely to be a loose assembly of independent components, each with varying levels of resilience, throughput, and availability.

How faults are handled depends on a number of factors: whether it's a business or system fault, was the service where the fault originated called synchronously or asynchronously, and whether the interaction between the client and the component detecting the fault is synchronous or asynchronous.

A business fault is loosely defined as one we know about in advance. It is defined as part of the service contract, and thus represents a legitimate state within the business process. How we handle a fault of this type is largely driven by business requirements, and so it makes sense to handle these within the context of the process.

A system fault conversely is one that is unexpected in nature and could typically occur to any component in the solution. Such faults are often caused by infrastructure problems, such as a network outage or a service being unavailable. Often these are temporary and can be handled by retrying the service at a later time.

The interaction between the client and the component detecting the fault also influences how we handle it. If asynchronous, the component has the time to resolve the problem. For example, if the fault occurred due to a service being unavailable, it can retry it later.

With synchronous interactions, we only have a small window in which to resolve the fault before the client times out waiting for our component, and raises its own fault. With this style of interaction, often all we can do is catch the fault, undo any partially completed activities so we leave the system in a consistent state, and then return a fault to the client.

In this chapter, we examine how to handle faults within our composite applications. We first examine the `catch` and `compensate` activities that BPEL provides, and how we can use them to handle business faults. Next, we examine the role of the Mediator in handling business faults, before looking at how to leverage the SOA composite fault management framework to simplify the handling of system faults within composites.

In the final section of this chapter, we look at the mechanisms the Service Bus provides for handling faults and how we can use these in our overall fault management strategy.

Business faults

A business fault is one that is defined in the **Web Service Definition Language (WSDL)** of the service. How we define the fault depends on whether a service is synchronous or asynchronous.

Defining faults in synchronous services

Synchronous services signal faults by returning a `fault` element in place of the defined output message for the service. These faults are defined in the WSDL of the service and are denoted by the `<fault>` element.

For example, the oBay application implements a dummy `CreditCard` service, which includes the operation `verifyCreditCard`. The definition of the operation is as follows:

```
<portType name="CardServices">
<operation name="verifyCreditCard">
<input     message="tns:verifyCreditCard" />
<output    message="tns:verifyCreditCardResponse"/>
<fault     name="invalidCreditCard"
                 message="tns:invalidCreditCardFault"/>
   </operation>
</portType>
```

As well as defining the standard input and output messages for the operation, it displays a fault message (highlighted in the previous code) that could be returned in place of the defined `output` operation. An operation can define zero, one, or many faults for an individual operation. It is similar in construct to an output message, except that it must also be named so that the client can distinguish which fault has been returned.

When a `soap:Fault` is generated, the `faultcode` will contain the fault name (`tns:invalidCreditCard` in the previous example), and the `detail` element will contain the content of the fault message.

Defining faults in asynchronous services

Asynchronous services don't explicitly support the concept of faults. This is because the result of an asynchronous service is returned in a separate `callback` operation. So to signal a fault, the service will need to define additional callbacks, typically one extra callback per fault. If we take our credit card example and rewrite is as an asynchronous service, we get the corresponding WSDL:

```
<portType name="CardServices"
<operation name="verifyCreditCard">
          <input message="tns:verifyCreditCard"/>
</operation>
</portType>
<portType name="CardServicesCallback"
<operation name="creditCardVerified">
          <input message="tns:creditCardVerified" />
</operation>
<operation name="invalidCreditCard">
          <input message="tns:invalidCreditCard" />
</operation>
</portType>
```

Here we can see that we've defined a second `callback` operation (highlighted in the previous code). This corresponds to the fault we defined in the synchronous operation. If we examine this, we can see that we've used the fault name as the operation name in the callback. Although we have two different messages, in reality they are identical, we have just used different names as we want to stick to our naming conventions.

It is still possible for the invocation of an asynchronous service to return a fault. This can occur when the system is unable to successfully deliver the invocation message to the asynchronous service, for example, when the network connection is down. We would treat this type of fault as a system fault as opposed to a business fault.

Handling business faults in BPEL

Within a BPEL process, any call to a partner link could result in a fault being raised. Other activities within a process can also result in a fault being thrown (for example, due to a selection failure within an `assign` activity), and in addition, the process itself may need to signal a fault.

When a fault occurs in a BPEL process, the process must first catch the fault, or else the process will terminate with a state of `Faulted`. Once caught, the next step is to decide whether the fault can be handled locally within the process or needs to be returned to the client.

If the interaction between the client and the process is synchronous, it provides a limited opportunity to correct the cause of the fault and retry the activity. For example, if the fault occurred due to a service not being available, we can retry the service in the hope that its outage was very temporary. But, if we wait for the service to come back up, then the client of our BPEL process is likely to timeout and raise its own fault.

With synchronous interactions, all we can really do is catch the fault, undo any partially completed activities so that we leave the system in a consistent state, and then return a fault to the client.

The client itself may be a BPEL process or another SOA component. Again, if the interaction between this component and its client is also synchronous, it will typically need to return its own fault, and so on up the chain until the interaction between a client and a component is asynchronous in nature.

With asynchronous interactions, we have a lot more flexibility to handle the fault within the context of the process, as the client is unlikely to timeout (however, we still need to take into account the fact that the client may not wait forever).

If the fault is temporary in nature, such as a service not being available, we can wait for the issue to be resolved and retry the activity later. However, this type of fault should be handled using the fault management framework (which we will cover later in this chapter). This allows us to focus on handling business faults within our BPEL process, which keeps our process simpler and easier to maintain.

Handling business faults is just a natural extension to the process, in that we need to model the process to cater to these types of scenarios. For example, if a fault occurred due to invalid data, then in a synchronous interaction, we would just return details of the fault to the client. However, in an asynchronous interaction, we could create a human workflow task for someone to capture the correct data so that the process can resume.

Catching faults

The first step in handling a fault is to catch it. Within BPEL, we do this using a `<catch>` branch, which can either be attached to a scope or the process. With a `<catch>` branch, we specify the name of the fault to be caught and the series of activities to be carried out in that event.

Once the `<catch>` branch has completed, processing will continue with the next activity following the scope in which the fault was caught, assuming of course another fault hasn't been thrown.

We can define as many `<catch>` branches as we want for a scope. In addition, we can also attach a `<catchAll>` branch, which will catch any fault that is not caught by any of the specific `<catch>` activities.

When a fault is raised, the BPEL engine will first check the current scope to determine a suitable `<catch>` or `<catchAll>` all branch. If the fault is not caught, the BPEL engine will then check the containing scope for an appropriate fault handler, and so on, up to the process level.

If the fault is not caught at this level, then the process will terminate with a status of `Faulted`. If the interaction between the client and the process is synchronous, then the fault will be automatically returned to the client. However, if the interaction is asynchronous, then the fault will not be returned, with the potential result being that the client may hang waiting for a response that is never sent.

Adding a catch branch

To demonstrate this, we will look at the `UserRegistration` process that needs to carry out a number of checks: for example, that the requested `userId` isn't already in use, that the supplied credit card is valid, and so on. Should one of these checks fail, we need to catch the fault and then return a reply to the client to indicate that an error has occurred.

To achieve this, we will place each validation step in its own scope and define a fault handler for each one. To add a `<catch>` branch to a scope, click on the **Add Catch Branch** icon for the scope; this will add an empty `<catch>` branch to the scope, as shown in the following screenshot:

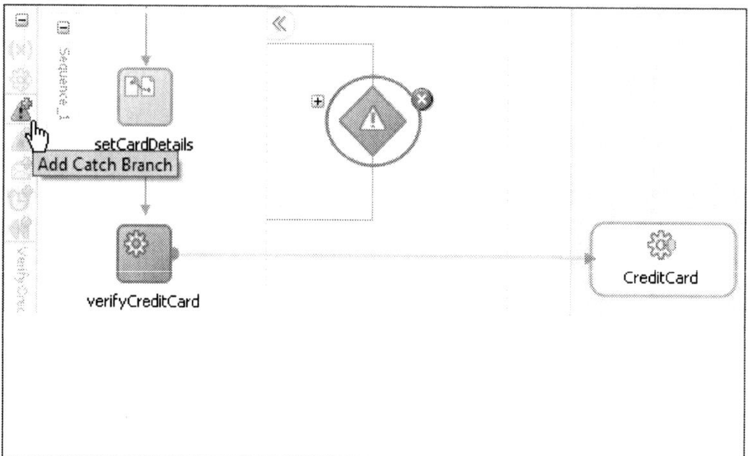

The next step is to specify the type of fault that you want to catch. To do this, double-click on the catch branch icon (circled in the previous screenshot). This will bring up the **Catch** dialog, as shown in the next screenshot:

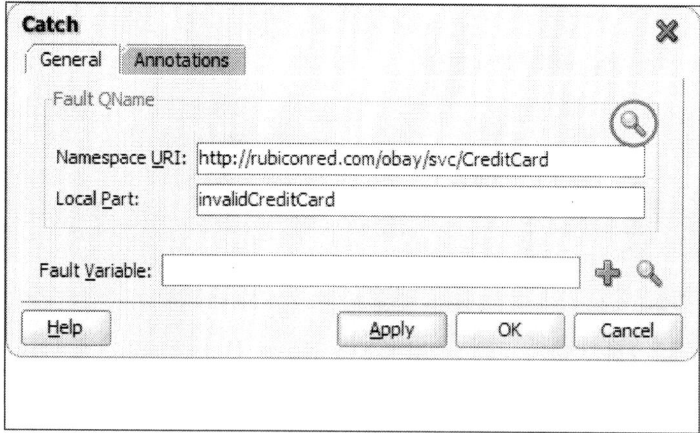

Click on the **search** icon for the **Fault QName** (circled in the previous screenshot), and this will launch the **Fault Chooser** dialog box. From here, you can browse to the fault that we want to catch, which, in our case, is the **invalidCreditCard** fault defined in the WSDL file of the **CreditCard Partner Links**.

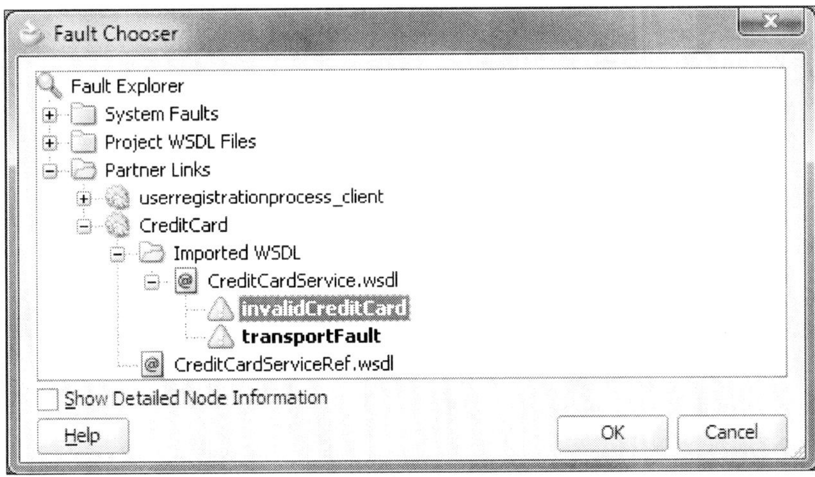

There is also the option to specify a fault variable to hold details of the fault returned. This should be of the type `Message` and match the message type defined for the fault, that is, `invalidCreditCardFault` for the case where the fault is `invalidCreditCard` (as defined in the WSDL file for this service).

Once we have caught the fault, we need to specify the activities to perform in order to handle the fault. In our case, we need to undo any activity completed in previous scopes using the `compensate` activity before we return the fault `invalidUserDetails` to the caller of this process.

However, the current scope is not the correct context for triggering the required compensation (we will see why in a moment), so our fault handler needs to capture the reason for the fault and throw a new fault that can be handled at the appropriate place within our process.

Throwing faults

To do this, expand the `<catch>` branch for the **Fault Handler** by clicking on the '+' symbol and drag a **Throw** activity into it.

To specify the fault we wish to throw, double-click the **Throw** activity to bring up the dialog to configure it, as shown in the next screenshot:

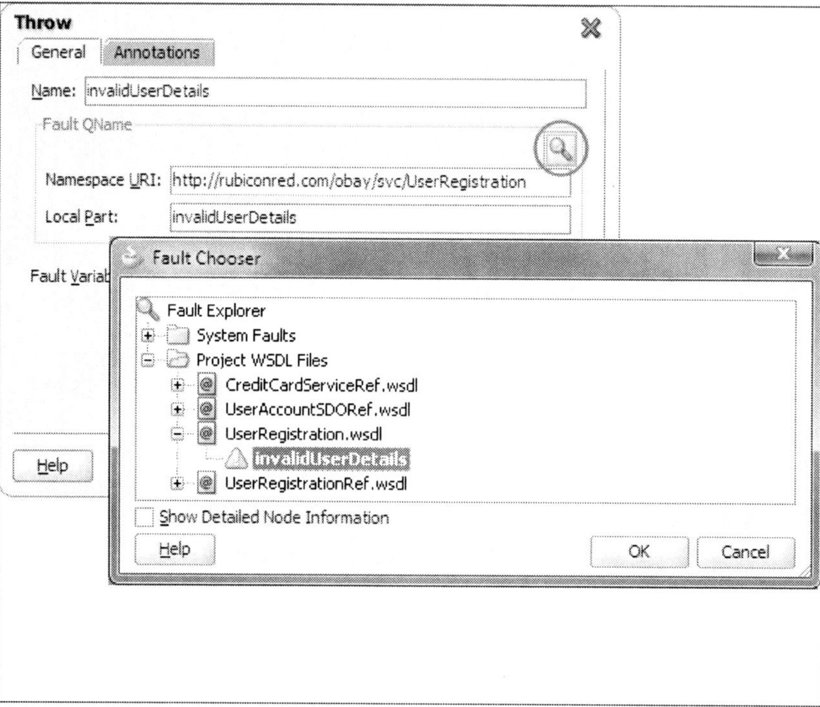

Next, click the **search** icon (circled in the previous screenshot) to bring up the **Fault Chooser**. This time we want to browse to the fault we wish to throw, which is the **invalidUserDetails** fault and is defined in the `wsdl` file for the **UserRegistration** process.

We also want to record the reason for the **invalidUserDetails**, so we need to define a fault variable to hold this. The simplest way to do this is by clicking on the **magic wand** icon to create a variable of the right type, though you should specify that the variable is local to the scope, as opposed to global.

Finally, we've added a simple `assign` activity before our **Throw** activity to populate our fault variable. So our final `<catch>` branch looks as follows:

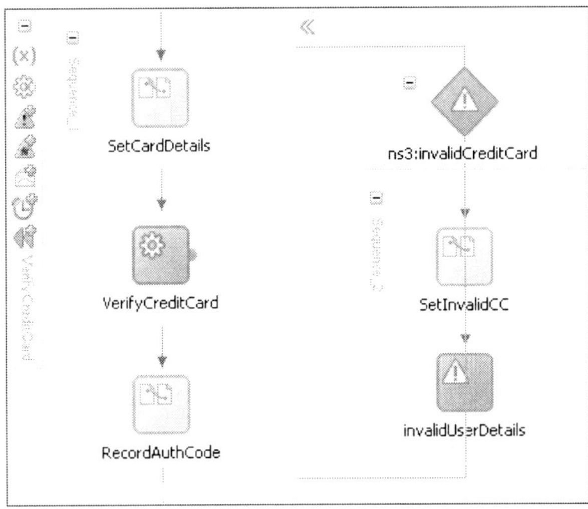

Compensation

As part of the user registration process, we need to check that the requested user ID is not already in use. We do this by attempting to insert a record into the `obay_user` table (where `userId` is the Primary Key).

If this succeeds, we know the `userId` is unique, and at the same time, we can prevent anyone else from acquiring it (on the off chance that two requests with the same user ID are submitted at the same time).

We do this before verifying the credit card, the result being that if the credit card fails verification, we end up with a user record for the specified user ID in the `obay_user` table. This will cause the next request to fail when the user resubmits their request with corrected credit card details.

An alternative approach would be to verify the credit card first before validating the user ID. However, with this approach, if the user chooses multiple user IDs that are already taken, their credit card would be validated several times, which could cause issues with the card company.

To prevent resubmission of user registrations from failing, we need to undo the creation of the user record. One way of achieving this is by using the compensation model provided by BPEL.

This allows us to break a BPEL process up into logical components using scopes. For each scope, we can define a compensation handler that will contain a sequence of one or more activities to reverse the effects of the activities contained within that scope.

In our case, we need to define a compensate handler on the `CreateUser` scope, which deletes the user record created by the scope.

Defining compensation

To define the compensation activities for a scope, click on the **Add Compensation Handler** icon for the scope, and this will add an empty compensation branch on the scope, as shown in the following screenshot:

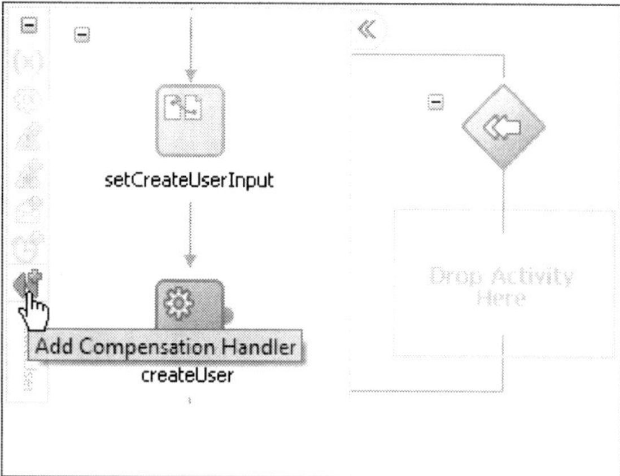

Once you've created your compensation handler, simply add the activities that need to be carried out to undo the effect of the scope. In our case, we just need to call the `deleteUser` operation on the `UserManagement` service.

Triggering a Compensation handler

Compensation handlers aren't triggered automatically, rather they need to be explicitly invoked using the `Compensate` activity, which can only be invoked from within a fault handler or another compensation handler.

When the `Compensate` activity is executed, it will only invoke the compensation handlers for those scopes directly contained within the scope for which the fault handler is defined. If invoked in a fault handler at the process level (as in our example), it will only execute the compensation handlers for the top-level scopes.

The compensation handlers will only be invoked for those scopes which have completed successfully and will be invoked in reverse order of completion. That is, the compensation handler for the most recently completed scope will be invoked first, and then the next most recent and so on.

If a scope whose compensation handler has been invoked contains scopes for which compensation needs to be performed, then it will need to call the `Compensate` activity within its own compensation handler.

Note:

If a scope doesn't have an explicit compensation handler defined for it, then it will have a default compensation handler that just invokes the compensate activity.

Adding a Compensate activity

For our purposes, we need to trigger the `Compensate` activity at the process level, so to do this, we have defined a fault handler on the process to catch the `invalidUserDetails` fault thrown by our previous fault handler.

Once done, we added a **Compensate** activity as the first activity within our fault handler. To configure it, double-click the **Compensate** activity to bring up the dialog box, as shown in the next screenshot:

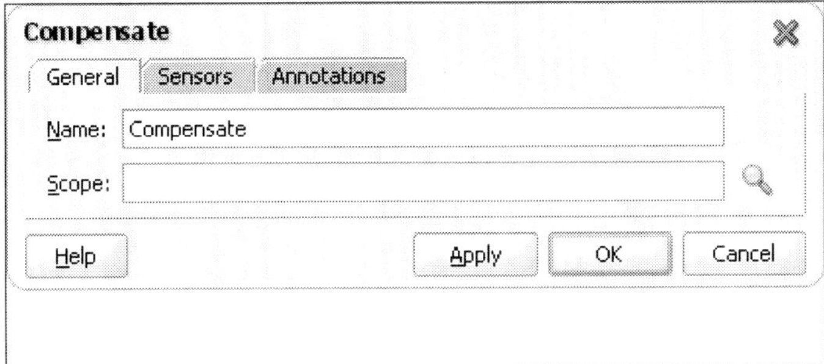

Here we have the option of specifying a scope **Name** to restrict it to invoking the compensation handler for that scope. For our purposes, we want to invoke the compensation handler for all top-level scopes, so we have left it blank.

Returning faults

If at runtime the `verifyCreditCard` operation returns a fault of type `invalidCreditCard`, then this will be caught by the `<catch>` branch we defined on the `VerifyCreditCard` scope.

This fault handler will throw an `invalidUserDetails` fault, which will get caught by the `<catch>` branch defined against our process. This will execute the `Compensate` activity triggering the compensation handler on the `CreateUser` scope, which will delete the previously inserted user record.

The final step is to return an `invalidUserDetails` fault to the caller of the BPEL process. To return a fault within BPEL, we use the **Reply** activity. The difference is to configure it to return a fault as opposed to a standard output message, as shown in the following screenshot:

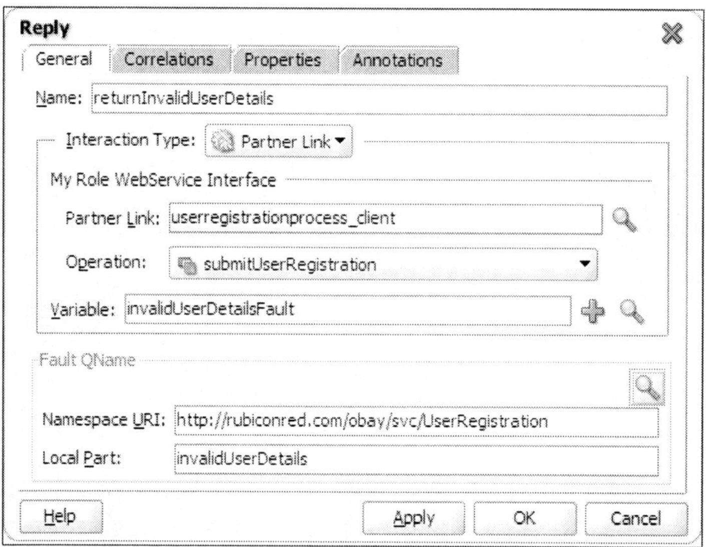

Here we have configured the **Partner Link** and **Operation** as you would for a standard reply. However, for the **Variable** we need to specify a variable that contains the content of the fault to be returned. In our case, this is the content of the fault caught by our process level fault handler (and populated by the fault handler for the `ValidateCreditCard` scope).

Finally, we need to specify that an `invalidUserDetails` fault should be returned. Specify this by clicking on the **search** icon in the **Fault QName** panel to launch the now familiar **Fault Chooser**. After returning the fault, the process will be completed.

If a fault had been triggered during the step of creating the user record (for example, because the `userId` was already in use), then an `invalidUserDetails` fault would have been thrown in the fault handler for this scope. The process would follow the same flow, as outlined previously, except that the compensation handler for the `CreateUser` scope would not have been triggered, as the scope never completed.

Asynchronous Considerations

As we pointed out earlier, asynchronous services don't explicitly support the concept of faults, so it's worth examining how we would manage the previous scenario if all the messaging interactions were asynchronous.

An asynchronous version of the `CreditCard` service would require two callbacks, namely, `creditCardVerified` and `invalidCreditCard`, which would be the equivalent of our fault in the synchronous example.

Within our `VerifyCreditCard` scope after our `invoke` activity, instead of having a `receive` activity to receive the callback, we would need a `pick` activity with two `onMessage` branches (one for each callback). The branch for `invalidCreditCard` would be the equivalent of our synchronous fault handler described previously and would contain the same activities as its synchronous equivalent (please take a look at *Chapter 16, Message Interaction Patterns* for more details on how to use the `pick` activity).

We would still have the fault handler defined for our process, which would catch the fault thrown by our `onMessage` branch for `invalidCreditCard`.

The activities of this fault handler would be similar to the fault handler in our synchronous version. We would still call the `Compensate` activity, but rather than use the `reply` activity to return a fault, we would now use the `invoke` activity to invoke the appropriate callback to signal invalid user details.

Handling business faults in Mediators

Handling business faults within Mediators is a lot simpler than in BPEL. This is due to the role it plays within a composite. It's primary role (as covered in *Chapter 10, oBay Introduction*) is to act as a proxy to the composite, which means that it is responsible for receiving all incoming messages for a composite, validating and optionally transforming them before routing them to the appropriate component within the composite, and then routing any response back to the initial caller.

A business fault, by our definition, is just another valid response that can be returned by a component. Therefore, the role of the Mediator is to transform that fault from a component-specific one to one defined in the WSDL of the composite service, which it can then return to its client.

Its secondary role is to act as a proxy for the composite to any external service called by a component within the composite. Here it is responsible for transforming the outbound message into one expected by the external service and vice versa for the response, which includes any business fault which might be returned.

The exact nature of how we handle a fault comes down to whether the Mediator provides a synchronous or asynchronous service. We will examine each of these cases.

Synchronous Mediators

With a synchronous Mediator, if we call a synchronous service that returns one or more business faults, then the routing rule will contain a **Fault** section (circled in the next screenshot), which allows us to map each business fault returned by the service to one defined in the WSDL of the Mediator.

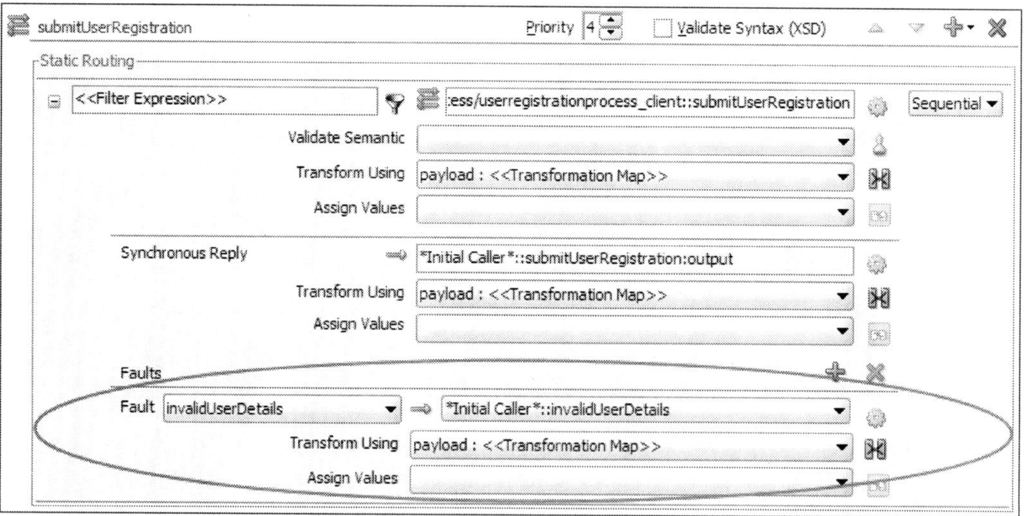

To define a fault routing, from the first drop-down list simply select from the list of faults returned by the `invoked` operation, and then in the second drop-down list select the fault that you want to map it to from the list of faults returned by the Mediator.

For example, in the previous screenshot, we've mapped the fault **invalidUserDetails** returned by the `UserRegistration` BPEL process to the equivalent fault that will be returned by the Mediator. Once we have defined our fault routing, we use the standard transformation tool to map the content of the service's fault to that returned by the Mediator.

If the `invoked` operation defines multiple faults, we should define a fault routing for each of them. To do this, just click on **Add another fault routing** (the green plus sign in the **Faults** section) and define as appropriate.

System faults

In the case of a system fault, the Mediator service will return the fault without modification directly to the client, and let it work out how to handle it. This is typically the desired behavior. The only potential problem with this is it doesn't provide us with the opportunity to transform the system fault.

The reason this can be an issue is that it often makes sense to define a standard set of system faults within our architecture that we map all other system faults to, as this can simplify the implementation of standardized error handling across our applications.

As faults originating from within the SOA infrastructure already conform to a standardized set of faults, the issue is more significant for system faults returned by external services. One solution to this is to invoke all such external services via the Oracle Service Bus and use this to map a nonstandardized system fault to one of our standardized faults (we look at how to do that later in this chapter).

Asynchronous Mediators

With asynchronous services, as we have already discussed, we don't have the concepts of business faults; rather the approach is to define additional callbacks, with each callback being the equivalent to a corresponding business fault returned by a synchronous service.

However, the Mediator component doesn't support multiple callbacks for a single operation. For scenarios where this functionality is required, an alternative approach is to use a BPEL process in place of the Mediator (see the section *Creating a proxy process* in *Chapter 16, Message Interaction Patterns* for details on how to do this).

Using timeouts

The only additional scenario we need to consider with an asynchronous Mediator is when we don't get a response back from the asynchronous service.

The default behavior of the Mediator is to wait forever, though we have the option of specifying a timeout period in which to receive a response, after which, the Mediator will send a response back to the initial caller (or to another service or event).

To specify a timeout period, click the **Browse for target service operations** icon, as shown in the next screenshot. This will bring up the **Target Type** window, where you can specify that the timeout should be routed back to the **Initial Caller**.

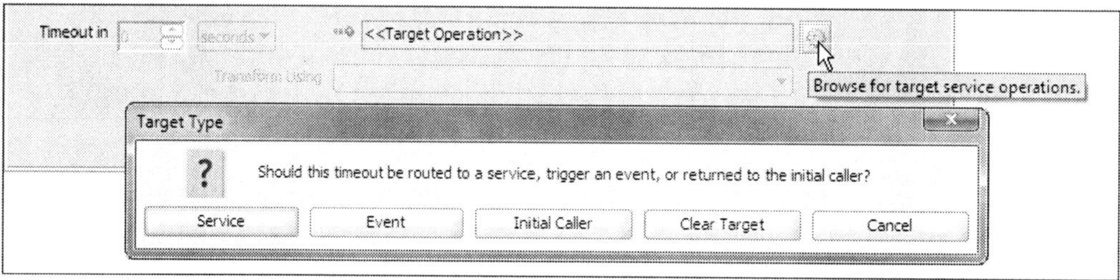

You will then be able to select from the **<<Target Operation>>** drop-down box, the asynchronous callback you want the Mediator to route the timeout to (exactly as you would for a standard callback).

You will also need to specify the time period, which can be specified in seconds, minutes, hours, days, months, or years. Finally, you need to specify the mapping file to generate the content of the callback.

The only other difference between this and standard callback mappings is that you don't have a response to map. In this case, the transformation will be based on the original payload used to invoke the Mediator.

Using the fault management framework

One of the advantages of the 11gR1 release of the Oracle SOA Suite is that it provides a unified framework for handling faults within BPEL processes and Mediator components.

The fault management framework allows us to define policies for handling faults. A policy consists of two basic components, namely, the faults that you wish to catch and the actions you wish to take once the faults are caught, such as retrying the service or performing manual recovery.

Once we have defined a policy, we can then attach (or bind) it to an SOA composite, a BPEL, a Mediator service component, or an external reference. This provides a flexible mechanism for attaching different polices to different components within a composite. For example, we could define a generic fault policy for a composite, but then override it for a specific component or external reference within that composite.

Although BPEL processes and Mediators leverage the same fault management framework, the application of the framework is slightly different for each.

Using the fault management framework in BPEL

Within BPEL, the fault management framework allows us to define policies for handling faults which occur when a BPEL process executes an **Invoke** activity.

When a fault occurs, the framework intercepts the fault before it is returned to the BPEL process. It then attempts to identify an appropriate fault policy to handle the fault. If it finds one, the policy is executed, and assuming the fault is resolved, the BPEL process continues as if nothing happened.

In the case where the framework is unable to identify an appropriate fault policy to handle the fault, the fault is returned to the BPEL process to handle.

This is fine for a business fault as we need to handle it in a way that is appropriate to the business process, as covered previously.

But for system faults, such as network problems resulting in a service becoming temporarily unavailable, implementing the handling of this at the process level can be protracted, often requiring the same fragments of BPEL to be implemented in every process.

For these scenarios, the fault management framework can greatly simplify the effort required to implement the appropriate error handling within BPEL.

Using the fault management framework in Mediator

The behavior of the fault management framework is slightly different for the Mediator. Firstly, we can only use it for operations which implement **parallel** routing rules. This means that we can only use it for asynchronous services.

Although at first this may seem like a strange restriction, it actually fits well with the strategy we laid out earlier for handling faults within a synchronous Mediator. That is not to handle the fault, but rather just propagate it to the client.

However, for an asynchronous operation that implements multiple routing rules in parallel, each of these routing rules has the potential to fail. In such scenarios, the fault management framework will attempt to identify an appropriate fault policy to handle the fault. If it finds one, the policy is executed, and assuming the fault is resolved, the routing rule will continue as if nothing happened.

Another difference with BPEL is that if the framework is unable to identify an appropriate fault policy, then the default behavior of the fault management framework is to invoke the human intervention action rather than return it to the Mediator.

The final difference is that unlike BPEL, it will also handle faults thrown by the Mediator itself in addition to handling faults returned by invoked services. These could be faults due to validation failures, transformation errors, and so on.

Defining a fault policies file

Fault policies for a composite are defined in the `fault-policies.xml` file, which should be placed in the same folder as the `composite.xml` file to which it applies. An example outline of a fault policy file is shown as follows:

```
<?xml version="1.0" encoding="UTF-8"?>
<faultPolicies xmlns="http://schemas.oracle.com/bpel/faultpolicy">
  <faultPolicy version="2.0.1" id="FaultPolicyA">
  ...
  </faultPolicy>
  <faultPolicy version="2.0.1" id="FaultPolicyB">
  ...
  </faultPolicy>
<faultPolicies/>
```

From this, we can see a fault policies file consists of the top level element `faultPolicies`, which contains one or more `faultPolicy` elements, each of which defines a specific fault policy.

Each `faultPolicy` element contains the attribute `id`, which is used to uniquely identify the policy (in the preceding example, we have defined two polices: `FaultPolicyA` and `FaultPolicyB`). We refer to these IDs when we bind a fault policy to a composite or a component using the `fault-bindings.xml` file (which we will cover later in this section).

Defining a fault policy

A policy consists of two basic components; the faults that you wish to catch and once caught the actions you wish to take, such as retry the service or perform manual recovery.

Let's re-examine the `UserRegistration` process at the point that it invokes the credit card service to verify the user's card's details. Apart from the business faults that could be returned, it could also return a system fault such as the following:

```
<soap:Body xmlns:soap="http://schemas.xmlsoap.org/soap/envelope"
           xmlns:flt="http://rubiconred.com/obay/xsd/fault">
    <soap:Fault>
        <faultcode>soap:Server</faultcode>
        <faultstring>Transport Run Time Error</faultstring>
        <detail>
            <flt:fault>
                <flt:code>380002</flt:code>
                <flt:summary>Connection Error</flt:summary>
                <flt:detail>
                    ...
                </flt:detail>
            </flt:fault>
        </detail>
    </soap:Fault>
</soap:Body>
```

Indicating that it's unable to call the service because of a transport problem, the code of 380002 indicating that this is probably due to a temporary problem. For this kind of scenario, we can define a fault policy to catch this error and retry the service.

The outline of the fault policy for our CreditCard service is shown as follows:

```
<faultPolicy version="2.0.1" id="CreditCardPolicy">
  <Conditions>
  ...
  </Conditions>
  <Actions>
  ...
  </Actions>
</faultPolicy>
```

From this, we can see that the fault policy is divided into two sections: the `Conditions` section, which defines the faults we wish to handle, and the `Actions` section, which defines the actions to take in order to recover from the fault.

Defining fault policy conditions

The first section of a fault policy defines the conditions that we wish to handle and contains a list of one or more `faultName` elements that we want our policy to handle. For the preceding example, we could define these as follows:

```
<Conditions>
    <faultName xmlns:soap="http://schemas.xmlsoap.org/soap/envelope/"
               xmlns:flt="http://rubiconred.com/obay/xsd/fault"
               name="soap:Server">
        <condition>
            <test>$fault.payload/flt:code="380002"</test>
            <action ref="ora-retry"/>
        </condition>
        <condition>
           <action ref="ora-human-intervention"/>
        </condition>
    </faultName>
    <faultName>
        <condition>
            <action ref="ora-human-intervention"/>
        </condition>
    </faultName>
    ...
</Conditions>
```

Specifying the <faultName>

A `faultName` element is used to define a specific fault which we wish to handle. It contains a single attribute `name`, which specifies the fault code (that is, `soap:Server` in the preceding example) of the fault to handle.

> Note that a `faultcode` is defined as a `QName` type, which has a format as follows:
>
> `prefix:faultName`
>
> Here `prefix` maps to a namespace, so within the `faultName` element, we need to define the namespace to which the prefix is mapped, otherwise we won't get a match.

We can also specify a `faultName` element without a `name` attribute, which will match all faults. This allows us to define a generic catch all policy for any fault not handled by a more specific policy.

Specifying the <condition>

The `faultName` element defines one or more conditions; each `condition` consists of an optional `test` element and an `action` reference.

The `test` element allows us to specify an `XPath` expression, which is evaluated against the content of the fault. If the `XPath` expression evaluates to true, then the condition is considered a match and the action referenced within the `action` element will be executed.

Otherwise, the fault management framework will look to evaluate the next condition, and so on, until it finds a match. A condition without a `test` element will always return a match.

When selecting data from the content of a fault, the `XPath` expression should follow the format:

```
$fault.<PartName>/<LocationPath>
```

Here, `<PartName>` is the name of the `<part>`, as defined in the `<message>` element of the fault (as specified in the WSDL for the service).

The expression `$fault.<PartName>` will evaluate to root node of the content of the `message` element. So `<LocationPath>` should be specified relative to this.

For example, the operation `verifyCreditCard` is defined as follows:

```
<wsdl:operation name="verifyCreditCard">
  <wsdl:input message="tns:verifyCreditCard"/>
  <wsdl:output message="tns:verifyCreditCardResponse"/>
  <wsdl:fault name="CreditCardFault" message="tns:CreditCardFault"/>
</wsdl:operation>
```

Here, the message `tns:CreditCardFault` is defined as follows:

```
<wsdl:message name="CreditCardFault">
  <wsdl:part name="payload" element="flt:fault"/>
</wsdl:message>
```

In order to refer to the content of this fault, we would specify `$fault.payload`, which would map to the root node within the `payload` part of our SOAP Fault, that is, `flt:fault`.

We can refer to the content of `flt:fault` by specifying the appropriate `XPath` relative to this location. In the previously mentioned policy, we have defined the following test for our first condition:

```
<test>$fault.payload/flt:code="380002"</test>
```

For the fault in our example, we will evaluate this to true, so the fault management framework would execute the action `ora-retry`; if `flt:code` contained some other value, then it would move to the next condition. As this doesn't include a `test` element, it will result in a match and execute the `ora-human-intervention` action.

> The `message` element for some faults, including the extension faults defined by BPEL PM, contains multiple parts. For example, `code`, `summary`, and `detail`. To evaluate the content of any of these parts, just append the part name to `$fault.`. Therefore, to check the content of the `code` part, you would specify `$fault.code`.

Defining fault policy actions

The second part of our fault policy defines the actions referenced in the `Conditions` section. This consists of an `Actions` element, which contains one or more `Action` elements.

Each **Action** element contains an `id` attribute, which is the value referenced by the action `ref` attribute within a condition. For the conditions defined in the preceding policy, we have defined two actions: `ora-retry` and `ora-human-intervention`, as shown here:

```
<Actions>
    <Action id="ora-retry">
        <retry>
            <retryCount>5</retryCount>
            <retryInterval>15</retryInterval>
            <exponentialBackoff/>
            <retryFailureAction ref="ora-human-intervention"/>
        </retry>
    </Action>
    <Action id="ora-human-intervention">
        <humanIntervention/>
    </Action>
</Actions>
```

The content of the `action` element is used to specify and configure the actual action to be executed by the fault management framework, which can be one of `retry`, `humanIntervention`, `rethrow`, `abort`, `replayScope`, or `javaAction`.

> The actions `rethrow` and `replayScope` cannot be used for the Mediator component.

Retry action

The **Retry** action instructs the fault management framework to retry a failed service invocation until it is successful or it reaches a specified limit. In the previous example, we have specified that we will retry the service five times, and if the invocation still fails after this, we have specified that we want to invoke the `ora-human-intervention` action.

The **Retry** action takes a number of parameters that allow us to configure how it behaves, and they are defined as follows:

- `retryCount` - This specifies the maximum number of retries before this action completes with a failure status.
- `retryInterval` - This specifies the period in seconds between retries.
- `exponentialBackoff` - This is an optional element, which takes no parameters. When specified, if a retry fails, the interval between this retry and the next retry is twice that of the previous interval. In the previous example, the first retry would occur after 15 seconds, the second after 30 seconds, the third after 60 seconds, and so on.
- `retrySuccessAction` - This is an optional element with a single attribute ref. This references another action to be taken upon successful retry of a service. This should only be used to reference a java action (see below), which we can use to generate an alert.
- `retryFailureAction` - This is an optional element with a single attribute ref that allows you to define the action to be carried out, should all retries fail.

For scenarios where the interaction between a BPEL process and its client are synchronous, we should only use small retry periods. This is because we are suspending the BPEL process between retries; thus if the retry period is too long, the client which invoked the BPEL process could timeout while waiting for a response.

Human intervention action

For errors which are more permanent, the `humanIntervention` action gives us the ability to suspend the routing rule or process where the fault is occurring. Once suspended, we can log into the Fusion Middleware Control Console in Enterprise Manager to manually handle the fault.

From within the console, we can perform a number of actions. These include manually retrying the service, with the option of modifying the input payload in case this is causing the error. Or, in the event that the service can't be called, we can get the process to skip the `invoke` activity and manually create the output that should have been returned by the service.

When using this action for a BPEL process, because we are suspending the process, we should only use this action if the interaction between the BPEL process and its client is asynchronous. Otherwise, the client will *timeout* while waiting for the problem to be resolved.

Abort action

This action causes the Mediator to abort the routing rule or the BPEL process to terminate. For BPEL, it's the equivalent of executing a `terminate` activity directly within the BPEL process.

An abort action takes no parameters and is defined as follows:

```
<Action id="ora-terminate">
  <abort/>
</Action>
```

Rethrow action

For errors that we don't want handled by the fault management framework, we can use the `rethrowFault` action to re-throw the fault to our BPEL process.

This is often useful when we have defined a generic fault handler to catch all faults, but want to exclude certain faults. For example, if we look at the fault policy defined previously, the final handler within our conditions section is defined as follows:

```
<faultName>
  <condition>
    <action ref="ora-human-intervention"/>
  </condition>
</faultName>
```

This will catch all faults that have not yet been handled. This is exactly what we want for any unknown system faults. However, we want business faults to be explicitly handled by our BPEL process.

The re-throw action allows us to do just this. We can define a fault handler that catches our business faults such as the following:

```
<faultName xmlns:tns="http://rubiconred.com/obay/svc/CreditCard"
           name="invalidCreditCard"
  <condition>
    <action ref="ora-rethrow-fault"/>
  </condition>
</faultName>
```

This will then invoke the following action:

```
<Action id="ora-rethrow-fault">
  <rethrowFault/>
</Action>
```

This will re-throw the fault to our BPEL process.

This action can't be used to handle faults within a Mediator component.

Replay scope action

This action causes the fault management framework to return a replay fault to the BPEL process. This fault will be automatically caught by the scope in which the fault is thrown and trigger the BPEL engine to re-execute the scope from the beginning.

A replay scope action takes no parameters and is defined as follows:

```
<Action id="ora-replay-scope">
  <replayScope/>
</Action>
```

This action can't be used to handle faults within a Mediator component.

Java action

This enables us to call out to a custom java class as part of the process of handling the fault. This class must implement the interface `IFaultRecoveryJavaClass`, which defines two methods:

```
public void handleRetrySuccess(IFaultRecoveryContext ctx );
public String handleFault( IFaultRecoveryContext ctx );
```

The first method `handleRetrySuccess` is called after a successful retry of an invocation, otherwise `handleFault` is called.

This class is not intended to handle a fault, but is more for generating alerts and so on. For example, you could use invocation of the method `handleFault` to generate a notification that there is a problem with a particular endpoint, and likewise, use the invocation of the method `handleRetrySuccess` to generate a notification that the problem with the endpoint has now been resolved.

The method `handleFault` returns a string value, which can be mapped to the next action to be invoked by the framework, for example, if we defined the following `javaAction`:

```
<Action id="ora-java">
   <javaAction   className="mypackage.myClass"
                 defaultAction="ora-human-intervention">
         <returnValue value="RETRY" ref="ora-retry"/>
         <returnValue value="MANUAL" ref="ora-human-intervention"/>
   </javaAction>
</Action>
```

The `javaAction` element takes two attributes: `className`, which specifies the java class to be invoked, and `defaultAction`, which specifies the default action to be executed upon completion of the java action.

Within the `javaAction` element, we can specify zero, one, or more `returnValue` elements, each of which maps a value returned by `handleFault` to a corresponding follow-up action to be executed by the fault management framework.

In the previous example, we have specified for a return value of 'RETRY'. The framework should execute the `ora-retry` action, and if a value of MANUAL is returned, then it should execute the `ora-human-intervention` action.

If no mapping is found for the return value, then the `defaultAction` specified as part of the `javaAction` is executed. This gives us the flexibility to calculate how we wish to handle a particular fault at runtime.

Binding fault policies

To put a fault policy into operation, we need to specify to what components within a composite that the fault policy is to be applied. This is known as binding.

Fault bindings for a composite are defined in the `fault-bindings.xml` file, which should be placed in the same folder as the `composite.xml` file to which it applies. An example outline of a fault binding file is shown as follows:

```
<?xml version="1.0" encoding="UTF-8"?>
<faultPolicyBindings version="2.0.1"
    xmlns="http://schemas.oracle.com/bpel/faultpolicy">

    <composite faultPolicy="UserAccountPolicy"/>
    <component faultPolicy=" UserRegistrationPolicy">
        <name>UserRegistration</name>
    </component>
    <reference faultPolicy="CreditCardPolicy">
        <name>CreditCard</name>
    </reference>
</faultPolicyBindings>
```

From this, we can see that we can bind fault policies to composites, components, or external references.

Defining bindings on the composite

The `composite` element is an **optional** element, which allows us to specify the default fault policy for a composite. It contains a single attribute `faultPolicy`, which contains the `id` of the fault policy to be used for the composite.

In the previous example, we had specified that the `UserAccount` composite should use `UserAccountPolicy` as its default fault policy.

Defining bindings on a component

After the composite binding, we can specify zero or more `component` bindings, each of which allows us to bind a fault policy to one or more Mediator or BPEL components. It contains a single attribute named `faultPolicy`, which contains the `id` of the fault policy to be used for this binding.

Within the `component` elements, we specify one or more `name` elements. The `name` element should contain the name of a component within the composite that we wish to bind the fault policy to.

Defining bindings on an external reference

After the component bindings, we can specify zero or more `reference` bindings, each of which allows us to bind a fault policy to one or more external references invoked by the composite. It contains a single attribute `faultPolicy`, which contains the `id` of the fault policy to be used for this binding.

Within the `reference` elements, we specify one or more `name` elements. The `name` element should contain the name of a reference within the composite that we wish to bind the fault policy to.

Binding resolution

At runtime, when a fault occurs, the fault management framework will attempt to find a condition with a corresponding action that matches the fault.

It does this by first attempting to locate an appropriate fault policy binding by looking for a binding in the following order:

- Reference binding
- Component binding
- Composite binding

Once it finds a binding, it will check the fault policy to find a matching condition and then execute its corresponding action. If no matching condition is found, it will then move to the next binding level. It will continue this process until either a matching condition is found or all binding levels have been checked.

Using MDS to hold fault policy files

Rather than create the `fault-policies.xml` and `fault-binding.xml` files in your composite project, which then get deployed with the composite into the runtime environment, you can actually reference files already deployed to MDS.

To reference policies deployed on MDS, we need to add the properties `oracle.composite.faultPolicyFile` and `oracle.composite.faultBindingFile` to the `composite.xml` file. These should be added directly after the `service` element and reference the location of your policy and binding files in MDS, as shown in the following code fragment:

```
<service name="proxy_ep" ui:wsdlLocation="UserAccount.wsdl">
  ...
</service>
<property name="oracle.composite.faultPolicyFile">
  oramds:/apps/com/rubiconred/obay/fltmgmt/fault-policies.xml
```

```
  </property>
  <property name="oracle.composite.faultBindingFile">
    oramds:/apps/com/rubiconred/obay/fltmgmt/fault-bindings.xml
  </property>
```

This has a number of distinct advantages. Firstly, you can share fault polices across multiple composites. Secondly, if you need to modify your fault policies, you simply need to update a single copy of your fault policy and redeploy it to MDS.

When deploying an updated version of the fault policy it will NOT be able to automatically pick up by any composite that uses it. Rather, you need to either re-deploy the composite or restart the server.

Fault policy and binding files are deployed to MDS in an identical way to XML Schemas, as covered in *Chapter 11, Designing the Service Contract*.

Human intervention in Fusion Middleware Control Console

To manage composites suspended pending human intervention, we need to log into the Fusion Middleware Control Console in Enterprise Manager. Once logged on, browse to the **Faults and Rejected Messages** tab. This, by default, will list all faults, if you select the checkbox **Show only recoverable faults** (shown in the next screenshot). This will list all recoverable faults, as shown in the following screenshot:

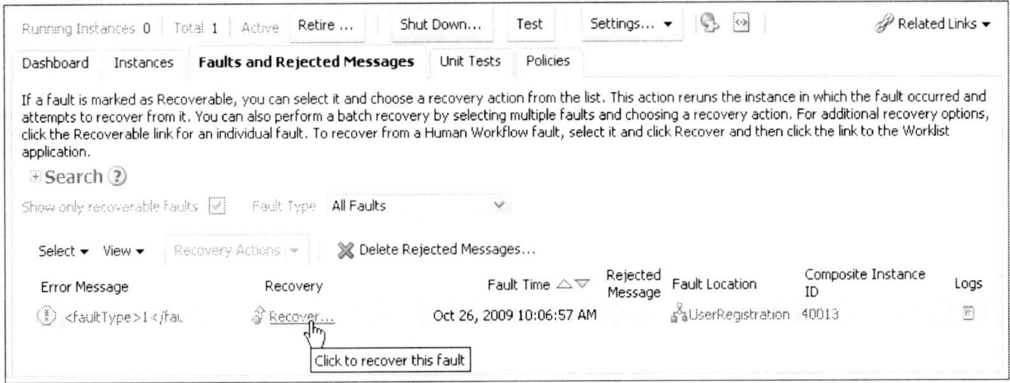

If you click on **Recover** for an individual fault, then the console will bring up the recovery screen for that instance of the composite, as shown in the next screenshot:

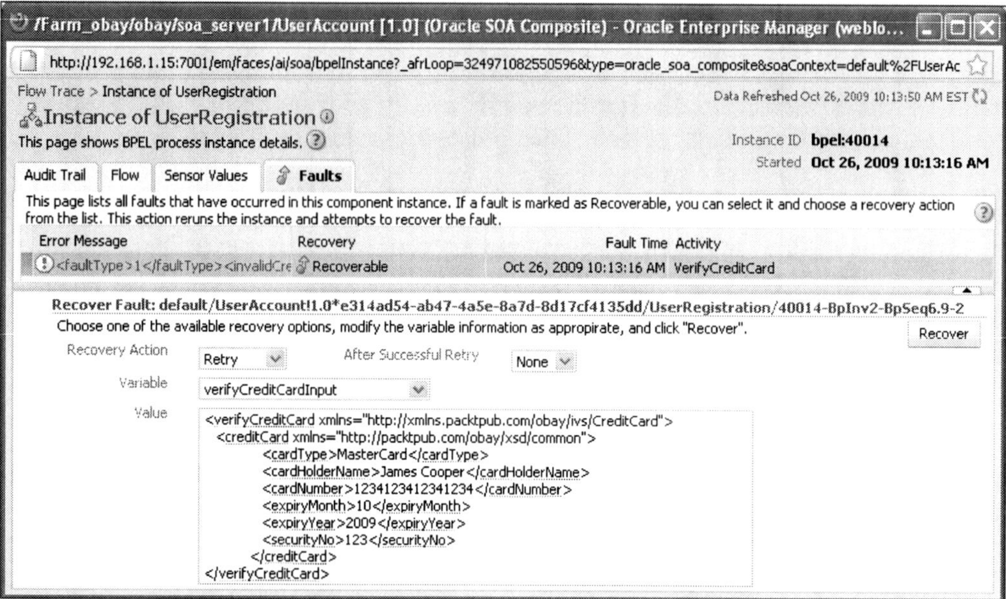

This will list all the faults that have occurred in that particular instance of the composite. If you select a recoverable fault (as shown in the previous screenshot), it will provide details of the fault and allow you to carry out any of the standard recovery actions available in the fault management framework, such as retrying the service, re-throwing the exception, aborting the component, or replaying the scope. It also provides the ability to skip the failed invoke by selecting the `continue` activity.

In addition, we can get the value of the payload or any BPEL process variable, like in the preceding screenshot, where we've fetched the variable `verifyCreditCardInput` that contains the message submitted to the failed `invoke` activity. From here, we can also update the content of this or any other variable.

This gives us a number of options for managing the fault, including changing the input variable and retrying the service or setting the output variable from a service and skipping the `invoke` activity.

Handling faults within the Service Bus

Before we look at how to handle faults inside a proxy service, it's worth taking a step back to revisit our SOA Architecture and the purpose of the virtual service layer.

Essentially, this layer provides a proxy service based on our canonical model, which is responsible for routing requests to the appropriate application service. In this process, it will validate and transform the input message into the one expected by the application service and vice versa for the response.

Within our proxy service, an error can occur at the validate stage (as discussed in the previous chapter, *Chapter 13, Building Validation into Services*), in which case the proxy service needs to generate and return an appropriate fault to the client.

In addition, when we call out to an external service, either to enrich the input message as part of the transformation or at the route stage, a fault could occur. This could either be a business or system fault.

A business fault, by our definition, is just another valid response that can be returned by our application service, so the role of the proxy service is to transform that fault from an application specific one, to one defined in the WSDL of the proxy service, which it can then return to its client.

In the case of a system fault, one option for the proxy service is to return the fault without modification directly to the client, and let it work out how to handle it.

However, it makes sense to define a standard set of system faults within our architecture that we map all other system faults to. This will simplify the implementation of standardized error handling for such faults across our applications.

With system faults that are temporary in nature, it may be tempting to build in the functionality to retry them. However, as we've already established, we only have a small window in which to resolve the fault before the client times out.

So we need to follow a strategy that avoids multiple layers in our composite application, retrying temporary errors as the role of the virtual service layer is to provide a standardized representation of the underlying service, including faults. As a guideline, we will not attempt to retry transient faults within this layer.

> One scenario, where it makes sense to retry a business service, is where it has multiple end points. In this scenario, if a call to one endpoint fails, the Service Bus can be configured to retry an alternate end point for the same business service.

Handling faults in synchronous proxy services

The basic strategy for handling faults within the Service Bus is essentially the same regardless of whether it is a business or system fault. That is to catch the fault, undo any partially completed activities so that we leave the system in a consistent state, and map the underlying fault to a *standard* fault, which is then returned to the client.

If we examine the `CreditCard` service used by the previous BPEL process, this is actually a proxy service implemented on the Service Bus. OBay accepts MasterCard and Visa, and in our scenario, each of these card providers offers its own service for card verification and payment processing.

The role of the `CreditCard` proxy is to provide a standardized service, independent of card type. It will then route requests to the appropriate service, based on the card being used.

As part of this process, the proxy service will transform the request from the oBay canonical form into the specific format required by the card provider and vice versa for the response.

If, during execution of the proxy service, an error occurs, the role of the proxy service is to intercept the fault and then map it to a specific type of fault, either a business fault defined by the proxy service or a standard system fault.

Raising an error

When an error occurs, the Service Bus performs a number of steps. First, it will populate the `$fault` variable with details of the error. Next, if the error was caused by the external service returning a fault, it will update the `$body` variable to hold the actual fault returned.

For example, if the `verifyMasterCard` operation returned the following fault:

```
<env:Body xmlns:env="http://schemas.xmlsoap.org/soap/envelope/">
  <env:Fault xmlns:mcd="http://xmlns.packtpub.com/MasterCard">
     <faultcode>mcd:invalidMasterCard</faultcode>
     <faultstring>business exception</faultstring>
     <faultactor>cx-fault-actor</faultactor>
     <detail>
      <declined xmlns="http://xmlns.packtpub.com/MasterCard ">
        <code>STOLEN</code>
        <desc>Card reported stolen.</desc>
      </declined>
    </detail>
  </env:Fault>
</env:Body>
```

This would be intercepted by the Service Bus, which would then populate `$fault` with the following:

```
<con:fault  xmlns:con="http://www.bea.com/wli/sb/context">
  <con:errorCode>BEA-380001</con:errorCode>
  <con:reason>Internal Server Error</con:reason>
  <con:location>
    <con:node>RouteToVerifyMasterCard</con:node>
    <con:path>response-pipeline</con:path>
  </con:location>
</con:fault>
```

Here, `errorCode` and its corresponding `reason` provide an indication of the type of error that occurred; common error codes include:

- BEA-380001 - Indicates an internal server error, including the return of a fault by a SOAP Service
- BEA-380002 - Indicates a connection error, such as the SOAP Service not being reachable or available
- BEA-382500 - Indicates that a service callout returned a SOAP Fault

We can also see from the content of the `location` element that the error occurred in the response pipeline of the `RouteToVerifyMasterCard` node. This information can be useful if we are implementing a more generic error handler at either the pipeline or service level.

In addition to populating the `$fault` variable, the `$body` variable will now contain the actual SOAP fault returned by the external service.

Finally, the Service Bus will raise an error, which, if not handled by the proxy service, will result in the Service Bus returning its own fault to the client of the proxy service.

Defining an error handler

The first step in handling an error is to catch it. Within a proxy service we do this by using an error handler, which can be defined at the route, stage, pipeline, or service level.

When the Service Bus raises an error, it will first look to invoke the error handler on the route node or stage in which the error occurred.

If one isn't defined or the error handler does not handle the error, then the Service Bus will invoke the error handler for the corresponding pipeline. Again, if the error isn't handled at the pipeline level, it will invoke the service level error handler, and if not handled at this level, then the Service Bus will return a `soapenv:Server` fault with the `detail` element containing the content of `$fault`.

A fault is only considered handled if the error handler invokes either a reply or resume action. The reply action will immediately send the content of `$body` as a response to the client of the proxy service and completes the processing of the proxy. A resume action will cause the proxy service to continue, with processing resuming on the next node following the node on which the error handler is defined.

For faults returned by external services, it makes sense to define our error handler as close to the error as possible, that is, on the route node, as we can handle the error in the context it occurred, thus simplifying the logic of our error handler.

For more generic errors, such as a connection error (for example, BEA-380002), we can define a higher level error handler at either the pipeline or service level.

In the case of our `CreditCard` service, this means defining an error handler on the route nodes for each endpoint to handle errors specific to each service callout and defining a generic error handler on the service itself.

Adding a route error handler

To define an error handler on a route node, click on it, and select the option **Add Route Error Handler**, as shown in the following screenshot:

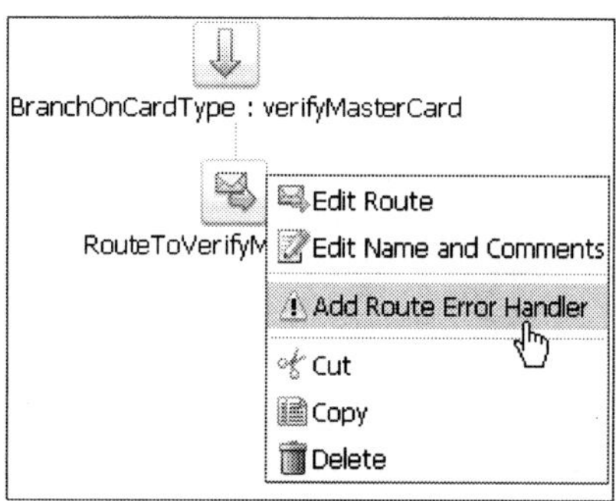

This will open the **Edit ErrorHandler; Route Node** window, where we can configure the error handler. An error handler consists of one or more stages, so the first we thing we need to do is to add a stage and name it accordingly (for example, **HandleVerfifyMasterCardFault**), as shown in the next screenshot:

The first step within our error handler is to check whether we have received a SOAP Fault or something more generic. To do this, we just need to add an `If... Then...` action, which checks if the value of `$fault/ctx:errorCode` is either BEA-382500 or BEA-380001.

Although the Service Bus reserves the error BEA-382500 for SOAP Faults, we find that when we return a custom SOAP Fault, the Service Bus raises an error of type BEA-380001. So we have to check for both error codes to be safe.

Checking the type of SOAP Faults

Next, we need to check the SOAP Fault returned (which will be in `$body`), so that we can handle it appropriately.

If we examine the WSDL for our `verifyMasterCard` operation, we can see that it could potentially return one of two faults: `mcd:declined` and `mcd:invalid`, each of which needs to be mapped to a fault returned by our proxy service.

At first glance, this all looks pretty straightforward. We just need to define an **'If... Then...'** action, with a branch to test for each type of fault returned and generate the appropriate fault to return.

For example, to test for a fault of type `mcd:declined`, we could define a branch with a condition such as the following:

```
$body/soap-env:Fault/faultcode = 'mcd:declined'
```

However, if we look at `faultcode` more closely, we can see its type is `QName`, with a format of prefix:faultName (for example, `mcd:declined`), where prefix is mapped to a namespace in the `soap:Fault` element (for example, `http://xmlns.packtpub.com/MasterCard`).

The issue here is that there is no guarantee that the same prefix will always be used, which could cause our condition to be incorrectly evaluated.

Getting the qualified fault name

To ensure that our test condition is correctly evaluated, we need to fully resolve the `QName`. We can do this by using the `XQuery` function `resolve-QName`. This takes two parameters. The first contains the `QName` that we wish to resolve (that is `faultcode`), the second contains an element in which the namespace prefix is defined (that is `soap:Fault`). This gives us a function call that looks likes the following:

```
fn:resolve-QName($body/soap:Fault/faultcode, $body/soap:Fault)
```

As we will need to test this value multiple times, rather than embed this within our if condition, we can use an **Assign** action to assign it to a variable (for example, `$faultcode`).

Our modified condition to test for a fault of type `mcd:declined` would now look like the following:

```
$faultcode = '{http://xmlns.packtpub.com/MasterCard}declined'
```

We can now define an **'If... Then...'** action, with one branch for each fault we want to test for, plus an else branch to cover any unexpected faults.

Creating a SOAP Fault

Once we know the fault returned by the external service, we can generate the appropriate fault to be returned by the proxy service and assign this to the `$body` variable.

The simplest way to do this is by creating an **Assign** action, and for the **XQuery Text**, we directly specify the actual SOAP Fault to be returned, as shown in the next screenshot:

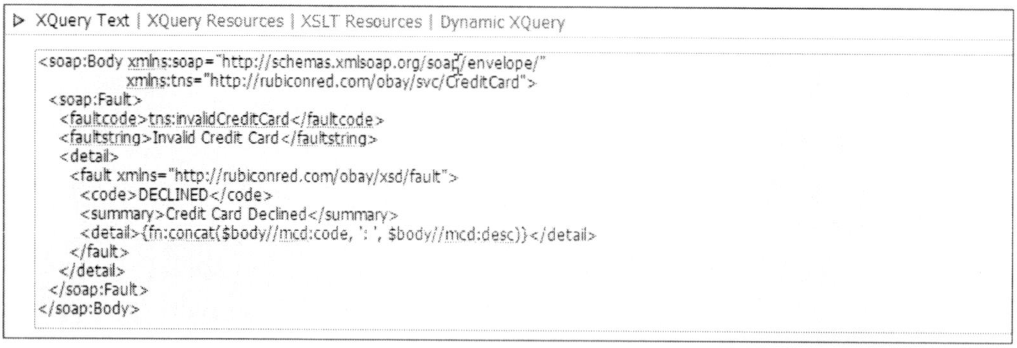

▷ XQuery Text | XQuery Resources | XSLT Resources | Dynamic XQuery

```
<soap:Body xmlns:soap="http://schemas.xmlsoap.org/soap/envelope/"
           xmlns:tns="http://rubiconred.com/obay/svc/CreditCard">
  <soap:Fault>
    <faultcode>tns:invalidCreditCard</faultcode>
    <faultstring>Invalid Credit Card</faultstring>
    <detail>
      <fault xmlns="http://rubiconred.com/obay/xsd/fault">
        <code>DECLINED</code>
        <summary>Credit Card Declined</summary>
        <detail>{fn:concat($body//mcd:code, ': ', $body//mcd:desc)}</detail>
      </fault>
    </detail>
  </soap:Fault>
</soap:Body>
```

Handling unexpected faults

In the case of unexpected faults, we have two choices: one is to return the fault as it is and let the client figure out how to handle it, the other is to return a generic fault indicating that an unexpected error occurred. Typically, we would recommend the latter approach as this will simplify error handling for the client.

It is often prudent to record details of the fault that occurred. For example, if it's occurring frequently, we may wish to add a specific branch to our error handler to manage a fault of this type, especially if it allows our client to make a more informed choice on how to handle the error.

One way of achieving this is to use the **Report** action. This takes two parameters: the first is the message we want to report, the second is zero, one, or more name value pairs that we can use to search for specific reports.

In the case of error handler, we have configured it to capture details of the actual fault message, with a single key of the format **BusinessService=$outbound/@name** (which will evaluate to `BusinessService=VerifyMasterCard`), as shown in the next screenshot:

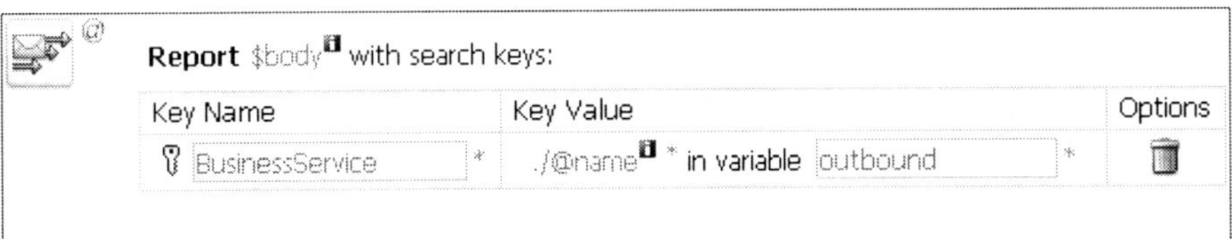

At runtime this will cause a record containing the specified information as well as additional metadata to be written to the Service Bus Reporting Data Stream. The metadata includes information such as the error code, inbound service name, URI, and operation and the outbound service, URI, and operation.

By default, the Service Bus is configured to write this data to a reporting data store, which can then be queried from the Service Bus console. To view the report data, click on the **Operations** tab, and then click on **Message Reports** (under **Reporting**).

This will bring up the **Summary of Message Reports**, where you can search for report entries against a number of criteria, including data range, inbound service name, error code, and the report key (defined in the Report action). From here, you can click on a report entry to view its metadata and the actual message.

The Reporting Stream can be configured to write data to a number of targets including JMS Queues, databases, files, and so on.

Returning a SOAP Fault

Once we have populated our `$body` variable with the appropriate SOAP Fault, the final step is for our proxy service to return it.

We do this to using a **Reply** action. The key here is to configure it to **Reply With Failure**, as shown in the next screenshot. This will cause the Service Bus to generate an HTTP 500 status, indicating a fault.

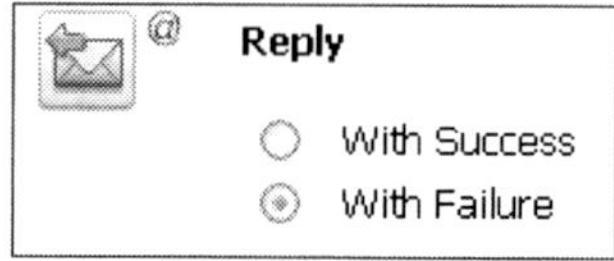

Once the reply has been sent, the processing of the request is completed and no further processing will be done.

This completes the definition of our error handler for our **RouteToVerifyMasterCard** node, which looks as follows:

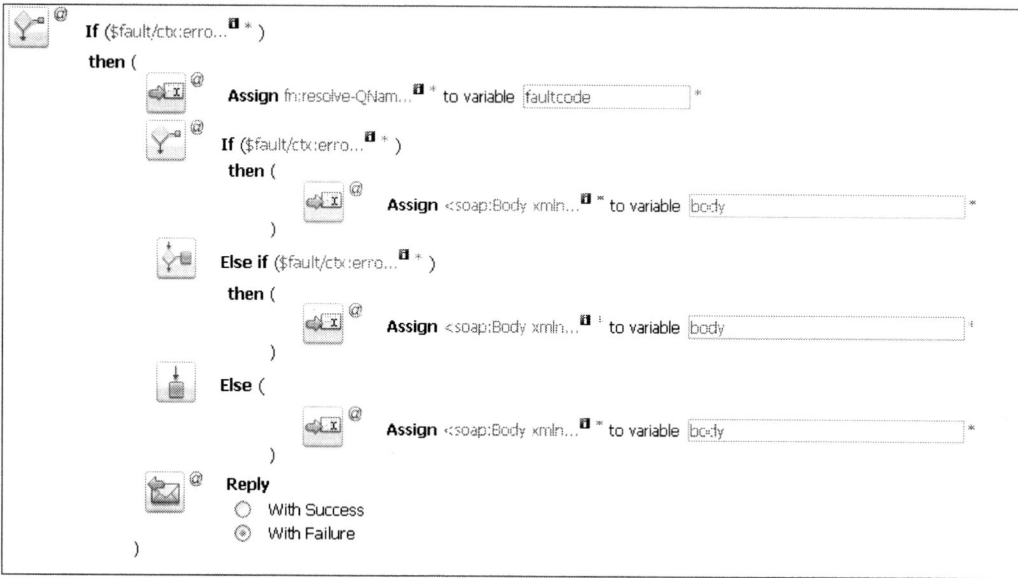

If an error other than a SOAP Fault occurs, then this handler will still be invoked, but because we don't handle it (that is, execute a `Reply` or `Resume` activity), the Service Bus will look to invoke an error handler on a higher level stage.

Adding a service error handler

For handling errors other than those caused by SOAP Faults, we typically want to define a generic error handler at the service level. To do this, click the **proxy service** icon and select **Add Service Error Handler**, as shown in the following screenshot:

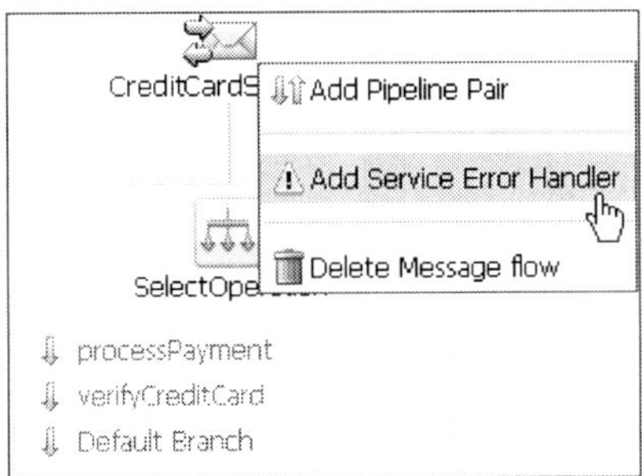

Here, we need to create a stage in which we define our error handling logic as we did for our route node error handler.

For errors which have been raised for a reason other than a SOAP Fault being returned by the external client, we just need to check the error code in `$fault` so that we can map it to an appropriate system fault.

When generating a system fault, rather than try and map a specific Service Bus error to a corresponding SOAP Fault, we need to think about how the client may handle the fault. This will be typically driven by whether it is a permanent or transient fault.

Handling permanent faults

Permanent faults are ones where the same submission will continue to cause an error. This could be due to a number of reasons, including invalid security credentials, erroneous data contained within the message payload, or an error within the actual service itself (that is, the request is valid, but for whatever reason the service is unable to process it).

For each type of error, a corresponding error code is defined by the Service Bus, which can be accessed in the `$fault` variable at runtime. These error codes are categorized into the following subsystems: Transport, Message Flow, Action, Security, and UDDI.

Within our generic service level error handler, we typically want to use an **If... Then...** action to check which error category the error code falls into and then map it to a corresponding SOAP fault. This follows a similar approach to the one we used for mapping business service faults to corresponding faults defined by the proxy service.

Once we have populated our `$body` variable with the appropriate SOAP Fault, we would then use a Reply action as before to return it to the client.

This ensures that any client of the proxy service will only have to deal with the business faults defined in the WSDL of the service and a handful of pre-defined system faults that any of the proxy services could return.

If we look at a BPEL process, this approach makes it very simple to write a fault policy for managing a small, well defined set of system faults, and within the BPEL process define fault handlers for the known business faults.

Generating alerts

When a permanent fault occurs, it may indicate that we have an underlying problem in the system. Therefore, in addition to returning a SOAP Fault to the client, we may wish to notify someone of the problem.

One way to do this would be through the report action we looked at earlier, but in some cases, we may have an issue that requires more immediate attention. For example, if we have an attempted security violation or if there is an error in the actual logic of a recently deployed proxy service.

For these situations, we can use the **Alert** action to publish an alert to an appropriate destination, which could be a JMS Queue, E-mail, SNMP Trap, or Reporting Data Stream.

To add an alert, click **Add an Action** | **Reporting** | **Alert**. This will insert an Alert action into our error handler, like the one shown in the following screenshot:

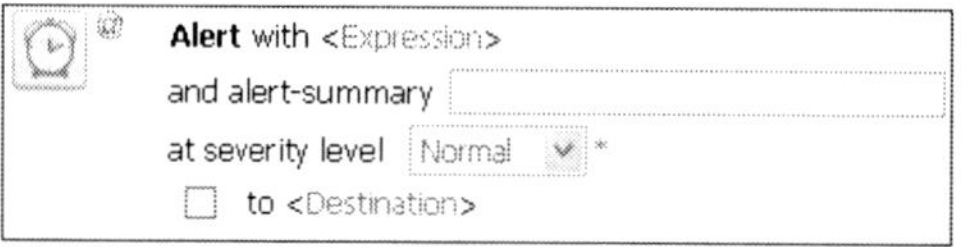

To specify the content of the alert, click on **<Expression>**. This will launch the XQuery expression editor, where we can define the alert body as required. We can also specify an optional **alert-summary**, which is presented according to the destination. For example, it will form the subject line for an e-mail notification. If this is left blank, then it defaults to **Oracle Service Bus Alert**.

The severity level can take a value of Normal, Warning, Minor, Major, Critical, or Fatal. These don't have specific meanings, so you can attach your definitions to each of these values. When we configure alerting for the proxy service (see below), we can opt to filter out alerts based on their severity level.

To specify the recipient of the alert, click on **<Destination>**. This will launch the **'Select Alert Destination**' window, where we can search for and select any previously defined destination.

Destinations are created and configured in the Service Bus console. This gives us the flexibility to change the actual recipient of the alert at a later point in time, just by re-configuring the destination appropriately.

Enabling alerts

In order for pipeline alerts to be generated, you must first enable them. Otherwise, Alert actions will just be skipped during the execution of the proxy service. Alerts need to be enabled in two places, first at the server level and then at the proxy service level.

To enable them globally, click on the **Operations** tab with the Service Bus console and then select **Global Settings**. This will display the **Global Settings** window. From here, ensure the option **Enable Pipeline Alerting** is checked.

Once enabled globally, we can then specify settings for a proxy service. Select the proxy service, and then click on the **Operational Settings** tab, as shown in the following screenshot:

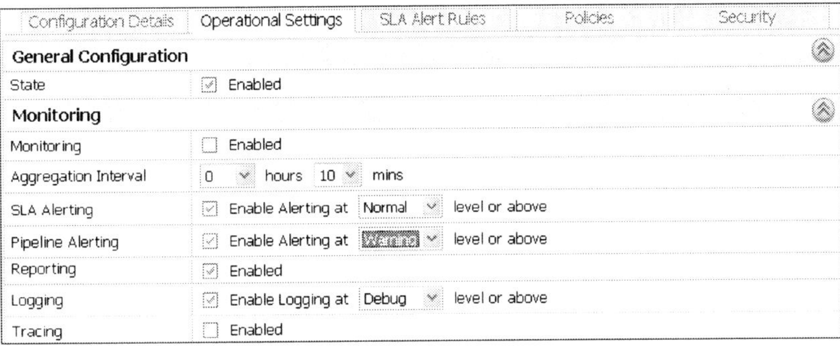

Select the checkbox for **Pipeline Alerting** and then from the **Enabling Alerting at** drop-down list select the level of alerting required. This will suppress the generation of any alerts with a lower severity. So in the preceding example, we have enabled alerting at the **Warning** level or above, so any alert actions in the proxy service with a severity level of **Normal** will be skipped.

Handling transient faults

Transient faults typically manifest themselves as non-responsive URIs (that is, no response is being received for a particular service endpoint), which the Service Bus indicates with the error code BEA-380002.

In this scenario, we have already established that for a synchronous proxy service, there is limited scope to take any corrective action. However, for services that provide multiple endpoints, one option is to retry an alternate endpoint.

Retrying a non-responsive business service

A business service allows you to configure multiple endpoints for a service, which it can load balance requests across (using a variety of algorithms). This can be useful when a particular endpoint becomes nonresponsive, as we can configure the business service to automatically retry an alternative endpoint.

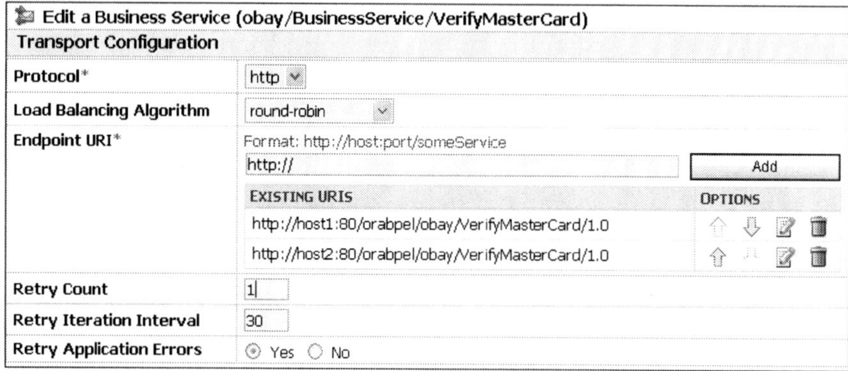

When we have multiple URIs specified for an endpoint, if the initial call to an endpoint fails, the business service will immediately attempt to invoke an alternate URI, and it will continue to do this until it is either successful, the **Retry Count** is reached, or all online URIs have been tried.

If, at this point, the retry count has not been reached, the business service will wait for the duration specified by the **Retry Iteration Interval** before iterating over the endpoints again.

Finally, you need to ensure that we set **Retry Application Errors** to **No**. Otherwise, any SOAP Fault returned by the business service will be treated as a failure and prompt the Service Bus to retry.

In the previous example, where we have defined two URIs, if the first call fails then the Service Bus will immediately call the second URI. If this fails, then it will have reached the retry limit and the underlying error will be returned to the proxy service. If the retry count was two, then it would wait for 30 seconds before attempting one final retry.

Handling faults in one-way proxy services

The Service Bus also allows you to define one-way proxy services, where the client issues a request to the Service Bus and then continues processing without ever receiving a response. This is often referred to as fire and forget.

The approach for handling errors for one way proxy services is quite different from that of synchronous services. For transient errors, it makes absolute sense to retry the business service until we are successful, as no one is going to timeout waiting for a response.

For permanent errors, we can't return a fault to the client and let them resolve it. Rather we need to alert a third party so that they can take some corrective steps to resolve the error, and then re-run the request.

One way to do this is to publish an alert notification to a JMS Queue. We could do this directly or go via the alerting mechanism, as described earlier. The content of the alert will typically need to contain details of the actual error so that we know what corrective action to perform, the proxy service invoked and its payload, so that we can re-invoke the proxy with the original payload once the issue has been resolved.

Once we've published the alert, we also need to implement something on the other end of the JMS Queue to process it. One approach would be to implement this as a BPEL process, containing a human workflow task to correct the error. Once corrected, the BPEL process could re-invoke the proxy service.

Summary

In this chapter, we've taken a detailed look at some of the key considerations we need to take into account when handling errors within an SOA-based application.

This includes whether the interaction between the components involved is synchronous or asynchronous, the error is a business or system error, and whether it's permanent or transient in nature. In addition, we've examined how the error and the handling of it are likely to impact other components at different layers within our composite.

With this is mind, we have outlined an overall approach for handling errors within our composite applications and how to implement this in composites and the Service Bus.

15
Advanced SOA Suite Architecture

In this chapter, we will examine some of the architectural features of the SOA Suite. We refer to them as advanced features because they are often ignored by developers, yet an understanding of how they work can give additional capabilities to our composite applications. We will begin by looking at how the BPEL component stores instance states during long running composite execution and then how it uses threads before moving on to examine where transaction boundaries occur. Finally, we will review how a cluster works, and how it may impact the way we design and build our composites. *Clemens Utschig* has been a great source of help in providing the information for this chapter.

Relationship of infrastructure to service engines

The **Software Component Architecture** (**SCA**) Assembly is understood by the core SOA Suite infrastructure, also known as **Fabric**. Fabric is responsible for routing messages to appropriate service components within a composite, for example, to a BPEL component or a Mediator component. How the message is processed is the responsibility of the service component and not Fabric. Fabric maps the incoming messages to the correct deployed composite and then within the composite to the correct service engine. It also routes messages between components in a composite. All the interesting work is done within the service engines themselves.

Fabric routes messages based on their incoming port type and endpoint to the correct composite. It does not route based on message content and it does not do any message transformation; these are features of the Mediator component.

Composite execution and suspension

Many composites will be long running, taking minutes, hours, or days to complete. To avoid unnecessary memory usage and to provide resilience in case of machine failure these composites will be persisted to the SOA Suite repository database. This process is known as **dehydration** and it involves storing the current execution state of the composite in the database. Usually this state is stored and managed by the BPEL component. When an event occurs that requires the composite to take some action, such as a timer expiring or a message arriving, then the SOA Suite retrieves the composite state from the database and schedules it for execution. A composite may be dehydrated multiple times during its life.

BPEL dehydration events

A BPEL process may be dehydrated at a number of different points. It is important to be aware of these when developing an application because, as we will see later, dehydration points affect the transaction boundaries of our composite.

Some of the key events that cause dehydration to occur are as follows:

- Waiting for an incoming message using a BPEL `receive` or `pick` activity
- Waiting for a specific time or a delay using a BPEL `wait` element
- After a non-idempotent call to another service
- Before a wait

For example, a BPEL process may be waiting for the response from an asynchronous interaction or a new inbound message as a result of a `pick` or `receive` activity. This will cause the process state to be written to the dehydration database.

When a composite is running on a server instance, in the event of server instance failure, a BPEL process will resume execution from the last dehydration point. A corollary to this is that if the composite is a request/response interaction with no dehydration points, then the composite instance will be lost.

Threading and message delivery in SOA Suite

There are a number of different thread pools used by the SOA Suite runtime. Some of them are used to run background tasks such as keeping track of which processes need to be woken after a BPEL `wait` activity or waiting for messages to arrive. Other threads are used to execute composites. In this section, we will focus on threads as they apply to the execution of our composite application. The SOA infrastructure obtains its threads from the underlying applications server but manages those threads itself.

Messages arrive in two distinct interaction patterns. They are either one-way messages, which are not part of an operation requiring a reply, or they are synchronous request/reply messages with a response message expected as part of the operation.

One-way message delivery

One-way interactions (messages that don't expect an immediate reply) are normally stored by the service layer prior to delivery, allowing them to be quickly accepted and then processed later. Effectively, they are enqueued by the incoming thread while a separate thread dequeues them and executes the associated composite. The messages themselves are not placed in a queue but stored in the database and only a notification that the message is available is placed on a queue. Synchronous request/reply messages are executed as part of the thread that made the request. For a web service request across HTTP, this will mean that they are executed as part of the servlet thread of the underlying application server. If the two-way request is from an adapter, then it will execute on the activation agent thread (note that normal operation is for activation agents to have a one-way interface).

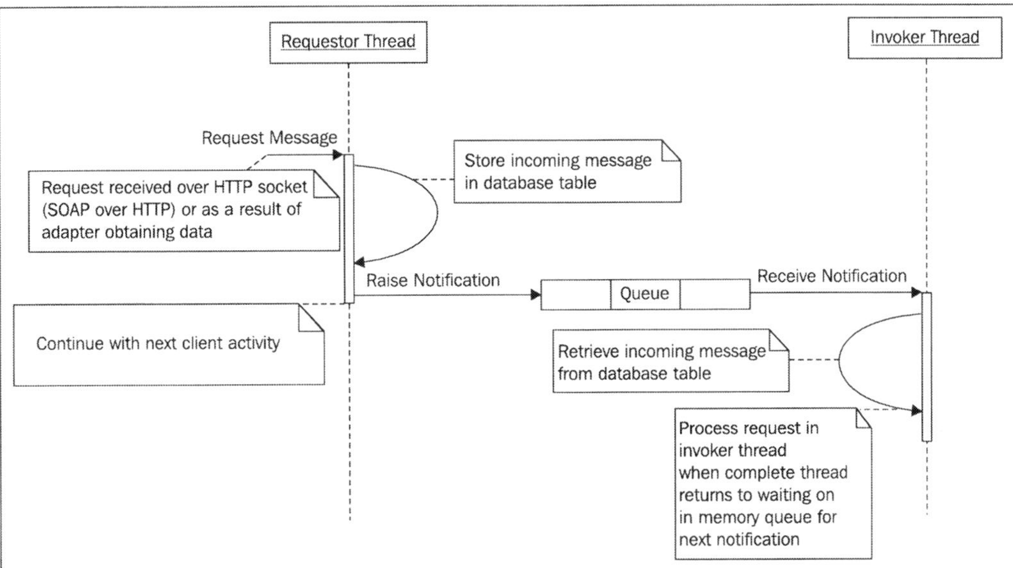

The previous diagram shows how a one-way message is processed. The example uses a SOAP binding example, but the request could be from another service engine in the same or a different composite, or from an adapter. The **Requestor Thread** places the message in the database and places a short notification message on a queue and then continues to do whatever it was doing before the request. Invoker threads (thread pools are explained later) in the BPEL engine will receive the notification message and retrieve the message from the database and execute the appropriate BPEL activities in the BPEL process.

Immediate execution of one-way messages in BPEL

As previously explained, the normal behavior of the BPEL and Mediator engines is to process a one-way message in a separate thread to the one on which it is received. This allows the engine more control over the scheduling of the request. However, sometimes we want our one-way message to be executed immediately using the incoming requestor thread. In that case, we can set a property on the BPEL component called `bpel.config.oneWayDeliveryPolicy`. This property has the following values:

bpel.config.oneWayDeliveryPolicy	Behavior
`async.persist`	Default behavior of storing message in database.
`async.cache`	Stores message in memory rather than database.
`sync`	Message not stored as it is processed directly on receiving thread.

Modifying the `oneWayDeliveryPolicy` allows us to trade-off reliability of delivery and coupling with the client for speed of delivery. Using the `sync` option offers the best performance, but the requestor will perceive that it took longer to post the message due to the increased coupling between the requestor and the target. Similarly, using the `async.cache` option reduces the performance overhead of storing the message in memory. However, if the server fails before the message is processed, it will be lost as it is stored in memory. The following sections outline the different types of threads used to process messages in the BPEL engine.

Activation agent threads

JCA adapters that support inbound messages (incoming messages to BPEL) have their own thread pools that are used to wait for incoming messages, often by polling, as in the case of the database adapter. When a message arrives, unless it is a two-way interaction, it will be enqueued for execution by a separate thread. It is possible to use the activation agent thread to process the request by changing the async interface into a synchronous (two-way) interaction by providing a dummy response in the WSDL. This is useful if we want any transaction associated with the adapter, such as JMS message removal or database update, to be included with the transaction used by a Mediator or BPEL component.

Dispatcher threads

There are a number of different dispatcher threads that manage execution of messages from the internal queue of messages to be processed. A number of these threads can be configured from the **BPEL Service Engine Properties** screen, accessed from the **soa_infra** | **SOA Administration** | **BPEL Properties** pop-up menu.

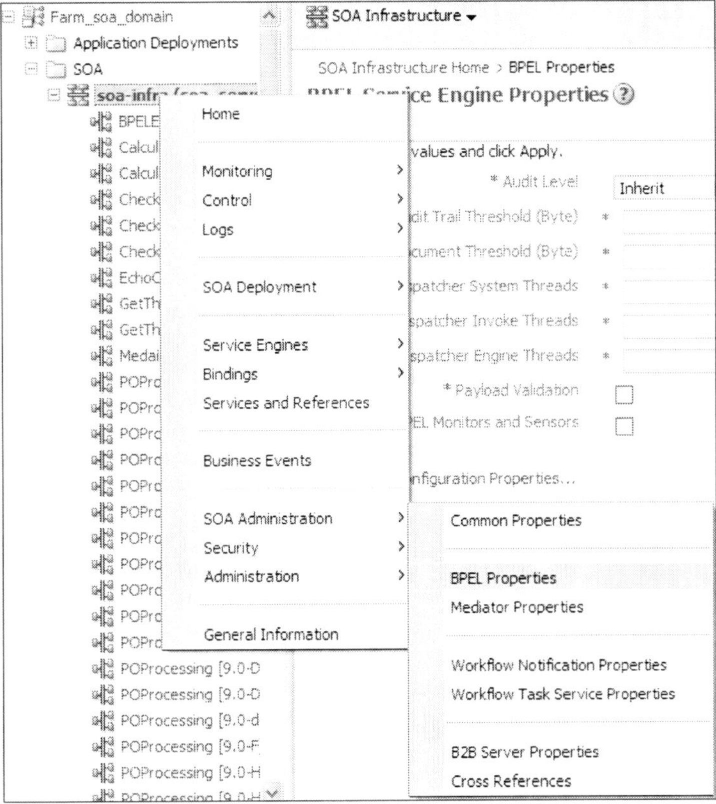

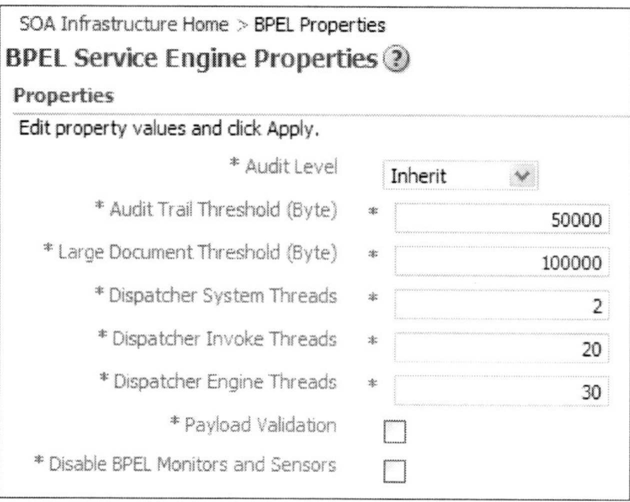

The previous screenshot displays BPEL properties. The **BPEL Service Engine Properties** screen also allows us to configure other BPEL engine properties besides the thread properties, outlined as follows:

- **Dispatcher System Threads**: These threads are used for cleanup activities by the engine.
- **Dispatcher Invoke Threads**: These threads are used to instantiate (create) new BPEL process instances as a result of messages arriving through one-way interactions. These are the invoker threads discussed earlier.
- **Dispatcher Engine Threads**: These threads are responsible for continuing processing of already created processes that have been suspended due to a wait or a receive. For example, when a BPEL process that has already been created receives a message, it will be processed using this thread pool.
- **Synchronous Invoke Threads**: Synchronous (request/reply) messages are processed on the thread on which they arrive, which may be a servlet thread for bindings that come through servlets, an **Enterprise Java Beans** (**EJB**) thread if the EJB invokes the service engine, and so on. These threads are managed at the application server level.

The next example shows how the requesting thread of a request/reply interaction is also used to process the BPEL activities associated with the process. The next example uses a SOAP binding but again it could be any client, including another service engine or an adapter. The example assumes that there are no dehydration points within the process and that it terminates after the `reply` activity.

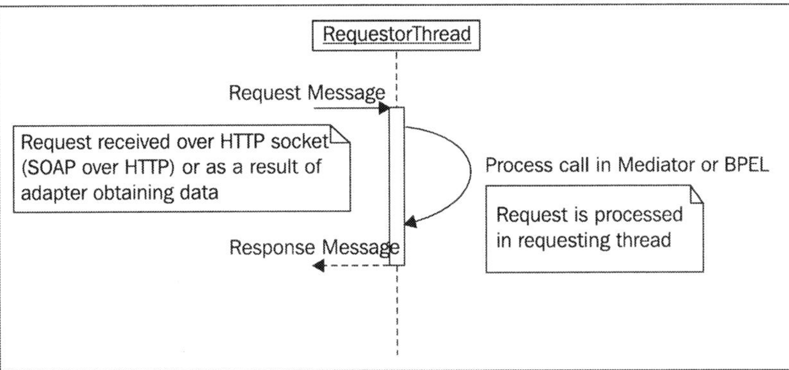

Transactions

Transactions are tightly coupled to dehydration points within a process. Composite interactions take place within a transaction context. That transaction context is committed when a dehydration point is reached in a composite. Any updates to the dehydration store are done in the context of the current transaction.

BPEL transactions

There are a number of ways to control the transaction within a BPEL process. Specific activities affect the transaction management as well as properties on partner links and composite components.

BPEL component properties

The transaction property of a BPEL component in `composite.xml` can be used to control the participation of the BPEL process in the calling entities transaction. This is similar to the way in which the author of an EJB can control the transactional behavior of the EJB. This allows the creator of the composite to control the transaction properties of their components.

The default setting is to have `transaction=requiresNew`, which causes the BPEL process to execute within its own transaction.

Component property	Target composite	Source process
`transaction=required`	Executes in the same thread and transaction. If no transaction exists one will be created that commits when the invocation completes.	Keeps the same thread and transaction.
`transaction=requiresNew` `(default value)`	Executes in the same thread but a separate transaction that commits when the invocation completes.	Keeps the same thread and transaction.

The following example shows how a component may be made to participate in the caller's transaction by editing the `composite.xml` file:

```
<?xml version="1.0" encoding="UTF-8" ?>
<!-- Generated by Oracle SOA Modeler version 1.0 at [3/6/10 11:16 AM].
-->
<composite name="TransactionThreadTest"...>
   ...
  <component name="GetThreadTxProcess">
    <implementation.bpel src="GetThreadTxProcess.bpel"/>
    <property name="bpel.config.transaction">required</property>
  </component>
  ...
</composite>
```

BPEL partner link properties

The following table identifies some ways in which the transaction behavior may be controlled in a BPEL process through the use of following partner link properties for synchronous interactions:

Partner link property	Target service	Source process
`nonBlockingInvoke=true` (default value is false)	Executes in a separate thread and transaction.	Under the covers, a receive is created to await the result from the invoke. This causes the current transaction to be committed and a new transaction to be started. It also results in suspension of the current thread and resumption of processing will occur on a different thread.
`idempotent=false` (default value is true)	Executes in the same thread and transaction.	After completion of the invocation, the transaction is committed and a new transaction is started. The same thread is kept.

When a transaction is committed and a new one has started, we refer to it as a dehydration point because the state of the process is committed to the database.

Partner link properties can be created and modified in JDeveloper by editing a partner link and selecting the **property** tab.

BPEL activities

The following table identifies some ways in which the transaction behavior in a BPEL process is influenced by certain activities:

Activity	Source process

`Receive`
`Wait`
`Pick`
	After the activity is set up, the transaction is committed and the thread is released to the pool. When the activity completes, the process will resume with a new thread and a new transaction. Note that a pick may be thought of as scheduling multiple receives and a wait, only one of which will complete.

`Flow` `FlowN`	The flow will execute in the same thread and transaction. It does not execute in parallel, but each branch may execute independently if there are activities to process. The use of other activities may cause the committing of the transaction and/or the scheduling of different threads, but the flow itself does not do so.

Parallel execution in a flow or flowN

Often, we may want to use a `flow` to fire off several request/reply invokes in parallel. We can achieve this by setting the `nonBlockingInvoke` partner link property on the target of the invokes to be `true`. This will cause the invoke to execute in parallel, rather than the default behavior of sequential execution. If each invoke may take 100s of milliseconds or more, then this can be a significant performance boost to our composites. In this case, the `flow` will stop processing the current branch after initiating the `nonBlockingInvoke` and look for another branch with activities to process.

Transactions and thread wrinkles in BPEL

Normally we think of async interactions as consisting of two one-way messages. However, we may have an async interaction that consists of a two-way message with a one-way callback. This would appear as a WSDL with two partner roles and an operation with `<input>` and `<output>` elements. In *Chapter 3, Service-enabling Existing Systems,* we used this same approach for a different purpose, to assist in throttling a file or FTP adapter. We may also have a BPEL process that continues after a reply.

Reply handling

We normally think of reply as causing the response to be sent back to the client, and if the transaction was initiated by the BPEL service engine, then it would be committed as part of the reply. In most cases, this is an accurate description of the end result, but this is not actually what happens. When a reply is reached, the response message is marked as available for returning to the requestor, but it is not returned to the requestor. Instead the BPEL engine will continue to process activities until it reaches a dehydration point. On reaching the dehydration point, the current thread (which was also the requesting thread) will return the reply message to the requestor. Note that this results in a delay in the returning of the result to the requestor, and it also causes the transaction scope to extend past the `reply` activity.

In SOA Suite 10.1.3, there was a partner link property `idempotentReply` that when set to true caused the transaction to be committed and the response returned to the requestor immediately after the `reply` activity. In 11*g*, this became a component property. The problem with this approach is that it applies to all operations of a partner link (and in the 11*g* patch, set 1 to all partner links in the component). Patch set 3 of SOA Suite 11*g* is expected to have a `checkpoint` activity which can be placed after the `reply` to force the thread to return the result immediately. The same effect can be achieved in patch set 1 and base 11*g* by using a Java `exec` activity with the `breakpoint()` call.

Oracle Service Bus (OSB) transactions

The OSB has a simpler transaction model than that of the BPEL engine. The way transactions are handled depends on the nature of the incoming request and the transaction characteristics of the partner service.

Transactional binding

If the incoming binding for the request to the Service Bus is transactional, then the proxy service will participate in that transaction, and any proxy services, or business services invoked by the proxy, will participate in the same transaction. Control of the transaction, in this case, rests with the client. An example of this is the EJB binding or the **Java Message Service (JMS)** binding.

In the case that a flow within a proxy invokes several transactional proxies and business services, they will all be enrolled in the initial inbound transaction and committed or rolled back as part of that transaction. Hence any transactional services invoked will all commit together or all roll back together.

Non-transactional binding

If the incoming binding for the request is not transactional, such as a SOAP request or a file transport, then the transactional behavior of the proxy depends on the type of proxy.

Non-transactional proxy

This is the default type of proxy and the only type of proxy that existed prior to 11*g*. In this case, if there is no incoming transaction then the proxy will not execute as part of a transaction. Any transactional proxies or business services that it invokes will each execute in their own transaction. This means that the invoked services will not necessarily be all complete or all roll back together. Some services may succeed and commit, others may throw an error and rollback.

Transactional proxy

A new feature in OSB 11*g* is the transactional proxy. A transactional proxy will start a new transaction if one does not exist in the request received. From this point on, the behavior is the same as the transactional binding case, with all transactional calls in a flow being part of the same transaction. In this case, the transaction is committed when the proxy flows have completed.

Comparison to EJB

Although OSB is not built using EJBs, the non-transactional proxy behaves transactionally in a similar way to EJBs with the transaction semantics of participates. If a transaction exists, they will participate in it, but they will not create a new transaction themselves.

The transactional proxy and BPEL processes with the transaction partner link property of `Required` behave in a similar way to EJBs with the transaction semantics of `Required`. If a transaction already exists, they will participate in it; if no transaction exists, they will start a new one.

BPEL processes with a transaction partner link property of `requiresNew` behave in a similar fashion to EJBs with transaction semantics of `requiresNew`. They will always start a new transaction rather than participate in any calling transaction.

Clustering

The SOA Suite and OSB both take advantage of the underlying clustering capabilities of the application server. A cluster can consist of one or more server instances running either the OSB, the SOA Suite, or **Business Activity Monitoring (BAM)**. When running on WebLogic, a domain may have no more than one OSB cluster, one SOA Suite cluster, and/or one BAM cluster.

A domain is a set of WebLogic servers with a central administration point (the Admin Server) and a central configuration repository (`config.xml`). A managed server is a WebLogic server instance running in a single JVM on a single machine with a targeted set of applications. A cluster has a number of managed servers that may be targeted at multiple physical machines and can be managed as a single entity.

> In SOA Suite 10*g*, domain was used to describe a logical collection of BPEL processes in a BPEL server. This could be used to give each developer their own environment (domain) in a single BPEL server instance on a single JVM. This facility is not available in 11*g* up to patch set 1. In patch set 2, this facility will be brought back under the new name of partitions. The name had to change because of the existing use of domains by the WebLogic server.

The best source of information on creating a cluster is the **Enterprise Deployment Guide** (**EDG**) in the SOA Suite documentation.

There are some key considerations to take into account when creating a cluster.

Load balancing

A cluster will require a load balancer to distribute inbound requests across machines in the cluster. A hardware load balancer such as an F5 Big IP machine will provide much better performance and resilience than a software load balancer. The address of the load balancer must be provided to the cluster to enable the correct creation of callback addresses and service endpoint references, as detailed in the EDG.

JMS considerations

Most components can be easily replicated in a cluster. However, JMS poses some challenges. JMS is used heavily by both the OSB and SOA Suite. WebLogic has the concept of distributed JMS, which allows for multiple servers to host a single logical queue. In this configuration, however, it is necessary for each server hosting part of the distributed queue to be set up for whole server migration. This WebLogic facility enables a server to be restarted on a different machine in the case of machine failure. This is important because without this, any messages in the portion of the distributed queue on the failed machine will not be available until that machine is brought back into operation.

When using a distributed queue, a shared filesystem such as a **Storage Area Network** (**SAN**) should be used to hold the distributed queue files so that they are available to the managed server when it is restarted on another physical machine.

WebLogic JMS also supports database queues. If stored in an Oracle **Real Application Clusters** (**RAC**) database these can provide a high degree of availability, but there may be contention issues for the queue tables when large numbers of managed servers are all accessing the same shared queue. Hence the Oracle recommendation is to use distributed queues with a resilient file-based backing store, ideally on a SAN, so that it can easily be shared between multiple machines.

Testing considerations

When testing a cluster, it is important to ensure that requests are distributed across the cluster in a fair manner. This is important to make sure that there are no unexpected behaviors when requests for the same composite instance are distributed across several nodes in the cluster.

Avoid IP stickiness

When using a load balancer during testing, it is important to avoid the use of a load balancer set up to use IP stickiness. IP stickiness is used to route requests to servers based on the IP address of the client. This is bad when testing, in particular, because the request will tend to come from a small number of load injectors, and this will cause all requests from a single injector to hit a single server. This can mask problems that only show themselves when the same composite is executed on multiple servers. Note that HTTP cookie stickiness is a good idea, however, as it allows correct operation of several components including the human workflow engine and the consoles.

Often, we will use a composite to test other composites. In this case, we need to make sure that the test harness composite makes external calls through the load balancer to all the services it invokes. We can do this by setting the endpoint address to be different from the configured property on a reference. This ensures that the test mimics the real world more closely. Failure to do this will mean that the test will be using the optimized internal transports and hence show better performance characteristics than might be expected in production.

Adapter considerations

Some of the adapters need to synchronize their access to shared inbound resources such as files, database tables, and message queues. The JCA adapters that require this communicate using cluster software called **Coherence** to run in *active-active* mode, meaning that all adapters are active at the same time but they co-ordinate their activities to avoid conflicts. This is configured by default and is a significant improvement over the active-passive adapter configurations that were required in SOA Suite 10*g*.

Metadata repository considerations

The repository is used not just to hold metadata, but also to persist runtime information such as BPEL process instance state. Hence it is important that this component is highly available to avoid outages due to database failure. Oracle Real Application Clusters can be used to provide a highly available database for the repository. Without the repository, the SOA Suite will not be able to operate so thought must be given to the availability characteristics of the database it uses.

Database connections

Although of a particular concern to the metadata repository, the number of database connections needed in a cluster is also relevant to application data sources. When sizing the database connection pools in the application server, it should be remembered that every dispatcher thread (invoker, engine, and system) will need at least one connection to the metadata repository. In addition, each concurrent request/reply message will require another connection.

When sizing the number of sessions and processes in the database, it is important to remember to size them based on the sum of the number of connections in the managed server pools multiplied by the number of managed servers, plus the number of connections in the connection pools of the Admin server.

Summary

In this section, we have examined how we can control the scope of transactions used in the SOA Suite. We have also looked at how these transactions interact with threads to provide different execution models for our composites. We concluded with a brief discussion of issues to consider when clustering SOA Suite. Oracle has produced a large document in the SOA Suite documentation, the Enterprise Deployment Guide, that explains in detail all the steps that are required to create a resilient cluster, and this document is worth a careful study before setting up any cluster.

16
Message Interaction Patterns

In every composite, messages are exchanged between participants. So far, we have only looked at simple interactions, that is, a single request followed by a reply, whether synchronous or asynchronous.

Asynchronous messaging adds additional complexities around the routing and correlation of replies. In this chapter, we look at how the SOA Service Infrastructure uses WS-Addressing to manage this, and in situations where this can't be used, examine how we can use correlation sets in BPEL to achieve the same result.

As a part of this, we look at some common, but more complex, messaging patterns and requirements such as:

- How we can handle multiple exchanges of messages, either synchronous or asynchronous between two participants
- How BPEL can be used to aggregate messages from multiple sources
- Although it is not strictly a message interaction pattern, examine one technique for process scheduling

Finally, as we explore these patterns, we take the opportunity to cover some of BPEL's more advanced features, including **FlowN**, **Pick**, and **Dynamic Partner Links**.

Messaging within a composite

Before looking at messaging patterns in detail, it's worth taking a moment to provide a high-level overview of how messaging is handled within a composite.

Within the SOA Suite, the messaging infrastructure consists of three distinct parts:

* **Service Engines**: They are responsible for executing the business logic within a composite (for example, BPEL PM, Mediator, Workflow, and Business Rules).
* **Binding Components**: They handle connectivity between composites and the outside world (for example, HTTP, JCA, B2B, ADF BC).
* **Service Infrastructure**: This is responsible for the internal routing of messages between service engines and binding components.

For example, the following diagram shows an external client invoking the **submitBid** operation against our **Auction Composite**.

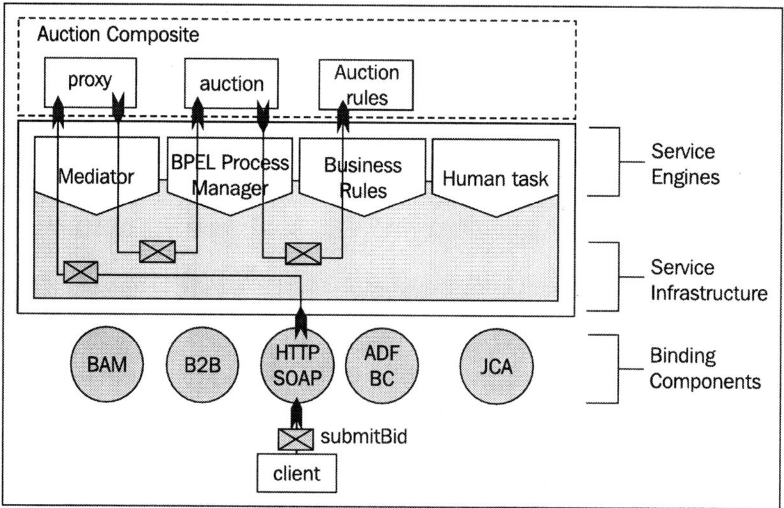

Here we can see the invocation is made using SOAP over HTTP via the corresponding binding component. The binding component handles receipt of the message over its corresponding transport protocol and then translates into a normalized form before forwarding it onto the **Service Infrastructure**.

The normalized form is an internal representation of the XML message, as defined by the service's WSDL contract.

The **Service Infrastructure** will apply the appropriate policies such as management and security (see *Chapter 21, Defining Security and Management* Policies for further details) against the normalized message before routing it to the appropriate service engine, as defined in the composite.

In the previous example, the **Service Infrastructure** will forward the request to the Mediator **proxy**, which will then route the request through to the **Auction** BPEL process. The BPEL process then invokes the rules engine to evaluate the bid. Each of these invocations between **Service Engines** goes via the **Service Infrastructure** (again applying any polices that we have defined).

After the bid has been successfully evaluated, the response is returned from the rules engine to BPEL to the Mediator to the Binding Component again via the Service Infrastructure, before the binding component returns the result to the consumer that sent the original request.

Processing of messages within the Mediator

The Mediator service engine on receipt of a new request message will instantiate a new instance of a Mediator to process the message. In the case of a synchronous operation, the request and response messages are evaluated in the same thread and transaction as the caller (that is, the binding component or service engine).

In the case of an asynchronous operation, the state of the instance will be persisted to the dehydration store awaiting the appropriate callback. On receipt of the callback, the Mediator will rehydrate the appropriate instance to handle the callback and send a response to the client.

Processing of messages within BPEL PM

In the case of a BPEL process, it is possible, as in the case of the auction process, to make multiple invocations against a single instance of a BPEL process (unlike the Mediator).

Thus, on receipt of a message, the BPEL engine will either instantiate a new instance of the process to handle it or route it through to the appropriate instance of an already running process.

Whenever a BPEL process reaches a point where it needs to wait for a message, for example, for an asynchronous callback or an incoming synchronous request, the state of the process instance is written to the dehydration store. On receipt of the message, the BPEL engine will rehydrate the appropriate instance to handle the message.

Thus, in the preceding example, each time a client invokes **submitBid** against the same auction item, the Mediator will create a new instance of the **proxy** Mediator to process the request, yet we will only have a single instance of the auction process.

The reason why this is important is because it places a number of requirements on the Service Infrastructure on how it handles the routing or addressing of messages between composites and the outside world, as well as internally within a composite.

Message addressing

As we have just covered, a key requirement in any message exchange is to ensure that messages are routed to the appropriate service endpoint. Initial web service implementations were built using SOAP over HTTP, primarily since HTTP is well understood and is able to leverage the existing Internet infrastructure.

Using this approach, a **URI** is used to identify a service endpoint, which can then be used to route a message using the HTTP protocol from the client to the provider. Additional information, such as the action to be performed at the endpoint is encoded in HTTP headers. While this is a simple yet powerful approach, it has a number of limitations.

Multi-protocol support

If we look at the following SOAP message sent over HTTP, we can see that the URI for the service endpoint is specified as part of the HTTP Request-Line, and the action to be performed at the service endpoint is specified in the HTTP header, `SOAPAction`.

```
POST /soa-infra/services/default/AysncB/client_ep HTTP/1.1
Host: www.rubiconred.com:80
SOAPAction: "process"
Content-type: text/xml; charset=UTF-8
Content-length: 356

<?xml version="1.0" encoding="UTF-8"?>
<env:Envelope xmlns:env="http://schemas.xmlsoap.org/soap/envelope/"
              xmlns:xsd="http://www.w3.org/2001/XMLSchema"
              xmlns:xsi="http://www.w3.org/2001/XMLSchema-instance">
  <env:Body>
    <HelloWorldRequest xmlns="http://rubiconred.com/HelloWorld">
      <input>Rubicon Red</input>
    </HelloWorldRequest>
  </env:Body>
</env:Envelope>
```

Now while this may seem trivial, it's important to recall that SOAP was never intended to be tied to a single transport protocol, rather SOAP messages could be transported via multiple transport protocols, such as JMS and RMI via the appropriate binding. Indeed, a single SOAP message may potentially travel over a number of protocols before reaching its final endpoint.

The impact of externalizing some of the message routing instructions within the HTTP header means that the job of dispatching the message is split between the HTTP layer and the SOAP layer.

This makes it difficult to switch from one transport protocol to another as this external information must be mapped to an equivalent property in the alternative transport layer, external to the SOAP message.

This hampers not only the adoption of alternative SOAP bindings, but historically has caused issues around interoperability, due to different vendors defining this header information in subtle different ways.

Message correlation

HTTP's other limitation is that it is stateless in nature, and thus provides no support for conversations requiring the exchange of multiple messages. With synchronous interactions, this is not an issue, as the response message for a particular request can be returned in the HTTP response.

However, with asynchronous interactions, this is a more serious limitation. To understand why, look at the following diagram, which shows a simple asynchronous interaction between two processes, A and B. In this case, the interaction is started by **Process A** initiating **Process B**, which does some work before sending a response back to **Process A**.

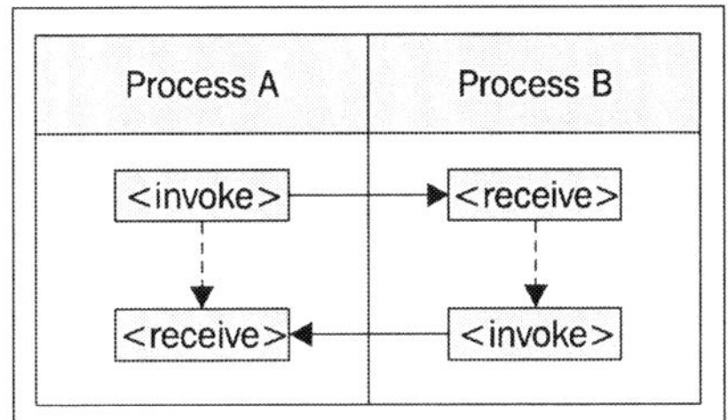

All of this looks pretty straightforward, until you consider how it actually works. The first thing to note is that this consists of two operations, one for the initial invocation and the other for the response. Each operation (or message) is sent as separate HTTP POSTs (with the HTTP response being empty).

This is where the complexity comes in. While this example shows **Process A** invoking **Process B**, it could potentially be invoked from multiple clients, for example, another process or an external client. So how does **Process B** know the service endpoint it needs to invoke for the callback?

Secondly, assuming that we have multiple instances of process A and B running at the same time, once we have routed the message to the correct service endpoint, how does the service engine at that endpoint know which instance of **Process A** to route the response from **Process B** to?

WS-Addressing

To solve these issues, the SOA Suite makes use of WS-Addressing, which provides a standardized way of including all the address-specific information as SOAP headers within a SOAP message.

With this approach, the transport protocol is just responsible for delivering the message to the appropriate binding component, which will then deliver the message to the Service Infrastructure. This will then route the message to the appropriate endpoint/service engine.

To demonstrate how WS-Addressing achieves this, let us look at the WS-Addressing headers the Service Infrastructure inserts into our request and response messages in the previous example.

Request message with WS-Addressing

The initial request sent by composite A, with WS-Addressing headers inserted, looks something like the following:

```
<env:Envelope xmlns:env="http://schemas.xmlsoap.org/soap/envelope/"
              xmlns:wsa="http://www.w3.org/2005/08/addressing"
              xmlns:ins="http://xmlns.oracle.com/sca/tracking/1.0">
  <env:Header>
    <wsa:To>http://hostname:8001/soa-infra/services/default/AysncB/
            client_ep</wsa:To>
    <wsa:Action>http://xmlns.oracle.com/AsyncA/AsyncB/BPELProcessB/
                BPELProcessB/process</wsa:Action>
    <wsa:MessageID>urn:62772860C2DE8F6A0634D09B</wsa:MessageID>
    <wsa:RelatesTo>urn:62772860C2DE8F6A0634D09B</wsa:RelatesTo>
    <wsa:ReplyTo>
      <wsa:Address>
        http://hostname:8001/soa-infra/services/default/AsyncA!1.0*
        2fc449a6-fa51-440a-afae-b143d9c26d88/BPELProcessB%23BPEL
        ProcessA/BPELProcessB
      </wsa:Address>
      <wsa:ReferenceParameters>
        <ins:tracking.ecid>…</ins:tracking.ecid>
        <ins:tracking.conversationId>…</ins:tracking.conversationId>
        <ins:tracking.parentComponentInstanceId>…
        </ins:tracking.parentComponentInstanceId>
      </wsa:ReferenceParameters>
    </wsa:ReplyTo>
  </env:Header>
  <env:Body>
    …
  </env:Body>
</env:Envelope>
```

The first header that has been added is `wsa:To`, which defines the URI address of the endpoint that the SOAP message should be delivered to. The other header related to this is `wsa:Action`, which specifies how the message should be processed, once delivered to the endpoint. In this respect, it is equivalent to the `SOAPAction` HTTP header we saw earlier.

The next header is `wsa:MessageId`, which is used to uniquely identify the message. The other header connected to this is `wsa:RelatesTo`, which contains the message ID of the first message exchanged in this interaction. As this is the first message in the exchange, it contains the same value as `wsa:MessageId`. As we will see in a moment, these headers are used to correlate the response message back to the original requestor.

The final header is `wsa:ReplyTo`, which contains the `wsa:Address` element. In the case of an asynchronous request, this will contain the URI address of the endpoint for the callback.

> You may have noticed that `wsa:ReplyTo` contains the additional element `wsa:ReferenceParameters`, which in turn contains a number of additional elements such as `ins:tracking.conversationId`. These are not part of the WS-Addressing specification, but rather an extension specific to the Oracle Service Infrastructure, which is used to maintain the invocation trace between all the different components involved in an end-to-end invocation of a service.

Response message with WS-Addressing

When sending an asynchronous response message, it will contain the same set of WS-Addressing headers as our request. What's of interest is the values in some of those headers and how they relate to the original request message.

```
<env:Envelope xmlns:env="http://schemas.xmlsoap.org/soap/envelope/"
              xmlns:wsa="http://www.w3.org/2005/08/addressing"
              xmlns:ins="http://xmlns.oracle.com/sca/tracking/1.0">
  <env:Header>
    <wsa:To>
      http://hostname:8001/soa-infra/services/default/AsyncA!1.0*
      2fc449a6-fa51-440a-afae-b143d9c26d88/BPELProcessB%23BPEL
      ProcessA/BPELProcessB
    </wsa:To>
    <wsa:Action>processResponse</wsa:Action>
    <wsa:MessageID>urn:62772860C2EBFB26F9ED8D4E</wsa:MessageID>
```

```
      <wsa:RelatesTo>urn:62772860C2DE8F6A0634D09B</wsa:RelatesTo>
      <wsa:ReplyTo>
        <wsa:Address>
          http://www.w3.org/2005/08/addressing/anonymous
        </wsa:Address>
        <wsa:ReferenceParameters>
          <ins:tracking.conversationId>…</ins:tracking.conversationId>
          <ins:tracking.parentComponentInstanceId>…
          </ins:tracking.parentComponentInstanceId>
        </wsa:ReferenceParameters>
      </wsa:ReplyTo>
    </env:Header>
    <env:Body>
      …
    </env:Body>
  </env:Envelope>
```

The first one of interest is `wsa:To`. This will contain the address specified in the `wsa:ReplyTo` endpoint reference of our request reference, which allows the Service Infrastructure to route the response to the appropriate endpoint.

In addition, if we look at the message above, we can see that the property `<wsa:RelatesTo>` contains the value of `wsa:MessageId` specified in the original request. It's this value that enables the endpoint to correlate the response back to the original request. In our case, this enables the BPEL engine to route the response from **Process B** back to the instance of **Process A**, which sent the original request.

In the preceding example, it's quite feasible for **Process A** and **Process B** to send multiple messages to each other. Any further exchange of messages between the two process instances will just contain the same `<wsa:RelatesTo>` property within the SOAP header.

Using BPEL correlation sets

For situations where WS-Addressing isn't appropriate or available, BPEL provides the concept of correlation sets. Essentially, correlation sets allow you to use one or more fields present in the body of all correlated messages (for example, `orderId`) to act as a pseudo conversation ID (equivalent to the `<wsa:MessageID>` and `<wsa:RelatesTo>` properties in WS-Addressing).

A correlation set consists of one more properties; these properties are then mapped using property aliases to the corresponding fields in each of the messages that are being exchanged. The combined value of these properties at runtime should result in a unique value (at least unique across all instances of the same process), which allows the BPEL engine to route the message to the appropriate instance of a process.

Using correlation sets for multiple process interactions

A common requirement is for a client to make multiple synchronous invocations against the same instance of a process. The first request is pretty much the same as a standard synchronous request, but all subsequent requests are subtly different as we now need to route these requests through to the appropriate instance of an already running process rather than initiate a new instance.

Take the `UserRegistration` process; this is a long running process which needs to handle multiple synchronous requests during its lifecycle. The first operation `submitUserRegistration` is called by the client to initiate the process, which validates all the provided user information and returns a confirmation of success or otherwise.

The only information that is not validated at this stage is the e-mail address. For this, the process sends an e-mail to the provided address containing a unique token which the user can use to confirm their address.

Once they have received the e-mail, they can launch their browser and submit the token. The web client will then invoke the `confirmEmailAddress` operation. It's at this point we need to use a correlation set to route this request to the appropriate instance of the `UserRegistration` process.

Defining a correlation set property

The first step is to choose a unique field that could act as a property. One approach would be to use the user ID specified by the user. However, for our purposes, we want to use a value that the user will only have access to once they have received their confirmation e-mail, so will use the token contained in the e-mail.

To create a property within the **Structure** view for the BPEL process, right-click on the **Properties** folder and select **Create Property...**, as shown in the following screenshot:

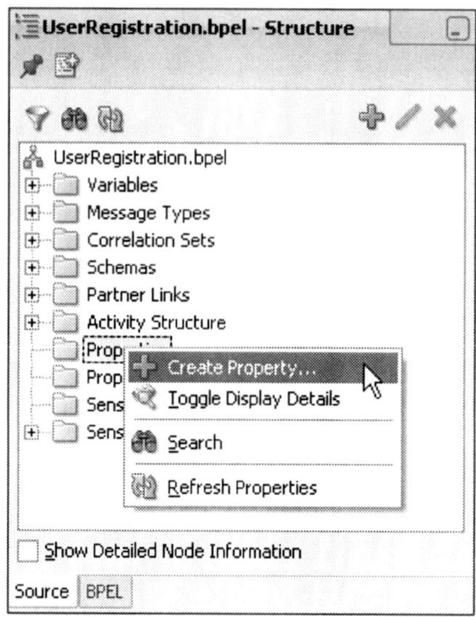

This will launch the **Create Correlation Set Property** window. Give the property a meaningful name, **EmailToken** for example, and then click the search icon to launch the **Type Chooser**, and select the appropriate schema type (for example, `xsd:string`), as shown in the following screenshot:

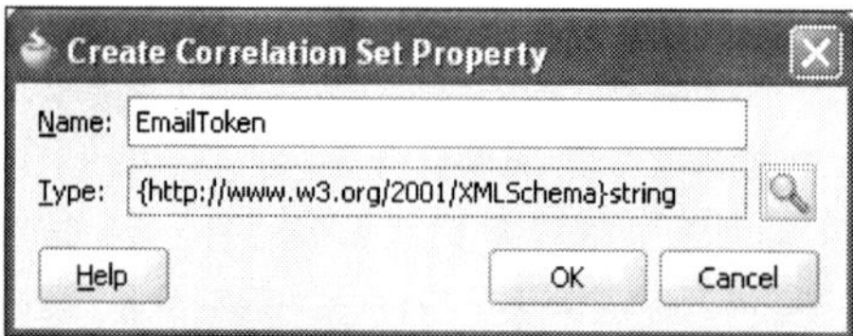

Defining correlation set

Once we've defined our correlation set property(s), the next step is to define the correlation set itself.

Correlation sets can be defined either at the process level or for a particular scope. In most cases, the process level will suffice, but if you need to have multiple correlated conversations within the same process instance, for example, iterations through a while loop, then we define the correlation set at the scope level.

Within the BPEL **Structure** view, expand the **Correlation Sets** folder, and then the **Process** folder, and right-click on the **Correlation Sets** folder. From the menu, select **Create Correlation Set...**, as shown in the following screenshot:

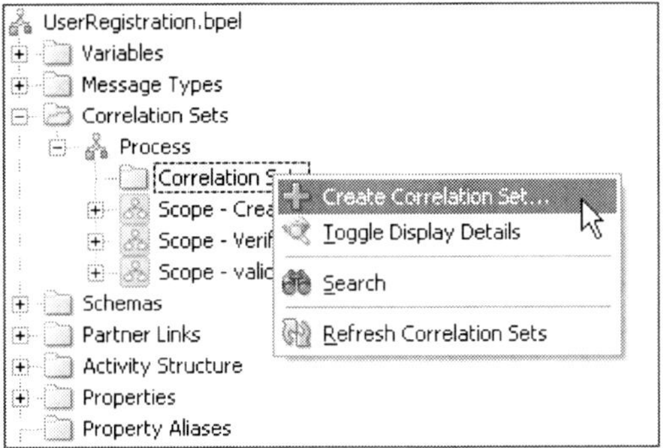

This will launch the **Create Correlation Set** window, displayed on the following page. Give the correlation set a meaningful name, **EmailTokenCS** in our case, and then select the **+** symbol to add one or more properties to the correlation set. This will bring up the **Property Chooser**, where you can select any previously defined properties.

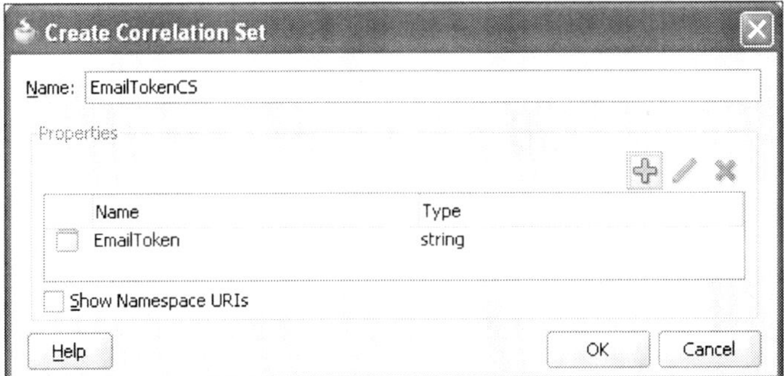

Using correlation sets

Next, we need to specify which messages we wish to route with our correlation set. For our purposes, we want to use the correlation set to route the inbound message for the operation `confirmEmailAddress` to the appropriate process instance.

To configure this, double-click the **Receive** activity for this operation to open the **Receive** activity window, and select the **Correlations** tab, as shown in the following screenshot:

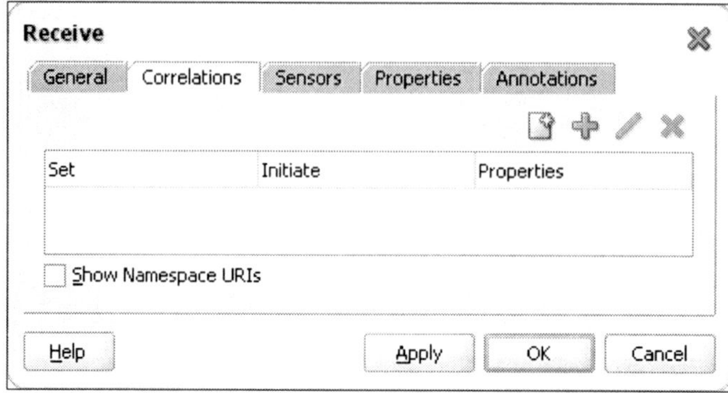

Next, select the **+** symbol; this will launch the **Correlation Set Chooser**, as shown in the following screenshot:

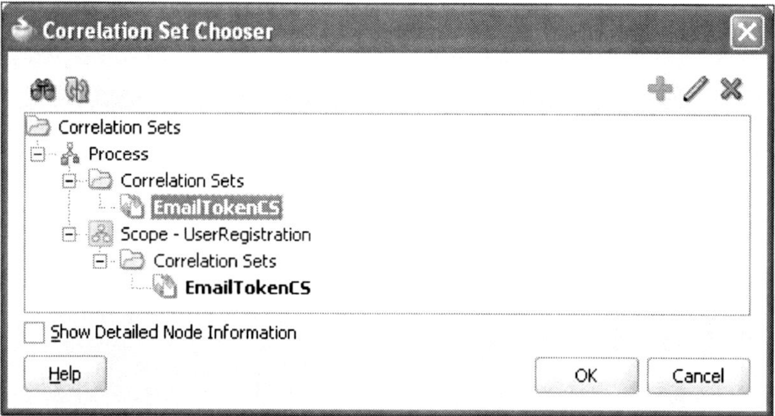

From here we can select the **EmailTokenCS** we defined previously. Click **OK**, and this will return us to the **Correlations** tab, showing the newly added correlation.

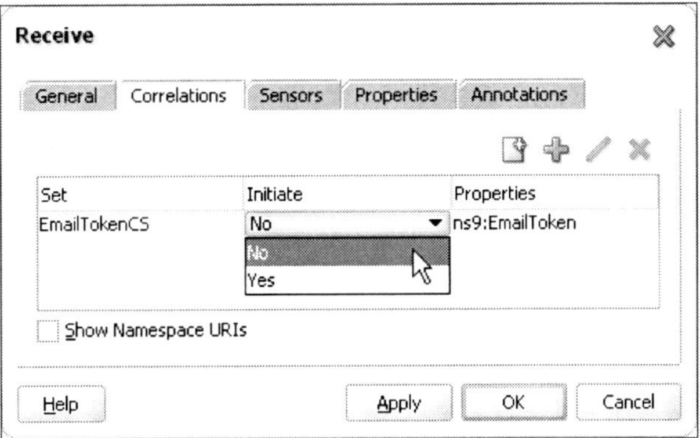

We can see here that we have to specify one additional property **Initiate**. This is used to specify which message should be used to initialize the correlation set.

Initializing the correlation set

As you would expect, the value of the property(s) contained in the first message exchanged in any sequence of correlated messages must be used to initiate the value of each property contained within the correlation set.

However, rather than implicitly initializing the correlation set based on the first message exchanged, BPEL expects you to explicitly define which message activity should be the first in the sequence by setting the **Initiate** property to **Yes**.

> If we try and initialize an already initialized correlation set or try to use a correlation set that isn't initialized, then a runtime exception will be thrown by the BPEL engine. Likewise, once initialized, the value of these properties must be identical in all subsequent messages sent as part of the sequence of correlated messages, or again the BPEL engine will throw an exception.

When initializing a correlation set, any outbound message can be used to achieve this. However, there are practical restrictions on which inbound messages can be used to initiate a correlation set, as the process must first **receive** the inbound message before it can use it to initialize a correlation set.

Essentially, if an inbound message is used to create a new instance of a process or is routed through to the process by another mechanism (for example, a different correlation set), then it can be used for the purpose of initiating our correlation set.

In our case, we are using the correlation set to route the inbound message for the `confirmEmailAddress` operation through to an already running process instance, so we need to initialize the correlation set in an earlier message. We can do this within the **Invoke** activity for the subprocess `validateEmailAddress`.

We define a correlation set for an **Invoke** activity as we would for any message-based activity, that is, we open its properties window, and select the **Correlations** tab, as shown in the following screenshot:

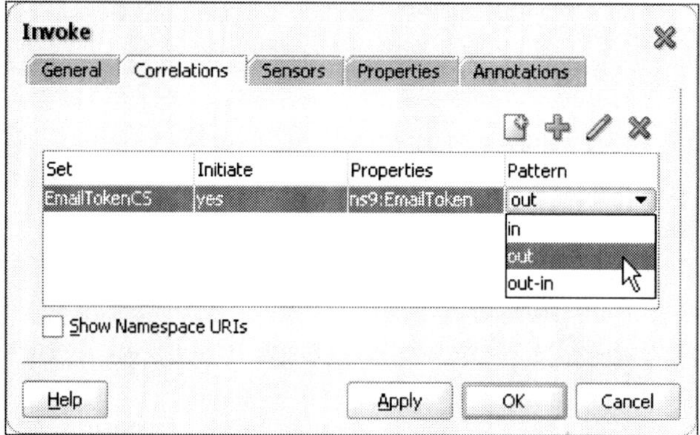

However, you may notice that when creating a correlation for an **Invoke** activity, we are required to set the additional attribute **Pattern**. This is because unlike any other message activity, **Invoke** can consist of two messages: the initial outbound request, and an optional corresponding inbound response. The pattern attribute is used to specify to which message the correlation set should be applied, that is, **out** for the outbound request, **in** for the inbound response, and **out-in** for both.

Since `validateEmailAddress` is a one way operation, we need to set the **Pattern** attribute to **out**.

Note that if you choose to initiate the correlation with an **out-in** pattern, then the outbound request is used to initiate the correlation set.

Defining property aliases

Once the messages to be exchanged as part of our correlation set have been defined, the final step is to map the properties used by the correlation set to the corresponding fields in each of the messages exchanged.

To do this, we need to create a property alias for every **message type** exchanged, that is, `validateEmailAddress` and `confirmEmailAddress`, in our user registration example.

To create an alias, within the **Structure** view for the BPEL process, right-click on the **Property Aliases...** folder, and select **Create Property...**. This will launch the **Create Property Alias** window, as shown in the following screenshot:

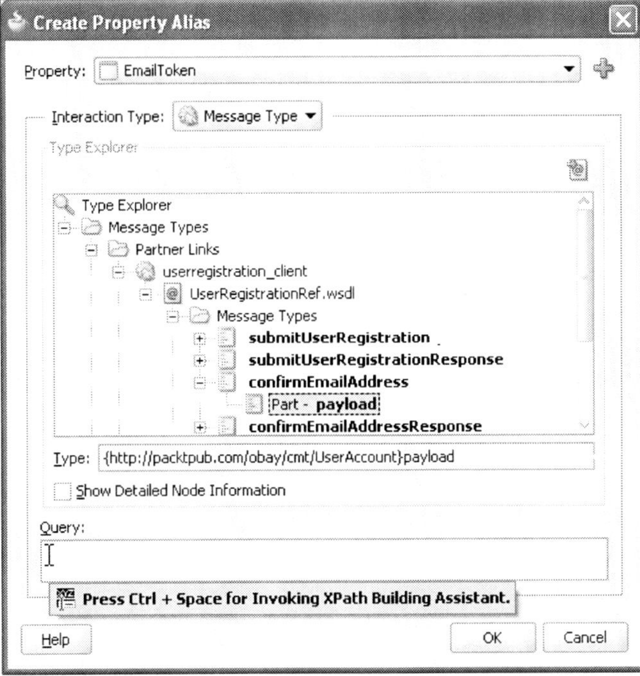

In the **Property** drop-down, select the property that you wish to define the alias for and then using the **Type Explorer**, navigate through the **Message Types**, **Partner Links**, down to the relevant **Message Types** and **Part** that you want to map the property to.

This will activate the **Query** field, where we specify the XPath for the field containing the property in the specified message type. Rather than type it all by hand, press *Ctrl* + *Space* to use the **XPath Building Assistant**.

Once we have defined an alias for each of the messages exchanged within our correlation set, we can view them within the **Structure** view of the BPEL process, as shown in the following screenshot:

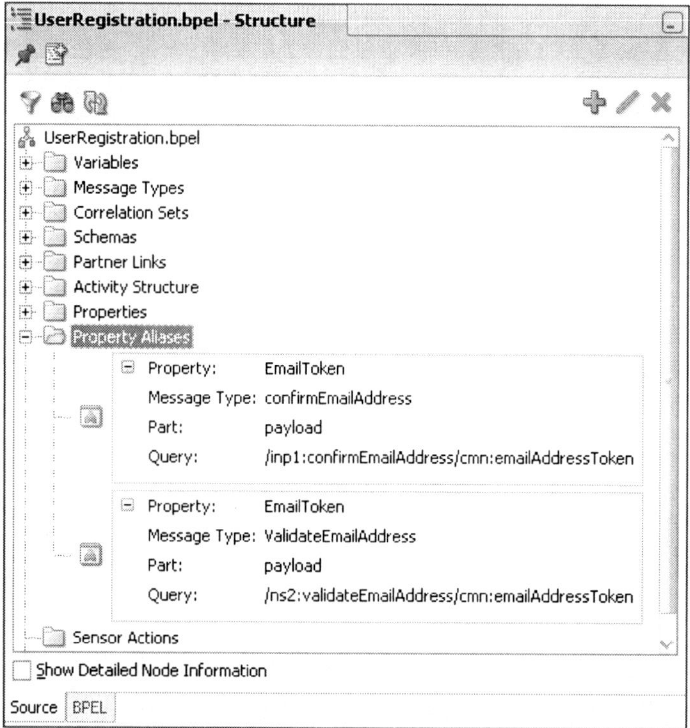

This completes the definition of our correlation set.

A BPEL process can define multiple correlation sets, and messages exchanged within a BPEL process can be exchanged in zero, one, or more correlation sets. When a message is involved in multiple correlations sets, it can be the same or different fields that are mapped to a corresponding property. You will of course require a separate property alias for each correlation set.

Message aggregation

A typical messaging requirement is to aggregate multiple related messages for processing within a single BPEL process instance. Messages are aggregated using a common correlation ID, in much the same way as we covered previously.

The other challenge is to determine when we have all the messages that belong to the aggregation. Typically, most use cases fall into two broad patterns:

- **Fixed Duration**: In this scenario, we don't know how many messages we expect to receive, so we will process all those received within a specified period of time.
- **Wait For All**: In this scenario, we know how many messages we expect to receive. Once they have been received, we can then process them as an aggregated message. It's usual to combine this with a timeout in case some messages aren't received, so that the process doesn't wait forever.

An example of the first pattern is the oBay auction process. Here, during the period for which the auction is in progress, we need to route zero or more bids from various sources to the appropriate instance of the auction, and then once the auction has finished, select the highest bid as the winner. The outline of the process is shown on the next page.

From this, we can see that the process supports two asynchronous operations, each with a corresponding callback. They are:

- **initateAuction**: This operation is used to instantiate the auction process. Once started, the auction will run for a preset period until it gets completed and then invoke the callback **returnAuctionResult** to return the result of the auction to the client which initiated the auction.
- **submitBid**: This operation is used to submit a bid to the auction. The operation is responsible for checking each bid to see if we have a new highest bid, and if so, it will update the current bid price appropriately, before returning the result of the bid to the client. The process then loops back round to process the next bid.

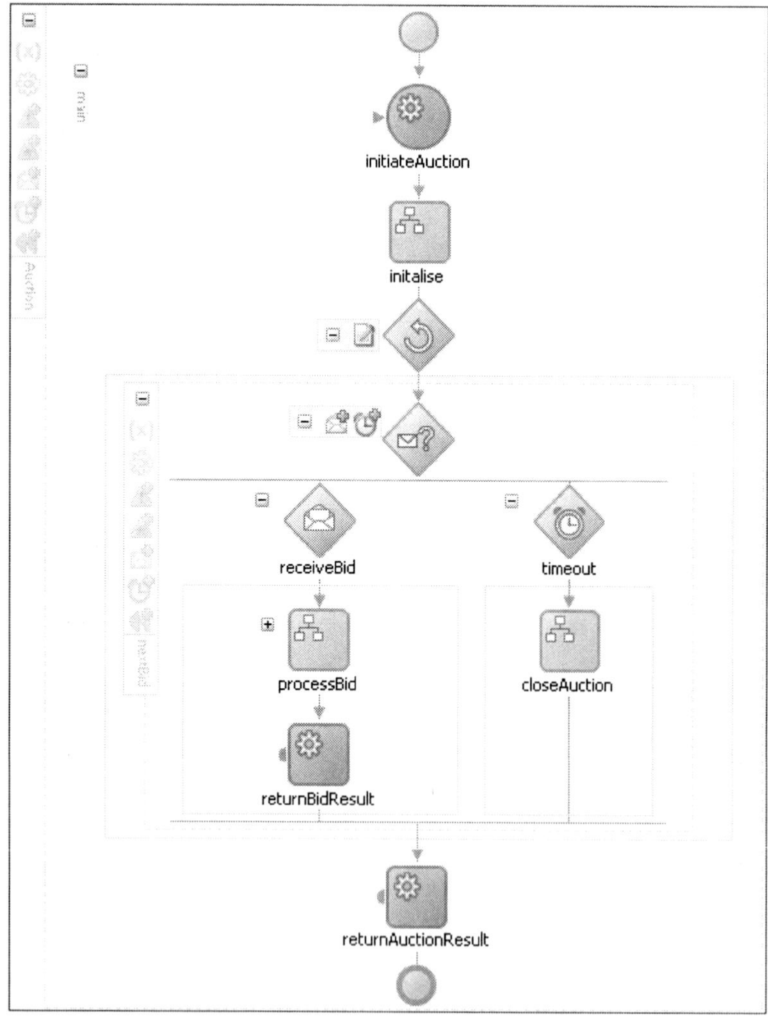

Message routing

The first task for the aggregator is to route bids through to the appropriate instance of the auction process. As with our earlier `UserRegistration` example, we can use a correlation set to route messages to the appropriate instance. In this example, we will create a correlation set based on the element **auctionId**, which is included in the message payload for **initateAuction** and **submitBid**.

At first glance, this looks pretty straightforward, as we can use correlation sets for aggregation in much the same way as we have already covered. However, this scenario presents us with an additional complexity; which is that a single instance of a BPEL process may receive multiple messages of the same type at approximately the same time.

To manage this, we need to implement a queuing mechanism, so that we can process each bid in turn before moving onto the next. This is achieved by implementing the interaction between the client submitting the bid and the auction process as asynchronous.

With asynchronous operations, BPEL saves received messages to the BPEL delivery queue. The delivery service then handles the processing of these messages; either instantiating a new process or correlating the message to a **waiting** `receive` or `onMessage` activity in an already running process instance.

If a process is not ready to receive a message, then the message will remain in the queue until the process is ready.

This introduces a number of complexities over our previous correlation example. This is because a BPEL process can only support **one inbound Partner Link** (for example, client), for which the BPEL engine generates a corresponding concrete WSDL. This defines all operations that can be invoked against that BPEL process (as well as any corresponding callbacks).

However, for any **single** instance of a BPEL process, the BPEL engine expects that any requests received via that partner link will always be from the same client, so upon receipt of the initial request, **initiateAuction** in the case of the auction process, it sets the conversation ID and the reply to address based on that request. These values are then fixed for the duration of that process.

Correlating the callback

The first complexity this causes is that whenever a client submits a request to the process via the **submitBid** operation, the BPEL engine, when sending a response, will set the value of `<wsa:RelatesTo>` based on the header contained in the **initiateAuction** request (not the value in the **submitBid** request). So we can't use WS-Addressing to correlate the response of the auction process back to the client.

Initially, the obvious answer might appear to be just to use the **auctionId** to correlate the result of the bid back to the client. However, while the **auctionId** allows us to uniquely identify a single instance of an auction, it doesn't allow us to uniquely identify a bidder. This, may seem strange at first, but recall we may have several clients calling the auction process at the same time, all waiting for a response. We need to ensure that each response is returned to the appropriate instance.

Thus the calling client will need to pass a unique key in the **submitBid** request message (for example, **bidId**) that the auction process can include in the response. Assuming we are using BPEL to implement the client, we then need to implement a correlation set based on this property in the calling process, so that the BPEL engine can route the response to the appropriate instance of the client process.

Specifying the reply to address

The second complexity is that whenever a client submits a request to the auction process, via the **submitBid** operation, the BPEL engine will ignore the `<wsa:replyTo>` and will attempt to send the reply to the client which initiated the auction.

This highlights the other issue, that our auction process supports two callbacks—one to return the auction result, the other to return the bid result. Yet the reply to address on the partner link is being fixed with the initial invocation of the process, forcing both callbacks to be routed to the same endpoint, which is not what we want.

Creating a proxy process

At this point, you may be thinking that all of this may be too complex. However, the solution is rather straightforward and that is to use a proxy process, which supports the same operations as the **Auction** process, as illustrated in the following diagram:

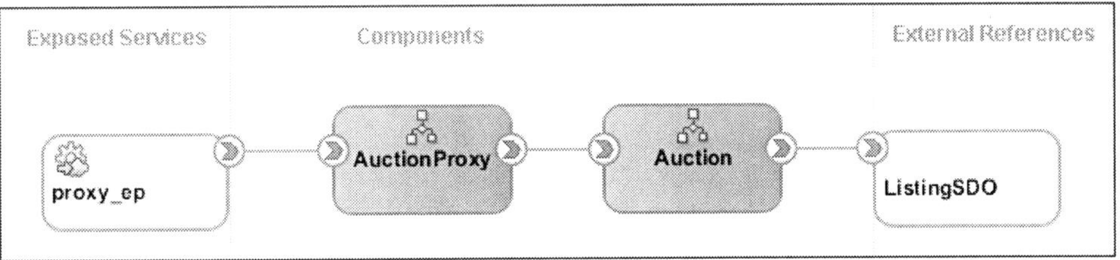

With this approach, the client invokes either the `initateAuction` or `submitBid` operation on the **AuctionProxy** process, which forwards the request to the **Auction** process. The **Auction** process then returns the result to the **AuctionProxy**, which then returns it to the original client.

This not only solves the problem of having a fixed reply to address, but has the additional benefit of shielding the client from having to use correlation sets, as it can use WS-Addressing to communicate with the proxy.

At this point, you may be thinking, why not use a Mediator as a proxy? While using a Mediator would allow us to address the issue of having a fixed reply to address, it doesn't address the correlation issue, as Mediators don't support the concept of correlation sets.

Using the pick activity

Our proxy process needs to support both operations, `initateAuction` and `submitBid`, as either operation can be used to **initiate** an instance of the proxy process. To achieve this we will use the `<pick>` activity at the start of our process in place of a `<receive>` activity.

A `<pick>` activity is similar to a `<receive>` activity. The difference is that with a `<pick>` activity, you can specify that the process waits for **one** of a set of events. Events can either be the receipt of a message or an alarm event (which we look at later in this chapter).

Each message is specified in a separate `<onMessage>` branch, with each branch containing one or more activities to be executed on receipt of the corresponding message. To use a **Pick** activity, drag a `<pick>` activity from the **Process Activities** list of the **Component Palette** on to your process.

As the <pick> activity is used to receive the initial message that starts the process, we need to set the createInstance attribute on the activity. In order to do this, double-click the <pick> activity to open the **Pick** activity window, as shown in the following screenshot, and select the **Create Instance** checkbox.

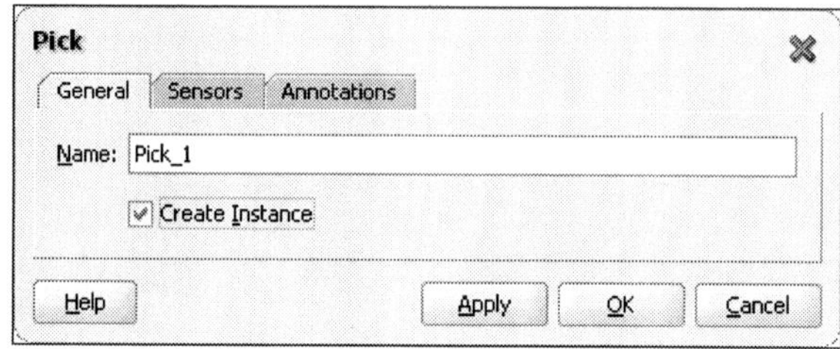

Next, within the process diagram, click on the **+** symbol to expand the <pick> activity. By default, it will have two branches, as illustrated in the following diagram:

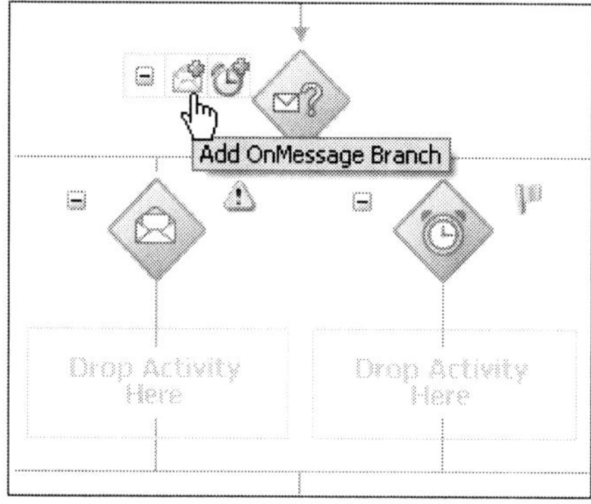

The first branch contains an <onMessage> component with a corresponding area where you can drop a sequence of one or more activities that will be executed if the corresponding message is received.

The second branch contains an <onAlarm> subactivity with a corresponding area for activities. It doesn't make sense to have this as part of the initial activity in a process, so right-click on the <onAlarm> subactivity and select **delete** to remove it

We require two OnMessage branches, one for each operation that the process supports, so click on the **Add OnMessage Branch** icon (highlighted in the preceding diagram) to add another <onMessage> branch.

The next step is to configure the `<onMessage>` branch. Double-click on the first branch to open the **OnMessage Branch** activity window, as shown in the following screenshot:

As we can see, an **OnMessage Branch** is configured in a similar fashion to a **Receive** activity. For the purposes of our proxy, we will configure the first **onMessage** branch to support the **initateAuction** operation (as shown in the preceding screesnhot) and the second **onMessage** branch to support the **submitBid** operation.

Each branch will just contain an **Invoke** and **Receive** activity to call the corresponding operation provided by the auction process, and a final invoke activity to return the result of the operation to the caller of the process.

Defining the correlation sets

For our proxy process, we need to define a correlation set for the `submitBid` operation to ensure that replies from the **Auction** process are routed through to the correct instance of the **AuctionProxy** process.

As mentioned earlier, this requires us to include a unique `bidId` within the `submitBid` message. To generate this, we can use the XPath function **generateGUID**, which is available under the category **BPEL XPath Extension Function** within the expression builder.

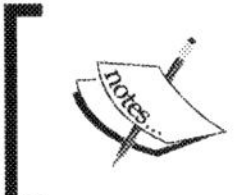

We do not need to define a correlation set for the **initateAuction** operation, as the corresponding operation on the auction process is still using WS-Addressing.

Completing the aggregation

All that remains is to add in the logic that enables the process to determine when the aggregation is complete. For a scenario where we know how many messages we expect, every time we receive a message, we just need to check whether there are any outstanding messages and proceed accordingly.

However, for scenarios where we are waiting for a fixed duration, as is the case with our auction process, it's slightly trickier. The challenge is that for the period over which the auction is running, the process will spend most of its time in a **paused state**, waiting for the `<receive>` activity to return details of the next bid.

So the only opportunity we have within the logic of our process to check whether the duration has expired is after the receipt of a bid, which may arrive long after the auction is completed or not at all (as the auction has theoretically finished).

Ideally, what we want to do is place a timeout on the `<receive>` activity, so that it either receives the next bid or times out on completion of the auction, whichever occurs first.

Fortunately, this can be easily accomplished by replacing the `<receive>` activity for the `submitBid` operation with a `<pick>` activity. The `<pick>` would contain two branches: an `onMessage` branch configured in an identical fashion to the `<receive>` activity and an `onAlarm` branch configured to trigger once the finish time for the auction has been reached.

To configure the **onAlarm Branch**, double-click on it to open the **OnAlarm Branch** activity window, as shown in the following screenshot:

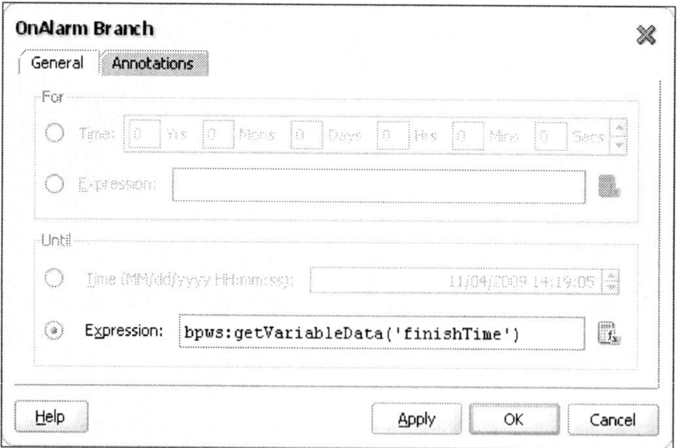

We can see that an **OnAlarm** branch is configured in a similar fashion to a `<wait>` activity, in that we can specify that the `<pick>` waits for a specified duration of time or until a specified deadline. In either case, we can specify a fixed value or specify an XPath expression to calculate the value at runtime.

For our purposes, we have pre-calculated the finish time for the auction, based on its start time and duration, and have configured the `<pick>` activity to wait until this time.

When triggered, the process will execute the activities contained in the **OnAlarm** branch and then move onto the activity following the `<pick>`. In the case of our auction process the branch contains just a single activity, which sets the flag `auctionComplete` to `true`, causing the process to exit the while loop containing the `<pick>` activity. Upon exiting the loop, the process calculates and returns the auction result before completing.

Scheduling services

A common requirement is to schedule a process or service to run at regular intervals. For example, the oBay `Billing` composite is required to be run once every night. One approach would be to use a scheduling tool. There are a number of tools available for this, including:

- **Quartz:** This is an open source Java-based scheduler; the advantage of Quartz is that it's already used internally by the BPEL engine for scheduling, so it's available for use as part of the SOA Suite platform. However, this approach requires knowledge of the API as well as Java.
- **Oracle Database Job Scheduler**: This is provided as part of the Oracle Database, and like Quartz it's available regardless of which platform you are running the SOA Suite on (assuming you are using Oracle as the backend database). However, it requires knowledge of PL/SQL.

While these are all perfectly valid approaches, they all require knowledge of components outside the SOA Suite. An alternate approach is to use BPEL to implement the scheduler.

One approach is to implement a BPEL process that continuously loops with the sole purpose of launching other scheduled BPEL process. However, as the process never dies, this will result in an ever-increasing audit trail, causing the objects persisted in the database as well as the in-memory size of the process to grow over time, which eventually will have a negative impact on the performance of the engine.

A better approach is to have an XML file that specifies a series of one or more services (or jobs) to be scheduled. We can then use the file adapter to read this file and trigger a scheduling process, which can invoke each of the scheduled jobs. Once all the jobs have been triggered, the scheduling process can be allowed to complete.

The trick to this approach is to recycle the scheduling file; that is, in the process of reading the file, the file adapter will move it to an 'archive' directory. To ensure that the scheduling process is rerun every day, we need to move the file back into the directory being polled by the adapter. We can do this using the scheduling process.

Defining the schedule file

For our oBay example, we are simply going to create a scheduling process that is run once at the start of the day. The schedule file will then contain details of each job to be run and at what time during the day. The schema for our scheduling file is as follows:

```
<?xml version="1.0" encoding="utf-8"?>
<xsd:schema xmlns:xsd="http://www.w3.org/2001/XMLSchema"
            xmlns="http://rubiconred.com/obay/xsd/schedule"
            targetNamespace="http://rubiconred.com/obay/xsd/schedule"
            elementFormDefault="qualified" >

    <xsd:element name="schedule"            type="Schedule"/>
    <xsd:element name="job"                 type="Job"/>

    <xsd:complexType name="Schedule">
        <xsd:sequence>
            <xsd:element name="startTime" type="xsd:time"/>
            <xsd:element ref="job" minOccurs="1"
                                   maxOccurs="unbounded"/>
        </xsd:sequence>
    </xsd:complexType>

    <xsd:complexType name="Job">
        <xsd:sequence>
            <xsd:element name="endpoint"  type="xsd:string" />
            <xsd:element name="startTime" type="xsd:time"/>
            <xsd:element name="jobDetail" type="xsd:anyType"/>
        </xsd:sequence>
    </xsd:complexType>

</xsd:schema>
```

The bulk of the schedule file is made up of the `Job` element, with each schedule file containing one or more jobs. The job elements contains three elements:

- `Endpoint`: Defines the endpoint of the service to invoke.
- `startTime`: Defines the time that the service should be invoked.
- `jobDetail`: Defined as `xsd:anyType`. It is used to hold details specific to the service being invoked.

For the purpose of our `Billing` composite, our schedule file looks as follows:

```
<?xml version="1.0" encoding="UTF-8" ?>
<schedule xmlns="http://rubiconred.com/obay/xsd/schedule">
  <startTime>0:2:55.125</startTime>
  <job>
    <endpoint>
      http://localhost:7001/soa-infra/services/default/Billing/proxy
    </endpoint>
    <startTime>T02:00:00</startTime>
    <jobDetail>
    </jobDetail>
  </job>
</schedule>
```

Using FlowN

To ensure that our schedule process supports the concurrent execution of jobs, we need to process them in parallel. If the number of branches/jobs was fixed at design time, we could use the `<flow>` activity to achieve this.

For our scenario, the number of branches will be determined by the number of jobs defined in our scheduling file. For use cases such as these, we can use the `<flowN>` activity. This will create N branches, where N is calculated at runtime.

Each branch performs the same activities and has access to the same global data, but is assigned an index number from 1 to N to allow it to look up the data, specific to that branch.

To use a **FlowN** activity, drag a `<flowN>` activity from the **Process Activities** list of the **Component Palette** on to your process. Double-click on it to open the **FlowN** activity window, as shown in the following screenshot:

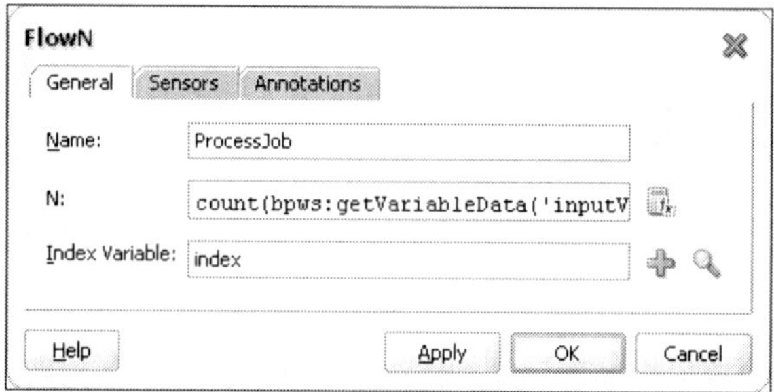

In addition to the activity **Name**, it takes two parameters. The first is **N**, which contains an XPath expression used at runtime to calculate the number of parallel branches required. This typically uses the `count` function to count the number of nodes in a variable. In our case, we need to calculate the number of `job` elements, so our expression is defined as follows:

```
count(bpws:getVariableData('InputVariable','schedule','/ns2:schedule/
ns2:job'))
```

The final parameter, **Index Variable**, is used to specify the variable into which the index value will be placed at runtime. While we have defined this as a global variable, each branch will be given its own local copy of the variable containing its assigned index number.

Accessing branch-specific data in FlowN

The first step within the **FlowN** branch is to get a local copy of the data that is to be processed by that specific branch, the **Job** in our case.

Before we do this, we need to ensure that we are working with local variables, otherwise each branch in the **FlowN** will update the same process variables. The simplest way to achieve this is by dropping a scope (which we've named **ProcessJob**) as the activity within the **FlowN** branch. Then define any branch-specific variables at the scope level and perform all branch-specific activities within the scope.

In this case, we have created a single variable **JobInputVariable** of type **Job**, which we need to populate with the job element to be processed by the flowN branch. To do this, we need to create an XPath expression that contains a **predicate** to select the required job based on its position with the node set, in effect, doing the equivalent of an array lookup in a language such as Java.

The simplest way to achieve this is by creating a standard **Copy** operation, as shown in the following screenshot:

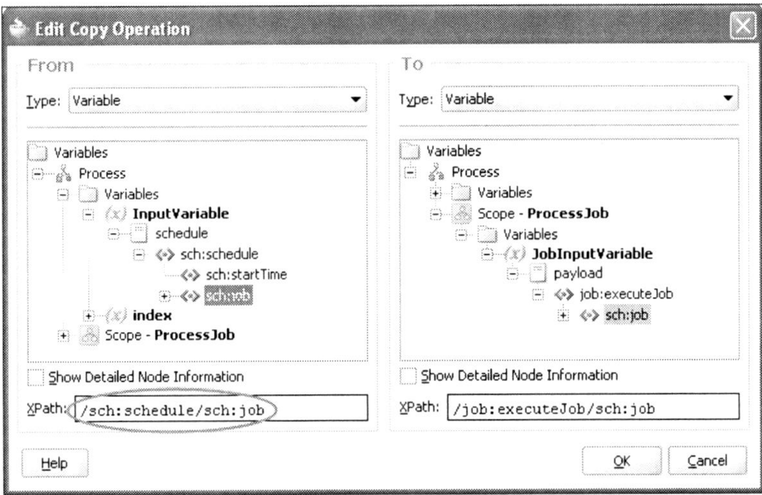

Next we need to modify the **From XPath** expression (circled in the preceding screenshot), so that we only select the required job based on the value of the index. To do this, modify the XPath to add a position-based predicate based on the index, to obtain an expression that looks something like the following:

```
/ns2:schedule/ns2:job[bpws:getVariableData('index')]
```

The next step within our branch is to use a <wait> activity to pause the branch until the startTime for the specified job.

Dynamic partner links

The final step within our branch is to call the service as defined by the endpoint in the job element. Up to now, we've only dealt in BPEL with static partner links, where the endpoint of a service is defined at design time.

However, BPEL also provides support for dynamic partner links, where we can override the endpoint specified at design time with a value specified at runtime.

Defining a common interface

While we can override the endpoint for a partner link, all other attributes of our service definition remain fixed. So to use this approach, we must define a common interface that all of our **Job** services will implement. For our purposes, we've defined the following abstract WDSL:

```
<?xml version="1.0" encoding="UTF-8"?>
<definitions name="Job">
  <types>
    <schema>
      <import namespace="http://rubiconred.com/obay/xsd/schedule"
              schemaLocation="../schedule.xsd"/>
        <element name="executeJob" type="client:ExecuteJob"/>
        <complexType name="ExecuteJob">
          <sequence>
            <element name="job" type="sch:Job"/>
          </sequence>
        </complexType>
      </schema>
    </types>

    <message name="executeJob">
      <part name="payload" element="tns:executeJob"/>
    </message>

    <portType name="Job">
      <operation name="executeJob">
        <input message="tns:executeJob"/>
      </operation>
    </portType>

    <plnk:partnerLinkType name="Job_PL">
      <plnk:role name="Job_Role">
      <plnk:portType name="tns:Job"/>
    </plnk:role>
  </plnk:partnerLinkType>
</definitions>
```

Examining this, we can see that we've defined a simple one-way operation (`executeJob`) that our scheduling process will invoke to initiate our job. For simplicity, we have defined the content of the input message to be that of the job element that we used in our scheduling file.

Defining a job partner link

Before we can define a job partner link within our schedule process, we need a WSDL file complete with bindings. The simplest way to do this is to deploy a default process that implements our abstract WSDL. To do this, create a composite process (for example, `JobService`) based on our predefined WSDL contract (as described in *Chapter 10, oBay Introduction*) containing just a single BPEL process. The process just needs to contain a simple `<receive>` activity, as it should never be called.

Note that for any other service that we wish to invoke as a job, we will need to create a composite based on our abstract WSDL, and then once created, implement the composite as required to carry out the job.

Once we've deployed our default `JobService` process, we can create a partner link and invoke it within our scheduler process, just as we would with any other service.

Creating an endpoint reference

To dynamically invoke the appropriate endpoint at runtime, we need to update the endpoint reference before invoking the service. To do this, we need to create a variable of type `EndPointReference` (as defined by WS-Addressing) containing just the `<Address>` **element** and populate this with the endpoint of the job service that we want to invoke.

This is important, as if we create an `EndpointReference` containing any of the other optional elements, then when we try and invoke the partner link, the BPEL engine will throw a fault.

To create a variable of type `EndpointReference`, you will need to import the WS-Addressing schema (located in MDS at: `oramds:/soa/shared/common/ws-addressing.xsd`).

To populate the address element, use a **Transformation** activity rather than an **Assign** activity, as shown in the following screenshot:

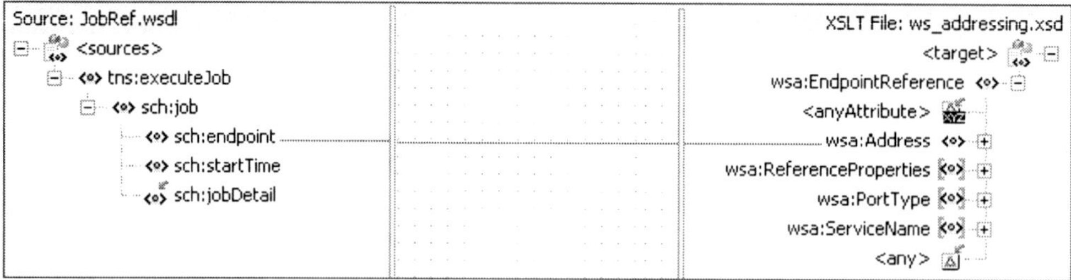

If we use an assign to directly populate the `<Address>` element, then BPEL, by default, creates an initialized `<EndpointReference>` element containing all the other optional elements (each with an empty value).

Updating the endpoint

Finally, we use another copy rule to dynamically set the partner link. The key difference here is that the **target** of the copy rule is the **JobService PartnerLink**, as shown in the following screenshot:

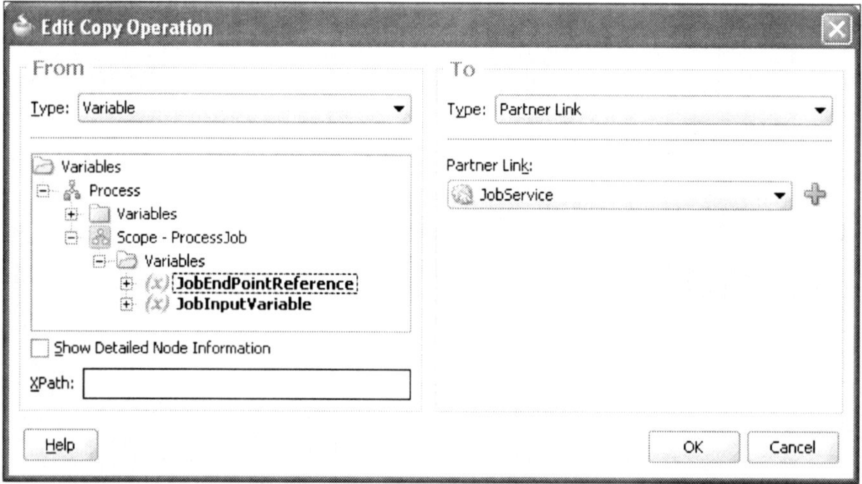

Now, when we invoke the **JobService**, via the **PartnerLink**, it will dynamically route the request to the updated endpoint.

Recycling the scheduling file

As we've already covered, the scheduling process is triggered by the file adapter reading in the `schedule.xml` file. As part of this activity, the file adapter will move it to an **archive** directory to ensure that the file is processed just once.

However, in our case, we actually want the file adapter to process the scheduling file on a daily basis, and to do this, we need to move the file back into the directory being polled by the adapter.

For this purpose, we have defined the following two directories:

```
<SOA_HOME>/scheduler/config
<SOA_HOME>/scheduler/execute
```

When creating our scheduling process, we have configured the file adapter to poll the `execute` directory on a regular basis (for example, every five minutes), and archive processed files to the `config` directory.

When the `schedule.xml` file is placed into the `execute` directory for the first time, this will trigger file adapter to pick up the file and launch the scheduler process, and at the same time, move the schedule file into the `config` directory.

Within the scheduler process, we then invoke the file adapter to move the `schedule.xml` file from the `config` directory back to the `execute` directory (see *Chapter 3, Service-enabling Existing Systems* for details on how to do this). However, rather than invoking the `moveFile` operation immediately, we have placed a `<wait>` activity in front of it that waits until the `startTime` defined at the head of the schedule file, as shown in the following code snippet:

```
<?xml version="1.0" encoding="UTF-8" ?>
<schedule xmlns="http://rubiconred.com/obay/xsd/schedule">
    <startTime>0:2:55.125</startTime>
    <job>
      ...
    </job>
</schedule>
```

This has a couple of advantages. The first is we use the `schedule.xml` file to control when the scheduling process is run, as opposed to configuring the file adapter to poll the `execute` directory once every 24 hours and then deploy the process at the right time to start the clock counting.

The other advantage is that most of the time the `schedule.xml` file resides in the `config` directory. Thus while the file is in this directory, we can go in and modify the schedule to add new jobs or update and delete existing jobs, which will then be picked up the next time the scheduler is executed.

Summary

In this chapter, we have looked at the more advanced messaging constructs supported by the Oracle SOA Suite, and how we can use this to support some of the more complex but relatively common message interaction patterns used in a typical SOA deployment.

We have also used this as an opportunity to introduce some of the more advanced BPEL activities and features such as the **Pick** and **FlowN** activity, as well as dynamic partner links.

While we have not covered every possible pattern, hopefully you should now have a good understanding of how the SOA Suite utilizes WS-Addressing, as well as how we can leverage correlation sets in BPEL to support message interactions that go beyond a single synchronous or asynchronous request and reply. You should now be able to apply this understanding to support your particular requirements.

17
Workflow Patterns

So far we've used workflow for simple task approval in conjunction with the worklist application. However, human workflows are often more complex, often involving multiple participants as well as requiring the task list to be integrated into the user's existing user interface rather than accessing it through a standalone worklist application.

In this chapter, we look at these common requirements. First, we examine how to manage workflows involving complex chains of approval, including parallel approvers and the different options that are available. Next, we look at the Workflow Service API, and how we can use that to completely transform the look and feel of the workflow service.

Managing multiple participants in a workflow

The process for validating items that have been flagged as suspicious, is a classic workflow scenario that may potentially involve multiple participants.

The first step in the workflow requires an oBay administrator to check whether the item is suspect. Assuming the case is straightforward, they can either approve or reject the item and complete the workflow.

This is pretty straightforward. However, for gray areas, the oBay administrator needs to defer making a decision. In this scenario, we have a second step in which the item is submitted to a panel who can vote on whether to approve or reject the item.

There are two approaches to modeling this workflow; one is to model each step as a separate human task and the other is to model it as a single human task containing multiple assignments and routing policies. Each approach has its own advantages and disadvantages, so we will look at each in turn to understand the differences.

Using multiple assignment and routing policies

For our `checkSuspectItem` process, we are first going to take the approach of combining the two workflow steps into a single human task. The first step in the workflow is the familiar single approval step, where we assign the task to the `oBayAdministrator` group.

The task takes a single non-editable parameter of type `suspectItem`, which contains the details of the item in question as well as why it has been flagged as suspect. The definition of this is shown as follows:

```
<xsd:element name="suspectItem"        type="act:tSuspectItem"/>

<xsd:complexType name="tSuspectItem">
  <xsd:sequence>
    <xsd:element name="item"          type="act:ItemType"/>
    <xsd:element name="reasonCode"    type="xsd:string" />
    <xsd:element name="reasonDesc"    type="xsd:string"/>
  </xsd:sequence>
</xsd:complexType>
```

Determining the outcome by a group vote

For the second step in the workflow, we are going to define a participant type of **Parallel**; this participant type allows us to allocate the same task to multiple participants in parallel with the final outcome being determined by how each participant within the group votes. The task definition form for the **Parallel** participant type is shown in the following screenshot:

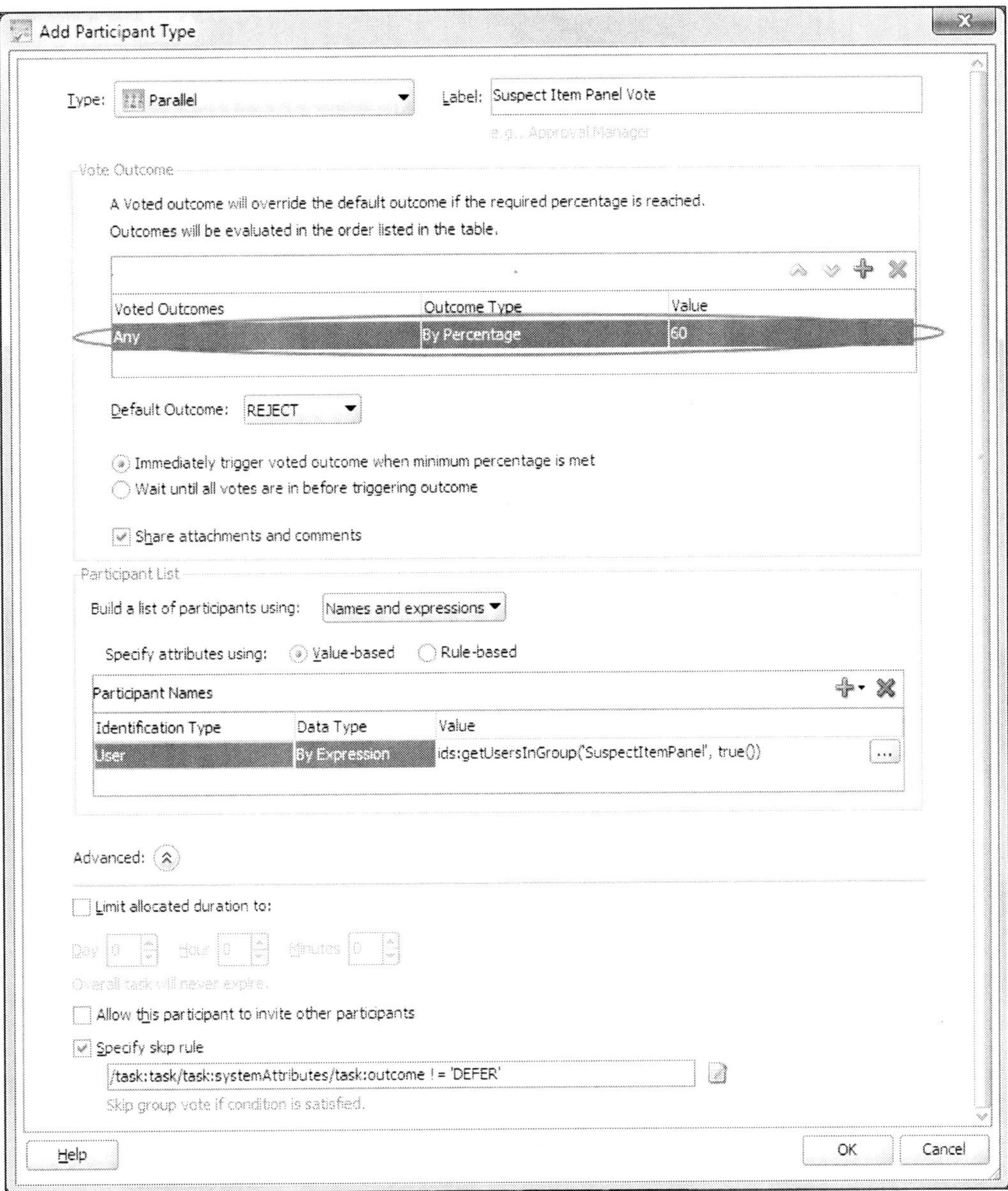
Add Participant Type
Type: Parallel
Label: Suspect Item Panel Vote
e.g., Approval Manager
Vote Outcome
A Voted outcome will override the default outcome if the required percentage is reached.
Outcomes will be evaluated in the order listed in the table.
Voted Outcomes
Outcome Type
Value
Any
By Percentage
60
Default Outcome: REJECT
Immediately trigger voted outcome when minimum percentage is met
Wait until all votes are in before triggering outcome
Share attachments and comments
Participant List
Build a list of participants using: Names and expressions
Specify attributes using: Value-based Rule-based
Participant Names
Identification Type
Data Type
Value
User
By Expression
ids:getUsersInGroup('SuspectItemPanel', true())
Advanced:
Limit allocated duration to:
Day
Hour
Minutes
Overall task will never expire.
Allow this participant to invite other participants
Specify skip rule
/task:task/task:systemAttributes/task:outcome != 'DEFER'
Skip group vote if condition is satisfied.
Help
OK
Cancel

Voting on the outcome

The first section, **Vote Outcome**, is where we specify the percentage of votes required for an outcome to take effect, such as a majority or a unanimous decision, as well as a default outcome in case no agreement is reached.

The size of the majority can be a fixed amount (for example, 60 percent as in our case), or can be based on an XPath expression, which could calculate this value dynamically at runtime (for example, if we wanted to calculate the percentage based on the number of voters).

We can specify the same value regardless of the outcome, as in our case, where we have specified **Any** (circled previously). Or, we can specify different thresholds for each outcome. When specifying different values for each outcome, the outcomes are evaluated in the order listed in the table.

In addition, we need to specify what the default outcome is if there isn't an agreement. In our case, we want to `'REJECT'` the item.

The final option we have is to specify whether all votes should be counted or if once we have sufficient votes on which to make a decision, the outcome should be triggered. In this scenario, any outstanding subtasks will be withdrawn.

In our case, the panel consists of three members, so as soon as two have approved the task, the required consensus will have been achieved and the third member will have their task withdrawn.

Sharing attachments and comments

When panel members are considering their decision, they may want to confer with one another. By default, anyone assigned a task will be able to see comments and attachments made by participants in previous steps of the task (that is, the oBay administrator). However, they won't be able to see comments made by other panel members.

To enable the sharing of attachments and comments between panel members, we've selected the **Share attachments and comments** checkbox.

Assigning participants

In the next section, **Participant List**, we need to specify the participants who are going to vote on the task. Our requirement is to assign the task to all users in the voting panel. To enable this, we've defined the group `SuspectItemPanel` in our user repository.

We don't want to allocate the task to the group, as this would only allow one user from the group to acquire and process the task. Rather, we want to allocate it to all members of the group. To do that, we can use the **Identity Service** XPath function `ids:getUsersInGroup`, illustrated as follows:

```
ids:getUsersInGroup ('SuspectItemPanel', true())
```

Doing this will effectively create and assign a separate subtask to every member of the group.

Skipping the second step

There is an issue with this approach so far, in that the second step of the workflow (that is, the Suspect Item Panel Vote) will always be executed regardless of what happens in the first step. To prevent this, we've specified the following skip rule:

```
/task:task/task:systemAttributes/task:outcome != 'DEFER'
```

The skip rule lets you specify an XPath expression, which evaluates to a `boolean` value. If it evaluates to true, then the corresponding participant will be skipped in the task.

In our case, we are testing the outcome taken by the oBay administrator in the previous step. If they didn't defer it, but chose to either accept or reject the item, then this step is skipped.

Using multiple human tasks

The other approach to this workflow is to model each step as a separate human task in its own right, each with a single assignment and routing policy.

With this approach, you get a lot more control over how you want to handle each step, since most of the runtime behavior of the human task is defined at the task level, allowing you to specify different parameters, expiration policies, notification settings, and task forms for each step in the workflow. In addition, on completion of every step, control is returned to the BPEL process, allowing you to carry out some additional processing before executing the next step in the workflow.

One of the drawbacks to this approach is that you need to specify a lot more information (roughly n times as much, where n is the number of tasks that you have), and often you may be replicating the same information across multiple task definitions as well as having to specify the handling of outcomes for multiple tasks within your BPEL process.

This not only requires more work upfront, but results in a larger, more complicated BPEL process that is not so intuitive to understand and often harder to maintain.

Linking individual human tasks

The other potential issue is that the second task doesn't include the comments, task history, and attachments from the previous task. In our case, this is important as we want the members of the panel to see any comments made by the oBay administrator before they deferred the task.

BPEL allows us to link tasks within the same BPEL process together. To do this double-click on the task in the BPEL process that you wish to link to a preceding task. This will open the **BPEL Human Task Configuration** window. From here, select the **Advanced** tab, and you will be presented with a variety of options.

If you select the checkbox **Include task history from:**, then you will be presented with a drop-down list of all the preceding human tasks defined in the BPEL process, as illustrated in the following screenshot.

By selecting one of these, your task is automatically linked to that task and will inherit its task history, comments, and attachments.

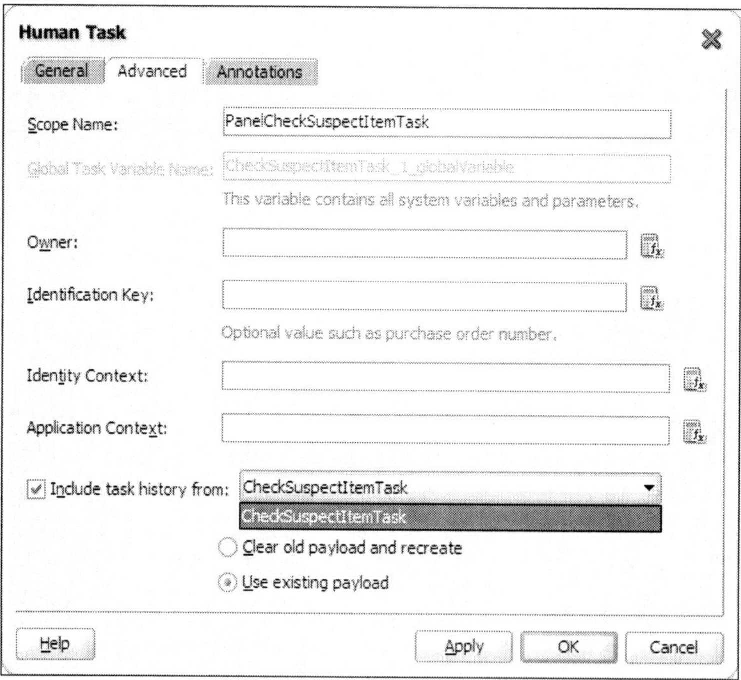

The final choice is whether you wish to use the payload from the previous task or create a new payload. This is decided by selecting the appropriate option.

Using the workflow API

If we look at the Order Fulfillment process, which is used to complete the sale for items won at an auction, it is a prime candidate for Human Workflow, as it will need to proceed through the following steps in order to complete the sale:

1. Buyer specifies shipping details (for example, address and method of postage)
2. Seller confirms shipping cost
3. Buyer notifies the seller that a payment for the item has been made
4. Seller confirms receipt of payment
5. Seller notifies the buyer that the item has been shipped
6. Buyer confirms receipt of item

You may recall from *Chapter 10, oBay Introduction* that we've decided to build a custom user interface for oBay's customers. As part of the UI, we need to enable users to perform each task required to complete the Order Fulfillment process.

One way to achieve this would be to use the worklist portlets and embed them directly within the oBay UI. However, oBay wants to make the user's experience a lot more seamless, so that users are not even aware that they are interacting with any kind of workflow system.

The workflow service provides a set of APIs just for this kind of scenario. These APIs are exposed as a set of SOAP-based web services, and there is an equivalent set of APIs for local and remote Enterprise Java Beans.

Indeed, the worklist application uses the same APIs. However, rather than invoking these APIs directly from our oBay UI, we are going to build our own **Task Based Business Service**, which acts as a façade around these underlying services. This will give us the architecture depicted in the following diagram:

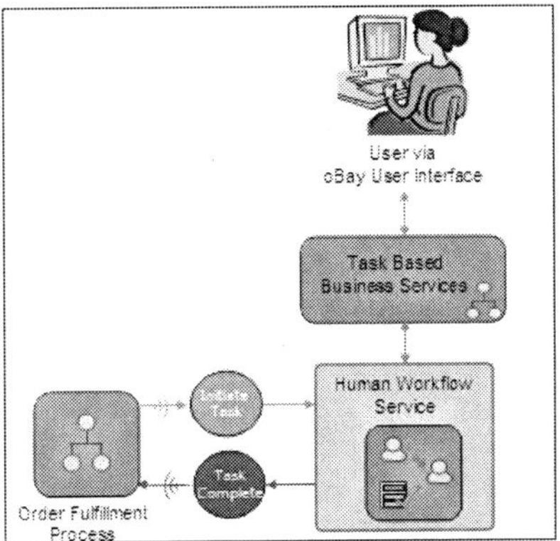

As we will be using BPEL to implement our Task Based Business Services, it makes sense to use the Web Service API (in the same way that any BPEL process containing a human task does).

If you compare this to our architecture outlined in *Chapter 10, oBay Introduction*, you will notice that we've decided not to wrap a virtual service layer around the workflow service; there are two key reasons for this.

First, if you look at the service description for the workflow services, they already provide a very well defined abstract definition of the service. Hence if you were to redesign the interface, they probably wouldn't look very different.

Secondly, whenever we include a human workflow task within our composite, JDeveloper automatically generates a lot of code which directly uses these services. Thus, if we wanted to put a virtual layer over these services, we would need to ensure that all our human workflow tasks also went via this layer, which is not a trivial activity.

So the reality is that adding a virtual services layer would gain us very little, but would take a lot of effort and we would lose a lot of the advantages provided by the development environment.

Defining the order fulfillment human task

For our `OrderFulfillment` process, we are taking the approach of combining all six workflow steps into a single human task (the `OrderFulfillmentTask.task`). Now this isn't a perfect fit for some of the reasons we've already touched on, so we will look at how we address each of these issues as we encounter them.

Within our task definition, we've defined two possible **Outcomes** for the task, either `COMPLETED` or `ABORTED` (where for some reason, the sale fails to proceed). In addition, in the **BPEL Human Task Configuration** window, we have configured the **Task Title** to be set to the item title and set the **Initiator** to be the seller of the item.

Specifying task parameters

A key design consideration is to decide on what parameter(s) we are going to pass to the task, taking into account that we need to pass in the superset of parameters required by each step in the workflow.

For our task, we will have a single parameter of type `order`, which contains all the data required for our task. The definition for this is shown as follows:

```
<xsd:element name="order"    type="act:tOrder"/>
```

```
<xsd:complexType name="tOrder">
  <xsd:sequence>
    <xsd:element name="orderNo"      type="xsd:string"/>
    <xsd:element name="orderDesc"    type="xsd:string" />
    <xsd:element name="itemId"       type="act:tItemId"/>
    <xsd:element name="sellerId"     type="act:tUserId"/>
    <xsd:element name="buyerId"      type="act:tUserId"/>
    <xsd:element name="orderDetail"  type="act:tOrderDetail" />
    <xsd:element name="shipTo"       type="act:tShipTo" />
  </xsd:sequence>
</xsd:complexType>

<xsd:complexType name="tOrderDetail">
  <xsd:sequence>
    <xsd:element name="orderDate"      type="xsd:date"/>
    <xsd:element name="orderStatus"    type="xsd:string"/>
    <xsd:element name="quantity"       type="xsd:int"/>
    <xsd:element name="itemPrice"      type="xsd:decimal"/>
    <xsd:element name="subTotal"       type="xsd:decimal"/>
    <xsd:element name="shippingPrice"  type="xsd:decimal"/>
    <xsd:element name="totalPrice"     type="xsd:decimal"/>
    <xsd:element name="lastUpdateDate" type="xsd:dateTime"/>
    <xsd:element name="nextAction"     type="xsd:string "/>
  </xsd:sequence>
</xsd:complexType>

<xsd:complexType name="tShipTo">
  <xsd:sequence>
    <xsd:element name="shippingName"           type="xsd:string"/>
    <xsd:element name="shippingAddress"        type="act:tAddress"/>
    <xsd:element name="additionalInstructions" type="xsd:string"/>
  </xsd:sequence>
</xsd:complexType>
```

Before we go any further, it's worth spending a moment to highlight some of the key components of this:

- **OrderNo**: Potentially we could have multiple orders per auction (for example, if oBay were to support a Dutch auction format at some point in the future), so every order will need its own unique identifier.

  As we have made the decision to have a single human task, we have a one-to-one mapping between an order and an `OrderFulfillment` human task, so will use the task number as our order number.

- **ShipTo**: This contains the details provided of where the item is to be sent to as well as the preferred delivery method. This needs to be specified by the buyer in the first step of the workflow.
- **ShippingPrice**: Once the buyer has specified the shipping details, the seller can confirm the cost of shipping. This needs to be added to the `subTotal` to calculate the `total` amount payable.
- **OrderStatus**: This field is updated after every step to track where we are in the order fulfillment process.

The most obvious problem from our requirement is that at each step in the process, we will need to update different fields in the `order` parameter and that some of these fields are calculated.

If we were using the default simple task forms generated by JDeveloper for the worklist application, then this poses a problem, since you can only specify at the parameter level whether the content of the payload is read-only or editable.

By default, whether the content of the payload is read-only or editable is the same at every step in the task. However, a new feature in 11gR1 allows us to configure different access levels for each participant in the task.

To configure this, select the **Access** tab in the **Task Definition** form and set content-level access to **Fine grained**. This will allow us to define different access rights (that is, Read or Write) for each type of content (for example, Payload, Comments, Attachments), for each participant in the task.

One workaround is to customize the generated form, which is definitely possible, if not entirely straightforward. However, in our scenario, we are developing our own custom built user interface, so this is not an issue.

Specifying the routing policy

For the `OrderFulfillment` task, we have specified six **Assignment and Routing Policies**, one for each step of the workflow. Each one is of type **SingleApprover** and is assigned dynamically to either the seller or buyer as appropriate, as illustrated in the following image:

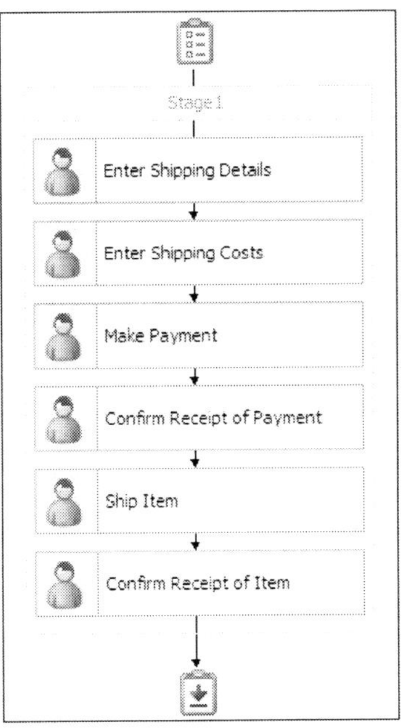

Notification settings

The only other potential issue for us is that we need to share generic notification settings for each step in the workflow. For our purposes, this is fine as we just want to send a generic notification to our seller or buyer every time a task is assigned to them to notify them that they now need to perform an action in order to complete the sale.

However, if we wanted to send more specific notifications, then we have two options. The first is to configure the task to publish a Business Event onto the Event Delivery Network whenever the task is assigned. To do this, select the **Events** tab on the task definition and select the **Trigger Workflow Event** checkbox, as shown in the following screenshot:

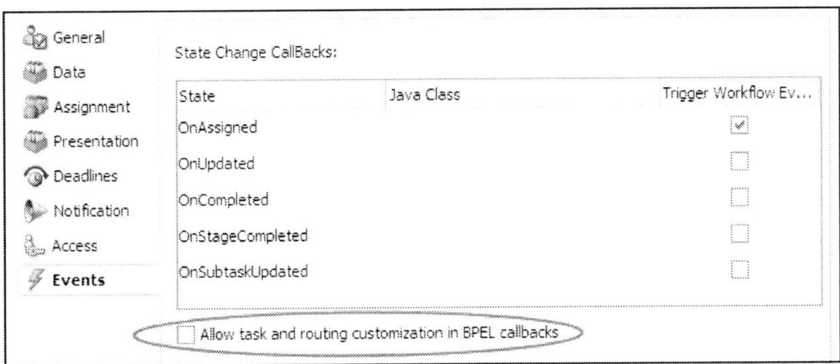

This will cause a business event to be sent whenever the task is assigned to another participant. The business event contains details of the task object, as well as a set of properties that are populated, based on the context of the fired event.

We can now write a simple BPEL process to subscribe to this event, which, on receipt of the event, can generate the required notification and send it using the **User Notification** service.

The other approach is to use the `OrderFulfillment` process to generate the notification. By default, the BPEL process will only receive a callback from the workflow service upon completion of the task.

However, if we go back to the **Events** tab and select the checkbox **Allow task and routing customizations in BPEL callbacks** (circled in the preceding screenshot), this will modify our BPEL process to receive callbacks when either a task is assigned, updated, or completed, as well as when a subtask is updated.

It does this by replacing the **Receive** activity, which receives the completed task callback with a **Pick** activity embedded within a **While** activity that essentially loops until the task is completed, as illustrated in the following diagram:

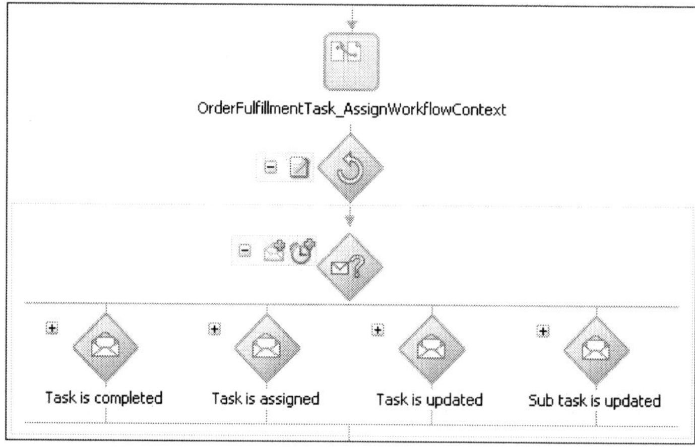

As you can see, the **Pick** activity contains an `onMessage` branch for each potential callback. You then just add any additional processing that is required to the appropriate `onMessage` branch.

In our case, we might add a switch to the **Task is assigned** branch to check where we are in the workflow and then based on that generate the appropriate notification.

Now that we have defined our **Order Fulfillment** task, the next step is to implement our task-based business services that will act upon it. If we look at the type of interactions that the user will have with our **Order Fulfillment** task, we can see that they are split into two categories. The first are query-based tasks, and the second are tasks that change the state of the workflow task. We will look at the query-based tasks first.

Querying task instances

By analyzing our requirements, we can see that we need to support the following query-based operations:

- `getSoldItems`: Returns a list of all items sold by the specified seller and provides details to those items which have an outstanding task assigned to the seller
- `getPurchasedItems`: Similar to the previous operation, but returns a list of all items bought by the specified buyer
- `getOrderDetails`: Returns detailed information about a specific order

It's worth noting that the first two operations are not just returning the current task list for either the buyer or seller, but a complete list of all applicable items, regardless of whether the task is currently assigned to the buyer or seller.

We are going to implement each of these operations as a separate BPEL process within our `OrderFulfillment` composite. To do so, we will make use of the **Task Query Service** provided by the Workflow Service. This provides a number of methods for querying tasks based on a variety of search criteria including status, keywords, attribute values, and so on.

> Instead of implementing each of the operations as a BPEL process, an alternative approach would be to perform the required transformation in the proxy Mediator and route the request directly to the **Task Query Service**.
>
> The advantage of this approach is that it's more lightweight and thus will be slightly more performant. However, the nature of the XSLT that we would need for the transformation isn't supported by the graphical mapping tool and thus would need to be handcoded.
>
> So in the interests of maintainability, we have decided to use BPEL and leverage the appropriate XPath within BPEL to perform the transformation.

Defining an external reference for the Task Query Service

The WSDL for the Task Query Service is located at:

```
http://<hostname>:<port>/integration/services/TaskQueryService/
TaskQueryService?WSDL
```

Here, `hostname` represents the name of the machine on which the SOA server is running and `port` represents the port number. If you inspect the WSDL, you will see that it defines two ports: `TaskQueryServicePortSAML` and `TaskQueryServicePort` each with its own corresponding endpoint, shown as follows:

```
<service name="TaskQueryService">
  <port name="TaskQueryServicePortSAML"
        binding="tns:TaskQueryServiceSOAPBinding">
    <soap:address location="http://localhost:8001/integration/service
                        s/TaskQueryService/TaskQueryService2/*"/>
  </port>
  <port name="TaskQueryServicePort"
            binding="tns:TaskQueryServiceSOAPBinding">
    <soap:address location="http://localhost:8001/integration/service
                        s/TaskQueryService/TaskQueryService"/>
  </port>
</service>
```

By default, the composite will always invoke the `TaskQueryServicePortSAML` endpoint, which, as the name suggests, expects a SAML token to authenticate the client invoking the service.

If you have configured your composite to require authentication and propagate identity (See *Chapter 20, Defining Security and Management Policies* for further details), then this should work as expected. However, if you are using the `authenticate` operation provided by the Task Query Service, then this will always result in a security exception.

For these scenarios, you need to invoke the `TaskQueryServicePort` endpoint. To do this, you either take a local copy of the WSDL and remove the `TaskQueryServicePortSAML` port definition, or update your `composite.xml` (using the source view) to remove the appropriate `binding.ws` entry, highlighted following code sample:

```
<reference name="TaskQueryService"
           ui:wsdlLocation="http://localhost:8001/integration/
           services/TaskQueryService/TaskQueryService?WSDL">
  <interface.wsdl interface="http://xmlns.oracle.com/bpel/workflow/
```

```
                taskQueryService#wsdl.interface(TaskQueryService)"/>
    <binding.ws port="http://xmlns.oracle.com/bpel/workflow/taskQuery
                    Service#wsdl.endpoint(TaskQueryService/TaskQuer
                    yServicePortSAML)"
                location="http://localhost:8001/integration/services/
                         TaskQueryService/TaskQueryService?WSDL">
    </binding.ws>
    <binding.ws port="http://xmlns.oracle.com/bpel/workflow/taskQuery
                    Service#wsdl.endpoint(TaskQueryService/TaskQuer
                    yServicePort)"
                location="http://localhost:8001/integration/services/
                         TaskQueryService/TaskQueryService?WSDL"/>
</reference>
```

User authentication

As with the worklist application, the Task Query Service will only return details of tasks for which you have access, such as if the task is assigned to you or you are the task owner or initiator (see *Chapter 6, Adding in Human Workflow* for details).

For authentication purposes (unless SAML is being used), the `authenticate` operation is provided. This takes an element of type `credential`, which consists of the following parameters:

- `login`: User ID, as defined to the underlying Identity Service.
- `Password`: Corresponding password for the specified user.
- `identityContext`: The identity service enables you to configure multiple identity repositories, each containing its own set of users. Each repository is identified by its realm name.

  The `identityContext` should be set to the name of the realm in which the user is defined. `jazn.com` is the realm of the sample user community.
- `onBehalfOfUser`: An optional element, which allows a user with administrative privileges to create a workflow context on behalf of another user by specifying their user ID here.

Upon successful authentication, a `workflowContext` is returned, which is then used in any subsequent calls to the workflow service.

If you are calling a single workflow service, you can provide the authentication details as part of that service invocation, instead of a separate call to the authentication service. This removes the overhead of having to make two calls to the query service.

Creating the credential element

When creating the `credential` element, we need to ensure that it doesn't include an empty `onBehalfOfUser` element, as the service will try and create a workflow context for this "*empty*" user, which of course will fail and return an error.

This is an easy error to make, since the first time we use an `assign` statement to populate any subelement of credential (for example, doing a copy to populate the `login` element), BPEL PM, by default, will create an initialized `credential` element containing all its subelements, including `onBehalfOfUser` (each with an empty value).

A simple way round this is to assign a fragment of XML, such as the following:

```
<credential xmlns="http://xmlns.oracle.com/bpel/workflow/common">
  <login/>
  <password/>
  <identityContext>jazn.com</identityContext>
</credential>
```

Directly to credential, this acts as a template into which we can copy the required values for `login` and `password`. We do this using a copy operation within an assign statement. The key difference is that we specify an **XML Fragment** as the **From Type**, as shown in the following screenshot:

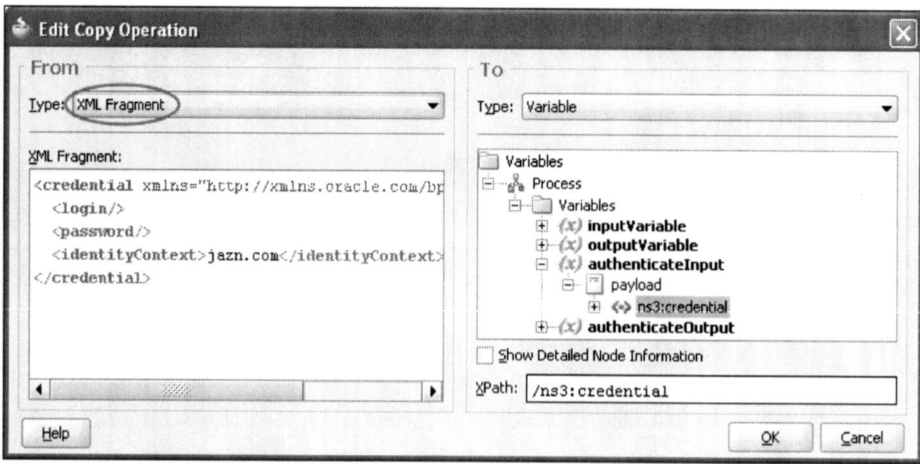

Note that we have specified the default namespace in the `credential` element so that all elements are created in the appropriate namespace.

Querying tasks

The `queryTask` operation returns a list of tasks for a user, which you can filter based on criteria similar to that provided by the worklist application. The following screenshot shows the structure of the input it expects:

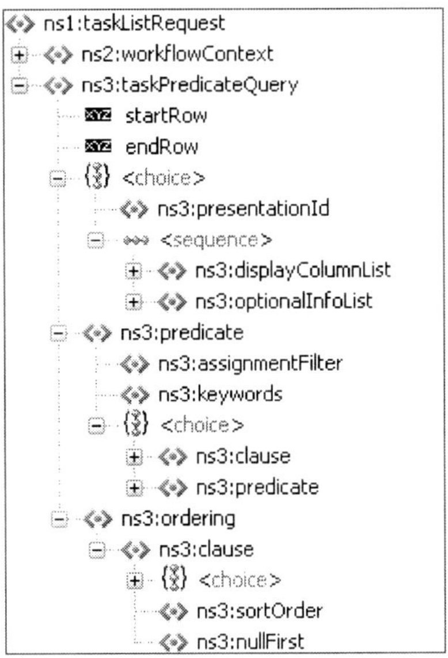

We can see that the `taskListRequest` consists of two elements: the `workflowContext`, which should contain the value returned by our authentication request and the `taskPredicateQuery`, which defines the actual query that we wish to make.

The `taskPredicateQuery` consists of the following core elements:

- `presentationId`: ID of a pre-defined presentation that specifies the columns, optional info, and ordering for the query. If specified, then the `displayColumnList`, `optionalInfoList`, and `ordering` elements should **not** be specified.
- `displayColumnList`: Allows us to specify which attributes of the task (for example, title, created by, created date, and so on) we want to be included in the resultset.

- `optionalInfoList`: Allows us to specify any additional information we want returned with each task, such as comments, task history, and so on.
- `predicate`: Used to specify the filter conditions for which tasks we want returned.
- `ordering`: Allows us to specify one or more columns on which we want to sort the result set.

Pre-defined presentations can be created and maintained via the User Metadata Service. When creating a presentation, we specify essentially the same information as defined by the `displayColumnList`, `optionalInfoList`, and `ordering` elements.

The two attributes `startRow` and `endRow` are used to control whether the entire result set is returned by the query or just a subset. To return the entire result set, set both attributes to zero. To return just a subset of the result set, set the attributes appropriately. For example, to return the first ten tasks in the result set, you would set the `startRow` to be equal to 1 and the `endRow` to be equal to 10.

Specifying the display column list

The `displayColumnList` element list contained within the `taskPredicateQuery` allows us to define which task attributes (or columns) we want returned by our query.

Simply include in here one `displayColumn` entry per task attribute that we want returned. Valid values include `TaskNumber`, `Title`, `Priority`, `Creator`, `CreatedDate`, and `State`.

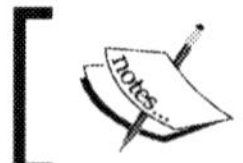

Display column names map directly to the columns names in the WFTASK table in the SOAINFRA database schema.

If we look at the WSDL definition for the `getSoldItems` operation, we can see that it returns the values `orderNo`, `itemId`, `orderDesc`, `buyerId`, `itemPrice`, `totalPrice`, `saleDate`, `orderStatus`, `lastUpdateDate`, and `nextAction`.

At first glance, only a couple of these match actual task attributes; when we created the task, we set the task `title` to hold `orderDesc` and the task attribute `updatedDate` maps to `lastUpdateDate`.

In addition, we have decided to use `taskNumber` for the `orderNo`, as this makes it a lot simpler to tie the two together.

However, the remaining fields are all held in the task payload, which we can't access through the `queryTask` operation. One solution would be to call the `getTaskDetails` operation for every row returned, but this would hardly be efficient. Fortunately, we have an alternative approach and that is to use flex fields.

Flex fields

Flex fields are a set of generic attributes attached to a task, which can be populated with information from the task payload. This information can be displayed in the task listing as well as used for querying and defining workflow rules in the worklist application.

Populating flex fields

The simplest way to initialize the flex fields is in the BPEL process, which creates the task. If you click on the **plus** sign next to a **Human Task** activity, this will expand the task, showing you the individual BPEL activities that are used to invoke it, as illustrated in the following screenshot:

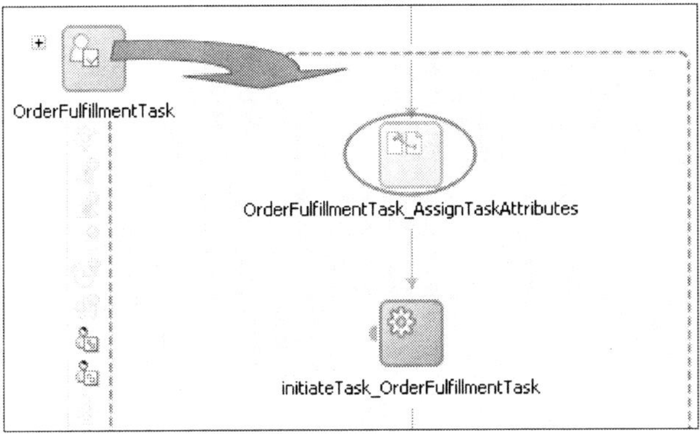

You will see that this starts with an **Assign** activity (circled), which is used to set the task attributes. To set the flex fields, simply open the **Assign** activity, and add an extra copy statement for each flex field required.

For our purposes, we will set the following flex fields in our **OrderFulfillmentTask**:

Flex field	Attribute
`textAttribute1`	`itemId`
`textAttribute2`	`buyerId`
`numberAttribute1`	`salePrice`
`numberAttribute2`	`totalPrice`
`dateAttribute1`	`saleDate`
`textAttribute3`	`orderStatus`
`textAttribute4`	`nextAction`

You will need to update the local variable `initiateTaskInput`, which will be defined in the scope with the same name as the Human Task (`OrderFulfillmentTask` in our case). The flex fields are located in the `systemMessageAttributes` element of the `task` element, as illustrated in the following screenshot:

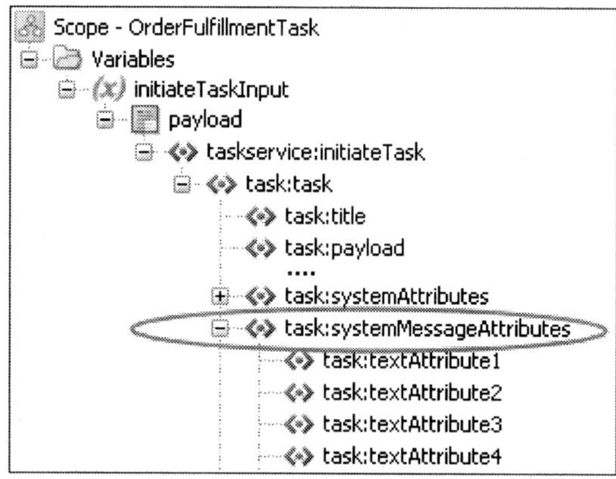

Accessing flex fields

Once we have populated the flex fields, we can access them in our query just like any other task attribute. This will give us a `displayColumnList` that looks as follows:

```
<displayColumnList
    xmlns="http://xmlns.oracle.com/bpel/workflow.taskQuery">
  <displayColumn>TaskNumber</displayColumn>
  <displayColumn>Title</displayColumn>
  <displayColumn>UpdatedDate</displayColumn>
  <displayColumn>TextAttribute1</displayColumn>
  <displayColumn>TextAttribute2</displayColumn>
  <displayColumn>NumberAttribute1</displayColumn>
```

```
    <displayColumn>NumberAttribute2</displayColumn>
    <displayColumn>DateAttribute1</displayColumn>
    <displayColumn>TextAttribute3</displayColumn>
    <displayColumn>TextAttribute4</displayColumn>
  </displayColumnList>
```

Specifying the query predicate

The next step is to specify the query `predicate` so that it only returns those tasks that we are interested in. We will first look at the query we need to construct to return all sold items for a particular seller.

The next screenshot shows the structure of the query `predicate`. The **assignmentFilter** allows us to specify a filter based on who the task is currently assigned to. Valid values are `Admin`, `All`, `Creator`, `My`, `Group`, `My+Group`, `Reportees`, `Owner`, `Previous`, or `Reviewer`.

For our purposes, we need to list all tasks related to items sold by the specified seller, so we will need to include those items which have tasks currently assigned to the buyer.

You may recall that when we defined our workflow, we assigned the initiator (or creator) of the task to be the seller, so we can use `Creator` as the **assignmentFilter**.

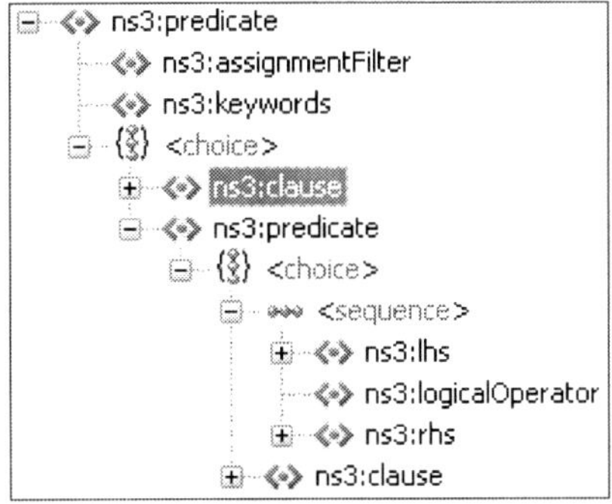

So far, our query will return all tasks created by the specified user, which could potentially include tasks created in other workflows, so we need to add an additional filter to further restrict our query.

One approach would be to use the **keywords** filter, which is an optional search string and if specified, will only return tasks where the string is contained in the task title, task identification key, or one of the task text flex fields. However, this probably won't result in the most efficient query. A better alternative is to implement a filter against the task definition name.

If we examine the structure of the query `predicate`, we can see that we have a choice between specifying a `clause` element (highlighted in the previous screenshot) or a `predicate` element. Either of these will allow us to achieve the same result.

However, the `clause` element (only the highlighted one) is deprecated in 11gR1 and is only there to provide backwards compatibility with SOA Suite 10.1.3.x. So, we will examine how we can use the `predicate` element to define our query.

> Looking at the previous screenshot, we can see there are two elements with the name `predicate`: the outermost one is of type `taskPredicateType` and the inner one is of type `predicateType`. This can be confusing as they have the same name, but a different structure. For the purposes of defining our query, we are using the innermost `predicate` element of type `predicateType`.

If we look at the structure of a `predicate`, we can see that we have a choice over its content. With the first option, the `predicate` is made up of the following sequence of elements:

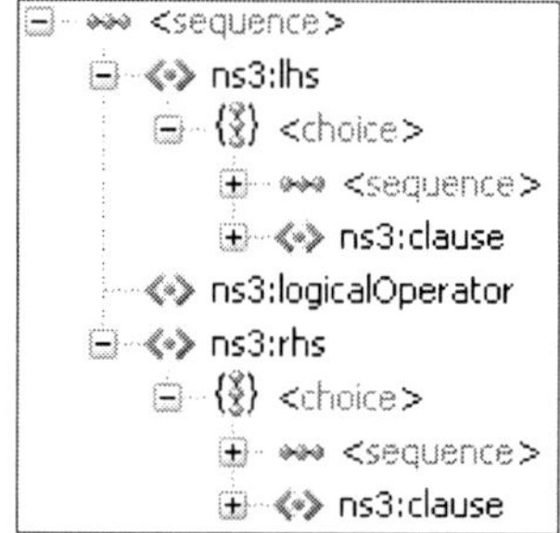

In this content model, both `lhs` and `rhs` are of type `predicateType`, with **logicalOperator** being able to take the value `AND` or `OR`. In other words, a `predicate` can be made up of two other predicates (and so on), each of which is evaluated separately with the results combined according to the logical operator.

Eventually, each of the leave predicates in the overall predicate tree must contain one or more clause elements, the structure of which is shown in the following screenshot:

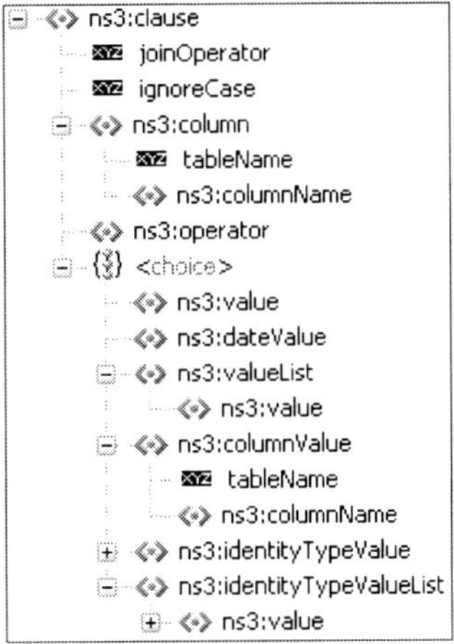

The `clause` element is made up of three core parts: the `column` element where we define the task attribute that we wish to query, the `operator` (for example, equal, not equal, and so on), and the value we want to compare it against.

The `column` consists of two parts:

- The attribute `tableName`: This should contain the name of the database table in the SOAINFRA schema that we wish to query. This will typically be the table WFTASK.
- The element `columnName`: This should contain the name of the column on the specified `tablename` that we wish to query (which, in our case, is `TaskDefinitionName`).

The `operator` specifies the type of comparison that we wish to carry out. The valid operators are as follows:

- **Standard operators**: `EQ` (Equal), `NEQ` (Not Equal), `GT` (Greater Than), `GTE` (Greater Than or Equal), `LT` (Less Than), and `LTE` (Less Than or Equal)
- **String operators**: `LIKE`, `NOT_LIKE`, `CONTAINS`, `NOT_CONTAINS`, `BEGINS`, `NOT_BEGINS`, `ENDS`, and `NOT_ENDS`
- **Date operators**: `BEFORE`, `AFTER`, `ON`, `NEXT_N_DAYS`, and `LAST_N_DAYS`
- **Value list operators**: `IN` and `NOT_IN`
- **Null operators**: `IS_NULL` and `IS_NOT_NULL`

The final part of the `clause` contains the value that we want to compare our task attribute against; here we have a choice of content, based on what we want to carry out. The valid options are as follows:

- `value`: Use this when we just want to compare the value of our task attribute against a single value.
- `dateValue`: This should be used in place of `value`, when the value we want to compare is a date.
- `valueList`: This can contain a list of one or more values, which we would use with either the `IN` or `NOT_IN` operator.
- `columnValue`: We would use this when we want to compare our task attribute against another task attribute. This has the same structure as the `column` element.
- `identityTypeValue`: We can use this to compare the value against an identity type (that is, user, group, or application role).
- `identityTypeValue`: This can contain a list of `identityTypeValue elements`, which we would use with either the `IN` or `NOT_IN` operator.

In addition, the `clause` element contains two attributes:

- `joinOperator`: This is only required when we have two or more clauses in the same `predicate`, and specifies how we want to chain additional clauses together. Valid values are `AND` or `OR`.
- `ignoreCase`: This takes a `boolean` value and allows us to specify whether string-based comparisons should be case sensitive.

In the case of our query, we want to restrict it to just return Order Fulfillment tasks. We can do that by querying on the column `TaskDefinitionName` in the table `WFTask`. Adding a clause to filter on this would give us the following predicate:

```
<predicate xmlns="http://xmlns.oracle.com/bpel/workflow/taskQuery">
    <assignmentFilter>Creator</assignmentFilter>
    <predicate>
        <clause>
            <column tableName="WFTask">
              <columnName>TaskDefinitionName</columnName>
            </column>
            <operator>EQ</operator>
            <value>OrderFulfillmentTask</value>
        </clause>
    </predicate>
</predicate>
```

Using flex fields in the query predicate

Specifying the query predicate for the buyer isn't quite so simple, as we want to list all tasks related to items bought by the specified buyer. So we will need to include those items which have tasks currently assigned to various sellers.

Unlike the seller's query, we can't use the `Creator` value as our assignment filter, and we can't use `My` either as this only returns tasks currently assigned to us. So the only option we have is to use `All` as our assignment filter. However, this will return all tasks currently in the system, so we need to find a way of restricting the list to just those tasks required by the buyer.

As you may recall, we have already defined the flex field `textAttribute1` to hold the `buyerId`, so we just need to add an extra clause to our predicate to test for this condition. This will give us a `predicate`, which looks as follows:

```
<predicate xmlns="http://xmlns.oracle.com/bpel/workflow/taskQuery">
    <assignmentFilter>All</assignmentFilter>
    <predicate>
        <clause>
            <column tableName="WFTask">
                <columnName>TaskDefinitionName</columnName>
            </column>
            <operator>EQ</operator>
            <value>OrderFulfillmentTask</value>
        </clause>
        <clause joinOperator="AND">
            <column tableName="WFTask">
                <columnName>TextAttribute1</columnName>
            </column>
            <operator>EQ</operator>
            <value>$buyerId </value>
        </clause>
    </predicate>
</predicate>
```

Here, `$buyerId` needs to be substituted with the actual `userId` of the buyer.

Ordering the data

The `ordering` element list contained within the `taskPredicateQuery` allows us to define which task attributes we want to order our result set by, the structure of which is shown in the following screenshot:

The `ordering` element can contain zero or more `clause` elements. When specifying multiple clause elements, the result set is sorted first on the first clause, then within that, on the second clause, and so on. The `clause` element contains the following elements:

- `column`: The column that we wish to sort on. It should be the name of one of the columns specified in the `DisplayColumnList`.
- `table`: The name of the table to which the ordering clause column belongs (this is nearly always `WFTASK`).
- `sortOrder`: Should be set to `ASCENDING or DESCENDING`.
- `nullFirst`: Takes a `boolean` value.

For our purposes, we want to order by sale date, which is held in `dateAttribute1`. This gives us an `ordering` element, which looks as follows:

```
<ordering xmlns="xmlns.oracle.com/bpel/workflow/taskQuery">
   <clause>
      <column>DateAttribute1</column>
      <table>WFTASK</table>
      <sortOrder>ASCENDING</sortOrder>
      <nullFirst>true</nullFirst>
   </clause>
</ordering>
```

> The simplest way to create the `taskPredicateQuery` is to create an **XML Fragment**, which can act as a template for the query and assign this with a single copy statement. Then just add any additional copy statements for those values which need to be specified at runtime in order to modify the template-generated value appropriately.

Getting task details

The final query-based operation we need to implement is `getOrderDetails`, which returns the order details for the specified `orderNo`. The Task Query Service provides two similar operations: `getTaskDetailsByNumber` and `getTaskDetailsById`.

As the `orderNo` corresponds to the `taskNumber`, it makes sense to call the `getTaskDetailsByNumber` operation. This just takes the standard `workflowContext` and the `taskNumber` as its input.

The only slight area of complexity is extracting the order from the task payload. This is because `payload` is defined as `xsd:any`, which means it can contain any value. Because of this, the XPath mapping tool can't determine the structure of the payload and thus can't visually map the **From** part of the operation.

Thus, you have to create the XPath manually. The simplest way to do this is to create a mapping from the task to your target variable using the visual editor and then modify the XPath manually, as shown in the following screenshot:

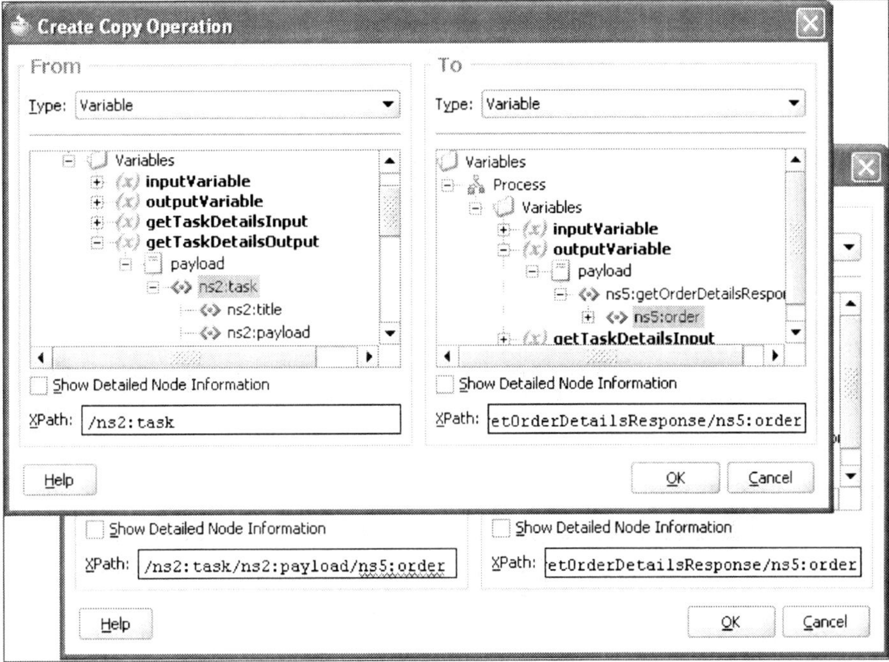

Updating a task instance

Our second category of task-based Business Service is one that allows the buyer or seller to perform actions against the workflow task. For the purpose of this section, we will look at the implementation of the `setShippingDetails` operation, though the other operations `submitInvoice`, `notifyPaymentMade`, `confirmPaymentReceived`, `notifyItemShipped`, and `confirmItemReceived` all follow the same basic pattern.

`setShippingDetails` is used to complete the first step in the workflow, namely, updating the task payload to contain the shipping name and address of the buyer as well as providing any additional shipping instructions. Finally, it needs to set the `outcome` of the current step to `COMPLETED` so that the task moves on to the next step in the workflow. The following screenshot shows the input fields for this operation:

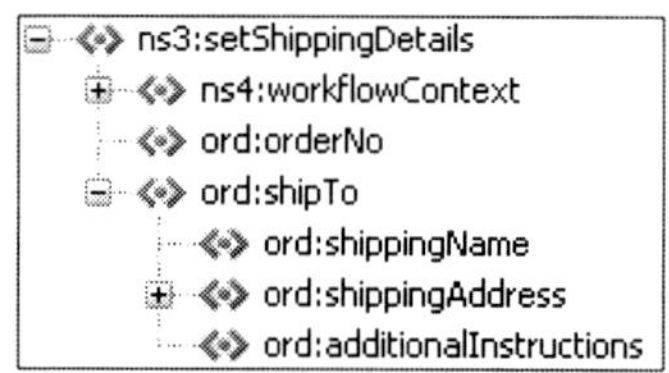

From this, we can see that it contains the buyer's `workflowContext`, which is required to authenticate with the Workflow Services, the `orderNo` that we will use to locate the appropriate Order Fulfillment task, and the actual `shipTo` details that we will use to update the task.

To implement this operation, we are going to make use of the `Task Service` provided by the Workflow Service. This provides a number of operations which act on a task.

The WSDL for the Task Service is located at:

```
http://<hostname>:<port>/integration/services/TaskService/
TaskServicePort?WSDL
```

Using the updateTask operation

Most of the tasks provided by this service are granular in nature and only update a specific part of a task. Thus they only require the `taskId` and the corresponding part of the task being updated as input.

However, our operation needs to update multiple parts of a task, that is, the order held in the task payload, the corresponding flex fields, and the task outcome. For this, we will use the `updateTask` operation. The following screenshot shows its expected input:

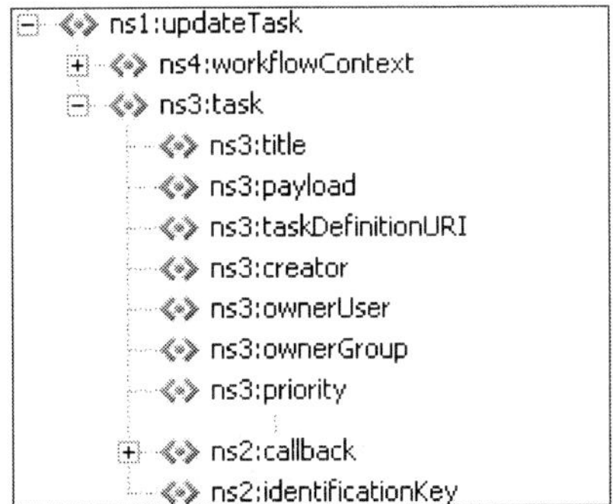

From this, we can see that it expects the standard `workflowContext` as well as the complete, updated `task` element.

The simplest way to achieve this is to use the Task Query Service to get an up-to-date copy of our `task`. We do this in exactly the same way we did for our `getOrderDetails` operation. Then, modify it as appropriate and call the `updateTask` operation to make the changes.

Updating the task payload

The only area of complexity is updating the `order` directly within the task payload. This is for the same reason we mentioned earlier when implementing the `getOrderDetails` operation; as the payload is defined as `xsd:any`, we can't use the XPath mapping tool to visually map the updates.

The simplest way to work around this is to first extract the `order` from the task payload into a local variable (which we do in exactly the same way that we did for our `getOrderDetails` operation).

Once we've done this, we can update the `shipTo` element of the `order` to hold the shipping details as well as update `nextAction` to **Enter Shipping Costs** to reflect the next step in the workflow.

Once we have updated the `order`, we must insert it into the task payload. This is essentially the reverse of the copy operation we used to extract it.

Updating the task flex fields

Once we have updated the task payload, we then need to update the corresponding flex fields so that they remain synchronized with the order. We do this using an **Assign** activity in a similar way that we used to set the flex fields when creating the task in our `OrderFulfillment` process.

Updating the task outcome

Finally we need to set the task outcome for the current step (this is effectively the same as specifying a task action through the worklist application). In our case, we have defined two potential outcomes: `COMPLETED` or `ABORTED`.

For `setShippingDetails` (as with all of our operations), we want to set the task outcome to `COMPLETED`, note this won't actually complete the task, rather it completes the current assignment, and in our case, as all our routing policies are single approver, it will complete the current step in the workflow and move the task on to the next step. Only once the final step is completed will the task complete and control be returned to the `OrderFulfillment` BPEL process.

To set the task outcome, we only need to set the `outcome` element (located in the task `systemAttributes` element) to `COMPLETED`. However, it isn't quite that straightforward; if you look at the actual task data returned by the `getTaskDetailsByNumber` operation, the `outcome` element isn't present.

Thus if we use a standard `copy` operation to try and assign a value to this element, we will get an XPath exception.

Instead, what we need to do is create the `outcome` element and its associated value and append it to the `systemAttributes` element. To do this within the **Assign** activity, use an **Append Operation**, as shown in the following screenshot:

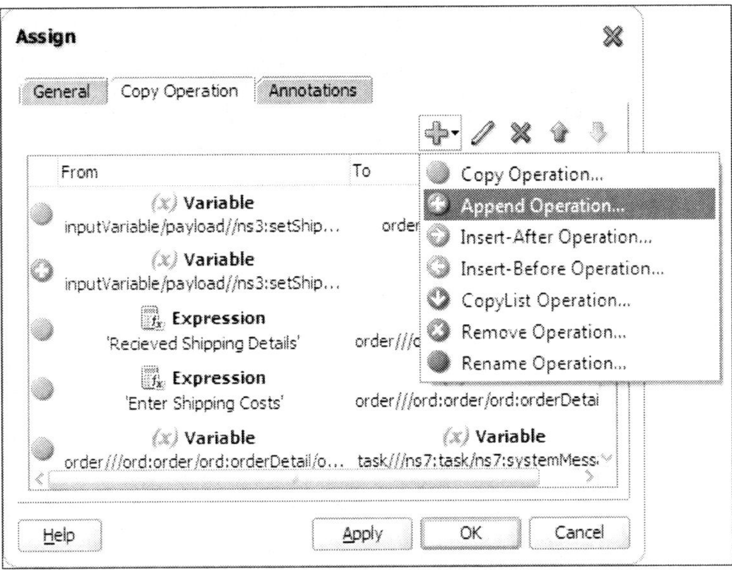

The simplest way to create the `outcome` element is to use an **XML Fragment** and append it to the `systemAttributes` element, as shown in the following screenshot:

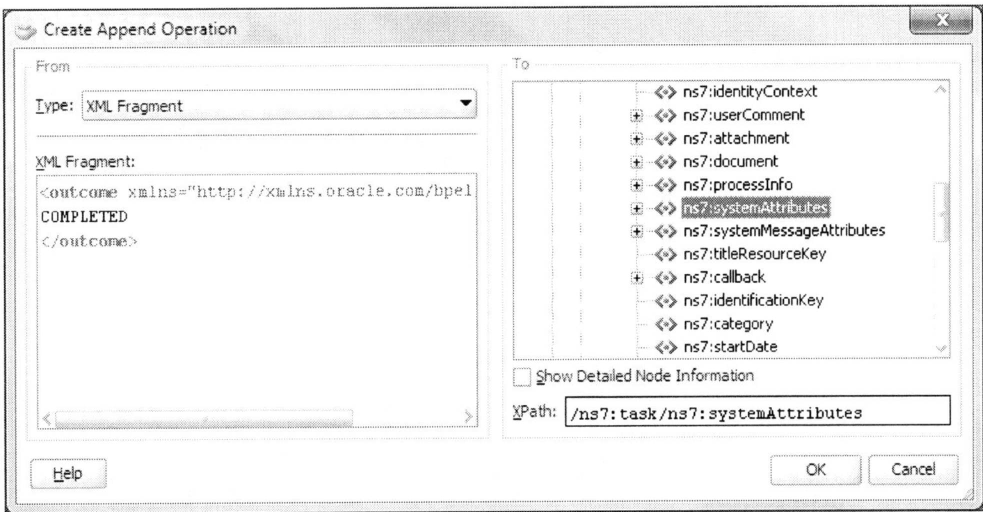

Once we've done this, we will have a completed task, so all that remains is to call `updateTask` to complete the operation.

Summary

Human workflow is a key requirement for many projects. Quite often, these are a lot more demanding than just a simple approval. In this chapter, we've looked at some of the more complex, yet common use, cases and shown how these can be addressed in a quite straightforward fashion by the workflow service.

In addition, we've demonstrated how we can use the Workflow API to completely abstract out the underlying Workflow Service and present a completely different appearance to the consumer of the service.

Although we have not covered every detail of the Workflow Service, you should now have a good appreciation of some of its more advanced features, the versatility this gives you, and more importantly, how you can apply them to solve some of the more common workflow requirements.

18
Using Business Rules to Implement Services

We have looked at how we can use the rules engine to define business rules that can then be invoked as a decision component within a composite. The examples we have used so far have been pretty trivial. However, the rules engine uses the Rete algorithm, which was developed by researchers into artificial intelligence in the 1970s.

Rete has some unique qualities, when compared to more procedural-based languages such as PL/SQL, C, C++, or Java, making it ideal for evaluating a large number of interdependent rules and facts. This not only makes it simpler to implement highly complex rules than would typically be the case with more procedural-based languages, but also makes it suitable for implementing particular categories of first-class business services.

In this chapter, we look in more detail at how the rule engine works, and armed with this knowledge, we write a set of rules to implement the auction algorithm responsible for determining the winning bid according to the rules set out in *Chapter 10, oBay Introduction*.

How the rule engine works

So far, we have only dealt with very simple rules that deal with a single fact. Before we look at a more complicated ruleset that deals with multiple facts it's worth taking some time to gain a better understanding of the inner workings of the rule engine.

The first thing to take into account is that when we invoke a ruleset, we do it through a rules session managed by the decision function (or service). When invoking the decision function, it first asserts the facts passed in by the caller. It then executes the ruleset against those facts, before finally retrieving the result from the rule sessions.

Within the context of this text, a **Decision Service** and a **Decision Function** is essentially the same thing. Within the rule editor, we define a **Decision Function**; we then expose that function as a web service, which can then be invoked within a composite as a **Decision Service**.

Asserting facts

The first step is for the decision function to assert all the facts passed by the client into the working memory of the rules sessions, ready for evaluation by the rule engine. Once the facts have been asserted into working memory, the next step is to execute the ruleset.

Executing the ruleset

Recall that a ruleset consists of one or more rules and that each rule consists of two parts; a rule condition, which is composed of a series of one or more tests, and an action block or list of actions to be carried out when the rule condition evaluates to true for a particular fact or combination of facts.

It's important to understand that the execution of the rule condition and its corresponding action block are carried out at two very distinct phases within the execution of the ruleset.

Rule activation

During the first phase, the rule engine will test the rule condition of *all* rules to determine for which facts or combination of facts the rule conditions evaluate to true. A group of facts that together cause a given rule condition to evaluate to true is known as a *fact set row*. A *fact set* is a collection of all *fact set rows* that evaluate to true for a given rule.

In many ways it's similar in concept to executing the rule condition as a query over the facts in working memory; with every row returned by the query equivalent to a fact set row, and the entire resultset being equivalent to the fact set.

For each fact set row, the rules engine will activate the rule. This involves adding each fact set row with a reference to the corresponding rule to the agenda of rules which need to be fired. At this point, the action block of any rule has *not* been executed.

When rule activations are placed on the rule agenda, they are ordered based on the priority of the rule, with those rules with a higher priority placed at the top of the agenda.

When there are multiple activations with the same priority, the most recently added activation is the next rule to fire. However, it's quite common for multiple activations to be added to the ruleset at the same time. The ordering of these activations is not specified.

Rule firing

Once all rule conditions have been evaluated, the rule engine will start processing the agenda. It will take the rule activation at the top of the agenda and execute the action block for the fact set row and the corresponding rule.

During the execution of the action block, the rule may assert new facts, assert updated facts, or retract existing facts from the working memory. As the rule engine does this, it may cause existing activations to be removed from the agenda or add new activations to the agenda.

When an activation is added to the agenda, it will be inserted into the agenda based on the priority of the rule. If there are already previous activations on the agenda with the same priority, the new activation will be inserted in front of these activations, that is, the set of new activations will be processed before any of the older activations with the same priority, but after any activation with a higher priority.

If a rule asserts a fact that is mentioned in its rule condition, and the rule condition is still `true`, then a new activation for the same fact set row will be added back to the agenda. So the rule will be fired again. This can result in a rule continually firing itself and thus the ruleset never completing.

Once the rule engine has completed the execution of the action block for an activation, it will take the next activation from the agenda and process that. Once all activations on the agenda have been processed, the rule engine has completed execution of the ruleset.

Retrieving result

Once the ruleset has completed, the decision function will query the working memory of the rule session for the result, specifically, the facts that we configured as outputs of the decision service, which the decision function will then return to the caller.

Note that for each fact that we have configured as an output of the decision function, we should ensure that just a single fact of that type will reside within the working memory of the decision service upon completion of execution of the ruleset. If zero or multiple facts exist, then the decision service will return an exception.

Session management

Before executing a ruleset, the decision service must first obtain a rule session. Creating a rule session involves creating a `RuleSession` object and loading the required repository that has significant overhead. Instead of creating a new `RuleSession` to handle each request, the decision service maintains a pool of shared objects that it uses to service requests.

When we invoke a decision function within a composite, the decision service will allocate a `RuleSession` object from this pool to handle the request.

In most scenarios, once the decision service has returned a result to the caller, the final step is to reset the session, so that it can be returned to the pool of `RuleSession` objects and be reused to handle future requests. This pattern of invocation is known as a stateless request, as the state of the session is not maintained between operations.

However, for invocations within a BPEL process, the decision service also supports a stateful invocation pattern, which enables you to invoke multiple operations within the same session when more flexibility is required.

For example, within the first invocation, you could assert some facts, execute the ruleset, and retrieve the results (without resetting the session). Based on the result, you may then take one of multiple paths within your BPEL process, at which point, you may re-invoke the decision service asserting some additional facts, re-execute the ruleset and retrieve an updated result, and then reset the rule session.

However, stateful sessions should be used with care as the state of the rule session is *not* persisted as part of the dehydration of a BPEL process, so it won't survive a server shutdown.

By default, when a decision function is created within the rules editor, it has the **Stateless** checkbox selected. You will need to deselect this if you want the function to support stateful invocations.

Debugging a ruleset

As the order in which rules and facts are evaluated are not specified for rules with equal priority, it can potentially be quite hard to debug when you don't get the result you are expecting. In these situations, it can be extremely useful to see what facts are being asserted, the activations that are being generated, and the rules as they are being fired.

Debugging a decision service with a test function

As we discussed in *Chapter 7, Using Business Rules to Define Decision Points*, it's a good idea to define one or more test functions to test your decision services. With this approach each test function will construct the input facts, submit them to the decision service, and then output the resultset.

In order to understand how the rules are being evaluated, the test function can instruct the rule engine to output details of these events by making the following function calls:

- `RL.watch.facts()`: Outputs information about each fact that it asserted, retracted, or modified within the working memory of a ruleset. As each fact is asserted it gives a numeric identifier prefixed with `f-`, which uniquely identifies that fact within the rule session.
- `RL.watch.activations()`: Outputs information about each rule activation as it's placed on the agenda (or removed from the agenda), including details of the facts in the row fact set for the activation.
- `RL.watch.rules()`: Outputs information about each rule as it fires, detailing the rule fired as well as the facts in the row fact set causing the rule to fire.
- `RL.watch.all()`: Outputs all of the mentioned information.

Debugging a decision service within a composite

To enable logging off the above mentioned events during execution of a ruleset within a composite, you need to set the logging level to TRACE for the rules logger as follows:

```
oracle.soa.services.rules.obrtrace
```

This will cause the output of `RL.watch.all()` to be logged to the SOA server diagnostic log, located in the following directory:

```
<WL_HOME>/user_projects/domains/<domain>/servers/<soa server>/logs
```

Here `<domain>` is the WebLogic Server domain in which you configured the SOA components, and `<soa server>` is the managed server on which you are running **soa-infra** (for example, soa_server1).

> See the Administrator's Guide for the SOA Suite for details on how to set logging levels via the Fusion Middleware Control Console. When set using the console, the settings take immediate effect, that is, you do not need to redeploy the composite.

Using the print function to add additional logging

Even with the available logging information, it can be useful to produce more fine grain logging within your ruleset. You can do this by calling the `print` function within your ruleset. This function can be used either within your own functions or called as part of the action block for a rule. Again, to enable these statements to be written to the SOA server diagnostic log, you need to set TRACE level logging for the rules logger.

Using business rules to implement auction

A good candidate for a service to implement as a ruleset is the oBay auction service. You may recall that we looked at the oBay auction process in *Chapter 16, Message Interaction Patterns*. What we didn't cover in this chapter is the actual implementation of how we calculate the winning bid.

In this scenario, our facts consist of the item up for auction and a list of bids that have been submitted against the item. So we need to implement a set of rules to be applied against these bids in order to determine the winning bid.

Defining our XML facts

The first step in implementing our business rules set is to define our input and output facts. We can create these using the `auction.xsd` that we defined as part of our canonical model for oBay, as shown in the following code snippet:

```
<xsd:element name="auctionItem"          type="tAuctionItem"/>
<xsd:element name="bids"                 type="tBids"/>
<xsd:element name="bid"                  type="tBid"/>
<xsd:complexType name="tAuctionItem">
```

```
    <xsd:sequence>
      <xsd:element name="auctionType"   type="tAuctionType"/>
      <xsd:element name="startTime"     type="xsd:dateTime" />
      <xsd:element name="endTime"       type="xsd:dateTime" />
      <xsd:element name="startingPrice" type="xsd:double" />
      <xsd:element name="reservePrice"  type="xsd:double"/>
      <xsd:element name="winningPrice"  type="xsd:double"/>
      <xsd:element name="winningBid"    minOccurs="0" type="tBid"/>
      <xsd:element name="bidHistory"    type="tBids"/>
    </xsd:sequence>
  </xsd:complexType>
  <xsd:complexType name="tBids">
    <xsd:sequence>
      <xsd:element name="bid" type="tBid" minOccurs="0"
                                          maxOccurs="unbounded" />
    </xsd:sequence>
  </xsd:complexType>
  <xsd:complexType name="tBid">
    <xsd:sequence>
      <xsd:element name="bidId"       type="xsd:string" />
      <xsd:element name="bidderId"    type="xsd:string" />
      <xsd:element name="bidtime"     type="xsd:dateTime"/>
      <xsd:element name="maxAmount"   type="xsd:double"/>
      <xsd:element name="bidAmount"   type="xsd:double"/>
      <xsd:element name="status"      type="xsd:string"/>
    </xsd:sequence>
  </xsd:complexType>
```

By examining this, we can see that this maps nicely to the facts that we have already identified; we have the element `auctionItem`, which maps to our auction fact. This has a start and end time during which bids can be received, a starting price and a reserve price (which defaults to the starting price if not specified), and an optional winning bid element, which holds details of the current winning bid for the auction, if there is one, as well as the bid history element, which contains details of all failed bids.

When we first create an auction, we won't receive any bids, so initially our `auctionItem` will not contain a winning bid and the bid history will be empty, as shown in the following code snippet:

```
<auctionItem>
<auctionType>STD</auctionType>
  <startTime>2010-04-01T15:45:48 </startTime>
  <endTime>2010-04-08T15:45:48</endTime>
  <startingPrice>1.00</startingPrice>
  <reservePrice>5.00</reservePrice>
  <winningPrice>0.00</winningPrice>
  <bidHistory/>
</auctionItem>
```

Against this, we need to apply one or more bids. This is contained within the fact `bids`, which contains one or more `bid` elements of type `tBid`.

As part of the auction process, as each bid is submitted to the BPEL process, it will assign a unique `id` to the `bid` (within the context of the auction), set the `bidtime` to the current time, and set the `status` of the bid to `NEW`, before submitting it to the auction ruleset.

So for example, if we submitted the following set of bids against the last item:

```
<bids>
  <bid>
    <bidId>1</bidId>
    <bidderId>jcooper</bidderId>
    <bidtime>2010-04-06T12:27:14</bidtime>
    <maxAmount>12.00</maxAmount>
    <bidAmount>0.00</bidAmount>
    <status>NEW</status>
  </bid>
  <bid>
    <bidId>2</bidId>
    <bidderId>istone</bidderId>
    <bidtime>2010-04-07T10:15:33</bidtime>
    <maxAmount>10.00</maxAmount>
    <bidAmount>0.00</bidAmount>
    <status>NEW</status>
  </bid>
</bids>
```

We would want the rule engine to return as an updated `auctionItem` fact that looked like the following code snippet:

```
<auctionItem>
  <auctionType>STD</auctionType>
  <startTime>2010-04-01T15:45:48 </startTime>
  <endTime>2010-04-08T15:45:48</endTime>
  <startingPrice>1.00</startingPrice>
  <reservePrice>5.00</reservePrice>
  <winningPrice>10.50</winningPrice>
  <winningbid>
    <bidId>1</bidId>
    <bidderId>jcooper</bidderId>
    <bidtime>2010-04-06T12:27:14</bidtime>
    <maxAmount>12.00</maxAmount>
```

```
      <bidAmount>10.50</bidAmount>
      <status>WINNING</status>
    </winningbid>
    <bidHistory>
      <bid>
        <bidId>2</bidId>
        <bidderId>istone</bidderId>
        <bidtime>2010-04-07T10:15:33</bidtime>
        <maxAmount>10.00</maxAmount>
        <bidAmount>10.00</bidAmount>
        <status>OUTBID</status>
     </bid>
    </bidHistory>
  </auctionItem>
```

Defining the business rule

Now that we have established our input and output facts, we are ready to create our auction rules. Open the `composite.xml` file for the auction composite, and then from the **Component Palette**, drag-and-drop a **Business Rule** onto the composite. This will launch the **Create Business Rules** dialog.

For the **AuctionRules** decision service, we need to pass in two facts, `auctionItem` and `bids`, and return the single fact `auctionItem`, as shown in the following screenshot:

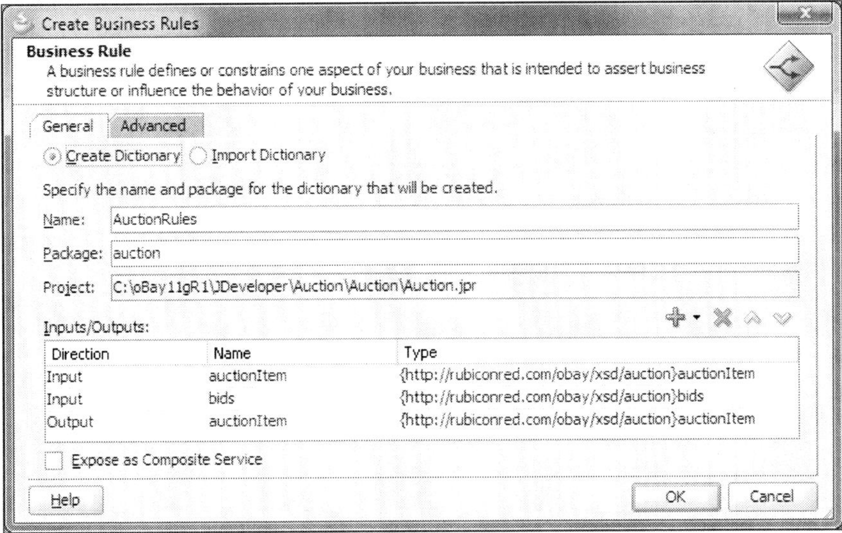

Configuring the decision function

Before we write our rules, we need to make some changes to the default configuration of our decision function. Within the rules editor, select the **Decision Functions** tab, next select `AuctionRulesDecisionService`, and click **Edit** (the pencil icon). This will open up the **Edit Decision Function** window, as shown in the following screenshot:

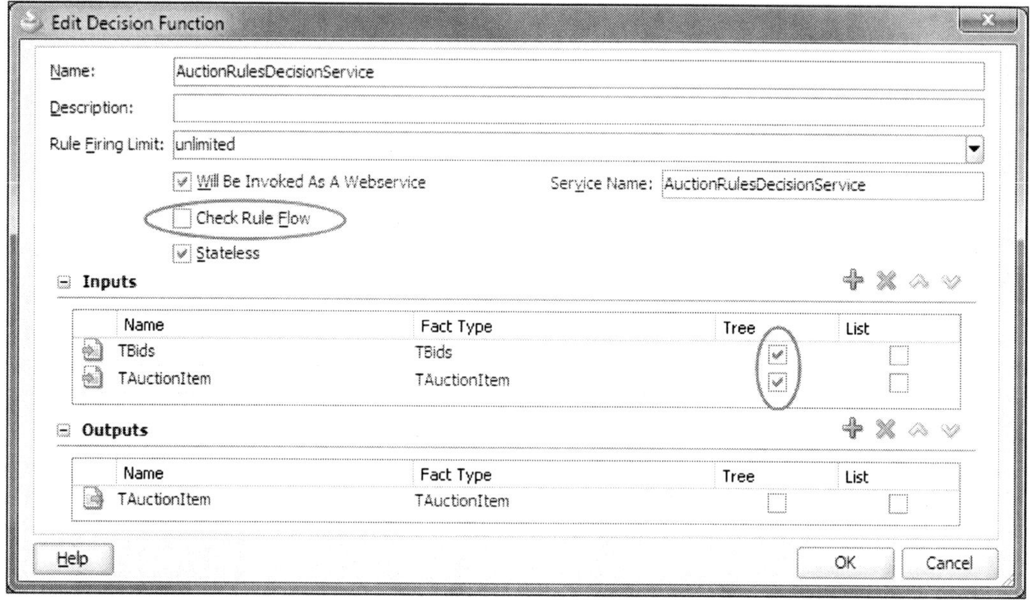

Deselect Check Rule Flow

First uncheck the option **Check Rule Flow** (circled in the preceding screenshot). By default, this is checked, which causes the rules author to check that all the input and output facts are *used* in the ruleset. By *used* it means that each fact is **directly** referenced by at least one rule in the ruleset and if not, the rule editor will flag an error that will prevent you from deploying the ruleset.

Within our ruleset, we are not going to make any direct reference to the **TBids** fact; rather our rules reference the **TBid** facts contained within the **TBids** fact.

Asserting the XML tree

The other subtlety we need to be aware of is that, by default, when you pass in an XML fact based on a complex type, and if that complex type contains other complex types, then it will only assert the top level XML element.

In our example, **TAuctionItem** contains `winningBid` and `bidHistory` (which contains `bid`), while `TBids` contains `bid`. As mentioned previously, we need to assert all the `bid` elements contained in `TBids`; we also need to assert the `winningBid` element contained in **TAuctionItem**. To do this, select the checkbox **Tree** (circled in the last screenshot) for each of these parameters. This will cause the decision function to parse the top-level element and assert all descendent facts.

At this point, we can actually save and run the ruleset from our auction process. Assuming everything works as expected, it will return a result containing details of the actual auction item that we passed in. All that remains now is for us to write the rules to evaluate our list of bids.

Using a global variable to reference the resultset

When we configure a decision service, we specify one or more facts that we want the decision service to **watch** (that is, `AuctionItem` in the previous example); these are often referred to as the resultset.

Many of our rules within the ruleset will require us to update the resultset. For example, every time we evaluate a bid, we will need to update the `AuctionItem` fact accordingly, either to record a bid as the new winning bid or add it to the bid history as a failed bid.

When a rule is fired, the action block is only able to operate on those facts contained within its local scope, which are those facts contained in the fact set row for that activation. Or put more simply, the rule can only execute actions against those facts that triggered the rule.

This means that for any rule that needs to operate on the resultset, we would need to include the appropriate test within the rule condition in order to pull that fact into the fact set row for the activation. So in the case of our Auction ruleset, we would need to add the following statement to every rule that needed to operate on the `AuctionItem` fact:

```
AuctionItem is a AuctionItem
```

This just adds an extra level of complexity to all our rules, particularly if you have multiple facts contained within the resultset. It's considered a better practice to define a global variable that references the resultset, which we can access within the action block of any rule and within any function we define.

Defining a global variable

To create a global variable from within the rule editor, select the **Globals** tab. This will present a list of the global variables currently defined to our ruleset (which at this point is empty). Click **Create** to bring up the **Edit Global** window, as shown in the next screenshot.

Here we have defined a variable of type **TAuctionItem** and given it a corresponding name. For the purpose of clarity, we tend to prefix all variables with **var** to indicate that it's a global variable.

If we check the box **Final**, the variable is fixed based on the value that we specify, allowing us to use it within the test part of a rule. However, as we want to be able to update the variable, we have left this unchecked.

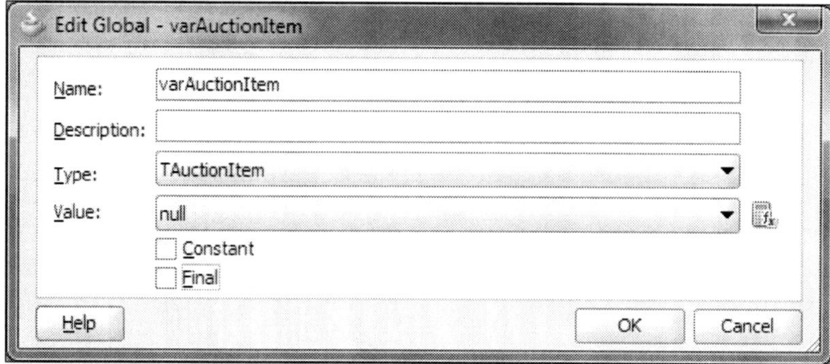

Finally, we can define an expression to initialize the variable. With XML facts you would often call a function to **create** the fact and initialize the variable. In our case, we want to initialize it to reference the `AuctionItem` fact passed in by the decision service.

As variables are created and initialized prior to asserting any facts, we will need to define a rule to do this once `AuctionItem` has been asserted. So, here we are just setting our variable to **null**.

Defining a rule to initialize a global variable

For this rule, we just need to test for the existence of a fact of type **TAuctionItem** (regardless of its content) and then assign it to our global variable. To do this, we need to use the rule editor in **Advanced Mode**.

Create your rule in the normal way, and then click on the **Show Advanced Settings** icon; the double chevron next to the rule name circled in the following screenshot:

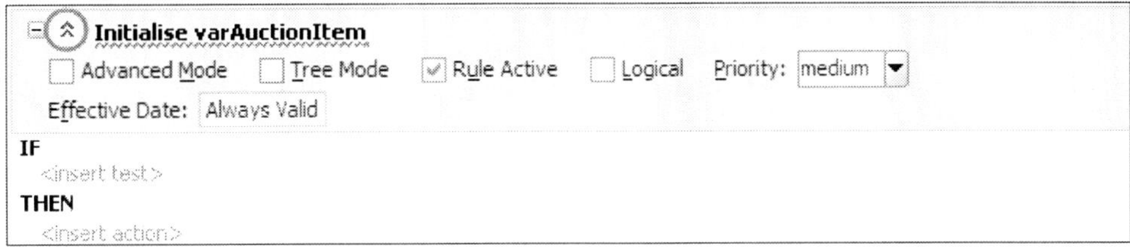

Next select **Advanced Mode**. This will expand the **IF** part of the rule, as we can see in the following screenshot:

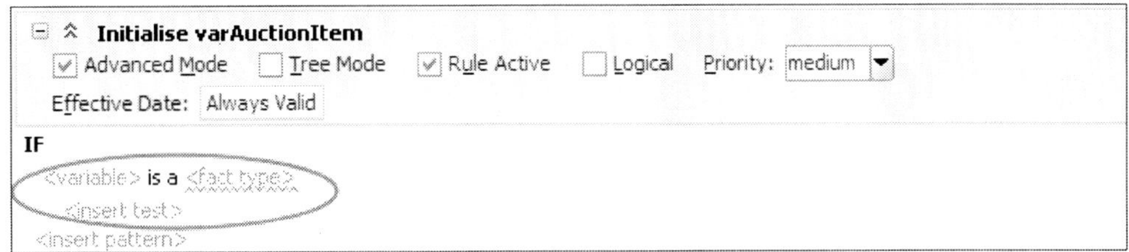

The circled part is called a **Pattern** and consists of two parts: the first is the type of pattern that we wish to test for, and the second is the tests we want to apply to the pattern. The rules engine supports the following patterns:

- **For each case where**: This is the *default* pattern, and is used to specify that the rule should be applied to each fact where the test evaluates to true
- **There is a case where**: With this option, the rules will only be triggered once, as long as there is at least one match
- **There is no case where**: With this option, the rule will be fired once if there are no matches
- **Aggregate**: This option allows you to write rule conditions based on the aggregate of more than one fact

When specifying the pattern, in addition to the pattern type, we need to specify the **fact type** that we wish to apply the pattern to as well as a **variable** name that we will use to reference the fact within the context of the rule (that is, within a test and/or an action).

Up to this point, whenever we have defined a rule, we have just been specifying the test part of the pattern. Behind the scenes, the rule editor has defaulted the pattern values, with the pattern type set to **for each case where**, the **fact type** set to the fact specified in the test, and the **variable** name set to the same name as the **fact type**.

For our rule, we just want to test for the existence of a fact of type **TAuctionItem**, so we will keep the default pattern (we will look at how to use a different pattern type in a moment).

To do this, click on **<variable>** and specify an appropriate name, next click on **<fact type>** and select **TAuctionItem** from the drop-down list, as shown in the following screenshot:

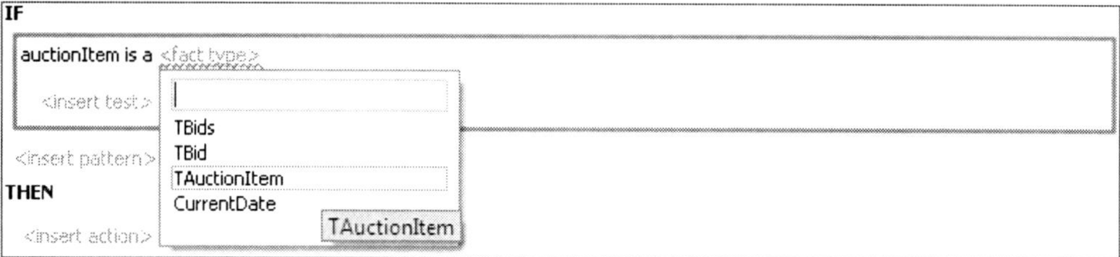

We don't need to specify a test as all we are doing is checking for the existence of the fact. The action part of the rule contains an **assign** statement to initialize our global variable. As you can see from the following screenshot, despite having to use **Advanced Mode**, the rule to initialize our global variable is pretty straightforward:

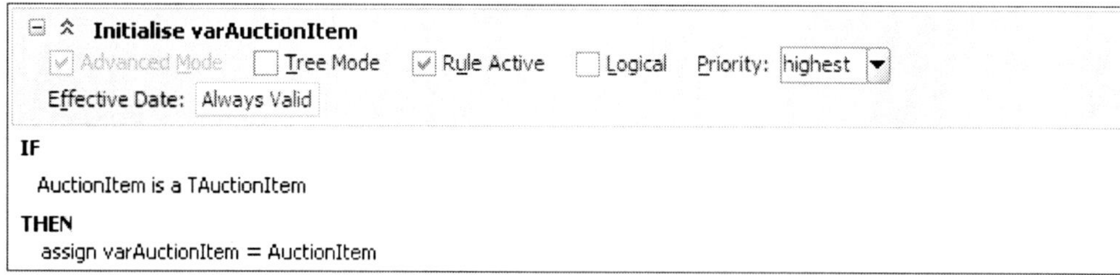

The other point worth noting is that we have specified a priority of **highest** (the default is **medium**) for the rule. This is to ensure that this rule is fired before any of the other rules which reference this variable.

Writing our auction rules

The next step is to write the rules to determine the winning bid. We could write a very simple rule to find the highest bid by writing a rule condition statement such as the following:

```
winningBid is a TBid
and
there is no case where otherBid is a TBid and
    otherBid.maxAmount > winningBid.maxAmount
```

This will match the bid which has no other bids with a greater bid amount. However, if we examine the bidding rules of an auction, we can see that the highest bid doesn't always win.

The reason being that once a successful bid has been placed, the next bid has to be equal to the winning amount plus a full bid increment, otherwise it's not a valid bid. In addition, if two maximum bids are equal, then the bid that was placed first is deemed the wining bid.

Evaluating facts in date order

In other words, we need to evaluate our bids in date order, the earliest first, and then the next, and so on. Once a bid has been processed, its status will be set to `WINNING`, `OUTBID`, or `INVALID` as appropriate.

So, we need to write a rule to select a bid with a status of `NEW`, which has an earlier `bidtime` than any other bid with a status of `NEW`, which we can then evaluate against our auction rules to determine its success or otherwise.

The first part of the rule condition is straightforward; we just need to implement a pattern such as:

```
nextBid is a TBid and
    nextBid.status == "NEW"
```

This will of course match all bids with a status of `NEW`.

Checking for non-existent fact

We need to define a second pattern, that checks to see if no other bids exist (with a status of `NEW`) with an earlier bidtime, in other words, we have to check for the non existence of a fact.

We do this by defining a pattern of type **there is no case where**, which will fire once if there are no matches, that is, no earlier bids.

To do this, click on **<insert pattern>** to insert the template for the second pattern into our **IF** clause. Then select the pattern and right-click on it. From the drop-down menu, select **Surround With**, as shown in the following screenshot:

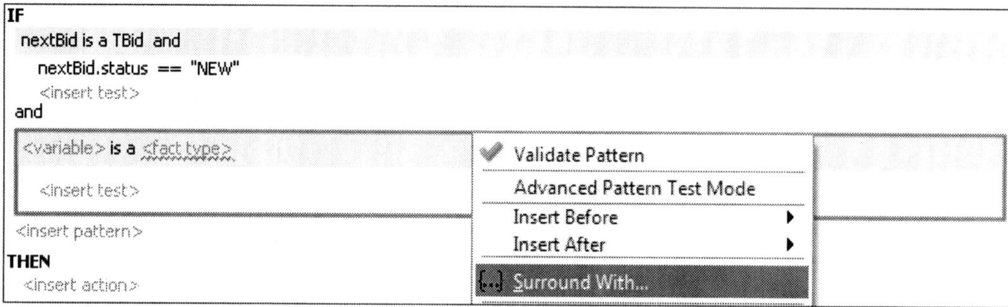

This will launch the **Surround With** dialog, from here, select **Pattern Block**. This will place our pattern within a pattern block, which allows us to specify which type of pattern we want to apply. This is shown in the following screenshot:

```
IF
  nextBid is a TBid  and
    nextBid.status == "NEW"
    <insert test>
and
(for each case where) {
   <variable> is a <fact type>
      <insert test>
 }  <insert test>
```

The final step is to click on the pattern type, and from the drop-down menu, select the type **there is no case where**, as shown in the following screenshot:

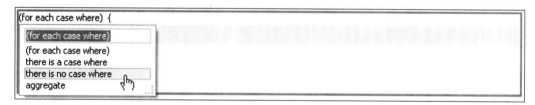

We can now implement the test within our second pattern to test for an earlier bid with a status of NEW. So our extended rule condition is implemented as shown in the following screenshot:

```
IF
  nextBid is a TBid  and
    nextBid.status == "NEW"
and
there is no case where {
   anotherBid is a TBid  and
      anotherBid.status == "NEW" and
      Duration.compare(anotherBid.bidtime, nextBid.bidtime) < 0
 }
```

This condition works as follows: the first test will select all the bids with a status of NEW. For each bid selected, it will execute the second test where it will select all other bids with a status of NEW and an earlier bidtime (using the function Duration). If no bids are selected then this test will evaluate to true and the rule will be activated and placed on the agenda.

When the activation is placed on the agenda, only the fact referenced by nextBid is included in the fact row set, as for the rule condition to be true, anotherBid won't actually reference any other bid.

Updating the bid status

Once we have located the next bid, we need to set its status to NEXT and reassert it. We do this with the following statements in our action block, shown as follows:

```
Assign nextBid.status = "NEXT"
Assert nextBid
```

An interesting side effect is that as soon as we assert our modified bid, the rule engine will reapply the test condition and potentially find another bid with a status of NEW, that is, the next bid to be processed after this one.

On finding this bid, it will place a new activation on the agenda for this rule referencing this new bid. To prevent this rule from firing before any of the rules which process bids with a status of NEXT, we have set the priority of this rule to **lowest**.

So, the complete rule to get the next bid is defined as follows:

```
GetNextBid
Advanced Mode   Tree Mode   Rule Active   Logical   Priority: lowest
Effective Date: Always Valid
IF
  nextBid is a TBid and
    nextBid.status == "NEW"
 and
 there is no case where {
    anotherBid is a TBid and
      anotherBid.status == "NEW" and
      Duration.compare(anotherBid.bidtime, nextBid.bidtime) < 0
 }
THEN
  assign nextBid.status = "NEXT"
  assert nextBid
```

Using inference

Once we have identified the next bid, we could then include the logic to determine the success or otherwise of the bid within the same rule. However, when processing a bid, we have to deal with the following three potential scenarios:

1. The next bid is higher than the current winning bid.
2. The current winning bid is higher than or equal to the next bid.
3. This is our first bid and thus by default it is our winning bid.

Before evaluating a bid, we also need to check that it's valid, specifically we must check that:

- The max bid amount is greater than or equal to the starting price of the item
- The max bid amount is greater than the current winning price plus one bidding increment

If we encompassed all these checks within a single rule, we would end up with a very complex rule.

For example, to write a single rule for the first scenario, we would need to write a rule condition to identify the next bid, validate it, and finally check if it is higher than the current winning bid. So we would end up with a rule condition like this one shown in the following code snippet:

```
nextBid is a TBid and
  nextBid.status == "NEW"
and
```

```
there is no case where {
  anotherBid is a TBid and
    anotherBid.status == "NEW" &&
    Duration.compare(anotherBid.bidtime, nextBid.bidtime) < 0
}
and
auctionItem is a TAuctionItem and
  nextBid.maxAmount >= auctionItem.startingPrice
and
winningBid is a TBid and
  winningBid.status == "WINNING" &&
  nextBid.maxAmount >= winningBid.bidAmount +
                       getBidIncrement (winningBid.bidAmount)&&
  nextBid.maxAmount > winningBid.maxAmount
```

We would then need to reimplement most of this logic for the other two scenarios.

Better practice is to use inference, that is, if A implies B, and B implies C, then we can infer from this that A implies C. In other words, we don't have to write all of this within a single rule; the rule engine will automatically infer this for us.

In our scenario, this means that writing a rule to get the next bid (as covered), and writing two rules to validate any bid with a status of `NEXT`. These rules will **retract** any invalid bids and update their status to reflect this. Finally, we need to write three rules, one for each of the scenarios identified previously to process each valid bid.

The only thing we need to take into account is that the validation rules must have a higher priority than the rules which process the next bid, so that they retract any invalid bids before they can be processed.

Processing the next valid bid

Using inference, we can now write our rules to process the next bid, on the basis that we already know which bid is next and that the bid is valid. Using this approach, the rule condition for the first scenario, where the next bid is higher than the current winning bid, would be specified as shown in the following code snippet:

```
nextBid is a TBid and
   nextBid.status == "NEXT"
and
winningBid is a TBid and
   winningBid.status == "WINNING" &&
   winningBid.maxAmount < nextBid.maxAmount
```

This, as we can see, is considerably simpler than the previous example.

If this evaluates to true for our next bid, then we will have a new winning bid and need to take the appropriate action to update the affected facts as well as the resultset.

The first action we need to take is to calculate the actual winning amount by adding one bidding increment to the maximum amount of the losing bid. So the first statement in our rules action block is as follows:

```
Assign nextBid.bidAmount = winningBid.maxAmount +
                           getBidIncrement (winningBid.maxAmount)
```

Here, `getBidIncrement` is a function that calculates the next bid increment based on the size of the current winning amount.

Next, we need to update its status to `WINNING` and reassert the bid in order for it to be reevaluated as a winning bid by our ruleset.

In addition, we need to update the status of our previous winning bid to `OUTBID` and retract it from the rule space, as we no longer need to evaluate it.

Using functions to manipulate XML facts

As part of the process of evaluating a new winning bid, we also need to update our resultset. When doing this, it's important to take into account that each XML fact (for example, `TAuctionItem`, `TBids`, and `TBid`) is implemented within the rules engine as a Java class, generated by the rules editor using JAXB 2.0.

When we pass a fact (such as `auctionItem`) into the rules engine, the decision function will instantiate an instance of the corresponding Java class (for example, `TAuctionItem`) to hold details of the fact. In addition, for each complex type embedded within the fact (for example, `winningBid` in `auctionItem`), it will instantiate a class of the appropriate type (for example, `TBid` in the case of `winningBid`), which will be referenced by `auctionItem`.

However, it will only do this if the complex type is actually present in the XML fact passed to the decision function. What this means is that when we update a complex type within an XML fact, we need to first check that this type exists, and if it doesn't, create it and update the XML fact to reference it.

For example, at the time we place our first bid, `auctionItem` won't contain a winning bid. So, we need to create a new element of type `TBid` and set `auctionItem.winningBid` to reference it, before updating the `winningBid` element with details of our new winning bid.

In the case of bidHistory, this is a collection of TBids, so every time we insert a new losing bid, we must create a new XML element of type TBid to hold the details of the losing bid and insert this into the bidHistory element.

Rather than performing this manipulation of the XML structure directly within the action block of our rules, it's considered best practice to implement this as a function that can then be called from our rule. This helps to keep our rules simpler and more intuitive to understand.

So, for this purpose, we need to define two functions: assertWinningBid and retractLosingBid.

Asserting a winning bid

To record details of a new winning bid in the resultset, we have defined the function assertWinningBid, which takes a single parameter bid of type TBid, used to pass in a reference to the winning bid. The code for this function is as follows:

```
// Update Status of Winning Bid
Assign bid.status = "WINNING"
assert bid

// Update result set with details of Winning Bid
assign varAuctionItem.winningPrice = bid.bidAmount

assign new TBid winningBid = varAuctionItem.winningBid

// Create Winning Bid if one doesn't exist
if (winningBid == null) {
    assign winningBid = new TBid()
    assign varAuctionItem.winningBid = winningBid
}

assign winningBid.bidAmount = bid.bidAmount
assign winningBid.bidNo     = bid.bidNo
assign winningBid.bidderId  = bid.bidderId
assign winningBid.bidTime   = bid.bidTime
assign winningBid.maxAmount = bid.maxAmount
assign winningBid.status    = bid.status
return
```

Looking at this, we can see that it breaks into two parts. The first part updates the status of the winning bid to WINNING, and asserts the bid. Now, this isn't actually updating the resultset, so rather than including these actions within the function, we could directly define them within the rule itself.

But as we need to process a winning bid in multiple rules, we have chosen to include this in the function, as it both simplifies our rules and ensures that we handle winning bids in a consistent way. Either approach is valid; it just comes down to personal preference.

However, to indicate to callers of the function that we are asserting the winning bid in the function, we have prefixed the name of the function with `assert`.

The second part of the function is used to update the resultset with details of the winning bid. The first line updates the element `winningPrice` to contain the bid amount of the winning bid.

The next set of code is more interesting; the line returns a reference to the winning bid element:

```
assign new TBid winningBid = varAuctionItem.winningBid
```

This may return `null`, as the `AuctionItem` may not currently have a winning bid (for example, if this is the first winning bid). In this scenario, we create a new `TBid` element and update `varAuctionItem` to reference this.

Finally, we update the winning bid element in `AuctionItem` to point to this newly created element as follows:

```
    assign varAuctionItem.winningBid = winningBid
```

Once we've done this, we update the details of the `winningBid` element with those of the `bid` element.

The final thing to note is that we are not asserting `varAuctionItem` or any of the elements we have added to it, so none of these changes will be visible to our ruleset, which is exactly what we want. This is because we are using the resultset as a place to build up the result of executing our ruleset and thus don't want it included in the evaluation.

Retracting a losing bid

To record details of a losing bid in the resultset, we have followed a similar approach and defined the function `retractLosingBid`, which takes two parameters `bid` of type `TBid` and `reason` of type `String`, which has the reason for the retraction (for example, `OUTBID`, `INVALID`).

The code for the function is as follows:

```
// Update Status of Losing Bid
assign bid.status    = reason
assign bid.bidAmount = bid.maxAmount
```

```
retract(bid);

// Record Details of Bid in Result Set
assign new TBid losingBid = cloneTBid(bid);


Call varAuctionItem.bidHistory.bid.add(0, losingBid)
```

Looking at this, we can see that, as with the previous function, it breaks into two parts. The first part updates the status of the bid and then retracts it. The second part of the function is used to record details of the retracted bid within the `bidHistory` element of our resultset.

The first line of this part calls the function `cloneTBid` to create a new element of type `TBid` and initialize it with the values of the losing bid using an approach similar to the one previously used to create a new winning bid element.

Once we've done that, we add it to the `bidHistory` element. The bid history itself is a collection of bid elements. JAXB implements this as a `java.util.List`. The attribute `bidHistory.bid` returns a reference to this list.

The final part of this function invokes the method `add` with an index value of `0` to insert the losing bid at the start of this list, so that the bid history contains the most recently processed bid at the start of the list.

Rules to process a new winning bid

With our functions defined, we can finish the implementation of the rule for a new winning bid, which is shown in the following screenshot:

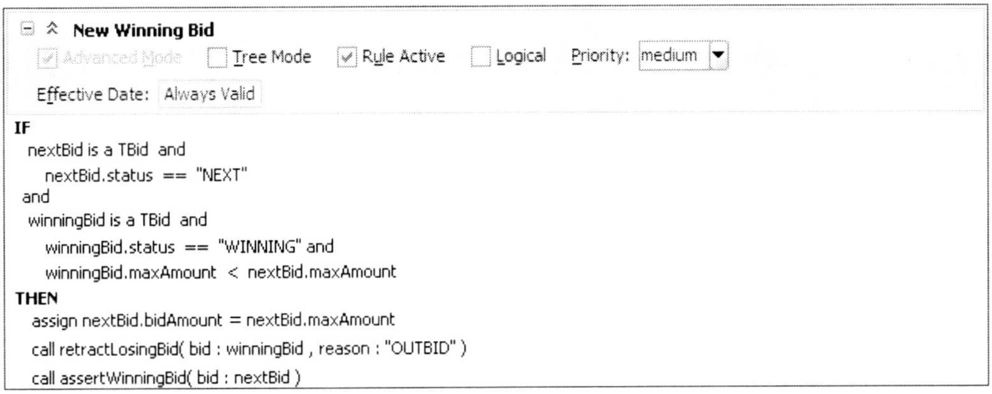

```
New Winning Bid
Advanced Mode   Tree Mode   Rule Active   Logical   Priority: medium
Effective Date: Always Valid
IF
  nextBid is a TBid and
    nextBid.status == "NEXT"
 and
  winningBid is a TBid and
    winningBid.status == "WINNING" and
    winningBid.maxAmount < nextBid.maxAmount
THEN
  assign nextBid.bidAmount = nextBid.maxAmount
  call retractLosingBid( bid : winningBid , reason : "OUTBID" )
  call assertWinningBid( bid : nextBid )
```

Due to the use of inference to simplify the rule condition and the use of functions to manipulate the resultset, the final rule is very straightforward.

The only thing we need to take into account is the priority of the rule, which we have set to **medium**. We need to ensure that the validation rules for a bid have a **higher** priority to ensure that they are fired first.

Validating the next bid

For the above rule to be complete, we need to define the rules which validate the next bid before we process it. The two conditions that we need to check are:

1. The maximum bid amount is greater than or equal to the starting price of the item.
2. The maximum bid amount is greater than the current winning price plus one bidding increment.

To validate that maximum bid amount is greater than or equal to the auction starting price, we have defined the following rule:

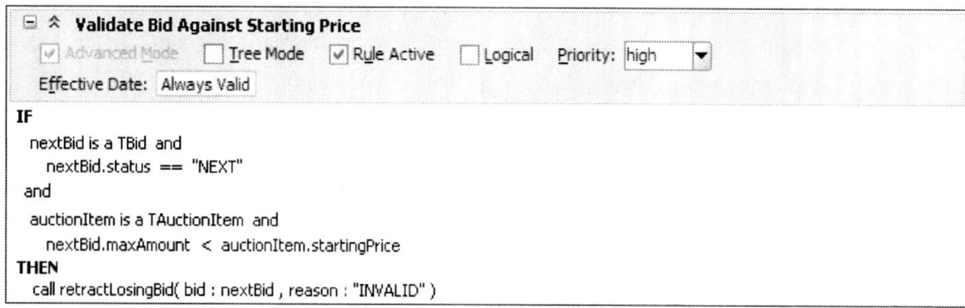

We have also defined a similar rule, `validateBidAgainstWinningPrice`, to validate that the maximum bid amount is greater than the current winning amount plus one bidding increment.

Each of these rules has a priority of **high**, which is higher than the rules for processing the next bid. This ensures that any invalid bids are retracted before they can be processed.

Rule to process a losing bid

The rules to handle other potential outcomes for the next bid, namely, where it's our first bid and thus by default a winning bid or a losing bid, are straightforward. However, there is an exception. The rule for the scenario where the next bid is a losing bid is shown in the following screenshot:

```
Losing Bid
Advanced Mode   Tree Mode   Rule Active   Logical   Priority: medium
Effective Date: Always Valid
IF
  nextBid is a TBid and
    nextBid.status == "NEXT"
 and
  winningBid is a TBid and
    winningBid.status == "WINNING" and
    winningBid.maxAmount >= nextBid.maxAmount
THEN
  assign winningBid.bidAmount = nextBid.maxAmount + getBidIncrement(nextBid.maxAmount)
  call retractLosingBid( bid : nextBid , reason : "OUTBID" )
  call assertWinningBid( bid : winningBid )
```

If we look at the first action that sets the bid amount of the winning bid equal to the maximum amount of the losing bid plus the next bid increment, there is a possibility that this could cause the bid amount to exceed the maximum amount specified.

For example, if the maximum bid was $10, with the current winning amount being $5, then, it would be valid for the next bid to be $10. This bid would fail but the new winning amount according to the above would be $10.50.

Capping the winning bid amount

To prevent this from happening, we need to write another rule to test if the winning amount of the bid is greater than its maximum amount, and if it is, then set the winning amount equal to the maximum amount. The rule for this is as shown in the following screenshot:

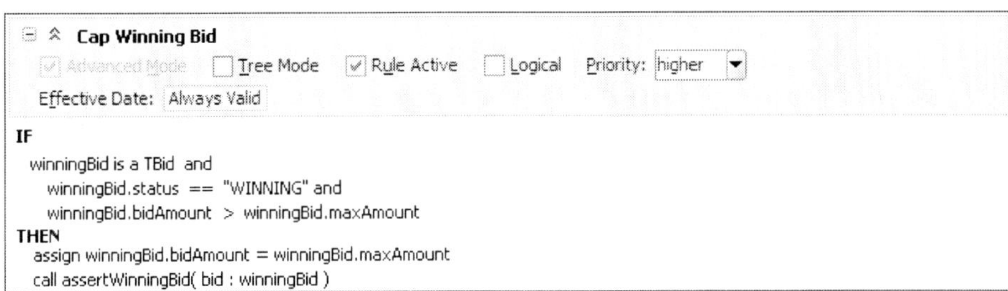

The rule itself is straightforward. But, as this rule is being used to correct an inconsistent state, we have given it a priority of **higher** so that it is fired even before the validation rules.

Complete ruleset

In total, we have eight rules within our auction ruleset. These rules are listed in the following table in order of priority:

Rule	Priority
`Initialise VarAuctionItem`	highest
`Cap Winning Bid`	higher
`Validate Bid Against Start Price`	high
`Validate Bid Against Winning Price`	high
`First Bid`	medium
`New Winning Bid`	medium
`Losing Bid`	medium
`Get Next Bid`	lowest

The first rule is just used to initialize the global variable that references the resultset. The next rule, `Cap Winning Bid`, ensures that we don't breach the maximum amount for a bid. The next two rules, `Validate Bid Against Start Price` and `Validate Bid Against Winning Price`, are just simple validation rules.

The majority of the work is done in the next three rules—`First Bid`, `New Winning Bid`, and `Losing Bid`—each of which deals with one of the three possible outcomes each time we have to process a new bid. With the final rule, `Get Next Bid` is used to ensure that we process each bid in date order.

An alternative approach to using priorities is to split the rules across multiple rulesets. As part of specifying multiple rulesets in a decision function, we also define their order on the stack, with the ruleset at the top taking priority and so on.

When activations for a decision function are processed, the activations for the ruleset at the top of the stack are processed first, followed by the activations for the next ruleset, and so on. If any of these activations result in new items being added to the agenda for higher priority rulesets, then those activations will be processed before those of the lower priority rulesets.

Performance considerations

In the previous example, we've been working on the basis that every time we receive a new bid, we add it to our list of bids received and then submit the auction and the entire list of bids to the ruleset for evaluation.

The obvious issue with this technique is that we are reevaluating all the bids that we have received from scratch every time we receive a new bid.

One possible solution would be to have a stateful rule session. With this approach, we would first submit the auction item to the decision service but with no bids. Then as we receive a bid, we could assert that against the ruleset and get the updated result back from the decision service.

The issue with this (as we discussed at the start of this chapter) is that when the BPEL process dehydrates, which in the case of our auction process will happen each time we wait for the next bid, the rule session is not persisted. Consequently, whenever the server is restarted we will lose the rules session of any auction in progress, which is clearly not desirable.

Managing state within the BPEL process

One alternative is to use the BPEL process to hold the state of the rule session. With this technique, we need to ensure that all relevant facts contained within the rule session are returned within the facts that the decision service is watching. The next time we invoke the decision service, we can resubmit these facts (along with any new facts to be evaluated) and reassert them back into a new rule session.

In the case of our auction ruleset, the relevant facts that need to be maintained between invocations are `auctionItem` and `winningBid`, which is contained within `auctionItem`.

With this approach, each time we receive a new bid, we just need to assert the `auctionItem` element as returned by the previous invocation of the ruleset and the new bid (within the `bids` element). As a result, each time we submit a new bid, rather than reevaluate all bids to determine the winning bid, we just need to evaluate the new bid against the winning bid, which is clearly more efficient.

To support this, we do not have to make any modifications to our ruleset, as we have implemented it in such a way that it supports either asserting all bids in one go or submitting them incrementally.

The only remaining drawback with this approach is that the ruleset will still assert all bid objects contained within the `bidHistory` element of `auctionItem` into working memory. While this won't change the outcome, it still means all these bids will be evaluated in the process of firing the rules, though none of them will cause an activation to happen.

When we have only a relatively small number of facts this doesn't really cause a problem, but if the number of facts is in the high 100s or order of 1000s, then this may make a noticeable difference.

Using functions to control the assertion of facts

The reason that all facts are asserted into the working memory of the rule session is that we specified (by checking the **Tree** checkbox) that the decision function should assert all descendants from the top-level element for each of our input facts.

This causes the function `assertTree` to be called for each fact passed in by the decision service (as opposed to `assert`), which causes all the descendants of the fact elements to be asserted at runtime.

An alternative is to leave this unchecked and write a function for each fact passed in that asserts just the desired facts. So, in our case, we would write a function to assert the `winningBid` element in `auctionItem` and all the `bid` elements contained in `bids`.

Summary

The business rules engine is built on a powerful inference engine, which it inherits from its roots in the Rete algorithm. We spent the first part of this chapter explaining how the rule engine evaluates facts against rules. The operation of the Rete algorithm can be a challenge to completely understand, so re-reading this section may be beneficial.

However, once you have an appreciation for how the rule engine works and can start "thinking in Rete", you will have a powerful tool not just for implementing complex business rules but also a certain type of service.

We demonstrated this by developing a complete ruleset to determine the winning bid for an auction. Looking at the final list of rules, we can see that we needed relatively few to achieve the end result and that none of these were particularly complex.

As is the case when implementing more typical decision services, we have the added advantage that we can easily modify the rules that implement a service without having to modify the overall application, giving us an even greater degree of flexibility.

Part 3

Other Considerations

Packaging and Deployment

Testing Composite Applications

Defining Security and Management Policies

19
Packaging and Deployment

In this section, we will look at how to package a set of SOA Suite components for deployment in different environments. We will also look at some of the deployment topologies that may be used at runtime to provide scalability. We will focus primarily on the SOA composite, as this has some of the more complex requirements for the mapping of services.

The need for packaging

When developing software, we generally use a local development environment to create our SOA artifacts. In some cases, this may be entirely on the developer's machine. At other times, the developer will have access to a shared development server. In either case, there will usually be the need to move the artifacts from the development environment into a test environment and eventually into a production environment.

Problems with moving between environments

Within our SOA artifacts, we have references to other artifacts such as service endpoint locations and rule repository locations. In addition, the configuration for some components, particularly adapter services, will probably be different between environments. For example, database locations and file locations may be different between different locations. We need to have a means of modifying these various environment-dependant properties.

Types of interface

Within the development environment, we will build many of the artifacts in a thick client design tool such as JDeveloper or Workshop and then deploy directly into the development runtime environment. As we move into test and/or production, we do not want our operators to have JDeveloper or other design-time environments; we would prefer that they had a set of command-line tools and/or web interfaces to deploy components. Often they will be unable to use JDeveloper to deploy because of firewall restrictions.

Web interfaces

Web interfaces are handy for rapid deployment of components into a new environment, and they generally make it easy to configure any changes that are required. However, web interfaces are not easy to automate and so are not ideal for deployment that has to be repeated across multiple stages, such as test, pre-production, and production environments.

Command-line interfaces

Command-line interfaces are often a little harder to work with, but have the huge advantage that they are easy to script, making it possible to have a repeatable deployment process. This is important enough for the move from test to production, but becomes even more important when we consider that we may wish to set up a data recovery environment or other multiple environments.

In a well-managed environment, the use of deployment scripts is essential to ensure a consistent way of deploying SOA Suite artifacts across different environments.

SOA Suite packaging

Unfortunately, the current release of SOA Suite is not consistent in the way in which it packages the different components. Each SOA Suite component, such as composites or the Service Bus, has a different way of packaging its artifacts for deployment. In this section, we will examine each component to see how it is packaged and how to manage deployment across multiple environments in the best way possible.

Oracle Service Bus

An **Oracle Service Bus** (**OSB**) project may be deployed from the Workshop IDE or imported from the Service Bus console by selecting the **System Administration** tab and then selecting the **Import Resources** link. In a similar fashion, it is possible to export resources from the Service Bus console by selecting the **Export Resources** link.

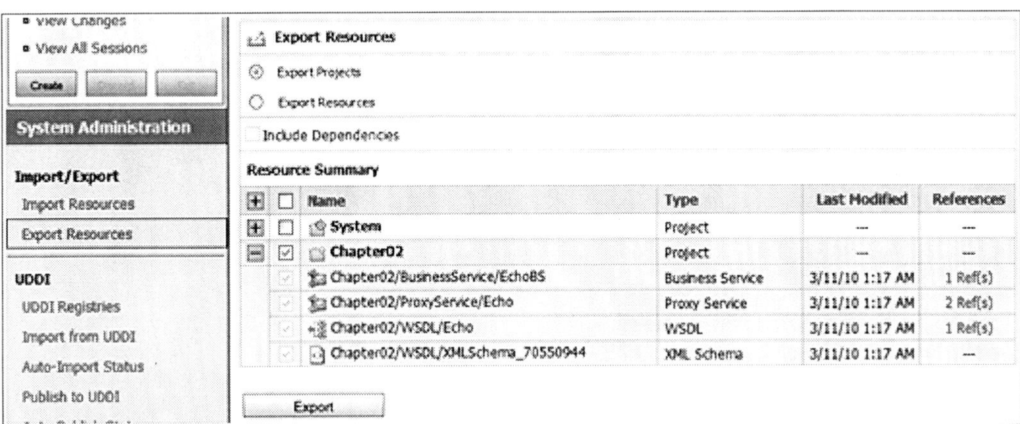

When exporting a project or group of projects from the Service Bus by clicking on the **Export** button, the project is exported in a `.jar` file package called `sbconfig.jar` by default, which may be saved from the browser.

The `.jar` file generated may be deployed to another Service Bus domain by importing it and then editing the project settings to have the correct configuration.

Unlike SOA composites, there is no concept of versioning in the Service Bus, and so once deployed, it is generally easier to maintain the existing deployment rather than replace it completely. However, complete projects may be replaced, if necessary. *Chapter 11, Designing the Service Contract* discusses how versioning may be applied in the Service Bus.

Individual service endpoint locations can be edited directly from within the Service Bus console. Potentially every business service may need modification for the correct environment.

It is also possible to use the **WebLogic Scripting Tool** (**WLST**) to migrate projects between environments. This provides the benefits of allowing automatic configuration of the settings for different environments.

Oracle SOA composites

The deployment unit of an SOA composite is the SCA archive file or a `.sar` file. The SCA archive may be deployed to an SOA Suite installation using the web interface accessed from the **soa-infra** home page of the EM Console. An SCA archive is generated when an SCA composite is deployed, either in JDeveloper or using an Ant task generated by JDeveloper. The location of the SCA archive is displayed in the deployment log during compilation. It is usually generated in the `$PROJECT_HOME/deploy` directory. When deploying from JDeveloper into SOA Suite, the SCA archive is used to transfer all the information required by the composite. The same is true whether we deploy the suitcase manually through the web interface or through an Ant task.

```
Deployment - Log
[02:19:58 PM] >>>>  Warning:  Unable to determine the target platform from the Profile.  Using default...
[02:19:58 PM] ----  Deployment started.  ----
[02:19:58 PM] Target platform is  (Weblogic 10.3).
[02:19:58 PM] Running dependenc Deployment messages
[02:19:58 PM] Building...
[02:20:04 PM] Deploying profile...
[02:20:04 PM] Wrote Archive Module to D:\Support\SOASuiteBook11gChapter19\Calculator\deploy\sca_Calculator_rev1.1.jar
[02:20:04 PM] Elapsed time for deployment:  6 seconds
[02:20:04 PM] ----  Deployment finished.  ----
```

Deploying a SCA composite via the EM Console

Clicking the **Deploy** link accessed from the **SOA Infrastructure** menu in the EM Console provides access to the EM deployer screen, as shown in the following screenshot:

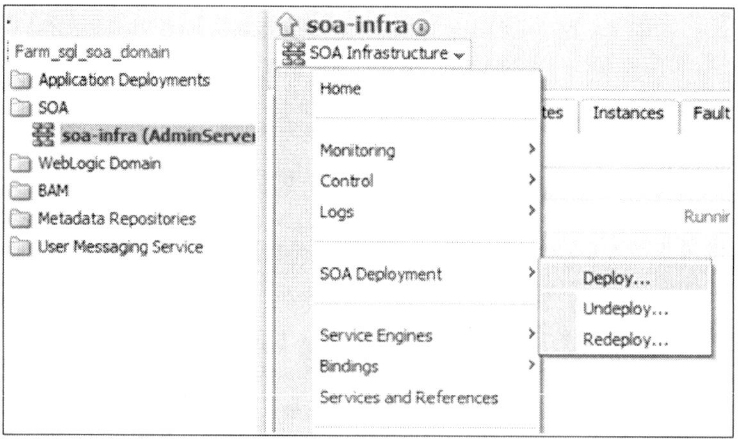

Here, we can browse for the SCA archive and then deploy it. We may also attach a configuration plan to the deployment, which will modify settings within the archive to adapt it to the target environment. We will discuss configuration plans later in this chapter.

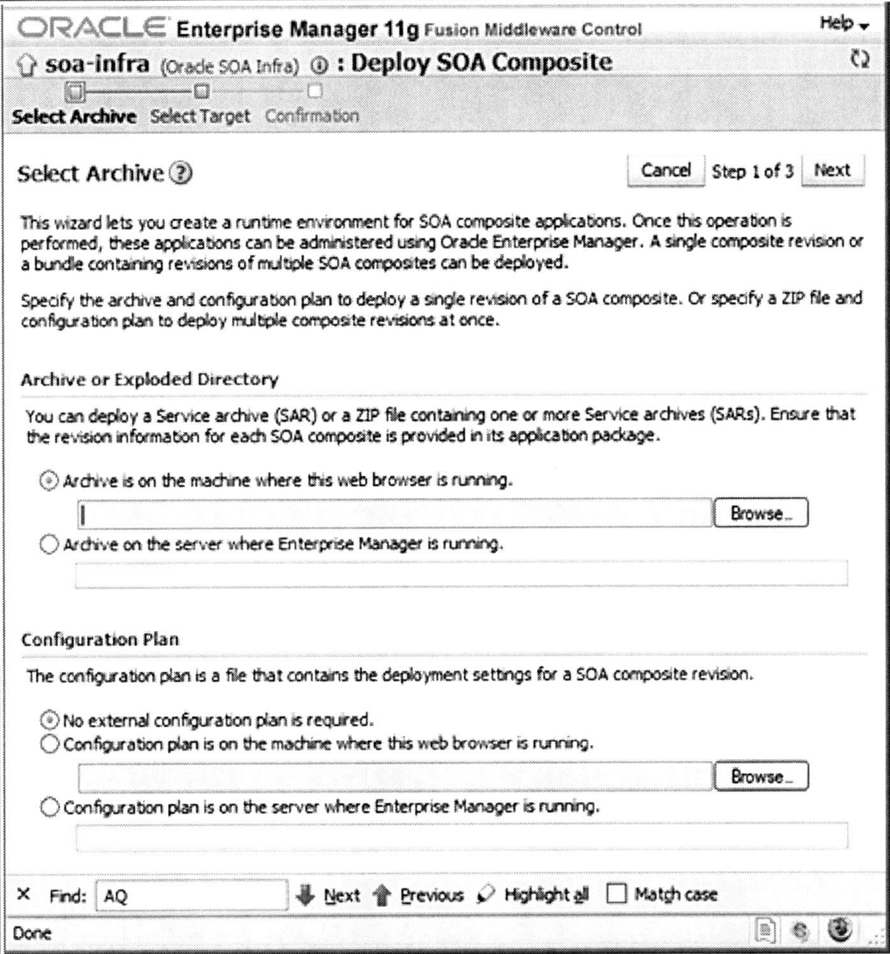

During the deployment process, we will be prompted for the target servers on which to deploy our composite. We will also be given the opportunity to set the revision being deployed as the default revision.

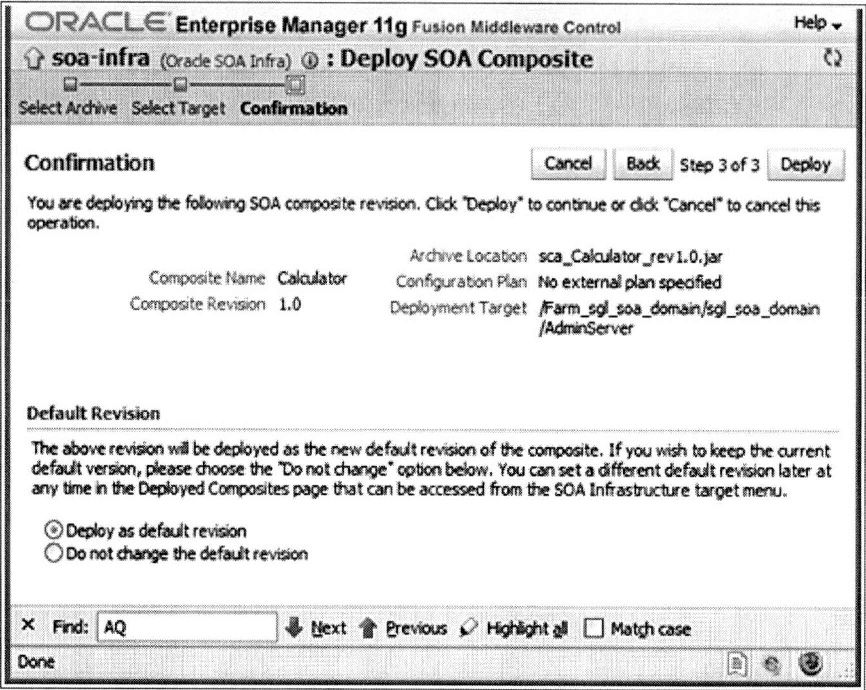

During deployment, we get a status screen informing us that the deployment is in process. After deploying the process, we are taken to the **Dashboard** tab of the newly deployed composite with a message at the top of the screen informing us that the composite was successfully deployed.

Deploying a SCA composite using Ant

JDeveloper and SOA Suite provide Ant scripts that may be used to deploy SCA composites and perform other lifecycle operations from the command line. This enables the scripting of tasks such as application deployment, making it easier for administrators to deploy applications across different environments and ensuring that composites are deployed in a consistent fashion.

The following key scripts are provided in the `$JDEVELOPER_HOME/jdeveloper/bin` directory for JDeveloper or the `$MIDDLEWARE_HOME/$SOA_HOME/bin directory` for SOA Suite.

- `ant-sca-compile.xml` compiles an SOA composite.`ant-sca-package.xml` generates an SAR file.`ant-sca-deploy.xml` deploys an SAR file to an SOA server. This may also be used to undeploy a composite or export a deployed SAR file and/or its post-deployment configuration changes.
- `ant-sca-mgmt.xml` controls the status of deployed composites, allowing them to be started, stopped, activated, and retired. These functions will be discussed later in this chapter.
- `ant-sca-test.xml` executes the test suites associated with a composite and writes the results to a directory.

Before executing these scripts, it is necessary to ensure that the environment is correctly set up. The PATH variable must have the Apache Ant bin directory (`$JDEVELOPER_HOME/modules/org.apache.ant_1.7.0` or `$MIDDLEWARE_HOME/modules/org.apache.ant_1.7.0`) prepended to it and the `JAVA_HOME` variable must point to a JDK such as `$MIDDLEWARE_HOME/jdk160_14_R27.6.5-32`.

Note that these scripts can be run with either a JDeveloper installation or an SOA Suite installation. JDeveloper is not required to run these scripts, meaning that test, production, and other environments only need to have SOA Suite installed in order to execute these scripts.

Execute these scripts from the directory where they are found. The scripts are executed using `ant`, as shown in the following command line:

```
ant -f <build-script> -D<parameter1>=<value1> -D<parameter2>=<value2> …
-D<parameterN>=<valueN>
```

`build-script` is one of the scripts listed here. Parameters are the inputs to the script. The following parameters are commonly used.

Compile parameters (ant-sca-compile.xml)

- `scac.input`: Name and location of the `composite.xml` file to validate/compile
- `scac.output`: File with results of compile
- `scac.error`: File with error messages, if any

```
D:\JDev\jdeveloper\bin>ant -f ant-sca-compile.xml
 -Dscac.input=%PROJ_DIR%\composite.xml
Buildfile: ant-sca-compile.xml

scac:
   [scac] Validating composite :
                'D:\Chapter19\Calculator\composite.xml'
   [scac] >>>>>>>>>>>>>>>>>>>>>>>>>>>>>>>>>>>>>>>>>>>>>>>
   [scac] >> modified xmlbean locale class in use
   [scac] >>>>>>>>>>>>>>>>>>>>>>>>>>>>>>>>>>>>>>>>>>>>>>>

BUILD SUCCESSFUL
Total time: 4 seconds
```

Package parameters (ant-sca-package.xml)

- `compositeName`: Name of the composite
- `compositeDir`: Directory of the project to be packaged
- `revision`: Revision/version of the composite

See the section on revisions and milestones later in this chapter for an explanation of versioning of composites. Default output will be a `.sar` file called `<compositeName>_rev<revision>.jar` in the `deploy` directory of the project.

```
D:\JDev\jdeveloper\bin>ant -f ant-sca-package.xml
     -DcompositeName=Calculator -DcompositeDir=%PROJ_DIR%
     -Drevision=1.2

Buildfile: ant-sca-package.xml
     [echo] oracle.home = D:\JDev\jdeveloper\bin/..

clean:
  [echo] deleting
         D:\Chapter19\Calculator/deploy/sca_Calculator_rev1.2.jar
  [delete] Deleting:
           D:\Chapter19\Calculator\deploy\sca_Calculator_rev1.2.jar
```

```
init:

scac-validate:
     [echo] Running scac-validate in D:\Chapter19\Calculator/
composite.xml
     [echo] oracle.home = D:\JDev\jdeveloper\bin/..

scac:
     [scac] Validating composite : 'D:\Chapter19\Calculator/composite.
xml'
     [scac] >>>>>>>>>>>>>>>>>>>>>>>>>>>>>>>>>>>>>>>>>>>>
     [scac] >> modified xmlbean locale class in use
     [scac] >>>>>>>>>>>>>>>>>>>>>>>>>>>>>>>>>>>>>>>>>>>>

package:
    [input] skipping input as property compositeDir has already
            been set.
    [input] skipping input as property compositeName has already
            been set.
    [input] skipping input as property revision has already been set.
     [echo] oracle.home = D:\Oracle\JDev11gPS1\jdeveloper\bin/..

compile-source:
    [mkdir] Created dir: D:\ Chapter19\Calculator\dist
     [copy] Copying 41 files to D:\ Chapter19\Calculator\dist
     [copy] Warning: D:\Chapter19\src not found.
      [jar] Building jar: D:\Chapter19\Calculator\deploy\sca_
Calculator_rev1.2.jar
   [delete] Deleting directory D:\ Chapter19\Calculator\dist

BUILD SUCCESSFUL
Total time: 12 seconds
```

Deploy parameters (ant-sca-deploy.xml)

- `serverURL`: Server on which to deploy the SAR file in the format `http://target-server:8001`
- `sarLocation`: Path to either a single SAR file or a ZIP file containing multiple SAR files
- `overwrite`: Replace an existing composite with the same name and revision/version (values are true or false, the default value)
- `user`: Username on SOA server, usually weblogic
- `password`: Credentials of the user on the SOA server

- forceDefault: Indicates if this revision is to be the default revision (values are true, the default, or false)
- configPlan: Configuration plan to be applied to this deployment

```
D:\JDev\jdeveloper\bin>ant -f ant-sca-deploy.xml
     -DserverURL=http://localhost:8001
     -DsarLocation=%PROJ_DIR%\deploy\sca_Calculator_rev1.2.jar
     -Duser=weblogic -Dpassword=welcome1
Buildfile: ant-sca-deploy.xml
      [echo] oracle.home = D:\Oracle\JDev11gPS1\jdeveloper\bin/..

deploy:
     [input] skipping input as property serverURL has already been
set.
     [input] skipping input as property sarLocation has already
been set.
[deployComposite] setting user/password..., user=weblogic
[deployComposite] Processing sar=D:\Chapter19\Calculator\deploy\
sca_Calculator_rev1.2.jar
[deployComposite] Adding sar file - D:\Chapter19\Calculator\
deploy\sca_Calculator_rev1.2.jar
[deployComposite] Creating HTTP connection to host:localhost,
port:8001
[deployComposite] Received HTTP response from the server,
                  Response code=200
[deployComposite] ---->Deploying composite success.

BUILD SUCCESSFUL
Total time: 10 seconds
```

See the section on revisions and milestones later in this chapter for an explanation of default revisions/versions. See the section on deployment plans later in this chapter for an explanation on how deployment plans allow the customization of SAR files for different environments.

Note that the deploy command takes a .sar file as input and so usually the deploy command is preceded by the package command.

The `deploy` command has the following sub-commands available:

- `undeploy` to remove a deployed composite. This command has the following parameters:
    - `serverURL`
    - `compositeName`
    - `revision`
    - `user`
    - `password`
- `exportComposite` to retrieve a deployed SAR file from a server, either with or without post-deployment configuration changes. This is useful for providing exact deployed configurations to Oracle support or for verifying changes needed in a particular environment. It has the following parameters:
    - `serverURL`
    - `compositeName`
    - `revision`
    - `updateType`: None includes no changes, all includes all changes, property includes only changes to properties and policies, and runtime includes only changes to items such as rules dictionaries and domain value maps.
    - `sarFile`: Location of the SAR file to be written containing export data
    - `user`
    - `password`
- `exportUpdates` allows configuration changes to the composite to be exported. This is useful for verifying changes needed in a particular environment or for creating a configuration file to be applied to the same composite in a different environment. It has the following parameters:
    - `serverURL`
    - `compositeName`
    - `revision`
    - `updateType`: Same as the `exportComposite` parameter
    - `jarFile`: Location of configuration `.jar` file to be written
    - `user`
    - `password`

- `importUpdates` is used in conjunction with the `exportUpdates` command and allows the import of composite configuration information. It has the following parameters:
  - `serverURL`
  - `compositeName`
  - `revision`
  - `jarFile`: Location of the `.jar` file containing configuration to import
  - `user`
  - `password`

Test parameters (ant-sca-test.xml)

- `scatest.input`: Name of the composite to test (test)
- `scatest.result`: Directory for test results (test)
- `jndi.properties.input`: JNDI properties file to use for server connection (test)

Tests are executed on the SOA server and the JNDI file contains the properties needed to connect to the server. A sample JNDI property file is as shown:

```
java.naming.factory.initial=weblogic.jndi.WLInitialContextFactory
java.naming.provider.url=t3://target-server:8001/soa-infra
java.naming.security.principal=weblogic
java.naming.security.credentials=welcome1
dedicated.connection=true
dedicated.rmicontext=true
```

The `test` command can be used to automate the initiation of test scripts. For example, allow test scripts to be run every evening against the latest build in the source repository and the test results will be available for the developers in the morning.

Revisions and milestones

When deploying a composite, we are required to provide a revision or a version number. The revision number is a sequence of numeric digits with '.' as separators. For example, the default revision in JDeveloper for a composite is '1.0'. Each revision number represents a different composite on the SOA server. For example, Calculator revision 1.0 and Calculator 1.1 are different composites. All the artifacts in a composite, including the rules, Mediator configuration, BPEL processes, and human workflow, are part of the versioning of the composite. The only exception is the custom UI components of the human workflow, which are not deployed as part of the composite and hence are not versioned with it. Redeployment of the UI portion of a human workflow will overwrite the previous version and therefore may break deployed versions of composites using them, unless the name of the human workflow UI artifacts are changed when they are redeployed.

Revisions may be thought of as major versions. It is also possible to specify milestones, which are sub-versions. This is done by appending a '-' to the version, as in Calculator 1.1-test6. The name of the milestone must start with an alphabetic character.

Version numbers can be used to keep distinct versions of the code separate in the server. Deployment of a new revision of a composite does not impact the execution of existing composite instances. Composite instances started with a particular revision of a composite will continue to execute on that revision.

If a revision is undeployed, then any instances associated with that revision will stop executing and will be marked as stale. This means that the data cannot be accessed because the metadata of the composite definition is no longer available to help interpret the composite instance data.

The default revision

There is a default revision associated with each composite name. When invoking a composite, it is possible to specify a revision number, in which case, that exact revision will be invoked. If no revision number is specified, then the default revision, which is in force at the time of invocation, will be used.

The default revision can be used to help manage migration between revisions. Imagine that we wish to deploy Calculator 1.1 alongside the currently deployed Calculator 1.0. We are concerned that we haven't tested Calculator 1.1 with real customers, so we would like to make it available as part of a beta program before making it our default composite revision. In this case, we can deploy Calculator 1.1, but leave Calculator 1.0 as the default revision. Users invoking the composite without a specific revision number will continue to invoke Calculator 1.0, but beta customers can be pointed at the specific 1.1 revision. When we are satisfied that Calculator 1.1 is a good revision, we can make it the default revision. Now all customers who do not specify a revision number will create instances of Calculator 1.1. Existing composite instances of Calculator 1.0 will continue to execute to completion.

Enabling web service endpoint and WSDL location alteration

If we are a using a UDDI repository to store the location of our WSDL and XSD artifacts, then when we deploy our composites to different environments, they will automatically pick up the appropriate endpoints by retrieving them from the UDDI server configured in the target container. However, some components may need additional modification such as JCA configuration files.

When deploying between environments, we typically want to modify the endpoint details to reflect the new environment, which will have different hostnames for its services. This can be done by editing the reference in JDeveloper by changing the **WSDL URL** to the new environment.

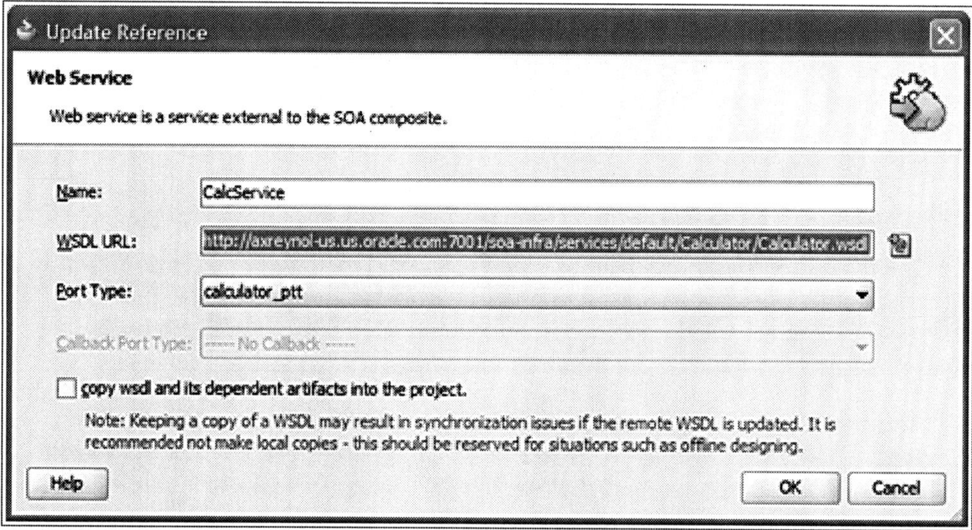

It is also possible to alter endpoint locations at runtime in Enterprise Manager. Select the composite to modify in EM and scroll down to the bottom of the **Dashboard** tab. In the **Services and References** section (see the following screenshot), click on the reference that you wish to modify.

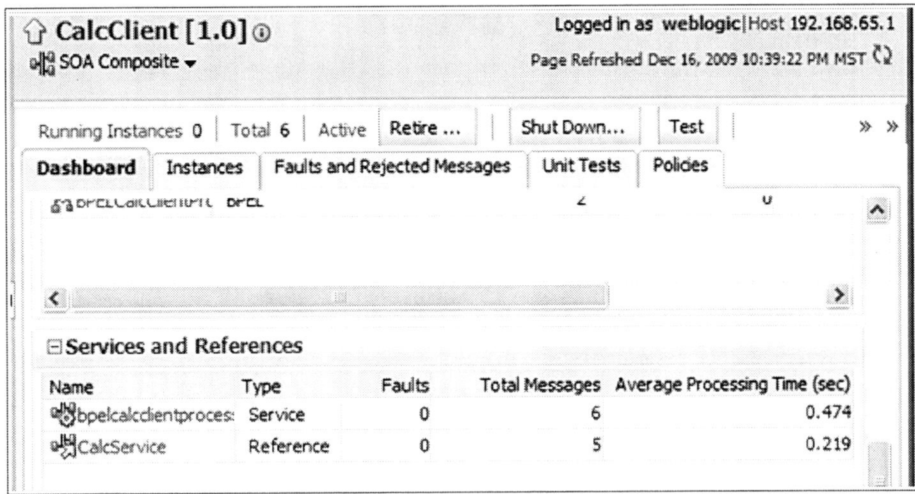

On the reference page, choose the **Properties** tab and set the endpoint location to be the correct value for the environment. Note that this is the target endpoint, not the WSDL location.

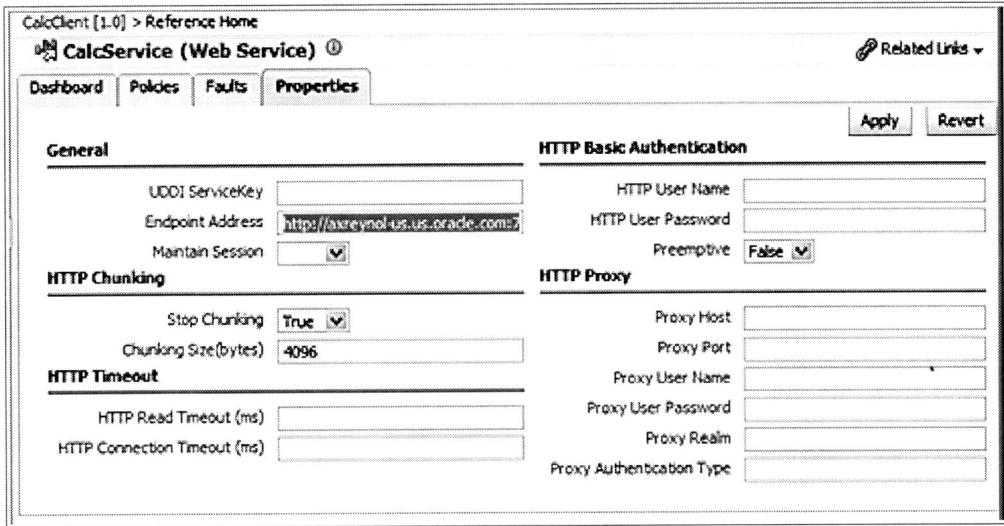

In the summary endpoint, the WSDL location changes can be handled by editing the reference in JDeveloper while the endpoint location changes can be handled in the Enterprise Manager.

Enabling adapter configuration

In addition to web service endpoints changing in different environments, we often want to modify the configuration of adapters. Many adapters make use of JEE resources, so the JEE container just needs to be correctly configured with the resource names. For example, the database adapter uses a JNDI lookup to find its data source. Similarly, the JMS adapter uses a JNDI lookup to find its queues. However, some adapters, such as the file adapter, do not have a JNDI lookup and have several properties that may require changing.

The adapter settings can be modified at runtime by editing the **Properties** tab in the reference screen. For example, the file adapter allows us to modify a number of settings to adjust the adapter to its environment.

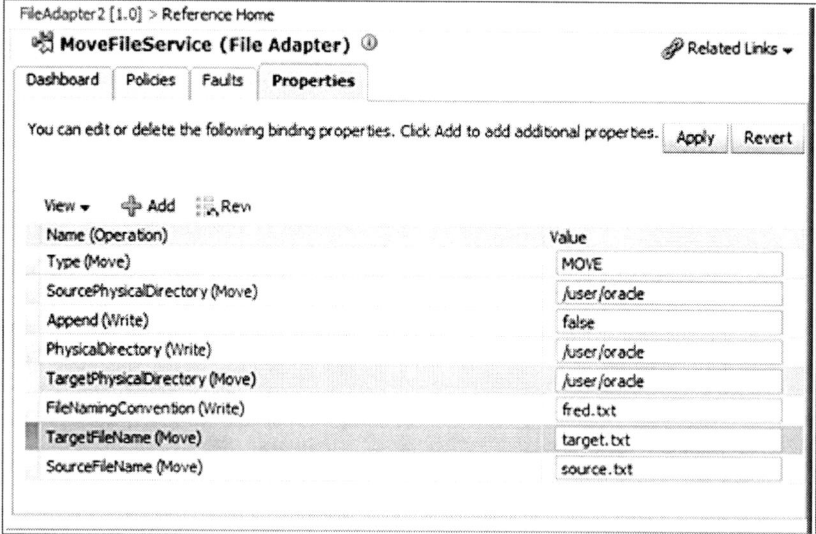

XML schema locations

XML schemas are often referenced via relative links from a WSDL file, in which case, updating the WSDL location will make the XML schema files available. However, sometimes the XML schema files are stored separately with their own URLs. In this case, the URLs will usually be embedded in the WSDL file referencing them, and each reference will need to be updated before redeploying the process to the correct environment.

XSL imports

Any XSL files that reference external schema will also need to be updated before deployment.

Composite configuration plan framework

Modifying the `composite.xml` file or altering locations through the console provides a degree of customization for different environments, but it is all done as a single property at a time and requires a lot of work for each environment, especially when it is considered that individual WSDL files may also need to be updated.

The configuration plan framework combines the SCA archive with a configuration plan that updates multiple files in the SCA archive with the correct values for the deployment environment. Different configuration plans can be created and maintained for each deployment plan.

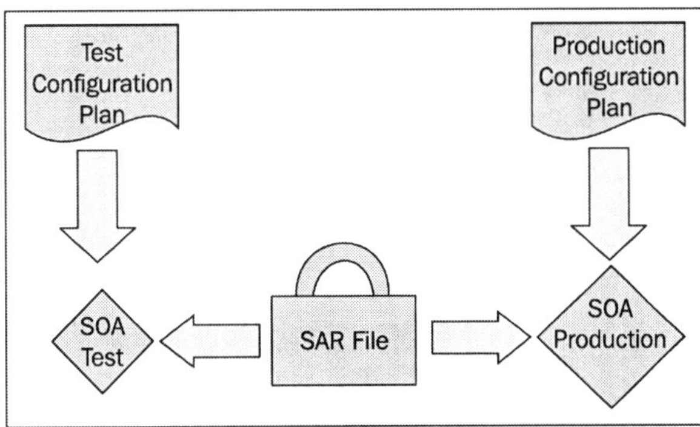

It is possible to generate a template configuration plan from a JDeveloper project, which can be customized and used with the base SCA archive at deployment time to update the various URLs and properties.

The steps to customize the SCA archive for each environment are as follows:

- Create a configuration plan template from within JDeveloper that will be used as the basis for the configuration plans
- Create a configuration plan based on the template for each target environment
- Attach the appropriate configuration plan to the SCA archive when deploying in the target environment

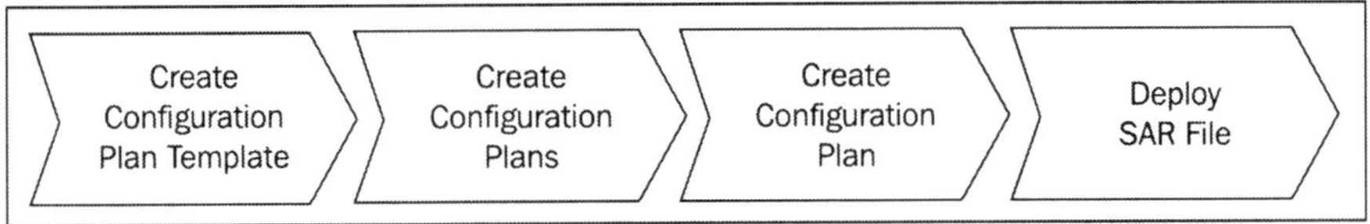

Creating a configuration plan template

There is no difference between a configuration template and a configuration plan, but the template is a useful concept as it forms the base configuration plan that must be modified for each environment.

To create a configuration plan, we can right-click on the `composite.xml` file in JDeveloper and select the **Generate Config Plan** option.

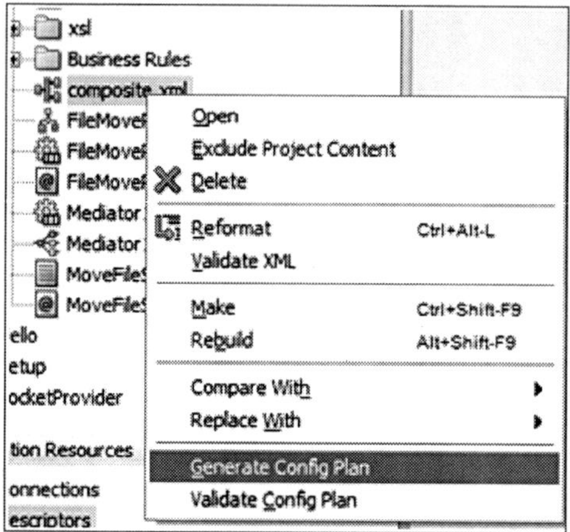

This takes us to the **Composite Configuration Plan Generator** dialog, where we can specify the name of the configuration plan to be generated.

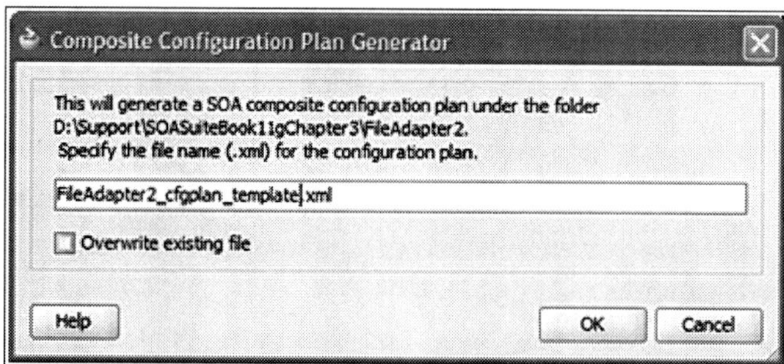

Clicking **OK** will create a new configuration plan and open it within JDeveloper. A sample configuration plan is shown in the code that follows. Note the use of two elements:

- `<replace>` is used to replace the value of a property
- `<searchReplace>` is used to `<search>` for a string and `<replace>` it with another string

The scope of the substitution is determined by the different elements within the configuration plan. The `<composite>` element controls changes within `composite.xml`. Individual elements within the composite can all be adapted for the target environment, including `<service>`, `<component>`, and `<reference>`.

```
<?xml version="1.0" encoding="UTF-8"?>
<SOAConfigPlan >
  <composite name="FileAdapter2">
    <searchReplace>
      <search>http://my-dev-server</search>
      <replace>http://my-test-server</replace>
    <searchReplace>
    …
    <service name="filemoveprocess_client_ep">
      <binding type="ws">
        <attribute name="port">
          <replace>http://xmlns.oracle.com /…</replace>
        </attribute>
         </binding>
    </service>
    <component name="*">
      <wsp:PolicyReference orawsp:category="management" orawsp:
status="enabled" URI="oracle/log_policy"/>
    </component>
    …
    <reference name="MoveFileService">
      <binding type="jca"/>
    </reference>
  </composite>
  …
  <wsdlAndSchema name="FileMove.wsdl|MoveFile.jca|xsd/FileMove.xsd">
    …
    <jca:property name="PollingInterval">
      <replace>10</replace>
    </jca:property>
    …
```

```
    <searchReplace>
      <search>http://my-dev-server</search>
      <replace>http://my-test-server</replace>
    <searchReplace>
  </wsdlAndSchema>
</SOAConfigPlan>
```

Creating a configuration plan

Having created a configuration plan to use a template, we can use this to create configuration plans for each specific environment. We do this by creating a copy of the configuration plan by selecting **Save As** from the `file` menu in JDeveloper and then editing the `<replace>` and `<searchReplace>` tags to match our target environment.

For example, we could search and replace all instances of our local development machine hostname, `w2k3`, with the name of our test server, `testserver`, across WSDL and XSD files. To do this, we modify the search and replace elements, as shown in the following snippet of code:

```
<wsdlAndSchema name="*">
  <searchReplace>
    <search>w2k3</search>
    <replace>testserver</replace>
  </searchReplace>
</wsdlAndSchema>
```

This will cause the SOA server to search all WSDL and schema files `"*"` in the suitcase at deployment time and replace the string `w2k3` with the string `testserver`. Note that it is possible to have multiple `<searchReplace>` elements.

Attaching a configuration plan to an SCA archive

Having created and saved a deployment plan specific to one or more environments, we will want to deploy our process into an environment. When deploying the composite, either through the command line, JDeveloper, or the EM Console, we have the option of attaching a configuration plan. When using JDeveloper, the configuration file is attached to the **Deploy Configuration** step of the deployment wizard. When using the command line, the configuration file is specified using the `configPlan` parameter.

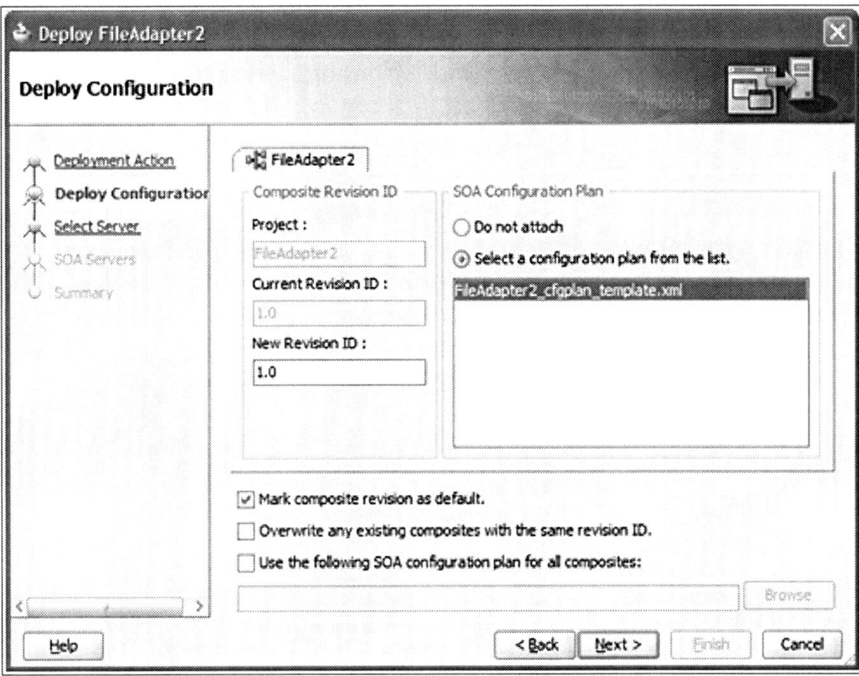

Web services security

We can export the policies from an SOA installation by going to the **Web Services Policies** screen. See *Chapter 21, Defining Security and Management Policies* for more information about creating and applying security policies. From the **Web Services Policies** screen, we can select the policy we wish to export and then click the **Export to File** link. This will give us the ability to save the policy to a local file, which can then be moved to another environment and imported using the **Import From File** link.

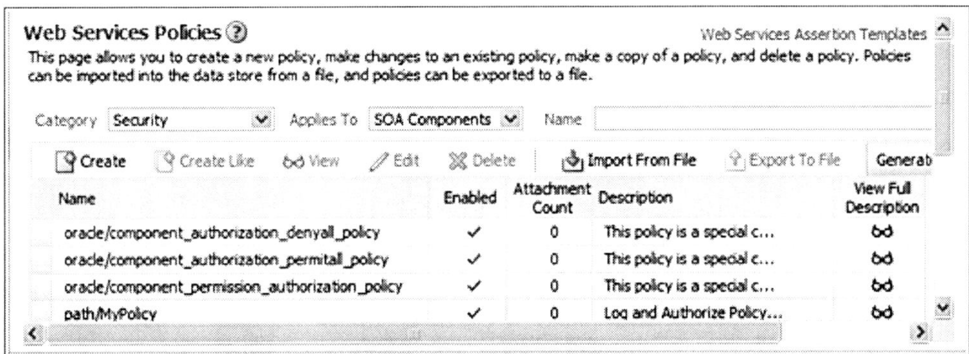

Oracle rules

Rules will generally not change between environments and can be deployed as part of the SAR file.

Business activity monitoring

Business activity monitoring (**BAM**) provides a command-line tool called `iCommand` to assist in exporting and importing BAM components such as data object definitions, reports, and data objects themselves. It is possible to select subsets of components, making it easy to move just the updated components from a development to a test and/or production environment.

Commands

`ICommand` allows a number of different operations through the `-cmd` parameter, which can take the following values:

- `export`: Exports the selected components and/or values
- `import`: Imports the selected components and/or values
- `delete`: Deletes the selected components
- `rename`: Renames components
- `clear`: Clears data from a given object

Selecting items

Items are identified using a file-like syntax such as `/Samples/Employees`. There are a number of parameters that may be used to select items in different ways, which are as follows:

- `-name`: Selects items explicitly by name, for example,`-name "/Samples/Employees"`
- `-match`: Selects items by using a DOS style pattern, for example,`-match "/Samples/*"`
- `-regex`: Selects items by using a regular expression, for example, `-regex "/Samples/[A-Za-z]* Sales"`
- `-all`: Selects all components

These queries may be combined with the following parameters to further restrict the items selected:

- `-type`: Restricts the items exported by type, for example, `-type Folder` or `-type DataObject`
- `-dependencies`: Includes dependent objects in the selection
- `-contents`: Includes (value 1 or unspecified) or excludes (value 0) the contents of a data object, for example, `-contents 0`
- `-layout`: Includes (value 1 or unspecified) or excludes (value 0) the data object type definition, for example, `-layout 0`

Using iCommand

Before using `iCommand`, we need to set the `JAVA_HOME` environment variable. If the BAM server is not running on port 9001, we need to edit the `BAMICommandConfig.xml` file found in the `$SOA_HOME/bam/config` directory and change the port number element `<ADCServerPort>`. We can also set the username and password in this file by adding the following elements:

```
<ICommand_Default_User_Name>weblogic</ICommand_Default_User_Name>
<ICommand_Default_Password>welcome1</ICommand_Default_Password>
```

Providing these elements in the configuration file avoids the need to provide the username and password when `iCommand` is run, which is useful if we are to script `iCommand`.

When migrating items between environments, we will generally not want to move the actual contents of the data, but only the layouts. For example, to export the layouts but not the contents for all the sales data objects, we issue the following command:

```
D:\ FMW11gPS1\SOA\bam\bin>icommand -cmd export -file SalesDataObjects.
xml -regex "[a-zA-Z]* Sales" -contents 0

Oracle BAM Command Utility [Build 7562, BAM Repository Version 2025]
Copyright 2002, 2009, Oracle and/or its affiliates. All rights
reserved.
Exporting of Data Object "/Samples/Film Sales" started
Data Object "/Samples/Film Sales" with "0" rows exported
Exporting of Data Object "/Samples/Media Sales" started
Data Object "/Samples/Media Sales" with "0" rows exported
Exporting of Data Object "/Samples/Product Sales" started
Data Object "/Samples/Product Sales" with "0" rows exported
"3" items exported successfully.
Items were exported to "1" files.
```

This generates a file that can be used to import the definitions into another BAM instance. The generated file `SalesDataObjects.xml` is in the following format:

```
<?xml version="1.0"?>
<OracleBAMExport Version="2025">
  <DataObject Version="14" Name="Film Sales" ID="_Film_Sales"
              Path="/Samples" External="0">
    <Layout>
      <Column Name="Region" ID="_Region" Type="string" MaxSize="100"
              Nullable="1" Public="1"/>
      ...
      <Indexes/>
    </Layout>
  </DataObject>
  <DataObject Version="14" Name="Media Sales" ID="_Media_Sales"
              Path="/Samples" External="0">
    ...
  </DataObject>
</OracleBAMExport>
```

Note that it is possible to edit the contents of the exported data files, and this can provide a means to batch load reference data from another system into BAM.

To import from a file `employees.xml`, we issue the following command:

```
D:\ FMW11gPS1\SOA\bam\bin>icommand -cmd import -file Employees.xml

Oracle BAM Command Utility [Build 7562, BAM Repository Version 2025]
Copyright 2002, 2009, Oracle and/or its affiliates. All rights
reserved.
Importing from file "D:\Oracle\FMW11gPS1\SOA\bam\bin\Employees.xml".
Data Object already exists, ID ignored.
Data Object already exists, Layout section ignored.
The contents of Data Object "/Samples/Employees" updated
Data Object imported successfully (3 rows).
"1" items imported successfully.Oracle BAM Command Utility
```

The `import` command will always import the full contents of the file into the target BAM instance.

Summary

The SOA Suite provides facilities for moving configurations between different environments, using either web-based tools or command-line tools. Generally, the use of command-line tools allows deployment to be more repeatable through scripting. Some properties must be modified during the move from one environment to another and configuration plan files make this easier.

20
Testing Composite Applications

In this chapter, we will focus on the tools in JDeveloper and the SOA Suite that will assist you in testing the components of your SOA application. The basic principles of testing are the same in SOA as in other software development approaches. You start by testing the lowest level components and gradually build up to a complete system test before moving into user acceptance testing. You may also be required to undertake some form of performance testing.

We will begin our discussion by looking at the manual testing of individual components and services in the SOA Suite. We will then investigate the importance of repeatable testing before moving on to discuss automated testing and the testing framework available in the Oracle SOA Suite. Finally, we will discuss how a system may be performance tested.

Tests can be run in either of the two fashions. They can be run manually by a dedicated testing team or there can be automated tests. Manual testing tends to run only when the software is deemed almost ready for release due to the cost of hiring people to run the tests. Automated tests are preferred as they potentially allow the test suites to be run on all the intermediate builds of software, providing management with a heartbeat of the robustness of the release under development. We will take a look at the support provided for both models of testing within the SOA Suite.

SOA Suite testing model

The SOA Suite has two distinct methods of testing SOA artifacts. They may be tested via a test service client or in a repeatable fashion through the SOA Suite test framework. In either case, it is necessary, at the very least, to generate the appropriate input data to the artifact being tested.

The following diagram shows a simple **Composite** service that is invoked by a **Client**, which in turn invokes two services before the **Composite** completes:

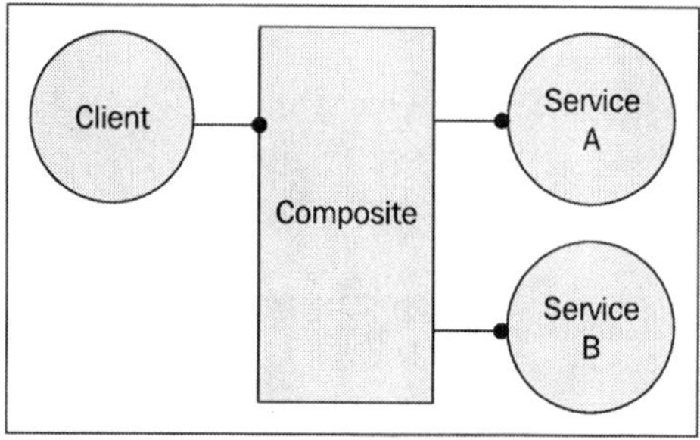

The details of the composite service are not relevant at this point, and the composite could consist of a Service Bus pipeline, a Mediator, a BPEL process, or all three. Note that the nature of the composite defines several interfaces; the composite exposes a client interface, and in turn makes use of interfaces exposed by the two services. We will use this simple example (previously shown) to explore how to perform different levels of the test.

One-off testing

Within a development environment, it is very useful to run a quick test of a composite or interaction to ensure that it behaves as expected. These one-off tests can be run from the **Enterprise Manager (EM)** Console and the Service Bus Console, as explained in the next section, *Testing composites*.

Testing composites

All deployed composites have a test client created for them. This is accessed by clicking on the composite in the EM Console and selecting the **Test** tab. The test client in the EM Console is very good when you want to quickly test whether the composite you have deployed is behaving as expected. It allows you to specify the input parameters through the web interface, including a choice of Tree or XML input formats. When switching between views, the data entered will be preserved. The next example from the EM console shows how the Tree format makes it very easy to focus on just the input fields required, rather than having to be concerned with the exact XML format required by the composite.

Posting the XML message will cause the composite to be invoked and any results will then be available through the console. Verification of the accuracy of the results must be done manually by the developer. Later in this chapter, we will examine how testing of results may also be automated.

If you have a very complicated interface, you may not want to have to enter the parameter values every time you test the composite. In 10*g*, there was a facility to set a default input to a BPEL process. Unfortunately, there is no such facility for 11*g* composites. In order to avoid retyping complex inputs, the input can be saved to a file and then pasted into the test dialog every time, as explained in the tip.

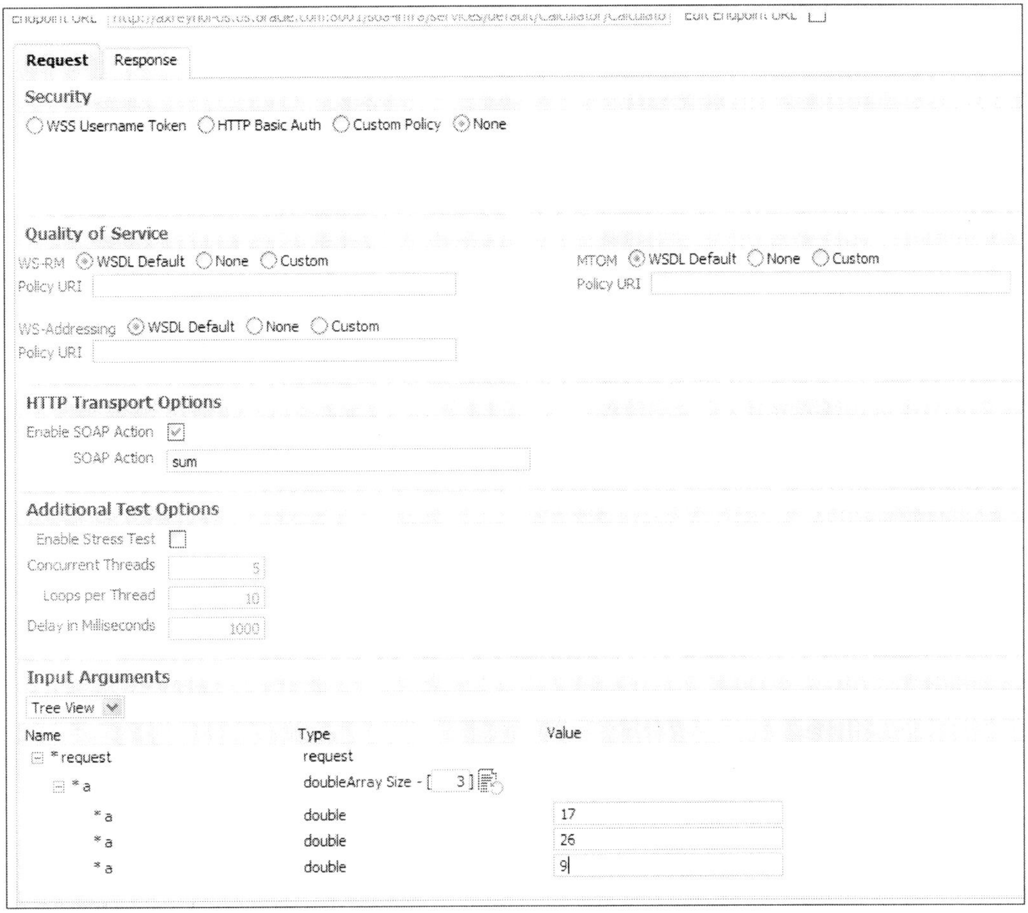

Providing Default Input

Enter the desired parameters in the **Tree View**. Switch to the **XML View** by selecting it from the drop-down list. You will now see a SOAP message constructed to contain the input to the composite that you entered in the **Tree View**. Copy the XML to the clipboard and then save it in a file. The contents of the file can then be pasted into the **XML View** to provide a default input.

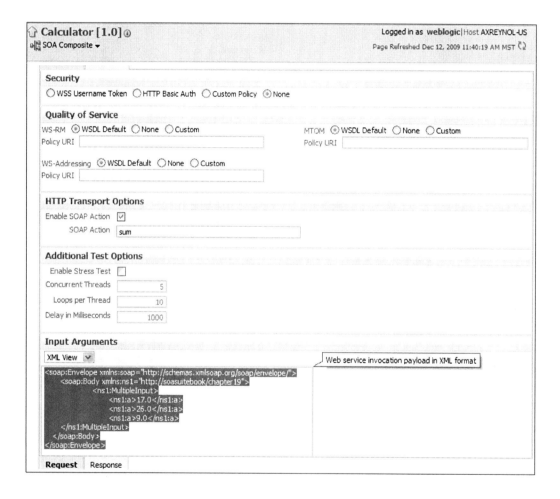

Calculator [1.0]
SOA Composite

Logged in as **weblogic** | Host AXREYNOL-US
Page Refreshed Dec 12, 2009 11:40:19 AM MST

Security

WSS Username Token HTTP Basic Auth Custom Policy None

Quality of Service

WS-RM WSDL Default None Custom
Policy URI

MTOM WSDL Default None Custom
Policy URI

WS-Addressing WSDL Default None Custom
Policy URI

HTTP Transport Options

Enable SOAP Action
SOAP Action sum

Additional Test Options

Enable Stress Test
Concurrent Threads 5
Loops per Thread 10
Delay in Milliseconds 1000

Input Arguments

XML View

Web service invocation payload in XML format

```
<soap:Envelope xmlns:soap="http://schemas.xmlsoap.org/soap/envelope/">
    <soap:Body xmlns:ns1="http://soasuitebook/chapter19">
            <ns1:MultipleInput>
                <ns1:a>17.0</ns1:a>
                <ns1:a>26.0</ns1:a>
                <ns1:a>9.0</ns1:a>
        </ns1:MultipleInput>
    </soap:Body>
</soap:Envelope>
```

Request Response

Use of the test client

The test client should not be part of the formal testing strategy. It should be used by developers to get immediate feedback on the correctness of their composite and not as part of a formal validation process.

Testing the Service Bus

The Service Bus also provides a simple client-testing interface. In EM, the only option is to test the entire composite, but in the Service Bus, we can test either the business service (the backend service) or the proxy service (the Service Bus Interface). After navigating to the folder containing the proxy or business service, the tester is invoked by clicking on the bug icon.

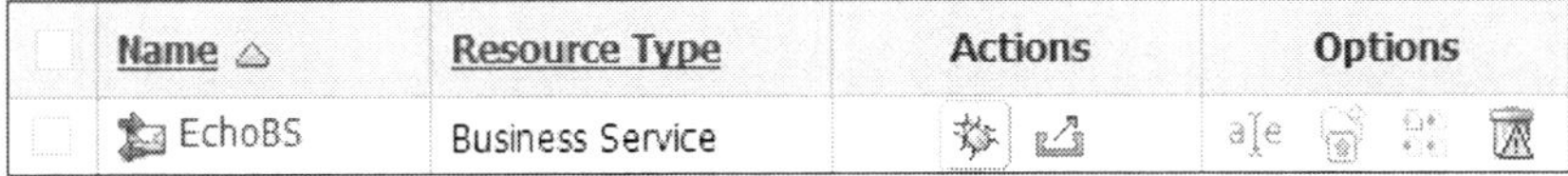

This brings up the test client. For a SOAP service, the test client allows the specification of the message parameters in the SOAP body through the payload textbox as well as the addition of any SOAP headers that may be required. When testing a proxy service, there are two options that control how the call is submitted and what additional information is collected. The **Direct Call** is normally used with the proxy service and allows additional information about the processing of the message to be collected through the use of the trace option. This can be invaluable in tracing problems in the Service Bus pipelines or routing services.

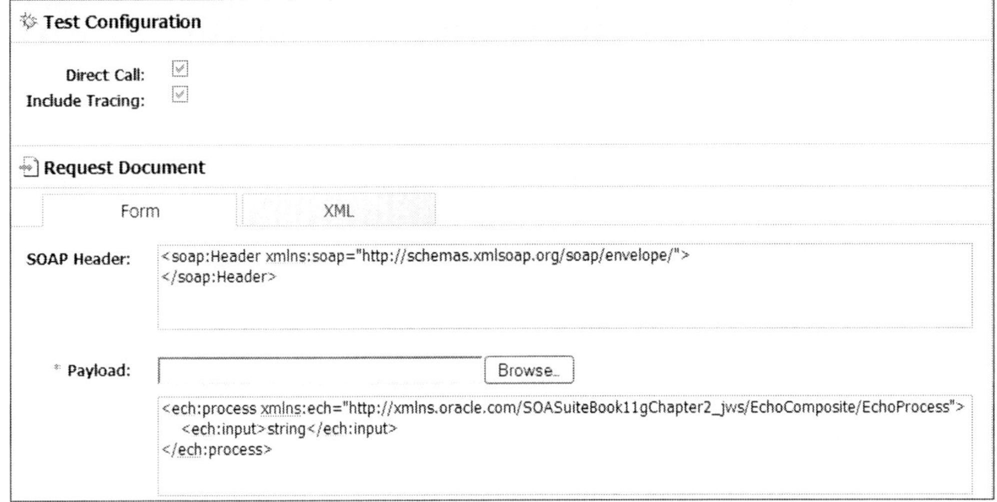

The output from the test client can be checked manually for correctness.

Automated testing

Up to this point, the testing we have investigated is manual-based and requires human intervention. For more extensive testing, we require an automated test framework, which is just what is included in the SOA Suite EM Console.

The composite test framework

The SOA Suite includes a test framework for composites that supports the following:

- Aggregation of multiple tests (called test cases) into a test suite
- Generation of initial messages
- Validation of input into and output from composites, references, and components
- Simulation of reference interactions
- Reporting of test results

The composite test framework may be thought of as similar to the Java unit test framework **JUnit**.

Composite test suites

Individual test cases are grouped into a test suite at the level of an individual JDeveloper project. Note that in the current release, this is only supported for a single composite. Multiple composites would require multiple test suites. Multiple test cases in a single test suite can be executed with a single request, automating a large part of the testing.

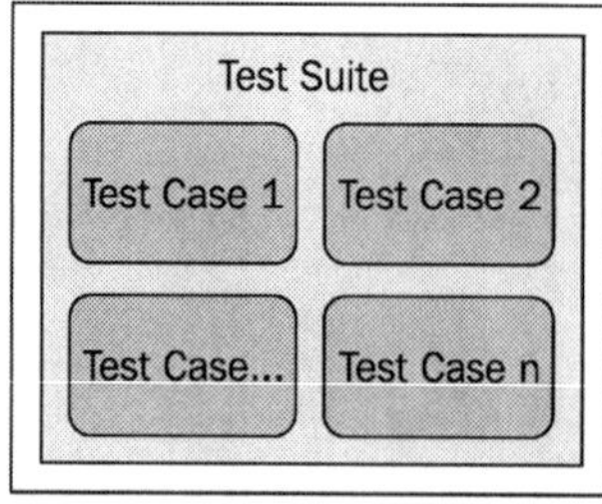

Individual test cases will be used to test different conditions. Each individual **Test Case** will result in a single instance of the composite being created. So a **Test Suite** with 100 test cases would have 100 composite instances created as a result of a single user request from the EM console.

To create a new **Test Suite** in JDeveloper, just right-click on the **Test Suites** folder in an SOA project and select **Create Test Suite**.

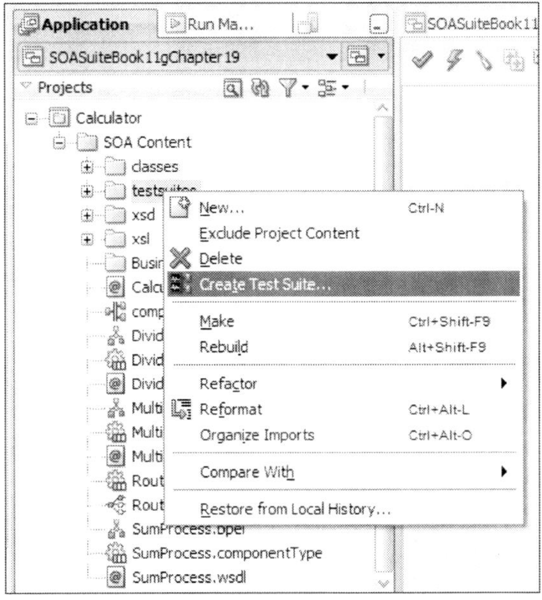

Name the **Test Suite**, and you will be prompted to create your composite test case. This is shown in the following screenshot:

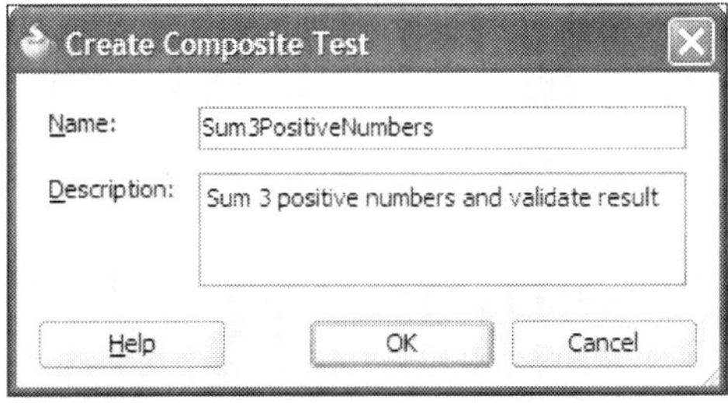

This gives us an empty composite test case to which we need to add an input message and some verification tests, as shown in the following screenshot:

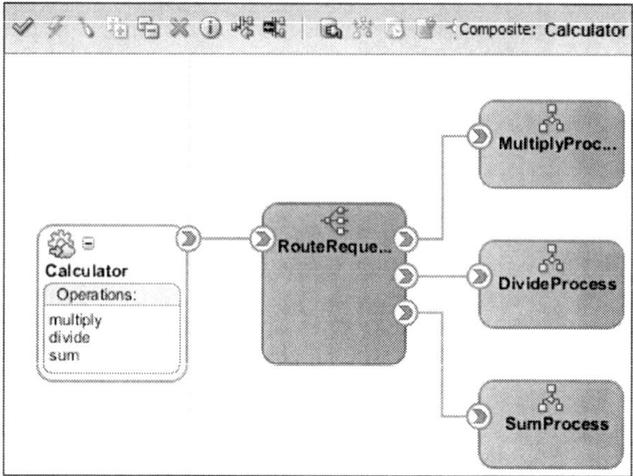

Injecting data into the test case

Firstly, we need to inject an initial message into our test case. We do this by right-clicking on the service in our test case diagram and selecting **Create Initiate Messages**, as shown in the following screenshot:

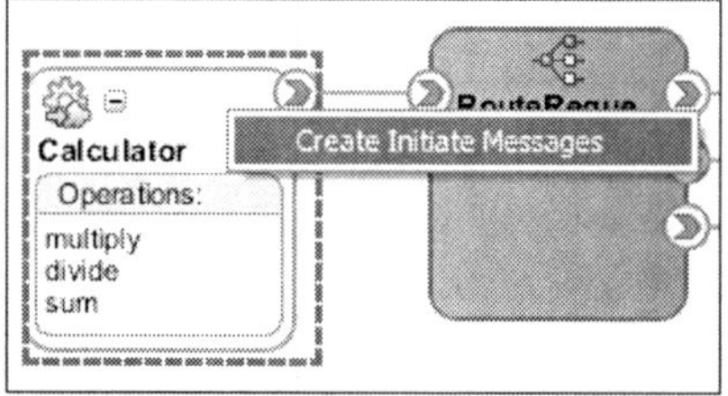

After selecting the operation we wish to test, we can have JDeveloper create a sample input message for us by clicking the **Generate Sample** button. This generates the XML input message, which we are then free to edit to drive the test down the paths that we want. Often, we will want to reuse an input message for different tests. For example, we may wish to have a test that completes successfully, another test that experiences an error in one of its references, and another test that experiences an error in a different reference. To reuse the input message for all these tests, we can click **Save As** to save the input as a file. We are prompted for a filename and the file is saved in the project, as shown in the following screenshot:

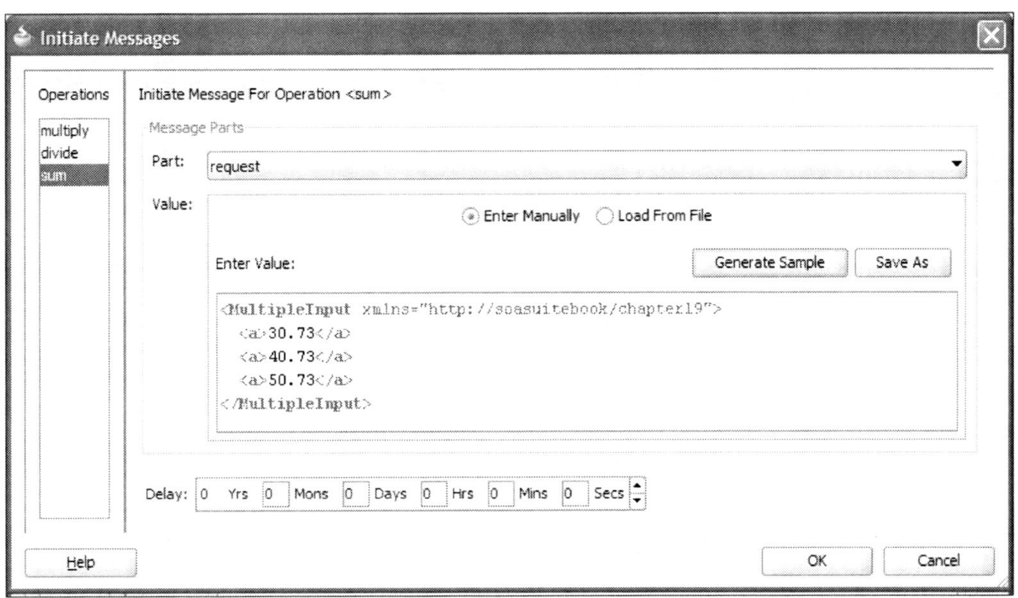

We can use an existing input file by clicking the **Load From File** radio button and using the **Browse** button to locate the input file we want to use, as shown in the following screenshot:

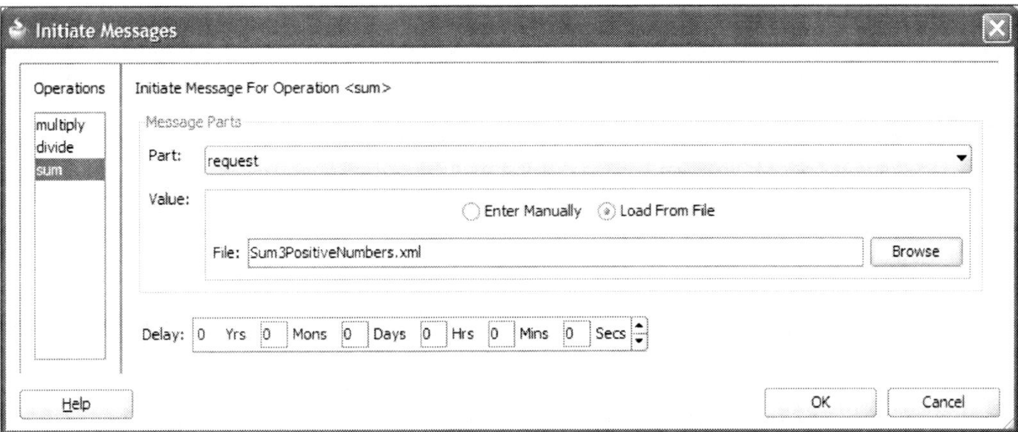

The **Delay** at the bottom of the screen does not make sense for an initiate message, but it is used for callback messages to specify the delay before the callback is invoked. Selecting **OK** will finish creating our initiate message, which is identified on the test diagram by an arrow on the service.

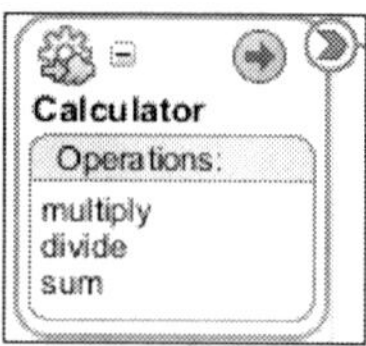

Note that in Release 1 of the 11*g* SOA Suite, it is not possible to test inner components. It is only possible to test at the composite level.

Data validation

The testing framework allows validation to be applied to the inputs and outputs of either the composite as a whole, or individual components, services, and references. Validation is performed through an assertion. An **assertion** is a statement about the expected behavior of the composite at this point. For example, an assertion may identify that the value of the output of a composite should be a particular value. When the test case is run, the actual value of the output will be compared with the expected value and if they do not match, the test case will fail.

We can add assertions to a test case to ensure that we get the expected result. We do this by right-clicking on a wire and selecting **Create Wire Actions** or by double-clicking the wire. This brings up the **Wire Actions** dialog, where we can specify assertions to be executed against input and/or output messages, or we can emulate the reply message from a component or reference. To validate the output from a component, we select the **Asserts** tab and ensure that we have selected the correct operation from the **Operations** list on the left of the dialog box.

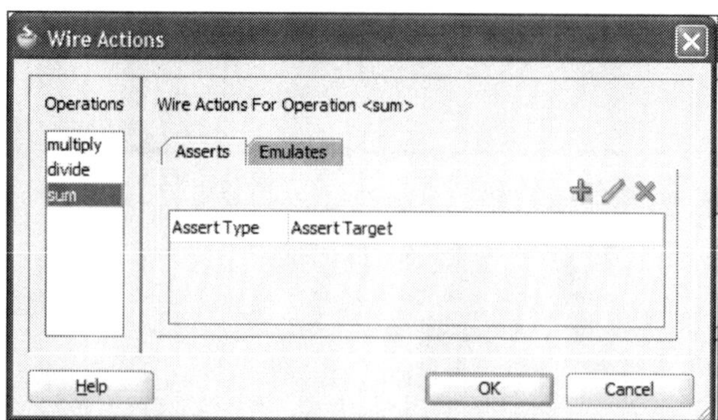

We can then add assertions to this wire by clicking on the green plus sign. This will bring up the **Create Assert** dialog box. Across the top, we can choose the type of assertion:

- **Assert Input** allows us to test the value of the input to the component or reference
- **Assert Output** lets us verify the response from a component or reference
- **Assert Callback** is used to check the value of an asynchronous callback
- **Assert Fault** tests the values of a fault thrown by a component or reference

When asserting faults, we can select the fault from a list of faults declared in the reference that the wire is connected to.

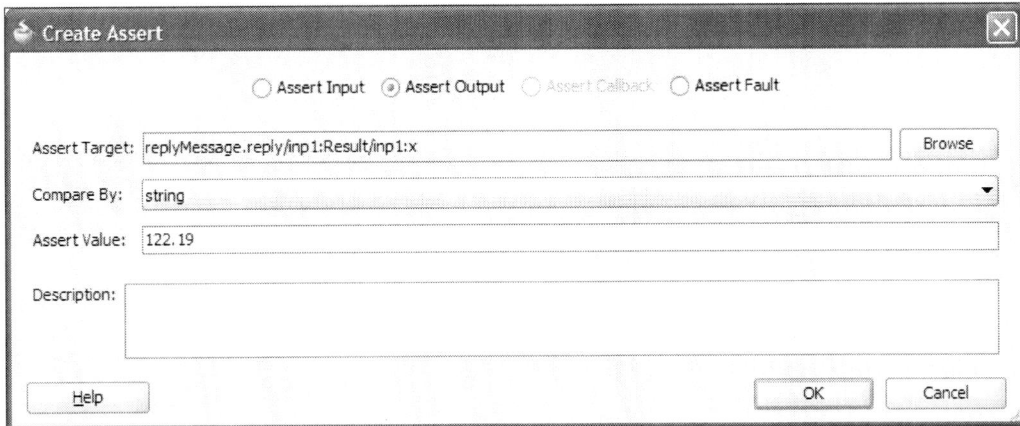

The **Assert Target** can be any XPath expression created by using the **Browse** button. Note that you cannot enter free form XPath expressions. This allows you to select either the entire message or a subset. Note that the XPath browser does not support repeating elements due to a `maxOccurs` property greater than 1, so you cannot select individual elements in an array. If the subset is a single element, then the comparison is done on a single value. If the **Assert Target** is the whole message, then a sample response can be generated using the **Generate Sample** button. If the **Assert Target** is a document fragment, then the **Generate Sample** button will be grayed out. Similar to the initialization message, it is possible to save the **Assert Value** to a file for reuse in other tests. When comparing documents and document fragments, it will generally be better to use the **Compare By** value of **xml-similar**, as this allows for different namespace prefixes to the same namespace and also allows attributes to be in different orders.

Emulating components and references

In addition to placing assertions through the **Wire Actions** dialog box, we can also emulate the behavior of a reference or component. This allows us to test different paths through our composite by emulating specific responses or faults instead of actually calling the component or reference. This is particularly useful for emulating external references and also for raising faults and error conditions.

We access the emulation capabilities through the **Emulates** tab of the **Wire Actions** dialog box. Clicking the green plus sign brings up the **Create Emulate** dialog box, which allows us to specify the output from our target component or reference. We can choose to emulate an out response, a callback message, or a fault. Similar to our initiate message, we can generate a sample response—enter one directly or load it from a file.

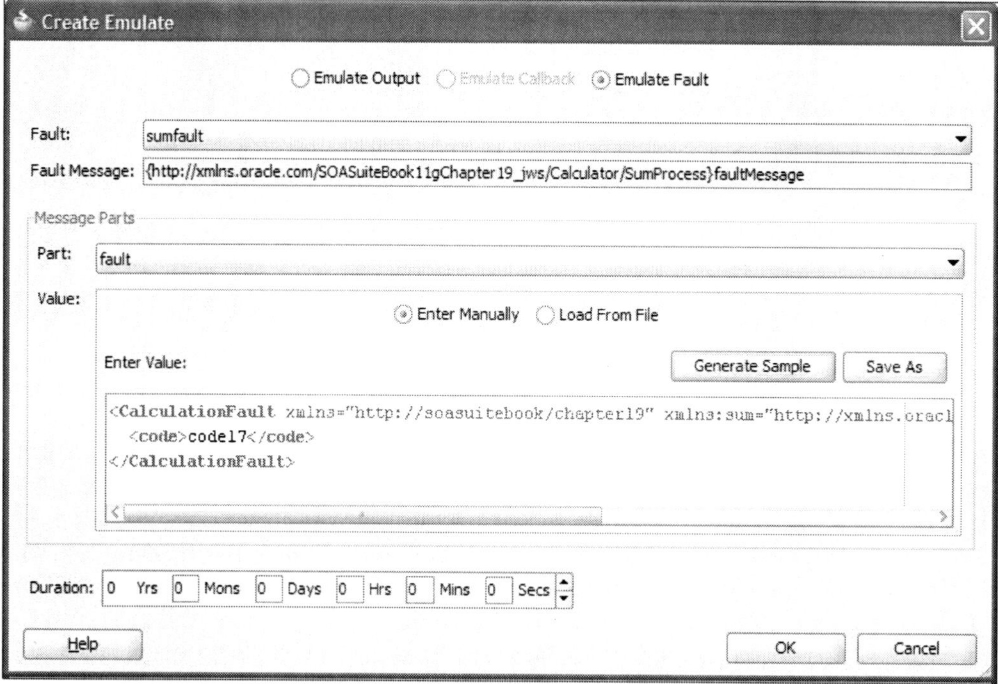

At the bottom of the screen, we can simulate the time taken in the reference or composite by specifying the **Duration** of the call. This is particularly useful if we want to test timeout logic in a callback. For example, there may be a `pick` statement in the BPEL process that calls our emulated component or reference, and we may wish to test the `onTimeout` branch.

When looking at our test case in JDeveloper, we can identify which wires have assertions and/or emulations associated with them by the green arrow pointing into a box that is overlaid on the wires with assertions and emulations.

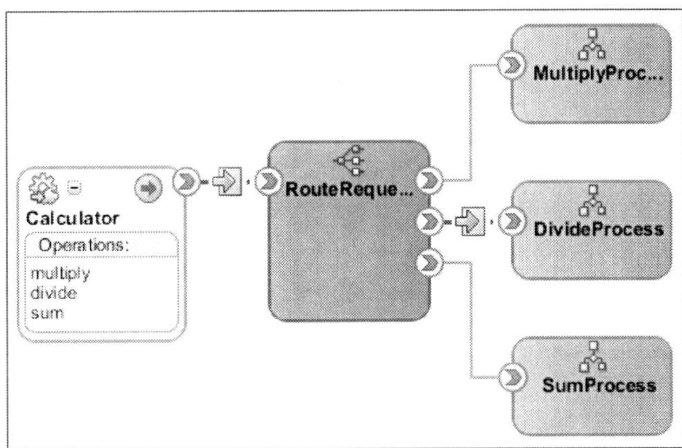

Deploying and running test suites

The test suites and their included test cases are all automatically deployed with the composite. The deployed test suites will appear in the EM console in the composite **Unit Tests** tab, as shown in the following screenshot:

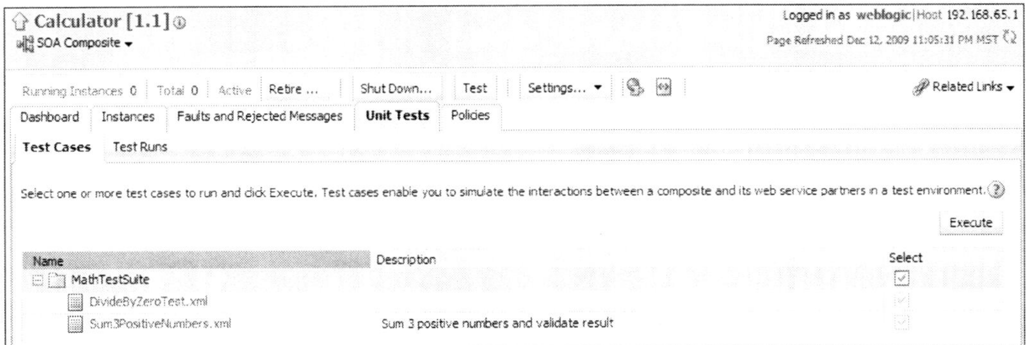

This interface allows all or a subset of tests to be selected and then executed by pressing the **Execute** button. This brings up the **Details of test run** dialog box, which allows us to specify this **Test Run Name**. The **Number of Concurrent Test Instances** field allows for concurrent execution of tests, as shown in the following screenshot:

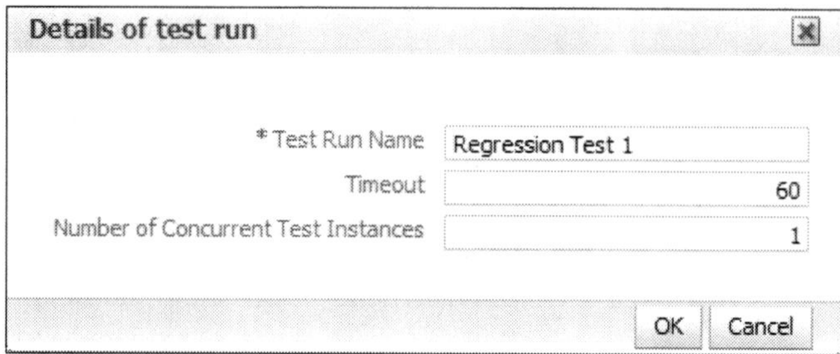

The results of the tests are displayed in the **Test Runs** tab. This provides details of the test runs and individual test results. It is possible to drill down into individual tests by selecting them in the **Results of Test Run** area of the screen and then clicking on the appropriate test instance in the **Assertion details** part of the screen to access the assertion values and also the execution history of the composite instance created during the test.

Note that it is possible to search for test runs by time, making it easy to pull up tests from a particular time period.

Non-executed Paths

If the composite does not generate a particular message across a wire, then the assertion will never fire for that message. For example, if a fault is expected and an assertion is created to test the fault but no fault is thrown, then the test will not fail because the assertion will never be executed. This can be guarded against on a single wire by ensuring that there are assertions for all possible outcomes. For example, in addition to the assertion for the expected fault, we can also create an assertion for a normal response with a value that will always fail if the fault is not thrown and a normal response is received instead.

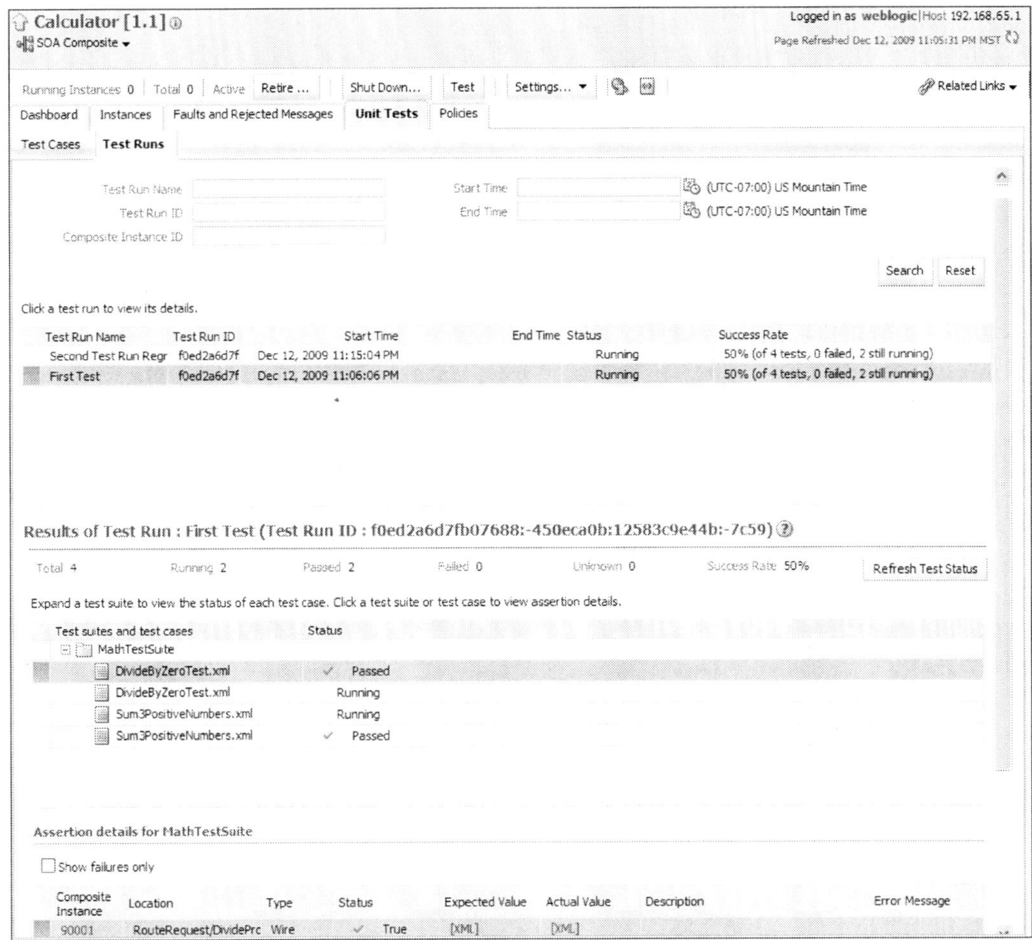

Regression testing

One of the hallmarks of an ongoing successful software system is regression testing. **Regression testing** is the process of creating a series of tests for a software system and then repeating those tests every time a new release of the software is produced. As defects are discovered in the field and fixed, test cases are produced, and these test cases are then added to the set of regression tests. This process helps to ensure that once fixed, the same defect does not reappear in future releases of the software. In this fashion, the number of tests to which a software system is subjected to increases over time. Note that regression tests should be performed at all levels of testing from unit testing up to system testing.

Use of Test Suites

Test suites should always be used to collect related tests on a BPEL composite. They can then be used to run multiple tests with minimal user intervention and so provide a useful regression testing environment.

System testing

Although the EM Console refers to **Unit Tests**, it is possible to test large portions of the system through the composite test framework. By creating a composite that exercises all external interfaces to the system, a large amount of system testing can be performed through the testing framework.

In the next example, the client injects a number of messages into the system, but then either no emulations, or minimal emulations that are performed to allow for the entire system to be exercised. This is because when no emulation is specified, the actual partner link will be invoked. This effectively tests both the individual services, which may be composites themselves, as well as the composite assembly itself. This type of testing only delivers high level success or fail information around individual use cases. Because many of the services will themselves be complex assemblies, it is not possible in this type of testing to drill down into the exact reason why an individual test case may fail. However, this type of testing does provide a high level of confidence that the whole system interacts correctly, because there is a minimum of emulation.

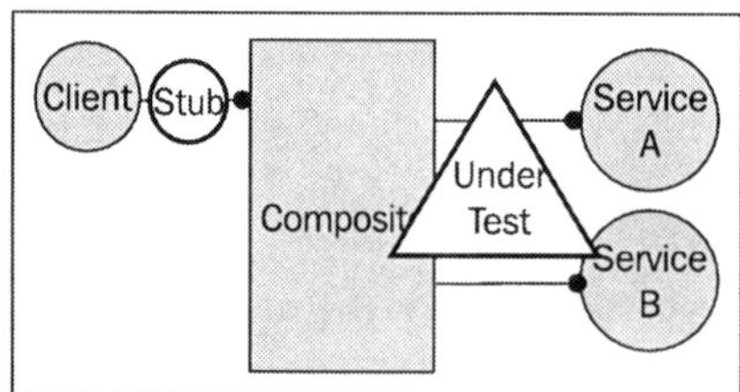

This type of configuration, as shown in the previous diagram, may also be used to test individual composites in the context of the actual services that they will use.

Composite testing

The problem with the system test is that it may fail for many reasons and often those reasons are unclear. Composite level testing allows us to isolate the individual composites and test them against their specifications. To do this, we inject requests from the client and emulate the references used by the composite, so that we have complete control over all interactions between the composite and the references it interfaces with.

This type of testing is good for identifying defects in the composite, but must be treated with care, as individual services may behave differently from the emulated versions of those services. Testing of a composite is shown in the following diagram:

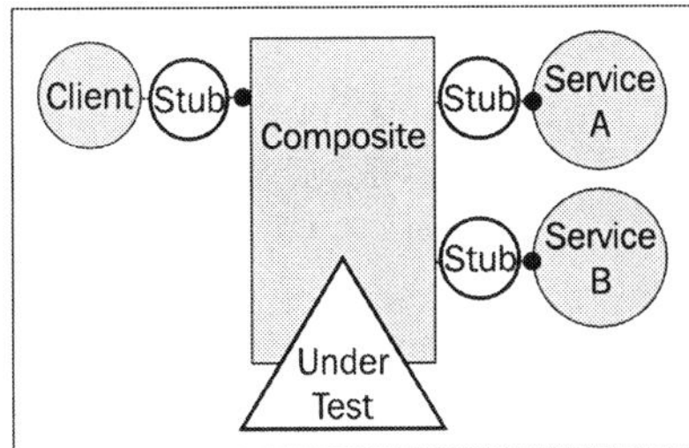

Component testing

The framework was designed for testing composites, but it may also be used to provide a test harness for individual services, as shown in the following diagram. In this case, a pass-through assembly is provided that allows injection of messages into the service. The BPEL **Composite** and the **Service** are then configured with suitable assertions to ensure that the service is behaving as expected.

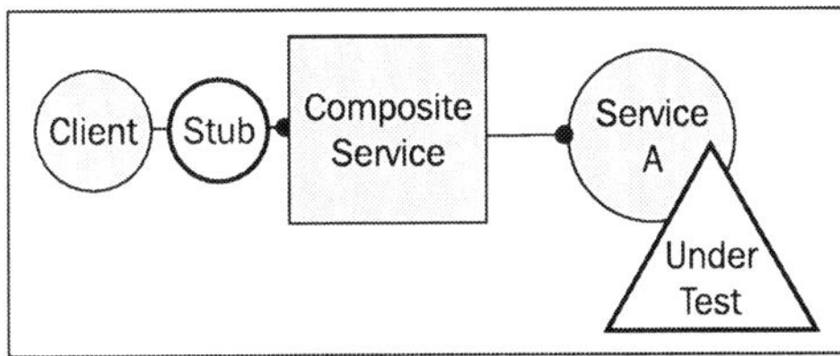

Unit testing

Unfortunately, the SOA Suite doesn't provide any specific low-level unit testing of individual components with the exception of XSL, although it may be emulated to an extent, as described in the previous section, *Component testing*. JDeveloper may also be used to run JUnit test cases, which can interact with low-level services. However, this is done outside the scope of the SOA Suite.

JDeveloper does have an XSL test tool that may be used to validate XSL transformations before deploying them as part of a Service Bus or BPEL deployment. This is invoked by right-clicking on the `xsl` file in the application navigator and selecting the **Test** option. This brings up the **Test XSL Map** dialog box that can be used to specify or generate a source XML file and then generate the output XML file, as shown in the following screenshot:

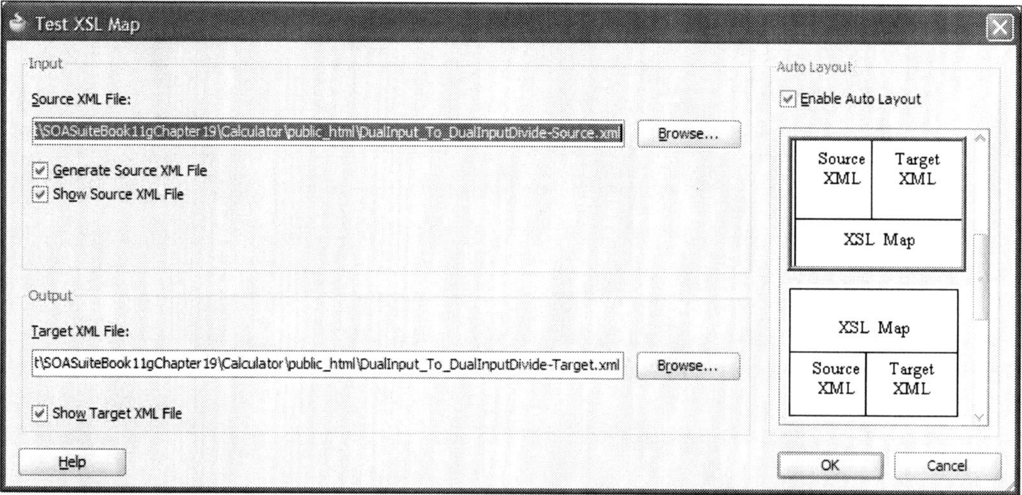

The default layout is to have two windows side-by-side with the input document on the left and the output document on the right, with the stylesheet being displayed in a separate window. The output document must be manually inspected to ensure that it is correct.

Performance testing

Although the SOA Suite, as part of the test client, provides the facility to run multiple queries concurrently against an interface, this should not be substituted for proper performance testing. The test client multiple thread interface has the following limitations:

- Single message input.
- All inputs to the service have the same input message. Depending on how the service is written, this may improve performance. For example, after the first request, all the data pulled from the database is available in memory rather than having to be fetched from disk.
- Limited scalability.
- The clients and servers are all part of the same system and run on a single machine. This is not a realistic scenario and precludes testing how well the system scales.
- Doesn't use test framework.
- The test framework provides detailed feedback on multiple types of tests, and this is missing from the simple client interface.

The test client interface is good for quick basic performance testing, but any real-world performance testing should use a more complete testing framework provided by Oracle Enterprise Manager testing tools or third parties such as HP LoadRunner. SoapUI is a popular test tool that can also be used to inject load into the SOA server and validate results.

User interface testing

The SOA Suite is focused on services rather than user interfaces and therefore any user interface interaction with the services must be driven from another test tool. Like performance testing, this is something for which other products should be used. Although there is a certain amount that can be tested by performing a system test, as described earlier, this does not fully test all the ways in which a web or thick client application may interact with the services exposed. There is no substitute for a proper end user interface testing tool to be used alongside the SOA Suite testing framework.

Summary

In this chapter, we have examined testing in SOA Suite, starting with simple one-off tests and then moving on to examine the composite test framework, which provides a repeatable testing framework for composites and any references called from a composite.

The SOA Suite testing framework can be used to provide a rigorous environment to support regression tests. In order to get the best out of this framework, it is necessary to invest effort in building test cases alongside the composites themselves. The following checklist may be useful:

- Always develop test cases alongside the composites
- Always develop test cases for standalone services by creating appropriate composites as test harnesses
- Add new test cases for defects discovered in the fields that were not caught by existing test cases
- Emulate references to allow test cases to focus on composites
- Directly call services (don't emulate) to allow test cases to interact with real endpoints

It is best to build tests when the components themselves are being built, as this allows us to validate our components incrementally and immediately.

Test early, test often!

21
Defining Security and Management Policies

In this chapter, we will investigate how service-oriented computing makes security and monitoring more complicated before exploring how to secure our service infrastructure and monitor it.

Security and management challenges in the SOA environment

Moving to service-oriented architecture brings with it a number of benefits that we have explored throughout this book, such as improved reuse, strong encapsulation of business services, and the ability to rapidly construct new composite services and applications. However, there is one area in which SOA makes life much harder, and that is in the area of security and management. By security, we mean the process of ensuring that individuals and applications can only access the information and invoke the processing which is allowed to them. By management, we mean the task of ensuring that a system is capable of delivering the required services when requested.

Evolution of security and management

The challenges that SOA brings to the security and monitoring space are made clearer when we look at the evolution of computing. The original computer systems provided a single centralized system with a single access mechanism via a terminal. These mainframe systems provided their own security and required external parties (users) to authenticate, at which point they were restricted in their access by the internal security protocols of the system. In a similar fashion, monitoring was a case of tracking the status of individual components within the central system. This made it very easy to provide strong centralized control of who could access resources, while also retaining a strong ability to monitor individual users as well as the health of the system.

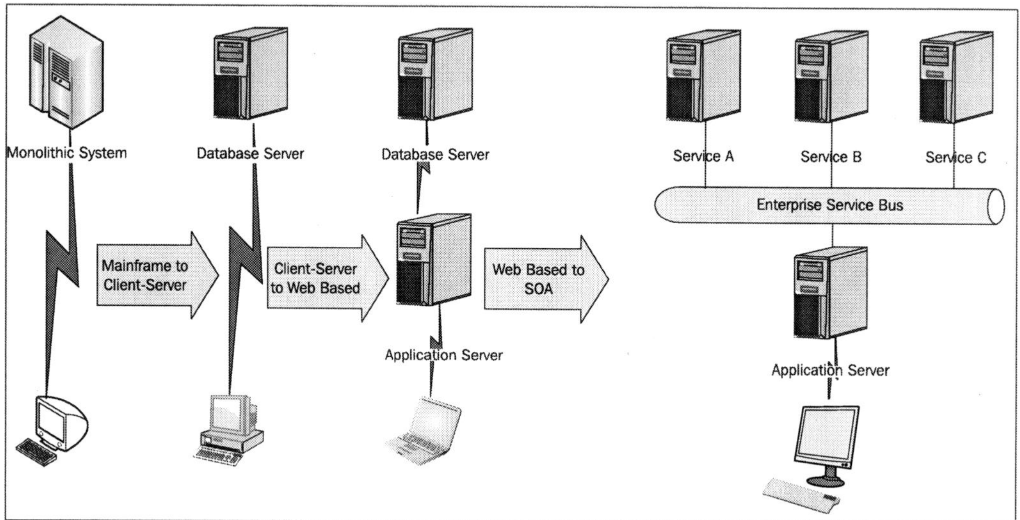

The move to client-server systems complicated things because now the actual processing was spread across two machines, the server, generally a database server, and a client, generally a personal computer. The central server was now required to provide external access at a more granular level, potentially protecting individual tables in the database rather than the broader brush application level that was required in the previous generation of centralized systems. This now introduced the problem of coordinating identity across two tiers. The client application would generally authenticate the end user against the server, providing a pass-through level of security. Hence the security model was more complex due to more demanding access control requirements, but the authentication model was not greatly different.

However, the move to a client server greatly increased the complexity of monitoring the solution. Moving processing off the central system and into the client meant that it was now necessary to monitor the health of components in the client and that the client was more complex than the terminals used in the previous generation. A particular problem in this environment was the unexpected interactions that different applications in the client could have with each other.

The problems of monitoring and managing the distributed client applications led to pressure to move the processing back into the data centre, which led to a third generation of solution architectures based around web/application servers and web browsers.

This led to a further complication of the security infrastructure, as applications now had to maintain links from many different clients and ensure that they enforced appropriate access controls on each individual client. It did, however, simplify the management environment by bringing the application back into the managed data centre environment. However, the end-to-end environment was now more complex to manage due to there being multiple tiers rather than a single tier, and problems in any one tier would impact the entire service offered by an application.

The move to service-oriented architectures can be thought of as a natural progression from the web deployment model, but with the additional complication that applications are now composed from services provided by many individual service providers, potentially on different machines. In some circumstances, the service may be provided outside the company by another company. In the next section, we will examine the management and security challenges that SOA brings.

Added complications of SOA environment

The SOA environment makes it harder to enforce a consistent security policy. It also has a number of moving parts that must be managed. Let us consider each of these challenges in turn.

Security Impacts of SOA

Consider a service that is invoked. In order to decide whether to service the request, it must determine if the requestor is allowed to access this service. Access may be controlled or restricted, based on the invoking code and also based on the originator of the request. Consider a composite application in which **User A** makes a request for **Application X**, which satisfies the request by making another request to **Service Y**, which in turn calls **Service Z**.

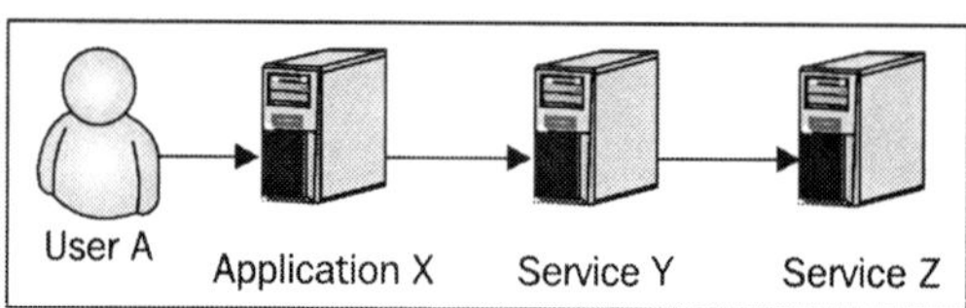

Application X has no more a difficult job in accepting the request in this environment than in a web application. It can require the user to authenticate, potentially via some form of secure certificate or biometric-based authentication. The challenges come when X starts to invoke services. **Service Y** must decide if it will honor the request. It has three basic ways it can do this:

- Accept requests: Effectively apply no security
- Accept requests from **Application X**: Effectively require the client application or service to be identified and authenticated
- Accept requests from **User A**: Effectively require some way of propagating the identity of **User A** through **Application X** into the service

Service Z has the same set of options, but instead of application A being the client in this case, it is **Service Y**. This potential chaining of services and potential requirements for propagation of identity makes it harder to effectively secure the environment. Later on, we will look at tools in the SOA Suite that can simplify this.

Management and monitoring impacts of SOA

In the same way that we have a more complicated set of security demands in the SOA environment, we also have a more complicated set of monitoring requirements. Have a look at the following diagram; it shows how a composite application makes use of services to satisfy users' demands:

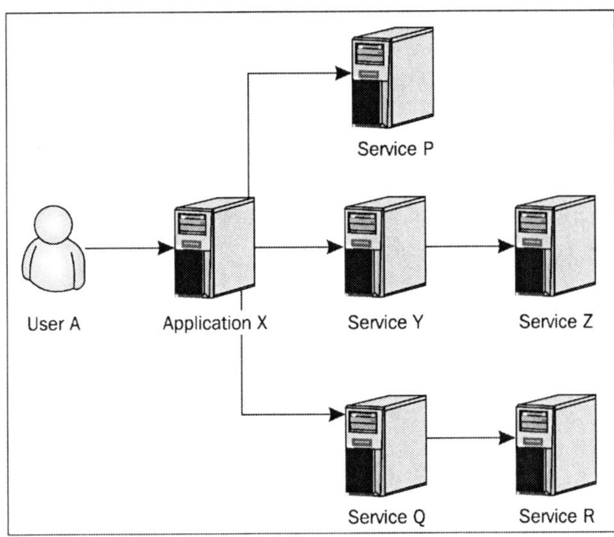

In this case, **Application X** makes use of five services either directly or indirectly to satisfy user requests. We need to monitor the individual services to get any idea as to why an application may be unavailable to an end user. However, this is not sufficient as some of the services may be required for execution and others may be optional.

For example, consider a shopping site. The catalog and order entry services must be available to provide a service to the end user, but the fulfillment and payment services need not be available, as they can do their work without the user being online at the time. In this case, if the fulfillment service is unavailable, then the application can still work, but it may have reduced functionality, such as being unable to provide an immediate delivery date.

Another aspect of service monitoring that must be considered is the throughput on individual services. This is important because individual services may be used by multiple applications. Therefore, it is possible that an application that previously gave excellent end-user response times may degrade its performance, because one of the services it depends on is under heavy load from other applications. Monitoring will allow this risk to be identified early on and corrective action can be taken.

Securing services

Having looked at the additional complications that SOA brings to the security infrastructure, let us examine how SOA Suite enables us to secure our services. We will look at securing services based on what application is calling them as well as securing services based on the end user for whom the request is being made. We will also look at the best places to apply security to our services.

Security outside the SOA Suite

There are several things we can do to secure our services without using the facilities available in the SOA Suite. The following are some of the ways in which we may provide security by configuration of the network and server environment in which our services execute.

Network security

An integral part of an SOA solution will usually be firewalls, which restrict access to different networks within the enterprise. A common model is to have a front-side network that receives requests from external clients and a back-side network that can receive requests from other services but cannot be accessed directly by external clients. Machines that need to be accessed externally will have access to both the front-side and the back-side networks and will act as application bridges between the two, as there is no network-level connection between them.

Preventing message interception

We can improve security by encrypting all messages between services by using **SSL (Secure Socket Layer)**. This requires the web servers hosting our services to be configured with certificates and only to accept requests across SSL connections. Basically, this means disabling HTTP access and only allowing HTTPS access to our servers. This has a performance overhead, as all messages must be encrypted before leaving the client machine and decrypted on arriving at the server machine. The server-side encryption may be reduced by the use of hardware accelerators, either embedded in the network card or in the network.

If all the machines are on the same physical switch, then messages between services are effectively secure because they can only be seen by the client and server machines. This allows us to configure our servers to accept HTTP requests from machines on the same switch, but only accept HTTPS requests from machines that are not on the same switch.

Restricting access to services

We may restrict access to machines based on the IP address of the caller. This is a quick, easy way to provide a layer of protection to our services. Configuring our HTTP servers to only accept requests from well known clients works well for internal networks, but doesn't work for external services. It also leaves us with the problem of reconfiguring our list of acceptable clients when a new client service is added.

Declarative security versus explicit security

A central tenet of service-oriented architecture is to abstract functionality into services that hide implementation details. When we come to security and monitoring, these are actually facets of a service and can also be provided in a service-oriented fashion. These two key concepts are worth exploring because they are central to making the best use of SOA Suite security and monitoring.

Security as a facet

We generally define our services in terms of the functionality (service) that they provide. These services also have attributes that may not be explicitly mentioned in their service data model but are nevertheless an important part of the service. These attributes include availability, response time, and security. Security is an attribute of a service that can be applied without altering the core functionality of the service. For example, a service may require that it is only invoked across SSL connections or that it may only be invoked by an authorized user.

Security as a service

Security is itself a service, which controls the following:

- Access control: Who may make requests of a service
- Authorization: Who is requesting the service
- Integrity: Can the data be read or altered to or from the service

We can think of security as a service that is applied as a facet to other services. This is the model that is applied within the SOA Suite. The Web Services Manager is the component embedded into the SOA Suite to provide security. Although it is a service, the developer always interacts with it as a property or facet of a service.

Security model

The web services manager allows security to be applied to services and operators to monitor services, without a need to modify the service. The model for this is shown as follows.

Access to services (access control) is always through a gateway or agent component supplied by the web services manager. The endpoint of the service is exposed as the gateway or agent endpoint. The agents embedded within SOA Suite are known as interceptors. Gateways and agents are explained later in this chapter.

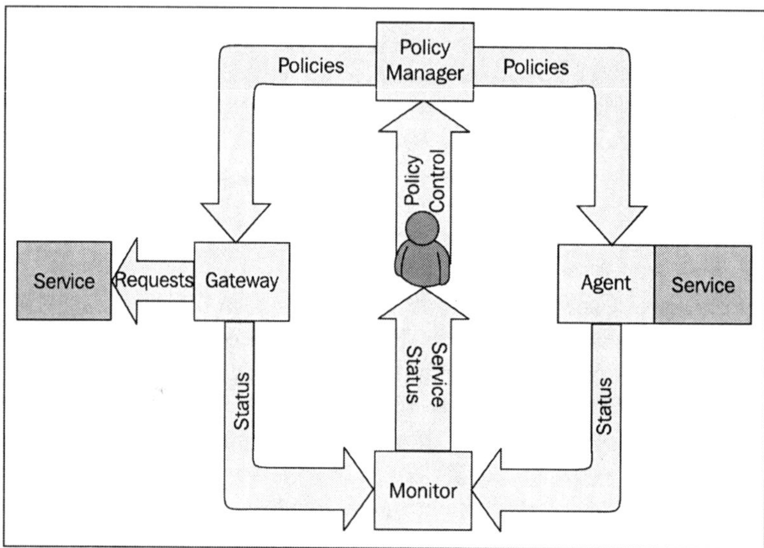

Rules for who can access the service (authorization), how they are authenticated, and the access they are allowed (access control) are determined by the policies provided by the policy manager component of the web services manager. These policies are pushed to individual agents and gateways.

Policies may also specify specific logging requirements or encryption requirements (message integrity) for the data.

Policies are determined by an administrator using the Enterprise Manager Console and enforced using policy enforcement points (interceptors). Policy enforcement points are provided by agents known as interceptors or by a gateway.

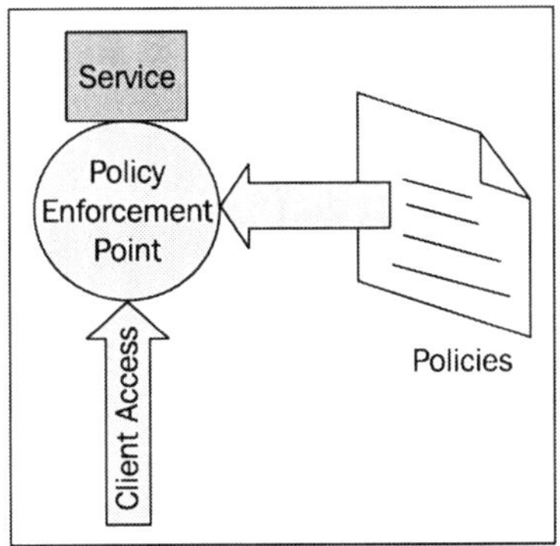

Policy enforcement points

Policies can be enforced at three distinct points:

- An external endpoint such as the entry point to a web service or an SOA Composite.
- An SOA Composite
- A client

The former two control policies for access to a service; the latter allows the policies to be applied as a message leaves the requestor.

Policies

A policy consists of one or more constraints applied to a service such as:

- Validate certificate of requestor
- Decrypt message
- Log portion of message

These constraints are known as assertions. A policy may consist of several assertions.

Multiple policies may be attached to an endpoint. Each request for a service must pass through the policies associated with that service. By defining a policy, we can have a consistent way of protecting a number of different services. For example, we may have the following distinct policies:

- Policy for Externally Accessible Services
- Policy for Services Making Financial Transactions
- Policy for Non Critical Services

The first policy may specify a need for encryption of data as well as authentication of clients. The second policy may require strong authentication of clients and special logging steps. The third policy may just perform some simple logging. An internally accessible payments gateway may make use of the second policy, while the same gateway configured for external access may be configured with the first and second policies.

Policies are applied to individual service endpoints.

Agents and gateways

From the preceding discussion, it is clear that gateways and agents are the key **Policy Enforcement Points (PEPs)** where the security facet is added to a service. Let's explore how these components differ.

Both gateways and agents are responsible for enforcing policies. The difference is in their physical location. Agents are physically co-located in the same container as the service they are protecting. This has the benefit that agents do not require an additional network hop or inter-process communication to deliver messages to the service. Because of this, the physical and logical layout of the agent is essentially the same, as shown in the following diagram. There is one agent per container that is hosting services.

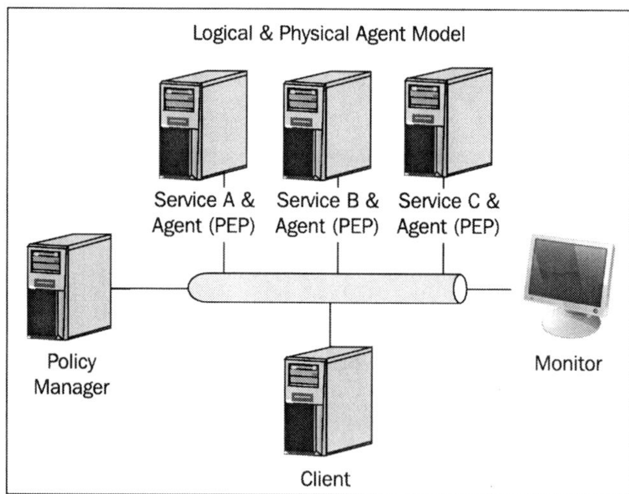

The gateway, on the other hand, is a centralized policy enforcement point. The service endpoint exposed is that of the gateway, not of the machine on which the service resides. All requests potentially incur an additional network hop as they must go through the machine on which the gateway resides. Although physically, the gateway is just another machine on the network, logically it sits in front of the services for which it enforces policies.

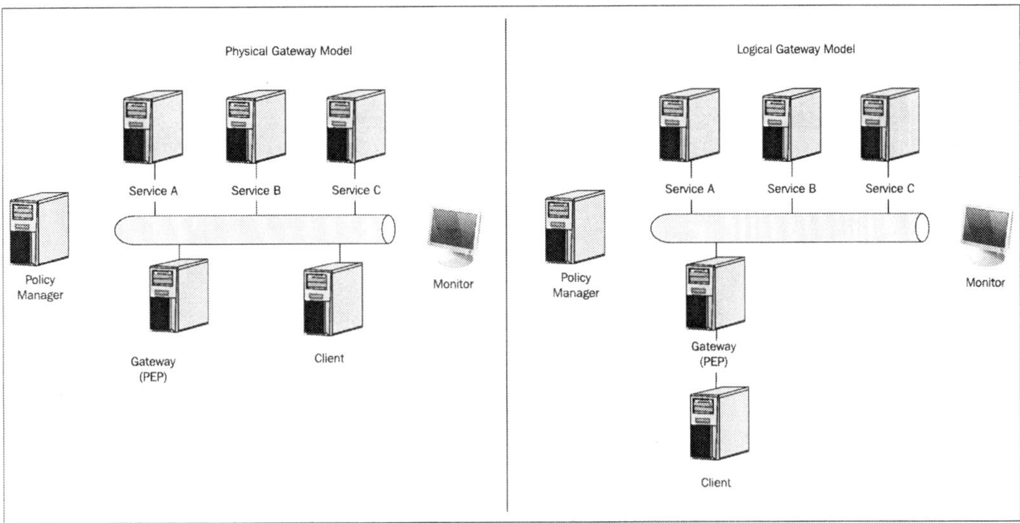

Note that in a production deployment, it is possible to have multiple gateways deployed so that a single gateway does not become a single point of failure in the service infrastructure.

Distinctive benefits of gateways and agents

Gateways and agents both achieve the same result of securing and monitoring services, but the different approaches they have provide different benefits. Both gateways and agents can be used together, with some endpoints protected by agents and others protected by gateways.

Benefits of gateways

- Can protect services running on platforms for which no agent is available, for example, a service implemented in Perl
- Does not require modification of service endpoints
- Less intrusive in an endpoint platform
- Supports message routing
- Supports failover

Drawbacks of gateways

- Clients must explicitly target gateway
- Services must be configured to only accept requests from gateways to avoid bypassing of gateway
- Service endpoints must be explicitly registered with gateway

Benefits of agents

- Provide true end-to-end security
- Cannot be bypassed by targeting the service directly
- Do not require changes to clients stored in service endpoint
- Potentially faster due to less latency

Drawbacks of agents

- Intrusive into services to be monitored / secured
- Cannot convert between transport protocols

The gateway dilemma

Note that the Service Bus can act in the role of a web services gateway, and it supports the same policy framework as OWSM. The 11*g* OWSM gateway is not yet available at the time of writing and the 10.1.3 gateway uses different policy descriptions that are not compatible with 11*g*. If a gateway is to be used, then a choice must be made between the 10.1.3 OWSM gateway and using the Service Bus in that role. The authors feel that the best solution for a gateway currently is to use the Service Bus in that role, as it will often be used for mediating access to/from external services. Therefore, this is a logical place to combine security policy enforcement with access to/from external services. In addition, the Service Bus supports the same policy model as the rest of the SOA Suite.

Service Bus model

The Service Bus model for securing and monitoring services is a gateway model in that the Service Bus sits between the client and the service and can apply policies and monitor performance of services. In the Service Bus model, the policy management server and the policy enforcement point are both parts of the Service Bus. In 11*g*, these policies can be set up using the Web Services Manager and thus provide consistency between the Service Bus and SCA environments, allowing the Service Bus to operate as a gateway.

Defining policies

Policies are defined using the Fusion Middleware Control Console. A policy (described in the standard WS-Policy) can be thought of as a pipeline of steps (assertions, some of which may be described using standard WS-Security) to be performed on a request response. There may be multiple policies in the pipeline, each with its own steps. The message passes through the steps of the pipeline on its way to the service, and in a synchronous interaction, the policies are applied in reverse order to the response message. Multiple policies may be concatenated together and applied in sequence to a given service. Some policies will only affect the pipeline in one direction. For example, authentication and authorization will only be part of a request pipeline but encryption and decryption may be part of a request and a response pipeline.

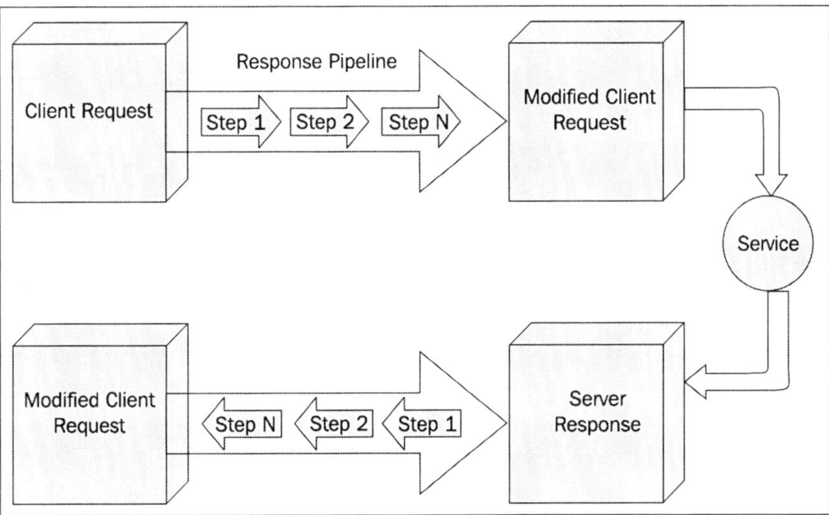

Policies may be used to partially or fully encrypt payloads, provide logging information, transform data, authenticate users, and authorize access or any number of other functions. It is worth noting that certain policies rely on information being made available by earlier policies. For example, an authorize assertion generally requires there to be an authenticate assertion to have been executed previously to identify the requestors identity.

This common pattern of authenticate and authorize reduces the number of valid users at each step. Up to the point that we extract credentials from a request, all users are authorized. The act of authentication restricts access to only authenticated users, while applying specific authorization policies restricts the user base further to only authorized users.

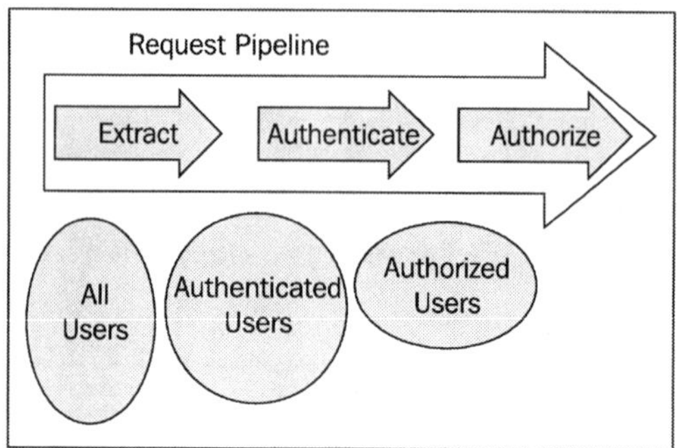

Creating a new policy to perform authentication and authorization

The easiest way to manage policies is to have specific policies that combine the various assertions into a single policy to be applied to multiple components. A policy is a centralized definition of the security and other steps to be applied to a service. As an example, we will create a policy that restricts access to users with a particular role, and a separate policy performs basic authentication with the username and password passed in a **Web Service Security** (**WSS**) header. The user credentials and roles are stored in the identity store provided by the SOA infrastructure, which in turn relies on the underlying WebLogic configured security. This policy could then be applied to provide protection for multiple service policies. The beauty of policy management is that if we need to change the policy, we can do it once and it will take effect on all the endpoints that have had the policy applied to them.

Creating the authorization policy

To create a new policy, we log on to Fusion Middleware Control, (whose security policy screens control the behavior of WSM), expand the Farm and WebLogic Domain folders, and right-click on the domain that has our SOA infrastructure. In the menu that appears, we select the **Web Services** item and choose the **Policies** item from the submenu.

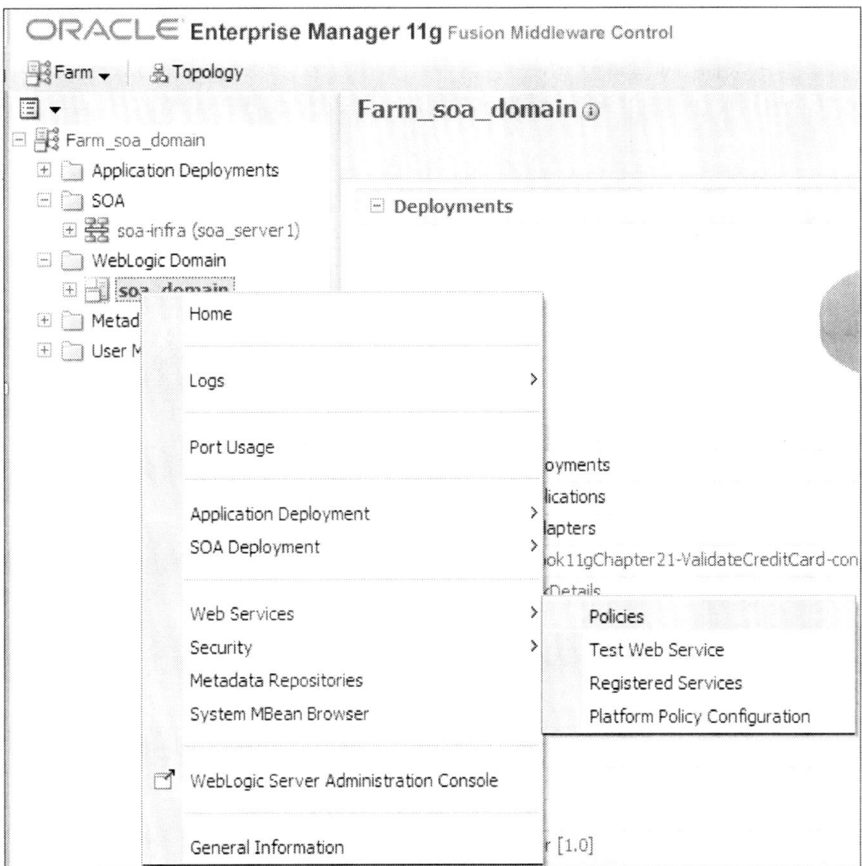

This takes us to the **Web Service Policies** screen, which allows us to list all the available policies in different categories and to create new policies.

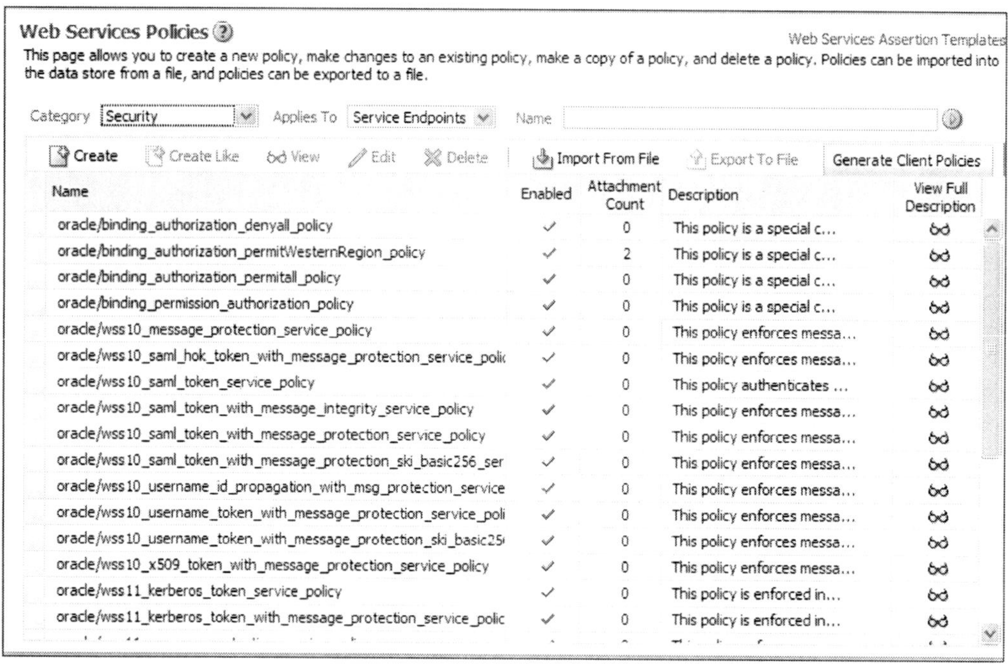

The **Category** drop-down list allows us to view only policies related to a particular category of policy, for example, **Security**, **Management**, or **Reliable Messaging**. The **Applies To** drop-down list filters the policies by the type of entity that they can be applied to, for example, **Service Endpoints** or **SOA Components**.

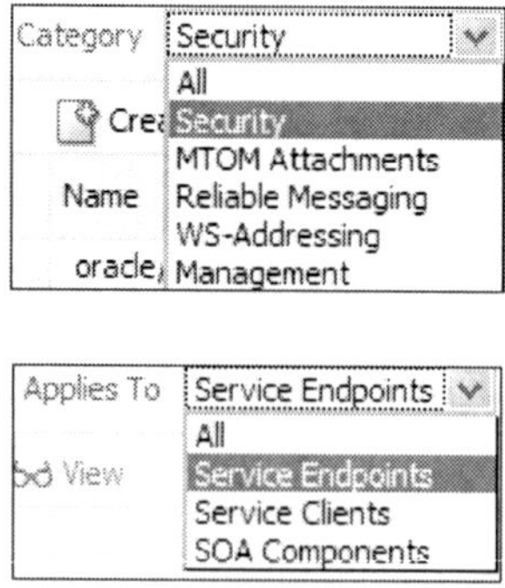

Some policies can only be applied to certain entities. For example, the authentication policies generally require access to the original message, including transport data, and so only apply to **Service Endpoints**.

Oracle-recommended naming conventions for polices

Oracle recommends the following naming convention for policies:

{Path Location}/{Web Services Standard}_{Authentication Token}_{Message Protection}_{Policy Type}

- Path Location is the directory to store the policy. It is recommended by Oracle that this be separate from the Oracle directory used by Oracle pre-configured policies.
- Web Services Standard is the appropriate standard being used, such as Web Services Security (WSS).
- Authentication Token is the means of identifying the requestor, for example, a SAML token or a username/password.
- Message Protection is the message integrity and encryption being applied.
- Policy Type is used to indicate if this is a policy or a template to be used in creating policies.

When looking at predefined policies and templates, this naming convention helps to identify what the policies do.

Creating the policy

To create a new policy that defines the security we wish to apply to several components, we can click the **Create** link to take us to the **Create Policy** screen. However, this screen requires us to create a policy from scratch by providing a series of assertions or policy steps. Generally, it will be better to select a policy that is similar to what we want and use the **Create Like** link to take us to the **Create Policy** screen, which is now populated with some initial assertions based on our earlier policy selection. In our case, we want to restrict access to an entity to only a specified individual, so we will select the **oracle/binding_authorization_permitall_policy** as our basis. We can then further restrict the individuals allowed to access our entity.

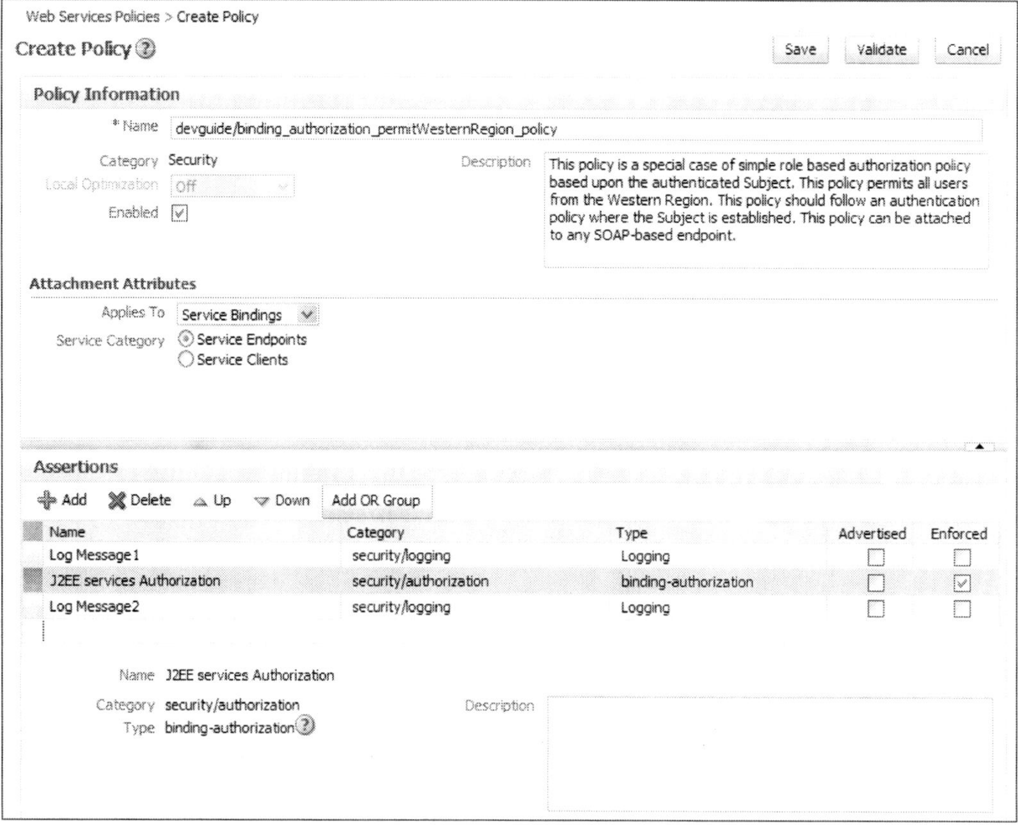

We need to edit the policy to reflect our changes. We begin by altering the name, setting it to a directory other than Oracle, and altering the security permission from **permitAll** to **permitWesternRegion** to make it clear what this policy does. Having changed the name, we will also want to alter the description to reflect what the policy will now be doing. We will then change the policy authorization restriction by choosing the **J2EE services Authorization** assertion and changing its **Authorization Setting** from **Permit All** to **Selected Roles**.

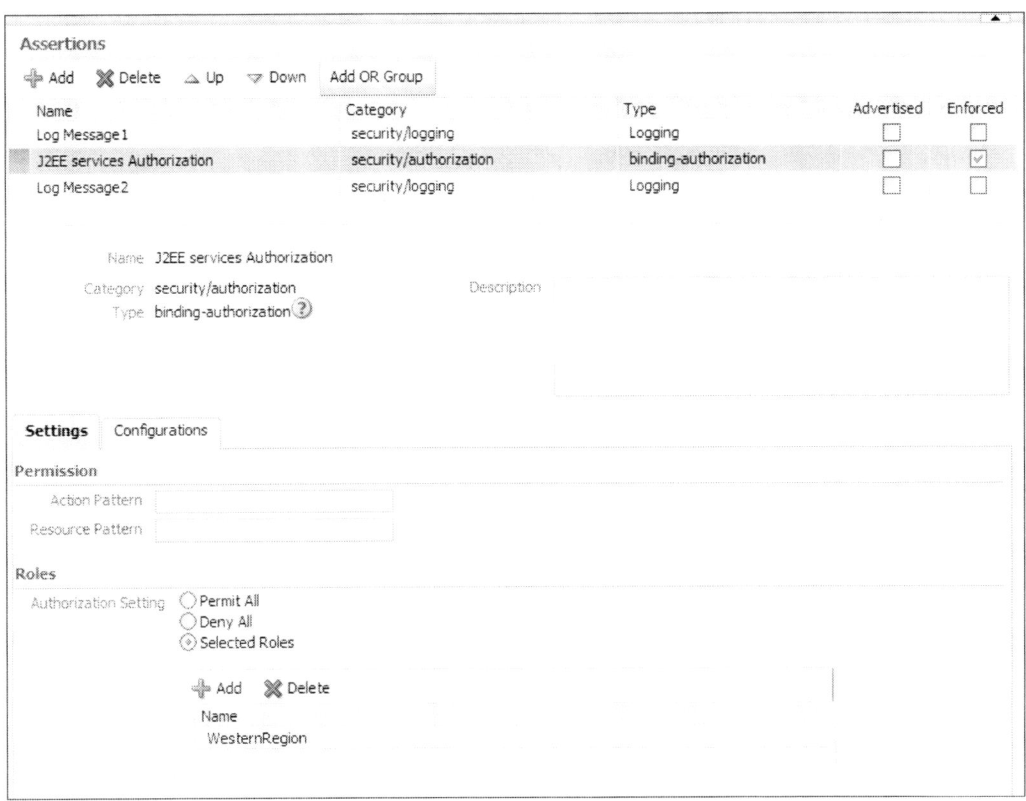

We want to restrict the authorized users to those who are part of the **Western Region**. This is using the SOA sample's user base that has been loaded into the WebLogic server. We do this by clicking the **Add** button and selecting and moving the **Western Region** role to the Roles Selected to **Add** List. After clicking **OK**, we can then check that our role now appears in the list of authorized roles for the **J2EE services Authorization** assertion.

This assertion means that only roles in the **Roles** list will be allowed access to the service the policy is applied to.

We can now save our policy by selecting **Save**, and the policy will be available to us for use.

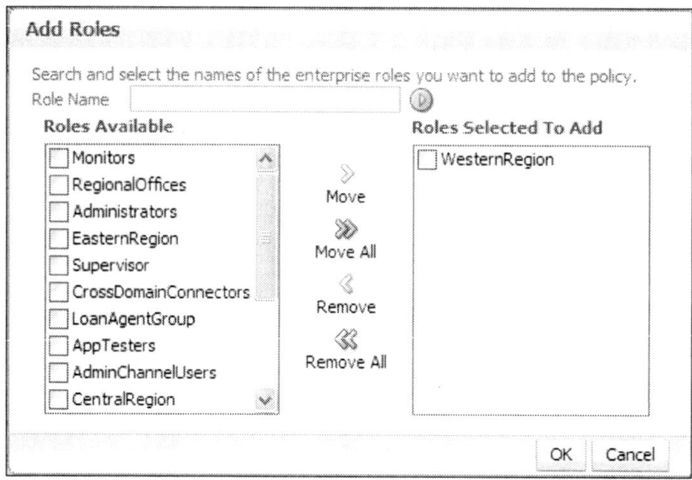

Applying a policy

Having created our policy, we can now use it to restrict access to services. To do this, we first choose the service we want to protect by navigating to it under the soa-infra section of the SOA folder in Fusion Middleware Control. Selecting the **Policies** tab for the service will show the current policies applied. In this case, we need to apply an authentication policy to identify the source of the user credentials and then our newly created authorization policy.

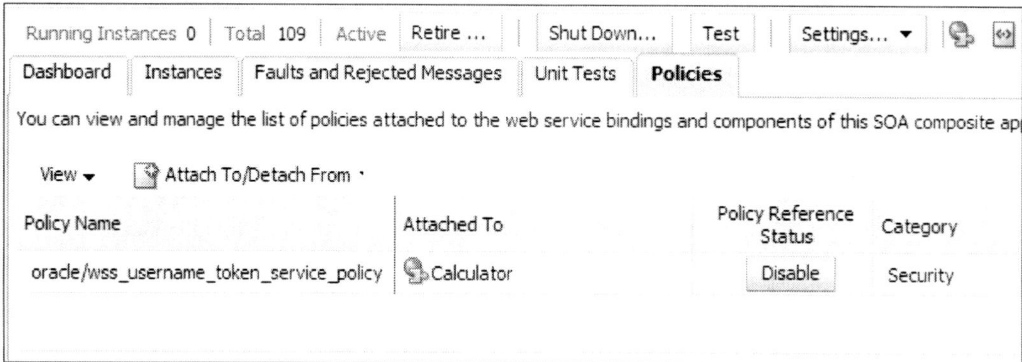

We select a policy to apply by clicking on the **Attach To/Detach From** menu, which presents us with a list of operations to which we wish to apply the policy. After selecting an operation, we are presented with the **Attach To/Detach From** policies dialog, which allows us to choose which policies to attach to the operation.

We can filter the available policies by editing the search settings and pressing the green arrow to the right of the search criteria to apply the filter.

We need to add an authentication policy to extract credentials from the inbound message. We choose the **oracle/wss_username_token_service_policy**, which extracts a username and a password from a Web Services Security (WSS) standard header. This policy will reject any requests to the operation that do not have a valid username and password in a WSS header. The username and password will be verified against the WebLogic user base, which will normally point to an LDAP server. The policy is attached by selecting it and pressing the **Attach** button.

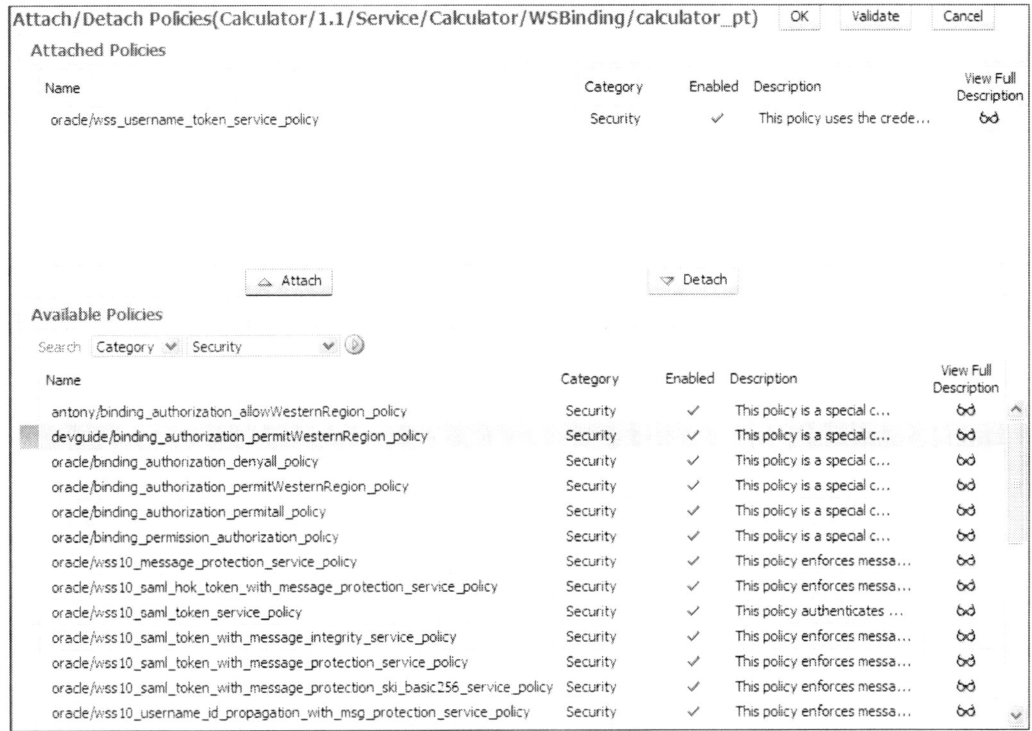

Having added the authentication policy, we have restricted access to only authenticated users. The next step is to apply our newly created authentication policy to restrict access only to users in the **Western Region** group. Having added the policies that we want to the list, we can apply them by clicking **OK**. This will take effect immediately.

Applying a policy through the Service Bus Console

The Service Bus can use Web Services Manager policies. In this section, we will briefly mention how the Service Bus may use OWSM policies. Policies are managed using the OWSM policy manager found in Enterprise Manager. Policies may be created and modified in the same way in Enterprise Manager for the Service Bus and the SCA container. We will look at importing a policy into Enterprise Manager and then see how a policy may be applied in the Oracle Service Bus. Remember that only the attachment of policies differs between the two environments.

Importing a policy

We can import a policy by going to the Enterprise Manager Console associated with the Oracle Service Bus installation. By right-clicking on the OSB domain under **WebLogic Domain** in the tree view, we can select the **Web Services | Policies** menu item.

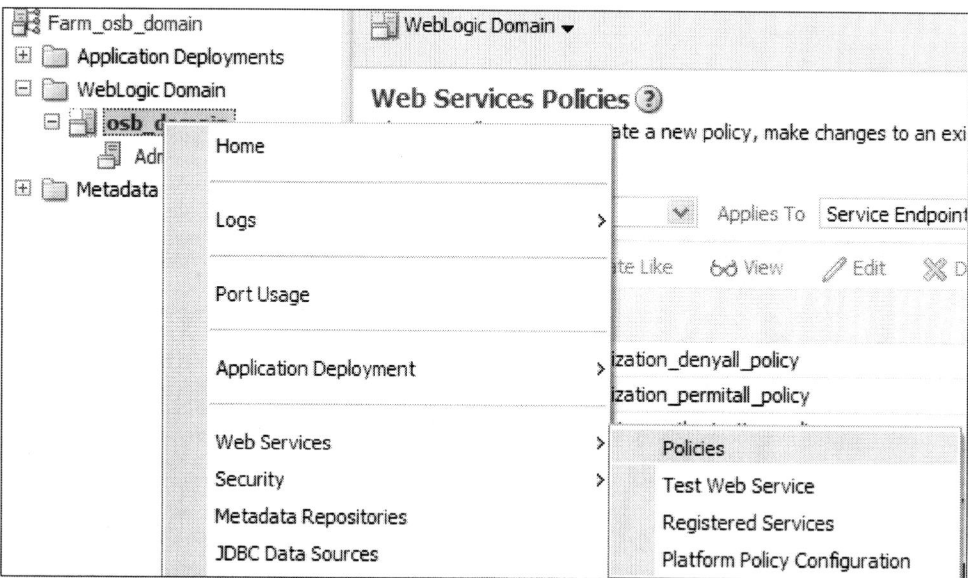

This brings up the **Web Services Policies** screen, where we can select **Import From File** to bring in policies that have been exported from another Service Bus installation or from the SCA container. After browsing to select a previously exported policy file and clicking **OK**, the policies in the file will be added to the existing **Web Services Policies**.

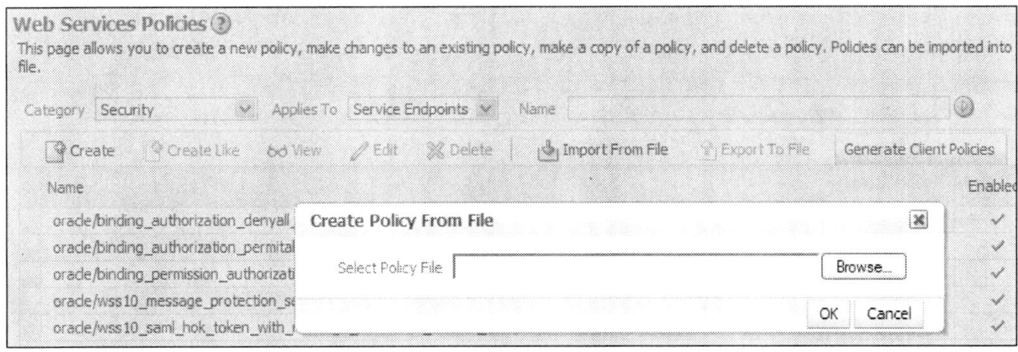

Once imported, the policies can be used in the same way as other OWSM policies, detailed as follows.

Applying OWSM policies in Service Bus

Policies are applied in the Service Bus console. Policies may be applied to a proxy service (inbound) or to a business service (outbound). Generally, in the proxy service we will apply policies that restrict access to the service, while in the business service we will apply policies that encrypt data or provide authentication tokens to the target service. To apply a policy to a service in OSB, we navigate to the proxy or business service we wish to apply the policy to and select the **Policies** tab. We can then press the **Add** button to bring up the list of available policies.

From the list of available policies, which may be filtered by **Category**, we can choose and apply the appropriate policy. For example, **oracle/wss_username_token_service_policy** expects a username and a password to be provided in a WS-Security SOAP header. After clicking on **Submit**, the policy will be attached to the service.

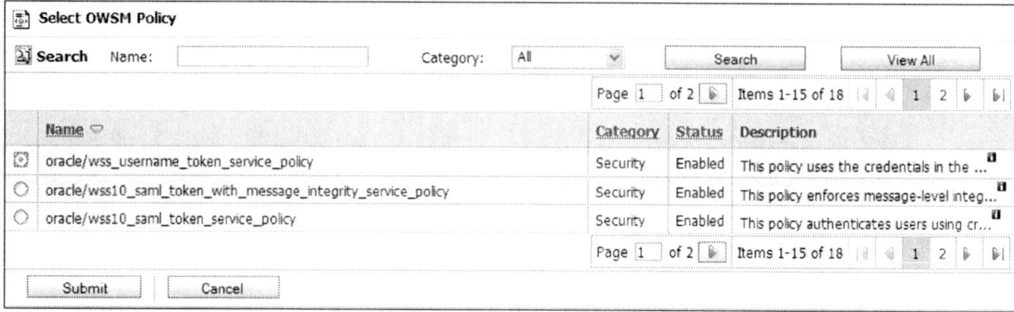

Because policies can be shared between OSB and the SCA-based service engines, it is possible to create a customized policy and apply it to services in both containers.

Final thoughts on security

The examples used in this chapter have been based on HTTP basic authentication or a simple username/password that does not require configuration of certificate stores. To properly secure services, it is recommended that a public key infrastructure is used in conjunction with an LDAP server to provide secure message delivery and centralized user management. The preceding steps are appropriate for use in development and test environments without access to an LDAP store or a PKI infrastructure.

Monitoring services

In addition to defining policies to be applied to requests, the Fusion Middleware Control Console can also monitor the performance of services.

Both Fusion Middleware Control and Service Bus can monitor services. Enterprise Manager is unique in being able to monitor the service directly by using an agent that resides in the same container as the target service. EM is also able to provide out of the box reports on the security aspects of service invocation, tracking the number of failed authentications or authorizations. The Service Bus provides an extremely capable monitoring and reporting framework for services that can be used alongside the EM reporting framework.

Monitoring service health in SOA Suite

There are several places in Fusion Middleware Control, apart from the home page, which show the overall health of the SOA system.

System up-down status

The general status of servers and individual SOA composites is indicated by the green up arrows on the initial Fusion Middleware Control page. This page is useful for checking that all expected composites and adapters are up and running. It also gives a snapshot of the status of individual servers in the cluster.

System throughput view

It is also possible to get more detail on overall system throughput by right-clicking the **soa_infra** menu and choosing the **Monitoring | Performance Summary** menu item. This displays a report showing throughput for the SOA system.

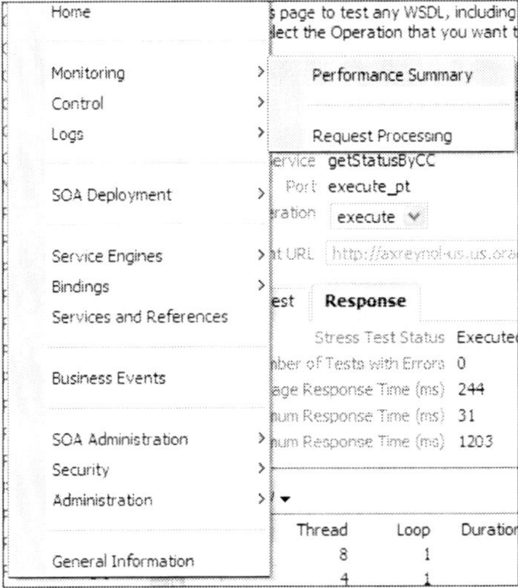

The report may be customized by pressing the **Show Metric Palette** button to add additional metrics to the report.

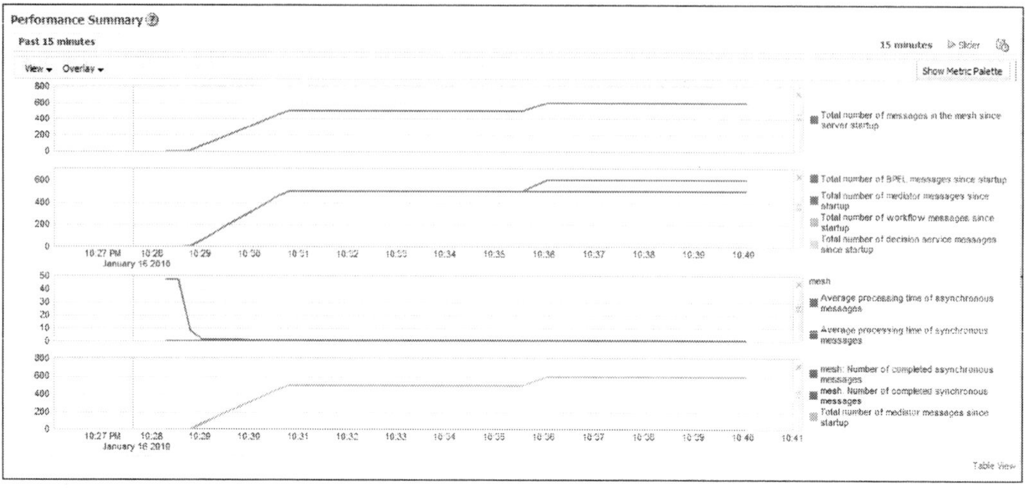

Monitoring SOA Composite performance

To get additional detail on which SOA composites are being used most or are performing the worst, we can use the tree view to navigate to a specific SOA server. Right-click on the server and choose the **Web Services** menu item. This takes us to the **Web Services** monitoring screen, where we may select the **SOA** tab to see a list of deployed SOA composites and the number of messages they have processed, the number of faults they have raised, and their average processing time.

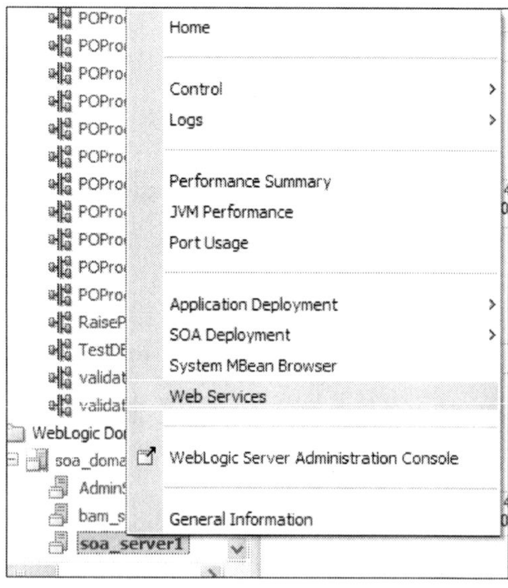

Note that the **Attach Policies** link provides an alternate way to attach policies to composites.

The **SOA** tab of the Web Services monitoring is a good place to look for composites that are being heavily used or taking a long time to respond.

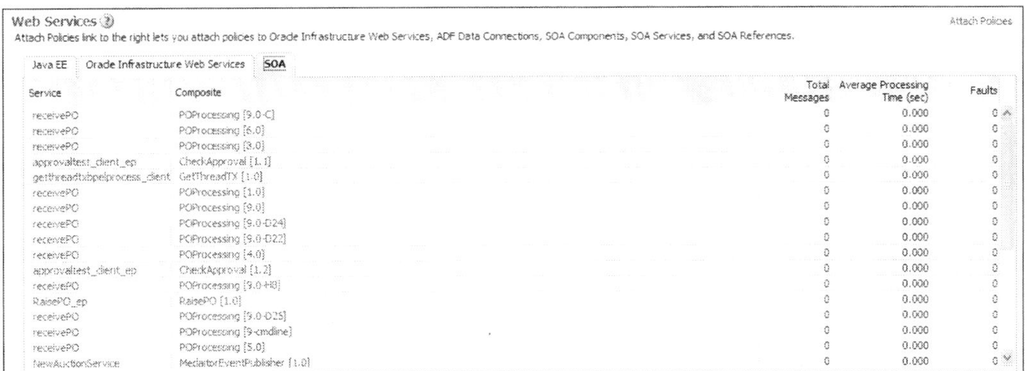

Clicking on a **Service** will take us to the **Web Service** monitoring page, where we can not only see the overall throughput for this service, but also look at the number of faults that it has encountered.

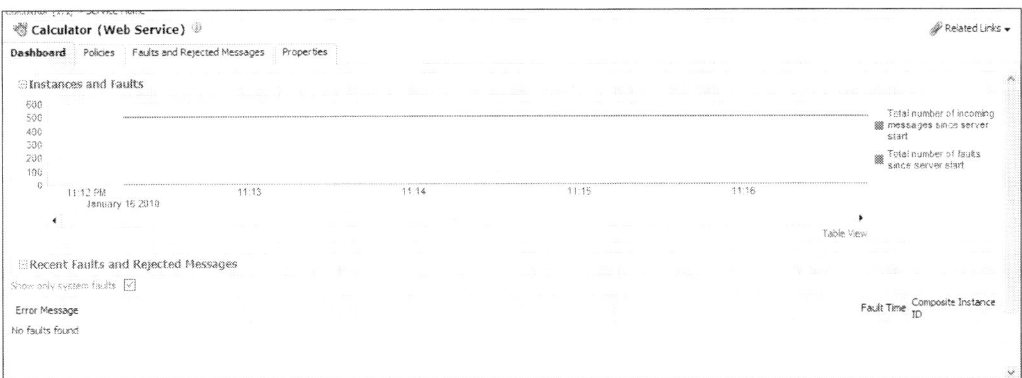

Monitoring in the Service Bus

The Service Bus is also able to monitor services. Like security policies, the Service Bus is not currently consistent with the rest of the SOA Suite in its service monitoring. Service Level Agreements can also be specified in the Service Bus.

Creating an alert destination

Any breaches of a service level in the Service Bus will cause an alert to be raised. An alert must be associated with a destination, so before we begin, we need to define an alert destination. This is done by adding an **Alert Destination** resource to our project in the Service Bus. Selecting **Alert Destination** from the **Create Resource** list takes us to the **Create Alert Destination** dialog.

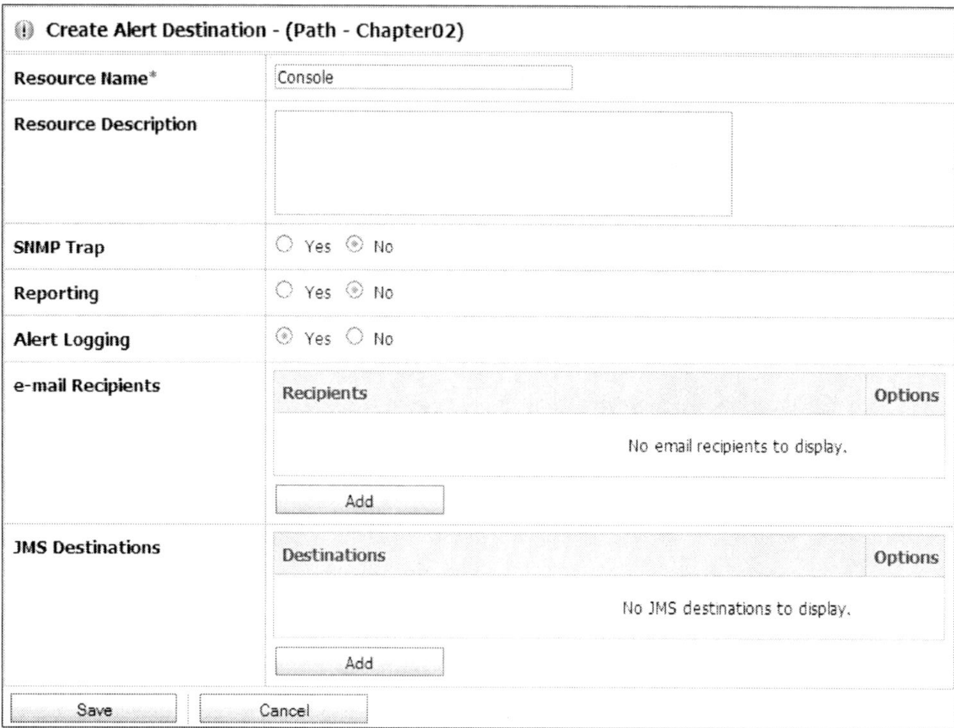

In this dialog, we need to provide a name for the alert destination and specify the targets for this destination. The console is always included as a destination, but we may also send alerts to SNMP for integration with system managements systems such as Oracle Enterprise Manager or HP OpenView. Other destinations include E-mail, JMS queues, alert logs, and internal reporting. Once we click **Save**, we have an alerting destination that can be used by many alerts.

Enabling service monitoring

To improve performance, by default, service monitoring is disabled for proxy services. To enable service monitoring, we need to go to the proxy service edit screen and select the **Operational Settings** tab.

After selecting the **Monitoring** checkbox to enable monitoring for this service, we can select the level of monitoring to perform (**Service** level, **Pipeline** level, or **Action** level) and then review the other potential properties. The **Aggregation Interval** is the rolling time period over which SLAs for this proxy will be monitored. **Alerting** and **Logging** specify the monitoring level at which events will be tracked. Reporting allows inclusion of this proxy service in reports on the console. Finally, **Tracing** can be enabled to help debugging the service. Selecting **Update** will save the new configuration.

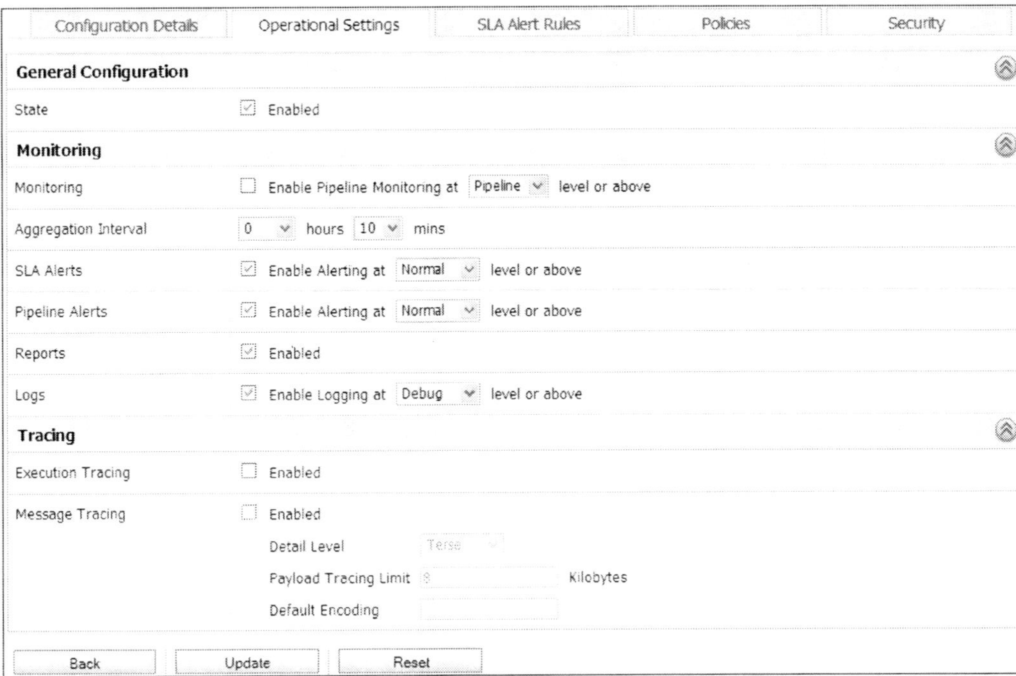

Creating an alert rule

Having enabled monitoring for our service, we can now create an alert rule by selecting the **SLA Alert Rules** tab. Selecting **Add New** takes us to the **New Alert Rule** dialog, where we can start configuring our rule.

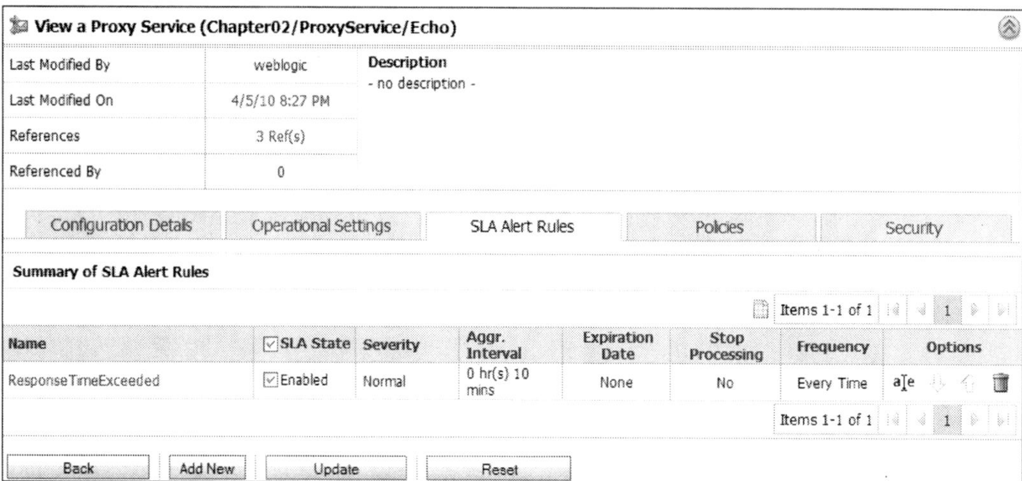

After providing a name for the alert rule, we need to specify the destination. It is possible to limit applicability of the rule by restricting the time window in which the rule applies by setting an expiry date or by explicitly suspending the rule by setting **Rule Enabled** to false. The **Alert Severity** indicates the importance of this alert. The **Alert Frequency** is used to control whether the alert works as an edge trigger, firing only when the threshold is first exceeded, or as a level trigger, firing whenever the metric is above the threshold.

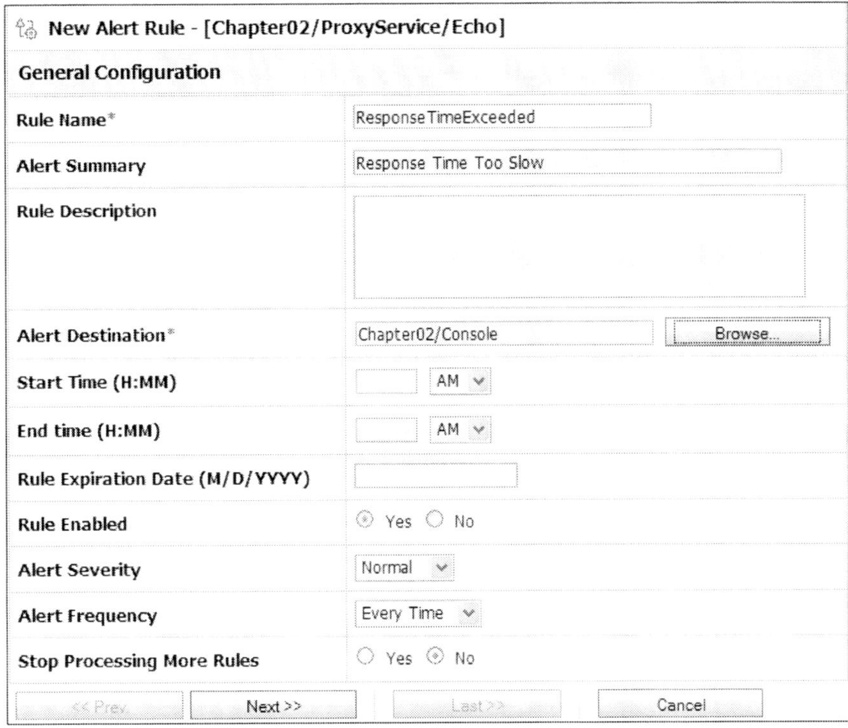

We also need to specify a destination for any alerts resulting from this rule. This is done by clicking the **Browse...** button next to the **Alert Destination** field and selecting an appropriate destination from the list presented in the **Select Alert Destination** dialog.

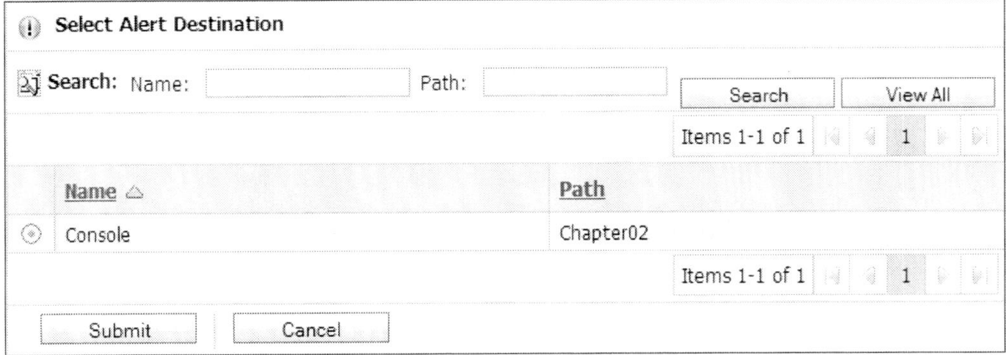

Having selected **Next>>**, we can now construct our rule by defining the expression or expressions that we wish to use as an SLA. Expressions are created by first selecting the type of expression and then selecting the actual measurement. The expression type may be a count, a minimum, a maximum, or an average. Actual metrics for count may be error or message counts and success or failure ratios. Metrics for minimum, average, and maximum may be response times. Multiple expressions may be combined with boolean operators. Expressions are added to the SLA rule by clicking **Add**.

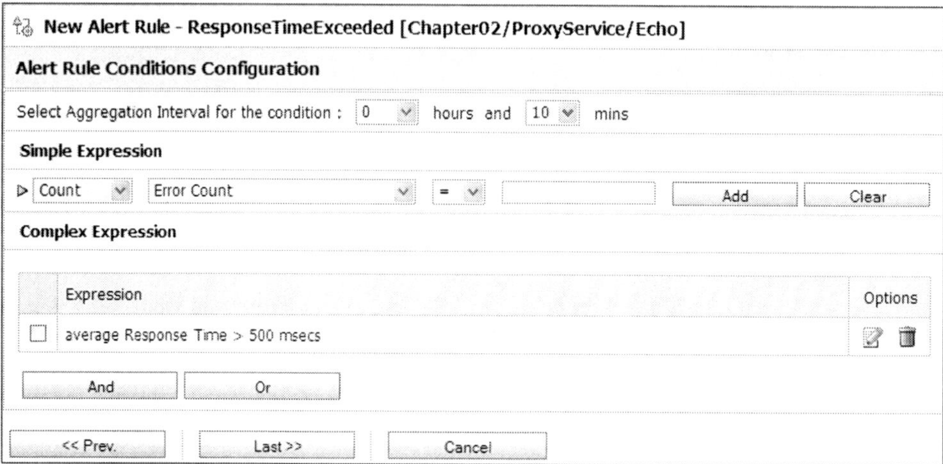

Clicking **Last>>** takes us to the summary screen where we can use the **Save** button to confirm our selections.

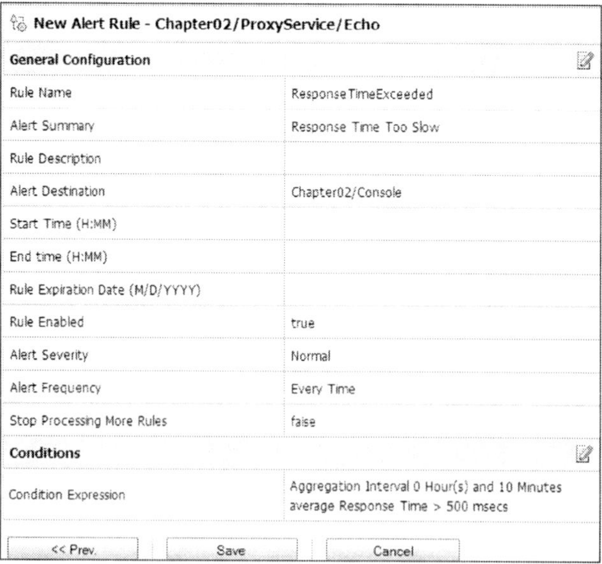

We can then do a final review of our modifications before selecting **Update** on the **SLA Alert Rules** tab. Remember to activate changes from the change center. Our SLA is now established and any violations will be reported.

Monitoring the service

We can monitor the health of our services by using the **Dashboard** tab found under the **Operations Monitoring** tab. This gives us an immediate overview of alerts generated within the last 30 minutes.

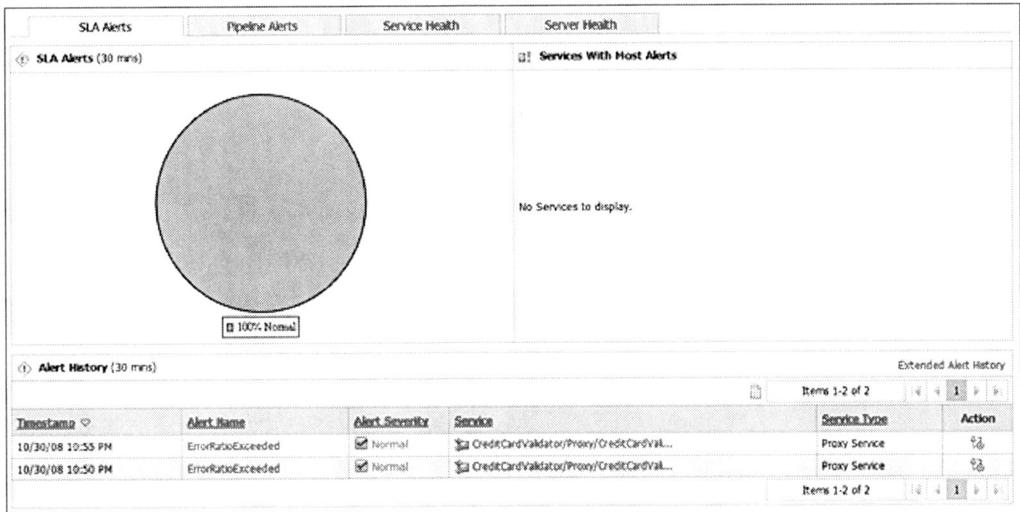

In addition to the dashboard, further information about the services can be obtained by examining the **Service Health** tab, which gives an overview of service behavior, throughput, error rates, and response times.

What makes a good SLA

SLAs should not be restricted just to report violations that are unacceptable. It can be good practice for a given metric to set two or even three SLAs. The worst SLA should be the one that is unacceptable and is the real SLA. The other SLAs should be used to warn that the metric has gone outside of normal operating bounds or to warn that it is approaching the worst SLA. These latter SLAs can be used to help operators diagnose problems and take corrective action before they become critical.

Summary

The Web Services manager and the Service Bus allow security and monitoring to be applied to services without modifying their core functionality. These policies may be applied consistently through the policy manager and enforced through the Service Bus, gateways, and agents. This model of security, as a service and as a facet that is applied to existing services, allows for new security standards to be easily incorporated into the SOA infrastructure. In addition, it is possible to monitor the health and performance of groups of services and of individual services, including monitoring for compliance with service-level agreements.

Index

B

D

E

F

N

O

P

S

Thank you for buying

Oracle SOA Suite 11*g* R1 Developer's Guide

About Packt Publishing

Packt, pronounced 'packed', published its first book "Mastering phpMyAdmin for Effective MySQL Management" in April 2004 and subsequently continued to specialize in publishing highly focused books on specific technologies and solutions.

Our books and publications share the experiences of your fellow IT professionals in adapting and customizing today's systems, applications, and frameworks. Our solution based books give you the knowledge and power to customize the software and technologies you're using to get the job done. Packt books are more specific and less general than the IT books you have seen in the past. Our unique business model allows us to bring you more focused information, giving you more of what you need to know, and less of what you don't.

Packt is a modern, yet unique publishing company, which focuses on producing quality, cutting-edge books for communities of developers, administrators, and newbies alike. For more information, please visit our website: `www.packtpub.com`.

About Packt Enterprise

In 2010, Packt launched two new brands, Packt Enterprise and Packt Open Source, in order to continue its focus on specialization. This book is part of the Packt Enterprise brand, home to books published on enterprise software - software created by major vendors, including (but not limited to) IBM, Microsoft and Oracle, often for use in other corporations. Its titles will offer information relevant to a range of users of this software, including administrators, developers, architects, and end users.

Writing for Packt

We welcome all inquiries from people who are interested in authoring. Book proposals should be sent to author@packtpub.com. If your book idea is still at an early stage and you would like to discuss it first before writing a formal book proposal, contact us; one of our commissioning editors will get in touch with you.

We're not just looking for published authors; if you have strong technical skills but no writing experience, our experienced editors can help you develop a writing career, or simply get some additional reward for your expertise.

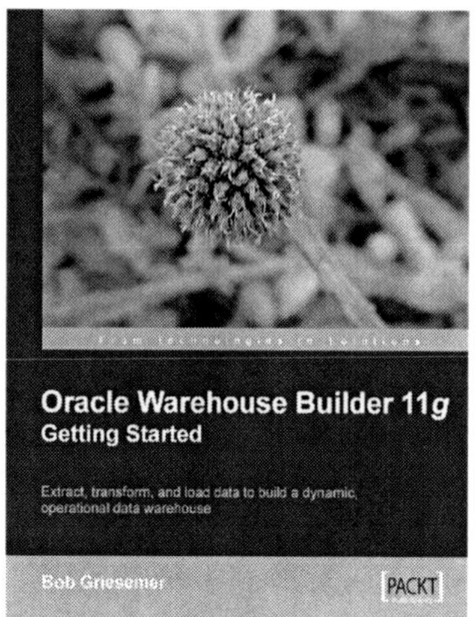

Oracle Warehouse Builder 11*g*: Getting Started

ISBN: 978-1-847195-74-6 Paperback: 368 pages

Extract, Transform, and Load data to build a dynamic, operational data warehouse

1. Build a working data warehouse from scratch with Oracle Warehouse Builder.
2. Cover techniques in Extracting, Transforming, and Loading data into your data warehouse.
3. Learn about the design of a data warehouse by using a multi-dimensional design with an underlying relational star schema.
4. Written in an accessible and informative style, this book helps you achieve your warehousing goals, and is loaded with screenshots, numerous tips, and strategies not found in the official user guide.

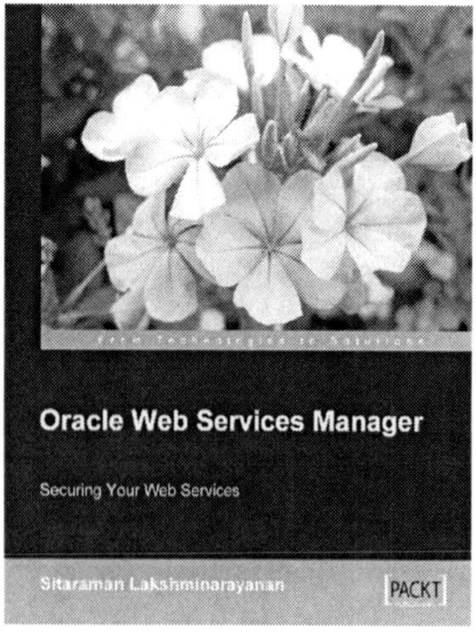

Oracle Web Services Manager

ISBN: 978-1-847193-83-4 Paperback: 236 pages

Securing your Web Services

1. Secure your web services using Oracle WSM
2. Authenticate, Authorize, Encrypt, and Decrypt messages
3. Create Custom Policy to address any new Security implementation
4. Deal with the issue of propagating identities across your web applications and web services
5. Detailed examples for various security use cases with step-by-step configurations

Please check **www.PacktPub.com** for information on our titles

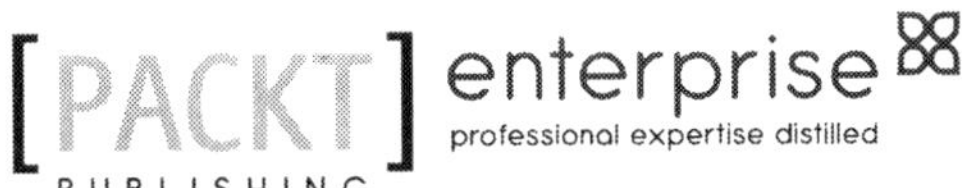

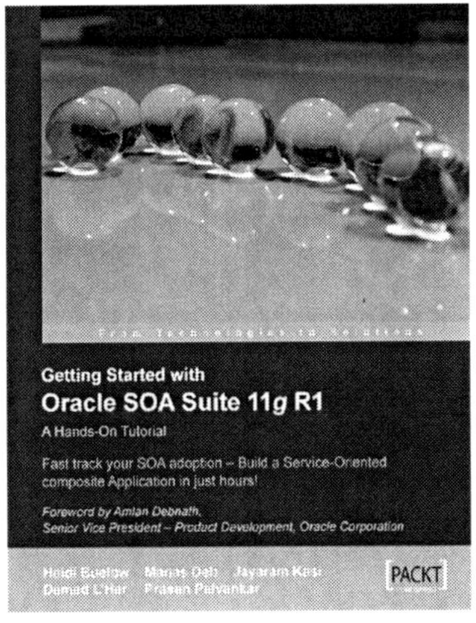

Getting Started With Oracle SOA Suite 11*g* R1 – A Hands-On Tutorial

ISBN: 978-1-847199-78-2 Paperback: 482 pages

Fast track your SOA adoption - Build a service-oriented composite application in just hours!

1. Offers an accelerated learning path for the much anticipated Oracle SOA Suite 11*g* release
2. Beginning with a discussion of the evolution of SOA, this book sets the stage for your SOA learning experience
3. Includes a comprehensive overview of the Oracle SOA Suite 11*g* Product Architecture
4. Explains how Oracle uses standards like Services Component Architecture (SCA) and Services Data Object (SDO) to simplify application development

---

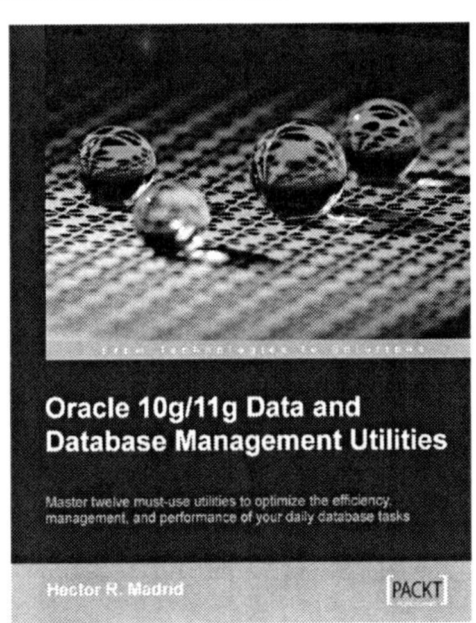

Oracle 10*g*/11*g* Data and Database Management Utilities

ISBN: 978-1-847196-28-6 Paperback: 432 pages

Master twelve must-use utilities to optimize the efficiency, management, and performance of your daily database tasks

1. Optimize time-consuming tasks efficiently using the Oracle database utilities
2. Perform data loads on the fly and replace the functionality of the old export and import utilities using Data Pump or SQL*Loader
3. Boost database defenses with Oracle Wallet Manager and Security

Please check **www.PacktPub.com** for information on our titles

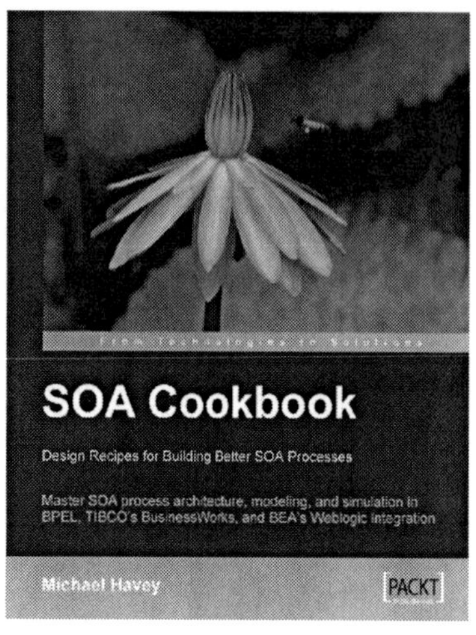

SOA Cookbook

ISBN: 978-1-847195-48-7 Paperback: 268 pages

Master SOA process architecture, modeling, and simulation in BPEL, TIBCO's BusinessWorks, and BEA's Weblogic Integration

1. Lessons include how to model orchestration, how to build dynamic processes, how to manage state in a long-running process, and numerous others
2. BPEL tools discussed include BPEL simulator, BPEL compiler, and BPEL complexity analyzer
3. Examples in BPEL, TIBCO's BusinessWorks, BEA's Weblogic Integration

---

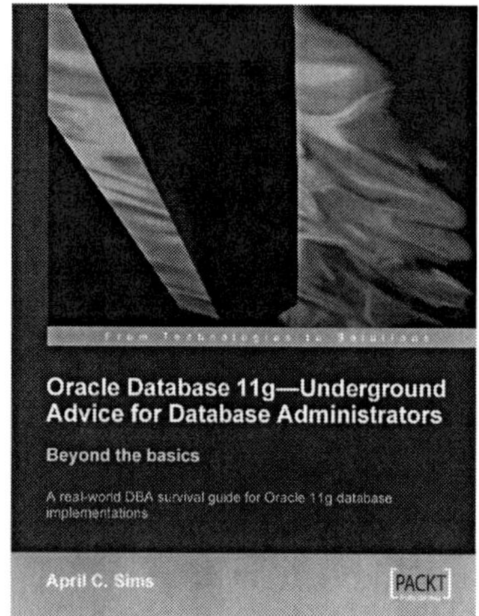

Oracle Database 11*g* – Underground Advice for Database Administrators

ISBN: 978-1-849680-00-4 Paperback: 348 pages

A real-world DBA survival guide for Oracle 11*g* database implementations

1. A comprehensive handbook aimed at reducing the day-to-day struggle of Oracle 11*g* Database newcomers
2. Real-world reflections from an experienced DBA – what novice DBAs should really know
3. Implement Oracle's Maximum Availability Architecture with expert guidance
4. Implement Oracle's Maximum Availability Architecture with expert guidance

Please check **www.PacktPub.com** for information on our titles

Oracle Modernization Solutions

ISBN: 978-1-847194-64-0 Paperback: 442 pages

A practical guide to planning and implementing SOA Integration and Re-architecting to an Oracle platform

1. Complete, practical guide to legacy modernization using SOA Integration and Re-architecture
2. Understand when and why to choose the non-invasive SOA Integration approach to reuse and integrate legacy components quickly and safely
3. Understand when and why to choose Re-architecture to reverse engineer legacy components and preserve business knowledge in a modern open and extensible architecture

---

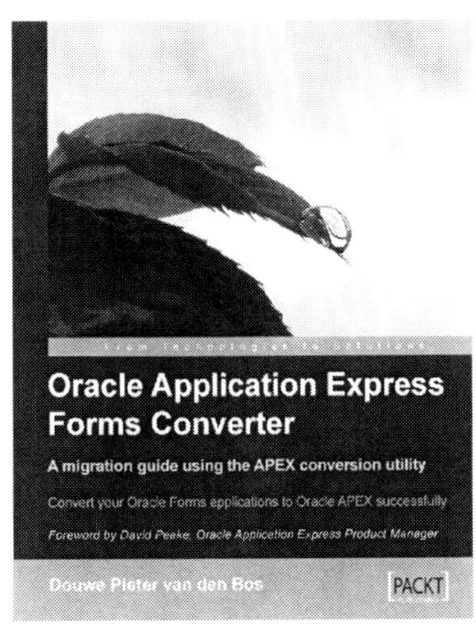

Oracle Application Express Forms Converter

ISBN: 978-1-847197-76-4 Paperback: 172 pages

Convert your Oracle Forms applications to Oracle APEX successfully

1. Convert your Oracle Forms Applications to Oracle APEX
2. Master the different stages of a successful Oracle Forms to APEX conversion project
3. Packed with screenshots and clear explanations to facilitate learning
4. A step-by-step tutorial providing a proper understanding of Oracle conversion concepts

Please check **www.PacktPub.com** for information on our titles

LaVergne, TN USA
09 April 2011
223413LV00003B/16/P